EDUCATIONAL REFORM AND INTERNATIONALISATION:

The Case of School Reform in Kazakhstan

Edited by **David Bridges**

CAMBRIDGE
UNIVERSITY PRESS

CAMBRIDGE
UNIVERSITY PRESS

University Printing House, Cambridge CB2 8BS, United Kingdom

Cambridge University Press is part of the University of Cambridge.

It furthers the University's mission by disseminating knowledge in the pursuit of education, learning and research at the highest international levels of excellence.

Information on this title: education.cambridge.org

© Cambridge University Press 2014

First published 2014
Reprinted 2014 (twice)

Printed in the United Kingdom by Printondemand-worldwide, Peterborough

A catalogue record for this publication is available from the British Library

Library of Congress Cataloguing in Publication data

Includes bibliographical references and index
ISBN 13-9781107452886 Paperback

To the children – the future – of Kazakhstan.

CONTENTS

ACKNOWLEDGEMENTS

This book is the product of several collaborations: between Nazarbayev Intellectual Schools, the University of Cambridge International Examinations and the University of Cambridge Faculty of Education on some of the education reforms that are the focus of the book; between Nazarbayev University Graduate School of Education, University of Pennsylvania Graduate School of Education, University of Cambridge Faculty of Education and Nazarbayev Intellectual Schools on the research project that has generated a core of the essays included here; and between these and Cambridge University Press (CUP) who agreed to publish our work.

At CUP we are especially grateful to Claudia Bickford-Smith and to the general editors of the series, Colleen McLaughlin and Michael Evans for their support, and to Paul Sloman and his team for their meticulous attention to the quality of our work and for seeing the text through to production.

We gratefully acknowledge the warmth of the welcome and hospitality that we received in schools in different parts of Kazakhstan and the willingness of school directors, teachers, students, local administrators and officers in the central arms of government to give generously their time in the cause of our research. To all of these we give many thanks.

The writing and editing of the book has also been very much a collaborative venture, and by rights we should probably have listed about twelve editors, though at the risk of discouraging anyone from ever referencing the book. The editor would like especially to acknowledge the work of Michael Neal on early drafts of the papers and the many forms of support offered in the Cambridge Faculty of Education by, in particular, Mike Younger, Laura Carnicero Carcedo, Chloë Gayer-Anderson and all the Kazakhstan research team, with whom it has been a privilege and pleasure to work.

The 'cut out' designs used in the front of each section of the book are by the National Hero of Kazakhstan Bauyrzhan Momyshuly, and are used here with kind permission of his grandson Yerzhan. The front cover uses a traditional Kazakh carpet design and is from a photograph by Mark Heard.

NOTES ON CONTRIBUTORS

Nazipa Ayubayeva (Nazarbayev Intellectual Schools) is currently completing her PhD at the Faculty of Education at the University of Cambridge. Since 2009 she has been a Deputy Chief Executive Officer of the Autonomous Education Organisation Nazarbayev Intellectual Schools. She has worked as a Manager of the JSC National Analytical Center under the Government and the National Bank of the Republic of Kazakhstan. She was a Human Resource Development Trainer with the TACIS Project 'Support of the Eurasian Center for Kazakhstan Civil Servants Training' led by the British Council, and has experience of working in regional projects for the European Commission, the American Agency on International Development and the World Trade Institute.

Bakhty Balgynbayeva (Centre of Excellence, Nazarbayev Intellectual Schools) started her career as a primary school teacher. She worked as Deputy Director of a secondary school, a methodologist, an inspector for a regional education authority and Head of Semey Municipal Education Authority. She was a coordinator of several educational international projects in the Republic of Kazakhstan. She worked as a Director of the Regional Scientific-Practical Center for Gifted and Talented children *Astana Daryny*, and as a Deputy Director of Department for Education Quality Assessment at AEO Nazarbayev Intellectual Schools. Since 2012 she has been a Deputy Director of Centre of Excellence at Autonomous Education Organisation Nazarbayev Intellectual Schools.

Darkhan Bilyalov (Nazarbayev University, Graduate School of Education) was, until the Autumn of 2013, the Head of the Office for Continuing Education, Development and Projects in the Graduate School of Education at Nazarbayev University (Nazarbayev University). He has extensive experience of working on education projects and initiatives, including those funded by the Kazakhstan Government, EU, World Bank, EBRD and UNDP. He was involved at the very first stages of the creation of several education institutions including Nazarbayev University and Nazarbayev Intellectual Schools. He earned his Master of Science in Education from Northwestern University (USA) and a teacher's qualification from Eurasian National University in Kazakhstan. He is currently working on his PhD in Higher Education at Pennsylvania State University.

David Bridges (University of Cambridge, Faculty of Education) is Director of Research (Kazakhstan and Mongolia) at the University of Cambridge Faculty of Education and an Emeritus Fellow of St Edmund's and Homerton Colleges. He is Emeritus Professor at the University of East Anglia (where he was previously

Pro-Vice Chancellor), holds an Honorary Doctorate of the Open University and is an Academician of the Academy of Social Sciences. He has been closely associated with educational reform in Kazakhstan since 2011, having previously worked on educational development projects in many parts of the world. He co-directs the collaborative research project between Cambridge and Nazarbayev University, is a board member of Autonomous Education Organisation Nazarbayev Intellectual Schools and an advisor to the Minister of Education on the development of the '2015–2020 Education Strategy'. His publications include: *Education, Democracy and Discussion*; *'Fiction Written under Oath': Essays in Philosophy and Educational Research*, and a number of edited or co-edited collections including *Autonomy Democracy and Education*; *Developing Teachers Professionally*; *Education and the Marketplace*; *Higher Education and Regional Development*; *Evidence-Based Education Policy: What Evidence? What Basis? Whose Policy?* and *Philosophy, Methodology and Educational Research*, as well as some 120 journal articles and book chapters.

Simon Brownhill (University of Cambridge, Faculty of Education) is a senior teaching associate in the Faculty of Education. He previously worked as a senior lecturer at the University of Derby on a range of education-based courses. As a class teacher Simon taught across the full 3–11 age range, leading as an Assistant Headteacher (3–6 years) in a large and culturally diverse inner-city primary school. His research interests include story writing, creative learning and teaching, cultural diversity, physical development, behaviour management and the male role model in the early years (the focus of his doctoral thesis). His research has been presented at many conferences including Limerick, Barcelona, Gothenburg, Quebec and Indonesia. He contributes substantially to the Centre of Excellence in-service teacher training programme in Kazakhstan on behalf of the Faculty of Education.

Makpal Dzhadrina (Nazarbayev Intellectual Schools) began her career as a teacher and then as a methodologist and researcher. In 1982–5 she completed full-time postgraduate studies at the Academy of Pedagogical Sciences in Moscow and defended her thesis on 'The Development of Subject Skills in Teaching Chemistry in Schools'. After her graduation she was appointed Head of the 'Didactics' laboratories and worked as a Deputy Director of the Institute of Secondary Education at Kazakh Academy of Education (KAE). In 2000 she defended her doctoral thesis on 'Didactical bases of the construction of content for variable education'. In 2001 she became a vice-president of the KAE and in 2006 she was Head of the Institute of Harmonious Development in the Education Center 'Bobek'. Currently, she works at Autonomous Education Organisation Nazarbayev Intellectual Schools. She has contributed to more than 150 publications.

Olena Fimyar (University of Cambridge, Faculty of Education) has a particular research interest in policy sociology, academic migration and comparative education more generally. Before embarking on her research and university teaching career, she worked for five years as an EFL teacher in Tsyurupynska Gymnasium, Kherson region, Ukraine. She holds an MPhil and PhD from the University of Cambridge, Faculty of Education. Prior to joining the Kazakhstan Projects team as a Senior Research Associate, she led a project on 'Return Academic Migration in Post-Communist Europe' at the Center for Area Studies, Free University Berlin, and prior to that, a study on the 'Sociology of Post-Communist Intellectuals' at the Collegium Budapest, Hungary. She has published extensively on education reform, actors and power in educational policy-making in Ukraine.

Michael Fordham (University of Cambridge, Faculty of Education) is a Senior Teaching Associate at the Faculty of Education, University of Cambridge. Prior to joining the Faculty, he read History at Fitzwilliam College, Cambridge, before training as a History teacher. As a practising History teacher and subject leader, he mentored trainee teachers and supervised MEd students writing theses on History Education, while pursuing his own doctoral research into the subject knowledge of History teachers in the UK. He is an editor of the journal *Teaching History* and is an Affiliated Lecturer at the Institute of Continuing Education, University of Cambridge, where he teaches the MSt in Advanced Subject Teaching (History), and he contributes to the teacher enquiry programme in Kazakhstan.

David Frost (University of Cambridge, Faculty of Education) is a member of the Leadership for Learning (LfL) group at the University of Cambridge Faculty of Education. He is one of the co-founders the LfL Network which is committed to developing democratic forms of leadership and learning. His ongoing research focuses on teacher leadership. Through partnerships with schools and local authorities he has developed strategies for supporting teachers as agents of change who play key roles in the creation and transfer of professional knowledge. He is currently the Programme Director for the HertsCam Network. Over a period of more than twenty years he has co-ordinated networks which support teachers as leaders of change and innovation. These have acted as test-beds for his ideas on teacher leadership and, since 2008, he has led the International Teacher Leadership initiative which has partner programmes in 15 countries around the world. He is the founding editor of the journal: 'Teacher Leadership'. He is co-author of: *Teacher Self-Efficacy, Voice and Leadership: Towards a Policy Framework for Education International,* a report for the global association of teacher unions. He is currently a member of the 'Internationalisation and Reform of Secondary Schooling in Kazakhstan' research team.

Svetlana Ispussinova (Nazarbayev Intellectual Schools) started her career as a History teacher before becoming a school director in Atyrar and then Head of Atyrau Regional Education Authority. She was Head of Unit, Head of Division and Director of Department at the Ministry of Education and Science in the Republic of Kazakhstan. In 2008 she started working at JSC *Orken*, later to become Autonomous Education Organisation Nazarbayev Intellectual Schools. Since October 2012 she has been a Deputy Chairperson of Autonomous Education Organisation Nazarbayev Intellectual Schools. She was involved at the very first stages of creation of the Centre of Excellence under the auspices of Nazarbayev Intellectual Schools.

Assel Kambatyrova (Nazarbayev University, Graduate School of Education) is a Manager at Nazarbayev University Graduate School of Education. She is responsible for administrative operations of the School as well as being part of the research team on 'Internationalisation and Reform of Secondary Schooling in Kazakhstan' in collaboration with the University of Cambridge Faculty of Education. She has been working in the education sector for six years, having earned an English Teacher's Diploma and an MA in Philology from Kazakhstani University. In 2013–14 she earned an MA in Education at the University of Sheffield (UK) in the framework of the International Scholarship of the President of the Republic of Kazakhstan *Bolashak*.

Yermek Kassymbekov (Centre of Excellence, Nazarbayev Intellectual Schools) is Director of the Centre of Excellence, Nazarbayev Intellectual Schools. He started his working experience as a teacher, then worked as Head of West-Kazakhstan, Almaty and Mangystau Regional Education Authorities, and Head of Secondary Education Department of the Ministry of Education in Kazakhstan. He was the Head of the Education Department in the Prime Minister's Office. As a Director he was involved at the very first stages (2011) of the creation of Centre of Excellence under the auspices of Nazarbayev Intellectual Schools.

Anel Kulakhmetova (University of Cambridge, Centre of Development Studies) received her BA in International Economics from the Eurasian Institute of Market, Kazakhstan and her MA in International Development from the University of Denver, USA, as a Fulbright Scholar. Anel worked with UNICEF Kazakhstan and ILO-IPEC as a national consultant on child protection and child labour monitoring, with Counterpart International as a Regional Reporting Coordinator, and she conducted research on protection mechanisms for working children in Central Asia at Justus-Liebig Universitat Giessen, Germany. Currently she is doing her PhD in Development Studies at the University of Cambridge, UK.

Kairat Kurakbayev (Nazarbayev University, Graduate School of Education) is Director of the Research Institute at Nazarbayev University Graduate School of Education, Astana, Kazakhstan. Prior to joining Nazarbayev University, he served as an acting director of the Office for Strategic Planning and a Deputy Director of the International Office in the Eurasian National University. His professional experience includes working as a school teacher in his home town of Pavlodar, a teacher educator and a higher-education administrator. He was awarded British Council and American Council academic scholarships in 2004 and 2008 respectively, and holds an MEd degree from the University of Exeter, UK. His research interests focus on teacher education, international policy borrowing and the globalisation of education.

Colleen McLaughlin (University of Sussex and University of Cambridge, Faculty of Education) is a Professor of Education and Head of the Department of Education at the University of Sussex. Prior to this she was at the University of Cambridge Faculty of Education. She has also been a teacher and local authority adviser. Her recent areas of work have been in educational reform and teacher learning. Other research projects have been on educational reform; HIV/AIDS and sexuality education; bullying and pupils with special educational needs and disabilities; the school's contribution to emotional wellbeing, and effective counselling interventions with children and young people. She is an editor of the *Educational Action Research Journal*. Recent publications include: McLaughlin, C. and Holliday, C. (2013), *Therapy with Children and Young People: Integrative Counselling in Schools and other Settings*. London: Sage; McLaughlin, C., Swartz, S., Kiragu, S., Walli, S. and Muhamed, M. (2012), *Old Enough To Know: Consulting Children on African Sexualities*. Cape Town, SA: Human Sciences Research Council Press.

Ros McLellan (University of Cambridge, Faculty of Education) is a Lecturer in Teacher Education and Development/Pedagogical Innovation at the Faculty of Education, University of Cambridge. She has a background in teaching Psychology and Mathematics in the secondary school sector in the UK and is committed to working collaboratively with schools to develop and refine strategies that make a real difference to teaching and learning in the classroom. She has recently become the coordinator of SUPER, a longstanding schools–university partnership that conducts research based on teacher enquiry that is useful to both schools and the university. Her research interests include teachers' professional development, student wellbeing, creativity, achievement motivation, attitudes and perceptions, self-efficacy, and issues related to gender and achievement.

Peeter Mehisto (University of London, Institute of Education) has worked internationally with a wide variety of stakeholders to develop and manage bilingual and trilingual programmes. Generating strategic plans and work plans, building teacher-training programmes, managing public relations and creating learning materials have been integral to these initiatives. He also has extensive experience working with teachers in the classroom to support the implementation of best practice in bilingual programmes. He has won several awards for his work. He has taught at the primary, secondary and university levels. Through the University of London, he has researched factors contributing to successful bilingual programme development, as well as potential barriers to their implementation. He has more recently been working with other contributors to this volume on the development of an Educational Development Strategy for Kazakhstan 2015–20.

Khalida Nurseitova (Nazarbayev Intellectual Schools and Gumilyov Eurasian National University) is an Associate Professor at Gumilyov Eurasian National University. She has participated in a number of projects aimed at developing and implementing innovative programmes in the teaching of linguistics. She is the author of a number of books and scientific articles in the field of linguistics and gender studies. She works extensively with teachers in secondary and higher education as the President of the English Language Teacher's Association. She has many grants in and awards for Excellence in Teaching from the Ministry of Education of the Republic of Kazakhstan and the US Embassy. She has been a co-researcher on the research project on 'Internationalisation and Reform of Secondary Schooling in Kazakhstan' in collaboration with Nazarbayev University Graduate School of Education and the University of Cambridge Faculty of Education.

Martyn Rouse (University of Aberdeen) is Professor Emeritus at the University of Aberdeen in Scotland, where, until his retirement, he held a Professorial Chair in Social and Educational Inclusion and Director of the Inclusive Practice Project. He was previously Senior Lecturer at the University of Cambridge Faculty of Education. He has undertaken research and development work on inclusion for local authorities in the UK and for several national and international agencies, including the European Agency for the Development of Special Needs Education, the OECD and UNICEF. Internationally he has been involved in work on inclusive education in Central Asia for the Soros Open Society Foundation, the 'Schools for All Project' in the Republic of Latvia, as well as development work on inclusion and the curriculum in Bosnia, Serbia, Georgia and Armenia. Among a long list of publications, mainly focused on inclusion, is a recent co-edited collection with Kate Lapham published under the title *Learning to See Invisible Children: Inclusion in Central Asia* (2013).

Cristina Rimini (Cambridge International Examinations) is the Lead Project Specialist at Cambridge International Examinations, where she oversees the collaborative projects between Cambridge and Autonomous Education Organisation Nazarbayev Intellectual Schools. Since joining Cambridge Assessment in 1999, she has had a number of roles related to curriculum and assessment development in international contexts and teacher professional development. She led the development of a multilingual assessment framework for England. She has a background in English language teaching and teacher training in a number of countries including Spain, Poland and Russia.

Alan Ruby (University of Pennsylvania) has a 40-year career in government, business, philanthropy and education ranging from classroom teacher to Australian Deputy Secretary of Education to Chair of the OECD Education Committee and World Bank human development expert. Currently a Senior Fellow at the University of Pennsylvania, he focuses on globalisation's effects on education, training policy and practice. He is an adviser to the leadership teams at Nazarbayev University and Nazarbayev Intellectual Schools and a Senior Fellow at the National Association for Study Abroad.

Aida Sagintayeva (Nazarbayev University, Graduate School of Education) is the Executive Director of Nazarbayev University Graduate School of Education, Kazakhstan. Prior to joining the Graduate School of Education, she was a Vice-

Rector for International Cooperation at the Eurasian National University, Astana. She has been involved in educational research projects at the Ministry of Education and Science (MoES) on gearing Kazakhstan's higher education system towards the European three-tiered degree system and has coordinated a ministerial initiative aimed at introducing Western PhD programmes in Kazakhstan. In 2008, she was awarded a Junior Faculty Development Programme Fellowship, funded by the US Department of State's Bureau of Educational and Cultural Affairs, and had her research internship at the George Washington University, US. She was formerly president of the Bolashak International Scholarship Office. Her research interests include internationalisation of education, comparative education and higher education governance.

Aslan Sarinzhipov (Nazarbayev University, Graduate School of Education) holds an Ed.D from the University of Pennsylvania Graduate School of Education. He began work on the Executive Committee of the Intergovernmental Council of Central Asia, and then, as a member of the Ministry of Foreign Affairs of the Republic of Kazakhstan, was appointed as a diplomatic attaché on economic issues to the Kazakhstan Embassy in Washington DC. He later became a Project Coordinator in the Department of Infrastructure and the Development of Finance and Private Markets with the World Bank. He became Deputy Chair of the National Analytical Center under the Government and National Bank in Kazakhstan, where he supervised fields of economic development, finance and education. From 2009 to 2013, he was the Chair of the Executive Council of Nazarbayev University. On 2 September 2013, by the official decree of the President of the Republic of Kazakhstan, he was appointed the Minister of Education and Science.

Kulyash Shamshidinova (Nazarbayev Intellectual Schools) is the Chief Executive Officer of Autonomous Education Organisation Nazarbayev Intellectual Schools. Prior to becoming CEO, she was on two occasions Vice-Minister of Education and Science of the Republic of Kazakhstan for a total of five years (2002–5 and 2007–9). She has also held the post of Director General of the Bobek National Scientific Practical Education and Health Centre, and has been the Deputy Mayor of Taldykorgan. Previously, she served as an adviser to the Party Committee of the Taldykorgan Region and as secretary of the same Committee. In addition, she has been the Deputy Director of the Taldykorgan Regional Extension Course Institute for Teachers, and earlier in her career, has worked as a Chemistry teacher and as a director of a secondary school in the Almaty region (1992–6).

Assel Sharimova (Centre of Excellence, Nazarbayev Intellectual Schools) is the deputy director of the Centre of Excellence, Nazarbayev Intellectual Schools. She received her teacher's qualification from Kazakh University of Law and Humanities in Kazakhstan and has experience of working as a teacher of foreign languages at university and private schools. Being a holder of an international scholarship *Bolashak* she earned her MA in Educational Leadership and Management from the University of Nottingham (UK). She was involved at the very first stages of the creation of the Centre of Excellence under the auspices of Nazarbayev Intellectual Schools and the development of the Centre of Excellence multi-level teacher professional development programme in cooperation with the University of Cambridge Faculty of Education.

Arailym Soltanbekova (Nazarbayev Intellectual Schools, Centre for Pedagogical Measurements) is a Project Manager in the Centre for Pedagogical Measurements, Nazarbayev Intellectual Schools. She holds an MA in Educational Leadership and Management from Warwick University (UK), and a teacher's qualification from Kazakh University of International Relations and World Languages, Kazakhstan. She is an official exam manager of Nazarbayev Intellectual Schools ESOL Exam Centre in Kazakhstan and currently leads the project on the monitoring system development for languages at Nazarbayev Intellectual Schools. Arailym has been a school teacher, a university educator and a Head of the research sector at the Centre for Pedagogical Measurements, Nazarbayev Intellectual Schools. Her areas of research interests include school leadership and management, educational assessment and evaluation.

Fay Turner (University of Cambridge, Faculty of Education) taught in primary schools for nearly 20 years and worked for the Cambridgeshire local authority as an Advisory Teacher in Mathematics prior to coming into teacher education, She has been involved in teacher education since 1999, firstly at Homerton College, then following reorganisation, at the Faculty of Education, University of Cambridge. Her teaching has focused on primary Mathematics but she has also taught on a number of undergraduate, postgraduate and MA courses which focus on pedagogy and general professional issues. Her work at the Faculty includes coordinating and teaching Primary PGCE Mathematics and teaching and supervising master's students working in the area of Mathematics. She has acted as an external examiner for the Primary PGCE courses and MA programmes at a number of UK universities. Since 2011, she has been heavily involved in the professional development of trainers and teachers in Kazakhstan. She has co-written and co-led an in-service professional development programme for primary and secondary teachers across Kazakhstan which focuses on general pedagogical approaches.

Madina Tynybayeva (Nazarbayev Intellectual Schools) is Deputy Director of the Department for Quality Assurance at Autonomous Education Organisation Nazarbayev Intellectual Schools. She has a BA in Teaching English and an MA in English Philology from the Innovative Eurasian University. In 2008 she graduated from Twente University, the Netherlands, obtaining an MA in Educational Science and Technology (Assessment). She worked as a lecturer in Methods of Teaching Foreign Languages at the university and as a manager at different levels at the *Bolashak* Scholarship Foundation Organisation under MoES. In the Department for Quality Assurance at Autonomous Education Organisation Nazarbayev Intellectual

Schools she is involved in developing assessment policy documents for international and Kazakhstani projects realized within the Nazarbayev Intellectual Schools network. Currently, she is a PhD student at Nazarbayev University Graduate School of Education.

Elaine Wilson (University of Cambridge, Faculty of Education) is a Senior Lecturer in Education and a Fellow of Homerton College. She was a secondary school Chemistry teacher and was awarded a Salters' Medal for Chemistry teaching while working in a Cambridge secondary school. She now teaches undergraduate students, Secondary Science PGCE students, coordinates a 'blended learning' Science Education MA course and supervises doctoral students. She has received two career awards for teaching in higher education in 2004; a University of Cambridge Pilkington Teaching Prize and a Higher Education National Teaching Fellowship. She is on the editorial board of the Educational Action Research Journal and has recently published papers in the area of social capital in school–university partnerships. The second edition of her edited book *School-Based Research: A Guide for Education Students* was published by SAGE in December 2012.

Liz Winter (University of Cambridge, Faculty of Education) is currently working as a Kazakhstan Project Development Officer. She started her career in Engineering Design and then retrained as a Chartered Academic Psychologist, taking an interest in social identities. She has taught across all levels from school to postgraduate qualifications and in a variety of higher education contexts. She is an active member of the British Psychological Society and sits on two committees: one that considers academic, teaching and research matters, and one that considers ethics. She has experience of course management and quality assurance in higher education, both at the University of Cambridge and ay her previous place of employment, the University of Leicester. She is a member of the Cambridge/Nazarbayev University research team.

Natallia Yakavets (University of Cambridge, Faculty of Education) is a Project Development Officer at the University of Cambridge Faculty of Education, and a member of the research team in the collaboration with Nazarbayev University. Prior to joining the Faculty of Education, she taught Research Methods at the Institute of Education, University of Warwick. She holds a PhD in Educational Leadership and Management and, having been a researcher at the UNESCO International Bureau of Education (Geneva, Switzerland), and the National Institute of Education, Ministry of Education (Minsk, Belarus), she has substantial experience of international collaborative research projects in the fields of educational policy, educational leadership and management, curricula reforms, teacher preparation and continuing professional development. Her research interests include: globalisation and school reform, gifted education, the historical dimensions of educational transformation in Eastern Europe and in Central Asia, international leadership practices, the role of social capital, leadership development and multi-agency partnership in school improvement.

SERIES EDITORS' PREFACE

The manifold dimensions of the field of teacher education are increasingly attracting the attention of researchers, educators, classroom practitioners and policymakers, while awareness has also emerged of the blurred boundaries between these categories of stakeholders in the discipline. One notable feature of contemporary theory, research and practice in this field is consensus on the value of exploring the diversity of international experience for understanding the dynamics of educational development and the desired outcomes of teaching and learning. A second salient feature has been the view that theory and policy development in this field need to be evidence-driven and attentive to diversity of experience. Our aim in this series is to give space to in-depth examination and critical discussion of educational development in context with a particular focus on the role of the teacher and of teacher education. While significant, disparate studies have appeared in relation to specific areas of enquiry and activity, the *Cambridge Education Research Series* provides a platform for contributing to international debate by publishing within one overarching series monographs and edited collections by leading and emerging authors tackling innovative thinking, practice and research in education.

The series consists of three strands of publication representing three fundamental perspectives. The *Teacher Education* strand focuses on a range of issues and contexts and provides a re-examination of aspects of national and international teacher education systems or analysis of contextual examples of innovative practice in initial and continuing teacher education programmes in different national settings. The *International Education Reform* strand examines the global and country specific moves to reform education and particularly teacher development, which is now widely acknowledged as central to educational systems development. Books published in the *Language Education* strand address the multilingual context of education in different national and international settings, critically examining among other phenomena the first, second and foreign language ambitions of different national settings and innovative classroom pedagogies and language teacher education approaches that take account of linguistic diversity.

Educational Reform and Internationalisation: The Case of School Reform in Kazakhstan is a landmark text as it is a detailed and rare account of the history of this reform process in Kazakhstan since independence. The national strategy has placed education centre stage in the move to develop Kazakhstan. The authors aim to examine the premises on which the reform is based, strategies of practice and policy borrowing and partnerships with external global partners. They examine the reform in relation to international debates, as well as country specific ones. The authors are a mixture of policy makers and academics. It provides rich research on education in Kazakhstan as well as making a significant contribution to international debates about educational reform.

Colleen McLaughlin and Michael Evans

FOREWORD

Shigeo Katsu (President of Nazarbayev University)

Conceiving, developing and implementing educational reform is a major – and continuous – undertaking for any country. It is even more daunting for a country such as Kazakhstan, which has undergone a societal upheaval that has been nothing short of a revolution as it has made the transition from a centrally planned economy under the Soviet Union system to a market-oriented one following its independence in December 1991.

I would like to start by congratulating the team of authors and the editor for pulling together in a single volume a succinct account of the history of this reform process in Kazakhstan since independence, followed by an in-depth discussion of underlying contexts and key trends, and concluding with a concise overview of the manifold challenges for development that lie ahead.

This book provides a clear articulation of the rationale for school-level education sector reforms in Kazakhstan. It also illustrates that the stakes are particularly high in this country. As President Nursultan Nazarbayev indicated in his seminal speech in December 2012 when he launched the Kazakhstan 2050 Strategy, human development – and in particular education – is considered the main instrument for catapulting Kazakhstan into the ranks of the top 30 most developed countries by 2050. Yet unfortunately, as recent international competency assessments have shown, the gap between Kazakhstan and the front-runners is substantial. Furthermore, the skills needed for Kazakhstan to prevail successfully in an ever-more competitive global economy are in short supply today. This situation mandates a modernisation of the education system with a sense of urgency, especially when we take into account the typical time lags inherent in education reforms before a tangible impact can be seen.

In this context, the discussion in the book of the evolution of Kazakhstan's education sector since independence reminds the reader of two characteristics that stand out when deliberating the direction of future reforms: the centrality, in the thinking of the nation's leadership, of education to any development strategies; and the country's openness to study, adopt and adapt international good practices, often in a fearless manner. I shall elaborate more on this later.

The book rightly argues that reforming teachers' education must be a core element of any reform, but also makes it clear that the demographic prospects over the next decade and a half, when the number of school children will swell by more than 50%, will translate into daunting challenges both in terms of the number of qualified teachers required and the availability of appropriately equipped schools. As if these challenges are not enough, Kazakhstan's education sector will over the coming years face other, equally important reform tasks such as the shift to student-centred education and the implementation of the policy of trilingualism, both of which are intimately linked to teachers' education. Kazakhstan has decided to switch the orthography of the national Kazakh language from the Cyrillic to the Latin alphabet by 2025; preparing for this important shift is another substantial challenge. Furthermore, the financing model for the education sector still needs more work, in particular to address the needs of communities in rural areas and secondary cities, and to ensure sustainability. The government is not shying away from these challenges, and has been discussing these and other education sector reform directions in the context of an evolving educational strategy reflected in the 'Roadmap 2014–2020'. This book provides the intellectual underpinning for this plan of action.

Understandably, within society in general and also within the political elite, there may be a sense of 'reform fatigue' after some 20 years of continuous reforms in almost all social and economic sectors. It is legitimate to ask whether one really needs to do more, whether one cannot step off the 'reform treadmill' and catch some breath before embarking on another demanding phase. In my mind the answer has to be a firm 'yes' for the *continuation* of reforms, especially when one reflects on the gap between the standing of the education sector today and the ambitious aspirations for the country articulated by President Nazarbayev.

Fortunately Kazakhstan's recent past and experience encourage me, and I hope others, to be quite optimistic about the prospects for the reform tasks discussed in this book.

First, Kazakhstan has a proven track record since independence of embarking on and implementing difficult socioeconomic reforms, and has exhibited a certain tenacity in doing so. It has established a system of monitoring progress (even though in the past the focus was primarily on inputs rather than outcomes), and increasingly has shown a willingness to learn from past failures as well as successes.

Second, Kazakhstan is a young and energetic country, 'hungry' enough to take on bold reform challenges – reforms that 'older' societies today would not even contemplate taking on, regarding them as politically not feasible.

Third, one observes an increasing awareness in Kazakhstan of where and what international 'cutting edge' benchmarks are with respect to excellence in the socio-economic sphere. This development is in itself a reflection of the enormous success of the government's *Bolashak* overseas study scholarship programme. Launched during the most difficult period post-independence, the programme celebrated its 20th anniversary in the autumn of 2013, and awarded its 10000th scholarship. This programme has also stimulated many other Kazakhstanis to study abroad. The *Bolashak* generation is now populating a broad range of public and private institutions with a clear understanding of international standards. Indeed, this generation will be called upon to become the driver for implementing President Nazarbayev's Kazakhstan 2050 Strategy.

Fourth, accompanying this willingness to reform is a remarkable appetite for experimentation based on international good practices. Taking just the education sector, this is repeatedly witnessed in some of the current signature reform initiatives such as the Nazarbayev Intellectual Schools (NIS) discussed in the book, my own institution, the Nazarbayev University, and KASIPKOR, a new-style Technical and Vocational Education institution. These are all designed with an eye towards internalising international good practices, scaling up and disseminating them throughout the country once the concepts have been tested and proven.

Fifth, reform designers recognise that the modernisation of the education sector has to be looked at in a systemic manner. For reforms in the sector to take root and be successful, all segments of education, from early childhood development through to tertiary and post-tertiary education including life-long learning, and research have to be addressed in an organic, intertwined manner. While this approach may create additional complexities, the pay-off in terms of sustainability and ability to adjust to evolving circumstances will be high.

Sixth, one cannot but admire the degree of commitment to reform initiatives in the core institutions tasked with their development and implementation. I see this commitment daily at our university, in faculty, staff and students, and I see this commitment in NIS. In November 2013 I attended portions of a large-scale workshop organized by NIS leadership to share NIS's progress and learning with a broad range of stakeholders that included not just NIS partners and teachers, but also the country's education community including the Ministry of Education and Science and leaders of schools throughout Kazakhstan. I was struck by the fervour, the thirst for information and 'buy-in' that was evident throughout all the sessions.

So, in summary, I am quite hopeful that the ambitious designs for modernising Kazakhstan's education sector will indeed translate into policies, programmes and actions; much more hopeful than I would be about the likelihood of this in the majority of emerging countries.

This present book establishes an important baseline for a holistic discussion of school education reforms in Kazakhstan, and will, without any doubt, serve as a source of reference for future generations of education policymakers and analysts alike.

Shigeo Katsu
President of Nazarbayev University

INTRODUCTION

David Bridges (University of Cambridge, Faculty of Education)
Aida Sagintayeva (Nazarbayev University, Graduate School of Education)

This book is intended as a contribution to at least two different conversations: one is the international conversation among researchers and policymakers about the processes of educational reform, 'policy borrowing' and the internationalisation of educational policy; the second is the conversation in Kazakhstan among researchers, policymakers and practitioners around the same issues, and especially those to do with the implementation of reform. Part of our ambition is to introduce these two conversational communities to each other: to engage colleagues in Kazakhstan with the international literature and research and to engage the international community with 'the case of Kazakhstan'.

These different readerships will require different introductions to the work that follows, so we hope that readers will skip through this introduction, selecting whatever is relevant to them. For international readers unfamiliar with Kazakhstan, a short introduction to the country is provided, followed by a summary of the main features of the education system today. A much fuller account of the history of reform since independence in 1991 is given in the opening chapters of the book. Then we provide a short account of the collaborative research project that underpins a core of the essays in this collection. Finally, we introduce the contributions to the book and their interconnected themes.

Introducing Kazakhstan

> 'Know anything about Kazakhstan?'
>
> 'Not much, no.' Next to nothing would have been a more honest answer: Genghis Khan and the Mongol hordes, the Silk Road, miles and miles of empty steppe. (Robbins 2007, 3)

Christopher Robbins's admission in his sympathetic presentation of Kazakhstan, *In Search of Kazakhstan: The Country that Disappeared*, is one that many in the international community would have to share. For those, we provide a very brief introduction to the country and its people.

Kazakhstan is the world's largest landlocked country by land area and the ninth largest country in the world. It is five times the size of France and four times that of Texas, and has a population of 17 million people. With 12% of its land area in Europe and the rest in Asia, Kazakhstan is the most central of all the Central Asian countries.

Kazakhstan has extensive land borders with Russia in the north and north-west, Turkmenistan, Uzbekistan and Kyrgyzstan in the south and south-west and China in the south-east. The total length of its frontiers is over 14000 kilometres, including 600 kilometres that border onto the Caspian Sea.

The country is rich in natural resources. It boasts giant deposits of oil and gas, coal and minerals. The current oil boom, which contributes around 78% of GDP, pays for the social infrastructure, including educational development. The country ranks first in the world in zinc, wolfram and barite output, second in uranium, silver, lead and chrome ore reserves, third in copper and fluorites, fourth in molybdenum and sixth in gold.

And apples came originally from Kazakhstan. And tulips, which bring brilliant colour to the steppes each spring. And, if the experience of this volume's editor is anything to go by, one of its greatest natural resources is the warmth and hospitality of its people.

Due to its long history and location at the junction of two continents, Kazakhstan presents a mix of different cultures. As a consequence of, in particular, Stalin's use of Kazakhstan as a dumping ground for communities he wanted out of the way and his use of the country as a major location for the notorious gulags, there are over 120 nationalities in Kazakhstan today with their own languages and historical and cultural values. The achievement of harmony and concord in inter-ethnic relations between peoples of different origins has been one of the long-term priorities of the government. The largest ethnic groups living in modern Kazakhstan are Kazakhs (63%), Russians (25%), Ukrainians (2.9%), Uzbeks (2.8%), Germans (1.5%), Tatars (1.5%) and Uyghurs (1.5%).

One of the most considerable achievements of world civilisation, the Great Silk Road, intersected the territory of Kazakhstan. It appeared as a trading artery in the 2nd and 3rd centuries BC. The networks of the caravan roads crossed Europe and Asia from the Mediterranean region to China and served as an important means of commercial relations and communication between cultures of the West and East. Kazakhstan, as part of the network, served as a region of exchange not only for goods but also for religions, cultures, scientific knowledge and customs. Chapter 14 offers the Silk Routes as a metaphor for the contemporary international exchange of policies in Kazakhstan.

In the beginning of the 18th century, the khans' decision to sign an assistance pact with the Russian Empire in order to get protection from the Zhungar tribes of western China led to what was initially a voluntary process of Kazakhstan's colonisation. However, the societal and cultural transformations that Russia tried to impose on the Kazakh nation caused numerous protests and a nationwide uprising in 1837.

The 20th century witnessed Soviet brutalisation of Kazakhstan. In response to the economic backwardness of the region, the USSR government introduced major reforms in Kazakhstan's economy and by 1941 its industrial output had increased eightfold in comparison with the period before 1913. However, as part of the Soviet plan to concentrate on large economic programmes, the land of nomadic herders was forcibly turned into a region for Soviet heavy industry, agriculture and cattle breeding. The campaign of the 1930s to collectivise the nomadic population led to famine. Many who could not survive without moving their herds from one place to another on the scanty steppe soils moved to China and neighbouring Central Asian countries. In 1931–34 about 1.5 million Kazakhs (more than 40% of the Kazakh ethnic population) died of hunger and related illnesses.

During the years preceding the Second World War and during the war, the national loss of indigenous population was soon replaced by large-scale deportations of whole communities of people including convicts and others that Stalin wanted out of the way. Between 1935 and 1940, the Poles from the Western Ukraine, Belarussia and Lithuania were deported (about 120000 people) to Kazakhstan. Germans from the Volga region and Chechens and Ingushs from Caucasus were forcibly resettled in Kazakhstan during the Second World War. Due to the development of the virgin lands in the 1950s and 1960s, more than one million inhabitants of Russia, Ukraine and Belarussia moved to Kazakhstan.

The fall of the Soviet Union in 1991 finally led Kazakhstan to national independence. The people of modern Kazakhstan now enjoy a period in which they are recovering or re-establishing their national identity, including their language and culture, which were suppressed and all but forgotten during the years of colonisation and oppression.

In 1995, to celebrate the history of Kazakhstan, the government established so-called 'friendship houses' in many regions (*oblasts*) as special venues to celebrate the diversity of nations and cultures living in that specific region of the country. In one of the nationwide forums, President Nazarbayev stated, 'we must work together to support the languages and cultures of all the peoples of Kazakhstan. No one should be discriminated against in their rights to use their own language and culture' (Tuymebayev et al., 2008, 459).

A 'trilingual' language policy has been part of this strategic development of the country (see Chapter 8). The first law on languages of Kazakhstan as of 22 September 1989 recognised Kazakh as the state language. Russian was initially considered to be a language of interethnic communication and is now recognised as an official language which is used on a par with Kazakh. One of the long-term strategic goals of the government is to increase the share of Kazakh-speaking citizens from 60% to 95% by 2020, and the share of Russian-speaking citizens is expected to reach 90%. The share of English-speaking citizens will constitute at least 20%.

Apart from developing national identity and national symbols of Kazakhstan, the government has been gradually breaking away from the planned economy of the Soviet regime. The nation has undergone multidimensional reforms in all fields of social and economic development. The strategy of economic growth has focused on developing a strong market economy (with an active role for government) and the attraction of foreign investment.

Developing a long-term vision for the nation, the government launched a number of strategic development programmes. One of them is the Industrial Innovation Development Strategy of the Republic of Kazakhstan for 2003–2015, which seeks sustainable development and economy diversification. The 'Kazakhstan 2030 Strategy' and the new '2050 Strategy' illustrate the longer-term strategic vision of the government. In 2000, the European Union recognised Kazakhstan as a market economy, and in 2002 this recognition was endorsed by the USA.

Emerging from this brutal past with a new-found identity and independence was itself no small political and economic achievement and is something that the country and its president look upon with justifiable pride. The achievements since independence in 1991 include the establishment of an independent currency, which broke Kazakhstan's dependency on the rouble; the declaration of Kazakhstan as a nuclear-free zone and the clearing out of one of the biggest stockpiles of nuclear weapons and materials in the world; the stamping out of the criminal gangs that for a period after independence terrorised many communities; a major economic recovery (following a period of economic collapse in the 1990s), which now makes Kazakhstan almost entirely independent of foreign aid; the adoption of a far-reaching programme of neo-liberal economic reforms; expanding investment in health and education (Kazakhstan now tops international league tables for participation in primary education); significant progress in rectifying one of the world's greatest environmental disasters, the drying up of the Aral Sea; and perhaps most impressively in a country with some 120 different nationalities, establishing the foundations for a culture of mutual respect between a diverse population – all in twenty years.

Notwithstanding all the achievements within the twenty years of national independence, there are questions in the minds of international observers as to the 'democratic' nature of Kazakhstan's political system. Not only this, but questions are posed about Kazakhstan's human rights record. It is also important, however, to bear in mind historical experience, the direction of movement and the challenges of any newborn state, let alone one with the sort of neighbours that surround Kazakhstan. As President Nazarbayev pointed out in a press conference following UK Prime Minister David Cameron's visit to Kazakhstan in July 2013:

> What should be taken into account is that . . . the first bill of rights was adopted in Great Britain in 1660, so parliamentary democracy is 300 years old . . . Of course our way should not be as long as that, but of course the direction of that way, of that path, I believe is very correct. So democracy is the outcome . . . the final goal, not the beginning. (Nazarbayev 2013)

These issues about Kazakhstan's political past and present and its future direction provide part of the context for educational reforms, but one of the convictions that is shared by all contributors to this book is the belief in the capacity of education to transform lives for the better; to equip people to think and to engage critically and creatively with society; to provide an intelligent and responsible political leadership for the future, to build the institutions that will expand people's 'capabilities' (Sen 1999), and enshrine their freedoms. The reforms we shall be discussing in this book include measures to expose Kazakhstan's teachers and young people to new ideas and experience and give them access to the best in international experience; to provide a new emphasis on developing critical thinking and on young people's capacity to think for themselves and apply the knowledge they have to novel conditions; measures to address the acknowledged inequalities in educational provision and achievement (especially those between rural and urban schools) as well as raising the overall level of achievement by international comparison; and to embed in people's minds and practices respect for the culturally and ethnically diverse population which makes up modern Kazakhstan. These seem to us to offer necessary if not sufficient conditions for progress towards a democratic as well as a flourishing society.

Kazakhstan's education system in brief

The development of the human capital of the nation through education is one of the priorities and challenges for Kazakhstan. According to UNESCO, the country reports adult and youth literacy rates of 99.7% and 99.8% respectively. Kazakhstan's primary and secondary education is free and mostly provided by public mainstream schools.

The role of preschool education is one of the urgent issues at hand. Political and educational leaders acknowledge that children who attend kindergartens are likely to be advanced at all levels of education and are more successful in life. As of 1 July 2010, the percentage of children receiving preschool education was about 40% compared to 90–100% in developed countries, but by 2013 this had risen to something in the region of 75%. The concern at this point is with the quality and not just the quantity of this provision.

In general, the private sector does not significantly occupy the education market; its share is merely 1.4% of all schooling organisations.

To date, there are 7667 schools in Kazakhstan with about 2.5 million pupils. 25% of schools are located in urban areas of the country which allocate almost a half of all pupils (48.3%), whereas 75% of rural schools account for another half. Upgrading school infrastructure is an important item on Kazakhstan's educational reform agenda. 146 new schools are going to be built in the near future in order to reduce the percentage of schools that are in an emergency condition from 3% to 1.5%. These new schools are also expected to reduce the percentage of schools which operate in three shifts from 1.3% to 0.1%. Rural schools will be provided with modern facilities and infrastructure.

There are different types of primary and secondary schools (in Kazakhstan these tend to be referred to together as 'secondary' education) which differ in terms of urban-and-rural classification and missions. Mainstream secondary schooling in Kazakhstan is made up for the most part of secondary comprehensive schools, gymnasiums and lyceums. There are also specialisation-oriented schools which have their specific missions of helping prospective school leavers towards their career choices. There is a network of schools for gifted children – the Darian schools – which has its branches in different regions of the country.

There are so-called ungraded schools, predominantly in rural areas, which represent mixed forms where, for example, fourth-graders would study in the same form with fifth-graders because there are not many pupils in each discrete grade. Almost every fourth teacher in Kazakhstan is working, and every sixth pupil is studying, in an ungraded school. It is recognised that the low quality of the education provided in many ungraded schools requires a strategic solution, and this has been emphasised in Kazakhstan's 'State Programme of Education Development for 2011–2020'.

Education in public schools is available through the medium of Kazakh, Russian and other languages represented by ethnic minorities. To date, half of schools (49.8%) use Kazakh as a medium of instruction and the rest are run in Russian (19%) and other mixed language programmes (31.2%).

The system of school education is experiencing a transition to a new paradigm of learner-centred approaches (promoted not least through the Centres of Excellence programme discussed in Chapter 5). According to new educational standards, school leavers should be able to search for and make meaning of information, be able to demonstrate critical thinking, and have skills for teamwork and independent lifelong learning.

The new network of Nazarbayev Intellectual Schools (NIS; see Chapter 4) has been established with the purpose of building schools of excellence supported by a state-funded, non-profit company and used for trying out new educational practices before their introduction in the public school system. NIS experience will be widely used in the coming years to update the school curricula content. A new educational programme will be introduced across mainstream schools starting at Grade 1 in 2015, and this will introduce new subjects such as 'Science Enquiry Projects' and elements of critical thinking skills. There will also be a strong focus on language (Kazakh, Russian and English) studies and ICT.

In accordance with the 'State Programme' the national testing system (see Chapters 6 and 7) has to be improved. Following the format of the Programme for International Student Assessment (PISA), exams will be aimed at the measuring of pupils' analytical skills rather than their demonstration of factual knowledge. The content of tasks, as well as the format of tests, of the national testing will be changed. The transition of national testing from knowledge-based assessment to competence-based assessment will be gradually carried out. The introduction of computer testing will be designed to reduce the room for cheating and other distorting factors.

The currently implemented reforms in the system, the current interest in raising standards to international levels and the pace of the development of education have created new requirements for teachers who can employ modern approaches to teaching, so a great deal of attention is being paid to the in-service training of teachers (see Chapter 5), and hopefully soon, pre-service teacher education.

To date, the majority (87.8%) of teachers out of the total number (286370, as of 2012) are holders of higher education degrees, whilst 11.7% completed only vocational training programmes. Annually, only 2.6% of new specialists join the young teachers' stream. One particular feature of the teaching workforce is that over 80% of the staff are women. Further, every fifth teacher in Kazakhstan is aged 50 or more, and 13% of teachers have up to 3 years of experience.

There are plans for the improvement of school governance by involving all stakeholders including pupils' families and the wider community, and by establishing boards of trustees and granting schools more autonomy. The Ministry of Education and Science (MoES) is also seeking to introduce a model of per-capita funding in place of the current financial system based on local taxes, which reinforces the gap between richer and poorer parts of the country. (The final chapter in the book sets out the next phase of educational development in more detail.)

One thing that becomes clear even from this brief outline is that schools in Kazakhstan are at the centre of a multiplicity of demands for change, most of them centrally driven, even if they are a response to locally expressed frustrations or dissatisfaction.

The collaborative research project

A number of core chapters in this book are derived from a piece of research carried out during 2012 and 2013 on 'School reform and internationalisation in Kazakhstan'. The research grew out of a partnership between the University of Cambridge Faculty of Education (FoE), University of Pennsylvania (UPenn) Graduate School of Education and the newly established Graduate School of Education of Nazarbayev University (NU) in Kazakhstan's capital, Astana. The university was and is being grown through international partnerships between the schools within the university and selected international institutions. The Cambridge FoE and the University of Pennsylvania Graduate School of Education advised the newly established NU Graduate School of Education on appointments, on course development and administrative process, admissions, and even the organisation and equipping of teaching spaces. The partners were also tasked to help build research capacity. They organised a few workshops, but decided at an early stage that the best way to achieve this was through a thorough collaboration involving NU staff at every stage of the development and conduct of research, through to conference presentations and publication. UPenn's contribution to the partnership focused on higher education and Cambridge's contribution, including the research, focused on the school system.

Membership of the school-focused research team fluctuated a little over the two years, but the core group consisted of six staff from the Faculty of Education, three to six staff from NU and, for fieldwork in 2013, three staff from NIS.

In 2012, most of the Cambridge team was new to Kazakhstan and they conducted a scoping study informed primarily by document research and interviews with key players around the central organs of educational administration. The aim was to understand something of the policy context and to identify the national and international sources of policy and their rationale. In 2013 the team decided to look at the system from the other end of the reform process, through the eyes and experience of teachers and school directors who had to implement the reforms, and those in the local administrative system and in-service training institutions who were part of the process of 'transmitting' or 'translating' messages from the centre to the periphery.

To this end the researchers divided into three teams and went to locations in three very different parts of Kazakhstan: to Shymkent in the south, deep in the heartland of the Kazakh people, to Pavlodar in the north (mainly Russian, but with, in one locality they visited, a significant Ukrainian population), and to Aktau in the west on the coast of the Caspian Sea. The researchers focused in each location on two schools, one urban and one small rural school, as well as on the administrative and training organisations that were the vehicles for translating national policy to them. The aim was to produce rough-hewn case studies of the schools in the context of educational reform in their localities. These would then be available to all members of the research team for cross-site analysis, leading to the production of thematic analytic papers grounded in the case material.

In advance of two periods of fieldwork in Kazakhstan the team agreed amongst themselves on the central research questions which they would seek to address through the research. These focused on:

- issues to do with the 'translation' of educational reform from the centre to the periphery of the educational system

- issues to do with the translation of educational reform into classroom practice
- the role of school leaders in the development and implementation of educational reform
- issues to do with the professional identity of teachers and their views of their roles in educational reform.

Each team agreed to collect data that would help members of all teams to address the research questions that most interested them. The data was in the form of documents, photographic evidence, transcripts of semi-structured individual and group interviews with people at all levels in the school and local system, and questionnaires administered to both teachers and students. With this substantial data set to hand (coded using NVivo software), they could then interrogate the material and write about the issues that interested them. Nine chapters in this book are drawn from this work.

The main themes and contributions

Part 1: The recent history of educational reform in Kazakhstan

The book begins with three chapters that put contemporary education in the context of the post-independence history of educational reform in Kazakhstan.

In Chapter 1, **Educational reform in Kazakhstan: The First Decade of Independence**, Natallia Yakavets provides an overview of education initiatives in Kazakhstan in the period immediately following the dissolution of the Soviet Union in 1991. The new state attempted to overhaul both the structure of its education system and much of the content of what was taught. Education policymakers wanted to 'nationalise' the curriculum to reflect the cultural and ethnic history of Kazakhstan, while simultaneously 'internationalising' it to enable the country to be competitive in a world economy – two themes that continue to shape educational policy in Kazakhstan to this day. However, the involvement of international organisations in education policy for the first time brought a clash between neo-liberal ideas and local traditions and practice. This chapter offers an account of these educational reforms and transitions, drawing on primary evidence from interviews with the key policymakers, scholars and others involved in educational reforms in the last two decades. This has been supplemented by examination of official educational policy documents, decrees published by the Ministry of Education and Sciences, laws, reports by international and bilateral organisations, reports from a number of studies, and available statistical information.

In Chapter 2, **Educational Reform in Kazakhstan: Entering the World Arena**, Natallia Yakavets and Makpal Dzhadrina take the history of school reform in Kazakhstan forward into the first decade of the 21st century. During this period, improving the quality of education was perceived as a key political priority for the country's economic development. The chapter highlights strong government intervention and substantial investment in educational initiatives. It offers a detailed analysis of the (anticipated) transition to a 12-year schooling model, revision of the curriculum and the effects of involvement in international monitoring studies. There is also a brief overview of the ideas underpinning the initiation of trilingual policy and the introduction of a new assessment system, namely the Unified National Test. The analysis draws on primary evidence from research interviews with key policymakers, scholars and international consultants, and data from previous surveys, as well as personal reflection by Makpal Dzhadrina on her involvement in some of these initiatives. The chapter ends with a discussion of the clash between the ambition to match world education standards and local realities inherited from the past.

In Chapter 3, **Educational Reform in Kazakhstan: The Contemporary Policy Agenda**, David Bridges, Olena Fimyar and Natallia Yakavets bring the story of school education reform up to the present. The chapter begins with a review of key strategic documents which provide the framework for contemporary policy and then introduces five key areas of contemporary development: the expansion of preschool education; the extension of secondary education up to 12 years; the implementation of trilingual education (see Chapter 8); the piloting of E-Learning; and a massive programme of in-service education focused on new approaches to teaching and learning conducted under the Centre of Excellence (CoE) programme (see Chapter 5). All these initiatives have been undertaken in the mainstream schools (albeit initially as pilot programmes in some cases), but a parallel and in some ways more radical set of developments are also under development in a suite of elite schools operated under what became the Autonomous Education Organisation NIS (see Chapter 4). As we write, NIS and MoES are addressing the not insignificant challenge of 'translating' its experience to the benefit of mainstream schools.

The first three chapters, then, provide a narrative of educational reform in Kazakhstan between 1991 and 2013 and thus a context for more detailed accounts of key elements of contemporary development that follow in the main body of the book.

Part 2: Changing educational culture and practices

This next section starts with what is in an important sense the flagship for contemporary educational innovation, which is the Autonomous Education Organisation, Nazarbayev Intellectual Schools. The title reflects both the high expectations that are vested in NIS and the speed of change that is required (and which has become a feature of its organisational culture).

Chapter 4, **Implementing Radical Change: Nazarbayev Intellectual Schools as Agents of Change**, by Kulyash Shamshidinova, Nazipa Ayubayeva and David Bridges, explains how what is effectively a parallel system of public schools came to be established in the wake of disappointment at the failure of MoES to introduce more radical change in the system, and discusses the significance of its status as an 'autonomous' educational organisation. It illustrates, in particular, the variety of ways in which, from the beginning, NIS drew on international experience and international partners in developing more radical approaches to change, while at the same time selecting and tailoring any imported material to valued or significant features of Kazakhstan's own educational, social and cultural traditions. (As ever we observe the dynamic of the twin demands for internationalisation and the cultivation of national identity). The chapter explains some of the key innovative features of education in the Intellectual Schools, features that might perhaps be extended to mainstream schools in line with NIS's mission. The authors acknowledge, however, that it will be neither possible nor perhaps desirable to 'translate' everything that has been developed in schools that are privileged centres for the education of the 'gifted and talented' to other schools that are much less well-resourced and designed to serve students with a much wider range of ability. The chapter ends with a short account of NIS's plans for this process of translation (the model for which is discussed in Chapter 14 on transferability and NIS schools).

Alongside NIS's development of a platform of innovative schools the same organisation has also initiated a large scale programme of in-service training for teachers across the system, designed to prepare them for significant changes in their approaches to teaching and learning: the CoE programme. The authors of Chapter 5 on **Centres of Excellence: Systemwide Transformation of Teaching Practice** have all been directly involved in the development and implementation of this programme, and some have also been involved in researching its progress. The CoE teacher education programme was designed to provide sustainable pedagogical changes that could be 'rolled out' from the centre to the periphery of the education system and reach the majority of children in classrooms across Kazakhstan. This involved a cascade model of training – a model that is sometimes seen as an unreliable one, but the chapter illustrates how the team sought to overcome the shortcomings of a cascade training model.

Central to the development of the CoE programme was the understanding that education reform 'at scale' means that deep and consequential changes need to take place in classroom practice. Deep changes go beyond simply tinkering with procedures and structures and usually involve altering teachers' beliefs about the norms and pedagogical practices of the classroom. It is these values and beliefs, embedded in a particular educational and professional *culture*, which the CoE programme sets out to change as a condition for changing more readily observable aspects of educational practice.

All the chapters in this section are occupied in one way or another with the challenge of changing not just superficial aspects of behaviour but a whole educational culture – and perhaps no force is more powerful in shaping that culture than the system of assessment, and more especially the high-stakes assessments that determine, for example, whether a student is able to proceed to higher education. Two laws of education have a universality which approximates to the laws of Physics: (1) that 'there is no curriculum development without teacher development', and (2) that 'assessment will trump curriculum in shaping the priorities of teachers and learners'. In Kazakhstan it is the UNT, in particular, that exercises this power (though the new entrance examination for NU is already functioning in a similar way) and progressively becomes the focus of the attention of teachers and learners, and this is why we give this and other key elements of the national testing system attention here.

In Chapter 6, **The Culture and Practice of Assessment in Kazakhstan: The Unified National Test, Past and Present**, Liz Winter, Cristina Rimini, Arailym Soltanbekova and Madina Tynybayeva focus in particular on the UNT (Unified National Test) taken at the end of secondary school. The chapter sets this in the context of wider considerations about assessment practices in Kazakhstan historically, socially and in relation to international practices. The UNT consists of 125 multi-choice questions that are expected to cover the whole range of the secondary school curriculum. It serves in particular as an entry qualification for higher education, but also acts as the most important record of a student's achievement in school (for those who continue to this point). In addition, teachers are appraised and a school's success is measured by students' UNT results. The chapter describes the UNT and compares it with other European qualifications. The comparison illustrates how it falls short in preparing students for lifelong learning and the development of 21st-century skills and competences. A short section on other forms of assessment within Kazakhstan is also included.

In Chapter 7, **The Culture and Practice of Assessment in Kazakhstan: an Alternative Model and the Future**, the same authors continue the discussion of the culture of assessment in Kazakhstan by contrasting what is happening in the mainstream schools with the radically different methods of assessment being developed within the NIS system. In NIS, a strategic international partnership has helped move thinking towards a whole new approach towards assessment. This includes criterion-based assessment, formative techniques, more extended responses and even some practical assessment assignments.

The chapter culminates with a discussion of how the UNT shapes behaviour in classrooms. In effect, it restricts not only students' critical thinking, free communication, creativity and methods of working, but also impacts badly upon the professionalism of teachers and undermines current reforms in pedagogy that are being promoted under, for example, the COE programme (Chapter 5). The chapter argues for better co-ordination between different departments of government, more consistency between these different initiatives and the wider dissemination of NIS assessment practices to the mainstream of education in Kazakhstan.

One of the key elements of national policy and by extension educational policy in Kazakhstan is its commitment to the development of its people's use and competence in three languages: Kazakh, Russian and English. In Chapter 8, **Three in One: Trilingualism in Policy and Educational Practice**, Peeter Mehisto, Assel Kambatyrova and Khalida Nurseitova address the educational dimensions of this area of policy and practice which is intimately associated with Kazakhstan's very identity, with its social cohesion and with its future prosperity.

The authors describe how over the past 100 years Kazakhstan has undergone a considerable demographic shift. Ethnic Kazakhs, after having been for decades a minority, are now again the majority. Demographics, among other factors, have influenced language knowledge. Kazakh is the state language, but in the majority of urban areas, Russian is the most widely-used language. Although the strengthening of Kazakh remains an important national objective, the government has set a target to achieve high levels of trilingualism. The target is for 95% of the population to speak Kazakh, 90% to speak Russian and 20% to speak English by 2020.

Ambitious plans are being implemented to meet these trilingualism targets. Two universities are mandated to take the lead in preparing teachers for trilingual education. A total of 130 centres have been created where people can learn both Kazakh and English. A 30-volume bilingual specialised dictionary is under development. A system has been created for assessing knowledge of the state language. A scholarship programme supports graduate and postgraduate students in studying abroad, and teachers in undertaking internships to improve their language skills. Education is expected to play a central role in achieving trilingualism targets. Trilingual education is currently being piloted in 200 preschools and two sets of secondary schools.

Government officials and stakeholders reported in three case studies in three regions of the country that they are generally speaking supportive of trilingual education. Many express concern about a shortage of qualified teachers, professional development opportunities and learning resources. Some schools are finding their own solutions to those challenges. When discussing trilingual education most respondents focus primarily on the learning of English. This suggests that Kazakh and Russian may require further attention. In addition, the authors of this chapter suggest, language learning targets could be better defined to guide the development of curricula and learning resources. Knowledge amongst officials and educators about the investments and practices required to achieve high degrees of trilingualism needs to be improved

The three reference points of the Soviet/ Russian, the Kazakh and the international, (the last mediated in particular today through the medium of the English language), shape national identity and, as we have seen in the previous chapter, language policy in Kazakhstan. They also shape educational understanding in interesting ways, as Olena Fimyar explains in Chapter 9, **'Soviet', 'Kazakh' and 'World-Class' in the Contemporary Construction of Educational Understanding and Practice in Kazakhstan**. This chapter offers an insight into the process of the construction of contemporary educational policies and practices in Kazakhstan by focusing on three interrelated concepts which often emerge in the discussion of educational issues in the country: the 'Soviet', the 'Kazakh' and the 'World-class'. Drawing on two strategic policy documents – 'State Programme of Education Development for 2011–2020' and 'Autonomous Education Organisation "Nazarbayev Intellectual Schools" 2020 Development Strategy' – and a series of research interviews, the chapter explores the meaning of, the effects of, and the relationships between the three concepts. The chapter is particularly interested in what processes, aspirations and ideas these concepts aim to represent and what meanings those working in different parts of the education service attach to them.

The chapter starts by reflecting on the changing nature of Kazakhstani society since independence, paying particular attention to growing disparities between educational opportunities in rural and urban areas. It then moves to analyse the *definitions of education* and the *model of the student* and the concepts of 'the Kazakh' and 'the World-class' embedded in these definitions. The references to the 'Soviet', which abound in research interviews, are explored, and the chapter concludes by providing an account of the relationships between the three concepts. The discussion provides opportunities for critique of the concepts that define the purpose of the educational transformation and an extension of the analysis of *policy rationalities* in the context of the Newly Independent States offered by the author in one of her earlier publications (see Fimyar 2010).

Some of the issues to do with equity and inclusion in Kazakhstan – notably those related to ethnic and linguistic diversity and those related to the gap in educational achievement between rural and urban areas – are clearly established on the political agenda even if there remain some major challenges. Kazakhstan has, however, been slower to engage with what are from most points of view outmoded and unjust approaches to the education of children with disabilities and special educational needs, who often remain stigmatised and excluded from mainstream educational institutions.

In Chapter 10, **Towards Inclusive Education: Swimming against the Tide of Educational Reform** Martyn Rouse, Natallia Yakavets and Anel Kulakhmetova explore some of the reasons why children continue to be marginalised from schooling in Kazakhstan. The authors draw on national and international reports on educational inclusion and diversity in Kazakhstan and on research evidence from recent small-scale research studies as part of the, 'School reform and internationalisation' project. The chapter starts with a brief overview of the terms 'inclusion' and 'inclusive education' developed in the international literature. Then the authors discuss the way in which, in Kazakhstan as well as in many post-Soviet countries, children with special education needs are educated within the traditional approach known as defectology. This involves education in special 'correctional' schools and/

or at home under the supervision of trained specialists called defectologists. There are still examples when children with special educational needs are stigmatised and socially excluded. There is an argument for changing the whole framework for responding to disability from one couched in terms of *defectology* to one conceived of in terms of *inclusion,* and that is seen as a new moral imperative. The chapter considers some of the substantial and competing forces that are currently affecting efforts to develop inclusive education in Kazakhstan and concludes with some tentative suggestions that might help the development of inclusion in Kazakhstan in the future. As with many of the issues discussed in this book, such changes require a radical reconceptualisation of the educational task and a change of educational culture.

It is sometimes tempting to examine the operation of educational policy from the relative comfort of the capital city and the offices of government, but no one can fail to acknowledge that any change emanating from the centre has ultimately to be interpreted and implemented (or not) at the local level in schools and classrooms – and in these domains it is the response and conviction of school directors and teachers that really matters. So the last two chapters of this section focus, first on the role of school directors and, then, on an innovative programme designed to engage teachers in the process of change.

In Chapter 11 David Frost, Olena Fimyar, Natallia Yakavets and Darkhan Bilyalov examine **The Role of the School Director in Educational Reform in Kazakhstan**. This chapter outlines an initial exploration of the role of school directors in the process of educational reform in Kazakhstan, and is based on data from research conducted between 2011 and 2013 in Kazakhstan. A scoping study in the capital of Kazakhstan, Astana generated an analytical framework for a more in-depth study conducted through two field visits to the three regions of the country. The research teams wanted to explore how the reform translated from the centre to the periphery and the challenges of disseminating key messages throughout the wide education system. The chapter examines the range of approaches adopted by school directors in responding to the challenge of managing change within the context of the current education reform programme. The chapter concludes by providing a number of suggestions for policy and practice.

In Chapter 12, **The Role of the Teacher in Educational Reform in Kazakhstan: Teacher Enquiry as a Vehicle for Change**, Colleen McLaughlin, Ros McLellan, Michael Fordham, with Andrew Chandler-Grevatt and Alison Daubney, examine a 'bottom up' approach to teacher professional development and change: a collaborative action research programme within the NIS schools. They present preliminary data and argue that there are signs of impact upon both collaboration and practice. Three elements affect the programme: cultural differences, the nature of professional learning and practice, and the reform process. Facilitators need to work in all three areas in order to understand and develop the practice of action research.

Part 3: The international and intranational translation of educational policy and practice

Running through the whole story of educational reform in Kazakhstan have been two themes: one to do with the *international* transfer or 'borrowing' of educational policy; the other, in what is still a highly centralised system as far as education is concerned, is the *intranational* transfer of policy and practice 'from centre to periphery'. We have seen too the major challenge that faces AEO NIS in taking its experience – much of it garnered from 'the global educational space' first into its own system and thence into the mainstream schools. The next section of the book offers three discussions of these 'transfer', 'translation' or 'transmission' practices.

In Chapter 13, David Bridges, Kairat Kurakbayev and Assel Kambatyrova offer an analysis under the title **Lost – and Found – in Translation? Interpreting the Processes of the International and Intranational Translation of Educational Policy and Practice in Kazakhstan.** This chapter addresses issues raised in both the international and intranational 'translation' of educational policy and practice. It examines, in particular, the changes that take place in such translation and the different ways in which these changes are interpreted and represented in the literature and in political discourse – as 'subversion', as 'policy hijacking', as 'brand-name piracy' but also as 'indigenisation'. The examination helps to explain, first, why such changes are inevitable, given the layers of interpretation through which they are filtered and the contested and unstable character of many of the policies and practices in the first place. But the chapter draws on first learning theory and then the theoretical work on literary translation to suggest a more positive response to what might be regarded as the 'co-construction' of meaning. In particular, it suggests, those near to the destinations of such translations can and do play a creative role in reshaping policies and practices in ways that are better suited to local circumstances. There is meaning to be found and new meanings to be created through acts of translation as well as meaning to be lost. Indeed this argues for retaining a place in educational development for exactly such local creativity and initiative.

In Chapter 14, **Transferability and the Nazarbayev Intellectual Schools: Exploring Models of Practice Transfer**, Alan Ruby and Colleen McLaughlin describe the way in which NIS, the network of publicly funded schools set up across Kazakhstan, are designed to act as what they describe as 'a beta site for innovation, experimentation and evaluation of educational practices'. In the tradition of Dewey's laboratory school they are to identify and model good practice. Once efficacy of a practice has been established it is to be transferred to the public schools of the nation. The chapter examines ways in which other educational innovations have been purposefully shared with large numbers of schools, offers a framework for the categorisation of different forms of dissemination or transfer and suggests which form is most suitable for NIS.

We stay with the theme of translation and change processes for the third chapter in this section in which Olena Fimyar writes of **Translating Pedagogical 'Excellence' into Three Languages or How Kazakhstani Teachers 'Change'**. Drawing on the works in policy sociology and comparative education, this contribution attempts to conceptualise and reflect on the process of 'change' and the translation of 'change' in the teaching profession in Kazakhstan. Using the establishment and operation of CoE – Kazakhstan's large-scale teacher professional development programme (see Chapter 5) – as an entry point for discussion, the chapter identifies critical turns in the discourse of teacher professionalism in Kazakhstan. The chapter is particularly interested in how macro-level change is experienced and enacted by the actors participating in the CoE programme. While keeping the focus of analysis on discourse and its enactment, the author continuously reflects on how the trilingual policy environment impacts upon the roles of the researcher, translators and the study participants. This contribution draws primarily but not exclusively on documentary data which includes trainees' accounts, official and media websites and publications. This is done with the view that the data produced in monolingual settings puts less pressure on the actors to perform the 'change' and speak *to* policy rather than reflect on 'change' and speak *of* policy. In advancing its argument the paper employs four categories of analysis: *the times of 'change', the model of 'change', the agents of 'change'* and *the experiences of 'change'*. These categories are then applied to the data collected in the three languages in order to demonstrate how the educational change is conceptualised and experienced by these three groups of participants. With its focus on the issues around language, translation and teacher professionalism, the paper contributes to the discussion of 'policy trilinguliam', which is a feature of any policy enacted in multilingual settings (Steiner-Khamsi 2012, 468).

The Way Forward

In the final chapter Aslan Sarinzhipov (the recently appointed minister of education, Republic of Kazakhstan) and Alan Ruby (University of Pennsylvania, Graduate School of Education and an advisor to the minister) look **Towards the Next Stages of Educational Reform in Kazakhstan**, though they remind us that the future is shaped by the past as well as being guided by the aspirations of its people. They identify the particular challenges offered by the increasing size of the school population and the demand for an expansion in the quantity of educational provision at the same time as the need for an improvement in the quality. This is a particular concern in the area of preschool education, where there is a requirement for some radical changes in approach, but little locally available experience of high quality preschool education on which to draw.

The next few years will see, as earlier chapters in this book have anticipated, the rolling out of a new curriculum for schools and new approaches to both in-school and end-of-school assessment. Layered over other curriculum changes will be a strong focus on the development of students' competence in three languages (Kazakh, Russian and English) which will include in some cases at least using all three languages as media of instruction.

There is widespread recognition of the gap between the opportunities available to students in urban schools and those available to students in what are often small, isolated and ungraded rural schools, and it will be a political and educational priority to do more to close this gap by enhancing what is available to rural students and the teachers who teach them.

Looking further ahead, the authors identify two key issues that are finance related. The first is the *stavka* system of teacher pay, which contributes to the low pay/low status culture of teaching but also provides disincentives to the sort of collaborative culture and extended professionalism that modern approaches to teaching and learning require. The second is the system which links school income to local taxation and hence reinforces the gap between richer and poorer parts of the education system.

Finally the authors turn to concerns about the character of initial or pre-service teacher education and its lack of engagement with the practicalities of teaching or with the forms of pedagogy demanded by the changing curriculum of schools. They urge the need for fresh thinking and alternative models of teacher preparation.

Conclusion

This book focuses attention on a unique setting for educational change, on the case of Kazakhstan – a country little known or understood outside its own region but one that is marking an increasing presence in international circles. The individual case provides, however, a window upon themes and issues which invite and receive much wider international attention from political scientists, economists and the field of cultural studies, as well as from education: the re-establishment of independent nation states after periods of colonial (and more particularly in this case, Soviet) domination; the cultivation of national identity amongst a linguistically and ethnically diverse population; the impact of neo-liberal economic policies on educational systems; 'entering the world arena'; 'policy borrowing'; and the management of change.

Our lens on these and related issues is provided by the recent and contemporary story of educational reform in Kazakhstan. We hope it is one that brings these wider issues into focus.

REFERENCES

MoES (Ministry of Education and Science) (2013). *National Report: Statistics of Education in the Republic of Kazakhstan*. Astana: Ministry of Education and Science of the Republic of Kazakhstan, National Centre for Educational Statistics and Assessment.

Nazarbayev (2013). 'Kazakhstan visit: Prime Minister's press conference with Nursultan Nazarbayev'. 1 July. www.gov.uk/government/speeches/kazakhstan-visit-prime-minis-ters-press-conference-with-nursultan-nazarbayev (retrieved 30 October 2013).

Robbins, C. (2007). *In Search of Kazakhstan: The Land that Disappeared*. London: Profile Books.

Sen, A. (1999). *Development as Freedom*. Oxford: Oxford University Press.

Steiner-Khamsi, G. (2012). 'The Global/Local Nexus in Comparative Policy Studies: Analysing the Triple Bonus System in Mongolia Over Time'. *Comparative Education* 48:4, 455–71.

Tuymebayev, Zh., **Atamkulov**, B., **Smirnov**, A., **Syzdykov**, M., **Tsarev**, D., **Tuyakbayev**, S., **Sagintayeva**, A., **Ordabayev**, S., **Syzdykova**, Ye., **Izbaskanova**, K., **Zhumagaliyeva**, A., **Sarazhanov** A. and **Eraliyeva**, A. (2008). *Kazakhstan: Country and People, Nature, History, Economy, Culture*. Almaty: Taimas Printhouse.

PART ONE:
The Recent History of Educational Reform in Kazakhstan

1 EDUCATIONAL REFORM IN KAZAKHSTAN: The First Decade of Independence

Natallia Yakavets (University of Cambridge, Faculty of Education)

Introduction

After the fall of the Soviet Union in 1991, Kazakhstan went through substantial changes in political, social and economic life which brought about changes in value orientations and educational expectations. Central here was the establishment of a market economy, and this was widely seen as having important implications for the education system, which still operated very much on Soviet lines.

The Soviet model had brought important benefits:

- free education for all children
- a well-developed infrastructure for educational provision and administration
- well-qualified teachers
- many research institutes, universities and regional scientific centres, encouraging high levels of Science and Mathematics knowledge.

One of the most distinctive features of the Soviet educational system at the pre-college level was the attempt to provide uniform Science and Mathematics instruction for all students up to the completion of secondary school (Ailes and Rushing 1991, 109–10). The content of education during the Soviet era, however, was highly specialised, driven by the employment demands of a massive command economy. Education was used to reinforce state philosophy in a much more narrow and insistent manner than is characteristic of broader notions of civics education. Mathematics and Sciences were emphasised, while the Humanities and Social Sciences were laden heavily with Marxist-Leninist ideology (Kanaev and Daun 2002). DeYoung (2006) notes that even Science was not immune to the ideological filter:

> Another critical component of Soviet educational philosophy was trust in the scientific method and of the teaching and learning of 'facts'. It was believed

that nature and society could be scientifically understood via the collection and presentation of data, and that the 'correct' interpretation was available via the teacher, who presented the facts armed with the theory of Marxism-Leninism (DeYoung 2006, 500).

Among other important features of the Soviet system was the role of the Russian language as a common bond uniting the multi-ethnic population of the USSR, Kazakhstan included. As Kreindler (1991, 219–31) describes, the Communist party supported Russian not only as a common *lingua franca*, but also as a key component of a common cultural foundation. Russian was assigned a central role in fostering rapprochement (*sblizhenie*) of the many nationalities inhabiting the USSR. According to official Soviet ideology, linguistic and other differences among nationalities in the USSR would progressively weaken and eventually lead to their merger (*sliianie*). In this regard, native languages and literature were seen as less important than Russian language and literature during the Soviet period. Despite the existence of a long liberal local tradition in pedagogical philosophy (e.g. Ushinsky 1949; Vygotsky 1978), there was uniform application of pedagogical practices. The creation of school lessons, textbooks and teaching manuals was highly centralised (DeYoung 2006, 500). As already noted, the educational emphasis was often on 'factology': the learning of facts and figures, rather than on creative thinking and problem solving (UNICEF 1999, 8). From the elementary level through to higher education, the Soviet educational process was heavily based upon prescriptive and rote learning. Questions directed to students generally sought to elicit 'correct answers' – in other words those found in the textbooks – not the students' interpretation or judgment with respect to the presented material (Ailes and Rushing 1991, 120). After independence, in Kazakhstan and elsewhere, this approach did not equip students with the practical skills required by the new market economy.

Challenges in researching educational reforms in post-Soviet and post-Socialist contexts

Educational reforms in the post-Soviet and post-Socialist contexts are somewhat difficult to research due to:

- challenges around conceptualising educational change within a context of societal transformation
- incomplete information and its unreliability
- variations in 'outsider' and 'insider' interpretations of events.

It is possible to distinguish between two broad categories of studies. The first applies particular models of educational change and concentrates primarily on understanding planned change at different organisational levels, such as those of the region, the district and the school (see Fullan 2001; Fullan 2003; Polyzoi and Dneprov 2003; Polyzoi and Nazarenko 2004; Elliott and Tudge 2007; Webster et al. 2011; Loogma et al. 2012). The second group of studies focuses on educational transfer, in particular the complementary practices of 'policy borrowing' and 'policy lending' (Steiner-Khamsi et al. 2006). Steiner-Khamsi (2004) interprets policy borrowing as a strategy that is used to re-solve protracted domestic policy conflict, and suggests that it results from a re-orientation in transnational educational space (Silova 2005). Furthermore, borrowing, whether at the level of discourse or actuality, has a certification effect on domestic policy talk (Steiner-Khamsi 2004). Phillips and Ochs (2003, 451–2) postulate 'borrowing' as a sequence of four director stages:

- cross-national attraction (impulses and externalising potential)
- decision
- implementation
- internationalisation/indigenisation.

They assert that policy borrowing refers to 'the conscious adoption in one context of policy observed in another' (Phillips and Ochs 2004, 774).

Steiner-Khamsi et al. (2006, 218) distinguish between three common phenomena:

- Very often the language of the reform is borrowed, but not the actual re-form (Steiner-Khamsi 2005)
- Borrowing occurs even when there is no apparent need; that is, when similar reforms already exist in the local context (Steiner-Khamsi and Quist 2000)
- If the actual reform is borrowed, it is always selectively borrowed and sometimes locally re-conceptualised to the extent that there is little simi-larity left between the copy and the original.

The second group also involves studies which examine the role of 'develop-ment assistance' in shaping, or at least striving to influence, educational re-form in the former Soviet countries (Gilbert 1998; Steiner-Khamsi et al. 2006; Asanova 2006; 2007; Silova and Steiner-Khamsi 2008; Takala and Piattoeva 2012). Silova (2005, 53), in her research on Central Asian states, claims that 'travelling policies have been "hijacked" by policy makers and used for their own purposes'. These studies are to a varying degree based on personal ex-perience, document analysis and interviews with key actors.

International observers who visited Central Asian countries in the immediate aftermath of independence from the Soviet Union argued that there were three general types of educational 'crises' in newly independent countries during the 1990s: expenditure decline, decentralisation and destabilisation, and 'structural anomalies' (Heyneman 1998). The next part of the chapter will explore these crises in turn.

Expenditure decline

In the Soviet Union, the central authorities played a vital role in the educational development of Kazakhstan, by supplying economic resources to these areas and by providing models and infrastructure for educational development (e.g. Silova 2005; DeYoung 2006; Asanova 2006; 2007a; Takala and Piattoeva 2012). Kazakhstan inherited a comprehensive educational system from the Soviet period which included: kindergartens, a network of comprehensive schools, boarding schools, vocational schools, special education schools and schools for gifted and talented children. Following Kazakhstan's independence, this educational network started to deteriorate as public expenditure on education rapidly declined. The first decade of independence in Kazakhstan witnessed a substantial decrease in economic performance, employment prospects, health services and gender equity, and there was also a general decline in public spending on education at a time when there was a need for the adaptation of education systems to the new economic and social structures (e.g. Asian Development Bank (ADB) 1995; Heyneman 1998; Silova 2005; DeYoung 2006; Shagdar 2006). One respondent in our research study in 2012 noted:

> There were difficult times because the system was ruined and a new system was going to be built . . . (Participant C, Nazarbayev Intellectual Schools; NIS)

Economic and fiscal crises during the process of transition led to severe cutbacks in education during the 1990s and it was difficult to provide basic education for all children, let alone undertake a fundamental reform of the system (ADB 1995; Silova 2005, 2009). As one respondent in our research interviews noted:

> . . . And in this situation, under great financial difficulties, when there was no money, we had to maintain our schools and support their heating. So, we encountered a problem of school closing . . . (Participant B, NIS)

Another respondent said:

> We had a problem with children in places where there were no schools. We organised transportation for children. We did not have any money, but we had to find them. (Participant J, NIS)

In Kazakhstan public expenditure on education as a proportion of gross domestic product (GDP) declined by more than half – from 6.8% in 1990 to 2.9% of a much smaller GDP in 1994 (ADB 2002), not exceeding 3.6% after 2000 (NHDR 2004). Predictably, a lack of investment in general secondary education was reflected in rundown facilities, shortage of school buildings and furniture, outmoded equipment, lack of educational materials for teachers and textbooks for students (Shagdar 2006; Silova 2009) and lower school participation rates. Teachers' salaries were very low; their payment was often delayed, and as a consequence many qualified teachers resigned. By 1993 one seventh of the teaching staff who were in the system in 1990 had left education, many of them to seek more lucrative employment elsewhere(ADB 1995; DeYoung and Nadirbekyzy 1997; DeYoung 2006). Government support for public schools fell from 8% of the nation's budget in 1990 to 3.6% in 1995 (Jurinov 1996). The monthly salary of a teacher with a normal teaching load in 1995 was 2700 tenge, or about US$41. Yet, teachers were rarely paid on time, and salaries were delivered two or three months late (DeYoung and Nadirbekyzy 1997, 76).

After the peak of the crisis (1991–4), the education system had to search for ways to overcome financial difficulties and diversify its sources of funding. New principles of financing were introduced by the government to improve the education system along market-economy lines, such as the introduction of a funding mechanism using a standard rate per student method and education grants and preferential credits for higher education students.

According to the ADB report, in Kazakhstan 'there was virtually no new construction and little maintenance of educational facilities and equipment' (ADB 1995, 4). In the 1990s, more than half of the country's schools were operating on two or even three shifts per day (ADB 1995). Resources were scarce for the import of textbooks, while a viable domestic textbook production capacity was slow to develop (80% of all textbooks and instructional materials were produced in Moscow before 1991).

The relatively high quality of education achieved prior to independence was being rapidly eroded. A respondent from our 2012 research study commented:

> The educational system, of course, did not perish, did not die . . . but it took some very unmanageable changes. (Participant B, NIS)

There was a decrease in the educational achievement of students and growing regional differences within the country. Students in rural and remote areas scored significantly lower than their counterparts in urban schools, school enrolment rates were decreasing, and student drop-out rates were rising (see UNDP Report 1996; Chapman et al. 2005; Silova 2005; Silova et al. 2007). The challenge for the new Kazakhstani government, with no prior experience of independence, was to avoid further disintegration of the education system and to recapture previous levels of educational access and quality, while at the same time adapting to new economic and political forms of organisation. As it was acknowledged:

> That is, it is as if there has been no conscious reform strategy in the first five to seven years. In this chaos was this slogan: 'The educational system ought to fit in the market economy' . . . The private educational establishments and new types of educational establishments, like gymnasiums, lyceums started appearing. (International Adviser, C)

During the same period state employment declined. In Kazakhstan, while nearly 2.2 million jobs disappeared in state enterprises and organisations, over 1 million jobs were created in the private sector, although many of them were part-time (ADB 1995).

Indeed, a 'transformational shock' after the collapse of the USSR was observed in many post-Soviet countries. At the same time there was a growing demand for skills in languages, computers, business, economy, banking and accountancy services. These tendencies demanded a general education system with a flexible curriculum and the capacity to provide pupils with skills required by the market economy.

Decentralisation and destabilisation

According to international observers, decentralisation and destabilisation emerged in most post-Soviet republics due to the disagreement among education and other government policy makers, some of whom called for radical change in administrative and governance practices (ADB 1995; Heyneman 1998).

The Law on Education (1992) established the Ministry of Education (MoE) as the central state body that defines and executes state policy in the field of education. (It later became known as the Ministry of Education and Science – MoES.) The ministry provides strategic planning and funding, including the preparation of draft education budgets and the setting of national guidelines and standards, curricula and syllabi; preparing state orders concerning the training of specialists; providing assistance in the organisation of the educational process in the Kazakh language and establishing international agreement on educational issues. In accordance with legislation, MoES supervises educational institutions funded from the regional budgets.

However, when calls for new practices were made, there were few funds to support different organisational strategies and little power at ministry level to prevail upon the remaining school bureaucracies at the regional levels (DeYoung 2006, 502). In Kazakhstan the ministerial portfolio changed hands several times between 1992 and the late 1990s. The frequent changes in the leadership of MoES resulted in staff attrition and reorganisations, affecting its capacity to co-ordinate and monitor a range of initiatives. 'One minister is a former university rector, the other – a secondary school teacher, and they change focus to their favourite subsectors', said a local expert (ICG 2011, 33). The ministry's division on secondary education alone saw dramatic cuts in staff from 220 in the early 1990s to 26 several years later (Asanova 2007a, 76).

The decentralisation of the school management system, begun in 1995, was viewed as an opportunity for delegating management functions from the central ministry to the local level. However, the decentralisation process suffered from an incomplete legal framework and was not supported by the necessary human resources. A serious constraint was the stock of qualified education administration at the local and school levels (ADB 2004, 33).

Structural anomalies

Another legacy of the Soviet system affecting the educational system in Kazakhstan, according to some commentators, was the presence of economic and structural anomalies (Heyneman 1998; DeYoung 2006). Soviet schools had been unconcerned with market forces or with efficiency or accountability. In addition, local education departments and individual schools did not have budget allocations or decision making power to rethink and reorient emerging curricular goals or staffing needs (DeYoung 2006). In Kazakhstan, partial devolution of financial responsibilities to province and district educational authorities resulted in huge cuts of funding from the educational sector. Regional education budgets reveal stark disparities. As a result, the challenge for school directors (i.e. headteachers) in Kazakhstan, many of whom started their careers in the Soviet era, was to learn how to raise and allocate funds for instructional purposes in their schools.

In the face of transitional difficulties, resource constraints and structural rigidity, the government initiated reforms in the mid-1990s with an effort to adjust the education system towards the needs of a market economy.

> Around 1997–1998 . . . various documents began to appear . . . the law on education was revised/modified. In our Law on Education from 1998, in which they have tried to assign . . . to give a role to the private sector for the first time . . . to reiterate that there will be general, all-inclusive secondary education . . . (Participant A, NIS)

Based on the analysis of the literature and data gathered so far, it is possible to summarise the following initiatives that were undertaken in the 1990s:

- legislative reform
- the creation of new structural institutions with the aim of providing scientific, consultative and organisational support (e.g. the Kazakh Academy of Education named after Altynsarin and the Republican Scientific Practical Centre, Daryn, for gifted children, amongst others)
- the revision of the general education curriculum with the aim of making it more flexible and responsive to learner needs in the context of economic transition (e.g. the learner-based curriculum)
- incorporation of a native language and culture in education – New Language and National History textbooks
- decentralisation of public spending on education (the role of *oblasts* and *raions* authority had changed)
- attempts to rationalise the education system to increase its external and internal efficiencies
- the creation of competition in the sector through the promotion of private education
- co-operation with international organisations and its impact.

In the overview of education policy-making in Kazakhstan in the 1990s, some major initiatives are distinguished and will be discussed in more detail.

Education policy framework in the 1990s

Since independence, public policy in the education sector has encountered two basic, interconnected problems. On the one hand, there was a desire to preserve and maintain positive aspects of the education system inherited from the Soviet Union. On the other hand, there was the need to develop the new approaches that must come with the economic and social reforms of a newly independent country. A respondent from the research study (2012) described that time: 'the process of survival was parallel with the process of the formation of state' (Participant F).

The chronology of education reforms in Kazakhstan in the 1990s is presented in Table 1 (only the key strategic policy documents are listed):

Table 1: Chronology of educational reform in Kazakhstan 1991–2000

Years	Legislation and legal framework	Focus
1991–1993	Law on Education (1992) Law on Higher Education (1993)	Formulation of legislation for the education system of an independent Kazakhstan
1994–1996	Constitution of the Republic of Kazakhstan (1995) Concept of Secondary Schools of the Republic of Kazakhstan (1996) A programme of preparation of textbooks and teaching materials for comprehensive schools (1996)	Conceptual revision of the content of education. Commencement of implementation of long-term national programmes in two strategic areas: new textbooks and the introduction of computers into schools.
1997–2000	Kazakhstan 2030: Prosperity, Security and Improvement of the Well-being of all Kazakh Citizens (1997) The State Programme of informatisation of the secondary education The Law on Languages (1997) Resolution of the Government 'On measures of further reform of the secondary education system in the Republic of Kazakhstan' (1998) Law of the Republic of Kazakhstan 'On Education' (1999) National Programme on Education (2000) The Government Resolution on a Guaranteed State Minimum for Educational Organisations' Network (2000)	Development and approval of the strategic documents. Changing from mainly Russian to Kazakh as the primary language of instruction. Restructuring and rewriting the curriculum of the Humanities (especially, a new History narrative). The reopening and modernisation of small schools that were closed as a result of the rationalisation process in 1995–97.

These laws ratify the democratic character of the education system and the administrative and financial decentralisation of educational institutions. The 1992 Law on Education determines the common purpose of education as follows: 'the main task of the education system is to create the necessary conditions for bringing up and developing individuals on the basis of national and common human values, and of specific and practical achievements' (p. 1).

According to Clause 30 of the Constitution of the Republic of Kazakhstan (1995), education is non-discriminatory and every child in Kazakhstan has the right to education and is guaranteed a free primary, general secondary and basic vocational education and free secondary and higher professional education on a competitive basis, regardless of origin, ethnicity, social and property status, gender, language, education, religious affiliation, place of residence, health status and other circumstances. Furthermore, the 'Kazakhstan 2030 Strategy: Prosperity, Security and Improvement of the Well-being of all Kazakh Citizens' states that 'health, education and well-being of citizens' are the main components of human development. An interviewee from the research study (2012) commented:

> . . . the legislation on education was quite progressive at that time because in each law there were points about competencies, the organisation of education process, and more practical approaches . . . (Consultant, International Organisation A)

Attempts were made to improve the structure and content of school education. The education system was founded on the principle of a continuous educational process through four levels: preschool education and upbringing, primary and secondary education, higher education and postgraduate education. Secondary education in Kazakhstan in the 1990s consisted of three stages: elementary (four-year programme, Grades 1–4); basic (five years, Grades 5–9) and senior secondary (two years, Grades 10–11). Secondary (basic) education was compulsory. In a subsequent update, the content of education was focused on the specification of educational domains and the refinement of subjects at each stage of school (*The Concept of Comprehensive Schools of the Republic of Kazakhstan,* 1996).

Daly (2008, 26) states that between 1989 and 2005, Kazakhstan lost two million of its six million Russian Soviet inhabitants. As a result of demographic recession, the number of schools was reduced. A respondent in the research study (2012) stated:

> . . . people from rural areas started moving to town. One part of the Russian speaking population started moving to Russia; the Germans started returning to Germany . . . A demographic problem, the birth-rate went down . . . The number of children at rural schools dropped down. (Participant C, NIS)

By 1999, the size of low capacity multi-grade schools dropped more than half (UNESCO-EFA 2000, 28).[1] The attendance rate decreased, and there was a severe understaffing issue. For example, due to the shortage of teachers, about 150000 pupils in 959 schools were unable to complete their studies of certain subjects – a factor which reduced the population's overall educational levels especially in rural areas. The facilities and technical resources of schools were not up-to-date. One in ten schools required a complete overhaul, while one in three were located in buildings that were not designed as schools. Because of the shortage of school space in 1997, as well as in previous years, classes were conducted in two or three shifts (UNDP 1998, 45), with the school open for extended hours and some lessons being taught in the evening. By 2000, over 30% of school buildings required major repairs.

Between 1991 and 2001 the number of schools in the education system reduced slightly from 8487 to 8309 while the number of pupils rose from 3145600 to 3247400.[2]

At the same time, private schools and institutions were emerging – by the school year 2000/1, private education institutions constituted 3% (217) of general education schools. However, the quality and appropriateness of their programmes needed to be ensured. As one respondent noted:

> . . . people found themselves in a very confusing situation, when too many educational institutions were opened. They sprang up like mushrooms after the rain . . . The variety of institutions was like in a very good supermarket . . . But some of them were bad quality. (Participant A, NIS)

Curriculum reform

Curriculum change has been a major issue in education since independence. The curriculum inherited from the Soviet Union was described as centralised, rigid, inflexible and overloaded (Steiner-Khamsi et al. 2006; Kalikova and Silova 2008, 144). In the 1990s, education policymakers in Kazakhstan wanted to 'nationalise the curriculum to reflect the cultural and ethnic history, while simultaneously "internationalising" it to enable the country to be competitive in a world economy' (Chapman et al. 2005, 522). Zhanabayeva and Isataeva (2004, 248) claim that 'sometimes our problems have resulted from the lack of new ideas and materials but, in other times, from the loss of some positive practices inherited from the Soviet model to unsystematic and fragmentary replacements.' They continue that 'the problems of secondary education result primarily from the lack of global experiences, untested new education methods, and inappropriate pedagogical foci . . . we still approach the pupil as an object, instead of the subject of an educational process. Teaching is still focused on "average" pupil, and we are overloaded with irrelevant subjects' (ibid., 248). As one respondent in the research study (2012) noted:

> . . . then we understand that the Soviet system was destroyed and something new needs to be built, but there is no time. So there is an assumption that since the West has already created something, why not borrow it, to get us fifty years ahead. But we have to consider to what extent we are ready mentally and to what extent the environment is suitable. These two things are absolutely not considered. (Participant B, NIS)

The literature suggests that curriculum challenges in many post-Soviet countries could be summarised in three categories (see Heyneman 1999; Chapman et al. 2005; DeYoung 2006; Shagdar 2006). Firstly, there was a challenge of pedagogy which involved a shift of emphasis from the content of teaching to the complexities of student learning. Secondly, there was the challenge of introducing new subject-matter which often had no precedent in the region – applied economics, accounting methods, principles of law, civil education and business administration. And thirdly, and by far the most complex, the challenges in the teaching of Social Studies, Languages and History (e.g. Heyneman 1999; Chapman et al. 2005; Shagdar 2006; Kennedy 2007; Silova 2011). It was noted by a respondent in the research (2012):

> In some schools in Kazakhstan, since the 1990s, there have been innovative changes related to introduction of student-centred methodology, the Elkonin-Davydov psychological theory of learning activity, active learning, and the competency-based approach. Also, many international organisations were quite active in supporting innovations in education. For example, the Soros Foundation-Kazakhstan and UNICEF introduced many international projects such as Reading and Writing for Critical Thinking. (Participant T, NIS)

The government sought to introduce more Kazakh-oriented programmes into the curriculum: more instructional hours were devoted to Kazakh History over World History, with a complementary increase in the number of hours scheduled for the study of the Kazakh language (DeYoung and Nadirbekyzy 1997; Kissane 2005). As one respondent in the research study (2012) acknowledged:

> . . . in Soviet times, the studies of Kazakh language were poorly developed, and such subjects as 'History of Kazakhstan' and 'Geography of Kazakhstan' occupied a very small share of the 10-years long education process . . . Therefore, we wanted to mend this situation, so we put more emphasis on such subjects. (Participant B, NIS)

Kissane (2005), researching Kazakhstan's History curriculum, observed that reforming History education after the dissolution of the Soviet Union became a 'multi-dimensional project' and History textbooks maintain a 'delicate balance' between ethno-nationalizing and recognition of multicultural identities. This period provided a critical opportunity for historians in Kazakhstan to re-evaluate Soviet history and reinterpret how Kazakhstan's history is portrayed in textbooks and classrooms. Post-independence Kazakh historiography focused on the human costs of Soviet rule, such as the deaths of millions during the famine and collectivisation (Matuszkiewicz 2010). Descriptions of the deeds of great *batyrs* – ethnic heroes of previous centuries – were displayed on the wall in schools across the country. The revival of Kazakh History means, in President Nazarbayev's words, that 'the spirit has been restored to the nation' (DeYoung and Santos 2004, 74). The sudden rush to revise content left the process open to criticism, debate, and many questions, including whether the writers of these new texts that asserted Kazakhstan's status as a nationalising state were threatening internal ethnic stability. Kissane (2005, 58) argues that 'History education received little support, influence, or advisement in the development of curriculum and methodology.' Teachers were asked to instil an interest in History and at the same time to foster a feeling of national identity in their students through the teaching of History.

All comprehensive schools followed the Basic Educational Plan of comprehensive schools (*Bazisnii uchebnii plan obscheobrasovatelnoi shkoli*) approved by MoES with a few modifications. It was an attempt to rationalise the curriculum through a reduction in the number of subjects, the introduction of integrated curricula, or reduction in the educational content so as to make schooling more efficient and effective. Nevertheless the curriculum remained 'outdated' and 'overloaded', which raised major concerns for the quality of education and the health of pupils. Curriculum issues became a major reform problem within schools. It was noted in the research study (2012):

> . . . in the 1990s, we were trying to make every author to write a textbook based not only on information but on action; yet, it was impossible to persuade them to do it.. . . in the end, we obtained a textbook which was overloaded with information . . . but the number of hours is limited, we have sanitary norms for them, and with these textbooks, the number of hours exceeds sanitary norms. If 39 hours is the highest possible number, we get it over 40–42 hours. We needed to get off this way. (Participant A, NIS)

Furthermore, some subjects (e.g. IT classes) were often added to the basic school curriculum without the necessary resources such as computers and new textbooks or other instructional materials. Thus, the 'computerisation' or 'informatisation' was another priority of the government at that time. The president's national 'Programme of Informatisation of the System of Secondary Education' was launched during the 1997/98 academic year which included the supply of computers to all schools in Kazakhstan during the period 1997–2002.

Language policy

Another problem that many post-Soviet countries faced related to the language of instruction and alphabets. Kazakh is a part of the Nogai-Kipchak subgroup of north-eastern Turkic languages, influenced by both Tatar and Mongol. In 1940, the Soviet Union mandated the use of Cyrillic throughout Central Asia, while previously Arabic (in the 1860s) and Latin (from 1929) alphabets were used, even though all but the Tajik language has a Turkish base. Linguistically, Kazakhstan was the most Russified of all the Central Asian republics. Largely because of migration, until the collapse of the Soviet Union, nearly all of Kazakhstan's *oblast* centres as well as other larger urban areas were inhabited primarily by non-Kazakhs, especially Russian and other Slavs.

At the end of the Soviet era, over 80% – and quite possibly over 90% – of Kazakhstan's total urban population was literate in Russian. In contrast, even though Kazakh had been declared Kazakhstan's single 'state language', the proportion of people who were literate in Kazakh was probably no higher than 10–15% (Fierman 2006, 101). Ethnological research on the urban population estimated that 60–75% of Kazakhs spoke Russian exclusively (Dave 2003; Dave 2004, 450). Olcott (2002, 17) claims that at the time of independence almost no non-Kazakhs, and not even all ethnic Kazakhs, spoke Kazakh. A respondent in the research study (2012) commented:

> ... in Soviet times, our school was closed. It was a dead-end. The Kazakh language since the year 1980 was taught until the 8th form. Afterwards it was not taught at all. Why was it so? Because there was no need for that, we all understood and became Russian-speaking. I finished a Kazakh school, but all that was required, to work, was in Russian. There were no universities, no Professional Training Schools ... we only had the faculty of Kazakh language and the faculty of History taught in Kazakh, the rest was in Russian, all was in Russian. (Participant B, NIS)

Fierman (2006) points out that knowledge of the Russian language during the Soviet time was seen as a valuable asset for upward educational and social mobility.

The 1995 Kazakh Constitution weakened the position of the Russian language, not giving it any legal status, but allowing it to be used on a par with the state language. The Kazakh language was thus proclaimed the sole state language. The government has declared a multicultural policy and a need to maintain ethno-cultural consensus as an important condition of progress and of Kazakhstan's prosperity (Concept, 1996). However, less than 1% of Kazakhstan's ethnic Russians (who comprised less than 40% of the nation's population) spoke Kazakh. They had appealed in an effort to restore Russian as an equal language under the new national constitution (DeYoung and Nadirbekyzy 1997). In addressing these calls the government adopted the Law on Languages (1997) and Kazakh became the state language, though Russian was recognised as the language for inter-ethnic communication. Any form of discrimination on the basis of not speaking the Kazakh or Russian languages was forbidden. Each citizen of Kazakhstan is now expected to know Kazakh, Russian and a foreign language, as outlined in state normative documents on education (*Kontseptsiya Obrazovaniya – The Concept of Education*).

Many urban Kazakhs, with a low proficiency in the Kazakh language, opposed rapid linguistic Kazakhisation, for example choosing schools that used Russian as a medium of instruction for their children. Matuszkiewicz (2010, 216) describes '*Kazakhization*' as a process of ascendance of Kazakhs as a national group at the expense of other national groups, mainly Russians. Data from research on Russian and Kazakh-language schools illustrate this point. The share of Kazakh pupils in Russian-language schools changed insignificantly between 1995 and 1999, from 19.8% to 18.7% (Fierman 2006, 117). Given the new legislation, one would have expected a much more dramatic fall in Russian-language schools' enrolments. Scholars researching the language policy in Kazakhstan argue that the state declared more than it could deliver (see Fierman 2006; Matuszkiewicz 2010). It lacked the competent staff and adequate provision for the language instruction required. The education authorities themselves criticised the quality of Kazakh language textbooks; the staff shortages were significant; teachers working through Kazakh were found to be not as efficient as the ones working through Russian.

Multilingual education at that time within Central Asia was mainly supported by external agencies; for example, the Soros Foundation's Open Society Institute (OSI) provided volunteer English teachers for schools all over Kazakhstan and recommended bilingual education in Central Asia with the argument that educating children from different nationalities in their own and their neighbours' languages increases social cohesion, reducing the risk of inter-ethnic violence.

The role of international agencies and local realities

In the 1990s, post-Soviet countries became a target for external assistance aimed at supporting the development of educational systems in transition and, as some international organisations claimed, saving 'a generation at risk' (ADB, 1998). At the same time, foreign aid was used by international institutions as a way to promote neoliberal educational reforms (Kalikova and Silova 2008). All Central Asian republics have received substantial financial and technical assistance from international organisations (e.g. the International Monetary Fund; the World Bank; the Asian Development Bank (ADB)), bilateral and multilateral donor agencies (e.g. the US Agency for International Development; USAID), European Union Institutions (e.g. the Technical Aid to the Commonwealth of Independent States (TACIS) programme), as well as the Canadian International Development Agency (CIDA), the Japan International Cooperation Agency (JICA), and various international non-governmental organisations (e.g. Open Society Foundations (OSF), known as the Open Society Institute (OSI) until 2011; the Aga Khan Foundation).

A number of studies of Western assistance in the post-Soviet countries have shown that 'external consultants had little knowledge of local conditions and lacked cultural sensitivity' and that this caused 'disillusionment' and 'consultancy fatigue' among the representatives of recipient governments (see Gilbert 1998; Rumer 2005; Kalikova and Silova, 2008; Silova 2011; Takala and Piattoeva 2012). Furthermore, Silova (2005, 53) suggests that 'travelling policies have increasingly clashed with a strong desire of education policy makers in the region to maintain Soviet education legacies and, in some cases, revive pre-Soviet traditions'. Drawing from Central Asian case studies, Silova (2005) argues that local education stakeholders may 'appropriate the language of the new allies', while not necessarily agreeing with or being willing to implement it' (2005, 52). As a result, 'travelling policies' have often not been fully implemented. Local educators do not always agree with donor approaches or goals (DeYoung 2007). Instead, communities at national, regional or local levels have begun to interact with and re-negotiate these 'travelling policies' and, in some cases, contest and resist them (Silova 2009, 313). Local education stakeholders may effectively internalise international discourses, while using them for their own needs such as legitimising contested educational reforms domestically, objectifying value-based decisions, or 'signalling' certain reform movements internationally (Silova 2005, 52). Not surprisingly, some reforms have become examples of institutional reform failure (see Kalikova and Silova 2008).

The role and the impact of international agencies in Kazakhstan represent an interesting case due to the fact that within one decade, 1991–2000, the country moved from being aid-dependent to being a donor-free country. Some international agencies (e.g. the ADB and OSI) were more vocal than others in shaping the trajectory of educational development in the country. The following discussion will focus on a few examples of projects initiated and supported by the ADB and OSI.

The ADB operated in Kazakhstan from 1994 until 2000, and Kazakhstan took loans in three tranches. In total, Kazakhstan received nearly 60 million US dollars in loans. As one respondent in the research study (2012) stated:

> The goal attached to one of the loans was to set up a system of education management in Kazakhstan . . . IMS – Information Management System. (Consultant, International Organisation A)

The Educational Rehabilitation and Management Improvement project, supported by the ADB, included the following components: provision of general educational equipment to 180 selected schools in Kazakhstan; development of textbooks and related instructional materials for a new learner-centred curriculum; development of computerised educational Management Information Systems; and in-country training of 950 school directors and teachers (ADB 1995). Overall, as some observers claim, the language of knowledge transfer and training, rather than capacity building, permeated the Bank's discourse. For example, Asanova (2006), in her study of the ADB's impact on education policy formation in Kazakhstan, found that ADB staff viewed policy dialogue as persuasion and the recipients as resistant to change. She noted that 'overall, the recipients were cautious about agencies' motives and their potential influence on the country's educational development' (659). Furthermore, the ADB promoted an educational policy framework grounded in an economic paradigm and advanced universal policies such as basic education, despite recipients' resistance to these. The ADB's 'rationalisation policy' (1995–98) is an example of developmental agencies' tendency to impose economic analysis on education.

According to ADB reports, the organisation of Kazakhstan's schools inherited from the Soviet period proved ineffective. As a consequence, the 'rationalisation policy' called for an integration of schools in rural areas to reduce administrative, maintenance and instructional costs. The recommendation was to increase class size by merging neighbourhood schools. Following this recommendation, during the four years of the reform the number of preschools was reduced by 3667 institutions – from 5226 to 1558, and the number of secondary general schools fell by 590 – from 8694 to 8104 (ADB 2002). As a result, many families in rural areas were left with the option of either migrating to areas where schools continued to operate or to keep school-age children at home. The reports published by MoES in 1997 showed that about 26900 eligible children did not attend schools. Furthermore, receiving schools were forced to operate in two to three shifts; class sizes and the number of mixed grade classes increased considerably, affecting the quality of education. The fact that Kazakhstan has a vast territory and is not densely populated meant that closing schools decreased access to schooling leading 'many children in sparsely populated areas to drop out of school or face the hardship of travelling longer distances in harsh weather' (Asanova 2006, 661). Kalikova and Silova (2008, 139) claim that 'these structural adjustment reforms were conceived by international consultants with little or no knowledge of Kazakhstan's education reform context.' The ADB changed its position after implementing the rationalisation policy. In its official evaluation report, the ADB acknowledged the validity of the recipients' arguments and the need to reopen rural (village) schools (ADB 2002, 5). In 2000, the school rationalisation reform was reversed by a government resolution, *Guaranteed State Minimum for Educational Institutions' Network*, which aimed at restoring the network of small rural schools in Kazakhstan (Kalikova and Silova 2008, 140).

The OSI, meanwhile, had identified certain pedagogical areas of concern. The OSI spent massive amounts of money introducing 'active learning', 'critical thinking', 'debate programme', and 'civic education' in Kazakhstan (Kalikova and Silova 2008, 141). School Parliament and English as a Second Language (ESL) programmes for schoolteachers sponsored by the Soros Foundation were also quite visible in secondary schools in Kazakhstan (DeYoung 2006). These 'pilot or demonstration projects' were intended to introduce new educational approaches, ideas, and concepts to Kazakhstan's educational system. For example, it was noted in the research study (2012):

> Soros [Foundation – OSI] had brought to Kazakhstan a lot of innovative programmes – critical thinking programme, debate programme, upgrading teachers' qualification programme, school as the focal point for the local community . . .

learning the innovative technologies at schools, preparation of new textbooks . . .
(Consultant, International Organisation A)

The assumption was that these demonstration projects would eventually be institutionalised in state education structures, with the Government of Kazakhstan assuming financial responsibility for their ongoing implementation (Kalikova and Silova 2008).

Despite a number of challenges in the education sector, the Government of Kazakhstan had reformulated policies regarding foreign aid. In December 1999, President Nazarbayev announced that Kazakhstan would substantially reduce the number of loans it accepted from international donors; it would instead finance education and health-sector reforms through internal resources. This has resulted in a substantial reduction in foreign aid and debt, making Kazakhstan one of the most donor-independent countries in Central Asia and the Caucasus. Furthermore, an important outcome was that the influence of international financial institutions on the government has also declined (Kalikova and Silova 2008, 138). The government has used its own resources for education reform, emphasising the need for closer collaboration with local experts. The shift in the foreign aid policy forced international institutions to revise strategies and approaches in their attempts to have an impact on educational development in Kazakhstan.

Conclusion

The main objective of this chapter is to provide an overview of educational reforms in Kazakhstan in the 1990s. In this period, educational policy-makers in Kazakhstan, as in other post-Soviet and post-Socialist countries, were trying to balance two tasks. First, they sought to restructure the education system for the purposes of nation-building, emphasising national distinctiveness as a means of establishing the identity of Kazakhstan as an independent country. Second, they were keen to develop a modern education system that would create a 'learning society', thereby addressing the demands of the 'knowledge-based economy' and meeting an 'elusive "international standard"' (Silova 2002; Chapman et al. 2005). In this context 'learning from elsewhere' was one of the central principles of educational transformation (Silova 2009).

However, during the 1990s education was not treated as the highest priority and was targeted as an area to cut costs in favour of private sector development (DeYoung and Suzhikova 1997). The main challenge of many state educational institutions at the time was merely to survive. Our own research undertaken in 2012 and evidence from national and international reports and studies indicate that, until the end of the 1990s, educational reforms had an incidental, fragmentary nature and were largely unsupported by any scientific programme of research. The numerous concepts, plans and programmes were not organically connected with each other; at times they contradicted one another, and represented a process of 'social improvisation'. As a respondent in this study commented: 'innovations remained on paper only' (Consultant, International Organisation). As Ball (1998, 126) puts it, 'national policy making is inevitably a process of bricolage: a matter of borrowing and copying bits and pieces of ideas from elsewhere, drawing upon and amending locally tried and tested approaches, cannibalising theories, research, trends and fashions and not infrequently flailing around for anything at all that looks as though it might work.' The debate over the direction and organisation of public schooling in Kazakhstan was marked by a lack of any consensus or unified course at the level of MoES, which was affected by a high staff turnover. Interestingly, the system of education remained highly centralised where major educational programmes and decrees were approved by President Nazarbayev.

The initial attempt to revise curriculum content and introduce new teaching methods was initiated but did not involve any major revision either in the existing curriculum or in teaching methods and was never really implemented. The curriculum continued to be overloaded with factual information and the number of subjects taught tended to increase. Many school directors and teachers still believed in 'education for the sake of education' and were unwilling to admit weaknesses in the curriculum inherited form the Soviet Union. Many practitioners still did not clearly understand the reasons for, and the methods by which, they were expected to teach children, whether the aim was to help them successfully enter the labour market or something else. Another important feature of educational transition in the 1990s was the role of international organisations. Various projects funded in this period were aimed at transferring know-how, technical assistance and policy advice, and were aimed at promoting democracy and facilitating institution building, 'open society values' (Silova 2008, 53), human resource development, rationalisation of institutional structure, and decentralisation, and to 'promote transparency, accountability and justice through capacity building. In the educational sphere the main funding was directed at curriculum reforms in line with the emerging market economy. However, some of these initiatives exemplified institutional reform failure. Notably, the ADB's 'rationalisation' policy, discussed above, was considered a fiasco, adding to education policy makers' wariness about external influences and insistence on the need to focus on developing the capacity of local experts. Overall, in the 1990s there was weak public participation and a lack of discussion of educational issues as part of the further development of education in Kazakh society. It was more common that teachers were regarded as technical implementers of centrally defined reforms not as key players in educational change (Azanova 2007b).

Despite a number of challenges and difficulties in the first decade after independence, there were some achievements in the education reform efforts. Particularly, a new and quite progressive legislative framework for the education system was established. The network of secondary schools was preserved. Furthermore, the 1990s was a time of learning how to write the first national textbooks.

Another important achievement of educational initiatives in the 1990s was the diversification of educational institutions through the establishment of specialised schools for gifted children and private education institutions such as the Kazakh-Turkish Lyceum (KTL) for boys and girls. Also established were some single-sex boarding schools for both boys and girls. The focus of the curriculum in KTL was on Mathematics, Science and languages: intensive Turkish, Kazakh, English and Russian language instruction. KTL were the first education institutions in Kazakhstan to use teaching materials published by Cambridge University Press and Oxford University Press. A few years later, in 1996, a strategically important document was signed by the president entitled *About the State Support and Development of Schools for Gifted Children* (MoES 1996). The document set tasks for creating the conditions necessary for the education of gifted young people. In 1998, a new research and practical centre *Daryn* ('Giftedness') under MoES was established with the aim of supporting the creative development of the most capable students in gymnasia, lyceums and secondary schools.

In short, education transformation in Kazakhstan in the 1990s was un-coordinated and piecemeal. Policy-makers were simultaneously struggling to maintain Soviet traditions, to revive pre-Soviet traditions (especially those associated with Kazakh culture and history) and to re-position the country closer to the West. We shall see in the following chapter and throughout this volume how these three reference points continue to shape the development of educational policy and practice in Kazakhstan.

REFERENCES

ADB (Asian Development Bank) (1995). *Report and Recommendation of the President to the Board of Directors on a Proposed Loan to the Republic of Kazakhstan for the Educational Rehabilitation and Management Improvement Project.* Manila: Asian Development Bank.

— (1998). 'A Generation at Risk: Children in the Central Asian Republics of Kazakhstan and Kyrgystan'. In A. Bauer, N. Boschmann, D.J. Green and K. Kuehnast, (eds), *A generation at risk: Children in the Central Asia republics of Kazakhstan and Kyrgystan.* Manila: Asian Development Bank.

— (2001). *Report on the Project "Regional Co-operation in the Field of Reform Management in the 'Educational Sector'.* Almaty: Asian Development Bank.

— (2002). *Project Completion Report on the Educational Rehabilitation and Management Improvement Project in Kazakhstan. Almaty: Asian Development Bank.* Available online: www.adb.org/sites/default/files/projdocs/2002/pcr_IN242-02.pdf (retrieved 24 October 2013).

— (2004). *Education reforms in countries in transition: Policies and Processes. Six Country Case Studies Commissioned by the Asian Development Bank in Azerbaijan, Kazakhstan, Kyrgyz Republic, Mongolia, Tajikistan, and Uzbekistan.* Manila: Asian Development Bank.

Ailes, **C.P.** and **Rushing**, **F.W.** (1991). 'Soviet Math and Science Educational Reforms During Perestroika'. *Technology in Society*, 13, 109–22.

Asanova, **J.** (2006). 'Emerging Regions, Persisting Rhetoric of Educational Aid: The Impact of the Asian Development Bank on Education Policy-making in Kazakhstan'. *International Journal of Educational Development*, 26:6, 655–66.

— (2007a). 'Seeing Near and Far: Balancing Stakeholder Needs and Rights in Kazakhstan's Educational Reform'. *Canadian and International Education*, 36:2, 71–90.

— (2007b). 'Teaching the Canon? National-Building and Post-Soviet Kazakhstan's Literature Textbooks'. *Compare: A Journal of Comparative and International Education*, 37:3, 325–43.

Bahry, **S.**, **Niyozov**, **S.** and **Shamatov**, **D. A.** (2005). 'Bilingual education in Central Asia', in J. Cummings and N.H. Hornberger, (eds), *Encyclopedia of Language and Education.* Springer Science+Business Media LLC, pp. 205–21.

Ball, **S.J.** (1998). 'Big Policies/Small World: An Introduction to International Perspectives in Education Policy'. *Comparative Education*, 34:2, 119–30.

Chapman, **D.W.**, **Weidman**, **J.**, **Cohen**, **M.** and **Mercer**, **M.** (2005). 'The Search for Quality: A Five Country Study of National Strategies to Improve Educational Quality in Central Asia'. *International Journal of Educational Development*, 25:5, 514–30.

Concept (1996). 'The Concept of Ethno-Cultural Education in the Republic of Kazakhstan', approved by the President Nazarbayev on June 15, 1996.

Constitution of the Republic of Kazakstan (1995).

Daly, **J.C.K.** (2008). *Kazakhstan's Emerging Middle Class. Silk Road Paper.* Central Asia-Caucasus Institute: Silk Road Studies Program.

Dave, B. (1996). 'National Revival in Kazakhstan: Language Shift and Identity Change'. *Post-Soviet Affairs*, 12:1, 51–72

— (2003). *Minorities and Participation in Public Life: Kazakhstan*. Commission on Human Rights, Sub-Comission on Promotion of Human Rights, United Nations. Working Paper, Paris.

— (2004). 'Entitlement through Numbers: Nationality and Language Categories in the First Post-Soviet Census of Kazakhstan'. *Nations and Nationalism*, 10:4, 439–59.

DeYoung, A.J. and **Suzhikova, B.** (1997). 'Redefining Post-Soviet Public Education: The Case of Kazakhstan'. *International Journal of Educational Reform*, 6:4, 441–54.

DeYoung, A.J. and **Nadirbekyzy, B.** (1997). 'Redefining Schooling and Community in Post-Soviet Kazakhstan'. *Journal of Education Policy*, 12:1, 71–8.

DeYoung, A.J. and **Santos, C.** (2004). 'Central Asia Educational Issues and Problems'. In S.P. Heyneman and A.J. DeYoung, (eds), *The Challenges of Education in Central Asia*. Greenwich: Information Age Publishing.

DeYoung, A.J. (2006). 'Problems and Trends in Education in Central Asia since 1990: The Case of General Secondary Education in Kyrgyzstan'. *Central Asian Survey*, 25:4, 499–14.

Education Law of the Republic of Kazakhstan (1992). Rus. Закон Республики Казахстан от 18 января 1992 г. No. 1153–XII Об образовании; online.zakon.kz/Document/?doc_id=1000964 (retrieved 22 November 2013.)

Education Law of the Republic of Kazakhstan (1999).

Elliott, J. and **Tudge, J.** (2007). 'The Impact of the West on Post-Soviet Russian Education: Change and Resistance to Change'. *Comparative Education*, 43:1, 93–112.

Fierman, W. (2006). 'Language and Education in Post-Soviet Kazakhstan: Kazakh-Medium Instruction in Urban Schools'. *Russian Review*, 65:1, 98–116.

Fullan, M. (2001). *The New Meaning of Educational Change*, New York: Teachers College Press.

— (2003). 'The Emergence of Conceptual Framework'. In E. Polyzoi, M. Fullan and J.P. Anchan, (eds), *Change Forces in Post-Communist Eastern Europe*. New York: RoutledgeFalmer.

Gilbert, K. (1998). '"Consultancy Fatigue": Epidemiology, Symptoms and Prevention'. *Leadership and Organisation Development Journal*, 19:6, 340–46.

Heyneman, S.P. (1995). 'Education in Europe and Central Asia Region: Policies of Adjustment and Excellence'. In F.J.H. Mertors, (ed.), *Reflections on Education in Russia*. Amersford: Acco.

— (1998). 'The Transition from the Party/State to Open Democracy: The Role of Education'. *Journal of Educational Development*, 18:1, 20–40.

— (1999). *From the Party/State to Multi-Ethnic Democracy: Education and Its Influence on Social Cohesion in the Europe and Central Asia Region*. The International Child Development Centre United Nations Children's Fund.

— (2003). 'One Step Back, Two Steps Forward: The First Stage of the Transition for Education in Central Asia'. In S.P. Heyneman and A.J. DeYoung, (eds), *The Challenges of Education in Central Asia*. Greenwich, CT: Information Age Publishing.

ICG (International Crisis Group) (2011). *Central Asia: Decay and Decline. Asia Report No. 201 – 3 February*. International Crisis Group, Bishkek/Brussel.

Jurinov, M. (1996). *About the Present Conditions and Development Perspectives Of the Higher education System Of the Republic of Kazakhstan*. Report to the Cabinet of Ministers, Almaty.

Kalikova, S. and Silova, I. (2008). 'From Educational Brokers to Local Capacity Builders: Redefining International NGOs in Kazakhstan'. In I. Silova and G. Steiner-Khamsi, (eds), *How NGOs Reach. Globalisation and Education Reform in the Caucasus, Central Asia, and Mongolia*. Boulder, CO: Kumarian Press, Inc.

Kanaev, A. and Daun, H. (2002). 'Nationalism and Educational Transition in Central Asia'. In H. Daun, (ed.), *Educational Restructuring in the Context of Globalization and National Policy*. New York: RoutledgeFalmer.

Kissane, C. (2005). 'History Education in Transit: Where to for Kazakhstan?' *Comparative Education*, 41:1, 45–69.

Kreindler, I. (1991). 'Forging a Soviet People'. In W. Fierman, (ed.), *Soviet Central Asia: The Failed Transformation*. Boulder, CO: Westview Press.

Loogma, K., Tafel-Viia, K. and Ůmarik, M. (2012). 'Conceptualising Educational Changes: A Social Innovation Approach'. *Journal of Educational Change*, 14(3), 283–301.

Matuszkiewicz, R. (2010). 'The Language Issue in Kazakhstan – Institutionalizing New Ethnic Relations after Independence'. *Economic and Environmental Studies*, 10, 211–27.

Nazarbayev, N. (1997). 'Kazakhstan 2030 Strategy: Prosperity, Security and Improvement of the Well-Being of all Kazakhstan Citizens'. Annual State of the Nation Address, Astana, October 1997. www.akorda.kz/en/category/gos_programmi_razvitiya (retrieved 20 November 2013).

NHDR (2004). *National Human Development Report. Education for All: The Key Goal for a New Millennium*. New York: The United Nations Development Programme.

Olcott, M.B. (1995). *The Kazakhs*. Stanford, CA: Hoover Institution Press.

Olcott, M.B. (2002). *Kazakhstan: Unfulfilled Promise*. Washington DC, Carnegie Endowment for International Peace.

Phillips, D. and Ochs, K. (2003). 'The Process of Policy Borrowing in Education: Some Explanatory and Analytical Devices'. *Comparative Education*, 39:4, 451–61.

— (2004). 'Researching Policy Borrowing: Some Methodological Challenges in Comparative Education'. *British Educational Research Journal*, 30:6, 773–84.

Polyzoi, E. and Nazarenko, T. (2004). 'A Comparative Analysis of Four Case Studies of Educational Reform in Russia: Strategies of Survival and Change'. *World Studies in Education*, 5:2, 65–80.

Polyzoi, E. and Dneprov, E. (2003). 'Harnessing the Forces of Change: Educational Transformation in Russia'. In E. Polyzoi, M. Fullan and J.P. Anchan, (eds), *Change Forces in Post-Communist Eastern Europe*. London: RoutledgeFalmer.

Resolution of the Government (1998). 'On Measures of Further Reform of the Secondary Education System in the Republic of Kazakhstan'.

Resolution of the Government (1999). 'On the Issues of Mandatory Pre-School Education for Children'.

Rumer, B. (2005). *Central Asia: At the end of transition*, Armonk, NY: M.E.Sharpe.

Šajmedrenov, E., Èbilova, G., Matyžanov, K., Orazov, N. and Tujaxbaev, T. (1999). *Yazykovaja politika v Respublike Kazahstan* (*Language policy in the Republic of Kazakhstan*). Astana, Kazakhstan: Ministry of Culture and Information.

Schatz, E. (2000). 'Framing Strategies and Non-Conflict in Multi-Ethnic Kazakhstan'. *Nationalism and Ethnic Politics,* 6, 71–94.

Shagdar, B. (2006). 'Human Capital in Central Asia: Trends and Challenges in Education'. *Central Asia Survey,* 25, 515–32.

Silova, I. (2002). 'Returning to Europe: Facts, Fiction, and Fantasies of post-Soviet education reform.' In A. Novoa and M. Lawn, (eds), *The Global Politics of Educational Borrowing and Lending.* New York, NY: TC Press.

— (2005). 'Traveling Policies: Hijacked in Central Asia'. *European Educational Research Journal,* 4:1, 50–59.

— (2008). 'Championing Open Society. The Education Logic of the Soros Foundation Network'. In I. Silova and G. Steiner-Khamsi, (eds), *How NGOs React: Globalisation and Education Reform in the Caucasus, Central Asia and Mongolia.* Bloomfield, CT: Kumarian Press.

— (2009). 'Varieties of Educational Transformation: The Post-Socialist States of Central/ Southeastern Europe and Former Soviet Union'. In R. Cowen and A.M. Kazamias, (eds), *International Handbook of Comparative Education.* Berlin: Springer Science + Business Media.

— (2011). *Globalization on the Margins: Education and Postsocialist Transformations in Central Asia.* Charlotte, NC: IAP – Information Age Publishing.

Silova, I., Johnson, M. and **Heyneman, S.** (2007). 'Education and Crisis of Social Cohesion in Azerbaijan and Central Asia'. *Comparative Education Review,* 51:2, 159–80.

Silova, I. and **Magno, C.** (2004). 'Gender Equity Unmasked: Revisiting Democracy, Gender, and Education in Post-Socialist Central/Southeastern Europe and Former Soviet Union'. *Comparative Education Review,* 48:4, 417–42.

Silova, I. and **Steiner-Khamsi, G.** (2008). *How NGOs React: Globalization and Education Reform in the Caucasus, Central Asia, and Mongolia.* Bloomfield, CT: Kumarian Press.

State Programme of Informatisation of Secondary Education (1997).

Steiner-Khamsi, G. (2004). *The Global Politics of Educational Borrowing and Lending.* New York, NY: Teachers College Press.

Steiner-Khamsi, G. (2005). 'Vouchers for Teacher Education (Non) Reform in Mongolia: Transitional, Post-Socialist, or Anti-Socialist Explanations?' *Comparative Education Review,* 49:2, 148–72.

Steiner-Khamsi, G., Harris-Van, K., Silova, I. and **Chachkhiani, K.** (2008). *Decentralization and Recentralization Reforms: Their Impact on Teacher Salaries in the Caucasus, Central Asia and Mongolia.* Geneva: UNESCO-IBE.

Steiner-Khamsi, G. and **Quist, H.** (2000). 'The Politics of Educational Borrowing: Reopening the Case of Achimota in British Ghana'. *Comparative Education Review,* 44:3, 272–99.

Steiner-Khamsi, G., Silova, I. and **Johnson, E.** (2006). 'Neoliberalism Liberally Applied: Educational Policy Borrowing in Central Asia'. In D. Coulby, J. Ozga, T. Seddon and T.S. Popkewitz, (eds), *World Yearbook on Education.* London and New York: Routledge.

Takala, T. and **Piattoeva, N.** (2012). 'Changing Conceptions of Development Assistance to Education in the International Discourse on Post-Soviet Countries'. *International Journal of Educational Development,* 32:1, 3–10.

UNDP (1996). *Kazakhstan Human Development Report 1996.* Almaty. www.undp.kz/ library_of_publications/files/58-31886.pdf (retrieved 20 May 2012).

— (1998). *Social Integration and the Role of the State in the Transition Period*. Almaty. www.undp.kz/library_of_publications/start.html?redir=center_view&id=295 (retrived 20 May 2012).

UNESCO-EFA (2000). *The Education For All 2002 Assessment*. UNESCO.

UNICEF (1999). *After the Fall. The Human Impact of Ten Years of Transition*. Florence: UNICEF, Innocenti Research Centre.

Ushinsky, K.D. (1949). *Sobranie socinenii (Collected Works)*, Moscow, USSR: Academy of Pedagogical Sciences.

Vygotsky, L. (1978). 'Interaction Between Learning and Development'. *Mind in Society*. Cambridge, MA: Harvard University Press.

Webber, S. (2000). *School Reform and Society in the New Russia*, New York: Palgrave Macmillan.

Webster, C., Silova, I., Moyer, A. and McAllister, S. (2011). 'Leading in the Age of Post-Socialist Education Transformations: Examining Sustainability of Teacher Education Reform in Latvia'. *Journal of Educational Change*, 12:3, 347–70.

World Bank (2000). *Partnership for Development*. The Creative Communication Group for the World Bank.

— (2003). *Lifelong Learning in the Global Knowledge Economy: Challenges for Developing Countries*. Washington: World Bank Report.

Zhanabayeva, S. and Isataeva, L. (2004). 'Secondary Education Reform in Kazakhstan'. In S.P. Heyneman and A.J. DeYoung (eds), *Challenges of Education in Central Asia*: Charlotte, NC: Information Age Publishing Inc.

Web resources

www.government.kz
www.e.gov.kz
www.edu.gov.kz
www.oecd.org

NOTES

1   Available statistics on educational enrolments or achievement in Central Asian Republics (according to some observers) are often inconsistent and politically manipulated. Schools usually provide 'official' data to the various regional and national ministries and, since data provided has the potential of being used to criticise school administrators and teachers (rather than to improve education), it is likely manipulated to avoid possible negative consequences. International data sets that rely on government statistics have similar problems, or usually come from regional samples. It is important to see that while situational analyses of national systems are underpinned by statistical information, these analyses are also political constructs. In the post-Soviet context a dramatic change has occurred, whereby the Ministries of Education have changed their rhetoric

from the previous emphasis on accomplishments ('plans have been completed success-fully' – or 'plan targets have been surpassed') to emphasise needs and even to convey a sense of crisis ('this is how far we lag behind international standards' (e.g. Silova and Steiner-Khamsi 2008, 14–16; Steiner-Khamsi 2008, 268–9; Asanova 2006, 663; Takala and Piattoeva 2012, 5).

2   Statistics Agency of the Republic of Kazakhstan www.eng.stat.kz/digital/Education/ Pages/default.aspx (retrieved 20 October 2012).

2 EDUCATIONAL REFORM IN KAZAKHSTAN: Entering the World Arena

Natallia Yakavets (University of Cambridge, Faculty of Education)
Makpal Dzhadrina (Nazarbayev Intellectual Schools)

Introduction

In the 2000s, rapid economic growth dramatically changed the prospects for education reform in Kazakhstan. At that time quality of education came to be seen as one of the key political priorities for the country's further economic development. In his speeches President Nazarbayev emphasised that Kazakhstan aspired to establish a high-quality education system, consistent with world standards, in order to improve the competitiveness of the country and its international standing. For example, the Address of President Nazarbayev to the People of Kazakhstan for 2005 emphasised that:

> . . . under the conditions of globalisation and tough global competitiveness the physical and intellectual capabilities of the Kazakhstan people are the key factors in the success of our intentions, the competitiveness of the country's economy and its survival in modern conditions. The nation's competitiveness is firstly determined by the level of its education.

The importance of education is made explicit with regard to both society and the individual. A key factor here is the identification of a 'skills gap' – an insufficient supply of qualified engineers, scientists, technicians and professional managerial specialists to supply the increasing demands of the economy. While Kazakhstan boasts a 99% literacy and school enrolment rate, there were concerns about the low quality of students' knowledge and skills and, as a result, a low demand for graduates from Kazakhstani schools on the labour market (ADB 2004; Tasbulatova and Belosludtseva 2007, 8). It was also argued that the curriculum was falling short of present-day goals to encourage the practical application of knowledge gained in the classroom, to promote the skills of learning, to make learning a lifelong pursuit and to prepare school leavers for employment and for an active role in society (ADB 2004, 37).

The following discussion focuses on the development of a legal framework in the early 21st century, the transition towards a 12-year schooling model and the revision of the school curriculum, especially in terms of the introduction of a trilingual model. In addition, developments of the national assessment model (the 'Unified National Test') will be considered, along with Kazakhstan's participation in international monitoring tests.

Education policy framework in the 2000s

Responding to the increasing criticism of the quality of the existing school system at the end of the 1990s, Kazakhstan's Ministry of Education and Science (MoES) announced a comprehensive school reform in 2001. Domestic pressure for reform came from higher-education administrations and academics, who had complained about the decreasing quality of graduates entering the universities (Kalikova and Silova 2008, 143). Having officially declared 2001 as the Year of Education, the Government of Kazakhstan initiated several substantive reforms in education. Key documents were published defining and regulating state policy in the field of education, as presented in Table 1.

Table 1: Key education policy documents and programmes 2000–2011

Years	Legislation and legal framework	Focus
2000–2004	2000 – State programme 'Education' (2000–2005) 2001 – Year of Education 2001 – Strategy of Educational Reform: Millennium Development Goals in Kazakhstan 2002 – State Educational Standards 2003 – Educational Standards for general secondary education of the Republic of Kazakhstan: Programme 'Rural School' (2003–5) 2004 – Concept of Development of the System of education in RK until 2015 2004 – National Education Development Programme	Determine key priorities of educational development for the medium and long term. Kazakhstan domestic 'quest for quality'.
2005–2008	2005 – State Programme of Education Development for 2005–2010 2007 – The new Law on Education 'Children of Kazakhstan' Programme for 2007–11	Set objectives for the provision of quality educational services in compliance with world standards.

Years	Legislation and legal framework	Focus
2009 to present	2010 – State Programme of Education Development for 2011–2020: *Balapan* pre-school education programme for 2010–14 2011 – The Laws 'On Science', 'On amendments to several legislative acts of Kazakhstan regarding the issues of education', 'On amendments to the Law of Kazakhstan 'On education' 2011 – The Law of the Republic of Kazakhstan 'On the Status of the Nazarbayev University, Nazarbayev Intellectual Schools, and Nazarbayev Fund'	Modernisation of entire system of education based on strategic partnership model with major international educational providers.
2004, 2005, 2006, 2007, 2009, 2012	Messages of the President to the People of Kazakhstan	Set priorities and objectives of education policy.

Education is presented as a key component of national goals and priorities. The main idea running through these documents is that more effective development of the country's human capital is a necessary condition of success. Furthermore, the ideology and principles stated in these documents gave a broad political framework and allowed a systematic approach to the development and implementation of programmes (national and regional) for particular areas of education system reforms. The emphasis is on the aim of 'entering the international educational arena' and compliance with 'world standards'. For example, the Education Reform Strategy (2001) specified assurance of resources, improved quality of outcomes and the efficiency of the education system as key objectives, stressing that the quality of education in Kazakhstan should be comparable to that of the developed countries of the world. The programme stated the extension of the duration of compulsory primary and secondary education from 11 to 12 years. Between 2000 and 2003 over 20 government orders were adopted on the reform and modernisation of various aspects of the secondary education system. Among these were the rules and regulations for the licensing of educational activity (2000), the plan of steps to realise the 'State Programme of Education Development for 2001' and the introduction of information and communications technology (ICT) in the education system of the Republic of Kazakhstan for 2002–4 (2001).

A further nationwide 'State Programme of Education Development for 2005–2010' was instituted following a presidential address to the nation on 4 March 2004, entitled 'Towards Competitive Kazakhstan, Competitive Economy and Competitive Nation'. The programme called for 'drastic changes' to upgrade the quality of education 'amidst [a] new economic and socio-cultural environment' and identified education as a national priority. Furthermore, it envisioned ambitious goals, including an increase in student enrolment from 73800 in 2001 to about 180000 in 2008, gradual decentralisation of the higher-education system, introduction of a western-style credit system, improvement of education standards, and an increase in international co-operation in the field of education.

In February 2007, the Annual Message of President Nazarbayev, entitled 'New Kazakhstan in the New World', specified and enhanced key priorities and principles of governmental policy in the field of education, aiming to ensure the further development of the system of education. It was stated:

> The main criterion of success of educational reform is to achieve such a level when any citizen of our country, having received appropriate education and qualification, can become a demanded specialist in any country of the world. (Nazarbayev 2007)[1]

The document also set the objective of providing quality education services throughout the country in compliance with world standards, quality assurance of education, vocational training and a 21st-century society. The new Law on Education was adopted in July 2007 and took into consideration international standards in the field of education in view of Kazakhstan's joining of the World Trade Organisation and integration with the Bologna Process, a Europe-wide agreement designed to ensure compatible standards of higher education qualifications. Asanova (2007, 76) argues that discourse on school reform in Kazakhstan became increasingly steeped in the language of 'world education standards'.

Seven laws in the sphere of education and Science were adopted in 2011 in Kazakhstan: the laws 'On the Status of the Nazarbayev University, Nazarbayev Intellectual Schools, and Nazarbayev Fund'; 'On Science'; 'On amendments to several legislative acts of Kazakhstan regarding the issues of education'; 'On amendments to the Law of Kazakhstan "On education"'; 'On ratification of the borrowing the project on modernization of technical and vocational education signed between Kazakhstan and the International Bank for Reconstruction and Development'; and 'On amendments to some legislative acts of Kazakhstan on the issue of children's villages of a family type'.

The president set an ambitious goal to develop Kazakhstan into a world-class centre of knowledge. In his speech at a Congress of Kazakhstan's Youth, President Nazarbayev said:

We are well aware that the country's prospects are not only oil and gas, not only industry giants, but the quality of education that we can give to the younger generation. One can judge the prospects of a country by its education system. (Nazarbayev 2011)[2]

State spending on education in the past ten years has increased 7.5 times, suggesting that these are not just words but a genuine development strategy. The spending was fuelled by rapidly rising energy export revenues and reached an equivalent of about US $4.7 billion in the 2008 fiscal year. Education expenditure in Kazakhstan in 2009 made up 4.4% of GDP and 4.1% of GDP in 2010. According to the UNESCO EFA Report (2010), Kazakhstan ranks fourth among 129 countries in its Education Development Index; in terms of literacy it is the 14th out of 177 countries (UNESCO EFA 2010, 285).

Secondary education in the 2000s

In the 2000s the education system in Kazakhstan became increasingly diversified through the establishment of private schools, academic lyceums, gymnasiums and colleges. According to the Republic of Kazakhstan State Statistics Agency (2001), there were 153 private schools and 265 schools of a new type, including 100 gymnasiums and 101 lyceums, in the academic year 2000–2001. The number of private schools decreased by 133 in the 2007–8 academic year. Private schools were operating in every region (Rus. *oblast*), but the largest number of them were located in Almaty (47 schools), Karaganda *oblast* (15 schools), Eastern Kazakhstan *oblast* (10 schools) and in Astana (10 schools). Most general secondary schools are under the jurisdiction of the local executive organs and the Ministry of Education and Science (MoES). Schools of the new type have become more competitive than standard schools, usually improving students' chances of entering higher education institutions. Although officially admission to such schools depends on the academic ability of a child, in practice it is often dictated by family income. Furthermore, as mentioned above, the majority of new-type and private schools are located in urban areas, thus reducing access to quality education for students from rural areas. Since 2005 the number of state schools decreased by 402 units, and in 2010/11 there were 7755 secondary schools in the country (see Table 2).

Table 2: The network of general secondary schools and number of students during the school year from 2001/2 to 2009/10

Years	Number of schools	Number of students
2001–2	8408	3084900
2002–3	8334	3115000
2003–4	8254	3044700
2004–5	8221	2935900
2005–6	8157	2824600
2006–7	8055	2715000
2007–8	7958	2627400
2008–9	7859	2561000
2009–10	7811	2534000
2010–11	7755	2534000

Source: The Agency of Statistics of the Republic of Kazakhstan[3]

According to the data of the MoES, 2522800 children were studying in 7706 day time secondary schools in 2011/12 (MoES 2012). More than 67% of schools were working in two or three shifts. In this connection, the government launched a construction initiative, '100 schools, 100 hospitals', which is also seen as an important step in the transition to a 12-year schooling model.

12 years of schooling

During Soviet times, basic education required 10 years of schooling. In 1985, as part of Gorbachev's political reforms of *perestroika* and *glasnost* ('reform' and 'transparency'), basic education was extended to 11 years of schooling to be closer to the Western standards of a 12-year education model.

In 2001, MoES initiated the extension of the duration of compulsory primary and secondary education from 11 to 12 years. In justification, government officials cited world education standards, particularly European education standards. In 1992, the Standing Conference on University Problems of the Council of Europe adopted the Declaration recognising 12-year schooling as the prevailing international education model. Thus, in accordance with the Declaration, the 12-year secondary education model is applied in 136 countries of the world including some post-Soviet countries such as Armenia, Georgia, Latvia, Lithuania, Moldova, Tajikistan, Uzbekistan, Ukraine, and Estonia.

However, the education system in Kazakhstan in the beginning of the 2000s faced a number of challenges. For example, in 2001 a working group of approximately 70 policy-makers, academics, teachers and representatives from non-governmental organisations initiated by the Soros Foundation-Kazakhstan (SFK) identified the following problems:

- The education system did not adequately reflect the new education paradigm, which emphasised individualisation and diversification and allowed upper secondary education students to make choices between academic studies and vocational paths (i.e. moving away from the Soviet centralised curriculum model).
- The curriculum was 'outdated' and 'overloaded', raising major concerns for the quality of education and the health of children. (For instance, Dzhadrina (2008) compared the weekly learning load of schools under the Soviet system, which had a standard curriculum for all republics including Kazakhstan, and found that the learning load had increased by 2002 not only because of the number of required subjects, but also because the hours for certain subjects had increased).
- Many secondary school graduates who did not enter higher education institutions faced difficulties finding employment after graduation due to their lack of basic vocational skills (Steiner-Khamsi et al. 2006).
- There was a growing concern over the quality of general secondary education, including a lack of child-centred teaching/learning methodologies and assessment systems (Steiner-Khamsi et al. 2006, 237).

In this context, the 12-year education reform was seen as an opportunity to improve the quality of education. However, promoting the extension of the length of study in basic/secondary education, and local re-conceptualisation of the reform idea, has resulted in an amalgam of different responses among the main education stakeholders (Silova 2005, 53). According to one of the surveys (Komkon-2 Eurasian 2002), the majority of education administrators (62% of government officials and 46% of school directors) supported the reform, while only 15% of education specialists, 19% of parents, 20% of present school students and 29% of teachers thought that there was a need for extending the number of years in basic/secondary education (Silova 2005, 53–4; Steiner-Khamsi et al. 2006). The results of another survey (Dzhadrina 2013) with teaching staff conducted in the Karaganda district of Kazakhstan also showed differences in opinions. Three groups of people were surveyed: in-service teacher training specialists (28), pre-school teachers (31) and the teachers of secondary schools (154). The total number of respondents was

213, with 37.5% of respondents having 13 years of teaching experience and 33.8% more than 8 years of professional experience. The majority (69.4%) of respondents thought that 12-year schooling needed to be implemented; 19.7% did not support the idea and 10.3% had never thought about this issue.

The evidence gathered in our research (2012) shows that there was a lack of clarity about 12-year schooling and the transition process. It was noted that:

> ... the transition to 12-years long secondary school education, [has] no single clear understanding in society. Some teachers also do not understand it, they are told that it should be carried out, but they have no inner, personal understanding of the need and the importance of this reform. And the people still live with the idea – 'why to change?' We used to have such a successful system of secondary education. (Consultant, International organisation A)

Some of the government officials suggested leaving the existing curriculum intact (11 years), while simply adding one year at each end of the existing education structure. There was a view that the first (additional) year would provide an opportunity for children to be better prepared for entering elementary schools, while the last (additional) year could be used for more intensive preparation for college. The most important task was to make sure that the society understands and is ready to accept the transition to a 12-year model of schooling. As one respondent stated:

> ... the 12-years long education is understood differently: some say that spending one more year at school, what for? In the Soviet Union, school education was 11 years long, and it was sufficient, and now we follow this American model, where children at school know nothing, and our children know everything. . . . So it is blind copying. . . . To be sure, it is not so, and I think many people understand it now. Today we pass to the 12 years-long system and there are no parents who would come and say: 'why are you doing it?'; we just informed everyone that it is necessary and everyone understood. (Participant K, NIS)

The initial deadlines to introduce 12-year schooling were postponed several times. The main reason was a lack of 'readiness' of human and material resources:

> ... reforming schools is a complicated process . . . it would not work like in a factory, where you replace the old equipment with a new one . . . here, we are dealing with people, so it is very complicated; we tried twice to implement the 12-years long education in schools, and we failed, because people were not ready; their mentality is not ripe . . . (Participant A, NIS)

According to the National Report (MoES 2011) about '62.3% schools do not have adequate learning environments for six year-old children and the transition to the 12-year schooling was postponed until 2015'. To facilitate the implementation of the 12-year reform, MoES studied the experience of Russia and the Baltic republics of moving to 12 years of schooling. In addition a pilot scheme of the move to 12-year education is being monitored in 104 schools in Kazakhstan including 45 in rural and 59 in urban areas. Overall, about 6813 students were involved in the experiment (4097 students in Kazakh language and 2716 students in Russian language of instruction).[4] However, some commentators (see Asanova 2006) argue that the pilot schools were selected on their 'material-technical base', and do not represent an average school in Kazakhstan. While a national research centre was created specifically to monitor the transition to 12 years of schooling it has been primarily concerned with developing probationary curricula and textbooks for Grades 1 to 5 in pilot schools.

The beginning of the transition to 12-year schooling is scheduled for 2015–16 with completion scheduled for 2020. The transition is seen as one of the most strategically important components of the educational modernisation programme and as an opportunity to set new goals and integrate the Kazakhstani education system into the international educational space. Furthermore, transition from 11 to 12 years of study was presented as a key to achieving recognition of Kazakhstan's secondary education certificates by universities internationally, thus 'enabling young people from Kazakhstan to continue their studies in the best universities abroad' (Steiner-Khamsi et al. 2006). The transition obviously requires a complex restructuring of the curriculum at all levels, an expansion of classroom space and the training of teachers in the new 12-year course. According to the data from the Ministry of Education, about 34 textbooks and 82 sets of teaching material have been developed for Grade 9 students within the transition to 12-year schooling. Furthermore, 468 teachers (71%) of 8th experimental grades undertook professional development courses between 2007 and 2011. Despite this preparatory work, there is a question about the capacity of the system to achieve the transition to 12-year schooling. The main obstacle, according to some respondents' comments in our study, is a lack of schools and teachers:

> Today the birth rate has grown by almost ten times. We saw it when we were working on the plan for a 12-year education program. There were, for example, 180,000 students of the same age group in the country, and now this number is reached 287000 or 290000. The drop is over now and we have a baby-boom. Now

to have 4–5 children is quite common for a young family . . . If before we had half-empty schools, now we have a lack of schools. They are not enough to launch a 12-year school program. (Participant D, NIS)

In addition the quality of textbooks in experimental classes was highly criticised by many respondents in this study, who argued that the 'books are very scientific . . . The material should be explained in a plain language. There are lots of terms now. It's hard for pupils to learn them by heart.' Another challenge to the transition to 12-year schooling is the fact that in the 2011/12 school year more than 67% of secondary schools worked in two or three shifts. Furthermore, one of the peculiarities of Kazakhstan's education system is the availability of ungraded schools, which make up 56.5% of the total amount of schools. In rural areas, it is about 68.6%. The Ministry of Education is planning to open about 160 supporting schools (i.e. resource centres for ungraded schools) (MoES 2010).

Revision of the curriculum

The New State General Educational Standard (Rus. GOSO – *Gosudarstvenii Obscheobyazatelnii Standard Srednego Obrazovaniya*) was approved in 2002, and until 2010 it was the key document for regulating secondary school education. This was a normative document which collected together all previously developed ideas (e.g. concepts, regulations, plans) and further developments (e.g. curriculum and textbooks). Despite the fact that the document was officially adopted in 2002, the launch of new curricula and textbooks had already begun during the 1996/97 school year. The implementation had been carried out gradually, one grade every year. The final implementation stage was completed in 2006/07 (Dzhadrina 2008). Textbooks used during the gradual implementation of the State Standard (GOSO) were updated and republished. However, textbooks were more theory-oriented with a lack of opportunity for students' creative independent work.

In its overall approach, the new State Standard still followed the former prescriptive model of content regulation, which defines items of knowledge, skills and capacities to be obtained in a large number of scientific domains (13–23 study subjects, depending on the level of secondary education). The annual classroom load for children in a group of 7–8 years old is 850 hours; for 9–11 years old 940 hours and for students 12–14 years 1190 hours; for students 16 years and older the annual classroom load is 1360 hours which is the highest among all countries in the world (Damitov et al. 2009, 141). The efforts of some teachers to integrate new learner-centred strategies of teaching and learning have not always been successful. It was challenging to integrate new ideas into the 'old' system of teaching and learning that was built on traditional methods. The existing system of teaching and curriculum for each subject in general focused on 'what to teach?' rather than 'learning how to learn'. As one respondent stated:

> . . . 20 years ago we were deeply convinced that the priority should be the content of each subject course, and we believed that if we provided students with systematic, fundamental knowledge in every field of education, then our education process would be complete. That is why the ten years of reform . . . ten years of searches have resulted, in 2002, in the appearance of the document entitled 'State Mandatory Standard for Secondary Education'. It is a framework document which determines the organisation of secondary education. And it contains our vision . . . we have put into order the content, the number of subjects, the number of academic areas; it introduced for the first time the notion of 'Differential Education'. When it was approved, this document served as the basis for developing educatory standards for various subjects, for a new generation of textbooks, which were made based on this document. (Participant A, NIS)

Although most education stakeholders were convinced of the need for a major education reform, there was still a lack of public support for the curriculum reform. This situation created a convenient entry point for the Soros Foundation-Kazakhstan (SFK) into the education policy scene (Steiner-Khamsi et al. 2006; Kalikova and Silova 2008). As mentioned above, in 2001, the SFK brought together a working group of policy-makers, academics, teachers and representatives from non-governmental organisations to discuss how the extension of secondary education could be used to revise the entire curriculum to address several specific educational issues. Furthermore, educational experts from different countries were involved (Steiner-Khamsi et al. 2006, 237). As a result, the analytical group prepared a policy paper, which outlined the dimensions of change in Kazakhstan's education and proposed a new, previously unarticulated solution for school reform – the introduction of outcome-based education (OBE) in the context of 12-year secondary education reform. As a respondent in our study commented:

> In the year 2001, was launched a project . . . as it seemed that, the reform should include a number of key steps . . . not just to provide a school with a grant, to train teachers, but it was a reform of school curriculum . . . It should be a systemic approach . . . Namely, it should be precisely about changing policy . . . and as a

result of such project, the qualification of experts was upgraded; before launching the project, the specialists examined the history of reforms in other countries, and adopted the conception of 'outcome-based education' and made use of the experience of Australia. Soros Foundation invited specialists from Australia, who organised training [courses] for the National Academy of Education that elaborates standards . . . (Consultant, International organisation A)

The policy paper presented OBE as 'an approach to systemwide improvement in education' which would define clear statements of expected outcomes to guide the organisation of the learning process, introduce learner-centred models, professionalise the role of teachers and increase community participation in the learning process (Steiner-Khamsi et al. 2006). Later some members of the analytic group were included in a working group organised by MoES, where they made key contributions to the development of the 'State Programme of Education Development for 2005–2010' (MoES 2004), and to a new policy paper 'General Secondary Education Standards in the Republic of Kazakhstan: Current Situation, Exploration, Alternatives' (2003). These two policy documents (known as the State Programme and Draft Standards) became the first policy texts that presented the idea of OBE in the Kazakhstani education context. The State Programme (2005–10), for example, underscored the importance of critical thinking, reasoning and reflection as some of the main goals of the teaching and learning process. In addition, the State Programme introduced the idea of national education standards 'oriented at student outcomes in a form of basic learner competencies' (MoES 2004, 29).

The existing system of secondary education has a notion called 'learning outcomes' (*Obrasovatelnii rezultat*), which specifies the knowledge, skills and competences that learners are to acquire (Rus. ZUN – *znaniya, umeniya i naviki*) in the course of the study of academic disciplines (or subjects). The focus on outcomes reflected an emphasis on the acquisition of subject-based knowledge that has its origins in the Soviet system of the 1930s.

Bearing in mind the philosophy of subject-based educational content, the system of secondary education in Kazakhstan is still answering the question: 'What shall be taught at school?' The list of compulsory subjects is defined and the scope of knowledge, skill and competences (ZUN) to be acquired from each subject is determined and written down in the State Educational Standard for secondary education, the standard curriculum for each subject and the subject specific teaching programmes (Dzhadrina 2004, 3–8).

Dzhadrina (2004) claims that current understanding of educational outcomes goes beyond the usual list of ZUNs correlated with learning the academic discipline. It would include knowledge and skills that are important and useful to students in their daily lives, as well as after graduation in order to be successful in life (Dzhadrina 2004, 3–8).

In Kazakhstan, research projects were conducted to increase the sense of values education and create a new model of education focused on outcomes. In addition, research has looked for ways to create a new approach that will increase the moral culture of the younger generation. For example, a project initiated by Sara Alpyskyzy Nazarbayeva on ethical development focusing on 'self-cognition' was widely supported by the teaching community and public. The key idea of this project was to facilitate the upbringing of a well-balanced individual through installation of personal qualities, this involving a value-based approach to understanding self, others, and the world. Learning objectives for 'self-cognition' as a subject were devised and content developed in the form of textbooks and study guides. Questions such as, 'How to use this concept to strengthen the value of education' were discussed in the context of this project. 'Self-cognition' can be considered as a structure-forming element, which in turn successfully cross-links all other components of educational content and integrates them.

To summarise, as Steiner-Khamsi et al. (2006, 239) argue, the introduction of OBE in Kazakhstan played a symbolic role, presenting itself 'as a drastic break from current educational practices and as a means of providing educational success for all students' (Capper and Jamison 1993, 427). Some commentators (e.g. Kalikova and Silova 2008) claim that the extension to 12-years schooling in combination with OBE was perceived as the most effective means for improving education quality, a necessary precondition for increasing Kazakhstan's competitiveness in the global market and a successful mechanism for 'entering the common world education space' (MoES 2004, 46).

The following sections will briefly focus on two important education initiatives in the first decade of the new millennium, namely a standardised national assessment – the Unified National Test (UNT) – and the development of trilingual policy (more information is given in the chapters devoted to the UNT and trilingual education).

Unified National Test

In the Soviet period, each higher education institute determined its own admissions policy and set tasks that were generally unique to their institution and, for some subjects, also relied upon oral interviews (Clark 2005). The co-existence of separate school exams and university entry exams created a number of tensions within the system (Minina 2010). Individual universities determined their own entrance exam procedure, minimal passing scores and grading criteria, and in practice had a monopoly and discretion over admissions (Osipyan 2009). As higher education was generally state-funded, many post-independent governments sought to exchange admission practices which were open to corruption or which were seen to be highly subjective with alternatives of their own overseen by a centralised body (Heyneman et al. 2008). In Kazakhstan, the Centre of National Standards in Education and Testing, otherwise known as the National Testing Centre (NTC), was set up in 1993 to develop a co-ordinated admissions policy and to report directly to the MoES. This resulted in the emergence of the first versions of a Unified National Test in 1999. After trials, a compulsory national version was adopted in 2004 which served as a school-leaving certificate as well as a means to assess candidates for entry to higher education (Drummond 2011). Those passing UNT gain an Attestat (Transcript) and Certificate which they can use to apply to universities. Since 2005, there has been held the intermediate state control of the level of knowledge of schoolchildren of 4th and 9th years of studies – ISC.

There are numerous disputes concerning the adequacy of the UNT. Proponents of the UNT maintain that, implemented alongside other reform measures, the UNT has the potential to create equal opportunities for access to higher education, to reduce corruption and to make higher education a more demand-driven industry. For example, the MoES states that the introduction of the UNT helped with 'improving the objectivity and reliability of educational assessment; providing some control over education quality and facilitating social justice in access to higher education' (MoES 2009). Opponents put forward serious objections to the universal use of the examination and point to new opportunities for malpractice, absence of public control and transparency in the exam administration and score reporting (Minina 2010, 122). The data from our research as well as results from other studies (see Asanova 2007) show that teachers had mixed reactions to the UNT as a graduation exam for secondary school leavers. Teachers stated that the UNT promoted rote learning and memorisation, as it assesses the knowledge of facts, not understanding of concepts, and narrows students' interests towards school subjects that are tested by the UNT. (For discussion of assessment, see Chapters 6 and 7 in this volume).

Trilingual policy

In Kazakhstan secondary education is provided in Kazakh, Russian, Uigur, Uzbek and Tajik languages of instruction. While schools with Kazakh and Russian as languages of instruction are spread evenly throughout the country, schools with Uighur, Uzbek and Tajik as languages are situated in the regions where these languages are mother tongues of a considerable percentage of students (Landau and Kellner-Heinkele 2001; Suleimenova and Smagulova 2005). The number of schools with Kazakh as the language of instruction has increased from 44.3% in 2000 to 45.9% in 2003, while the number of schools where Russian is the only language of instruction has decreased from 29.4% to 26.8% (UNESCO-IBE 2007). The issue of having Kazakh-medium or Russian-medium instruction in schools is politically sensitive. It was noted in our research:

> . . . the quality of teachers' training and the conditions in which operate Russian language and Kazakh language schools definitely are different. . . . Because Russian language schools receive information not only from Kazakhstan sources, but also from the Russian market . . . they can use the textbooks. . . . It is not so much about textbooks, but about supplementary readings, materials for upgrading professional skills, for the professional development of teachers, themselves. The teacher in a Russian language school is in a more favorable situation. (Consultant, International organisation A)

Over the last decade the role of the English language in general education and as an important skill for young children has been widely discussed in Kazakhstan. For example, Asanova (2007) recalled that in 2001, Bekturganov, a former Minister of Education, proposed a three-language education programme that would have entailed teaching academic subjects concurrently in three languages: Kazakh, Russian and English (e.g. Mathematics in Russian, Geography in English, and History in Kazakh) amongst students of 12 years and older. However, at that time other educators and officials were against this approach on the grounds of fiscal unfeasibility and competing priorities in a resource-scarce environment (Asanova 2007, 85). A few years later, in October 2006, President Nazarbayev proposed a project called Trinity of Languages. It was stated:

> Kazakhstan must be considered a highly developed country all over the world, where three languages are used. They are: Kazakh is a state language, Russian is a language of international communication and English is the language of integration into the global economy. (Nazarbayev, October 2006)[5]

Thus, the 'trinity of languages' is seen as an indicator of the competitiveness of the country. However, due to strong and efficient Russification, the Kazakh language has the reputation of being a backward language, and many Kazakhs are reluctant to switch to Kazakh in communication (Schatz 2000; Dave 2003). This attitude has emerged despite the changing language laws, as the Kazakh language becomes compulsory in documents and political institutions, in education and the media. The laws set high standards and demand a full use of the Kazakh language, yet few sanctions have been put in place to implement the change (Matuszkiewicz 2010). In reality, Russian is still widely used, even by the state officials. President Nazarbayev's restraining influence on language was manifested in a speech in which he criticised attempts to replace Russian with Kazakh too rapidly, noting:

> . . . it is the Russian language that unites our nation [*natsiya*], all citizens of our country. This is the way things developed historically, and this is no one's fault. We will need time in order for the Kazakh language to begin to fulfil this unifying role, and things should not be rushed. (N. Nazarbayev 2004)[6]

For a discussion of multilingual education, see Chapter 8 in this volume.

Participation in international monitoring studies

Three international testing programmes measure student performance in Reading, Maths and Science on a regular basis. The Trends in International Mathematics and Science Survey (TIMSS), a test of Science knowledge in Grades 4, 8, and 12, and the Progress in International Reading Literacy Study (PIRLS), a test of 4 Grade 4 literacy, are produced by the International Association for the Evaluation of Education Achievement (IEA). The Programme for International Student Assessment (PISA), produced by the OECD and administered every three years, measures performance in Maths, Science and Reading for 15-year-olds.

The need for Kazakhstan to take part in international monitoring studies was first discussed in 2001–4, and was initiated by the Soros Foundation-Kazakhstan as part of the 'Development of National Standards of General Secondary Education in the Conditions of the Changing World' project (OSI) discussed earlier. In 2007, Kazakhstani students took part for the first time in TIMSS. Kazakhstan was the only Central Asian country to participate in the survey, and only did so at the Grade 4 level. A total of 4271 Grade 4 pupils from 150 schools in all regions of the country took part. The performance of Kazakhstani students was particularly remarkable in Mathematics, ranking highest among post-Soviet countries and fifth highest internationally, both on the mean score and on the proportion of students reaching the advanced international benchmark (see TIMSS 2007, 35). In Science, Kazakhstani students also performed well, ranking third in the group of post-Soviet states, following Russia and Latvia, and eleventh internationally. However, the TIMSS study showed that while students were able to solve educational problems, they were not taught to apply their knowledge in life.

Kazakhstan first took part in PISA in 2009 The programme is aimed at 15-year-old pupils in each participating country. In Kazakhstan this included pupils from 184 general educational schools (with instruction in Russian and Kazakh) and 16 colleges and vocational schools (MoES 2011, 57). In December 2010, the Organisation for Economic Co-operation and Development (OECD) published the PISA 2009 results. Kazakhstan ranked 59th place out of the 65 countries that took part in PISA 2009. In addition to a general rating of the country, the report contains comparative tables reflecting the so-called contextual factors, such as influence on students' performances, teachers' qualifications, discipline in the class and so on. Even though on some of these indicators Commonwealth of Independent States (CIS) countries – including Kazakhstan – fared better than other countries, this does not change the general picture. Kazakhstan is among a group of countries whose results are far below the OECD average. For example, analysis of the results of the literacy levels of reading showed that Kazakh students were unable to cope with the tasks on the 6th level of difficulty, and only 0.4% of students were able to solve the tasks of the 5th level of difficulty (MoES 2011, 57). Kazakhstani students found it difficult to work with multiple texts, and finding and using information from various sources. All this was interpreted as indicating that the process of learning in secondary education in Kazakhstan was not sufficiently focused on practical tasks and, according to MoES (2011), not related to the realities of life. The results of the international test of scientific literacy also showed a poor performance on the part of Kazakhstani students in tasks that required a review of the results of Natural Science research and providing evidence for their point of view (MoES 2011, 60).

Table 4: The overall results of Kazakh students in PISA results in 2009

	The number of points accrued	Rank (out of 65 countries)
Reading literacy	390	59
Mathematical literacy	405	53
Scientific literacy	400	58

Source: OECD PISA, 2009

The results of these studies are usually widely discussed and have a direct impact on the formation of educational policy in the participating country. It is difficult to overestimate the importance of Kazakhstan's participation in international comparative studies to assess the educational achievements of pupils. Clearly the below-average achievement results in PISA of Kazakhstani students have generated pressure for reform and have led to educational experts in Kazakhstan being sent to visit other countries in order to learn how to refine its educational policies. It was also acknowledged that:

> If we were more or less ahead in terms of results, it does not really matter. The most important thing is that we get a certain place, which is a good sign. It is a good sign that our schools, our teachers are trying to change . . . (Participant A, NIS)

Between 3 and 30 April 2012, Kazakhstani students participated in the PISA 2012. Around 5000 students from 218 education organisations in all 16 regions of Kazakhstan participated in the study. It was conducted according to the schedule drawn up jointly with the Education Departments of the provinces (*oblast*) and the cities of Astana and Almaty. President Nazarbayev, while delivering his annual address to the Nation 'Socio-economic modernisation – main direction of development of Kazakhstan', charged the government to develop the National Action plan for 2012–16 aimed at the development of the functional literacy of students. In this regard, the holding of independent monitoring studies of academic achievements including the participation of Kazakhstani students in the international studies such as PISA and TIMSS is a real effective measure in this direction.

Conclusion

This chapter has explored some of the factors that have had an impact on the trajectory of educational development in the country such as rapid economic growth and the Soviet legacy, the commitment to building Kazakhstan's competitiveness as a nation and the goal of reaching world educational standards. It has highlighted a strong government intervention and substantial investments in the process of educational reform in that period. Despite this, the highly centralised Soviet-style management created a situation in which education authorities at most levels of the system had neither the power nor the incentives to make key operating decisions. Furthermore, the legacy of the 'Soviet insistence on planning' (Steiner-Khamsi et al. 2006, 223) was still observed in five- or ten-year plans in all areas of economic, social and educational development in Kazakhstan.

The driving force behind secondary education reform in the 2000s was the creation of a new education space, symbolising Kazakhstan's movement to new, European education standards (Chapman et al. 2005; Silova 2005; Steiner-Khamsi et al. 2006). This phase of initiatives in education covers the period when the application of neo-liberal ideas and values started to become evident. The transition to a 12-year schooling model was seen as a strategically important precondition for realigning both the primary and higher education systems toward world standards. However, it took over 10 years for the entire education community to understand the importance of this transition and the fundamental change from the old model it implied. To date, some issues remain controversial, such as the internal structure of 12-year schooling: an addition of one grade to primary school, or middle school or high school. Other issues relate to the capacity of the system. Systemic imbalances in educational quality and provision between rural and urban schools are found on almost every educational indicator. Salient issues include: declining achievement and completion rates, the deteriorating school infrastructure, a shortage of qualified teachers and differentiated access to high quality education (HDR 2004). Regional differences were also significant.

The extension of secondary education to 12 years was presented as an opportunity to revise the Soviet-style curriculum which, according to Steiner-Khamsi et al. (2006, 235), 'resulted in the emergence of outcome-based education (OBE), signalling Kazakhstan's desire to join the Western alliance and increase its competitiveness on the global market'. Interestingly, OBE was not entirely new in the post-socialist context, but rather revitalised a practice that had been quite common in socialist times. As a result, OBE resonated well with the post-socialist policy-makers (Steiner-Khamsi et al. 2006, 235).

However, the introduction of OBE played a largely symbolic role in the 2000s. The content of the school curriculum remained overloaded and the amount of required learning materials increased every year. The curriculum still did not have clear methods for setting expected results as indicators of the consistency of expectations of individuals, society and the state. The education process was still not strongly focused on encouraging students' independent learning. The success of students was measured primarily in terms of the quantity of acquired knowledge rather than in terms of a wider spectrum of skills and competencies.

The role of international organisations within the country changed in this period. For example, during the 1990s the Open Society Institute (OSI) and its parent organisation, Soros Foundation-Kazakhstan, focused their efforts on implementing 'demonstration' projects to model best practice at the school level. During the second phase OSI shifted its strategy to ensure greater sustainability of the 'demonstration' projects and to increase the systematic impact of its education initiatives (Silova 2008, 52). Within the third phase, during the 2000s, OSI made concentrated efforts to get involved in national education policy-making to influence reform on a larger scale through a combination of carefully designed 'demonstration' projects, systems-reform activities and education advocacy initiatives (Silova 2008, 52).

As this illustrates, curriculum reform in Kazakhstan provides an interesting example of collaboration between the community of international organisations and the state. The involvement of nationally recognised educational experts was an important strategy which demonstrated that the reform was initiated by local experts who commanded high regard and respect among academics, professionals and politicians nationally (Kalikova and Silova 2008). The goal was not educational borrowing per se (or adopting best practice from abroad), but rather the development of a basic framework and the creation of favourable conditions that would help policy-makers to assess, understand and address national educational issues in a broader comparative context (Kalikova and Silova 2008, 148). A range of conferences and workshops were organised with the aim of developing local capacity and knowledge and influencing the thinking of 'Soviet-bred' specialists by providing opportunities to learn about different philosophical approaches to curriculum organisation, the relationships between curriculum and teaching/learning, as well as techniques and approaches to education reform.

Overall, during the 2000s across Kazakhstan, there was an increase in teacher and public participation in discussions, conferences and workshops about various issues related to education reform. There were a number of opportunities for teachers to share their experience about the use of new strategies, teaching methods, research techniques, lesson plans and plans of extra-curricular activities in educational journals such as *Kazakhstan Schools, Primary School, Open School, Creative Pedagogy* and others. It is important to acknowledge that the creative work of teachers was focused primarily on improving methods, forms and tools; they had little input into the key driving elements of education such as learning objectives and the specified content of certain subjects. This resulted not only from the centralised command and control system predominant in secondary education, but also from the traditional knowledge-based paradigm, which was still the key philosophy of education in school in the 2000s. As explained above, the traditional way of teaching was based on a standard regulation which determines how the education process should be administered in schools (e.g. 'State Standards for General Education in Kazakhstan' 2002). The knowledge-based paradigm was seen as a key factor in the success of the Soviet school and was therefore still supported not only by the education community but also by the adult population as the main value of education.

The key strategic step towards 'entering' the world education arena was Kazakhstan's participation in international studies (e.g., PISA and TIMSS). Importantly, the results have raised some issues that key policy makers and educational officials were not able to ignore and were forced to address in the light of international attention.

There is a lot of uncertainty in the context of globalisation and internationalisation about how educational initiatives mesh with national, regional and local contexts. The distinctiveness of Kazakhstan lies in the fact that there is a strong modernising project underway, that this is well-financed, and that it is operating on a system that had already been subject to central reform through Russification, but also one in which there remains a strong commitment on the part of some sections of society to preserve Kazakhstani traditions. However, change was already underway, and from 2008 onwards a new stage of education reform began, which will be discussed in the next chapter.

REFERENCES

ADB (Asian Development Bank) (2004). *Education Reforms in Countries in Transition: Policies and Processes. Six Country Case Studies Commissioned by the Asian Development Bank in Azerbaijan, Kazakhstan, Kyrgyz Republic, Mongolia, Tajikistan, and Uzbekistan.* Manila: Asian Development Bank.

Asanova, J. (2006). 'Emerging Regions, Persisting Rhetoric of Educational Aid: The Impact of the Asian Development Bank on Education Policy-Making in Kazakhstan'. *International Journal of Educational Development,* 26:6, 655–66.

— (2007). 'Seeing Near and Far: Balancing Stakeholder Needs and Rights in Kazakhstan's Educational Reform'. *Canadian and International Education,* 36:2, 71–90.

Capper, C. and Jamison, M. (1993). 'Outcomes-Based Education Reexamined: From Structural Functionalism to Poststructuralism'. *Education Policy,* 7:4, 427–46.

Chapman, D.W., Weidman, J., Cohen, M. and Mercer, M. (2005). 'The Search for Quality: A Five-Country Study of National Strategies to Improve Educational Quality in Central Asia'. *International Journal of Educational Development,* 25:5, 514–30.

Clark, N. (2005). 'Education Reform in the Former Soviet Union'. *World Education News and Reviews.* City.

Dave, B. (2003). *Minorities and Participation in Public Life: Kazakhstan.* Paris: Commission on Human Rights, Sub-Commission on Promotion of Human Rights, United Nations. Working Paper.

Damitov, B.K., Ermekov, N.T. Bekenova, A.B., Mozhaeva O.I., Absamatov, A.U. et al. (2006). *National Report on the Status and Development of Education.* Astana: National Center for Assessment of the Quality of Education.

Damitov, B.K., Ermekov, N.T., Bekenova A.B., Mozhaeva, O.I., Absamatov, A.U., Golovataya, G.I. and Gabdulina A.V. (2007). *National Report on the State and Development of Education* (Short Version). Astana: MoES and National Center for Assessment of the Quality of Education.

Damitov, B.K., Ermekov, N.T., Mozhaeva, O.I., Bekenova, A.B., Bekish, R.M., Golovataya, G.I., Egimbaeva, Z.K. and Bondar, L.A. (2008). *National Report on the Status and Development of Education.* Astana: MoES and National Center for Assessment of the Quality of Education.

Damitov, B.K., Ermekov, N.T., Mozhaeva, O.I., Golovataya, G.I., Egimbaeva, Z.K., Nogaibalanova, S.Z., Suleimanova, S.A., Mahmetova, G.P. and Tekesheva, T.U. (2009). *National Report on the Status and Development of Education in the Republic of Kazakhstan.* Astana: Ministry of Education and Science and National Center for Assessment of the Quality of Education.

Drummond, T. (2011). 'Higher Education Admission Regimes in Kazakhstan and Kyrgyzstan'. In I. Silova, (ed.), *Globalisation on the Margins.* Charlotte, NC: Information Age Publishing.

Dzhadrina, M. (2004). 'Problems of Identifying Multi-Level Learning Outcomes in School'. *Open School,* 8:33, 3–8. Rus. Dzhadrina, M. (2004). 'Problema opredeleniya mnogourovnevoi sistemi ozhidaemih rezultatov obucheniya v shkole'. *Otkritaya shkola,* 8:33, 3–8.

— (2008). 'Opportunities for Strengthening the Value Relevance of Education in the Context of Globalization'. International conference, 'The development of a national system of education in the context of globalisation', 20–21 October 2008. Rus. Dzhadrina, M. (2008). 'Vozmozhnosti usileniya cennostnoi znachimosti obrazovaniya v usloviyax globalizacii. Mezhdunarodnaya nauchno-prakticheskaya konferenciya Altinsarinskie chteniya Razvitie nacionalnoi sistemi obrazovaniya v usloviyax globalizacii', 20–21 Oktyabrya 2008.

— (2013). 'Educational Reforms in the End of the 2000s: Innovations in the System of School Education'. Unpublished paper, Astana, September 2013. Rus. 'Obrazovatelnie reformi v konce 2000-h godov', Astana Sentyabr 2013.

HDR (2004). *Education for All: The Key Goal for a New Millenium.* Human Development Report. www. hdr.undp.org/en/reports/national/europethecis/kazakhstan/kazakhstan_2004_en.pdf

Heyneman, S., **Anderson**, K. and **Nuralieva**, N. (2008). 'The Cost of Corruption in Higher Education'. *Comparative Education Review,* 52:1, 1–25.

Kalikova, S. and **Silova**, I. (2008). 'From Educational Brokers to Local Capacity Builders: Redefining International NGOs in Kazakhstan'. In I. Silova and G. Steiner-Khamsi, (eds), *How NGOs Reach: Globalisation and Education Reform in the Caucasus, Central Asia, and Mongolia.* Bloomfield, CT: Kumarian Press.

Landau, J.M. and **Kellner-Heinkele**, B. (2001). *Politics of Language in the Ex-Soviet Muslim States: Azerbaijan, Uzbekistan, Kazakhstan, Kyrgyzstan, Turkmenistan and Tajikistan.* Ann Arbor, MI: University of Michigan Press.

Matuszkiewicz, R. (2010). 'The Language Issue in Kazakhstan: Institutionalizing New Ethnic Relations after Independence'. *Economic and Environmental Studies,* 10, 211–27.

Minina, E. (2010). 'The Unified National Test for Student Admission to Higher Education in Russia: A Pillar of Modernisation? From Past to Present'. In E.M. Johnson, (ed.), *Politics, Modernisation and Educational Reform in Russia.* Oxford: Symposium Books.

MoES (Ministry of Education and Science) (2004). 'State Programme of Education Development for 2005–2010'. Astana: MoES.

— (2009). *System of Higher Education in Kazakhstan: Achievements and Perspectives of Development.* Country Report. Astana: MoES.

— (2010). 'State Programme of Education Development'. Astana: MoES.

— (2011). *National Report on the Status and Development of the Republic of Kazakhstan* (Concise Version). Astana: The National Center for the Education Quality Assessment.

Nazarbayev, N. (2008). 'Improving Welfare of the Citizens of Kazakhstan – The Main Goal of the State Policy'. 6 February 2008. *Kazakhstanskaya pravda,* 7 February 2008, N26 (25473). Rus. 'Povishenie blagosostoyaniya grazhdan Kazakhstana - glavnaya cel gosudarstvennoi politiki. Poslanie Prezidenta Respubliki Kazakhstan narodu Kazakhstan'. Astana, 6 Fevralya 2008. *Kazakhstanskaya pravda,* N26 (25473).

OECD (2009). *PISA 2009 Results: What Makes a School Successful? Resources, Policies and Practices.* IV, 304.

Osipian, A.L. (2009). 'Corruption Hierarchies in Higher Education in the Former Soviet Bloc'. *International Journal of Educational Development,* 29, 321–33.

Schatz, E. (2000). Framing Strategies and Non-Conflict in Multi-Ethnic Kazakhstan. *Nationalism and Ethnic Politics*, 6, 71–94.

Schwab, K. (2012/13). *The Global Competitiveness Report*. The World Economic Forum

— (2013/14). *The Global Competitiveness Report*. The World Economic Forum.

Silova, I. (2005). 'Travelling Policies: hijacked in Central Asia'. *European Educational Research Journal*, 4(1), 50–59.

— (2008). 'Championing Open Society: The Education Logic of the Soros Foundation Network'. In I. Silova and G. Steiner-Khamsi, (eds), *How NGOs React: Globalisation and Education Reform in the Caucasus, Central Asia and Mongolia*. Bloomfield, CT: Kumarian Press.

— (2011). *Globalization on the Margins: Education and Postsocialist Transformations in Central Asia*. Charlotte, NC: Information Age Publishing, Inc.

Silova, I. and Steiner-Khamsi, G. (2008). *How NGOs React: Globalization and Education Reform in the Caucasus, Central Asia, and Mongolia*, Bloomfield, CT: Kumarian Press.

Steiner-Khamsi, G., Silova, I. and Johnson, E. (2006). 'Neoliberalism Liberally Applied: Educational Policy Borrowing in Central Asia'. In D. Coulby, J. Ozga, T. Seddon and T.S. Popkewitz, (eds), *World Yearbook on Education*. London and New York: Routledge.

Suleimenova, E. and Smagulova, J. (2005). *Yazikovaya Situatsiya v Kazakhstane [The Language Situation in Kazakhstan]*. Almaty: Qazaq Universiteti.

Tasbulatova, S. and Belosludtseva., V. (2007). *Skills Development and Poverty Reduction in Kazakhstan. ETF working document*. European Training Foundation.

TIMSS (2007). *TIMSS 2007 International Mathematics Report: Findings from IEA's Trends in International Mathematics and Science Study at the Fourth and Eighth Grades*. Boston: IEA, TIMSS and PIRLS International Study Center, Lynch School of Education, Boston College.

UNDP (2004). 'Human Development Report. Education for All: the Key Goal for a New Millenium'. Kazakhstan: Pilot TC.

— (2011). 'Human Development Report, Kazakhstan'. www.un.kz/en/articles/1/41.jsp.

UNESCO EFA (2010). 'Education For All Global Monitorin Report. Reaching the marginalized'. Paris. www.unesco.org/new/en/education/themes/leading-the-international-agenda/efareport/reports/2010-marginalization/.

UNESCO-IBE (2007). 'World Data in Education'. UNESCO-IBE, www.ibe.unesco.org.

— (2011). 'World Data in Education'. UNESCO-IBE, www.ibe.unesco.org.

NOTES

1   Address of the President of Kazakhstan Mr. Nursultan Nazarbayev to the Nation of Kazakhstan New Kazakhstan in the New World, March, 2007. www.kazakhembus.com/document/presidents-2007-address (retrieved 30 October 2013).

2   Address of the President of Kazakhstan Mr. Nursultan Nazarbayev on 28 January 2011. www.kazakhembus.com/document/presidents-2011-address (retrieved 30 October 2013).

3   www.eng.stat.kz/digital/Education/Pages/default.aspx.

4   Source: www://spy.kz/2010.

5   www://centralasiaonline.com/en_GB/articles/caii/features/2008/08/04/feature-03 (retrieved 30 October 2013).

6   Speech of N. Nazarbayev on III Congress of educational and Science specialists. Kazakhstanskaya Pravda, 13 October 2004. Available at: www.kazpravda.kz/ (retrieved 12 April).

3 EDUCATIONAL REFORM IN KAZAKHSTAN:
The Contemporary Policy Agenda

Olena Fimyar, Natallia Yakavets and David Bridges
(University of Cambridge, Faculty of Education)

The intention of this chapter is to review the contemporary state of educational reform in Kazakhstan, as a preliminary to the discussion of more specific features of the process that follow. In Kazakhstan, however, the 'contemporary', the 'present' and the 'today' are peculiarly fleeting moments given the speed with which new reforms are introduced, so we should perhaps locate ourselves more precisely in time. We are writing in the autumn of 2013 at what might turn out to be a pivotal moment in the reform process. It is pivotal, first, because a new Minister of Education, Aslan Sarinzhipov, was appointed in September with a clear mandate from government to secure rapid change. Sarinzhipov is co-author of the final chapter in this book, 'The way forward'. By the end of November 2013 the minister will have received an action plan for educational reform developed by a team of international advisors (including several contributors to this book). International reference and benchmarking remains firmly on the agenda, even if, as is sometimes politely suggested, such advice is 'an expensive way to confirm what we already know'! In parallel with this, different departments of the Ministry of Education and Science (MoES) are developing their plans. Already in the last few weeks government has approved an ambitious plan developed by Nazarbayev Intellectual Schools (NIS) for the mainstreaming of their educational practice and experience. In the meantime the in-service training programme associated with the Centre of Excellence (CoE) will, by the end of 2013, have already reached some 20000 teachers. Of course a flurry of activity emanating from the centre does not in itself mean any radical change in what happens in schools, and a monitoring and evaluation programme will be implemented in 2014 designed to assess the impact so far of at least the CoE programme.

These and other changes are, however, framed by some wider strategic objectives both for the country as a whole and for the health, education and social services sector. We shall rehearse here some of the key features

of the policy documents that are shaping the contemporary education reform agenda before turning to more specific and immediately visible developments within the sector.

The strategic vision for educational development: A review of policy documents

The 'Kazakhstan 2030' and 'Kazakhstan 2050' strategies provide a framework for a number of state programmes including the 'State Programme of
Education Development for 2011–2020'.[1] This section reviews strategic priorities for education outlined in four policy documents: (1) the 'Kazakhstan
2030 Strategy' (approved in October 1997); (2) the 'Strategic Plan Kazakhstan
2020' (approved on February 1, 2010); (3) the 'State Programme of Education
Development for 2011–2020' (approved on 7 December, 2010) and (4) the
'Kazakhstan 2050 Strategy' (delivered as an annual Presidential address on
14 December, 2012).

Kazakhstan 2030 Strategy: A new vision of a new state

The 'Kazakhstan 2030 Strategy' provides a political vision and rationale for
reforms in various sectors of economy and society. The document is different
in style and presentation from the other documents reviewed in this chapter.
It combines elements of political analysis, allegory and historical narrative. A
number of proverbs and quotes from different cultures and epochs are used
as a leitmotif for each section and incorporated in the main text. These reflect a particular Kazakhstani world view and trace Kazakhstan's search for
its place – historical, cultural, conceptual – among other nations, cultures
and civilizations.

This emblematic document starts by mapping out the horizons of 'our
epoch' (p. 17) and drawing a clear line between the previous stages of development and a new era of reform and prosperity in Kazakhstan. The documents states that:

> [W]e have parted with our former political and economic system for good and
> all. I mean the system that for seventy years dominated our lives. Today we have
> an altogether new state, and an utterly different political and economic system is
> at work now. (Nazarbayev 1997, 5)

The Strategy stresses the sense of urgency of the reforms through the phrases such as: '[t]ime has come to say once and for all what future we want to build' (p. 2), 'we cannot afford putting off solutions [...] for tomorrow' (p. 3), 'we cannot afford waiting' (p. 3), 'it was too early yesterday but it might be too late tomorrow' (p. 3), '[in] this race we cannot afford lagging behind' (p. 28). The document is infused with a sense of pride and confidence that 'by the year of 2030 Kazakhstan would have become a Central-Asia Snow Leopard [as opposed to Asian Tigers] and would serve a fine example to be followed by other developing countries'. Allegorically the document describes how '[It will be] a Kazakhstani Snow Leopard with inherent elitarianism [sic.], sense of independence, intelligence, courage and nobleness, bravery and cunning' (p. 11). The 'Kazakhstani Snow Leopard would also possess western elegance multiplied by the advanced level of development, oriental wisdom and endurance' (p. 12). (See Chapter 9 on 'Soviet, Kazakh and the World' for a more in-depth treatment of the topic of policy construction in Kazakhstan).

The document is infused with a strong moral purpose, which calls for an almost parental responsibility of the present generation towards future generations. Examples of this include: 'what future we want to build for us and for our children' (p. 2), 'our generation bears tremendous responsibility to future generations, it is in fact responsibility of parents and grandparents to their children and grandchildren' (p. 2), '[w]hat will our children and grandchildren be - the way we want to see them in that remote future - when they are our age? Will they be well-off, well-fed, healthy and well-educated? Will they live in a prosperous and democratic society? Will they live in peace?', (p. 2) '[y]et only we, none other than we, are capable of coping with this enormous work which is indispensable for the implementation of our dream of and hope for building the Kazakhstan, which our children and grandchildren will be proud of when they are our age' (p. 3), [y]et, we do all this not only for our own benefit but for the benefit of our children and grandchildren, first and foremost. (p. 5).

The vision for education in the 'Kazakhstan 2030 Strategy' is captured in the paragraph stating that:

> [Our children] would be well-educated and healthy. They would be prepared to work in conditions of modern market economy sticking though to the traditions of their forefathers. They would have an equally good command of the Kazakh, Russian and English languages. They would be patriots of their peaceful, prosperous, rapidly growing country well-known and respected all over world. (Nazarbayev 1997, 12–13)

However, alongside the bright vistas for the future the document stresses the problem of Soviet legacies which prevent a number of Kazakhstani citizens from adapting to the conditions of market economy (pp. 20–21). The document also emphasises a growing gap between the rich and the poor in Kazakhstan which runs along the rural/urban divide in the country:

> The countryside of today has become an epitome of major social problems: non-payment of wages and pensions, backwardness, poverty and unemployment, poor ecology, poor infrastructure, education and health care. Meanwhile the country-side manifests the highest demographic potential. Badly needed resources laboriously 'collected' at the central level don't reach the country-side accumulating in the city. (Nazarbayev 1997, 22)

The Strategic Plan 2020: A focus on pre-school education, curriculum and inclusion

The 'Strategic Plan 2020' details the first phase of implementation of the 'Kazakhstan 2030 Strategy'. It has an extended section on education (pp. 32–4) which stipulates that '[b]y the year 2020 a radical modernisation of all levels of education – from pre-school to higher education – will be completed' (p. 32). It is stated that the state will 'provide opportunities for pre-school education to all children regardless of locality and family income' (p. 32), 'the transition to 12-year schooling [. . .] will be completed'. The document puts emphasis on developing competencies and expanding life-long learning opportunities. The central mission for the modernisation of the system of secondary education is delegated to the Nazarbayev Intellectual Schools, which are conceptualised as 'experimental grounds for development, implementation and piloting of curriculum for kindergartens, pre-school and 12-year education sectors' (p. 32). It is envisaged that the new curriculum 'will combine the best Kazakhstani traditions [in teaching] and best international practices' (p. 32). The state will continue to expand access to education for vulnerable groups of children: children with special needs and low income families. By 2015 the Plan envisages the implementation of the new Educational Standard, also known as GOSO (Rus. GOSO – *Gosudarstvenii Obscheobyazatelnii Standard Obrazovaniya*), and per-capita financing of schools [with the exception of ungraded schools] (p. 34). Important for the discussion presented later in the chapter (and also in chapter 9) is the view of the student advanced in the document. A Kazakhstani student is regarded as 'educated, with high moral values, critical thinking, physically and spiritually developed citizen of Kazakhstan, striving for self-development and creativity' (p. 34).

Kazakhstan 2050 Strategy: A continuous focus on pre-school education and curriculum reform

The 'Kazakhstan 2050 Strategy',[2] which was delivered by the President as the Address to the Nation in December 2012, outlines key strategic developments in different sectors of economy and society including education. Reporting on the implementation of the long-term development strategy 'Kazakhstan 2030: Prosperity, Security and Improvement of the Well-Being of Kazakhstan's Citizens', the 2050 Strategy states that: '[s]ince 1997 we have built 942 schools and 758 hospitals across the country' (p. 7). The document confers the 'progressive' implementation of a 'policy of affordable and high-quality education' (p. 7). The coverage of children by early and pre-school education – two policy areas which are under continuous close control of the government – is reported to reach 65.4% and 94.7 % respectively. In the framework of the *Balapan* (in Kazakh, 'Chicken') programme, '3956 new kindergartens and mini-centers', aimed at 'equaliz[ing] the starting opportunities of our children', were opened across the country (p. 21). The 2050 Strategy advocates the shift to new methods in pre-school and secondary education, the introduction of online and distance education, the establishment of public-private partnerships, obligatory practice for high school students in industry and enterprise ventures, and updating the existing school curriculum. The importance of developing entrepreneurship skills and fostering innovation is reflected in the need to 'create entrepreneurship oriented curricula, educational courses and institutions' (p. 21).

The above strategic documents provide a broad framework for development in various areas including education. This strategic vision is then translated into the State Programme of Education Development, which is the object of analysis in the next section.

The State Programme of Education Development: Problems, target indicators and solutions

The 'State Programme of Education Development for 2011–2020' (MoES 2010)[3] was approved by the Decree of the President of the Republic of Kazakhstan No. 1118 on 7 December 2010. It specifies priorities, sets target indicators and offers solutions to problems in all areas of education including secondary-level education, higher education and technical and vocational education. This section reviews the initiatives and issues in secondary-level education.

The State Programme as a whole is underpinned by a strong economic imperative, which views education as a means to economic competitiveness. This rationale is reflected in the goal of the programme, which seeks 'to increase the competitiveness of education and the development of human capital through ensuring access to quality education for sustainable economic growth' (MoES 2010, 2). Similarly, the references to 'educational services', 'public-private partnership', 'implementation of corporate governance principles [in educational management]', and 'development of competitive human capital for economic prosperity, 'in accordance to the requirements of industrial-innovative economic development' demonstrate the commitment of the policy-makers to the economic development agenda.

In providing the rationale for a set of measures for 'investment in human capital', the document makes references to the vision of national development outlined in 'Kazakhstan 2030 Strategy'. In particular, the programme re-states that 'by 2020 Kazakhstan will have become an educated country with a smart economy and highly qualified labor force' (MoES 2010, 6). In the opinion of policy-makers the successful implementation of the Programme will be ensured 'due to understanding of the importance of human capital development by the country's top officials and all-round support rendered while initiating reforms in the education sector' (p. 7).

The *Analysis of the current situation* section deserves particular attention. After listing a number of educational initiatives including the development of the Quality Assurance System, investment in internet and IT technologies, Science laboratories and multi-media classrooms, the successful results of the 2007 TIMSS International Comparative Study, the piloting of the 33 trilingual schools and the network of NIS schools, the Programme admits that 'the education sector of Kazakhstan remains uncompetitive' (MoES 2010, 9).

In secondary-level education the programme identifies the following areas which call for immediate attention. The first problem area is the *critical state of the school infrastructure*. In particular, according to the 2010 data, out of 7576 schools throughout the country '37.4% of schools do not have access to drinking water'; 'every fifth school lacks either a dining room or canteen'; '26.4% of schools do not have gyms' (MoES 2010, 10.). These and other factors resulted in postponing the implementation of the 12-year education in the country. Another problem area is the number of *ungraded schools* in the sparsely populated areas of the country. According to the programme, the number of ungraded schools constitutes 56.5% of the total number of schools in the country (for comparison, 52% in 2005). In rural areas 68.6% of schools are ungraded schools and 'every fourth teacher is working and every sixth pupil is studying in ungraded schools' (MoES 2010).

The increase of number *of students with disabilities* from 124000 in 2005 to 149000 in 2010 is viewed as another problem area. The issues of the *ageing* and *feminisation of teaching profession* whereby 'every fifth teacher in Kazakhstan is aged 50 or more' and '81.3% of teachers in Kazakhstan are women' (MoES 2010), also call for immediate attention. The reason behind these tendencies is low wages (approximately 60% of the national average), which fuel another troubling tendency of the growing number of teachers who choose to leave the profession. This negative dynamic persists despite that fact that 'since 2000 the wage of education sector employees has grown by 400%' (ibid.); yet 'it remains one of the lowest' across the country. Furthermore, the educational institutions and the children's organisations 'have not fully used their upbringing potential yet' and their existing activities are 'ineffective' (MoES 2010, 11).

Importantly, the 'Secondary Education' section of the programme (pp. 10–11) is critical of 'outdated methodology' and 'information overload' in school. These factors, in the opinion of the authors of the Programme, result in a 'decrease in learning motivation and deterioration in the health of students' (ibid.). The section concludes by a sweeping statement that 'the education sector focuses today on formal results but not on personality development' (ibid.).

In order to address the above problems and achieve the 'cardinal modernization' of education (p. 6), the Programme sets a number of target indicators to be reached by 2020. These include the transition to 12-year schooling, raising the number of students successfully completing Science and Mathematics programmes from 60% in 2015 to 70% in 2020, improving the results of participation in international studies of student assessment from the 50–55th place in 2015 PISA to the 40–45th place in 2020 PISA; from the 10–15th place in 2015 TIMSS to the 10–12th place in 2020 TIMSS, and 10–15th in 2020 PIRLS (p. 35). In the areas of inclusive education the programme sets an indicator to ensure that 30% of schools in 2015 and 70% in 2020 are accessible to students with special needs (p. 35).

Under the heading '[The] solution of the problems of ungraded schools' the Programme lists a set of measures aimed at raising education quality in ungraded schools. Among those measures are:

- opening the National Centre for Development of Ungraded Schools at Altynsarin National Academy of Education, which will provide methodological support for 14 regional centres for teacher professional development;
- launching a free school bus programme;
- installing broadband internet and widening e-learning opportunities in all ungraded schools with 10 and more students.

The document advocates the opening of supporting schools in regional centres, which will function as resource centres for ungraded schools. The Programme specifies that:

> There will be several ungraded schools assigned to each resource centre. The students of ungraded schools study for 10 days three times a year in the supporting school (at the beginning, in the middle and at the end of the academic year) and pass intermediate and final examination there. During the inter-session period the teaching-learning process in ungraded schools is conducted with the participation of teachers from supporting schools and with the help of distance technologies. Thus, resource centers will provide the students of ungraded schools with the access to quality education. (MoES 2010, 38)

It is envisaged that 160 supporting schools will be opened across the country.

The problems of demand and availability of resources faced by secondary-level education set a critical and ambitious tone to the programme. By providing a detailed analysis of the current situation and vision for the future, the document underlines that the most pertinent problem of educational development in the country remains the gap between rural and urban schools in terms of access to educational facilities, transportation and living conditions. The last two factors are not entirely solvable by the efforts of the Ministry of Education and Science alone and will, no doubt, remain a matter of national priority for the years to come.

Current developments

Education has a high priority in Kazakhstan government policy, though the level of funding for education still has some way to go before it compares with that of international competitors. Five developments in mainstream education are perhaps especially noteworthy at this time.

1. Expansion of pre-school provision

In the 1990s many kindergartens were closed, destroyed, or were sold off as, in the face of high unemployment, there was no demand for them. Today Kazakhstan has over 1 million children under the primary school starting age of seven, but not all of them receive any sort of early years education.

The government is trying to close the gap between the demand for and supply of pre-school education through *Balapan* program. It includes an accelerated kindergarten school building initiative; the streamlining of pre-schools' licensing and significant government subsidies paid to private pre-schools for each pupil that they enrol. Since the initiation of the programme the total number of pre-schools has increased by more than five times, and the proportion of children aged one to six attending some form of pre-school has risen from 23.2% in 2005 to 41.6% in 2012 (MoES 2013). The 'Kazakhstan 2050 Strategy' sets out ambitious targets for the expansion of early education, specifying that by 2020 there will be access to pre-school and upbringing organisations for 100% of children aged three to six.

According to data from MoES (2013), about 71.5% of children from three to six year old were attending pre-school in 2012. The teacher-child ratio in pre-school was 1:23 in 2012, which is higher than in other OECD countries (which is 1:14). Furthermore, there are some other troubling issues, which are widely discussed in public documents, including: the poor quality of teacher training, the lack of high quality teaching staff (only 57% of pre-school teachers have attended higher education institutions); and the slow development of inclusive education in early years (less than a third of young children with disabilities have access to pre-school education; MoES 2010). Another issue of concern is the increase in the number of private kindergartens being set up without any formal licensing process and with relaxed inspection procedures and different types of organisation. The differences that exist in funding, resources, personnel and monitoring procedures make it difficult to assure consistent quality across the system. (Ayubayeva et al. 2013, 21).

2. Extension of secondary education to 12 years of schooling and review of assessment

The extension of schooling to 12 years is one of the major aims of the government, which is stated in the 'State Programme of Education Development for 2011–2020'. The transition of the whole system to this model is expected to be completed in 2020, but many challenges remain. Importantly, 12-year schooling requires a complex restructuring of the curriculum at all levels. This could be seen as an opportunity to introduce more intellectually engaging and demanding material and move away from a knowledge-based paradigm, with an emphasis on memorisation and facts rather than, for example, critical thinking and problem solving. The 'Concept Paper' which was developed in 2010,[4] includes some encouraging messages. In it the rationale is clearly stated with the aim to: 'overcome traditional re-productive learning style and the transition to a new developmental, struc-tural model of education providing cognitive activity and independence of thought'. The document makes reference to the development of a competence based approach to the design of the curriculum. However, the document fails to adopt a competence-based approach when it begins to describe what the curriculum should consist of. The evidence from the research project 'Internationalisation and Reform of Secondary Schooling in Kazakhstan', conducted in 2013, suggests that there is a tendency to pack more and ra-ther technical information into the programme. Furthermore, teachers that are already introducing 12-year education were very critical of the quality of textbooks to support a new curriculum which were overloaded with scientific information inappropriate for a school level.

Moreover, there are ongoing debates about the effectiveness of an existing assessment system in Kazakhstan. The Unified National Test (UNT) is often described as 'dysfunctional' from a number of points of view (Ayubayeva et al. 2013, 21). The major criticism is about the tests themselves, which are based on the recall of a selection of factual information. The UNT, which serves as a school leaving certificate, is strongly criticized by the higher edu-cation institutions because the tests based on five subjects do not take into account the peculiarities of various (tertiary-level) majors. Furthermore, UNT results are often used to 'measure' teachers' performance and enter into the process of awarding performance based pay – a task for which they are singularly unsuited.

Under plans for the 12 years of schooling it is proposed that there will be two tests following completion of Grade 12: one test providing as it were a statement of achievements at the point of leaving school; another being a new university independent entrance examination. (See Chapters 6 and 7 for a fuller discussion of issues of assessment).

3. Piloting trilingual education in the mainstream

Trilingual education is seen as an important strategy for boosting a country's competitiveness. Speaking about Kazakhstan's trilingual policies, President Nazarbayev stated:

> I think that knowledge of three languages, teaching young people three languages, is the right thing to do, because it is an imperative of our time, our geographic location demands it, and technological development is closely linked to it. (N. Nazarbayev, 20 October 2013)[5]

According to data provided by the National Centre for Educational Statistics, in 2012 about 58.8% of students were in Kazakh-medium schools in comparison to 57.9% in 2011. Furthermore, 200 pre-schools and 33 secondary schools are piloting trilingual education. Starting from September 2013, schools in Kazakhstan were expected gradually to introduce English-language learning from the first grade. However, problems arose from a lack of suitably qualified teachers (particularly in rural areas), and appropriate textbooks and teaching materials. Despite the fact that 32 higher educational institutions in Kazakhstan have already begun training 5500 teachers in English for different subjects, there is an urgent necessity for training more specialists. The evidence collected in the research project in 2013, provided some useful insights into how participating schools were responding to the requirements to teach Science and Mathematics through the medium of English. For instance, in one urban school a teacher of English taught Science but this was supplemented by additional instruction in children's first language (e.g. Kazakh or Russian). In addition, the school had to provide a special course in the translation of technical and scientific terminology. Overall, that school showed remarkable resilience in improvising solutions to teach in English as a medium of instruction. This example suggests that there is a need for a more careful strategy of introduction and a systematic management of new programmes in schools. (See Chapter 8 for a fuller discussion of Kazakhstan's trilingual policy).

4. Piloting E-Learning

According to strategy outlined in the 'State Programme of Education Development for 2011–2020', the government initiated a national E-Learning project in 2011. The aim of the project was to 'ensure an equal access for all participants of educational process to the best educational resources and technologies' (MoES 2010). In January 2013, a new state programme, 'Information Kazakhstan 2020', was approved by the government. The programme aims to create conditions suitable for the transition to the information society. Furthermore, the key objectives of the programme are:

- to ensure efficiency of the state administration system
- to ensure accessibility of information and communication infrastructure
- to establish an information environment necessary for social, economic and cultural development of the society
- to develop the national information space

(National 'Information Kazakhstan 2020' Programme; Rus. 'Informatsionnii Kazakhstan 2020')

The implementation of the E-Learning project was scheduled in two phases: 2011–2015 and 2016–2020. As part of the project, schools are to be equipped with new computers, digital educational resources and broadband internet. Students are expected to keep personal portfolios, calendars and diaries in computerised systems; teachers are expected to fill in electronic registers with lesson and term plans, take class registers and use emails in communication with parents.

The findings of research in 2013 suggest that few teachers have grasped the possibilities that web-based learning might offer. In classroom observations teachers still tend to use E-Learning resources as an extension of the textbook rather than as something offering a much more diverse, interactive and challenging resource for learning. In rural schools we observed only limited access to internet, and in many others, no access at all. The Kazakhstan 'digital divide' risks exacerbating the already significant gaps in educational opportunity and achievement between rural and urban schools.

5. Developing pedagogy through the Centres of Excellence programme

In the spring of 2011 the government set up the Centres of Excellence (CoE) – an in-service programme of teachers' training and professional development system (NIS Annual Report 2011a, 94). Since August 2011 CoE has been working with their strategic partners: the University of Cambridge Faculty of Education and Cambridge International Examination (See Chapter 5). The focus of the programme is on generic aspects of pedagogy (including assessment

for learning, active and interactive learning; individualised and student centres teaching, a stress on critical thinking and the application of knowledge),
and it will reach, in some form, virtually all teachers in Kazakhstan.

The programme operates on the basis of a cascade model of in-service
training for teachers: a core of expert trainers are trained, and they in turn
then go out to the regions to train teachers. The successful completion of
each of three levels by a teacher will lead to salary increase (Level Three 30%;
Level Two 70% and Level One 100%). The current CoE programme does
not provide training of a subject-specific nature in the requirements of the
new curriculum or the subject related assessment. The programme has been
scaled up through *Orleu* and CoE branches in every region in Kazakhstan.
Furthermore, with an aim to support the change agenda in schools, the programme of professional development for school directors (head teachers)
was initiated in August 2013 within the CoE framework. Plans are currently
under development to monitor its impact.

All five of the developments described in this section have been taking
place in *mainstream* schools, though in the case of 12 year curriculum, trilingual education and E-Learning this has so far been only in so-called experimental' or 'pilot' schools). In the meantime, however, a perhaps more
radical programme of change has been taking place in a newly established
suite of schools distributed across the regions of Kazakhstan, the Nazarbayev
Intellectual Schools (NIS).

Development through two parallel systems in the later 2000s

On some accounts the government grew tired of the failure of MoES to grapple in any fundamental way with the requirements for change, and so in May
2008 the government launched a project aimed at establishing twenty schools,
one in each regional centre and in Astana and Almaty – the Autonomous
Education Organisation Nazarbayev Intellectual Schools (AEO NIS). In a
speech in 2011, President Nazarbayev stated:

> Special attention in the education sphere will be paid to projects on establish-
> ment of unique education institutions similar to those established in Astana –
> New International University, Special Fund and Intellectual Schools. I agreed to
> give them my name. We should exert every effort to help them become the flag-
> ships of the national education system, main platforms for development and ap-
> probation of advanced educational programs. (N. Nazarbayev, 19 October 2011)[6]

NIS was established with its own board and direct funding, which made it independent of MoES, effectively creating a parallel system of state education. The schools have a highly selective entry of highly motivated students and especially selected staff. All schools are located in new specially constructed buildings which are equipped with the latest technology, study-labs and libraries. Fifteen NIS were in operation in October 2013. Among key distinctive features of the NIS is an academic freedom, which includes: its own admission, own curriculum and assessment, an opportunity to hire staff (including international teachers), and its own payroll system. NIS embodies many of the progressive principles that form part of the reform agenda with newly developed curricula and examinations designed to international standards (Cambridge International GCSE and the International Baccalaureate have been particular points of reference), criterion based assessment, a focus on critical thinking, problem solving, communicative skills and knowledge application, use of ICT and trilingual education are all central to their programmes.

Despite all the features that make NIS unlike their mainstream counterparts they are nevertheless expected to provide a model for mainstream schools to follow. (The tension between these disparate conditions and the expectation that other schools may be able to follow the example of NIS has not escaped sceptical attention). Chapter 14 in particular discusses the model of change which is reflected in this strategy.

Kazakhstan seems to be at a pivotal moment. Writing in late 2013, even in the last few weeks an elaborate and ambitious plan for the 'translation' of NIS experience to the mainstream has been approved by the government, paving the way for an energetic programme of reform starting in January 2014 with the revision of the standards that underpin curriculum, assessment, textbooks and pedagogy. The process of translation will shortly begin in earnest, and, again, the outcome will be observed with interest.

Earlier in 2013 we were asking ourselves how, politically as well as practically, the two parts of the parallel developments might come together. In an important sense the question was answered by the appointment of Aslan Sarinzhipov (who was an influential figure behind the establishment of both AEO NIS and another AEO, Nazarbayev University) as Minister of Education. One of his first tasks – working with Kulyash Shamshidinova, Chairperson of NIS – was to bring NIS practices (or those regarded as appropriate for this purpose) into the mainstream of educational reform even before all the planned NIS schools had been constructed and before any child (or teacher) had had a full experience of the new curriculum and assessment.

The agenda for change does not stop with the translation of NIS curriculum and assessment and other practices. There are teasing issues to do with, for example, developing a more equitable approach to school finance; the inclusion in mainstream schools of children with disabilities and special educational needs; the preparation of teachers for the new curriculum and pedagogies; raising the status of the teaching profession; and the transition from 12 years of schooling to higher education. Aslan Sarinzhipov and Alan Ruby will look at these in the final chapter, 'The Way Forward'.

REFERENCES

Ayubayeva, N., Bridges, D., Drummond, M.J., Fimyar, O., Kishkentayeva, M., Kulakhmetova, A., McLaughlin, C., Mehisto, P., Orazbaeyv, S. and **Shinkarenko, V.** (2013). *Development of Strategic Directions for Education Reforms in Kazakhstan for 2015–2020: Final Report of the Early Years and Secondary School Working Group*. Astana: Nazarbayev University.

Concept Paper (2010). Concept Paper on Government Resolution No. 681. *On Approval of the Action Plan for the Transition to 12-Year Secondary Education*, 19 July 2006.

GOSO (2008). *State Compulsory Educational Standard. Primary Education. Secondary Education*. GOSO RK 2.003 – 2008. Astana. (ГОСО, Государственный общеобязательный стандарт образования Республики Казахстан. Начальное образование. Основное среднее.Общее среднее образование. Основные положения. ГОСО РК 2.003 – 2008, Астана GOSO).

MoES (Ministry of Education and Science) (2012). *Radical Modernisation of the System of Teacher Professional Development has a Systemwide Implicaiton for Modernisation of Education*. [Rus.] *Korennoe preobrazovanie sistemy povyshenia kvalifikatsii uchiteley imeet obschesistemnoye znacheniye dlia modernizatsii obrazovaniya*. Astana. www.edu.gov.kz/ru/news/?tx_ttnews[tt_news]=3960&cHash=7f5dcf670deb82555fba8027df207205 (retreived 19 Nobember 2013).

— (2010). 'State Programme of Education Development in the Republic of Kazakhstan for 2011–2020'. Decree of the President of the Republic of Kazakhstan No. 1118, 7 December 2010. Astana: MoES.

— (2011). 'National Report on the Status and Development of Education of the Republic of Kazakhstan (Concise Version)'. Astana: MoES.

— (2013). 'Statistics of the System of Education of the Republic of Kazakhstan: National Collection'. Rus. 'Statistika Sistemy Obrazovaniya Respubliki Kazakhstan: Natsionalnyj sbornik'. Astana: MoES.

National Report (2011). 'National Report on the Status and Development of Education of the Republic of Kazakhstan'. Astana: MoES.

Nazarbayev, N. (1997). 'Kazakhstan 2030 Strategy: Prosperity, Security and Improvement of the Well-Being of all Kazakhstan Citizens'. Annual State of the Nation Address, Astana,

October 1997. www.akorda.kz/en/category/gos_programmi_razvitiya (retrieved 20 November 2013).

— (2012). 'Kazakhstan 2050 Strategy: New Political Course of the Established State'. Annual State of the Nation Address. Astana, December 2012. www.kazakhstan.org.sg/content/intro.php?act=menu&c_id=43 (retrieved 19 November 13).

— (2013) 'National Information Kazakhstan 2020 Program'. Decree of the President of the Republic of Kazakhstan No. 464, 8 January 2013. 'On National "Information Kazakhstan 2020" Programme'. www.ortcom.kz/en/program/program-infokaz/text/show and www.mtc.gov.kz/index.php/en/gosudarstvennaya-programma-informatsionnyj-kazakhstan-2020 (retrieved 20 November 2013).

Nazarbayev Intellectual Schools (NIS) (2011). *Autonomous Education Organisation 'Nazarbayev Intellectual Schools' Annual Report*. Astana: AEO NIS.

NIS (2012). *Annual Report of the Autonomous Education Organisation 'Nazarbayev Intellectual Schools'*. Rus. *Годовой отчет Автономной Организации Образования 'Назарбаев Интеллектуальные Школы'*. Astana: AEO NIS.

NOTES

1   www.akorda.kz/en/category/gos_programmi_razvitiya (retrieved 19 November 2013).

2   www.akorda.kz/en/page/page_poslanie-prezidenta-respubliki-kazakhstan-lidera-natsii-nursultana-nazarbaeva-narodu-kazakhstana- (retrieved 17 November 2013).

3   www.edu.gov.kz/en/legislation/state_program_of_education_development_in_the_republic_of_kazakhstan (retrieved 17 November 2013).

4   The legal basis for the introduction of 12 years of schooling still rests on the Government Resolution N681 On approval of the Action Plan for the transition to 12 year secondary education, 19 July 2006.

5   en.tengrinews.kz/politics_sub/Kazakhstan-President-calls-people-to-learn-English-and-eye-Chinese-and-Russian-23449/ (retrieved 4 October 2013).

6   www.primeminister.kz/program/event/view/784?lang=en (retrieved 19 November 2013).

PART TWO:
Changing Educational Culture and Practices

IMPLEMENTING RADICAL CHANGE: Nazarbayev Intellectual Schools as Agents of Change

Kulyash Shamshidinova (CEO Autonomous Education Organisation
Nazarbayev Intellectual Schools), Nazipa Ayubayeva (Deputy CEO, Nazarbayev
Intellectual Schools and University of Cambridge, Faculty of Education)
David Bridges (University of Cambridge, Faculty of Education)

Nothing is as remote as yesterday,
Nothing is as close as tomorrow.
Kazakh proverb

In times of globalisation and growing competitiveness, governments, educators and researchers are challenged to educate future generations to be competitive in a constantly changing world. This is the case in Kazakhstan, which opened its borders to the world in 1991 after gaining its independence. In 1997, in his State of the Nation Address 'Kazakhstan 2030 Strategy: Prosperity, Security and Improvement of the Well-Being of all Kazakhstan Citizens', the President of the Republic of Kazakhstan, Nursultan Nazarbayev, defined the strategic priorities for the development of the country until 2030 and stressed that the driving forces for economic and social progress into the coming century were 'the people themselves, their will, energy, persistence, and knowledge' (Nazarbayev 1997). Later, in 2006, the president talked about the nation's competitiveness as the major principle for the development of the society in the 21st century, and stressed that 'educational reform is one of the most important tools to ensure the real competitiveness of Kazakhstan' (Nazarbayev 2006).

It was a short step from this emphasis on education for economic competitiveness to the adoption of the language of 'human capital' to refer to the 'products' of that education. The development of 'human capital' was identified as one of the top priorities of the long-term 'Kazakhstan 2050 Strategy' (Nazarbayev 2012) and the quality of 'human capital' was identified as one of the crucial elements of the country's competitiveness (Decree of the President of the RK No. 1118 2010). In pursuit of this aim, the president proposed to implement a national project under the title of 'Intellectual Nation 2020' (Nazarbayev 2008). He specified three essential points in his proposal: the innovative development of the educational system; a powerful information revolution; and (in deference perhaps to more traditional values) the spiritual education of young people. The ultimate goal of the initiative, he said, was 'the upbringing of a new breed of Kazakhstani youth and the transformation of Kazakhstan into a country with competitive human capital' (Nazarbayev 2008).

Efforts to reform and modernise the secondary education system in Kazakhstan have been in progress since 1991 (see Chapter 1), including the introduction of new administrative and legislative changes and the enactment of a new national curriculum. However, the changes have been neither radical nor revolutionary. Still affected by the legacy of the Soviet system, they have proceeded with caution. This has been an essentially bureaucratic approach to reform, the central part of the reform being 'new norms and legislation' rather than a change of practice.

Perhaps this is not surprising, since neither officials nor practitioners had prior knowledge or experience of running an independent educational system. Thus, it required time and space not only for the educationalists, but also for the specialists in different economic and social sectors, to learn from the experiences of other countries, relying initially on donor organisations' knowledge and consultancy in order to gain confidence in running an independent educational system, and an independent country. As President Nazarbayev explained in his first State of the Nation Address:

> Sure enough, we may and ought to study the experience of other countries and take advantage of auspicious tendencies in the world community. Yet only we, none other than we, are capable of coping with this enormous work which is indispensable for the implementation of our dream of and hope for building the Kazakhstan, which our children and grandchildren will be proud of when they are our age. Why is it particularly today that we set this task? It is because we were not ready for this yesterday, we were short of both experience and knowledge, we could hardly afford it because of unfavorable circumstances and all sorts of instabilities. And the task itself was quite different. (Nazarbayev 1997)

The increasing realisation was that after two decades spent trying to grapple with the complexities of establishing an independent educational system really very little had changed for the better, and this perception was reinforced by Kazakhstani students' weak results in the 2008 PISA tests. The Ministry of Education and Science (MoES) appeared to be tied up in its own bureaucracy of norms and legislation and seemed unlikely to deliver real change. A more radical initiative was required which was freed from these requirements.

The search for a more effective way of achieving secondary educational reform and the objectives set out in 'Intellectual Nation 2020' led to the implementation of the project 'Twenty intellectual schools for gifted and talented children' aimed at the education and upbringing of 'a new generation of intellectual elite' (Nazarbayev 2009). But what was recognised from an early stage was that if these schools were to break with the old ways, they needed the freedom to experiment, to depart from existing 'norms' and to pioneer new practice. This was a radical departure from previous experience and deserves closer examination.

The idea of establishing the Nazarbayev Intellectual Schools: school autonomy and academic freedom

The first step towards giving the 20 Intellectual Schools a measure of autonomy was to establish them in 2008 as a State owned joint-stock company, *Orken*. The status of the joint-stock company and the word 'Orken' had a considerable significance for the project. The legal status of a joint-stock company was granted in order to provide the Intellectual Schools with some autonomy 'to test modern educational programmes, verify their effectiveness and develop technical solutions for their further integration into the national educational system, and to seek additional funds, and new forms of financing in a form of public–private partnership' (Uteulina 2009). The word 'Orken' (meaning 'sprout' or 'shoot' in Kazakh) was used as the name for the grant to be awarded to the students selected to study in the network of Intellectual Schools on a competitive basis. The development of the network of Intellectual Schools came under the direct control of the very powerful decision-making board of directors chaired by the Deputy Prime Minister of the Republic of Kazakhstan, with members consisting of the representatives of the office of the President of the Republic of Kazakhstan, MoES, the Ministry for Economy and Budget Planning, the Ministry of Finance, the CEO of the managing company and three independent directors.

However, very soon it became evident that the partial autonomy in the form of awarding a legal status of a joint-stock company was not an effective way to initiate educational innovations. First, the very concept of *partial* autonomy meant that the Intellectual Schools could decide on some things (such as teacher hiring and student selection) but not others (such as educational standards, national assessment and accountability regimes and the pay of teachers). Secondly, on these terms there were few observable differences between the Intellectual Schools and already existent experimental schools.[1] Thirdly, partial autonomy could not fulfil the main task for the Intellectual Schools 'to become the flagship of the national educational system and engage in the development and testing of state-of-the-art educational programmes with their further distribution across the country' (Nazarbayev 2010).

Consequently, a new law[2] 'on the status of the Nazarbayev Intellectual schools' was passed. Under this law, Intellectual Schools received a new legal status and became the Autonomous Education Organisation Nazarbayev Intellectual Schools[3] (AEO NIS), and by this means were guaranteed full autonomy and academic freedom. In accordance with the new law 'the principle of academic freedom is the autonomy of the Intellectual Schools in the design and adoption of educational programs, forms and methods of educational activities, directions for research' (Law of the RK No. 394-IV 2011).

In order to realise fully this new academic independence, the principle of a collective decision making management system was introduced and a Supreme Board of Trustees (chaired by the president himself) and a Board of Trustees (chaired by the deputy prime minister) were created. The seniority of the membership of these boards simultaneously provided the Intellectual Schools with powerful support in their attempts to go beyond the limitations of the past, access to plentiful central government financial support and very direct lines of accountability to the centre of political authority in Kazakhstan.

Combining 'the best traditions of Kazakhstan education and international best pedagogic practice'

The role of the network of 20 Intellectual Schools was reflected in the Strategic Plan for the development of the Republic of Kazakhstan until the year 2020,[4] and the 'State Programme for the Development of Education for 2011–2020'[5] set two main tasks. The first task was, as it were, integral to what had soon become formally approved by the president as the Nazarbayev Intellectual School (NIS) system:

> . . . Nazarbayev Intellectual Schools project shall become one of the key projects facilitating modernization of the secondary education system. These schools are to become the experimental sites for the development, introduction and testing of educational programmes for kindergarten and pre-school, as well as educational programmes for 12-year secondary education. These programmes shall combine the best traditions of Kazakhstan education and international best pedagogic practice, providing profiled preparation of students by Physics and Mathematics, Chemistry and Biology directions, and encouraging advanced study of languages, i.e. 'the main site for testing the polylingual educational model and educational innovations. (Decree of the President of the RK No. 922 2010)

The elimination of legislative barriers and the autonomy enjoyed in designing and adapting the educational programme provided by NIS opened the doors to new possibilities. Shamshidinova (2011), the CEO of the NIS managing company, writes:

> Creating a network of intellectual schools allowed us to study in detail the existing content of secondary education in Kazakhstan and to compare it with international educational programs of secondary schools. (Shamshidinova 2011)

The pursuit of international best practice has led NIS staff to many parts of the globe and itself provides an interesting example of what is sometimes, misleadingly, called 'policy borrowing' but which is really more like an extensive self-directed inquiry across many national and cultural divides. Re-tracing the (ongoing) inquiry is a reminder of how one connection led to another, of leads that went nowhere, of passing relationships and enduring collaborations, and of serendipity as well as purposeful selection in the pathways chosen. Singapore's experience was an early focus of NIS attention, given the evident achievement of its own educational system since independence, but this inquiry led NIS to Cambridge International Examinations (CIE), an organisation that has played a central part in educational development in Singapore for the last twenty years. The link with CIE, and also, independently, the recommendation of Anne Lonsdale, provost of the newly established Nazarbayev University and a former pro-vice-chancellor at Cambridge, led NIS to the University of Cambridge Faculty of Education, which has played a major part in the development of NIS's in-service teacher education in Kazakhstan (see Chapter 5). NIS has however consistently tried to consider and test out alternative options, and its investigation of alternative curriculum models led it not just to CIE but also to the International Baccalaureate offices in Geneva and to IB schools in Luxembourg, the UK, the USA and Italy. Cambridge University Press is involved in support for the production of new textbooks, as is, more recently, the London Institute of Education. When the identification of 'talented and gifted' children was the challenge, NIS sought guidance from CITO in the Netherlands and the Centre for Talented Youth at Johns Hopkins University in the US. In the US again, the University of Pennsylvania contributed to the training of the NIS leadership. On trilingual education, NIS were led to make study visits to Estonia and later to Quebec. Most recently they have been visiting and referencing pre-school education policy and practice in Italy, New Zealand and the UK. Beyond all this there have been the conference presentations, the web searches and the stream of visitors from across the globe.

Nor has the absorption of international experience been restricted to the senior levels of NIS. All NIS schools have themselves an international staff, responsible for bringing international approaches to teaching and learning directly into the schools through their own teaching and through collaboration with other staff. There are more than 200 international teachers serving in nine NIS schools and the number is increasing with the opening of new schools. Students of NIS schools have also enjoyed international experience through (i) their links with other schools arranged through the British Council, the American Council and the Faculty of Education of the University of Cambridge (ii) summer language schools in the UK including some offered by the Bell Language School and the International House Belfast English language School and (iii) attendance at the famous Christmas lectures of the Royal Institution in London and participation in the Institution's Science laboratory workshops. Most significantly, perhaps, they have become accustomed to (iv) the use of the international language of English as not only a language to be learned in English lessons but also as the medium of instruction in Mathematics and Science lessons.

Through all these channels (and more) NIS has served to bring international practice, experience and thought to bear on the development of education, first through NIS and thence into the mainstream of education in Kazakhstan. This is not to say, however, that that the 'international' has been allowed to displace what remains important in Kazakhstan's own cultural and educational tradition. NIS has, for example, insisted on high levels of competence in both Kazakh and Russian for all children; it continues to offer Kazakh History alongside World History and taught through the medium of Kazakh; it promotes Kazakhstan's own cultural diversity in music, dance and arts; and it protects important parts of personal, social and civic education, of 'upbringing', alongside academic education. Not only this but

NIS has firmly asserted its own judgement, for example on matters of curriculum and assessment against that of international partners when it has felt that these have failed to take local context, traditions, values or problems sufficiently into account. On assessment, for example, outsiders have not always understood the critical importance in Kazakhstan of having a system that is as proof as possible against cheating and corruption. In all of this, of course, there has been a balance to strike between what (in the terms discussed in Chapter 13) might be thought of as 'indigenisation' of reform and its 'hijacking'.

What are the innovative practices being implemented in Nazarbayev Intellectual Schools?

In terms of the curriculum structure as a whole, perhaps the most obvious features of NIS are the concentration on achieving advanced use of three languages, Kazakh, Russian and English, including their use as a medium of instruction for different purposes. The other feature of the curriculum is its focus from Grade 7 onwards on Science (with specialist options), Mathematics and ICT. The 'human capital' to which Kazakhstan attaches such importance is especially defined in terms of scientific and technological capability. Once it is decided that these six subjects are to be taught to an advanced level, this of course fills a substantial part of the curriculum, but NIS also includes a range of other subjects including Kazakh History, World History, Geography, a new course called 'Global Perspectives' and Creative Arts in the remaining time. As a result, NIS schools struggle, as do mainstream schools, with a curriculum which is almost certainly overcrowded, and this is an issue that needs to be addressed.

In a sense the innovative nature of education in NIS becomes more apparent when you start to look at what is taught and how it is taught within this curriculum framework. The direction for this change was signalled in a 2008 presidential address:

> . . . it is necessary to consider the influence of the processes of globalization, which we should contrast with the strengthening of national-cultural values and morality of the young generation . . . We need to strive for our young people to learn both how to gain and create new knowledge. Today the most valuable quality is creativity, ability to process knowledge to generate new solutions,

technologies and innovations. This requires new forms of teaching, new professionals. (Nazarbayev 2008)

There is much more emphasis in NIS on what might broadly be referred to as 'skills', on what students can do rather than on (as in most mainstream schools) information and what they can remember and recall. So across the curriculum there is emphasis: on applying knowledge in unfamiliar conditions; on interpreting (text, graphs, photos, maps and so on); on explaining why and how; on investigating (individually and as part of a team); on communicating; on working creatively and critically. The focus on the development of these abilities is the mark of the 'intellectual', and this is what really makes the NIS experience something different.

And once these kinds of abilities are focused upon, a lot more follows in terms of the requirements for teachers and teaching, on resources and textbooks and on assessment. Briefly:

- Teachers need to adopt different approaches to *teaching and learning* that are more student centred, more interactive, more inquiry based and so on (and these are reflected in, in particular, the Centres of Excellence (CoE) in-service education programme described in Chapter 5).
- These kinds of approaches need a *resource rich environment* that permits student investigation, creativity and practical work – and, of course, in this age that also means full access to web-based resources and communicative spaces. (The extra resources that are immediately evident to any visitor to an NIS school are not just a luxury; they are essential to the kind of learning that NIS is seeking to develop).
- *Textbooks* need to be developed which are not just stocks of information to be absorbed but which are stimuli to inquiry and active learning.
- They need different approaches both to the continuous *monitoring of students' progress* against mutually recognised criteria and to *high stakes assessment* – approaches that allow students to demonstrate not just what they can recall, but their ability to solve problems, evaluate evidence, develop an argument, explain a process, interpret data and so on.

In these ways, then, innovation in terms of educational and curriculum objectives have demanded innovation in every other aspect of the work of NIS schools.

The 'transfer' of Nazarbayev Intellectual Schools' experience to mainstream schools

According to the 'Strategic Plan for the Development of the Republic of Kazakhstan until the year 2020', and the 'State Programme of Education Development for 2011–2020', the Intellectual Schools had two main tasks, the first of which was to develop in these schools themselves best practice informed both by international experience and what was valuable in Kazakhstan's own educational tradition. The second task was to transfer the lessons of its own experience to other schools in the system.

As stated by the first CEO of the JSC *Orken* (managing company) Khafiza Uteulina, the aim of establishing a joint-stock company to manage NIS was to provide schools with some autonomy 'to test modern educational programmes, verify their effectiveness and develop technical solutions for their further integration into the national educational system, and to seek additional funds and new forms of financing in a form of public–private partnership' (Uteulina 2009).

In other words, NIS was expected from the start not just to provide a privileged environment for a highly selected group of children, but, having enjoyed the opportunity to depart from what were sometimes referred to as 'the old ways' and to be innovative, they were expected to be the engine room for the reform of the wider system.

NIS was not in the event given very long to switch into this new role. By 2013 the pressure on NIS to demonstrate this wider benefit in return for the substantial investment that the schools had enjoyed was becoming very powerful, even though a number of the schools had not yet even opened, and even those that had been open longest (the first NIS was opened in January 2008, and the 10th to 15th schools were opened in 2013) had hardly had chance to accumulate the considered experience that might have provided a firm basis for wider dissemination. Communities and their representatives in parliament were asking why the Intellectual Schools had the privilege of selecting the best teachers and the best students over the ordinary schools in the country and why they enjoyed such a significant share of Republic funding for education. Kate Lapham, Senior Programme Manager for the Open Society Education Support Programme writes:

> NIS seems set up to be much better resourced than ordinary schools, which will make them attractive to the best teachers in the system. Thus, rather than knowledge and good practice trickling down into the general education system, it is

more likely that talent will trickle up, leaving the general education system worse off than before. (Bartlett 2012)

Indeed one of the Gymnasia that featured in the Nazarbayev University/ University of Cambridge research featured elsewhere in this book complained that the newly established NIS school in the same city had poached the teachers that it, as an experimental school, relied on to teach Science and Mathematics through the medium of English and that it was now poaching its most able students.

Therefore, in the autumn of 2013, AEO NIS sought and received government endorsement for its action plan for the wider implementation of key elements of its practice. Aslan Sarinzhipov, Minister of Education and Science, in his 2013 speech about reform to the educational system in Kazakhstan, proposed:

> . . . to use of Nazarbayev Intellectual schools' experience to renew the content of secondary education in the form of: (i) the introduction of a new educational programme across all subjects starting from Grade 1 in 2015; (ii) the partial introduction of a new subject, 'project work in Maths and Science subjects' and elements of critical thinking in existing 11 year schooling, and (iii) revision of in-depth study of languages (Kazakh, Russian and English) and ICT. (Sarinzhipov 2013)

The action plan combined what by Kazakhstan's standards was a relatively measured approach to more radical change in the whole curriculum and assessment process with some quicker changes in certain aspects of mainstream school practice.

The more measured part of the roll-out of NIS involves the introduction to mainstream schools of a new curriculum and assessment *adapted* from the NIS model, starting in 2015. This will proceed one year at a time starting with Grade 1. The point about adaptation is critically important. NIS will be reviewing the suitability of its existing curriculum even for its own highly selective students. It already looks too overcrowded to allow for the more inquiring approaches to learning that it seeks to foster. No-one supposes that you can simply take a curriculum designed for an intellectual elite and transfer it into schools for all, though there may be important features of it that can and should be part of the educational experience of *all* and not just an elite.

Clearly this approach to change is going to take some time (12 years, of course) to work through the system as a whole, and it may be important that some changes are introduced more quickly. The NIS Action Plan provides for, among other things, earlier introduction of improvements in language learning with more of a focus on all four language competences. There will be work too on criterion-based assessment. The CoE programme will continue to expand to reach tens of thousands of teachers across the system and the assessment system will be reviewed in anticipation of a progressive movement towards examinations that test a wider range of student competences.

NIS learned quickly from international research and experience that, as it is often expressed: 'there is no curriculum development without teacher development' and continues to invest heavily in the training of teachers. It also learned that these teachers need the support of school directors if they are to implement change in their classrooms, and so NIS introduced training for school directors and, by extension, officers from *rayon* and *oblast* level. The AEO is also acutely aware of the risks of educational change running ahead of the support and understanding of parents and the community, and plans activity aimed at ensuring that all members of the community understand the importance of the changes taking place and the benefits they will bring their children.

Introducing innovative practice in 20 newly established schools is one thing: introducing change across a system with 7348 schools (MoES of the RK 2013, 25) and 292064 teachers (MoES of the RK 2013, 69), many of them, 4145 schools or 56.4% (MoES of the RK 2013, 27), in small and isolated rural communities, is an altogether more ambitious challenge. It is, however, one which NIS is determined to meet.

REFERENCES

Bartlett, P. (2012). *Kazakhstan: Elite Schools May Limit Opportunities*. 22 February 2012. Retrieved from www.eurasianet.org/node/65035.

Law of the Republic of Kazakhstan No. 394–IV. (2011, 19 January). *On the Status of Nazarbayev University, Nazarbayev Intellectual Schools and Nazarbayev Fund*. Astana.

MoES (Ministry of Education and Science) (2013). *Statistics of Education System of the Republic of Kazakhstan*. Astana: MoES.

Nazarbayev, N. (1997). 'Kazakhstan 2030 Strategy: Prosperity, Security and Improvement of the Well-Being of all Kazakhstan Citizens'. Annual State of the Nation Address, Astana, October 1997. www.akorda.kz/en/category/gos_programmi_razvitiya (retrieved 20 November 2013).

— (2006). 'Strategy to Enter the Club of 50 Most Competitive Countries in the World. Kazakhstan on the Threshold of a New Leap Forward in its Development'. Annual State of the Nation Address. Astana, March 2006.

— (2008). *Speech of the President of the Republic of Kazakhstan at the Forum of the Bolashak Programmes's Scholars.* 30 January, 2008. www.akorda.kz/.

— (2009). 'Kazakhstan in Post-Crisis World: Intellectual Breakthrough to the Future'. Lecture at Kazakhstan National University after Al-Farabi, Almaty, October 2009.

— (2010). 'New Decade – New Economic Expansion – New Opportunities for Kazakhstan'. Annual State of the Nation Address. Astana, January 2010.

— (2010). 'The Strategic Plan for Development of the Republic of Kazakhstan until the Year 2020'. Decree of the President of the Republic of Kazakhstan No. 922, 1 February 2010.

— (2010). 'The State Programme of Education Development for 2011–2020'. Decree of the President of the Republic of Kazakhstan No. 1118, 7 December 2010. Astana: MoES.

— (2012). 'Kazakhstan 2050 Strategy: New Political Course of the Established State'. Annual State of the Nation Address. Astana, December 2012. www.kazakhstan.org.sg/content/intro.php?act=menu&c_id=43 (retrieved 19 November 13).

Sarinzhipov, A. (2013). Speech of the Ministry of Education and Science of the Republic of Kazakhstan at the Government meeting, 29 October 2013. www.zakon.kz/4583456-zasedanie-pravitelstva-rk-ot-29.html.

Shamshidinova, K. (2011). JSC 'Nazarbayev Intellectual School': Development Strategy. *Sovremennoe obrazovanie* 1:81.

Uteulina, K. (2009, 9 December). *Interview '20 Intellectual schools are to become part of the Kazakhstani education'.* www.zakon.kz/128149-20-intellektualnykh-shkol-stanut.html.

NOTES

1   Since 1991 Kazakhstan secondary education has created many experimental platforms to introduce some minor and major changes and innovations to the system. For example, 33 schools became experimental platforms to implement trilingual education; there are 104 experimental platforms for gifted and talented students; another 200 have the status of experimental schools to pilot 12 year education; 200 schools are experimenting to introduce e-learning. Analysis of these experimental platforms showed that these schools had to introduce innovations that are outside the existing system while complying with the existing system at the same time.

2   Law of the Republic of Kazakhstan No. 394–IV LRK on January 19, 2011. 'On the status of Nazarbayev University, Nazarbayev Intellectual Schools and Nazarbayev Fund'.

3   Decree of the Repubic of Kazakhstan No. 647 on June 9, 2011. 'On reorganization of non-profit joint-stock company "Nazarbayev University" and JSC Nazarbayev Intellectual Schools'.

4   Decree of the President of the Republic of Kazakhstan No. 922 on February 1, 2010. 'On approval of the Strategic plan for development of the Republic of Kazakhstan until the year 2020'.

5   Decree of the President of the Republic of Kazakhstan No. 1118 on December 7, 2010. 'On approval of the State Programme of Education Development for 2011–2020'. Astana: MoES.

5 CENTRES OF EXCELLENCE: Systemwide Transformation of Teaching Practice

Fay Turner, Elaine Wilson (University of Cambridge, Faculty of Education)
Svetlana Ispussinova (Nazarbayev Intellectual Schools)
Yermek Kassymbekov, Assel Sharimova, Bakhty Balgynbayeva
(Centre of Excellence, Nazarbayev Intellectual Schools)
Simon Brownhill (University of Cambridge, Faculty of Education)

Introduction

In May 2011 the Government of the Republic of Kazakhstan approved new approaches to the training and professional development of Kazakhstani teachers and ordered the establishment of the Centre of Excellence (CoE) under the auspices of the Autonomous Education Organisation (AEO) Nazarbayev Intellectual Schools (NIS) to develop and deliver these new approaches. The primary aim of the CoE teacher development programme was to equip teachers to educate citizens of the 21st century, i.e. to help pupils become independent, self-motivated, engaged, confident, digitally competent, responsible and critically reflective learners, able to communicate in Kazakh, Russian and English. The strategic plan included a target of training 120000 teachers by 2016, that is approximately 40% of comprehensive school teachers of the Republic of Kazakhstan. A further aim of the CoE programme was to build capacity within the education system through establishing a network of professional development centres. It was intended that the centres would provide leadership throughout the regions of Kazakhstan so that the development process would be sustainable beyond the initial stages of training. In August 2011, the University of Cambridge Faculty of Education (FoE) and Cambridge International Examinations (CIE) were commissioned to produce a programme of in-service training and assessment in cooperation with AEO NIS. To this end, in October and November

2011, a FoE team worked with colleagues from Astana to develop a bespoke training course including assessment procedures. Concurrently, the CIE team designed a trainer accreditation process. Training began in January 2012 and is ongoing. This chapter describes the development and implementation of the programme and will illustrate in particular the issues of 'rolling out' pedagogic change from the centre to the periphery of an educational system, drawing on research evidence to reflect on the issues that have arisen during its implementation.

Cascade models of teacher professional development

A cascade model of professional development was adopted for the CoE programme in order to reach as many teachers as possible in the shortest timescale (Gilpin 1997). Hayes delineates the benefits of this model for bringing about large-scale change. He suggests that it is 'cost-effective, does not require long periods out of service, and uses existing teaching staff as co-trainers' (Hayes 2000, 137). However, the problems associated with the cascade model have aslo been well documented (Solomon and Tresman 1999; Kennedy 2005). A principle concern is that of dilution and distortion of the messages of programmes as they are passed down the line. There are also concerns about the nature of training usually associated with the cascade model. Kennedy (2005) and Solomon and Tresman (1999) argue that the cascade model is ineffective because it 'supports a technicist view of teaching, where skills and knowledge are prioritised over attitudes and values' (Kennedy 2005, 240). However, other researchers (Hayes 2000; Bax 2002) have suggested that it is the transmissive style of training, encouraged by a focus on skills and knowledge, that is responsible for the shortcomings of the cascade model rather than the model *per se*. In order to address problems associated with cascade training and to overcome potential conservatism in the Kazakhstani system, the CoE development team consulted evidence from a range of international educational development programmes, particularly where large-scale innovative projects had been shown to be successful in bringing about change (Levin 2002). This evidence informed the development and implementation of a cascade model of training within the context of Kazakhstan.

In evaluating the development and implementation of the programme we will draw on Hayes's (2000) framework for effective cascade training. Hayes proposed five criteria and seven related principles for effective cascade training shown in Table 1 below.

Table 1: Criteria and project principles

Criteria	Project training principles
The method of training must not be transmissive but experiential and reflective	Context sensitivity Normative re-educative models of training Reflexivity
The training must be open to reinterpretation rather than expecting rigid adherence to prescribed ways of working	Context sensitivity Normative re-educative models of training Reflexivity Flexibility and responsiveness to local needs
Expertise should not be concentrated at the top but diffused through the system as widely as possible	Participative development Collaboration Continuing professional development
A cross-section of stakeholders must be involved in the preparation of training materials	Participative development Collaboration
Decentralisation of responsibilities within the cascade structure is desirable	Flexibility and responsiveness to local needs Collaboration

Source: Hayes 2000, 141

This framework, along with the findings of other research concerned with professional development programmes, provides criteria against which to evaluate the roll-out of the programme to date.

Development of the programme

Central to the development of the CoE programme was the understanding that education reform 'at scale' means that deep and consequential changes need to take place in classroom practice. Such deep changes go beyond simply tinkering with procedures and structures and usually involve altering teachers' beliefs about the norms and pedagogical practices of the classroom. Therefore, in developing the programme, knowledge and skills were not prioritised over beliefs, values and attitudes (Solomon and Tresman 1999; Kennedy 2005) but rather the opposite. This is illustrated by Figure 1 below which is included in the teachers' handbooks and underpins training activity.

Figure 1: Teachers' beliefs underpin attitudes, decision making and actions

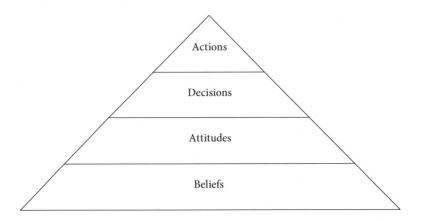

The structure of the CoE programme was informed by the findings of Pedder et al. (2009) who suggested that the conditions necessary for teacher learning to be transformative are that 'training activity' must be context specific and embedded in a real classroom. Furthermore, it ought to involve a reflective stage where teachers think deeply about what they are doing and why. The 'training activity' must also be sustained over an extended period of time, and include some form of collaborative enquiry-based practice supported by more knowledgeable critical friends. This suggested a three-stage programme at each of the levels of training: a first face-to-face stage (F2F1) where ideas are introduced and modelled; a stage in schools where ideas are tried and evaluated, and a second face-to-face stage (F2F2) where the implementation of ideas in practice is reflected upon and discussed. Table 2 indicates how this pattern is repeated at each level of the CoE programme.

Table 2: Pattern of activities during each stage of the programme for each of the three levels

Stage of programme	Activity during stage of training
Face to face 1 (F2F1) 2 weeks trainers 4 weeks teachers	Demonstrating, modelling, participation in and discussion of: Pedagogic approaches (Levels 3, 2 and 1) Coaching and mentoring of colleagues in pedagogic approaches (Levels 2 and 1) School development planning for introducing pedagogic approaches (Level 1)
School-based period 4 weeks trainers 4 weeks teachers	Trying out and evaluating: Pedagogic approaches – 'Action Research' (Level 3, 2 and 1) Coaching and mentoring of colleagues in pedagogic approaches (Levels 2 and 1) Cross-school development in pedagogic approaches (Level 1)
Face to face 2 (F2F2) 2 weeks trainers 4 weeks teachers	Reflecting and reporting on the implementation of: t approaches – Action Research (Level 3, 2 and 1) Coaching and mentoring of colleagues in pedagogic approaches (Levels 2 and 1) Cross-school development in pedagogic approaches (Level 1)

A major challenge for the Cambridge team in developing the programme was a lack of familiarity with the Kazakhstani educational system. To overcome this, the FoE team worked closely with Kazakhstan-based experts from the inception to the realisation of the programme. These experts included teachers and 'would-be' trainers as well as current CoE employees. This was consistent with Hayes's criteria for effective cascade training, one of which states that *a cross-section of stakeholders must be involved in the preparation of training materials.* Colleagues from Kazakhstan worked alongside FoE developers for a month to determine the structure and content of the programme. The medium for production of programme materials was the subject of some discussion in the development period. Hayes's principle of *participative development* underpinned an early key decision that although outlines for each training session would be produced in hard copy, training materials and resources would only be accessible online in order that these might easily be added to, amended or replaced as they were trialled by Cambridge and local trainers in Kazakhstan.

The development of the CoE programme at all levels was underpinned by the principles associated with Hayes's criteria that training should be experiential and reflective. The CoE approach was also developed to be consistent with the principle of *context sensitivity* since active participation during F2F1 enables participants to bring their knowledge of context to ideas presented, the school-based period involves trying out ideas in context, and F2F2 involves reflection on the implementation of these pedagogical approaches in the contexts of Kazakhstani classrooms and schools. The *normative re-educative models of training* principle requires training to involve critically evaluating existing practice as well as examining the principles underpinning pedagogic approaches, and making changes to practice in the light of these considerations. The three stages of the CoE programme were designed to include all these processes.

Development of structures and communication

In parallel with the development of programme materials and activities, a great deal of effort and resources were focused on developing structures and lines of communication that would support the roll-out of the programme.

CoE has opened its branches in all 16 regions of Kazakhstan, where CoE trainers deliver the three levels of the programme. However, in order to reach as many teachers as possible in the shortest timescale it was decided that an organisation with responsibility for teacher professional development that already existed in Kazaksatan would be involved in the CoE programme. Therefore, the National Center for Professional Development *Orleu* (NCPD *Orleu*) is also delivering the CoE programme (Level 3 and Level 2 only). With the aim of having a rigorous assessment system within the training provided by CoE and NCPD *Orleu* there is a Centre for Pedagogical Measurements under the auspices of AEO NIS (CPM).

So far, we have focused on the development of the programme. We have explained how we aimed to overcome problems associated with cascade training and suggested how research into teacher professional development programmes informed the structure and content of the programme. In the remainder of this chapter we consider evidence relating to the achievement of these aims. We draw this evidence from the second phase of the cascade process, i.e. the training of teachers, rather than from the training of trainers, since it is here that dilution effects are likely to be more visible.

Evaluation of programme roll-out at the 'train the teachers' phase

In terms of numbers trained, there is no doubt that the aims of the programme roll-out have been achieved. In the first year (2012) 7347 teachers were trained at Level 3 and 300 at Level 2. However, this does not answer the question of whether the programme has achieved its aims. Such a question can only be fully answered over the long term by examining the classroom practice of teachers and the learning of students. However, the second phase can be reviewed in relation to what is known about successful teacher development programmes. Some evidence for this review comes from post-training teacher evaluations carried out by CoE. However, the most useful source of insight comes from visits by FoE mentors to training centres across Kazakhstan. FoE was commissioned by CoE to provide mentoring for trainers during the roll-out of the programme to teachers. Ten two-week visits were agreed for the first year of the roll-out in which pairs of mentors from Cambridge worked for a week in two different branches of CoE. Mentors observed the training sessions and gave constructive feedback to trainers. The length of time that mentors worked with individual trainers varied from five full days to a little over one half day depending on the number of training groups in each centre. Mentors produced daily written feedback reports for each trainer with whom they worked, as well as an overall report of what they observed during their visits. The following evaluation draws on this documentation which involves six training centres where five different mentors worked with 26 trainers.

Focus on beliefs

As discussed previously, in order for cascade training to be effective, it needs to address values or beliefs as well as skills and knowledge (Solomon and Tresman 1999; Kennedy 2005). Feedback from teachers collected by CoE provided direct evidence of trainers' perceptions of changes to their beliefs. CoE monitoring and evaluation of the quality of the programme and training process included summaries of teachers' comments. Teachers who had undertaken Level 3 training said that it had 'changed their mind-set, their attitude to the profession and made them re-think educational strategy.' Teachers trained at Level 2 suggested that 'the key ideas of the programme not only improved their methodological, theoretical and scientific competence, but also changed their mind-set to work in class and school.' These teachers also commented that this course was 'qualitatively different from traditional teacher professional development programmes.'

Views of mentors about the impact of the programme on the beliefs of trainers and teachers were strong if inferential. All mentors reported seeing training that was 'supportive of the aims and principles of the programme' (Pair 2, Centres 3 and 6). Mentors frequently reported on trainers' enthusiasm and conscientious way of working and from this made inferences about their belief in the ideas promoted in the programme. Comments included:

> Discussions with trainers as well as observations of practice clearly indicated that they strongly believed in the importance of continued professional development for themselves and for teachers. Furthermore there was a strong belief that this programme provides trainers and teachers with good opportunities for learning and development of practice. (Pair 1, Centres 7 and 8)

> The enthusiasm of the trainers underlined their belief in the importance of continuing professional development and moreover the value of the training programme. (Pair 4, Centre 9)

A criticism of cascade training is that it focuses on skills and knowledge rather than encouraging reflection on underlying principles and on encouraging criticality. This same criticism is made in relation to education in Kazakhstan and suggests that Kazakhstani trainers need to change their beliefs about teaching and learning developed from experience in the system. Although the training of trainers explicitly attempted to address this, there was a danger that the emphasis on reflection and criticality might be diluted or lost in the next phase. Mentors provided some insight into the amount of reflection and criticality happening in the training of teachers. A number of comments similar to those below were found in their reports:

> Some teachers were starting to ask and to answer the questions 'why' and 'how', and to question aspects of the programme more deeply. (Pair 3, Centres 4 and 9)

> There were genuine attempts to encourage teachers to think more deeply about their learning. Many trainers were skilled at encouraging self-reflection in their groups. (Pair 4, Centre 9)

However, this was an area felt by two mentors to be underdeveloped in the training:

Trainers were encouraged to ask the questions 'why' and 'how' more often particularly in relation to the use of the seven strands. Some had started to do this, but this area needs to be developed further. (Pair 1, Centres 7 and 8)

A mentor who had worked with eight trainers commented:

Far too few trainers fostered an atmosphere of criticality in their training sessions. The use of probing questions – 'why' and 'how' – was not widespread and, as such, some trainers failed to adequately challenge and extend the learners' learning and practice. Seldom did a trainer push teachers to give evaluative rather than descriptive responses to questions. (Pair 4, Centre 9)

One aspect of changes to beliefs that was frequently mentioned by mentors was that relating to inclusion. The approach to inclusion taken within the training programme was quite different to that previously experienced by trainers and teachers in Kazakhstan. Soviet-based pedagogical approaches tend to treat teaching groups as homogeneous except when identifying 'gifted and talented' students through competitions such as Olympiads. The concept of inclusion involving differentiation for the learning of all students, and identifying needs and talents in all students required significant shifts in thinking. Mentor reports suggest that trainers had incorporated ideas about inclusive teaching into their own practice and worked hard to ensure that all teachers in their groups were able to learn the ideas and to implement changes in their practice.

Trainers prioritised inclusivity in their sessions and went out of their way to ensure that teachers had equal access to the programme. (Pair 2, Centres 3 and 6)

Trainers genuinely cared about the prospects of the teachers in their group; on several occasions during the feedback sessions a significant period of time was spent discussing specific teachers in the groups and their personal barriers to learning. (Pair 5, Centres 1 and 4)

Mentor reports offer some cause for optimism in relation to the programme's aim of changing beliefs. That trainers were committed to the aims of the programme and worked hard to promote them does not seem to be in doubt. There is some evidence in their practice of shifts in the beliefs of trainers, such as in relation to beliefs about inclusion. However, evidence that trainers have developed beliefs in the importance of encouraging reflection and criticality in learners is less clear. Although examples of this were seen, this was an area in which mentors found it necessary to give support to trainers.

Constructive working environments: Participative, experiential and reflective training approaches

A training environment which facilitates openness and critical reflection is crucial for bringing about deep and lasting changes to beliefs and practice. Participative, experiential and reflective training approaches can only work within a trusting and positive training environment. Therefore, Cambridge trainers put an early emphasis on developing warm and constructive relationships during the train the trainer phase. All mentor reports suggest that trainers had understood the need to develop constructive working environments and that they used approaches that were similar to those they had experienced in their own training. The following are representative of many comments made by mentors:

> We observed all the trainers carrying out activities designed to establish fair, respectful, trusting, supportive and constructive relationships with and between the teachers. Observations of training sessions suggested that such relationships had been established. (Pair 2, Centres 3 and 6)

> It was obvious in all groups that a culture of trust and an atmosphere of mutual respect had been inspired. In such a comfortable setting, teachers were prepared to receive critical advice from the trainer and fellow teachers and the enthusiasm of all trainers had a positive effect on the motivation and learning of the teachers. (Pair 4, Centre 9)

However, the environments were not always as consistently positive as might be hoped and mentors commented on specific strategies that they saw being used to remedy this:

> A particularly successful strategy used by one trainer followed a day when a few teachers had been particularly negative. Having re-sorted groups to isolate and re-integrate the teachers concerned, she used a psychological activity which focused all individuals in reflecting on themselves and their relationship with others. The result was a visible surge in positive group work. (Pair 4, Centres 7 and 8)

A feature of constructive working environments, and a principle underpinning three of Hayes's criteria for effective cascade training, is collaboration. Trainers encouraged collaboration through group work as suggested by comments above. Mentors also reported on a number of specific active or reflective training strategies involving collaboration that they thought had been particularly successful:

Activities that developed learners' creativity and ability to think critically included the preparation and presentation of a collaborative environment through role-play, a gallery walk and dialogic teaching also through role-play. (Pair 1, Centres 7 and 8)

A variety of teaching and learning strategies were observed that engaged all learners, e.g. hot seating was used to good effect as was the encouragement of thinking skills in groups. (Pair 5, Centres 1 and 4)

Although group work was generally regarded as a positive learning approach it was not without difficulties. One mentor noted:

The predominance of group work among sessions presented certain problems not least the oft-seen occurrence of one or two individuals dominating the discussion, overshadowing the contributions from more introverted members, and/or more reluctant individuals sitting back and letting the others do the work. (Pair 2, Centres 3 and 6)

Trainers tried to develop environments that would support participative, experiential and reflective training approaches and mentor reports suggested that such approaches were the norm in training sessions. It was clear that trainers valued and made much use of group work and that they were skilled in promoting good relationships and facilitating collaboration.

The training materials and tasks: openness to reinterpretation

A focus of mentors' observations was the closeness with which trainers adhered to the programme, since a concern associated with cascade training is that the messages will become diluted (Solomon and Tresman 1999; Kennedy 2005). Mentors noted that trainers were all very knowledgeable about, and stayed close to, the programme; they were seen to adhere to the programme learning outcomes and made appropriate use of the materials. Comments such as those below were common in the reports.

All trainers were following the Cambridge programme, using resources, documents and materials provided. (Pair 3, Centres 4 and 9)

Good use was made of the programme materials and of approaches modelled in the train the trainer courses to bring consistency to the learning environment. (Pair 5, Centres 1 and 4)

Although many of the activities seen by mentors mirrored those used in the train the trainers courses, innovative activities and new resources were also seen. This was encouraging and consistent with Hayes's criteria for effective cascade training that 'training must be open to reinterpretation'. A very strong theme in the mentor reports was that trainers amended materials and developed training activities of their own to suit the context and the needs of their particular group of teachers. There were many comments in mentor reports similar to the following:

> Trainers often modified teaching appropriately to suit the needs of learners. I saw trainer prepared resources used, or in some cases new materials that had been prepared by a group of trainers. (Pair 3, Centres 4 and 9)

> Cultural and contextual modifications to the materials and activities available on the portal fostered in trainers a feeling of ownership and made the training sessions more relevant and engaging for teachers. (Pair 1, Centres 7 and 8)

However, one mentor found that not all trainers felt able to make amendments to the programme:

> Surprisingly, despite the fact that some trainers' changes to the programme had been very successful, other trainers appeared unsure whether modifying the provided activities and materials to suit their learners was permitted. (Pair 4, Centre 9)

When developing the programme a decision was made to store training materials online in order that they might more easily be amended and supplemented. During the train the trainers phase, Cambridge trainers emphasised that trainers could and should amend materials and activities to suit the Kazakhstani context and the needs of learners. Insight into the training of teachers, provided by mentoring visits, suggests that the principles of 'context sensitivity', 'flexibility and responsiveness to local need' and 'participative development' (Hayes 2000) continue to underpin training at this phase and that the criteria for successful cascade training that 'training must be open to reinterpretation' appears to have been achieved.

Development of conceptual understanding: diffusion of expertise throughout the system

Hayes (2000) suggested that for effective cascade training, expertise should be 'diffused through the system rather than concentrated at the top'. Some evidence relating to the conceptual understanding of trainers and teachers was found in an analysis of mentor reports. Mentor comments relating to the way trainers questioned and challenged the teachers suggested that trainers had deep conceptual understanding and had therefore become experts in the system.

Some trainers succeeded in challenging and extending the teachers' learning through asking higher order questions of presenters or audience members, or asking for examples of their assertions from their own teaching experience after group presentations in class discussions (Pair 2, Centres 3 and 6).

There was also evidence that teachers too had become experts within the system. The CoE evaluation data indicates that teachers who had completed the Level 3 training courses thought the programme had 'promoted and enhanced their methodological arsenal'. Teachers who had completed the Level 2 programme felt that 'key ideas of the programme improved their methodological, theoretical and scientific competence.' Mentor reports supported the teachers' self-reported developments in understanding. Most mentors commented on observations of teacher presentations. These focused on work done in classrooms during the school-based period and provided evidence of developing conceptual understanding of teachers and, by implication, of their trainers. There were many comments in mentor reports similar to that below:

> We saw many collaborative and individual presentations from teachers during our mentoring visit and these clearly demonstrated successful teacher learning. It was especially gratifying to see how the teachers had applied ideas and approaches promoted through the programme in their classrooms. We saw very effective management of the reflection process by the trainers and witnessed a great deal of critical reflection by teachers about the implementation of ideas into their practice. (Pair 4, Centres 8 and 9)

One area of programme content that was found to be particularly important for bringing about change to learning and teaching in Kazakhstan was that of criterion-based formative assessment. Such assessment is very different to that used throughout the Kazakhstani education system and therefore presented a significant conceptual hurdle. It is therefore worth considering evidence of trainers' and teachers' understanding of this theme. Criterion-based assessment is modelled throughout the programme in relation to assessment of both trainer and teacher assignments. Much use was made of peer- and self-assessment during the train the trainer courses and mentors made many observations of how these processes had been 'rolled-out' in the training of teachers. The following are typical mentor comments:

> All trainers frequently used formative assessment methods to support and monitor the teachers' learning. Teachers were engaged in peer- and self-assessment to support their own learning on many occasions. Methods were varied and innovative at times but clearly well-practiced with teachers. (Pair 1, Centres 7 and 8)

> Often teachers were observed discussing the criteria for use in peer-assessment and also reviewing the results. Teacher conversations confirmed that teachers were confident about the effectiveness of the use and value of formative assessment. (Pair 2, Centres 3 and 6)

However, not all trainers and teachers appeared to have a depth of understanding about how to use criterion-based formative assessment. A lack of criticality and of reference to criteria when giving feedback on presentations was noted by several mentors in relation both to peer and trainer feedback:

> . . . peer feedback did not always relate to the requirements of the presentation and the programme key criteria. (Pair 2, Centres 3 and 6)

> Some peer evaluations were still not sufficiently critical, but this was improving under the direction of trainers. (Pair 5, Centres 1 and 4)

> They all [trainers] however, failed at times to take the opportunity to raise specific learning points with teachers to develop their own learning, particularly in relation to group presentations and individual feedback. (Pair 3, Centres 4 and 9)

Critical reflection on practice is integral to the CoE programme. However, writing reflective accounts and making changes to practice was an area of expertise which appeared to prove difficult to diffuse through the system. This had been an issue for trainers during the train the trainers courses and continued to be an issue in the training of teachers. The CoE monitoring of the teachers' courses revealed difficulties in carrying out and reporting on action research. The summary of responses of Level 2 teachers within CoE monitoring, and evaluation on the quality of the programme and training process, suggested that 'teachers needed further development of skills in order to use action research and lesson study to improve practice'. Mentor reports also suggested that the reflective account of a small-scale action research study required of Level 2 teachers appeared particularly difficult. Mentors commented:

> Many trainers were concentrating on reflective writing as some teachers are still finding this a difficult area. (Pair 3, Centres 4 and 9)

> At Level 2, increasing worry and stress was noted in those teachers who said they were not used to the academic demands of the action research report. (Pair 4, Centres 8 and 9)

Mentor reports suggest that the aspect of writing about their action research or their coaching and mentoring that teachers found most difficult was presenting rigorous evidence for the effectiveness or otherwise of changes to practice:

> One particular aspect of the training that teachers appeared to find difficult was presenting evidence of pupil learning or of teacher-colleagues learning from coaching and mentoring. (Pair 2, Centres, 3 and 6)

The success of the programme in bringing about change to learning and teaching across Kazakhstan will clearly be diluted if understanding of key concepts is not effectively passed from Cambridge trainers to Kazakhstani trainers and on to teachers. The end of course assessment of trainers and teachers involves them demonstrating an understanding of key ideas, the application of these ideas to practice, and the ability to reflect on this implementation. The course pass rate and the scrutiny of a small sample of trainer and teacher assessment portfolios by FoE trainers suggests that understanding is being 'passed down'. However, insight from mentor reports suggests that retaining a depth of conceptual understanding at each phase remains a concern and should be a focus for support.

Decentralisation of responsibilities within the cascade structure

Hayes (2000) suggested that 'decentralisation of responsibilities within the cascade structure is desirable' for effective cascade training. Interviews with Kazakhstani trainers suggested that by the end of the train the trainers course, they felt responsible for taking the programme to the next phase, even though some of them were unsure of their ability to fulfil this responsibility. Observations by mentors provided some insight into how far trainers and teachers took on responsibility as the programme was rolled out. Analysis of mentor reports revealed five themes relating to the decentralisation of responsibilities: hard work and enthusiasm; evaluation of practice; development of independent learning; relationships; and communication.

The conscientious manner in which trainers approached the training courses and the amount of work they put in may be interpreted as evidence that they were taking on responsibility for the programme. All mentors comment on this in relation to various aspects of the trainers' work. For example:

> All trainers worked long hours planning and preparing materials and resources for their groups. They were all highly conscientious in their work, despite demands relating to the production of their own portfolios, problems relating to Centre management of the learning environment and their personal life. (Pair 3, Centres 4 and 9)

Mentors expressed some surprise and concern about the workloads of trainers, which were thought to be excessive by UK standards:

> The only concern was in the excessive number of hours all three trainers were spending in preparing for each day including reading and providing written feedback to teachers on their draft accounts. (Pair 5, Centres 1 and 4)

Although we suggest that the conscientious work of trainers suggests that they were taking responsibility for the success of the programme, we must also recognise that the work culture in Kazakhstan is not the same as that in the UK and that the observed trainers' work ethic may not be exceptional in the Kazakhstani context. It is also possible that there may be consequences for trainers who 'fail to succeed' in their training of teachers which might also explain their efforts. However, comments in mentor reports suggest that it was internal rather than external motivation that sustained the trainers. Mentors commented on the concern demonstrated by trainers that the teachers in their groups should succeed in the programme.

> Trainers genuinely cared about the prospects of the teachers in their groups and were obviously working very long hours, and weekends as well, to ensure they gave their best to the teachers. (Pair 3, Centres 4 and 9)

> All trainers had the learning and development of their teachers in mind and were prepared to work long hours to support their teachers in any way. (Pair 1, Centres 7 and 8)

Mentors also commented on teachers' enthusiasm for the programme, which like the enthusiasm of the trainers, might be considered a measure of the responsibility felt for their role in its dissemination:

> Teachers were very enthusiastic and receptive of the content of the course and enthusiastic about the results they had achieved in school. (Pair 4, Centres 8 and 9)

> All teachers maintain their enthusiasm for the programme and the majority are looking forward to returning to classrooms and overcoming the problems they know await them. (Pair 2, Centres 3 and 6)

However, some mentors also noted that some teachers did not seem to take responsibility for their own learning and therefore for their role in the programme:

> Such instances (of poor standards of teacher behaviour) included use of mobile phones in the rooms and instances of latecomers to sessions. (Pair 1, Centres 7 and 8)

Self-evaluation may be considered a clear indicator of taking responsibility for the success of the programme. Mentors frequently commented on how trainers evaluated their practice and how they used these evaluations to improve their training. The following comment is similar to many others in the reports:

> Trainers frequently evaluated their learning sessions by analysing information from a variety of sources. These included teacher shared comments, verbal comments from teachers as well as written and visual reflections from teachers. Trainers used the outcome of evaluation to plan future improvements to their learning and their own practice. (Pair 3, Centres 4 and 9)

By acting on evaluative feedback from their teachers, trainers not only demonstrated their own responsibility for the programme, but also enabled teachers to play a part in the programme by encouraging them to see themselves as responsible players in the programme roll-out:

> Addressing the issues of their group, gleaned from post-it notes at the end of activities, fosters an atmosphere of mutual trust and respect between trainers and teachers and means that learners become very receptive to ideas and advice. (Pair 4, Centres 8 and 9)

> Teachers appreciated that their feedback had been acted on in the development of new and improved learning activities. This was clearly evidenced in interviews with teachers. (Pair 5, Centres 1 and 4)

Just as it was felt to be important that trainers should have some autonomy in the development and use of programme materials, it would seem important that teachers are given some level of ownership so that they feel responsible for the success of the programme:

> There could have been more instances where teachers were made more directly aware of how useful their contributions had been to changes in the trainers' learning plans. (Pair 4, Centres 8 and 9)

Although not universal, it seems that some trainers gave teachers a level of autonomy by acting on their evaluations. Mentors also commented on other ways in which trainers disseminated responsibility for the training programme to teachers:

> The trainer altered her original plan in response to the request from a teacher to lead the forthcoming session on 'age-related learning' taking the role of mentor and recording much of the session for future planning. (Pair 2, Centres 3 and 6)

> One group used a very experienced ICT teacher to teach the remainder of the group how to use hyperlinks for including video in their PowerPoint presentations. (Pair 1, Centres 7 and 8)

In order for the decentralisation of responsibilities within the programme to occur, it is perhaps necessary for all participants (trainers, teachers and ultimately students) to feel they have some autonomy in relation to their own learning. A concern for the development of independent learners is integral to the programme and one mentor commented that trainers were 'practicing what they preached' in attempting to give responsibility to the teachers for their own learning:

> Many [trainers] said that they wished to develop the teachers as self-regulated learners and were giving teachers the opportunity to develop their own learning skills. (Pair 4, Centres 8 and 9)

The CoE evaluation of the Level 3 teachers' courses supported the notion that trainers attempted to make teachers independent learners. The summary of teachers' responses presented in CoE monitoring and evaluation on the quality of the programme and training process, suggested that the teachers felt the programme provided support for 'the formation of self-education skills, self-regulation, self-determination of own professional development trajectory', as well as 'increase[d] motivation' and changes in 'the position of teacher from a passive listener to an active involvement in the process'.

There would appear to be some evidence for the decentralisation of responsibilities at each phase of the programme. The enthusiasm and hard work of trainers as well as their conscientious evaluation of, and consequent amendments to, their training clearly suggests that they took responsibility for their part in the programme. Evidence for responsibility being passed down to teachers is less clear from the mentor reports. However, there was evidence that teachers were enthusiastic about the programme and that trainers were encouraging autonomy and independent learning in teachers.

Two final areas relevant to the decentralisation of responsibility commented on by mentors were those of relationships and communication. Without the support of good relationships and effective communication it is difficult to see how responsibility for bringing about and sustaining changes to learning and teaching in Kazakhstan could be shared throughout the system. Mentor reports give some useful insight into relationships and communications between course leaders (directors), trainers and teachers at 'the chalk face' or operational level which suggest that networks are being built up which can help sustain changes to teaching and learning.

There are a number of both UK and Kazakhstan based organisations involved in the programme, i.e. FoE and CIE in the UK and CoE, CPM and the NCPD *Orleu* in Kazakhstan. Good relationships and effective communication were essential for successful roll-out. An organisational relationship that might have led to problems in its roll-out is that between the two organisations (CoE and NCPD) carrying out the training of teachers. Although mentoring visits were originally planned only for CoE centres, some mentors were also able to visit and work with trainers at NCPD *Orleu*. Since there had been some earlier concern over the quality of training not under the direct control of CoE, these visits were highly welcomed. Mentors who visited these centres reported seeing very similar training in NCPD as in CoE centres and were particularly encouraged by the level of communication between directors of the centres.

> We were happily surprised by the level of communication and collaboration between the CoE and Orleu centres. The relationships between staff were particularly strong in [name] where the director had previously worked in *Orleu*. In both cities there had been cooperation between organisations in putting on seminars and conferences and there were plans for further cooperation. We recommend that the cooperation between them should be encouraged in any way possible. (Pair 2, Centres 3 and 6)

Many comments in mentor reports concern relationships and communication between people within the centres visited. Mentors frequently commented on the warmth of relationships between all people working in the centres, a warmth which was extended to the mentors themselves:

> CoE centres were characterised by constructive and warm relationships between all people working there. The directors of CoE branches were approachable and held in high esteem by their colleagues. (Pair 5, Centres 1 and 4)

> The friendly and welcoming atmosphere in the centres we visited made the mentoring process both enjoyable and constructive. We were overwhelmed by the level of warmth of relationships and the support received during our mentoring visits. (Pair 3, Centres 4 and 9)

Good relationships support good communication and the warmth and openness of relationships observed by mentors suggested a real desire to move forward and to share expertise and experience. Mentors commented positively on the communication between trainers within centres:

> All trainers we saw in the CoE and its branches were keen to collaborate and did so when possible. However, circumstances made this easier for some than others. In the NCPD *Orleu* the large number of trainers enabled 'team teaching' and a great deal of collaboration and support between trainers. (Pair 2, Centres 3 and 6)

> Trainers clearly believed that communicating and collaborating effectively with colleagues helps to develop and improve their own and others' practice. (Pair 4, Centres 8 and 9)

Mentor reports suggest that trainers understood the need for strong communication networks and frequently commented on the efficient communication systems set up by trainers:

> Both trainers kept in touch with the teachers during the school-based period by email and Skype. One trainer set up a system whereby four teachers who were IT specialists acted as a conduit for around six teachers. The trainer made regular contact with the group leaders who passed on any issues. This trainer expected her teachers to make contact each evening following training in order to address any issues and to monitor their progress. (Pair 2, Centres 3 and 6)

> All trainers had maintained contact with teachers during the school-based period, which enhanced this part of the programme, and many were hoping to maintain links with teachers after completion of the course. (Pair 3, Centres 4 and 9)

The ability to keep in touch was however sometimes hampered by the lack of technology or expertise in using technology:

The trainers in [name] also attempted regular contact with teachers during their school-based period. Here, 25% of teachers were from villages and the rest were NIS teachers from the local school. Village teachers did not have good access to technology and were not able to keep in touch with the trainers by email and Skype as were the city teachers. However, they were in weekly contact by phone. (Pair 2, Centres 3 and 6)

The emphasis of the programme on developing good communications through structures and networks at the organisational level was also apparent at the operational level in the train the teachers phase of the programme. Mentors generally reported good relationships within and between training centres as well as with the central CoE organisation. The development of sustainable relationships and communication between trainers and teachers was observed being put into practice. Use of ICT, and particularly of the internet, plays a large role in the ability of trainers and teachers to communicate. The extension of internet access to all parts of Kazakhstan will therefore be important for the sustainability of the programme roll-out.

Conclusion

There would seem to be much cause for optimism about the cascading of the programme to the train the teachers phase. However there are also indications that some aspects of the roll-out need further attention. There are a number of themes relating to successful cascading that have arisen from previous research into large-scale teacher development programmes as well as from the evaluation of this programme. This summary addresses each of these themes in turn.

Recognised as central to the success of the programme is the need to change beliefs as well as to develop knowledge and skills. Beliefs in the ideas and approach of the programme appear to have been successfully cascaded to trainers as evidenced by their enthusiasm and hard work. Most trainers also appear to understand the need to address the beliefs of teachers within the programme as evidenced by their questioning and challenging of teachers. However, not all trainers were seen to deepen teachers' thinking and challenge beliefs by asking 'why' questions and this is seen as an aspect of training that needs to be developed.

The participative training approaches modelled in the training of trainers were clearly visible in the training of teachers. Many active approaches used in the first phase were repeated or amended and used in different contexts. Kazakhstani trainers clearly recognised the need to develop trusting and constructive learning environments for their teachers. They made much use of group work and demonstrated skills necessary to support co-operation and collaboration between teachers.

The content of the programme did not appear to suffer from 'dilution' as it was rolled out to teachers. Trainers adhered to the learning outcomes specified in the training session plans. However, consistent with one of Hayes's criteria for effective cascade training that *training must be open to reinterpretation,* most trainers made context-specific amendments to training materials and some introduced new tasks to achieve the learning outcomes.

Diffusion of expertise throughout the system depends on both trainers and teachers having secure understanding of concepts central to the programme. Trainers generally demonstrated such understanding in their training of teachers, and teacher presentations provided some evidence that secure conceptual understanding was being passed on to teachers. However, focussing on criterion-based formative assessment as a specific aspect of conceptual understanding suggested that not all trainers and teachers had the level of understanding necessary for deep and consequential change to practice. Trainers and teachers also appeared to need further support in the writing of accounts that demonstrate critical reflection on practice.

There is much evidence to suggest that responsibility for the success of the programme has been rolled out to trainers, as demonstrated by their hard work and enthusiasm and by their conscientious evaluation of their own practice. Many trainers are also supporting the decentralisation of responsibility to teachers by helping them to become independent learners and by responding to teacher evaluations. It is clear that trainers and teachers have developed networks using technology that enable them to continue to take responsibility for developing and promoting the programme.

REFERENCES

Bax, S. (2002). 'The Social and Cultural Dimensions of Trainer Training'. *Journal of Education for Teaching*, 28:2, 166–78.

Coburn, C.E. (2003). 'Rethinking Scale: Moving Beyond Number to Deep and Lasting Change'. *Educational Researcher*, 32:3, 3–12.

Gilpin, A. (1997). 'Cascade Training: Sustainability or Dilution?' In I. McGraph, (ed.), *Learning to Train: Perspectives on the Development of Language Teacher Trainers*. Hemel Hempstead: Prentice Hall.

Hayes, D. (2000). 'Cascade Training and Teachers' Professional Development'. *English Language Teaching Journal*, 54:2, 135–45.

Kennedy, A. (2005). 'Models of Continuing Professional Development: A Framework for Analysis'. *Journal of In-Service Education*, 31:2, 235–50.

Levin, B. (2002). *How to Change 5,000 Schools. A Practical and Positive Approach for Leading Change at Every Level*. Cambridge, MA: Harvard Education Press.

Pedder, D., Storey, A. and Opfer, D. (2009). *Schools and Continuing Professional Development in England: The State of the Nation, Synthesis Report*. London: Training and Development Agency.

Solomon, J. and Tresman, S. (1999). 'A Model for Continued Professional Development: Knowledge, Belief and Action'. *Journal of In-Service Education*, 25:2, 307–19.

6 THE CULTURE AND PRACTICE OF ASSESSMENT IN KAZAKHSTAN: The Unified National Test, Past and Present

Liz Winter (University of Cambridge, Faculty of Education)
Cristina Rimini (Cambridge International Examinations)
Arailym Soltanbekova (Nazarbayev Intellectual Schools)
Madina Tynybayeva (Nazarbayev Intellectual Schools)

Introduction

This chapter is primarily focused on a high-stakes assessment known as the Unified National Test (UNT). Currently, students who complete 11 years of school take this at the end of their schooling, and for them it serves both as a school leaving exam and, more importantly, as the determinant of which course, if any, they may enter at which higher education institution. Not surprisingly, given this significance, it plays a major role in shaping what young people learn in school and how this is taught. It is perhaps one of the most powerful drivers of behaviour in the school system.

An assessment of the UNT is useful as it is also indicative of the greater problems behind the understanding and construction of assessment *per se* in Kazakhstan. Certainly, this particular life-changing appraisal of a candidate's eligibility for funding and entry to higher education not only matters to individuals but poses very fundamental questions about education more widely. Are the arguments of the past for the particular form of assessment represented by the UNT still valid? Is Kazakhstan currently operating an educational meritocracy fit for the 21st century? Where does the balance of power behind educational reforms lie and, connected to this, are decision makers listening to stakeholders? Indeed, this leads to the very questions that will be answered to some extent in the next chapter: are new approaches to assessment needed and, if so, what are the alternatives?

Why a Unified National Test?

In the Soviet period, each Higher Education Institution (HEI) determined its own admissions policy. This would typically involve application to a single university; travel for on-site, institutionally provided tests; and, for some subjects, oral examination (Clark 2005; see also Chapter 2 in this volume). Although corruption existed, political monitoring of quotas from Lenin through Stalin to Brezhnev maintained a level of trust in the system; or, at least, indicated centralised political oversight of what constituted the criteria for entry to higher education (Chabe 1971).

Following independence, higher education was opened up to the private sector. This led to diverse entry criteria to institutions including some of dubious quality; so uncertainty reigned in the Kazakhstani higher education sector. A senior figure within NIS describes how stakeholders such as parents, employers, the students themselves and the universities struggled in a chaotic economic situation to decide what best to do in order to make the right choices and to secure a personal, let alone national, future.

> While in the Soviet Union, people were sure that tomorrow they would have a job, at least some kind of job, and they would not be unemployed. But then we encountered the problem of unemployment. This problem was new for us and we were confused. People were confused. That is how we came to an understanding that good education was something very important. There was no chance to get a job without it. A good education and professional competence were necessary for an employer to believe in you and offer you a job. People found themselves in a very confusing situation when too many higher educational institutions were opened. They sprang up like mushrooms after the rain. Parents had to make a decision where to send their children, to which institution. . . . From one side, those students, who would not have got a place to study at a higher educational institution before, because their knowledge was insufficient, got a chance to study there now. If their parents would pay, they would study. But there was another question, whether after receiving this kind of diploma they would actually be employed . . . (Senior manager within NIS)

Amidst all this turmoil and anxiety there was a need for a mechanism to allow fair access to higher education – a national system, a transparent and objective system and one that was relatively immune from corruption and which ensured therefore that entry to higher education was on merit alone. This was the demand that the UNT was primarily designed to meet.

Whatever our current critiques of the UNT, it should be acknowledged that in its time it was a reforming initiative.

The National Testing Center[1] was set up in 1993 to oversee content, format and overall construction of several forms of national assessment in schools and higher education. Advice upon the project for a higer education selection test was invited from internationally respected experts in educational measurement such as the Soviet academic Dr Vadim Avanesov (2005) and the World Bank. This led to the first versions of a UNT for Kazakhstan (Единое Национал'ное Тестирование) in 1999 which was designed to replace each university's own Complex Testing Exam (Комплексное Тестирование). Trials ensued until a compulsory national version for all Grade 11 school leavers was adopted in 2004. Including the 2013 figures, 1.24 million people have taken the UNT, making up 80% of all Kazakhstani school leavers over the last nine years.[2]

How does the UNT operate?

In terms of qualifications, children in Kazakhstan in 2013 may leave school either after nine or eleven years with a Basic School Attestation at Grade 9 or a Diploma of Secondary School at Grade 11. The certificate of basic schooling requires no external evaluation but is based upon within-school marks with only the most excellent students' work (predominantly marks of '5' in the student record from Grades 5 to 11) moderated externally. This moderation is conducted by experts within the regional education department's methodological unit. For students continuing in secondary schools beyond Grade 9, the Diploma of Secondary School comprises two elements: marks from School-Based Assessment (SBA) and, if taken, the score from the UNT. The Diploma at Grade 11 can be given at one of three levels: Blue Attestation (which the majority of school-leavers obtain); Red Attestation (externally moderated at regional level and indicative of an excellent student) and Altyn Belgi (the Golden Award) which requires every mark to be excellent (5) throughout Grades 5 to 11 plus an outstanding UNT score.

Rules for taking the UNT are published by the Ministry online (MoES 2013a) and make clear the mechanics of the process for all students. As decreed in 2008 and amended in 2011, there are 154 testing centres where students can sit the UNT. Most of these sites are at universities or other 'neutral' locations rather than in the schools themselves and serve to offer a standardised and assured environment for the UNT. Practice papers are available each year on the government electronic portal along with the precise locations of the test sites (MoES 2013b). Parents and schools are also free to purchase practice papers which others such as the Kazakh-Turkish Lycea, a private collection of 28[3] schools operating under licence in Kazakhstan, sell for profit.

Despite efforts to the contrary, corruption and a culture of attempted dishonesty remains a problem. Each year substantial numbers of students have materials confiscated with, for example, 28000 confiscations of items such as mobile phones and cheat-notes from candidates in 2013 (Central Communications Service 2013a). MoES staff (1500 employees in 2013) plus CCTV surveillance cameras and metal detectors are used as a matter of course to check fair execution of the tests. The UNT is considered to have the status of a 'state secret' and its contents are protected from disclosure by the highest powers of legal enforcement possible (Tempus 2012).

What are the contents of the UNT?

The UNT in 2013 was a three-and-a-half hour Multiple Choice Question (MCQ) test consisting of 125 questions with five options per item. It covers five subjects split into 25 question-blocks on each of the following: language of instruction (Kazakh or Russian); History of Kazakhstan; Mathematics; second state language (Russian in Kazakh schools or Kazakh in Russian schools) and a fifth 'profile' subject of choice from the following options: a foreign language (English, French or German); Geography; Physics; Chemistry; Biology; World History; Russian or Kazakh Literature (MoES 2013c).

Alongside the UNT, more subject specialist study at TVET colleges leads to a diploma of specialist secondary education (Диплом о Среднем специальном Образовании) to which a new form of centrally controlled Complex Testing of Applicants (CTA) adds a further national measure towards selection for higher education. Students retaking the UNT, those from rural schools that do not teach beyond Grade 9, those from abroad or young people from non-Kazakh or non-Russian speaking sectors of Kazakhstan are the ones most likely to take the CTA. The CTA follows the same format as the UNT but with the section on the state language (Kazakh or Russian) other than that of the test omitted, thereby making it 100 questions and of two-and-a-half hours' duration.

A typical selection of factual questions from the 2013 compulsory Mathematics section of the UNT is shown in Figure 1, with typical questions from the optional profile subjects of English, Chemistry, World History and Geography shown in Figure 2.

The reader can draw their own conclusions upon the style of questioning in Figures 1 and 2 to conclude what the UNT is and has been essentially testing. However, since 2009, part of the development of the UNT by MoES has been to add new types of questions to supposedly examine cognitive ability, critical thinking and the everyday application of knowledge. Examples of this new type of 'logical' question for the Mathematics section are shown in Figure 3.

Figure 1: 2013 UNT Variant 1, selected Mathematics questions.

Mathematics (2013, variant 1)

1. Solve the equation: $\dfrac{2x + 5}{2x - 1} = \dfrac{5}{3}$

  A) 1
  B) 2
  C) 6
  D) 5
  E) 3

24. The area of an equilateral triangle, which lies at the base of a right prism, is equal to $16\sqrt{3}$ cm^2. Calculate the volume of the prism, if the total area of its lateral surface is $100\sqrt{3}$ cm^2.

  A) 300 cm^3
  B) 248 cm^3
  C) 250 cm^3
  D) 200 cm^3
  E) 320 cm^3

Figure 2: 2013 UNT Variant 1, selected profile subject questions.

English (2013, variant 1)

1.   Выберите правильно написанное слово (*Choose the correct written word*):
      A) Cryed.
      B) Cryied.
      C) Cryeid.
      D) Cried.
      E) Cred.

Chemistry (2013, variant 1)

25.   What is the volume of natural gas (80% CH4, 10% SO2, 10% N2) required for
      obtaining the same amount of carbon oxide (IV) to that which is released during the
      combustion of 28 litres of propane containing 20% of incombustible impurities?
      A) 54 litres
      B) 24 litres
      C) 34 litres
      D) 84 litres
      E) 44 litres

World History (2013, Variant 1)

10.   Which person is associated with starting an era of enlightened absolutism?
      A) Peter I
      B) Elizabeth I
      C) Catherine II
      D) Paul I
      E) Alexander II

Geography (2013, variant 1)

4.   Characteristics of an equatorial race are:
      A) yellow skin and eyes wide open.
      B) elongated skull and fair skin.
      C) a narrow nose, narrow slit eyes.
      D) narrow nose, curly hair.
      E) dark-skinned, curly hair.

Figure 3: 2013 UNT Variant 1, selected Mathematics and English questions to reflect the new 'real life' and 'logical' type of items.

Mathematics (2013, Variant 1)

23.   A boat set off from Pier 1 towards Pier 2 at 12 km/h. A half hour after it, in the same direction, a steamer set out at 20 km/h. What is the distance between the piers if the steamer arrived 1.5 hours before the boat?
A) 62 km. B) 60 km. C) 61 km. D) 64 km. E) 63 km.

English (2013, variant 1)

24.   Прочитайте текст и выполните задание после текста (*Read the text and complete the task after it*):

London parks are the most beautiful areas of the city. In the summer you can sit in St. James's Park by the side of the lake and listen to the band playing music. Green Park is a different kind of park. It is a quiet, wooden (sic) place. Hyde Park was once part of a forest. Nowadays, Speakers' Corner of the park is always a centre of activity. Sunday is the most popular day and you will usually find some people standing on their soap-boxes and making speeches. There is a boating lake, and skating in the winter if the ice is 10 centimetres thick. There is an open-air theatre where plays are put on in the summer, and a rose garden and a restaurant.

Ответьте на вопрос (Answer the question):

Where do the speakers usually stand making speeches?

A) At the boating lake.
B) In a wooden (sic) place.
C) In a rose garden.
D) On the soap-boxes.
E) At the open-air theatre.

What does the UNT test and what does it fail to test?

As can be seen from the examples of the UNT questions given previously, they primarily reward factual knowledge. There is no opportunity for candidates to show how they have reached their answers or any way in which they can communicate using anything other than a shaded response box. The questions described as 'logical' that are being introduced do not work; and are not so much invoking problem solving as attempting to translate the curriculum to real life settings in a rather stilted manner.

So, for the example of the Mathematics and Chemistry papers, an error in arithmetic, even if the calculation method is known, gains no more marks than a guess at the answer. Additionally, as no formulae are supplied, Mathematics and other Science questions require a student to first recall these to conduct any calculations. Whether an incorrect answer originates from never having known the answer in the first place, inaccurate recall, simple arithmetical error or misinterpretation of the question is unknown. Hence, even the more difficult Mathematics questions do not necessarily extract a demonstration of skill or competence. Any application of knowledge in selecting an appropriate method for the solution in the case of some of the Mathematics and Science questions is within a very demanding timeframe of an average of 100 seconds per answer. This challenges even good mathematicians to respond appropriately under pressure. One teacher asked how critical thinking and logic can begin to be tested effectively if there is no opportunity to expand beyond a quick tick.

> They are afraid of the tests because of the time limits. They cannot fully express their potential and just tick. Those who have less ability are usually successful. I cannot say that the test checks their knowledge; much depends on fortune. They should pass exams which makes them think: process and produce something. Critical thinking cannot be tested in the UNT; you cannot justify your tick. (Mathematics teacher, rural secondary school)

The UNT format does not test depth of thinking; and questions are not linked to difficulty or any considered marks scheme that rewards progressively more complex tasks. Although the English paper attempts to locate the language in national cultures and involves some comprehension exercises and wider factual questioning around this, it is unclear whether the context is a North American or a British one. Asking factual questions about landmark buildings or national emblems may be a first attempt at cultural sensitivity to language but whether this is necessary or appropriate in measuring language proficiency is highly debatable. As with the Russian, Kazakh and all other language sections of the UNT, no oral component to testing means that skill and competence in listening or speaking are entirely neglected and most would argue this is a serious omission (e.g. Bachman 1990). It is not likely to predict those most able to actually communicate in any language other than in a written form and even then, only in a formulaic, non-spontaneous and inflexible manner, with comprehension being only minimally examined. This approach is not limited to the UNT, as the comment below from a vice director demonstrates. A lot of assessment in Kazakhstan appears to be record-keeping. Also, just having numbers is not enough; there must be meaning behind them. That said, the interviewee's keen interest in monitoring and marking for progression is remarkable and indicative of what professional teachers do: and, might be able to contribute at a national level. Notably the interviewee's records include language skill assessment such as dictation which is, of course, never tested in the UNT:

> I presented the results on Russian Language Testing, as you can see - type of task on the test, here there was a dictation task and we assessed the quality, the grammar task part. You see here the grade for the second Quarter of the year. Five '5s' in total and nine '5s' for the dictation. It is clear from the results, what the problem is. We compared the Quarter grades and the final test results. Whether they were objective. These were done in relation to all the classes, the Kazakh and the Russian ones. We work as a team. (Vice Director, Professional Lyceum)

As recognised by a teacher quoted below, learning through practice gives real insight and acquiring practical skills extends beyond languages towards Science subjects as well. The pressure of a fact-heavy curriculum, and assessment through the UNT designed to test rote-knowledge, does not allow understanding or time to pursue Science in a more interesting manner, let alone allow students with good laboratory skills to shine:

> . . . for example, in one of the Chemistry lessons, which actually involved drawing out the chemical processes and also the practical mixing of chemicals, with burning, we could see the interest of children. We saw children learning and understanding through practice. Of course, other children, who do not have such practice, will not understand how the processes go in reality . . . we have to give more hours for such practice lessons. The problem is that we have a lot of theory; even some practical lessons only involve verbal discussions and not actual practice. So, if we are talking about choosing future professions, children have to know the basics through practice. (Teacher focus group upon assessment, Lyceum school)

The World History and Geography papers are entirely based upon factual recall and simplistic interpretations of the subject that lack any level of sophistication. Interpretation by students or the demonstration by students of connection or understanding of events to include causal factors or the underlying directors behind natural or economic phenomena is completely untested. There is no visible reward for original thought or the creative, intelligent interpretation of knowledge and learning from History or Geography towards application in a modern world and, as described below, no system to place a genuinely interested and capable student ahead of one with a good memory.

> Oh, this (UNT) needs change and modifications. In practice we see that two different students, the one who does everything superficially and the one who does everything seriously are ultimately assessed as equal. In this sense, it is a bit unfair. (Teacher of Kazakh History, rural secondary school)

Another very real problem with the UNT is the number of subjects that students can choose. Only one profile subject beyond the four required subjects is allowed, forcing students to concentrate upon one subject to the neglect of others. Hence, scientists have to choose between Physics, Chemistry and Biology for their 'profile' option. Linguists must choose English, French or German and those interested in the Humanities must choose either History or Geography.

Who sits the UNT and who gains funding for higher education?

The UNT plays a part in a great number of lives. Between 3 and 7 June 2013, around 95000 people from the national cohort of 143000 secondary school students took the UNT. Of these, 71.2% ($\approx$ 65000) achieved the threshold value of 50, making them eligible for entry to higher education; 11.1% (11167) achieved a score of over 100 and thereby prioritisation to receive state funding.

By comparison, there were 78758 entries for the CTA in 2013 formed from: 43425 college graduates who began studying after their Grade 9; 17568 college graduates who began studying after their Grade 11; and 17765 school leavers (Central Communications Service 2013b). CTA tests were held at 39 centres around Kazakhstan from 19 to 22 July and although no national data are available, it appears, based upon the results announced for Astana, that around 28% typically pass the threshold to become eligible for a place within higher education (Akimat of Astana 2013).

Therefore, as an approximate calculation of the numbers eligible in total for study at universities in 2013, around 22000 derive from taking the CTA and 65000 from the UNT making a total of 87000 eligible candidates. There is state funding for 35000 places, which leaves the remaining eligible candidates to self-fund or seek out regional sponsors such as their local Akimat's (Mayor's) office (Central Communications Service 2013a).

Figures for 2012 indicate that there are around 610000 higher education students in total (320000 at public and 290000 at private HEIs) at 146 universities in Kazakhstan (Tempus 2012). This tends to suggest, with a typical four-year Bachelor programme, that there are currently more students at university than are deemed eligible on the basis of UNT scores alone. It has to be remembered, therefore, that the UNT criteria scores apply to state institutions only. Indeed, HEIs in Kazakhstan still have varying reputations, and it is one of the MoES's aims to reduce the total number of universities to one hundred by 2018 and so allow the ratio of higher education places to be six universities per million residents.[4] This would bring the ratio somewhat closer to other countries, with one example of this being the UK which has a total of 130 universities[5] against a domestic population of 53.5 million.[6] Consequently, selection for places within state HEIs will need to become even more discriminatory in the future and the performance of the UNT will be all the more critical.

Details of the part that CTA and UNT results play in funding are described in the 'Terms of Awarding Educational Grants to pay for Higher Education', with cut-off scores being the most significant factor (MoES 2012a). Some recognition of students' backgrounds is made by the use of quotas whereby candidates from rural schools have closed competition for 30% of the grants awarded and open general competition for the remaining 70% with, in the case of equal scores, preference being given to children or parents with disabilities, orphans and those lacking parental support (MoES 2012a). Additionally, some universities have competitive sponsorship schemes of their own to attract good students and involve private-funding initiatives to offer grants (Tempus 2012). Funding is also prioritised around subjects, with limited funds available for non-priority subjects and what funding there is available going to the very highest UNT achievers. This is exemplified in the comment form a teacher below.

> Well children already have some choice in UNT testing by choosing the subjects they want to take, but maybe they need more freedom of choice . . . at the moment there are, all in all, 12 children, who have chosen the subject Geography as an

option for UNT. Not many children chose Geography because . . . usually you won't be able to get a scholarship with the subject Geography. There are very few of them, probably one or two universities offer them. As a result when a student chooses Geography, they consider whether they can pay (for university) or not. Those who can't afford usually choose Physics or some other subject, where you get more scholarships. (Teacher of Geography, Professional Lyceum School)

Official commentary on the 2013 and 2012 results

Very little official commentary exists for UNT results for 2013 beyond the raw publication of some descriptive test statistics. What there is (Central Communications Service 2013b) indicates 70% Kazakh and 30% Russian versions of the test were taken, supporting the consistent slow drift away from Russian as the language of instruction in Kazakhstani schools. The average score was 74.5 (out of 125) with improvement from the previous year most marked in those candidates taking the Kazakh versions of the test; the average score for this group rose from 68.2 in 2012 to 72.8 in 2013. In 2013, 11.7% scored over 100, with seven students (three from one school) gaining full marks of 125. This compared to 9% in 2012, when only three individuals achieved the maximum score, all from different schools. The pass criteria for university has remained the same for 2013 as it was under the 2012 scheme which is as follows: 50 out of 100 points (on the total of the four compulsory sections), with the fifth elective subject score being no less than 7 points and no one section scoring below 3 points (MoES 2012b).

Additional commentary on UNT results

Introducing 'logical' items has a history of surprising some schools and students, so this adaption of the UNT has not been without problems. As indicated below, different variants of the test had differing proportions of these new types of logic test items and so introduced an element of chance in whether a student came across them or not:

We had changes last year (2012), and in 2008–9 as well. 2009 was a little bit difficult. Last year, there were changes in Maths and History. Assignments for logic and thinking were added to the test but not to every variant. In some variants there are 2–3 changes all in all, some do not have any. To those who had these changed variants, it was difficult to solve them . . . some students had these new questions in their variants . . . three (out of 25), one or none. It depended. (Director, rural secondary school)

The element of chance in encountering different variants of the UNT is backed up by the published data (MoES 2013d). For the six days of UNT variants in operation in 2013, the proportions achieving a score above 100 on days one to six (3 June 3 to 9 June 9 2013) varied as follows: 11.4% of 24152 (3 June); 8.4% of 21794 (4 June); 12.6% of 25646 (5 June); 13.5% of 10339 (6 June); 12.3% of 9309 (7 June); 26.7% of 1586 (8 June); 7.9% of 2661 (9 June); giving an overall value of 11.7% from the total of 95487. Unless there is some rationale behind which students sit which papers on which day, it is remarkable that of those who sat the UNT on 8 June, over 1 in 4 scored above 100; whereas of those who sat it the next day, the chances of scoring over 100 were around 1 in 12.

The results for students with Kazakh as their language of instruction have been consistently lower than those with Russian as the language of instruction up until and including 2013 (MoES 2013d). There are many compounding factors to this such as there being far more urban, lyceum and gymnasium schools represented in the Russian group. There may be socio-economic factors as well, but what appears certain is that there are complexities to taking the test in Kazakh that do not exist if taking the test in Russian. For instance, there are many more textbooks and other resources available in Russian beyond the state-supplied materials and many teachers will have been educated themselves in Russian and so use terminology and explanation consistent with their own understanding. The effect of language of instruction was most marked in 2012 when despite the proportion of those sitting the UNT from Kazakh-medium schools being 68% and those from Russian-medium being 32%, those failing it were 74% Kazakh-medium against 26% Russian. Russian-medium students achieving scores over 100 were also remarkably over-represented at 44% compared to their overall candidates' figure of 32%. What is even more surprising is that the second state language, other than the language of instruction, scores were radically different in 2012; with the 80941 Kazakh-medium students only achieving an average score of 13.41 in Russian whereas the 36392 Russian medium students had an average score of 18.06 in Kazakh. This alone may have been sufficient to depress the overall performance of all Kazakh-medium students, yet no accommodation or adjustment for this seems to have publically been recorded or taken place. No open inquiry as to the potential causes of this, such as a shortage of Russian teachers in Kazakh schools, has been recorded either. The complexities of having two state languages is further illustrated by a shortage of Russian-speaking History of Kazakhstan teachers so that this compulsory subject within the UNT is often taught in Kazakh but for students at Russian-medium schools, the UNT questions upon it will be in Russian, as described by a student below:

> This is the same issue as with the History of Kazakhstan. We learn the subject in Kazakh, and because we are a Russian-language class, the subject is very difficult for us. And at UNT, all examinations are in Russian. (Grade 11 student within a Student Focus Group, rural secondary school)

The UNT compared with international qualifications

As Kazakhstan is looking towards internationalisation, it may be helpful to make some direct comparisons between the UNT and some international assessments. To do this, Table 1 illustrates the expectations of the European Qualifications Framework (EQF) in terms of qualifications below those of higher education with Level 3 being the one required as suitable preparation for entry into higher education. As can be seen within Table 1, there are three essential components in preparing students for higher education: knowledge, skills and competences. Students should not only be equipped with knowledge in a specific field of study but they should also understand its conceptual framing (under the remit of 'knowledge'); be able to apply it towards appropriately solving problems (under the remit of 'skills'); and act adaptively with a certain level of independence and autonomy (under the remit of 'competence').

Table 1: Supposed knowledge, skills and competences for pre-tertiary qualifications as key elements within European Qualifications Framework Levels 1 to 3 (EQF, 2008)

'Qualification' means a formal outcome of an assessment and validation process which is obtained when a competent body determines that an individual has achieved learning outcomes to given standards.			
	Knowledge	**Skills**	**Competence**
Key definitions	'Knowledge' means theoretical and/or factual.	'Skills' means the ability to apply knowledge and use know-how to complete tasks and solve problems. In the context of the European Qualifications Framework, skills are described as cognitive (involving the use of logical, intuitive and creative thinking) or practical (involving manual dexterity and the use of methods, materials, tools and instruments).	'Competence' means the proven ability to use knowledge, skills and personal, social and/or methodological abilities, in work or study situations and in professional and personal development. In the context of the European Qualifications Framework, competence is described in terms of responsibility and autonomy.
Expectations for Level 1	Basic general knowledge	Basic skills required to carry out simple tasks	Work or study under direct supervision in a structured context
Expectations for Level 2	Basic factual knowledge of a field of work or study	Basic cognitive and practical skills required to use relevant information in order to carry out tasks and to solve routine problems using simple rules and tools	Work or study under supervision with some autonomy
Expectations for Level 3	Knowledge of facts, principles, processes and general concepts, in a field of work or study	A range of cognitive and practical skills required to accomplish tasks and solve problems by selecting and applying basic methods, tools, materials and information	Take responsibility for completion of tasks in work or study. Adapt own behaviour to circumstances in solving problems

For comparison with those sitting within a National Qualification Framework, and to attempt to locate UNT in terms of European standards, Figure 4 illustrates typical questions in a UK Mathematics paper. This paper forms part of a larger examination used for selection for higher education. Marks are shown on the paper, as awarded for various elements, and for a demonstration of known method as well as ultimately giving the correct answer. These questions illustrate Level 3[7] of EQF through a General Certificate of Education: Advanced Level (GCE A Level) awarded at the end of further education in England, Wales and Northern Ireland (for those, generally aged 18 years, following an additional two years of study beyond the end of compulsory schooling). A major A Level reform[8] is to take place in the UK in 2013–14, but the demands of the GCE A Level qualification, as shown in Figure 4, should remain intact. The awarding organisation for the examples in Figure 4 is OCR[9] (Oxford, Cambridge and Royal Society of the Arts Examinations, part of Cambridge Assessment, a department of the University of Cambridge), which is a nationwide, independent self-governing entity, regulated to provide such qualifications by the independent governmental agency Ofqual[10] (Office of Qualifications and Examinations Regulations). Ofqual ensure the integrity and parity of qualifications from several such awarding organisations in England, Wales and Northern Ireland as ratified against the EQF by the self-certification documents submitted by the UK government (see Figure 4).[11]

Appropriate grades in several subject-specific GCE A Levels allow application to enter higher education and undergraduate programmes directly through UCAS[12] (Universities and Colleges Admissions Service) which is funded by contributions from HEIs in the UK. As shown in Table 2, the duration of the examination and overall number of marks awarded for the UNT and these qualifications in England, Wales and Northern Ireland for Levels 1 to 3 are very different. In terms of the number of marks, using Mathematics as an example, the UNT requires 25 MCQ responses for entry into a Mathematics Bachelor programme in Kazakhstan (along with an overall satisfactory UNT score) whereas for a UK undergraduate programme, progression has to be shown through the various levels ultimately totalling another 9 hours examination on top of the EQF Level 2 (Higher tier) GCSE, deemed to have most parity to UNT. Connected to that is the difference in rewarding skills through marks for method and a much more sophisticated marking scheme overall that requires trained markers and co-ordination of these markers, as opposed to computerised processing of MCQ responses. Hence universities can have some confidence in candidates' ability to understand and apply their knowledge and that they have transferable skills for generic use in a multiplicity of other arenas such as medicine or engineering. The opportunity for greater discrimination between candidates exists by means of a check of progress through the levels and a philosophy of thorough preparation for higher education by ensuring students have a good set of skills and the capacity for independent study. This also relates to making higher education selection decisions of one candidate against another to reflect potential as well as performance.

Figure 4: Comparison with OCR Mathematics GCE A2 paper (Level 3 EQF)

A2 GCE Mathematics Unit 4723 Core Mathematics 3 14 June 2012: Question 4

Retrieved 1 October 2013 from www.ocr.org.uk/Images/136131-question-paper-unit-4723-core-mathematics-3.pdf.

and

A2 GCE Mathematics Unit 4734 Probability & Statistics 3 31 May 2012: Question 3

Retrieved 1 October 2013 from www.ocr.org.uk/Images/136161-question-paper-unit-4734-probability-and-statistics-3.pdf.

'Your answers should be supported with appropriate working and *marks will be given for correct method even if the answer is incorrect.'*

Two Core 90 minute examinations in Pure Mathematics as typified by Q4:

4   (a) Show that $\int_0^4 \frac{18}{\sqrt{6x+1}}\, dx = 24$.   [4]

     (b) Find $\int_0^1 (e^x + 2)^2\, dx$, giving your answer in terms of e.   [4]

One optional 90 minute examination in either Mechanics, Statistics and Probability or Decision Mathematics as typified by Q3:

'Your answers should be supported with appropriate working and *marks will be given for correct method even if the answer is incorrect.'*

3.   It is known that on average one person in three prefers the colour of a certain object to be blue. In a psychological test, 12 randomly chosen people were seated in a room with blue walls and asked to state independently which colour they preferred for the object. Seven of the 12 people said they preferred blue. Carry out a significance test, at the 5% level, of whether the statement "on average one person in three prefers the colour of the object to be blue" is true for people who are seated in a room with blue walls **[7 marks]**

Reproduced with permission © OCR.

Table 2: Comparison of test/examination times for Mathematics component of UNT and Level 1, 2 and 3 Mathematics qualifications in the UK

The example of Mathematics national assessment				
	UNT	OCR GCSE (Foundation tier Mathematics B)	OCR GCSE (Higher tier Mathematics B)	OCR GCE Advanced GCE (7890)
Educational level	End of 11-year schooling	End of 12-year compulsory schooling	End of 12-year compulsory schooling	End of additional 2 years of Further Education
Number of exam papers	1	2	2	6
Total time of subject exams	42 minutes	2×1 hour 30 minutes (one paper with and one without a calculator)	2×1 hour 45 minutes (one paper with and one without a calculator)	6×1 hour 30 minutes
Marks available	25	200	220	432
Grades possible	2 to 5	C (Level 2) D–G (Level 1)	A* to E	A* to E or U
EQF level	?	1 or 2[13]	2	3

To confirm the status of UNT as an EQF Level 1 to Level 2 qualification, UK NARIC[14] (which offers services to universities alongside UCAS) assessed the test in 2004 and deemed a pass equivalent to several good grades at a UK GCSE (OECD 2007). Level 2 would prohibit progression for most Kazakhstan-educated school leavers into higher education programmes outside Kazakhstan. The OECD Review of Higher Education in Kazakhstan (OECD 2007) also suggests the UNT would not be able to 'demonstrate' the appropriate levels of knowledge, skills and competences shown in either the Baccalaureat in France, the Abitur in Germany or many other school-leaving qualifications in Europe.

Another factor that separates UNT from the UK qualifications is that, in line with the NQF, the awarding organisation (OCR in the example above) publishes aims, learning outcomes, assessment objectives and performance descriptions. This transparency assists in defining transferable skills that form part of a lifelong learning paradigm.

What is wrong with the UNT?

The following sections propose various perceived limitations to the current UNT relating to: its reliability and validity; different language versions of the test; its multiple functions; its fitness for purpose as preparation and selection for higher education; the lack of a well-implemented NQF; and, its removal from teachers and their professional development.

Problems of reliability and validity of test items affecting the overall scale

A student's UNT score is valid only until the end of the calendar year of its award. Since the year-on-year performance of the UNT is unchartered, this is probably wise, as more general test-retest data is not freely available. No internal reliability measures, evidence of Rasch modelling, other scaling statistical algorithms or more general psychometric performance data for the UNT have been published. As the UNT is not independently calibrated, or otherwise adjusted, to ensure that a pass score or a given mark is associated with the same level of knowledge and ability from year to year, this undermines its credibility as a psychometric measure and hence in having meaningful population parameters. Many suggest the quality of the tests themselves is suspect with errors in the questions and, as illustrated earlier, published data on different variants of the test suggest irregularities in performance across sometimes very large cohorts, which is troubling.

Problems of language

This represents the equivalence of state language versions and problems of multilingual education. This includes the availability of resources to satisfy the demands of teaching the curriculum in a certain language of instruction whilst simultaneously facing the confounding demands of assessment in another language within the UNT.

As discussed previously, official data indicates performance differentials in Kazakh and Russian variants of the UNT. Whether this is a lack of test equivalence or a true effect is impossible to determine for a variety of reasons. However, the trilingual policy is likely to only make this effect worse as teaching takes place in English, yet UNT testing takes place in Kazakh or Russian. Requiring students to frequently switch from one language of study to a different one for assessment concerns those already trialling a trilingual approach:

> You know, every year, there are two to three meetings at which I always speak. I always raise the problems of UNT, problems of teachers and textbooks. They always give us textbooks from Turkey, Cambridge etc. for comparison; however, their standards do not comply with our standards. Therefore, we translate our Russian textbooks into English, which is also not right. There are many such problems that I raise. So, last year, we had the first trilingual programme graduates, in 2012. They studied Chemistry in English and we were lucky, because not all of them chose to write the Chemistry exam. Mathematics and other UNT test, they wrote in their own language. Now, this year, Grade 10 students are studying Mathematics in English, but they will have to write it during UNT in Russian, which means that they will have to translate the problems before solving them. It is a big problem. (Director, urban Gymnasium)

Problems of using the UNT to measure many different things

Strong criticism exists that the UNT is trying to do too much and that its multiplicity of purpose not only damages test construction but also affects other facets of the educational system. Determining teachers' pay and regional performance appraisals based upon UNT results not only places an unfair burden on some teachers where students' performance may be beyond their control but also opens up conflicts of interest. These may affect conduct around implementation of the UNT and open it up to corruption. The comment that follows takes the perspective of a teacher, supporting the criticism of how UNT results are used to detrimental effect for teacher appraisal:

> The (UNT) results are equal to an academic competition, the contest 'Teacher of the Year', and if, say, the UNT results turn out to be poor, since in our countryside the children are not prepared, then who is to blame? The child lives in the village and has practical household chores, such as wood and coal, and we cannot force them to concentrate at school. We are generally equated to our students' UNT rating; if they pass then we are appreciated. Last year, children were well prepared and passed; but, here, two years ago, it was not alright. It is for the UNT results I am afraid; because all my (teaching) services beforehand, they are crossed out. Republican achievements will be lost because the child gets a very low grade. In rural schools, it is a big problem with UNT. Urban schools do not have so many teachers and classes. So, it is not rewarding, and it is a huge stress for people . . . now I have 11 classes, I work all the time and have no vacation. We

must all be prepared for UNT. (Russian-speaking teacher as part of a Teacher Focus Group, village secondary school)

The Ministry of Education and Science (MoES) acknowledges many faults with the UNT and is making moves to improve it, not only by revision to its content but also by better recognition of the impact that the multiple roles it is asked to perform may have. For example, using it as a mechanism to allocate and prioritise funding to students alongside a performance measure of teachers and regional education organisations may affect the integrity of those involved in its delivery or reporting, as described by a senior figure within the MoES:

> The UNT has too many functions: it is the summative annual assessment of the school system; it is the opportunity for the receipt of a distinction diploma, the *Altyn Belgi*, which enables entry to higher education institutes without exams or competition; access to higher education in general; the state scholarship; the assessment of the teacher's work; school assessment; region assessment; so finally, it gets very tempting to intervene (at the level of the) UNT. The UNT performs too many functions . . . this is why the situation pushes local authorities to violate UNT procedures. It is easy to solve all problems after 3½ hours of the UNT by just 'making up' incorrect results. As a result, the UNT has not always been an objective instrument: (for example), some rural schools showed better results than our elite schools. This year the results of the UNT were more objective as a consequence of the regional departments of quality control that we created. (Senior figure at MoES)

Furthermore, such a singular high-stakes measure of students, teachers and schools places individuals under intense stress and strain. The UNT acts to indicate almost the entirety of one's success at school and thus to determine lifelong educational opportunities based upon one day's performance. No account is made of extenuating circumstances, and no attempt made to assess the student in a more holistic way:

> On National Testing, some pupils cannot show all their knowledge; some of them are not ready from a psychological point of view. For instance, we have one student, Z, she is an excellent learner. When she came to the 11th grade, during preparation for National Testing, her mother died. She is under great stress as an adult child with two little children in her family. Being in such a condition; we also need to think about National Testing. In my opinion, it was very difficult for her. If she cannot get the Diploma with Honours, I will say that nobody dies, but she should do it. I will motivate her, she has studied very well during all her time

at school but with such upset; she may forget everything. (Director, professional Lyceum)

Problems of unfitness for purpose as preparation for higher education

It is universally acknowledged that the UNT does not act well to select or prepare students for later specialised study at university. Insufficient depth of enquiry or choice of subjects as preparation for students to study within higher education are recognised in this typical statement from a teacher:

> There are a lot of haters/opponents of the UNT. According to the diplomas, our children have to study 22 disciplines, but only five of them really matter because of the UNT, so the students don't pay sufficient attention to other disciplines. They pay their whole attention to these five disciplines to pass the UNT in order to get free university grants. Thereby, such disciplines as Chemistry, Literature are rejected. The students don't read any Literature nowadays because they don't have to pass the UNT on Literature. There are a lot of such nuances. And I think that the student should have the right of choice, that is to say career guidance should be inculcated in the fifth to sixth grade. For example, some students are inclined to engineering, botany, medicine. They have to determine with their career guidance in advance. The things they do best. Sometimes, we have students who don't know what kind of discipline they should choose in 11th grade, as a fifth UNT option because they don't know which profession they will choose in the future. We have to work on this matter to teach our children in order to help them choose the right profession before the sixth, seventh, eighth, ninth or tenth grade. (Director, urban Gymnasium)

Again, this is something that MoES recognises as a shortcoming of the UNT. The comment below endorses the previous teacher's analysis almost exactly but unfortunately does not provide any solutions to the problem.

> At the same time, the UNT has several systematic problems. For example, there are a limited number of subjects on which tests are based. As a result, teachers and children prepare for the tests in five subjects only and they ignore their other subjects. The higher education system also criticises the UNT because the tests based on five subjects do not take into account the peculiarities of various (tertiary-level) majors. Of the five subjects, only one is an elective, also, the tasks address the reproduction of knowledge without demonstrating key competencies. (Senior figure at MoES)

Arguably a general education with breadth of subjects covered and assessed at Grade 9 leading onto specialism within the school during Grades 10 and 11 may be one solution. However, how this will fit with the move from 11-year to 12-year schooling then becomes another question to be answered. The next section, dealing with the somewhat unstructured approach across the whole educational system, discusses this point further.

Problems stemming from no (as yet) enacted National Qualifications Framework

The European paradigm of lifelong learning that develops skills and competences alongside the accruement of knowledge is set upon the premise of a national, structured suite of qualifications. The UNT is currently the first and only NLSA in Kazakhstani schools, which means that for those not taking the UNT and leaving school at Grade 9, no national qualification is offered for recognition in the labour market (Damitov et al., cited in OECD 2007). Pursuant to this, the UNT is not located in a National Qualifications Framework and hence has no defined level of attainment. No transparently defined preparation for the UNT or transparently defined competences for others to ascribe to candidates holding a successful UNT score exist. The UNT sits in isolation as the only pre-tertiary national measure and, as illustrated previously, tests knowledge with little intent to reward the selection and application of appropriate knowledge in a skilful or competent manner. There is minimal direction towards students' autonomy of study, independent thought or capacity to critique. In particular, the sole means of testing by use of one MCQ test precludes examination of: practical skills; more extended reasoning; or the ability to communicate effectively. This is recognised below by MoES as improving scores on international measures of school students' performances cannot be done without engaging in a fundamental shift in ideas around the very purpose of education:

> In terms of the content of school education, the main issue is to move from knowledge-centred education to competency-based education. International comparative research, PISA and TIMSS, demonstrate that our children are not able to apply the knowledge they have; they are not able to work independently, to analyse, or to forecast. (Senior figure at MoES)

Problems resulting from taking assessment out of the hands of the profession

Teachers are undertaking new pedagogical training and continuing professional development towards embracing more modern styles of teaching. Yet they have to contend with the UNT that precludes group-work as students need to study towards learning large libraries of knowledge to recall as individuals in a non-discursive format. In addition, teachers assess students within schools but are not involved in the national process of assessment other than by submitting questions on an ad hoc basis for inclusion in the overall test-bank. They do not mark papers or receive feedback upon their students' performances other than a summative subject by subject score. The possibility for professional development of teachers therefore does not exist within the current set up of the UNT.

What is the culture of assessment, based upon the UNT, in Kazakhstan, past and present?

To summarise the assessment culture in Kazakhstan, there seems to be a total disconnect between what professional teachers are doing within schools and what the NTC provides as a means to identify the most suitable Grade 11 students for funding and study within higher education. The school Attestat, which in general is not cross-moderated from school to school, appears detached from the UNT score within it and plays little part in the process of student appraisal by universities. What HEIs want themselves in terms of specialist study is also neglected; as are the needs of those leaving school without attempting the UNT. From an external viewpoint, the type of test NTC are providing appears to be a fairer mechanism than what went before; but still allows a great deal of corruption to exist. The sheer number of students turning up with the means to cheat indicates that there is a social norm around national testing that needs a serious shift in the mind-set to address. There seems to be a lack of creative thought around alternatives to the UNT and although there appears to be slow improvement in the quality of test items, the fundamental principal of whether a MCQ and a single test (or even two similar tests) is a good idea appears relatively unchallenged from within NTC. It may require further transformational thinking to implement a life-long learning paradigm alongside transparent learning outcomes to provide meaningful year-on year comparisons. The concept of teacher involvement in the marking of NLSA appears very alien. It is the absolutism, as exemplified by a MCQ format, which is perhaps most worrying within the current culture of educational assessment as this prevents discussion, creative and questioning ambiguity or any communication of originality.

Conclusion

This chapter set out to ask whether the arguments of the past for the particular form of assessment represented by the UNT are still valid and if Kazakhstan is currently operating an educational meritocracy fit for the 21st century. From the problems listed with the UNT above, it appears the answer to both of these questions is 'no'.

Problems of misconduct and corruption still exist. Waiting for a NQF to define required levels of knowledge, skills and competences throughout the educational system is critically damaging a strategic redesign of all national assessment practices in Kazakhstan geared towards having a population equipped with 21st-century skills. The UNT, as it is, appears unreliable and different versions of it may not have parity or reflect the difficulty some schools have in being equipped to prepare students fully for it. It is failing to prepare students with the skills and specialist knowledge required for higher-education study; it limits study of certain subjects and fails to reward or promote students' higher order cognitive skills.

The third question posed at the start of this chapter was: Where does the balance of power behind educational reforms lie and, connected to this, are decision makers listening to stakeholders? This clearly connects to the culture of assessment in Kazakhstan. Based on the evidence presented thus far, the authors would argue that it is top-down, highly summative and concerned with relatively simple fact-checking rather than working with the teaching profession to appraise students more holistically and fairly. Even within schools this appears to be the case, with directors and vice directors leading assessment decisions. The fact that the UNT seems to operate for reasons of administrative conveience on a single turn-round day rather than on a pattern indicated by educational research, practice or theory is of concern. However, as the next chapter will address, this is perhaps more a historic view and inherited perspective from the past rather than necessarily a current attitude as evidenced by the open, willing way that flaws in the UNT are acknowledged by MoES.

The next chapter further discusses drawbacks to the current UNT and sets them against alternative models and prospects for the future. It also explores how this particular national policy surrounding UNT colours the culture of assessment more generally in schools that intuitively seem to adopt more sophisticated types of assessment than the national ones, albeit generally still of a dictated, well-documented, summative nature.

REFERENCES

Akimat of Astana (2013). *28% of Applicants Overpassed the Threshold of the Complex Testing in Astana.* Press release published 11 June 2013 by Akimat of Astana. www.astana.kz/en/modules/material/1851.

Avanessov, V.S. (2005). *Theory and Practice of Educational Measurements.* (Proceedings of publications in open sources and Internet). Prepared by the DH and the ICE Ural State Technical University. viperson.ru/data/200812/jbjejbjxjklmjuje.pdf (retrieved 1 October 2013).

Bachman, L.F. (1990). *Fundamental Considerations in Language Testing.* Oxford: Oxford University Press.

Central Communication Service (2013a). *Education Minister Informed President about UNT Results.* Press release published 14 June 2013 by Central Communication Service of Kazakhstan. ortcom.kz/en/news/education-minister-informed-president-about-unt-results.1513.

— (2013b). *Complex tests for school leavers begins in Kazakhstan.* Press release published 11 June 2013 by Central Communication Service of Kazakhstan. ortcom.kz/en/news/complex-tests-for-school-leavers-begins-in-kazakhstan.1740.

Chabe, A.M. (1971). 'Soviet Educational Policies: Their Development, Administration and Content.' *Association for Supervision and Curriculum Development,* 525–31. www.ascd.org/ASCD/pdf/journals/ed_lead/el_197102_chabe.pdf (retrieved 1 October 2013).

Clark, N. (2005). 'Education Reform in the Former Soviet Union.' *World Education News and Reviews,* December. www.wes.org/ewenr/PF/05dec/pffeature.htm (retrieved 10 September 2012).

ENIC (2013). *ENIC-NARIC.net: Country Pages: Kazakhstan.* Hosted by Lifelong Learning Programme/NARIC action of the European Union. enic-naric.net/index.aspx?c=Kazakhstan (retrieved 1 October 2013).

EQF (2008). *Documents Agreed by the EQF Advisory Group: Criteria and Procedures for Referencing National Qualifications Levels to the EQF.* Brussels: European Commission. ec.europa.eu/eqf/documentation_en.htm (retrieved 1 October 2013).

MoES (Ministry of Education and Science) (2012a). *Terms of Awarding Educational Grants to Pay for Higher Education.* www.edu.gov.kz/ru/activity/abiturient_2012/pravila_prisu-zhdenija_obrazovatelnogo_granta_dlja_oplaty_vysshego_obrazovanija/ (retrieved 1 October 2013).

— (2012b). *Uniform National Testing (UNT).* e.gov.kz/wps/portal/Content?contentPath=/egov-content/education/edu_heis/article/abiturient_2012&lang=en (retrieved 1 October 2013).

— (2013a). *Approved by Order of the Minister of Education and Science Republic of Kazakhstan '18' March 2008 No. 125 Amended and Supplemented by Order Minister of Education and Science on January 20, 2009 No. 14.* www.educontrol.kz/en/uniform-national-test/list-of-places-of-uniform-national-testing/ (retrieved 20 November 2012).

— (2013b). *e.gov Public Services and Information Online: Entrant 2013.* e.gov.kz/wps/portal/Content?contentPath=/egovcontent/education/edu_heis/article/abiturient_2012&lang=en (retrieved 20 November 2012).

— (2013c). *Committee for Control of Education and Science.* www.educontrol.kz/en (retrieved 1 October 2013).

— (2013d). *Statistics of Education within the Republic of Kazakhstan, National Collection using Data from the Ministry of Education and Science of the Republic of Kazakhstan and the Agency of the Republic of Kazakhstan Statistics (Minutes of the NMS number February 2013, Astana).* www.edu.gov.kz/fileadmin/user_upload/deyatelnost/obrazov_monitoring/Nac_sbornik_06_03_13.pdf (retrieved 1 October 2013).

Nazarbayev, N. (2012). 'Socio-Economic Modernization as Main Vector of Development of Kazakhstan'. Address by the President of the Republic of Kazakhstan. The Official Site of the President of the Republic of Kazakhstan, 27 January 2012. www.akorda.kz/en/page/address-by-the-president-of-the-republic-of-kazakhstan-nursultan-nazarbayev-to-the-people-of-kazakhstan-27-01-2012_1341926486.

OECD (2007). *Reviews of National Policies for Education: Higher Education in Kazakhstan 2007.* Paris: OECD and The International Bank for Reconstruction and Development/ The World Bank.

Tempus (2012). *Higher Education in Kazakhstan.* Brussels: Education, Audio-visual and Culture Executive Agency (EACEA). eacea.ec.europa.eu/tempus/participating_countries/reviews/Kazakhstan.pdf (retrieved 1 October 2013).

NOTES

1. kazakhtest.kz/en/about/.
2. www.edu.gov.kz/ru/news/?tx_ttnews%5Btt_news%5D=5226&cHash=1377fa0288915f7e6eb26631f54d7386.
3. engnews.gazeta.kz/art.asp?aid=283866.
4. centralasiaonline.com/en_GB/articles/caii/features/main/2013/06/20/feature-02
5. www.hesa.ac.uk/content/view/1897/239/.
6. www.ons.gov.uk/ons/rel/pop-estimate/population-estimates-for-uk--england-and-wales--scotland-and-northern-ireland/mid-2011-and-mid-2012/index.html
7. ofqual.gov.uk/help-and-advice/comparing-qualifications/.
8. ofqual.gov.uk/qualifications-and-assessments/qualification-reform/a-level-reform/
9. www.ocr.org.uk/.
10. ofqual.gov.uk/.
11. ec.europa.eu/education/lifelong-learning-policy/doc/eqf/ukreport_en.pdf.
12. www.ucas.com/.
13. ec.europa.eu/eqf/compare/uk-eni_en.htm#comparison.
14. ecctis.co.uk/naric/.

7 THE CULTURE AND PRACTICE OF ASSESSMENT IN KAZAKHSTAN: An Alternative Model and the Future

Liz Winter (University of Cambridge, Faculty of Education)
Cristina Rimini (Cambridge International Examinations)
Arailym Soltanbekova (Nazarbayev Intellectual Schools)
Madina Tynybayeva (Nazarbayev Intellectual Schools)

Introduction

The previous chapter described past and present national assessment practices in Kazakhstan, primarily for school leavers seeking entry to higher education by means of the Unified National Test (UNT). It highlighted several problems with this particular assessment and its operation. This chapter explores where assessment within Kazakhstani schools may be heading in the future. It aims to provide insight into possible ways to improve the current system and to modernise the assessment culture more generally so that wider educational reform initiatives can occur unhindered.

A World Bank summary of current assessment practices in Kazakhstan

One important source of description of all types of assessment in Kazakhstan comes from the SABER (Systems-based Approach for Better Educational Results) Review (World Bank 2012). This draws its data from questionnaire responses of Ministry of Education and Science (MoES) personnel to provide an overview of assessment practices currently in operation. From its top-down perspective, it examines the four areas of: ILSA (International Large Scale Assessment); NLSA (National Large Scale Assessment); Examinations; and CBA (Classroom Based Assessment). With regard to ILSA, Kazakhstan has taken part (2009 and 2012) in PISA[1] (Programme for International

Student Assessment) and (2007 and 2011) in TIMSS[2] (Trends in International Mathematics and Science Studies). Kazakhstan's students' performances in ILSA are beyond the scope of this chapter; suffice it to say that as new PISA and TIMSS results are published, they will be seen by many as an obvious signal of how successful the heavy investment in educational reform has been. National forms of assessment, however, are discussed here, starting with NLSA.

Tests or qualifications to assess school leavers nationally?

There are essentially three choices in assessing students as they leave school: local school examinations and attestations; a national test(s) or a national qualifications system. Kazakhstan has one NLSA, the UNT. Many other nations including the USA, China and several post-Soviet nations also have national tests, for example, the Azerbaijan National Test[3] (TQDK), Kyrgyzstan National University Entrance Examination[4] (ORT), Russian National Final School Exam[5] (EGE) and Ukrainian External Independent Testing[6] (EIT). In contrast, Europe operates a qualifications system for life-long learning.

The key point here is that Kazakhstan is committed to following a European approach through its 2010 signature of the Bologna Process (EHEA 2010a). Implicitly this assumes a student-centred qualifications framework at all levels, including a suite of qualifications that starts by recording the levels of attainment of students at the end of compulsory schooling. This then moves towards transitioning qualifications to provide access onto qualifications conferred by Higher Education Institutes (HEI) and other professional or vocational bodies. By retaining national testing as the sole form of NLSA, Kazakhstan may therefore run the risk of developing a dysfunctional mix of two systems: non-European and European. In doing this it may then fail to meet the obligations as stated in the signatory document (EHEA 2010b) that it has undertaken in order to be a full member of the European Higher Education Area (EHEA).

Dominant features of assessment in Kazakhstan

The UNT dominates the assessment landscape in Kazakhstan. This is reinforced by the very public nature of the way in which results are declared

– both in terms of named individuals and the identity of their schools. Indeed there is continuing argument as to whether individuals' results should be declared in public and treated with no regard for confidentiality. However, putting that to one side, the impact of a school's UNT results on parents is demonstrated starkly by the remarks below that refer to 2010 results. These represent the first public impressions of an unknown school, newly created and following an untested format.

> At the time when the students were taking National Unified Test, and at 6 pm, next to the university where the students had been sitting the test in the morning, they were announcing everyone's results by calling students' names. There was a large crowd of students, coming from 10 or 15 schools; and it happened that the results of our NIS students were announced at the very end. Students and their parents were standing on a square in front of the university. It was raining. So, when they started announcing the last results, many children and parents were already leaving. But when they started hearing the high scores obtained by our students . . . the highest possible score was 125, while they were getting 120, 122, 119 . . . students and parents started coming back to ask 'What school is that? What school is that?' . . . I was at the school, participating in the admission of new students, the next day after that happened to be the last one to deposit documents to apply to our school. So, since early morning, there were real crowds of children and parents rushing to apply documents to get entry into the 7th, the 8th and the 9th Grade. [Overnight]the information spread that this school had obtained the best results in the final test. (Senior manager at NIS)

The school in question was one of the newly established and selective Nazarbayev Intellectual Schools (NIS; of which more below) but the account illustrates the importance which communities attach to UNT results and hence the power of the test within the school environment.

There are however, other elements of the assessment system and culture and it is to these that we now turn.

Academic Olympiads play an important role in schools and in the process of student assessment in Kazakhstan. The winners of Olympiads are exempt from UNT and get funding plus priority for places at universities, second only to the *Altyn Belgi* awardees. *Altyn Belgi* is 'The Gold Medal', a ratified recommendation from school alongside an exceptional UNT score. Teachers are highly instrumental in preparing their students for these and are rewarded financially for success as well as having teaching Olympiads of their own. Teacher Olympiads similarly operate at regional, national and international levels; often with the higher levels offering substantial prizes such as cars and even an apartment.

Classroom assessment is conducted after every lesson as a teacher records a value from 2 to 5 (1 is never used) on the register that is then put on the electronic platform (and school record) for parents and those within the school to see. This is a laborious process for teachers and record-keeping is a large part of their job. Hence there is a large quantity of assessment but very little depth or quality. Apart from doing this, with perhaps meaningless regularity, the problems of reducing all assignments and class contributions to such a limited scale is described below by a school director of a rural secondary school.

> If there are six mistakes in grammar and three in spelling, then the student will receive a '3'. It is easy to evaluate a Maths exam, but harder to evaluate compositions. You should give two grades for the composition: first grade for the composition, and the second one for the grammar. . . . Our system of assessment is known as a 5-point grading system. But grade '1' is never given to anyone. Thus our scoring system is seen as a 4-point scale. In some assessments it seems that these grades are not enough to assess. Because you give a '3' to the child, even if the child deserves a point higher than '2' you give him a '3' and even to the child who deserves a full '3' you give a '3'. In the past, the elders used to say 'a fat 3' and 'a thin 3'. And here the issue is that these two are different grades. Thus, this assessment system, generally nowadays sometimes seems insufficient. (School director, rural state secondary school)

However, it could be argued that all this record-keeping is a legacy from the Soviet era (e.g. Brofenbrenner 1962; Aviram and Milgram 1977; and Runco 2004). Then, a strict marks-scheme, albeit interpretatively applied within and between schools, was a useful mechanism: to control schools through their record-keeping; to punish non-compliance, and to ensure the ideologies of hard work and productive labour were disseminated in line with Communist principles. The same commentators see the last 60 to 80 years as crippling in terms of acting to constrain independent thought and creativity in schools throughout the USSR. Furthermore, they appear instrumental in reversing a more enlightened and burgeoning approach to student-centred learning. It may be argued, therefore, that current assessment practices are a legacy from the '1936 liquidation of Soviet pedology under Stalin' (Byford 2013, 212).

The teacher attestation process sets such a tone that it challenges anyone involved with schools to construe assessment as anything beyond a checking and compliance process. Individual teachers are inspected against MoES standards, so the focus is on meeting thresholds and imposing sanctions rather than guidance and support for improvement. Some teachers gain financial rewards for exceptional performance by their students in Olympiads or the UNT, but clearly this requires having students for whom this is a possibility. So, primarily, the focus of any inspection of school documents is to make sure teachers complete their records and describe students in line with given marking parameters. No-one formally analyses these teachers' records or appraises them for meaning at school or regional level unless the student is a candidate for special attestation; even then it is on a case-by-case basis rather than a feature of a proper moderation procedure. The school director collates teachers' portfolios as part of the school attestation process but the student portfolios are never collectively appraised or analysed since each tutor keeps their students' records separately. Therefore, there is little cross-fertilisation, critique or learning with regard to assessment practices from one teacher to another or from one school to another. This results in a piecemeal, idiosyncratic approach existing within a climate of concern to retain accreditation, both for individual teachers and the school overall.

Formative, peer- and self-assessment received little mention in the data collected by ourselves or other colleagues in the research team who visited six schools in Kazakhstan in 2013 and spoke with dozens of teachers and students. Assessment appears, on the whole, to be something that is done to you from above – as a teacher or as a pupil – for external purposes such as monitoring, perhaps, but mainly for accreditation purposes or competitive selection. Assessment is rarely seen as formative reflection on practice or study. Self-improvement, mentoring and more effective learning and teaching for educational improvement are not in the common mind-set. These are, however, concepts that are being introduced into Kazakhstan: notably through the agreed adoption of a student-centred approach from the Bologna Process in Higher Education, the Centres of Excellence in-service school teachers and school directors training programme (see Chapter 5) and through the pilot programme of NIS (see Chapter 4 and below). From these, there is at least a chance of a change in the culture of assessment as well as the more straightforward necessary technical improvements. However, the legacy of hierarchies and expectations around the measurement and control of society as well as the social norms regarding levels of autonomy are deeply, embedded in people's popular, as well as professional, consciousness. Changing the assessment culture will not be easy.

School improvement and inspection sits under national protocols to evaluate schools. These were originally based upon a mechanism called Interim State Control (ISC). From 2011, this has been replaced by a new scheme, again staffed and organised by MoES, called External Evaluation of Educational Achievements (EEEA, Внешняя оценка учебных достижений,

ВОУД) which examines student performances in Grades 4 and 9. In Grade 9, two-hour Multiple Choice Question (MCQ) tests in the Kazakh Language and three other subjects take place (MoES 2013a). Schools are not notified beforehand about the nature of the three other subjects, which are rotated annually with the intention to cover all taught subjects over time. For example, the three subjects for April 2012 were the History of Kazakhstan, Chemistry and Algebra. Only some schools take part in this each year, being told of their participation at the start of the academic year. Regional results are published online (MoES 2013b) to indicate differences across regions. Individual schools' results within each region are fed back to be discussed within local education departments.

Assessment ought to be an important tool for school improvement if appropriate methods are applied in an appropriate way. A useful source on the role of assessment in school improvement comes from Mary James (James 1998). James's book, written as guidance for policy-makers, argues forcefully that a balance needs to exist between assessment and record-keeping. Assessment cannot act merely as a control mechanism of the state but should also act as a means to provide informative feedback to stakeholders (James 1998). Trajectories of performance and improvement, both between schools and within schools, are important only if they are based upon proper and meaningful measurement resulting from good pedagogy. In essence, it seeks to encourage a two-way approach whereby policy-makers should 'develop and implement effective systems at school level which promote good practice at classroom level' (James 1998, 1). Of course, to this end, uniform national tests or examinations are necessary to make situational and temporal comparisons possible, but they should not have a negative impact on what is happening in the classroom. As discussed in the previous chapter, the apparent lack of reliability and face validity of the UNT diminishes its usefulness for within-school or even between-school comparisons. A cross-sectional analysis of school results also lacks enough detail from UNT scores to provide meaningful feedback on teaching and learning. Furthermore, multiple choice questions that neither prompt nor reward students who show a worked solution make teaching the art of problem-solving less attractive or riskier than rote learning. This makes the development of forms of assessment for younger students such as Grade 4 and Grade 9 even more critical since a child's trajectory is often apparent then, if not well before.

In order for students to reach their full potential and to give guidance on school improvement, Kazakhstan set up NIS to identify the academic elite and provide them with excellent facilities, teaching and resources. These schools, as described elsewhere in this book, act as 'experimental platforms' to inform how best to improve mainstream schools. As part of this, NIS have their own curricula and assessment systems, as discussed below.

An alternative model of assessment in Kazakhstan: what is happening in NIS?

The development of different forms of assessment in NIS

Chapter 5 described how what was almost a parallel system of education was established in Kazakhstan under the Autonomous Education Organisation NIS to pilot innovative practice. What did NIS have to offer by way of a change in the practice and culture of assessment?

Until 2012 NIS students were obliged to take the UNT. But in parallel during 2010, NIS also began to introduce criteria-based assessment. This was, among other things, to address the supposed impact of the Bologna Process on secondary education with the vision of setting up a high quality education working to international standards for elite students (NIS 2012). This has since been developed further through the application of an Integrated Criteria-Based Assessment Model (ICBAM), a product of the international partnership that NIS enjoys and which has been specifically designed to connect to the new curriculum and NIS system of schooling. This model was introduced in 2013.

The main distinction of this model compared with the mainstream schools' norm-based assessment approach, according to an internal document from the international partner, is that it is 'based on the principle that teaching, learning and assessment are interrelated and form a coherent approach to learner progress and achievement'. The progress of a student is captured through three strands of assessment:

- classroom assessment (throughout each school term)
- internal summative assessment (at the end of each of the four terms)
- external summative assessment (at key assessment points according to a curriculum and assessment model in certain subjects).

Though such concepts of assessment are in their early stages, NIS teachers confirm the beginning of changes in the culture of assessment in NIS. Comparing their previous experiences in mainstream schools, they highlight the main differences to be: students' developing self-assessment practices; better feedback given and received from students; increased teacher-student-parent involvement; more transparency, with a decrease in bias and subjectivity; and an ability to plan developments ahead, both for teachers and students. Alongside pedagogic matters, teachers' record-keeping routines are shaped by the electronic register which automates the recording of students' attendance and charts their academic progress. Teachers submit their formative assessment comments, together with the marks arising from criteria-based tests, both of which are used to calculate an overall grade. These become part of the student's overall profile (NIS 2013).

Second-phase reactions to NIS

NIS is recognised by employers as a 'Breakthrough project in the sphere of education' (KAZENERGY 2013) and appears to be reforming the culture of assessment in Kazakhstan by example, turning a generally subjective, summative culture in schools towards an acceptance of different and more transparent forms, such as criteria-based marking schemes and formative assessment practices. With praise for NIS approaches coming from the employment sector, mainstream schools will no doubt look at what NIS are doing, and the changes that have already occurred, not just in the more obvious ways such as using an Integrated Criteria-Based Assessment Model, but also by teachers taking on a more active role in thinking about the purposes of checking students' learning and the means by which to do it. These ideas are being spread by teachers who have completed professional development courses, also being run through the international partnership.

NIS in relation to the mainstream system

Before the NIS experience can be transferred to a larger scale, mainstream platform, more extended research on school-based assessment and how it is culturally constructed in Kazakhstan appears necessary. A close working partnership with an international partner may not be on hand to guide every school in this very large educational system through the process. Inevitably training in assessment plays a vital part in changing embedded practices and switching from normative practices of assessment to criteria-based ones. Familiarity with the concept of assessing academic achievement through specified and stratified levels of attainment is currently very limited; although it should develop further once the National Qualifications Framework (NQF) becomes better acknowledged and operational. However, as Tempus (2012, 21) indicates; thus far only the first step of five is complete with regard to the operation of a NQF. The first step, 'Decision taken. Process just started', has occurred but the second step 'The purpose of the NQF has been agreed and the process is under way including discussions and consultations' has only just been initiated through the establishment of various committees, so the process is ongoing. The next two stages: 'The NQF has been adopted formally and the implementation has started' and 'Redesigning the study programmes is ongoing and the process is close to completion' are not yet begun.

NIS external assessment systems for entry into higher education and monitoring other student transitions such as for Grades 5 and 10

NIS students are now exempt from UNT, but NIS have developed their own system in order to provide an overall measure which will satisfy external parties such as universities. This effectively sits outside a NLSA system. It operates as a standardised local school suite of examinations across the network of all NIS. In effect, students at NIS sit internal NIS examinations that are then mapped onto an equivalent UNT score. The system of external examining that is being developed by NIS is operated in conjunction with their international partner through a 'strategic partnership'. It is being developed and implemented alongside the rolling out of the new curriculum, the ICBAM described previously, and a new system of school education that includes 12-year schooling. The 12-year schooling model utilises a '5+5+2' approach; meaning five grades in primary school, five grades in secondary school and two grades in high school. External assessment will take place after each stage of schooling – in Grades 5, 10 and 11–12.

As the new curriculum has only been rolled out so far in Grades 1, 7, 8, 11 and 12, the first new type of external assessment is expected to occur in 2014 for Grades 11 and 12. The NIS affiliated Centre for Pedagogical Measurements (CPM) was established in 2012 specifically to fulfil the purposes of developing and administrating this. It is highly innovative for Kazakhstan to create a new type of assessment within the secondary school education system. The international strategic partnership allows the CPM to build up a new assessment system in two ways: by receiving direct assistance in the development of new types of test items; and by tackling the problem from a more fundamental perspective by building capacity. Capacity will be built through a series of training programmes for cohorts of CPM developers in order to furnish them with a solid understanding of what constitutes a valid and reliable assessment instrument. This should help to address an issue mentioned previously within the SABER report (World Bank 2012) that one of the reasons why the UNT did not carry out its full function was that there were no well-trained specialists who could develop reliable assessment tools. Another operation CPM oversees is the actual administration of the test. This starts from the development of test items through to secure printing and handling of test papers, quality assured conduct of examinations, dissemination of confidential results and the final issuing of certificates.

The question papers include up to three components formed from practical elements and experiments for Science subjects and examination in four language competences (reading, listening, writing and speaking) in the state-recognised languages of Kazakh (L1/L2) and Russian (L1/L2). Graduates of NIS will be tested not only on their knowledge and understanding of subjects taught at school but also their skills in applying this in different contexts. Various examination formats will be employed such as: open-ended questions requiring answers of different extension; course work; project and research writing and oral presentations.

The role of strategic international partnerships in developing assessment systems within NIS

A significant part to the NIS work on assessment is the close working international partnerships it has forged as a key part of developing and adopting examination processes and administrative procedures that are both truly innovative and fit for purpose yet remain culturally appropriate through input from local personnel. The international partners allow NIS access to the experience and expertise that enables them to make rapid progress by adopting established effective practices. But for the successful implementation of new practices and sustainable development, it is of critical importance that working with international partners results in a model that can be integrated into the national context. It is not simply a case of importing a foreign model wholesale, but there needs to be due regard on both sides to underlying beliefs about the nature, role and practices of assessment. It is also essential to identify and disseminate tacit knowledge so that there is a common understanding of the intended outcomes, the steps that need to be taken and the challenges that will be faced. Such co-development requires close collaboration, with open and trusting communication. One objective for NIS, as an experimental platform, is to select nurture, produce and prepare students for the best universities in the world. But AEO NIS, as an organisation, has a second objective. It is also committed to sharing its experience more widely in Kazakhstan.

The new assessment model for NIS is being implemented alongside a skills transfer programme for CPM. This is taking a phased approach to development in which the international partner starts by modelling practices, followed by a cycle of joint working, leading to a cycle where the international partner takes on a mentoring and quality assurance role. Through this structured approach the aim is to implement high quality, innovative assessments while simultaneously building the required capacity in Kazakhstan which will enable the country to continue these developments unaided. This is happening alongside the development of the infrastructure required for examination.

Although working with international partners enables rapid development, it is not without its challenges. A pre-requisite is to establish the context for effective working relationships as mentioned above. From a practical perspective, working through the medium of two or three languages imposes huge challenges in providing accurate and meaningful translations of ideas about assessment, the practices of assessment and actual assessment items that are essential for building a shared understanding and for successfully implementing a new assessment model. More significantly, consideration needs to be given to the extent to which a model designed for a relatively small cohort of elite students in a restricted context, can be shared with the wider country. Without a doubt, capacity building is important in increasing understanding of alternative assessment practices in Kazakhstan, but taking this to a larger scale in the face of the sort of established cultural assumptions about assessment described in this chapter will be challenging.

The continuing impact of the UNT in its current format

Before considering how another shift in the culture of assessment will be translated, we must remember that the UNT places huge demands on teachers and students, yet is generally seen as fairer than what went before. There are many reasons why high-stakes multiple choice question tests may or may not be the best form of assessment (see Noddings 2004; Berliner 2011; Stobart and Eggen 2012 for brief general discussions of this) but the UNT's initial remit was a first step towards meeting a strong national need to introduce qualifications that minimise corruption and to include those for whom Kazakh or Russian is not their native language (Sackett et al. 2001).

In terms of what makes a fair university admissions system, Heyneman (2004) argues that three principles apply: available resources; logistical challenges and level of public accountability. Clearly a system needs trained markers and moderators for examinations more sophisticated than the computerised marking of multiple choice questions, and this is a matter of resources, but more important than this is the likelihood of dishonesty that potentially could annihilate confidence in the whole educational system. Indeed, NCEQA (NCEQA 2013) acknowledge the benefits of testing with multiple choice questions as 'test technologies are more economical and easier operationally to arrange, as well as in the processing of results'. Multiple choice questions are exceptionally efficient at checking facts, and the limitations to test potential are certainly recognised as a current problem with the UNT along with its duality of functions (NCEQA 2013).

To counter the reliance upon a single 3 ½ hour multiple choice test, the temporal offset of the UNT (taken in May) and the Complex Testing of Applicants (CTA) (taken in July) means that this affords a ready opportunity for splitting the current UNT into two separate tests and thus to address the dual function it attempts to perform. In 2014, students will be taking two tests: one entitled the 'National Test' to add to the school Attestat and one entitled the 'Complex Test' that screens applicants' suitability and allocates priority for funding (Central Communication Service 2013). MoES are indicating that these will include psychometric measures of critical thinking and the application of knowledge, in effect testing for 'aptitude (способностей отличается)' rather than 'achievement (достижений)'. This marks a 'new direction (является новым направлением) for Kazakhstan' (NCEQA 2013), but the question which remains unanswered is the role of new types of assessment being developed in NIS which are specifically designed to prepare students for HE and which go beyond multiple choice questions (MCQs) in testing practical skills in Science and languages. Furthermore, the suggestion that MCQ formats are spreading further and are being used to examine school improvement and the performance of younger children is of grave concern, especially as the assessment innovations in NIS run counter to this. If this is a policy, where has it come from and how is it justified?

International involvement in the development of the UNT

The developments to UNT (and its two replacements) described above are being conducted under the acknowledged guidance of the World Bank and individual consultants with expertise from the USA and Russia (NCEQA 2013). The main focus appears to be on the improvement of test items and MCQ test reliability. The SABER report (World Bank 2012) has no mention of: the alignment of school assessment with HE reform in Kazakhstan towards a student learning approach; to any NQF; or to what is happening in NIS. No alternative models of assessment or measures to include national assessment by those involved in the delivery of the curriculum are proposed. This appears a dangerous disconnect from what is happening elsewhere in Kazakhstan, not only in terms of assessment per se but also in terms of the professional role of teachers.

Teachers and the current culture of assessment in Kazakhstan

Effectively, a UNT format perpetuates a divide between teachers and markers with the implicit distrustful suggestion that teachers cannot be involved in the national assessment process. The fact that MCQs are marked by computer means that teachers cannot learn from the process of marking students' examination papers, and seeing how students have responded to the teaching of the curriculum. Teachers do not even have the opportunity for professional development that would be afforded through reading published marking schemes or being employed as markers in their own right. Test papers are closely guarded until marks are distributed and then, after a few days for appeal against the score, they are destroyed. So, very little feedback is given to teachers on their teaching other than individual student scores on various sections of the test. Raising the status of teachers is a stated aim within Kazakhstan (Akorda 2012), and computer marking of UNT clashes with the educational reform on pedagogical practices evident elsewhere, particularly in NIS and through the Centre of Excellence training (chapter 5) which involves tens of thousands of teachers throughout Kazakhstan aspiring to become 'reflective practitioners'.

Furthermore, the obsession with MCQs means alternatives that reduce corruption are not being considered apart from within NIS. Monitoring and inspection of schools or other premises where examinations take place, as well as of staff, would, as in the case of NIS, devolve responsibility for correct administrative procedures to schools and to individuals, albeit with clear repercussions if matters went awry. This would not only develop professional integrity, but also cultivate norms of behaviour that most likely would then pass down to the students themselves. Without some initial trust, social norms of honesty are unlikely ever to evolve, so starting with teachers seems a good point at which to endorse the message that cheating is unacceptable, morally wrong and punishable. As a further means of achieving this, an academic profile and multiple points of measurement mean that cheating is easier to spot on an individual student-by-student basis.

Assessment and the development of 21st-century skills

The European Commission (2012) Eurydice report 'Developing Key Competences at School in Europe: Challenges and Opportunities for Policy' indicates that a national strategy is key for educational reform to ensure the objectives of improvement in curricula: teacher education and professional development plus that 'clarification of the learning outcomes associated with each relevant curriculum area is considered to be particularly important'. In addition, 'assessment can play a significant role in improving the quality and relevance of the skills that are acquired at school' with 'assessment methods which can capture the complexity of the whole range of key competences and can measure students' ability to apply their knowledge in context' (European Commission 2012, 9). Furthermore, until a NQF becomes evident and integrated throughout the assessment system in Kazakhstan, how can anyone from one sector understand someone from another? Without centralising the role of the NQF how can professionals or anyone guide people through a structured and integrated lifelong educational experience? Additionally, without transparent qualifications and professional standards, how can stakeholders understand the whole process and where individuals sit within it? How does one person with a UNT score of 65 from 2012 compare with someone scoring 75 in 2013? The lack of a fully operational NQF appears to be a hot political topic (Kazakhstan News Agency 2013) but why has there been so little progress so far and in particular why have plans to revise UNT not addressed these issues?

The role of stakeholders in assessment

The lack of involvement of stakeholders and the question around UNT's fitness for purpose for HE selection is recognised within the SABER report, which states the following:

> No systemic mechanisms are currently in place to monitor the consequences of the examination. The Center and the National Testing Center analyzes the results of the UNT. However, the analysis is usually limited to descriptive nature, and no studies on the impact or predictive validity take place. (World Bank 2012, 33)

There is, however, a very encouraging development from the NTC. In April 2012 it conducted a national survey (NTC 2012) across all 16 administrative districts in Kazakhstan to collect the opinions about UNT of 1750 stakeholders (750 students (Grade 11 and first-year undergraduate students); 500 parents of students in Grade 11 and 500 educational professionals (teacher and local administrators within schools, university academics and MoES employees)). The results are freely available on the internet and not only give overall results but also present data for sub-groups of stakeholders, for example in terms of rural-urban divides and the income levels of the participants. General opinion can be best summarised by saying that there are some benefits of the UNT in its present form, and that there is no overriding wish to split it into two similar forms and that school assessment grades should be included in some way in applications to HE. In addition, there are serious concerns over corrupt practices and the psychological pressure placed upon students taking the test. Several conclusions were forthcoming, many of which have, by an independent route, been discussed earlier in this chapter. The most significant recommendations made by NTC from the survey are listed below:

- Align schooling to the requirements of higher education institutions and their teaching methods
- Adjust the school curriculum and national testing to give preparation in a range of specialties
- Low-income families should receive funding to access the same test preparation materials as others
- Increase surveillance before, during and after UNT administration and also impose severe penalties for misconduct
- Set up an appeals process
- Provide better counselling and support opportunities for students at psychological risk
- Make HE selection decisions using school grades in some way (t.b.d.) as an essential supplement to the UNT score
- Seek out ways in which creativity can be assessed for appropriate specialist subjects

- *The use of UNT results for evaluating the performance of teachers, schools and regions should cease.* (Our emphasis)

Those working in schools and HE at every level, plus representatives of national testing, national qualifications and national accreditation organisations, as well as other stakeholders such as employers, students and parents, need to discuss all these issues. It is vitally important that people talk to each other and work to remove conflicts of interest, as illustrated by the last point in the list above whereby teachers' (and entire schools' or regions') integrity may be compromised by students' UNT scores influencing the way in which they teach, behave and are perceived. Teacher performance and school improvement need a more effective and sophisticated measure than simply relying upon student performances on national tests (James 1998), especially if the tests themselves have questionable validity. Universities and employers need to record what they would like students to bring and school teachers must state what they would like to see at the end of schooling and what would they would like to contribute towards assessing their students' success. Students need to reflect upon their experiences and speak out about overlaps and gaps in their education, as well as what they feel are necessary criteria for selection and preparation for HE and the workplace.

Stakeholders need to feel invested in the assessment process so that it does not seem to be inflicted upon them. Assessment must go beyond decanting knowledge into students and forcing teachers to 'teach to test' and in so doing potentially undermining professional obligations to equip students with autonomy, problem-solving skills and a sustainable lifelong approach to learning. By encouraging ownership of the system, all stakeholders from students and teachers through to NTC and MoES should feel more motivated to take collectively a more active role in outing cheats and suggesting improvements more generally.

Translating NIS experiences in assessment to mainstream settings

NIS experiences and practices need tailoring to meet the needs of mainstream schools that may have less well-equipped facilities, fewer resources and a broad mix of abilities. Again, there needs to be discussion and dialogue about what has worked within NIS, why it has worked and why it may not readily transfer, plus what has been gained from strategic partnerships that have sought to locate Kazakhstani schools in an international context. Some of the answers are beginning to emerge in NIS and given time, patience and understanding they may go some way towards removing the current anomaly that is the UNT and also the national external assessment more widely.

Conclusion

At the moment the UNT is holding back reforms within the pedagogical and teaching profession and allowing only a trickle of the innovation to flow forwards into the universities. This is not a new finding. High-stakes MCQ entrance tests for HE are described in the context of a similar but older test in Iran (Salehi and Yunus 2012) as the effects of 'washback' (Smith 1991; Wall and Alderson 1993) that directs teaching and learning as students prepare for the test. It also holds back and limits the possibilities for students to show fully what they know, can do and can express. If it has to remain as a MCQ, it would work best in conjunction with school-based appraisals of students. Most critically of all, it has to be located in a NQF if Kazakhstan is to follow a qualifications approach and hold to the Bologna Process later on. The UNT is holding back new ideas and hanging on to outmoded values of rote learning that curtail pedagogical advances within schools that technology and the internet have generally made obsolete.

Our argument, therefore, is that too much emphasis has been placed upon computer-marked MCQs as the sole answer to national school assessment in Kazakhstan. The NTC still does not seem to countenance supplementing these with alternatives to form qualifications. Instead they seem to be placing this burden back upon school assessment systems which are not standardised. It is also worth questioning what place such a strategy has in terms of alignment to a National Qualifications Framework, to, European higher education systems and to the development of 21st-century skills. The subtlety in the differences between testing and examining people needs far more discussion by everyone to resolve this.

REFERENCES

Aviram, A. and **Milgram, R.M.** (1977). 'Dogmatism, Locus of Control and Creativity in Children Educated in the Soviet Union, the United States and Israel.' *Psychological Reports*, 40, 27–34.

Berliner, D. (2011). 'Rational Responses to High Stakes Testing: The Case of Curriculum Narrowing and the Harm that Follows.' *Cambridge Journal of Education*, 41:3, 287–302.

Bronfenbrenner, U. (1962). 'Soviet Methods of Character Education: Some Implications for Research.' *American Psychologist*, 17:8, 550–64.

Byford, A. (2013). 'Parent Diaries and the Child Study Movement in Late Imperial and Early Soviet Russia.' *The Russian Review*, 72, 212–41.

Central Communication Service (2013). *Experiment of Dividing UNT into Two Stages to be Held in 2013.* Press release published 28 January 2013. www.ortcom.kz/en/news/experiment-of-dividing-unt-into-two-stages-to-be-held-in-2013.359.

EHEA (2010a). *Budapest-Vienna Declaration on the European Higher Education Area.* Brussels: Education, Audio-visual and Culture Executive Agency (EACEA P9 Eurydice). www.ond.vlaanderen.be/hogeronderwijs/Bologna/2010_conference/documents/Budapest-Vienna_Declaration.pdf (retrieved 1 October 2013).

EHEA (2010b). *Report Submitted by the Republic of Kazakhstan as Part of the Application for Membership of the Bologna Process.* Bucharest: Romanian Bologna Secretariat. www.ehea.info/Uploads/Documents/Kazakhstan_national_report_2010.pdf (retrieved 1 October 2013).

European Commission (2012). *European Commission/EACEA/Eurydice, 2012. Developing Key Competences at School in Europe: Challenges and Opportunities for Policy. Eurydice Report.* Luxembourg: Publications Office of the European Union. eacea.ec.europa.eu/education/eurydice/documents/thematic_reports/145EN.pdf (retrieved 1 October 2013).

Heyneman, S.P. (2004). 'Education and Corruption'. *International Journal of Educational Development*, 24:6, 636–48.

James, M. (1998). *Using Assessment for School Improvement.* Oxford: Heinemann.

Kazakhstan News Agency (2013). *Kazakhstan need National Qualifications Framework, Nazarbayev.* Press release published 10 July 2013 by Interfax-Kazakhstan. www.interfax.kz/?lang=eng&int_id=expert_opinions&news_id=1104.

KAZENERGY website (2013). 'Nazarbayev Intellectual Schools: A Breakthrough Project in the Field of Education'. www.kazenergy.com/ru/4-48-2011/2527-2011-10-14-11-37-38.html (retrieved 27 October 2013).

MoES (2013a). *Committee for Control of Education and Science.* www.educontrol.kz/en (retrieved 1 October 2013).

— (2013b). *Statistics of Education within the Republic of Kazakhstan, National Collection using Data from the Ministry of Education and Science of the Republic of Kazakhstan and the Agency of the Republic of Kazakhstan Statistics (Minutes of the NMS Number February 2013, Astana).* www.edu.gov.kz/fileadmin/user_upload/deyatelnost/obrazov_monitoring/Nac_sbornik_06_03_13.pdf (retrieved 1 October 2013).

Nazarbayev, N. (2012). 'Socio-Economic Modernization as Main Vector of Development of Kazakhstan'. Address by the President of the Republic of Kazakhstan Nursultan Nazarbayev. Official Site of the President of the Republic of Kazakhstan, 27 January 2012. www.akorda.kz/en/page/address-by-the-president-of-the-republic-of-kazakhstan-nursultan-nazarbayev-to-the-people-of-kazakhstan-27-01-2012_1341926486.

NCEQA (2013). *Logical Tests of Character. (Тесты логического характера).* www.naric.kz/index.php-option=com_content&view=article&id=18&Itemid=19&lang=Rus.htm (retrieved 1 October 2013).

NIS (2012). *Conception for Student Achievements Criteria-Based Assessment System Implementation in Autonomous Education Organisation 'Nazarbayev Intellectual Schools'.* Astana. nis.edu.kz/en/programs/criter-eval/leg-doc/ (retrieved 23 October 2013).

— (2013). *Regulations for Student Achievements Criteria-Based Assessment in Autonomous Education Organisation 'Nazarbayev Intellectual Schools'.* Astana. nis.edu.kz/en/programs/criter-eval/leg-doc/ (retrieved 23 October 2013).

Noddings, N. (2004). 'High Stakes Testing: Why?' *Theory and Research in Education,* 2:3, 263–9.

NTC (2012). *The Attitude of the Public towards the External Assessment of Knowledge (Public Attitudes towards the UNT).* www.testcenter.kz/?tab=download&idd=73 (retrieved 29 October 2013).

Runco, M.A. (2004). 'Creativity'. *Annual Review of Psychology,* 55, 657–87.

Sackett, P.R., Schmitt, N., Ellingson, J.E. and **Kabin, M.B.** (2001). 'High-Stakes Testing in Employment, Credentialing, and Higher Education: Prospects in a Post-Affirmative-Action World'. *American Psychologist,* 56:4, 302–18.

Salehi, H. and **Yunus, M.M.** (2012). 'University Entrance Exam in Iran: A Bridge or a Dam'. *Journal of Applied Sciences Research,* 8:2, 1005–8.

Smith, M.L. (1991). 'Meaning of Test Preparation'. *American Educational Research Journal,* 28, 521–42.

Stobart, G. and **Eggen, T.** (2012). 'High-Stakes Testing – Value, Fairness and Consequences'. *Assessment in Education: Principles, Policy and Practice,* 19:1, 1–6.

Tempus (2012). *Higher Education in Kazakhstan.* 'Brussels: Education, Audio-visual and Culture Executive Agency (EACEA)'. eacea.ec.europa.eu/tempus/participating_countries/reviews/Kazakhstan.pdf (retrieved 1 October 2013).

Wall, D. and **Alderson, J.C.** (1993). *Examining Washback: The Sri Lankan Impact Study.* Language Testing, 10, 41–69.

World Bank (2012). *Systems Approach for Better Education Results: Kazakhstan Student Assessment.*wbgfiles.worldbank.org/documents/hdn/ed/saber/supporting_doc/CountryReports/SAS/SABER_SA_Kazakhstan_CR_Final_2012R.pdf (retrieved 10 October 2013).

NOTES

1   www.oecd.org/pisa/home/.

2   www.timss.bc.edu/.

3   www.tqdk.gov.az/en/.

4   www.eacea.ec.europa.eu/tempus/participating_countries/reviews/kyrgyzstan_review_of_higher_education.pdf.

5   www.eng.kremlin.ru/news/3687.

6   www.mon.gov.ua/ua/activity/68/nakazi_zno/.

8 THREE IN ONE?
Trilingualism in Educational Policy and Practice

Peeter Mehisto (University of London Institute of Education)
Assel Kambatyrova (Nazarbayev University Graduate School of Education)
Khalida Nurseitova (Gumilyov Eurasian National University)

Introduction

By 2025, the Government of Kazakhstan wants Kazakh to be spoken by 95% of Kazakhstan's citizens (Government of Kazakhstan 2012). Moreover, it is expected that Kazakh will take on a 'lead role in all spheres of life' (ibid.). This is considered to become 'the most important achievement' of the state, 'something that binds the nation and cements it' and central to the 'state's sovereignty' (ibid.). In addition, a goal has been set for young people to learn 'Russian and English equally well as Kazakh' (ibid.). The term 'equally' implies very high levels of proficiency in these languages.

In order to understand what has led to these goals, this chapter traces the socio-political context of Kazakhstan from Russian conquest through to the first 22 years of independence. It also discusses education in independent Kazakhstan, and language-learning options offered through the education system. The chapter analyses self-declared language knowledge and use, and reviews some of the numerous government policies and measures aimed at supporting the country's citizenry in achieving high levels of proficiency in three languages. Finally, based on notes from interviews with government officials, the analysis of government documents and three case study reports, the chapter examines how schools, and the agencies/institutions that manage these schools and train teachers, are interpreting and seeking to meet the trilingual challenge set forth in the 'Kazakhstan 2050 Strategy'.

Socio-political context: From Russian conquest to independence

Kazakhstan was a largely nomadic culture until the lands that today constitute Kazakhstan were conquered and colonised, gradually over many decades, by Czarist Russia beginning in 1731 (Kassymova 2012, 7). Although some formal instruction such as Islamic schools already existed prior to the Russian conquests, it was the Russian governors who began to develop a national network of schools, which stressed Russian history and the Russian language (DeYoung and Balzhan 1996, 3–4). Russian-medium education would be further strengthened by continued immigration from Russia, which placed the Kazakh language and culture under increased pressure. The inward migration of Russian settlers was facilitated by Russian agrarian reform and supported by the introduction of railways in 1906. As more and more settlers established farms on traditional pasturelands and used scarce water resources, the Kazakh nomadic culture came under even greater pressure. By 1917, close to a million Russians were living in Kazakhstan, constituting 30% of the country's population (Kassymova et al. 2012, 230).

For two-and-a-half years beginning in late 1917, part of what today makes up Kazakhstan had a period of relative independence known as the 'Alash Autonomy'. In 1919, the Alash Autonomy aligned itself with the Bolsheviks in return for an amnesty of Alash Party members and a promise to create a national state for the Kazakhs. With the consolidation of Soviet power in 1920, the Alash Party was disbanded. Significant numbers of Kazakh intellectuals, including former Alash Party members, worked in the Soviet administration (Kassymova et al. 2012, 24), as well as in schools and universities, and they continued to promote Kazakh autonomy (DeYoung and Balzhan 1996, 4–5).

The requisitioning of foodstuffs by the Soviet authorities in 1921–22 for their war effort led to famine and large-scale loss of life (Amanzholova 1994). By the late 1920s and early 1930s, print-based instruction became ubiquitous in Kazakhstan, but at the same time repressions of educators and others who had any association with the Alash Order party took place (DeYoung and Balzhan 1996, 6; Kassymova et al. 2012, 24). In the early 1930s famine related to collectivisation led to extensive loss of life. Abylkhozhyn et al. (1989, 67) estimate the death toll to be about 1.75 million people. The famine also caused considerable damage to the education system. In particular, rural schools were abandoned and often broken up for firewood (DeYoung and Balzhan 1996, 7).

At the end of 1936, after having been a Kazakh Autonomous Socialist Soviet Republic within the Russian Soviet Federative Socialist Republic, Kazakhstan became a Soviet Socialist Republic. Russification intensified during most of the Soviet period (1920–91). Secondary and university education were offered primarily in Russian. In 1939, the Latin script, which had replaced the Arabic script in 1929, was in turn replaced with Cyrillic for the writing of Kazakh (Abdakimov 1994, 135). Inward transfers of population mostly from elsewhere in the Soviet Union took place, largely as a result of Stalinist repressions in the 1930s and 1940s, and the transfer of industry during World War II (Kassymova et al. 2012, xxix, 230).

By 1959, Kazakhs constituted 30% of the population (see Table 1). In urban environments that figure was considerably lower. In addition, during the Soviet period, 'language shift' – the decline in the status and use of a language (Fishman 1991) – had occurred, with the majority of Kazakhs in urban environments becoming Russian dominant. Furthermore, the majority of urban Kazakhs were choosing Russian-medium primary education for their children as it was considered to be of better quality.

Table 1: Percentage breakdown of total population of Kazakhstan according to national census

Ethnicity	1959	1970	1979	1989	1999	2009
Kazakhs	30.0	32.4	36.0	39.7	53.5	63.1
Russians	42.7	42.8	40.8	37.8	29.9	23.7
Ukrainians	8.2	7.2	6.1	5.4	3.7	2.1
Germans	7.1	6.5	6.1	5.8	2.4	1.1
Tatars	2.1	2.2	2.1	2.0	1.7	1.3
Uzbeks	1.5	1.6	1.8	2.0	2.5	2.9
Others	8.4	7.3	7.1	7.3	6.3	5.8

Source: Zimovina 2003; CIA 2013

After the establishment of independence in 1991, the percentage of ethnic Kazakhs in the population continued to grow, as did the status of the Kazakh language. By 1999, the national census reported that ethnic Kazakhs constituted 53.5% of the population. In 2009, that figure stood at 63.1% (see Table 1). However, in most urban environments Kazakhs remained a minority. At the national level, the demographic shift in favour of ethnic Kazakhs was primarily due to the departure of ethnic Russians, Ukrainians, Germans and other nationalities to their ancestral homelands, and to a lesser extent the repatriation of Kazakhs from countries such as China, Mongolia, Russia, Turkmenistan and Uzbekistan (Commission on Human Rights 2012).

Finally, the ethnic Kazakh birth rate remains positive, being about twice as high as the birth rate among ethnic Russians, who are experiencing a negative birth rate (see Table 2). If the trend is maintained the percentage of ethnic Kazakhs in Kazakhstan will continue to rise.

Table 2: Birth rates and natural increase among ethnic Kazakhs and Russians

	Per 1000 people								
	Index of birth rate			Index of death			Natural increase		
	2009	2010	2011	2009	2010	2011	2009	2010	2011
Kazakhs	25.4	25.7	25.6	5.9	5.8	5.7	19.5	19.9	19.9
Russians	12.9	12.8	12.8	14.4	14.9	14.6	-1.5	-2.1	-1.9

Source: Agency of Statistics of the Republic of Kazakhstan 2013a

Education after the establishment of independence

In the mid-1990s, in stark contrast to the Soviet period, Kazakh parents began increasingly to choose Kazakh-medium education. Kolstø and Malkova (1997) suggest that in September 1996 just over 40% of Kazakhs and virtually all non-Kazakhs were choosing Russian-medium schools for their children. In 2013, the Agency of Statistics of the Republic of Kazakhstan (2013b) reported the percentage of students studying in Kazakh-medium classes as 64.2% and the percentage in Russian-medium classes as 32%, with the remaining 3.8% of students studying through other languages (see Figure 1). No ethnic breakdown of students was available. Kazakh- or Russian-medium classes can be in Kazakh or Russian-medium schools respectively or in mixed schools, with some students studying primarily through Kazakh and others primarily through Russian. In addition to Kazakh-medium, Russian-medium and mixed schools, in 2013 there were 60 Uzbek-medium, 14 Uyghur-medium and 2 Tajik-medium schools. Also, 79 other schools offered some content classes in Uzbek, 49 in Uyghur and 10 in Tajik (MoES 2013a). A number of private schools use English as a medium of instruction. As this chapter focuses on Kazakh, Russian and English, and since issues pertaining to the Uzbek, Uyghur and Tajik schools merit a chapter of their own, these schools will not be further discussed in this chapter.

Figure 1: Number of students (in thousands) per language of instruction

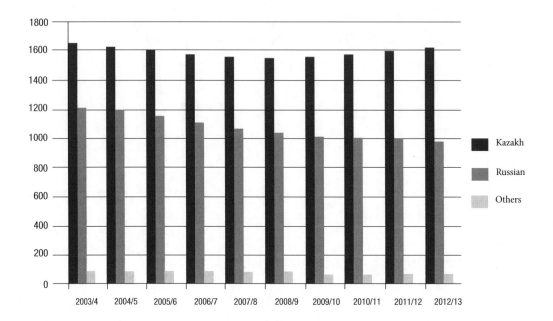

Source: Agency of Statistics of the Republic of Kazakhstan 2013b

The quality of education in Kazakh-medium classes is widely perceived as being poorer than that delivered through Russian. The Programme for International Student Assessment (PISA) (OECD 2013, 52) scores from 2009 indicate that students in Kazakh-medium classes are performing considerably less well than students in Russian-medium classes with, for example, 66% of Kazakh language students reading below Level 2 versus 27% of Russian language students reading below Level 2 (see Table 3). According to the National Centre for Education Statistics and Assessment, in some regions students are on average achieving higher scores on the Unified National Test (UNT) in Kazakh-medium classes; however in general, students in Russian-medium classes are outperforming students in Kazakh-medium classes (see Figures 2 and 3). Despite the fact that the UNT currently primarily tests memorisation skills as opposed to critical thinking (Ayubayeva et al. 2013, 18, 19; OECD 2013, 60), the UNT is broadly considered to drive the decision-making of parents and probably older students in relation to their education and training. It remains a gatekeeping mechanism for access to further education. In addition, educators report that Kazakh-language professional development materials and learning resources for students are often of poor quality in terms of language (Ayubayeva et al. 2013, 28). The underperformance of Kazakh-medium education is placing the growth of Kazakh-medium education at risk.

Table 3: Reading, Mathematics and Science performance of students in Kazakh and Russian-medium classes

Language of instruction	Reading Mean Score	Reading % Below Level 2	Reading % Levels 5+6	Mathematics Mean Score	Science Mean Score
Kazakh	362	66.1	0.3	383	375
Russian	453	27.1	4.5	453	457
Difference (R-K)	91	-39.0	4.2	70	82

Source: OECD 2013, 52 based on PISA results for 2009

Figure 2: Distribution of UNT results between Kazakh- and Russian-medium urban schools

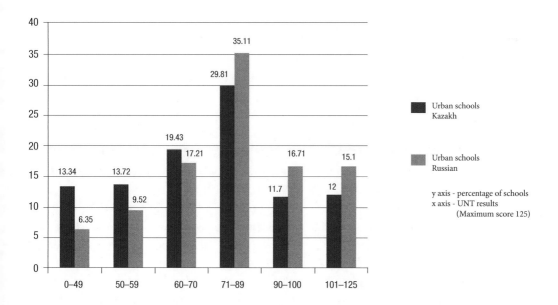

Source: MoES 2012a, 51

Figure 3: Distribution of UNT results between Kazakh and Russian-medium rural schools

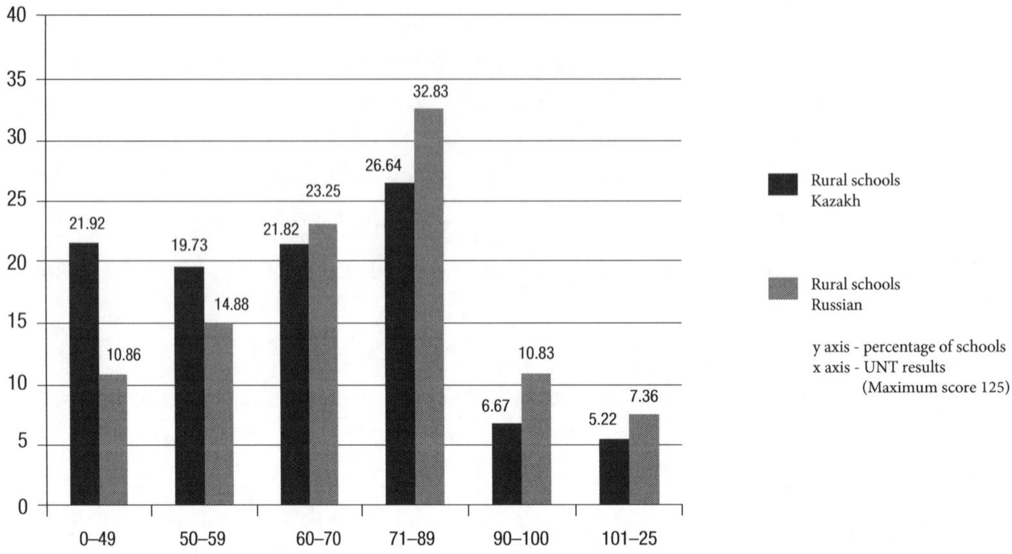

Rural schools
Kazakh

Rural schools
Russian

y axis - percentage of schools
x axis - UNT results
(Maximum score 125)

Source: MoES 2012a, 56

Language learning options

All schools are expected to support the implementation of the government's trilingual policy. The *Standard Subject Plan for 2012–2013* foresees that all schools teach at least three languages (MoES 2013b). Kazakh-medium schools/classes are expected to teach two 45-minute periods of Russian language arts per week, beginning in Grade 3 and continuing through to Grade 11. In Grades 5 to 11 an additional period is accorded to Russian literature. Small variations in requirements exist among schools depending on their specialisation. In Russian-medium schools/classes there are two periods of Kazakh per week in Grades 1 to 2, three periods per week in Grades 3 to 4 and four periods per week throughout the remaining grades. In addition, there is one lesson of Kazakh literature per week in Grades 5 to 11. Some variation exists depending on the school's area of specialisation. The learning of a third language begins in Grade 1 with one period a week. In Grades 5 to 7, two periods are devoted to the foreign language whilst in Grades 8 to 9 those figures vary from two to four periods and in Grades 10 to 11 they vary from two to six periods depending on the school's specialisation. Since this current subject plan is unlikely to lead to high levels of trilingualism, the government has launched several more ambitious initiatives. These include 200 pre-schools that are piloting trilingual education, the 29 Kazakh-Turkish Lyceums, 31 trilingual schools and 15 (soon to be 20) Nazarbayev Intellectual Schools (NIS).

The Kazakh-Turkish Lyceums (Grades 7 to 11) are managed directly by the Ministry of Education and Science (MoES) and the KATEV International Foundation for Education and Culture. These schools have been purpose-built, with the first school opening in 1992. History, Geography, Physical Education and Military Preparations are to be taught through Kazakh. Physics, Mathematics, Biology, Chemistry and Computer Science are to be taught through English. Turkish and Russian are only to be taught in Language Arts classes. These schools are intended for gifted and talented students (KATEV 2013).

The 31 trilingual schools were designated as such from amongst existing schools by MoES. They were launched in 2007. Their work is supposed to be co-ordinated by the government-financed Daryn Centre which has a mandate to create conditions that will allow gifted and talented children to realise their potential. In these 'trilingual' schools, one or more subjects from the Natural Sciences or Mathematics are to be taught through English, beginning in Grade 7. In Russian-medium schools/classes, Kazakh language and literature and the history of Kazakhstan are to be taught through Kazakh, whilst in Kazakh-medium schools/classes, Russian language and literature are to be taught through Russian. The Daryn Centre reported during a Roadmap Project interview that the network of 31 trilingual schools will be expanded to 700 schools by 2020.

The NIS project was launched in 2008 (AEO NIS 2013, 3). These Intellectual Schools offer a trilingual programme from Grades 7 to 12, with the exception of two of its schools that offer primary education as well. AEO NIS has developed its own curricula and educator training programmes, and is also in the process of developing its own learning materials. To ensure that its educational programmes meet international standards NIS co-operates extensively with, among others, Cambridge University, Johns Hopkins University and the International Baccalaureate Organisation (see Chapter 4). Of the three types of schools that have been designated as trilingual this is the only type that teaches content classes through three languages – Kazakh, Russian and English. The Intellectual Schools are expected to serve as a model for the reform of the entire education system.

Languages of instruction in higher education

The languages of instruction available in higher education can act as an extrinsic motivator that influences the choice of languages studied and the attention paid to a given language in secondary education. In 2000, 32% of students (85 300 individuals) in universities were studying primarily through the medium of Kazakh and 68% (181 000) through Russian (Decree of the President of the Republic of Kazakhstan 2001). In 2009, 50.7% were studying primarily through Russian, 47.6% primarily through Kazakh and 1.6% primarily through English (Agency of Statistics of the Republic of Kazakhstan 2013c). During the 2012–13 academic year, 54.8% of technical and vocational college students were studying primarily through Kazakh, and 45.1% through Russian (Agency of Statistics of the Republic of Kazakhstan 2013d). Concomitantly, two Roadmap Project respondents reported that some university courses that are designated as Kazakh-medium continue to be taught in Russian as the lecturers feel more confident teaching through Russian.

Language knowledge and use

The previous sections have traced demographic shift, the use of Kazakh, Russian and English as media of instruction, and the teaching of Kazakh, Russian and English. This section explores whether those changes are reflected in language use outside of the education sphere. A shift in language knowledge and use in the work and private lives of citizens has taken place over the past few decades, although this does not fully mirror the demographic shift or the increased use of Kazakh and the decreased use of Russian in education. The northern part of the country has long been primarily Russian-speaking. The majority of urban environments tend to be linguistically speaking Russian-dominant. Russian remains the most widely spoken language, with 94.4% of the nation's population indicating during the 2009 census that they understood spoken Russian and 84.8% indicating that they can read and write the language. This contrasts with 74% reporting that they understood spoken Kazakh and with 62% reporting that they could read and write Kazakh. However, the census did not clearly define levels of language proficiency and people may have been overly generous in assessing their language knowledge. According to a survey in 17 cities, there appears to be a preference for Russian, whether that be for media consumption or for communication at work, with friends or in the home (Association of Sociologists and Political Analysts of Kazakhstan 2007 as referred to by Aminov et al. 2010, 2; see Table 4). This suggests that in addition to the cities being Russian dominant, schools offering Kazakh-medium education in urban areas must at the same time teach large numbers of students arriving with little Kazakh whilst taking into account the needs of those who are fluent in Kazakh (cf. Fierman 2006).

Table 4: Primary language used by percentage of population for various purposes

Purpose or context	Kazakh	Russian	Other
watching TV and reading newspapers	29	79	2
in public places	35	79	2
place of work, be that companies or learning institutions	33	73	3
with friends	36	72	3
in family	44	60	6

Government policies and initiatives

Language use is heavily influenced by the political and economic environment. This section discusses government policies and initiatives that seek to support trilingualism. A 1987 Soviet Socialist Republic of Kazakhstan (SSRK) decree *On Improving the Study of the Kazakh Language in the Republic* signalled the beginning of a shift in the status of Kazakh and introduced mechanisms designed to facilitate the learning of Kazakh. This was followed in 1989 by a major milestone in the attempt to turn the tide of Russification – the SSRK's Law on Languages. This law declared Kazakh as the official language of the country but, seeking to maintain inter-ethnic harmony, it also forbade discrimination against anyone due to their lack of knowledge of the state language. The law made the learning of Kazakh and Russian obligatory in all schools, and aimed to guarantee access to Kazakh-medium education at all levels of the system. In 1995, however, the newly adopted constitution accorded Russian the status of an 'official' language 'on a level with the state language'. A new Language Law adopted in 1997, which is still in force today, states that all citizens are to learn the state language, but it does not include any sanctions for those who do not learn the language, and allows for Russian to be used in and with national, regional and local government. In the sphere of education, there is no requirement for school directors or teachers to learn Kazakh or Russian.

The Migration Act of 1997, amendments to it in 2002 and the Migration Law of 2011 have all facilitated the repatriation of the *Oralman* or ethnic Kazakhs. By October 2011, 860 400 Kazakhs had been repatriated mostly from China, Mongolia, Turkmenistan and Uzbekistan (Commission on Human Rights 2012, 9). Repatriates tend to speak Kazakh, but not necessarily Russian. Non-Russian speakers would probably also be unfamiliar with the Cyrillic script used to write Kazakh. Bokayev et al. (2012), using a survey of 1000 repatriates, report that the overwhelming majority of those being repatriated from China, Mongolia, Tajikistan, Turkmenistan and Uzbekistan speak Kazakh either fluently, or speak and read it without writing it, or speak, write and read it with some difficulties. Repatriates from Russia reported low levels of Kazakh language knowledge. Repatriates from Mongolia and China in particular indicated low levels of Russian language knowledge (ibid.) – a language of considerable economic and political power in the Kazakhstan of 2013. At the same time these repatriates have high levels of fluency in the official language of their countries of former residence.

The Presidential decree on 'The Development and Functioning of Languages in the Republic of Kazakhstan for 2011–2020', alongside the action plan for 2011–13 designed to implement the decree, seeks not only to stimulate the learning, use and perceived status of Kazakh, but also to preserve the existing linguistic diversity of the nation while fostering the learning of English and other foreign languages. Kazakhstan is a multi-ethnic state with over 130 nationalities (Office of the President 2013). The decree sets targets for 95% of the population to speak Kazakh, 90% to speak Russian and 20% to speak English by 2020. Also by 2020, Kazakh-language content in public media is targeted to reach 70%. In addition, 100% of civil servants and 100% of employees in organisations providing public services are expected to take the Kaztest (see below) and receive a prescribed level of qualification. The number of new television projects in Kazakh is to increase by 10% annually. Kazakh-language translations and the publication of encyclopaedias, as well as scientific, business, art and other literature are to be fostered. Other targets refer to the development of terminology in Kazakh, the training of teachers and the creation of language learning materials. Over 19.1 billion tenge (19.2 million EUR) were allocated for the implementation of the *Action Plan for Languages for 2011–2013*.

Co-ordination of the national language policy is the responsibility of the Language Committee of the Ministry of Culture and Information.

Responsibility for the implementation of the language policy is divided among numerous government bodies including MoES, the Ministry of Communications and Information, the Ministry of Industry and New Technologies, the Ministry of Foreign Affairs, the Agency for Land Management, the National Assembly, the World Association of Kazakhs, the People's Democratic Party 'Nur Otan' and the Inter-Ministerial Commission. Non-governmental organisations (NGOs) and private businesses are also expected to help implement the language policy.

In 2011, the Tildaryn Centre was established to foster the learning of the state language and to introduce effective and new methods for teaching Kazakh, English and other languages. Ablai Khan University and Karaganda University have been accorded a leadership role in preparing teachers for trilingual education. A total of 130 centres (state and private) have been created where people can learn both Kazakh and English. A 30-volume specialised Kazakh-Russian and Russian-Kazakh dictionary is under development, with at least 10 volumes already in circulation. A system has been created for assessing knowledge of the state language – the Kaztest. Top grade civil servants are required by law to pass the advanced level of the Kaztest. The President's *Bolashak* scholarship programme, founded in 1993, supports Master's, postgraduate 'aspirantura' and PhD students studying abroad, but as of 2011, undergraduates are no longer awarded scholarships. *Bolashak* scholarships are also available for medical internships, and teachers can apply to go abroad for up to 18 months to improve their language skills and to undertake placements in foreign schools. Between 2005 and 2012, 8448 *Bolashak* scholarships were awarded (JSC 'Center for International Programs' 2013). The Ministry of Foreign Affairs (2013) reported that in 2012, 100 motion pictures were in production and that there were about 40 Kazakh language newspapers and magazines, 13 television channels and 10 radio stations. In short, the Kazakhstani government has put in place ambitious plans, and backed these up with mechanisms, only some of which have been named here, to support their realisation.

What it all means on the ground

Having discussed government intentions expressed through the education system, strategic planning documents, initiatives and policies, this section now focuses on how government intentions regarding trilingualism are perceived by various stakeholders, drawing on data from case studies of educational reform conducted in six schools in three different regions of Kazakhstan. The regions will be referenced as Location A, Location B and Location C. (Due to obligations of confidentiality to participants in this research, the case studies themselves are only available to members of the research team). The case studies describe the schools in their local contexts and include quantitative and descriptive information about staff and students, facilities, ethnicity, language of instruction and so on. They also refer to news reports, and government websites and documents. They rely substantially on interviews with local and regional government officials, with people in positions of authority at pre- and in-service teacher training institutions, and with headteachers and their deputies, teachers and students. Teacher and student interviews took place in focus groups in a total of six schools (three rural and three urban). Interviews focused on perceptions of planned reforms including in the areas of trilingualism, curriculum, learning resources, e-learning, learning environments and teacher training, as well as on perceptions of central government. The extensive case study reports were reviewed to understand how educational reform was perceived at the local level. A sub-component of the studies examined the coherence between the government goal of achieving high degrees of trilingualism among the population and the readiness/preparedness of schools, teacher training institutions, and local and regional government to support the achievement of that goal.

In addition, this discussion draws on data from the final report of the *Development of Strategic Directions for Education Reforms in Kazakhstan for 2015–2020* project ('Roadmap Project'). In its initial phase the project aimed to diagnose the *problems* in education in Kazakhstan that need to be addressed in the next stage of the development of the education system in preparation for the creation of a detailed roadmap for education for 2015–20. One of the authors of this chapter was part of the Roadmap team and as such was able to draw on notes from meetings with education officials.

Officials and educators in all three regions were all aware of the government's trilingual policy as were the officials and educators interviewed for the Roadmap Project. In general, support was expressed for the teaching of three languages. The overwhelming majority of respondents characterised the government reform as logical, important, necessary and/or needed. The few people in the case studies expressing dissatisfaction with the trilingual policy purported not to be against the learning of three languages, but expressed concern about launching the teaching of subjects through English without sufficient qualified staff and professional development. Respondents stated:

> We have a shortage of personnel that could fully teach English subjects. Before introducing these innovations, we first need to train personnel. (Teacher responsible for upbringing, School G, Location C case study)

> Acute is the problem of shortage of teachers and staff . . . (Deputy headteacher, School F, location C case study)

> The main problem is the personnel. All subjects providing general education, except foreign languages, should be taught by a person who knows a foreign language fluently. Only 4% of our teachers in Kazakhstan are able to teach in foreign languages. . . . [teaching through English] all depends on the pedagogue and his logic, thus this is the main problem. (Government official, Location A case study)

Reinforcing the same point, one case study respondent stressed that a lack of English language knowledge could ultimately have a negative impact on student learning.

> Suppose we teach Biology in English, but the teacher is not a Biology teacher, but a teacher of English . . . Therefore, lack of the deep knowledge of the subject exists. We have a shortage of personnel that could fully teach English subjects. Before introducing these innovations, we first need to train personnel. So, personally I am against doing it right now, because children receive incomplete and inappropriate knowledge. (Teacher on upbringing, school G, location C case study)

Roadmap Project respondents pointed to the low salaries of education workers as a major reason why schools lack well-qualified staff. Citing the Agency for Statistics of the Republic of Kazakhstan, the Roadmap report (2013, 48) states that in June 2013 '[o]n average teachers [were] paid 80 386 Tenge (US $535) per month which is below the average salary in Kazakhstan which is 109 970 Tenge (US $733)'. This point of view was reinforced by one case study respondent who stated:

> For example teachers of English language, they were giving up the job to work for oil companies as interpreters and translators. Only the patriots stay at school – those who love to work as a teacher and love to work with children. (Deputy Director, School D, Location B case study)

In addition, Roadmap Project respondents expressed concern about the quality of Kazakh-language professional development materials. This may serve as one indication of the many possible reasons why, as argued earlier in the chapter, students in Kazakh-medium education may be disadvantaged.

Kazakh-language teacher training materials are very poor. [Several other teachers concurred] (Kazakh Language Teacher, Roadmap Project, teacher focus group)

There was little evidence of case study teachers having received training specific to trilingual education. One case study respondent did refer to a course on trilingualism, but found the course too short. Also, the quotation below implies that professional development in trilingualism is being perceived as 'teaching through the medium of English' as opposed to defining pedagogies appropriate for trilingual education such as translanguaging, the rich scaffolding of language input and output, or supporting students in developing generic language learning skills.

[Courses on trilingualism] were very short. Literally within a week, there were really good teachers coming, they were teaching in English and offered their ways of work. Just for trilingual education. It was a good course, but it was only a week long. (History Teacher, School G, Location C case study)

A Roadmap Project respondent working in teacher education said the courses her institution offered in trilingualism were primarily focused on the normative aspects of trilingual education as opposed to pedagogy. This implies a lack of awareness by the teacher educator of how pedagogy would need to be adapted in trilingual education contexts. Furthermore, when referring to trilingual education, case study teachers expressed a need for further language training in English, although it was not always clear who should be trained. However, several respondents pointed to the need for subject-area specialists to teach content classes.

. . . we need to train personnel first. For example, for a teacher of Physics to teach Physics in English, it is very difficult. And, a teacher of English will not be able to become a physicist. Maybe this teacher knows English, but he might not know Physics at all. (Government official, Location B case study)

The quality of existing learning resources, and the lack of age- and grade-appropriate learning resources for the teaching of content subjects through English were frequently cited as major concerns. Here again, despite being asked questions about trilingual education in general, English was often the focus of the responses.

Next problem is lack of resources. We do not have enough textbooks . . . (Government official, Location A case study)

> Everywhere the problems are the same: absence of textbooks and teachers. (Deputy Director, School G, Location C case study)

> As we said before, elementary grades started to study in English. But we don't have enough didactic materials, for example, we don't have Kazakh-English dictionaries and textbooks. (Teacher, School B, Location A, focus group, case study)

> We need textbooks for elementary school written in the appropriate manner for children of first grades. (Deputy headteacher, School F, Location B)

There was also concern that too little time was allocated to the teaching of English both in primary and secondary school and that that time allocation was insufficient for students to learn the language.

> . . . I will be learning English one hour per week and I will probably forget everything I learned on Wednesday before the next Wednesday, and what English is. Is it worth it? I do not see any point of doing so and having one hour English class per week in the first Grade. (Headteacher, School G, Location C case study)

> One hour of English lessons per week during four years is not enough. (Deputy Director, School G, Location C case study)

> Because in the high school, the number of hours allocated to English is only two a week. It is not enough at all. It is only 90 minutes a week. (English teacher, School C, Location A case study)

Moreover, a couple of teachers expressed concern that the learning of a third language would prove difficult for students who had not yet mastered two.

> As a teacher of the History of Kazakhstan, I would like to say that our students have just started to learn the Kazakh language, but if they start learning the English language, then it will be difficult for the students. (History Teacher, School B, Location A, focus group, case study)

Similarly a headteacher stopped teaching a subject through Kazakh due to a belief that students would not perform well on the UNT in Russian. This suggests that government intentions may be undermined by a lack of understanding of the teaching and learning strategies suitable for trilingual education contexts. It also reinforces the power of UNT-related perceptions.

> Also, one of our projects for the Grade 9 for example we had History of Kazakhstan in Kazakh language, which we have to close up now, because there is UNT in a couple of years, which will be in Russian. Of course all the UNT questions will be in Russian, so we just have to take such actions. (Headteacher, School G, Location B case study)

All of the schools in the three regions were teaching Kazakh, Russian and English, or were planning to start teaching English at the primary level in 2013 or 2014. Faced with the above concerns, one school in Location C reported using the following solutions. They stream students so only one class enters the trilingual programme per year. As the children entering Grade 5 are deemed as not having an adequate level of English to undertake English-medium instruction in Grade 7, the school provides a special intensive class for those children choosing the trilingual stream. As the Science teachers do not speak English, the English teacher has had to learn Science and teach the subject, but students also receive supplemental instruction in their primary language of instruction. As Science textbooks are not in English, teachers spend long hours translating materials and collecting additional learning resources. In order to prepare students for the UNT, which is either in Kazakh or Russian, students who have been taught Science mostly through English are also provided with a special course in the translation of scientific terms and additional Science lessons in the language of the UNT. A trilingual school visited in the framework of the Roadmap Project (2013) also reported using many of the same strategies. Other coping strategies reported by other respondents included having parents purchase additional English language tuition from the private sector, and having schools provide extracurricular activities in English or extra lessons in English. An English teacher from Location C, who became the Physics teacher, also reported needing to rely on a parent who was a Science teacher to prepare for the job, and wondering if it would have otherwise been possible to prepare for this new role. The teacher expressed concern about the personal sacrifice involved:

Teacher: . . . it is very time-consuming work, so you get little sleep. It really is a deadly job . . .

Interviewer: So, you started this work without having any material as a base or training?

Teacher: It is true. The only thing was, I was warned in advance, I was warned in March, and in April, just before the start of the programme.

Interviewer: But you were already working in this school?

Teacher: Yes, of course, I was working here, I was teaching English. And these 4–5 months before the start of the year, I sacrificed to the programme, to study Physics and every holiday I was gathering information to use it later on. Plus, this is what always gets updated, and has to be

> added to and so on, i.e. Summer is spent on preparation for the next year. (Physics Teacher, School G, Location C)

This suggests that insufficient support was made available, at least to this school, from regional or national authorities and institutions in terms of professional development, mentoring and access to learning materials. The broad range of concerns expressed across respondents suggests that leadership of the trilingual initiative may be insufficient. One case study respondent reinforced this view:

> Another problem is the immobility of the bureaucratic system. The officials have not enough practice and experience. We have already discussed that ... Officials don't want to hear what people are saying to them. (Deputy Director, School G, Location C case study)

Some teachers also expressed concern for the development of the students' language skills in Russian. The following extracts from interviews belie a comment made by a national senior education official that all Kazakhs speak both Kazakh and Russian:

> ... there is not a single Russian in our area. I come to the lesson three times a week, I speak Russian during the lessons three days – and then, all children forget what the Russian language is. (Teacher of Russian language and literature, School F, Location C case study)

> I see the difficulties in the regions, such as we have 90% of the students knowing the Kazakh language and we are proud of it, but they know the Russian language worse. (Teacher, School F, Location C case study)

One Location C respondent, who also referred to the lack of Russian language knowledge, stressed that some students spoke English better than they spoke Russian. This may be an indication that in this location the status of English may be on the rise and this to the detriment of lcoal Russian language knowledge. Furthermore, this respondent refers to the possibility that teachers who are supposed to teach their classes through Russian may resort to using Kazakh because of the students' weak Russian language knowledge. The following text also reveals possible tensions among languages and that at least in this teacher's view the use of Kazakh in the home and on the street is a 'most terrible problem'. Personal beliefs will need to be drawn out and addressed as required in the shift to trilingual education.

> ... little children are far from the Russian language. Of course, they get closer in the 7th Grade; we adapt them to the Russian language. It does not come

immediately. The most terrible problem for me is that the children, both at home and on the street and in the school speak Kazakh. There are even children who know English better than Russian. They study English very thoroughly and English teachers are much respected for their English kids, who speak very well. And the History of Kazakhstan in Russian classes is taught in Kazakh. We have colleagues who teach Kazakh in Russian classes. Of course, they also have difficulties and do not get everything at once, but gradually they move toward the goal. (Teacher, School G, Location C case study)

It is apparent that the linguistic profiles of both students and, to a lesser extent, staff across the three regions, vary greatly. Whereas in Location C students appeared to be Kazakh dominant and there are few native speakers of Russian, this is not the case in other locations. Moreover, students in Kazakh-medium programmes may not necessarily speak Kazakh as a first language, and Russian-dominant students may find it a challenge to learn Kazakh:

So we teach the Kazakh language and literature, this is the official language. Our burden is much heavier than that of others. Our Kazakhs do not really stand out for their knowledge of the Kazakh language. As well, we have a Russian-speaking audience, to which we teach Kazakh as a foreign language. (Teacher, School C, Location A case study)

In total we have 60 classes, of which 31 are Russian classes and 29 Kazakh classes. However, in Russian classes, we have a majority of Kazakh children. (Headteacher, School G, Location B case study)

Our students remain Russian-dominant despite studying primarily in Kazakh and English. (Teacher, Astana, Roadmap Project)

The above also imply a need for a more thorough understanding of the pedagogy appropriate for trilingual education. This point is further illustrated by the following statement:

However, there are good conditions for teaching Kazakh; there is a three-times-a-week norm for early grades . . . There is also division between teaching Kazakh grammar and literature. (Government official, Location A case study)

The official's comment may represent wishful thinking as the investment in time reflected in the quotation is unlikely to lead to high degrees of fluency in Kazakh among these primarily Russian-speaking students. There was also evidence that schools base their decision on which subjects would be taught through English on the availability of teachers and the perceived ability of students to cope with English-medium instruction. This was reported by two schools visited under the Roadmap Project and is evidenced by the following quotations:

Interviewee: For example, in the 7th Grade, there is Physics two times a week in English, and two times a week in Kazakh. (Physics Teacher, School G, Location C case study)

Interviewer: They start English as a medium of instruction in all Science subjects at Grade 7?

Interviewee: We tried to, but it was extremely difficult for students. We started for example Biology and Chemistry at once and it was very difficult for the children. So we stopped this practice and we study only one subject now. (Deputy Director, School G, Location B case study)

Data from two student focus groups implies that a variety of subjects may be taught in English.

Interviewer 2: How many subjects are taught in English in your case?

Interviewee 2: Business English and Algebra

Interviewer 2: You are the students of the 9th Grade, right? So, Algebra, Business English.

Interviewee 2: Some classes have Biology in English.

Interviewee 1: It is other classes.

Interviewee 2: In 10th Grade we study Business English, Technical Translation, Biology. That's all. (Focus Group with Students, School G, Location C case study)

Interviewee 1: We are Kazakh group.

Interviewee 2: I know that in the 7th Grade they learn Physics in English, and Geography

Interviewee 3: In our classes. In Grade 8 when I was we learned Geography of the USA. (Student Focus Group, School G, Location C case study)

What appears under-represented in the discourse of the case studies and in the meetings for the Roadmap Project is a complex view of trilingualism where the learning of all three languages is discussed and planned for as an integrated task. What is completely missing from that discourse, except in interviews with the management of NIS, is learning from education systems elsewhere in the world that seek to support students in becoming trilingual.

By extrapolation, this would suggest that planning for trilingual education is taking place with insufficient knowledge about the investments and practices required to achieve high degrees of trilingualism within a society. In addition, interviewer questions almost always evoked a response about measures taken to support schools in teaching and/or students in learning English. Furthermore, the three languages were presented from a monoglossic perspective, as three separate entities. Little evidence was apparent outside of the NIS network that pedagogy might need to change in bilingual or trilingual education. No definition of trilingualism or of trilingual education was mentioned as a common reference point.

The levels of fluency to be achieved in each language appear to be insufficiently and inconsistently defined. Fluency is the ability to speak and/or write a language with ease and accuracy. One government document speaks of all students achieving 'fluency' in the state language (MoES 2012b). This is probably an unrealistic target, at least in the short-term. Moreover, without defining what is meant by fluency this target would be difficult to measure. By contrast, another document sets a target for all high school graduates to reach a B1 level (Common European Framework of Reference for Languages (CEFR)) in the state language. Targets are not differentiated according to native speakers and those who are learning Kazakh as an additional language. Native speakers would be expected to achieve much higher degrees of fluency than non-native speakers. Moreover, the CEFR is not intended as a reference point for measuring fluency in a native or first language, and the CEFR descriptors of competences would need to be operationalised for trilingual education so that learning could be better planned and student achievement better measured. Although the CEFR offers a set of descriptors, it does not give precise indications about how these are to be measured. The lack of clear language targets would likely complicate curriculum renewal, and the development of learning resources and educator professional development programmes.

Conclusion

Kazakhstan is steadily shifting towards becoming linguistically-speaking a Kazakh-dominant society whilst seeking also to foster the learning and use of Russian, English and minority languages. However, that shift is far from being assured. For Kazakh to take a 'lead role in all spheres of life', the quality of Kazakh-medium education needs to be improved and people will have to choose to use Kazakh more often in their work and private lives. There is general agreement amongst respondents in the case studies and the Roadmap Project that students need to learn three languages with the support of government initiatives; however, not all educators believe this is possible in the current circumstances. Still, respondents generally speaking expressed concern about a lack of teachers who can teach through English. Respondents also argued that there is a lack of high-quality language learning materials, in particular for teaching Kazakh and English, and for teaching through English. This has not deterred some schools from demonstrating considerable initiative and resourcefulness in finding their own solutions to offering English-medium instruction. However, the lack of awareness of the results that have been achieved elsewhere in the world in trilingual education and how that has been done, coupled with a lack of agreement on what levels of language proficiency will be achieved in each of the three languages and how, suggest that planning for trilingual education is taking place with insufficient knowledge about the investments and practices required to attain high degrees of trilingualism within a society. Further investment appears to be required into the leadership and management of trilingual education.

REFERENCES

Abdakimov, A. (1994). *History of Kazakhstan (From Ancient Times to the Present Day)*. Almaty: Almaty.

Abylkhozhyn, Zh.B., Kozybayev, M. and Tatimov, K. (1989). 'Kazakhstan Tragedy'. *Questions of History* 7, 53–71.

Agency of Statistics of the Republic of Kazakhstan (2013a). *Demographic Indexes for the Period 2007–2013.* www.stat.gov.kz/faces/wcnav_externalId/homeNumbersPopulation?_afrLoop=646668534986623&_afrWindowMode=0&_afrWindowId=06bviu6ut_59#%40%3F_afrWindowId%3D06bviu6ut_59%26_afrLoop%3D646668534986623%26_afrWindowMode%3D0%26_adf.ctrl-state%3D06bviu6ut_75 (retrieved 10 October 2013).

— (2013b). *Number of the Pupils in General Education Schools by Kind of Studying Language.* www.kaz.stat.kz/digital/naselsenie_kz/Pages/default.aspxminside (retrieved 10 November 2013).

— (2013c). Archive 2009. *Higher Educational Institutions in The Republic of Kazakhstan. Number of Students According to the Language of Instruction.* www.stat.gov.kz/faces/wcnav_externalId/publBullS13-2009?_afrLoop=195820972285196&_afrWindowMode=0&_afrWindowId=12xkdli1f8_211#%40%3F_afrWindowId%3D12xkdli1f8_211%26_afrLoop%3D195820972285196%26_afrWindowMode%3D0%26_adf.ctrl-state%3D12xkdli1f8_227 (retrieved November 2013).

— (2013d). at.gov.kz/faces/wcnav_externalId/homeNumbersEducation?_afrLoop=304983236968484&_afrWindowMode=0&_afrWindowId=ykqopd3ku_11#%40%3F_afrWindowId%3Dykqopd3ku_11%26_afrLoop%3D304983236968484%26_afrWindowMode%3D0%26_adf.ctrl-state%3Dykqopd3ku_100 (retrieved 25 November 2013).

Amanzholova, D.A. (1994). *Kazakh Autonomy and Russia. History of Alash Movement.* Moscow: Rossiya Molodaya.

Aminov, K., Jensen, V., Juraev, S., Overland, I. Tyan, D. and Uulu, Y. (2010). 'Language Use and Language Policy in Central Asia'. *Central Asia Regional Data Review*, 2:1.

Ayubayeva, N., Bridges, D., Drummond, M.J., Fim'yar, O., Kishkentayeva, M., Kulakhmetova, A., McLaughlin, C., Mehisto, P., Orazbaeyv, S. and Shinkarenko, V. (2013). *Development of Strategic Directions for Education Reforms in Kazakhstan for 2015–2020: Final Report of the Early Years and Secondary School Working Group.* Astana: Nazarbayev University.

Bokayev, B., Zharkynbekova, S., Nurseitova, K., Bokayeva, A., Akzhigitova, A. and Nurgalieva, S. (2012). 'Ethnolinguistic Identification and Adaptation of Repatriates in Polycultural Kazakhstan'. *Journal of Language, Identity, and Education*, 11, 333–43.

CIA (Central Intelligence Agency) (2013). *CIA Factbook: Kazakhstan.* Washington: CIA. www.cia.gov/library/publications/the-world-factbook/geos/kz.html (retrieved 24 November 2013).

Commission on Human Rights under the President of the Republic of Kazakhstan (2012). *Special Report on the Situation concerning the Rights of Oralmans, Stateless Persons and Refugees in the Republic of Kazakhstan.* Astana: President's Office.

Decree of the Soviet Socialist Republic of Kazakhstan (SSRK) (1987). *Decree 'On Improving the Study of the Kazakh Language in the Republic'.*

DeYoung, A.J. and **Balzhan, S.** (1996). *Issues in Post-Soviet Secondary School Reform: The Case of Kazakhstan.* Report Education Resources Information Center (ERIC).

Drummond, T. (2010). 'Higher Education Admissions Regimes in Kazakhstan and Kyrgyzstan: Difference Makes a Difference'. In I. Silova (ed.), *Globalization on the Margins: Education and Post-Socialist Transformations in Central Asia.* Charlotte, NC: Information Age Publishing.

Fierman, W. (2006). 'Language and Education in Post-Soviet Kazakhstan: Kazakh-Medium Instruction in Urban Schools'. *The Russian Review* 65, 98–116.

Fishman, J.A. (1991). *Reversing Language Shift.* Clevedon, England: Multilingual Matters Ltd.

Government of the Republic of Kazakhstan (2011). *Bylaw #878 on Approval of the Action Plan for 2011–2013 for the Implementation of the State Programme of Functioning and Development of Languages for 2011–2020.*

JSC 'Center or International Programs' (2013). www.bolashak.gov.kz/index.php/en/.

Kassymova, D., Kundakbaeva, Zh.B. and **Markus, U.** (2012). *Historical Dictionary of Kazakhstan.* Maryland: Scarecrow Press, Inc..

KATEV International Foundation for Education and Culture (2013). www.katev.kz/?p=content&cl=hakkimizda&i=59 (retrieved 20 August 2013).

Kolstø, P. and **Malkova, I.** (1997). 'Is Kazakhstan Being Kazakified?' *Analysis of Current Events* 9:11, 1 and 3–4.

Law of the Republic of Kazakhstan (1997). *Law on Languages in the Republic of Kazakhstan.* www.online.zakon.kz/Document/?doc_id=1008034 (retrieved 24 November 2013).

Law of the Soviet Socialist Republic of Kazakhstan (SSRK) (1989). *Law on Languages in the Kazakh SSR.* www.online.zakon.kz/Document/?doc_id=1005765 (retrieved 24 November 2013).

MoES (Ministry of Education and Science) (2012a). *Results of Student Enrolment to the Higher Educational Institutions of the Republic of Kazakhstan in 2012.* Astana: Ministry of Education and Science and the National Testing Centre.

— (2012b) *Ministry of Education and Science in Figures and Facts, Results of 2012.* Astana: Ministry of Education and Science.

— (2013a). Personal email communication.

— (2013b). 'Standard Subject Plan'. www.edu.gov.kz/ru/activity/doshkolnoe_i_srednee_obrazovanie/srednee_obrazovanie/standarty_i_uchebnye_programmy/ (retrieved 24 November 2013).

Ministry of Foreign Affairs (2013). www.mfa.gov.kz/en (retrieved 12 September 2013).

Nazarbayev, N. (2001). 'On the State Programme of Functioning and Development of Languages for 2001–2010'. Decree of the President of the Republic of Kazakhstan No. 550.

— (2011). 'On the State Programme of Functioning and Development of Languages for 2011–2020'. Decree of the President of the Republic of Kazakhstan No. 110.

— (2012). 'Kazakhstan 2050 Strategy: New Political Course of the Established State'. Annual State of the Nation Address. Astana, December 2012. www.kazakhstan.org.sg/content/intro.php?act=menu&c_id=43 (retrieved 19 November 13).

— (2012, December). 'Kazakhstan 2050: New Political Course of the Established State'. Annual State of the Nation Address.

NIS (2013). *Autonomous Education Organisation 'Nazarbayev Intellectual Schools' 2020 Development Strategy*. Astana: NIS.

OECD (Organisation for Economic Cooperation and Development) (2013). *Kazakhstan*. Paris: OECD.

Office of the President (2013). www.akorda.kz/ru/page/page_v-kazakhstane-v-druzhbe-i-soglasii-prozhivaet-bolee-130-narodnostei-i-natsionaln_1348723760 (retrieved 12 September 2013).

Valyaeva, G. (2006). 'Standardized Testing for University Admissions in Kazakhstan: A Step in the Right Direction?' Paper presented at the Central Eurasians Studies Conference, University of Michigan, Ann Arbor, MI.

Zimovina, E.P. (2003). 'Population Dynamics and Ethnic Composition of Kazakhstan in the Second Half of the 20th Century'. *Demoscope Weekly*, 3–16 March, 103–4.

9 'SOVIET', 'KAZAKH' AND 'WORLD-CLASS' in the Contemporary Construction of Educational Understanding and Practice In Kazakhstan

Olena Fimyar (University of Cambridge, Faculty of Education)

Introduction

In the last decade Kazakhstan has experienced rapid growth in all spheres of social life including education. The 'Kazakhstan 2030 Strategy' sets up an even greater goal of the country becoming one of the 50 most competitive world economies. In line with this objective a multi-billion dollar investment in highly selective English-medium Nazarbayev University (NU) and Nazarbayev Intellectual Schools (NIS) has created the so called 'points of growth' (Rus. *tochki rosta*) which will provide a 'model' for the whole education system to follow. This is the story of one Kazakhstan, urban, modern, mobile, ever changing and rapidly growing. However, there is also another Kazakhstan – rural, remote, traditional and crying out for investment in basic hygiene facilities and infrastructure. The level of educational achievements and educational opportunities open to children in these two Kazakhstans differ sharply across these divides.

Educational thought in the country also presents an interesting mixture of old and new, national and international, influences and agendas. On the one hand, there are strong sentiments for the achievements of the Soviet past, among which are, just to name a few, the almost universal literacy rate, a high level of investment in education, provision of pre-school education and gender-equal participation in education. On the other hand, international comparative studies of student achievement (e.g. TIMMS, PISA) are gradually gaining greater importance as international rankings themselves are becoming the major drivers for educational reform. Against this background Kazakh culture, literature and language, the opportunities for the development of which were tragically curtailed during Soviet times, are now at the centre of the state policies and are going through a period of major development.

All these socio-economic factors, 'points of growth', inter-cultural influences, and divides are important for understanding the construction of contemporary educational theory and practice in Kazakhstan. Drawing on the analysis of documentary and interview data, this chapter traces the construction of educational discourses and follows Kazakhstan's attempts to recreate itself and find its place in the world arena.

The changing nature of Kazakhstani society since independence: Migration, demography and growing class disparities

While the political leadership of oil-rich Kazakhstan has remained stable for more than two decades, the social fabric of Kazakhstani society is constantly changing. The economic collapse of the early 1990s set in motion processes which were beneficial for some, but which left the majority, especially in rural areas (WHO/UNICEF 2013), economically disaffected and marginalised (Tengri News 2012). The opening of the borders soon after independence witnessed a large number of ethnic Russians and Germans returning to their homelands (Daly 2008, 26; Osipian 2009, 189). These emigration processes were paralleled with the return migration of ethnic Kazakhs (*oralmans*), who came from China, Mongolia and the Central Asian Republics of the Former Soviet Union on the invitation and sponsorship provided by the Kazakhstani government (Bokayev et al. 2012). One of our interviewees described how these migration and mobility processes affected the school intake during these years:

> In the early 90s many people left for Russia, now 80% of our students are repatriates from Mongolia. During the restructuring, the rural population, mainly Germans, Russians and Ukrainians began to move to the city. (Interviewee A,[1] Vice-head of upbringing, mid-career professional, School B, Location A)

The rise of the middle class in Kazakhstan from the mid-1990s onwards created a demand for private education, English language provision and opportunities to study abroad. The government-sponsored *Bolashak* programme has also contributed to the growing numbers of Western-educated professionals joining the ranks of the aspiring middle class in Kazakhstan. However, Kazakhstani teachers, especially those working in the state sector, could hardly consider themselves part of a middle class. According the recently completed *Development of Strategic Directions for Education Reforms in Kazakhstan for 2015–2020* report, the average salary in education of US $535 per month remains below the national average of US $733, and far below average salaries in the science and technology (US $1329), mining (US $1317) or even catering (US $621) sectors (Ayubayeva et al., 2013, 54).

Apart from growing disparities in income distribution throughout the country, demographic change has been another factor shaping the nature of Kazakhstani society (Osipian 2009, 189). The drastic decline of the birth rate during the early 1990s was reversed in the early 2000s, and now the birth rate throughout the country, especially in the southern regions, has reached a record high. These changes have important and direct implications for the education system and teaching profession. The high birth rate has created unprecedented demand for kindergarten and pre-school places throughout the country. In Almaty, for example, where the current capacity of the kindergarten and pre-school sector can only accommodate 45 000 children, over 48 000 children are on a waiting list for placement allocation (Bolatbek 2013). According to the 'State Programme of Education Development for 2011–2020', as of 1 July 2010 the coverage of pre-school children throughout the country was 40% (MoES 2010, 8), which makes the Almaty case rather representative. Demographic changes coupled with low pay have affected the composition of the national teaching corps, which is now increasingly 'dominated by women and greying fast' (International Crisis Group 2011, 35–6). To capture this tendency in numbers, 'every fifth teacher in Kazakhstan is 50 years and older', while the annual inflow of graduates into the teaching profession remains under 2.6% (ibid.).

Educational initiatives as responses to socio-economic transformations: Exemplar schools and persisting rural/urban disparities

The Ministry of Education and Science (MoES) has responded to these socio-economic challenges with a number of initiatives, including the structural adjustment policies of the early 1990s; a number of curriculum reforms; the changing of the language of instruction in schools from predominantly Russian to Kazakh; the transfer of a share of the financial responsibilities from the national to the regional levels; the introduction of Unified National Testing (UNT); the piloting of the trilingual system (Kazakh, Russian, English); the introduction of ICT in schools; and the piloting of 12-year education and other government-led initiatives. For a comprehensive discussion of the first decade of educational reform see Chapter 1 in this volume. In the early 2000s the emphasis of reform shifted from curriculum to teacher education and teacher professional development. A number of international organisations active at the time, including the Soros Foundation, the Asia Development Bank and others, organised professional development workshops on critical thinking, debate and a communicative approach to teaching English. The network of private schools for gifted and talented students, including Miraz, Daryn and Kazakh-Turkish Lyceums, was encouraged in order to diversify the system of educational provision and meet the growing demands of the middle class for better educational opportunities for their children. For a detailed overview of the second decade of educational reform see Chapter 2 in this volume.

For the purposes of this chapter, however, it is important to mention two post-2010 educational initiatives: the establishment and operation of Nazarbayev University (NU) and Nazarbayev Intellectual Schools (NIS). Both of these institutions are built on the model of partnership with world top-ranking universities or other international educational providers and both are catering for less than one per cent of the same year student cohort in the country. In part to justify the level of investment in these two initiatives, a three level programme of teacher professional development for mainstream schools was established on the basis of the NIS Centre of Pedagogical Excellence (CoE). NIS is also working on the schedule of rolling out its curriculum to mainstream schools starting from 2014. In 2011–12, the development and provision of the CoE programme (see Chapter 5) was carried out through the involvement of the University of Cambridge Faculty of Education (FoE) and Cambridge International Examinations (CIE). The programme is now being scaled up through *Orleu*, a nationwide network of in-service teacher training institutes, and regional CoE. The successful completion of each of the three levels by the teachers is linked to a salary increase of 30%, 70% and 100% respectively. The programme of professional development for school directors, also through the involvement of FoE and CIE is currently in operation. In parallel, NU is offering a nine-month (in 2013, six-month) teacher professional development course and is launching an MSc in Educational Leadership and a PhD in Education starting from the 2013–14 academic year.

These and other initiatives demonstrate the aspirations and commitment of Kazakhstani leaders to transforming Kazakhstan into a strong player in the global economic and educational arenas. Citing the Foreword of the 'National

Report of the State and Development in Education – 2007': 'the President of the Republic of Kazakhstan N. Nazarbayev has set up a global task for the Ministry of Education and Science . . . the need to provide [quality] services of education at the level of the world standards' (Damitov *et.al.* 2007, 1). However, despite the efforts to date, the authors of the 'State Programme of Education Development for 2011–2020' admit that 'the [mainstream] educational sector in Kazakhstan remains uncompetitive' (MoES 2010, 9). This revelation is supported by more disturbing figures which state that '201 schools [out of 7576] are in poor condition', '25.1% of schools need an overhaul', '37.4% don't have access to drinking water', there are '70 three-shift schools and one four-shift school' (ibid.). Further, it is stated that:

> Every fifth school lacks either a dining room or canteen. Depreciation of equipment and inventory in school canteens is 80%. 26.4% of schools do not have gyms. . . . Ungraded schools make 56.5% of the total number of schools (52% in 2005). In rural areas this figure makes 68.6%. (ibid.)

What is particularly disturbing is that the above disparities in educational provision and school infrastructure are disproportionately evident in rural areas. For example, the recent figures from MoES suggest that in rural areas there are 4.5 times more schools without gyms, 4.5 times more schools working in three shifts and 13.2 times more schools in shabby buildings as compared to the number of schools in same conditions in urban areas (MoES 2013). Such acute disparities make the task of closing the rural/urban divide a matter of national priority, because disaffected and unemployed youth, which are yet again disproportionately present in rural areas, can pose a serious threat to national security if not dealt with properly and competently.

The discussion above has aimed to map out a diverse and highly unequal educational landscape in Kazakhstan, which many policy makers, including the authors of the 'State Programme of Education Development for 2011–2020', recognise as problematic and in need of radical change and intervention. Viewed as one of the most effective sites of intervention, the newly established NU, NIS and NIS/CoE are delegated the task of sharing their practices with mainstream education. It is envisaged that such strategy will result in radical overhaul of the educational system as a whole. However, as the above analysis demonstrates, in Kazakhstan's attempt to 'catch up' with the developed West, national challenges and disparities will require the close attention of policy makers for years to come.

Having presented a broad overview of the critical issues in Kazakhstani education, the chapter now moves to analyse the references to 'Kazakh' and 'world-class' in the *definitions of education* and the *model of the student* advanced in two policy texts under analysis.

'Kazakh' and 'world-class' in the definitions of education and the model of the student: Insights from documentary data

> '[An] intellectual individual, who perfectly combines patriotism with common human values and ethnic-cultural values . . .' (NIS 2011, 5)

> 'Formation of an intellectually, physically and spiritually developed citizen of the Republic of Kazakhstan.' (MoES 2010, 1)

This section explores the meaning of the terms 'Kazakh' and 'world-class' in the *definitions of education* and the *model of the student* advanced in two strategic policy documents, the 'State Programme of Education Development for 2011–2020' (hereafter 'State Programme') and the 'Autonomous Education Organisation "Nazarbayev Intellectual Schools" 2020 Development Strategy' (hereafter 'NIS Strategy'). Both documents are available in English and can be downloaded from the official websites. Table 1 and Table 2 present a selection of the most representative definitions of education advanced in the two documents. The definitions of education are mapped against three categories – i.e. principles, goals and standards – which broadly correspond to the categories of values, objectives and reference points in education. This categorisation is not exhaustive and is used here to demonstrate the inscription of the categories under analysis in textual data.

Table 1: Definitions of education in the 'State Programme'

Principles	Goals	Standards
'The basic principle of the new content will be creation of humane educational environment in each school stimulating development of moral and spiritual features of an individual: self-cognition, self-determination and self-realization. The high level of moral and spiritual culture will be achieved in educational organisations and in families.' (p. 34)	'Integration into the global educational space.' (p. 2) 'Establishment of national education statistics with consideration of international requirements.' (p. 2) '[To achieve the] ranking of the students of Kazakhstan's general education schools in international comparative surveys: the OECD PISA, 40–45th; TIMMS, 10–12th; PIRLS, 10–15th.' (p. 4).	'Conforming to the world's best practices in education.' (p. 1) 'joining European educational space.' (p. 13) 'As international experience shows, investment in human capital . . . results in significant benefits for economy and society.' (p. 5) 'The indicators of national education statistics do not comply with the requirements of international statistics.' (p. 12)

Table 1 demonstrates that the 'State Programme' views the creation of 'stimulating' and 'humane' educational environments as a core value in education. The document also places importance on the values of self-discovery, morality and spirituality, responsibility for the development of which is shared between the state and the family. Adherence to 'the world's best practices in education' is established at once as a goal of educational development and a measure of success in the progression towards the goal of 'integration into the global educational space'. Such double positioning of 'world-class' as a goal-oriented and judgement-forming category intensifies the grasp of the 'catching up' logic in educational discourses in Kazakhstan.

Table 2: Definitions of education in the 'NIS Strategy'

Principles	Goals	Standards
'An innovative polylingual educational model combining classical traditions of Natural and Mathematical Sciences-oriented education and contemporary achievements of Kazakhstani and world teaching practice.' (p. 4) 'Teaching pupils flexibly, readiness for innovation, critical attitude and creative thinking' (p. 11)	'To create an innovative model of general secondary education that combines the best traditions of Kazakh and international educational systems, gives pupils the opportunity of research and experimental activities.' (p. 1) '[To create] an innovative environment that promotes the development of teaching staff of new formation, pupil environment with the motivation for learning and self-improvement.' (p. 1) 'The purpose of the Intellectual Schools is to act as experimental sites for development, monitoring, research, analysis, validation, introduction and implementation of advanced models of educational programmes for different levels (including pre-school development and education), secondary school and high school.' (p. 3)	'Necessity for transfer to the competence-oriented school with up-to-date content, select methods and constantly improving educational technologies.' (p. 3) 'It is necessary to develop a special infrastructure . . . and introduce innovative educational programmes meeting the global educational standards.' (p. 4)

In comparison with the definitions of education advanced in the 'State Programme', the 'NIS Strategy' places emphasis on polylingual competencies, research, innovation, and critical and creative thinking. The role of NIS in this process is largely viewed as being that of an authoritative institution, which 'combines the best traditions of Kazakh and international educational systems' and transmits its practices into mainstream education. The quotations above provide examples of discursive devices whereby 'Kazakh' and 'world-class' are joined together to form 'Kazakh world class'. Such discursive moves work to orient Kazakhstani education towards a new future. The insistence on the 'new', 'innovative', 'advanced' and 'constantly improving' models of education and teacher professionalism secures the position of NIS as an authority in the field of educational innovation and technology transfer in Kazakhstan.

Table 3 presents the models of the student advanced in the two documents under analysis.

Table 3: Model of the student in the 'State Programme' and 'NIS Strategy'

'State Programme'	'NIS Strategy'
'Formation of an intellectually, psychically and spiritually developed citizen of the Republic of Kazakhstan . . . satisfying his/her needs in obtaining education, in order to ensure success in a rapidly changing world; development of competitive human capital in the country.' (p. 1)	'Highly educated person with an active life position that can compete at international leve.l' (p. 1)
	'Highly literate and creative individuals actively participating in the development of the country and improvement of its competitiveness' (p. 1)
'Encouragement of active citizenship, social responsibility, patriotism, high moral and leadership skills among young people.' (p. 2)	'Each civilized society perceives gifted children as the national asset entitled to special social rights.' (p. 2)
'All children, pupils, students and teaching employees will master the fundamentals of self-cognition, universal human values development.' (p. 34)	'Educated individuals with high moral values, critical thinking, physically and spiritually gifted, striving for self-development and creative activity.' (p. 4)
	'Intellectual individual, who perfectly combines patriotism with common human values and ethnic-cultural values, who can adapt to the society and maintain competitiveness, who is ready for lifelong learning, who can speak three languages and has good knowledge of IT.' (p. 5)
	'development of effective communication skills allowing pupils to communicate with various types of audience; training of pupils as people ready to serve their native country with commitment and integrity.' (p. 11)
	'combine common human values with ethnic and cultural values, show functional literacy and competitiveness in any life situation.' (p. 12)

The two models of the student in Table 3 have a lot in common. They put equal emphasis on 'competitive human capital' as a pre-condition for individual and national success in a 'rapidly changing world'. Equally important are the values of 'patriotism', 'morality', 'self-development'/'self-cognition' and 'leadership'. However, there is one important difference. In comparison with the 'State Programme', the 'NIS Strategy' defines its students as 'gifted children', a special category of children, who are a 'national asset entitled to special social rights'. Phrased in a rather contentious manner the definition seeks to legitimise itself by suggesting that '[e]ach civilized society perceives gifted children' as such. Another feature that sets NIS students apart from their peers in mainstream schools is the adverb 'highly' in the description of qualities and characteristics that NIS students are to demonstrate. Examples include 'highly educated', 'highly literate' and 'with high moral values'. The emphasis on 'functioning literacy', 'speak[ing] three languages' and 'good knowledge of IT' is what also sets NIS students apart from their peers. To conclude, at the level of policy texts 'Kazakh' and 'world-class' operate in close conjunction with each other and each provide resources for policy makers to legitimise the policy options aimed at aligning national standards and practices with elusive 'world-class' ideals.

As the analysis turns to interview data, the references to 'Kazakh' and 'world-class' are overshadowed by recurrent references to another concept, which continues to define interviewees' understanding of the reform process. This is the concept of the 'Soviet', which is the object of analysis in the next section.

Coming to terms with the 'Soviet': Insights from interview data

'We had Sputnik, . . . but we lost our [Kazakh] language.'
(Interviewee B, early-career professional, NIS)

'Do you have any questions?'
'Yes, why do you think the Soviet Union collapsed?'
(Interviewee C, Geography teacher, late-career professional, School B, Location A)

In the course of the study, research participants expressed rather ambivalent attitudes towards the Soviet past. They would start their interviews with a statement acknowledging the achievements of Soviet education. This statement would be followed immediately by another more revealing account which would unravel the inadequacies and failings of the Soviet system. This ambivalence towards the past is very well captured in the account of one interviewee who acknowledges that, on the one hand, 'we had Sputnik, Soviet education was successful' yet, on the other hand, 'we lost our [Kazakh] language' (Interviewee B, early-career professional, NIS). Indeed, during

Soviet times titular languages of the nations other than Russia, suffered great losses and neglect (Shturman 1988, 211–12; Fierman 1998). The quotation continues:

> When it comes to the Kazakh language, there was a stagnation. During the Soviet time this language was not developing as academic language, because everyone was using Russian. (Interviewee B, early-career professional, NIS)

Another interviewee recalled the situation with the use of languages in higher education:

> We only had the Faculty of Kazakh Language and the Faculty of History which taught in Kazakh, the rest was in Russian, all was [taught] in Russian'. (Interviewee D, late-career professional, NIS)

The use of languages of instruction in secondary schools was also severely imbalanced:

> In [an] especially difficult situation are now schools with the Kazakh as the medium of instruction, because they were severely affected during the Soviet time. There was a very small number of Kazakh-language schools left in the Soviet time. As an example, in Almaty [with approximately 250 thousand inhabitants of ethnic Kazakh origin] there was only one school with the Kazakh language of instruction. All others switched to Russian, because if you didn't know Russian then you will not have your career at that time. (Interviewee E, mid-career professional, international organisation A)

The lasting legacies of the neglect of the Kazakh language in Soviet times continue to affect the quality of teaching and provision of textbooks in the Kazakh-medium schools. As one of the interviewees indicated, the problem was particularly acute at the beginning of the country's independence:

> And this problem of closeness and isolation [of the language] . . . it manifested itself in everything once we became independent. We had no textbooks written in our language, we did not have any teaching methods . . . Kazakh language as a method, as a discipline was underdeveloped; it was developing in isolation, it was not used in practice, there was no opportunity to use it in everyday life. (Interviewee D, late-career professional, NIS)

Some interviewees admitted that their limited knowledge of Kazakh is also the so-called 'product', and the lasting legacy, of Soviet education:

> Unfortunately, I am not reading or writing in Kazakh . . . so you can see me as the 'outcome' of the Soviet education system. (Interviewee E, mid-career professional, international organisation A)

And this interviewee is not alone: Fierman (1998, 174) uses the 1989 census to illustrate how severely imbalanced the use of languages in Kazakhstan was at the time. According to census data, over 80% of Kazakhstan's population reported either native or close to native fluency in Russian. Yet, this did not mean they were bilingual, because while over 60% of ethnic Kazakhs claimed fluency in Russian, only less than 1% of Russians claimed fluency in Kazakh. Other numbers from the census were even more disturbing, with only 40% of ethnic Kazakhs claiming fluency in their native language.

During the years of independence the situation with the use of the Kazakh language has improved significantly. Now Kazakh as a state language enjoys a wider use on a par with the Russian language. Recently, the importance of English as a language of globalisation has captured policy-makers' attention. The importance of all three languages for increasing the economic competitiveness of the country was embraced in the model of trilingual education which is now piloted in the newly established NIS, with a view to it being implemented in the whole country.

The remainder of this chapter focuses on examples of how 'Soviet' was mobilised as critique of the view of knowledge and approaches to teaching.

'Soviet' as critique of knowledge

Soviet education prided itself on its use of theory and a systematic approach in all areas, from curriculum, assessment and pedagogy to the organisation of extra-curricular activities and school timetables. Everything was considered to be a part of a greater system, an end-point of which was the holistic, all-round development of Soviet citizens. All school lessons and planning objectives were prefixed with the 'systemic approach', 'system of procedures aimed at' and similar phrases postulating the primacy of the systemic, i.e. the scientific foundations of education.

In the organisation of school subjects and selection of subject knowledge, preference was given to material which was systematic and organised in blocks susceptible to explanation through rules or exceptions to these rules. Knowledge itself was viewed as solid and fixed in time. Teaching preference was given to classical texts, formulae and algorithms. The overall purpose of education was viewed as an orderly, systematic, well-organised process of acquiring and consolidating knowledge through formal instruction in fairly large classrooms (Muckle 1988, 188).

> Twenty years ago we were deeply convinced that the priority should be given to the content of each subject, and we believed that if we provided students with systematic, fundamental knowledge in every subject, then our educational objectives would be achieved. (Interviewee D, late-career professional, NIS)

In the literature on education reform in Commonwealth of Independent States (CIS) countries and the wider region several attempts have been made to grasp conceptually the shift from the traditional, Soviet, teacher-centred view of education to the more innovative, liberal/Western and student-centred approaches. Fimyar (2010), for example, puts forward the term 'changing rationalities' of post-communist education reform. Drawing on a different country context, Cheng (2008, 14–15) proposes the term 'paradigm shift toward the third wave', by which he means the movement towards world-class standards in education. Borytko's (2005, 38–39) conceptualisation of educational change as the move from a *sciento-technocratic* to a *humanistic*[2] paradigm is also useful in this respect. Drawing on the earlier work by Kolesnikova (1991), Borytko (2005) identifies the differences between the two paradigms, which are presented in Table 4 below.

Table 4: Changing educational paradigms: from a sciento-technocratic to a humanistic model

Paradigm name	Sciento-Technocratic	Humanistic
Motto	'Knowledge is power'	'Learning is power'
Core value	Cognitive experience	Mode of knowledge acquisition
View of knowledge	Fixed, fundamental, theoretical	Fluid, multiple, constructed
Teaching and pedagogy	Rote learning, memorisation, teacher-centred	Activity-based experience, student-centred
Assessment	Identifies 'gaps' in knowledge, lack of knowledge leads to inadequacy, incompetence, weakness	Assessment for learning, focus on what students already know, not the 'gaps' in their knowledge
Outcomes	Well-informed students with encyclopaedic knowledge	Students able to argue, interpret, synthesise

Adapted from Borytko 2005, 38

This is how, in the opinion of one interviewee, learning occurred under the *sciento-technocratic* paradigm:

> In the Soviet system, when I studied at school we were given for example, for math – 50 problems and tomorrow is the lesson. And all you do is *zareshivanie* [cramming/solving a lot of math problems]. This does not make any sense, because I

know, you solve one similar problem 10–20 times – you are becoming automatic at it, it does not involve thinking. (Interviewee F, early-career professional, NIS)

'Soviet' as critique of teaching methodology

'The teacher tries to fill students with all this knowledge, practically, by chewing it for them.'
(Interviewee G, Chemistry teacher, early-career professional, Teachers focus group, CoE training)

An increasing number of studies are now analysing the experiences, identities and changes that the transformations in the CIS, and particularly in Central Asian countries, brought to teachers and the teaching profession (see for example DeYoung 2006, 2008; Niyozov and Shamatov 2010; and the most recent studies in Part II of *Globalisation on the Margins: Globalisation and Postsocialist Transformations in Central Asia* (Silova 2011). The majority of these studies, however, focus on teachers' experiences and coping strategies in response to the devastating consequences of economic decline and major socio-political transformations. Only a few of the studies actually engage with the analysis of teachers' professional beliefs (e.g., Niyozov 2011, 287–313). This section advances this line of inquiry.

Soviet education was notorious for producing conceptual binaries which many of its prominent thinkers and theorists were aiming to overcome. Two such binaries which continue to structure educational debate in Kazakhstan and other CIS countries are *theory and practice* and *education and upbringing* (Rus. *vospitanie*). In the interview process, frequent references were made to the disjuncture between theory and practice. As mentioned earlier in the chapter, the Soviet curriculum was often criticised for being too overloaded and knowledge-based. On the other hand, this theoretical density is something that many of the respondents take pride in as one of the greatest achievements of Soviet education. This is how one of the respondents explains why theory was important and how successfully theory and practice were integrated in the Soviet schooling and university settings.

The material and technical base of schools at the Soviet times were very well supported. The students at schools did practical experiments in Physics and Chemistry with various chemical substances, as well as optics. We could see all these in practices and do the experiments. Our curriculum always had practical assignments side by side with learning the theory. The same was true about the funding and support for universities. For example, I studied mineral and raw materials, the stage between the mining and metallurgy. Our department had all the necessary devices, mechanisms and units, which would be found at any factory. We had the same machineries, maybe of a smaller size, for example, for the process of flotation. We used the same chemical reagents and obtained the same process but in its smaller size. Approximately until the year of 1996 we had this base. But after this time everything started collapsing, universities closed or were united, and everything was lost. Buildings were sold and bought, and the base which supported the theory was lost. (Interviewee H, Physics teacher, mid-career professional, Teachers focus group, CoE training)

However, another respondent views this legacy of theoretical overload of the curriculum as counter-productive for teaching and learning.

In our system of education we learn a lot of theory, and then what happens is that a teacher tries to fill students with all this knowledge, practically by chewing it for them. And then students go to university and they cannot apply any of that knowledge there. They do not know how to work independently; they do not know how to find useful information in textbooks and other sources. After this they graduate and go into profession. And there they do not know how to deal with any arising question or task. (Interviewee G, early-career professional, Teachers focus group, CoE training)

The next section concludes the discussion by exploring the relationships and effects of the 'Soviet', 'Kazakh' and 'world-class' triad in the construction of contemporary educational policies and practices in Kazakhstan.

Conclusion: 'Soviet', 'Kazakh' and 'world-class' as discursive resources and categories of analysis

In commonplace usage the terms 'Soviet', 'Kazakh' and 'world-class' represent the historical and geo-political trajectories Kazakhstan has followed in the course of its development. In line with this logic, 'Soviet' not only represents the period when Kazakhstan was a part of the Soviet Union, but is also often mobilised by practitioners as a critique of contemporary educational practices. In this context, 'Soviet' represents the legacies of the previous education system, which are evident in present day approaches to teaching and learning in Kazakhstan. The chapter, and the more extended treatment of this topic in Fimyar and Kurakbayev (forthcoming), demonstrate that 'Soviet' remains a highly ambivalent category which encompasses, on the one hand, the strengths of Soviet education and its long-lasting legacies, which manifest themselves in the prevalence of rote learning, levels of corruption and lack of critical and independent thinking as reported by our interviewees and various observers (Niyozov 2011; Silova 2010, 2011; Osipian 2009).

The second category of analysis, often mentioned in the discussion of educational policies, is the references to the 'Kazakh'. This category stands for pre-Soviet and post-independence developments in education, economy and society and encompasses ethnic Kazakh and national values in approaches to education and upbringing. In this meaning 'Kazakh' is often used interchangeably with 'national' and 'ethnic', the opportunities for the development of which, according to the post-independence history narrative, were severely curtailed during Soviet times. To restore historical justice and 're-capture' the past (cf. Fimyar 2010, 85), a whole range of disciplines prefixed with 'ethnic' – as in 'ethno-cultural education', 'ethno-pedagogy', 'ethno-politology [from Political Sciences]', 'ethno-sociology', 'ethno-philosophy' and 'ethno-cultural studies' (Kozhakhmetova 2011, 31) – have been mobilised to inscribe ethnic Kazakh values in educational, social and political discourses (see Kozhakhmetova 2011, Baubekova 2011 as examples of such inscriptions in education).

Importantly, pre-Soviet 'Kazakh' and post-independence 'Kazakh' differ in their meaning and in the way they are mobilised by policy makers as resources in support of existing and future policies. While pre-Soviet 'Kazakh' encompasses the layers of culture and historical wisdom of Kazakh thinkers, modern-day 'Kazakh' reflects the efforts of the Kazakhstani leaders to align 'Kazakh' education with elusive 'world-class' standards. The ultimate goal of such a discursive shift is to create a desired semantic unit – i.e. 'Kazakh world-class', which will signal a high quality education in Kazakhstan both regionally and globally. In the opinion of policy makers the improvements in the country's ratings in international comparative studies such as PISA, TIMMS, PIRLS and various International Competitiveness Indexes will be visible, powerful and traceable indicators of the country's movement towards 'world-class' standards.

Interestingly enough, the references to 'world-class' are relatively new in the educational domain. As Yakavets demonstrates, preoccupation with international ratings became pronounced in political and policy discourses from the early 2000s (see Chapter 2). Despite its relatively recent appearance in Kazakhstani political and educational discourses the term 'world-class', which is now used interchangeably with 'international' and 'quality', has established itself as a proof of commitment of Kazakhstani leaders to transform Kazakhstan into a strong regional and global player. Given this dynamic, the analysis of the references to 'world-class' in educational and policy documents is central for understanding the process of the construction of contemporary educational policies and practices in Kazakhstan.

It is however, easy to think in the language of 'world class' when one moves among the glamorous architectural monuments of Astana, but not difficult to apply the normative discourse of 'third world' in some of the 'shabby' rural schools where 200 and more children and teachers share a bucket of drinking water and a tin mug. The rural/urban divide remains one of the biggest obstacles to the realisation of the Kazakh/world-class dream.

REFERENCES:

Ayubayeva, N., Bridges, D., Drummond, M.J., Fimyar, O., Kishkentayeva, M., Kulakhmetova, A., McLaughlin, C., Mehisto, P., Orazbaeyv, S. and Shinkarenko, V. (2013). *Development of strategic directions for education reforms in Kazakhstan for 2015–2020: Final Report of the Early Years and Secondary School Working Group*. Astana: Nazarbayev University.

Bolatbek, A. (2013). 'Approximately 48 thousand pre-school children do not have access to kinder-gartens'. www.zakon.kz/kazakhstan/4570183-okolo-48-tys-almatinskikh-detejj-ne.html (Russian, retrieved 15 November 2013).

Baubekova, G.D. (2011). *Dukhovnaya kultura kak vazhnyj component natsiolalnogo vospitaniya* (in Russian) / 'Spiritual Culture as an Important Component of National Up-bringing'. *Bilim-Education*, 4:58, 48–52.

Bokayev, B., Zharkynbekova, S., Nurseitova, Kh., Bokayeva, A., Akzhigitova A. and Nurgalieva, S. (2012). 'Ethnolinguistic Identification and Adaptation of Repatriates in Polycultural Kazakhstan'. *Journal of Language, Identity & Education*, 11:5, 333–43.

Borytko, N.M. (2005). 'Values and Education: Russian Perspective'. In *Edited Collection of the Institute of Pedagogy and In-service Training, Volgograd State Pedagogical University*. Available at: www.doiserbia.nb.rs/img/doi/0579-6431/2005/0579-64310502 035B.pdf (retrieved 15 November 2013).

Cheng, Y.C. (2008). 'New Learning and School Leadership: Paradigm Shift towards the Third Wave'. In J. MacBeath and Y.C. Cheng, (eds), *Leadership for Learning: International Perspectives*. Rotterdam: Sense Publishers.

Daly, J.C.K. (2008). *Kazakhstan's Emerging Middle Class*. 'A Silk Road Paper. Washington: Central Asia-Caucasus Institute & Silk Road Studies Program / A Joint Transatlantic Research and Policy Center'. www.silkroadstudies.org/new/docs/silkroadpapers/ 0803daly.pdf (retrieved 15 November 2013).

Damitov, B.K., Ermekov, N.T., Bekenova A.B., Mozhaeva O.I., Absamatov, A. U., Golovataya, G.I. and Gabdulina A. V. (2007). *National Report on the State and Development of Education* (short version). Astana: MoES and National Center for Assessment of the Quality of Education.

DeYoung, A.J. (2006). 'Problems and Trends in Education in Central Asia Since 1990: The Case of General Secondary Education in Kyrgyzstan'. *Central Asian Survey*, 25:4, 499–514.

— (2008). 'Conceptualizing Paradoxes of Post-Socialist Education in Kyrgyzstan'. *Nationalities Papers: The Journal of Nationalism and Ethnicity*, 36:4, 641–57.

Fimyar, O. (2010). 'Policy Why(s): Policy Rationalities and the Changing Logic of Educational Reform in Post-Communist Ukraine' (1991–2008). In I. Silova, (ed.), *Post-Socialism is Not Dead: (Re)Reading the Global in Comparative Education*. Bingley: Emerald Publishing.

Fimyar, O. and Kurakbayev, K. (forthcoming). *Soviet in the Memories and Teachers' Professional Beliefs: Points for Reflection for Reformers, Educational Consultants and Practitioners*.

Fierman, W. (1998). 'Language and Identity in Kazakhstan: Formulations in Policy Documents 1987–1997'. *Communist and Post-Communist Studies*, 31:2, 171–86.

International Crisis Group (2011). *Central Asia: Decay and Decline*. Asia Report No. 201 – 3 February. Bishkek/Brussels: International Crisis Group.

Kolesnikova, I.A. (1991). 'Theoretical and Methodological Preparation of the Teacher for Upbringing Work Across the Disciplines'. Rus. 'Teoretiko-methodologicheskaya podgotovka uchitelia k vospitatelnoj rabote v tsikle pedagogicheskih disiplin'. Unpublished doctoral dissertation, St Petersburg State University.

Kozhakhmetova, K. Zh. (2011). 'The development of ethno-pedagogy as science and curriculum subject in post-independence Kazakhstan'. Rus. 'Razvitiye etnopedagogiki kak nauki i uchebnoj distsipliny za gody nezavisimosti Kazakhstana'. *KazhNU Newsletter, 'Pedagogical Sciences' series*, 3:34, 30–35.

Mitter, W. (1986). 'Bilingual and Intercultural Education in Soviet Schools'. In B.J.J. Tomiak, (ed.), *Western Perspectives on Soviet Education in the 1980s*. London: Macmillan, in association with the School of Slavonic and East European Studies, University of London.

MoES (Ministry of Education and Science) (2010). 'State Programme of Education Development for 2011–2020'. Astana: MoES. www.akorda.kz/upload/SPED.doc (in English, retrieved 15 November 13).

— (2013). *Strategic Directions of Education and Science Development for 2014–2016*. Document for internal circulation. Astana: MoES.

Muckle, J. (1988). *A Guide to The Soviet Curriculum: What the Russian Child is Taught in School*. London, New York, Sydney: Groom Helm.

NIS (2011). 'Autonomous Education Organisation "Nazarbayev Intellectual Schools" 2020 Development Strategy'. Astana. nis.edu.kz/site/nis/repository/file/%D0%A1%D0%A0% 202012-2020%20%D0%B0%D0%BD%D0%B3%D0%BB.pdf (in English, retrieved 15 November 13).

Niyozov, S. (2011). 'Revisiting Teacher Professionalism Discourse Through Teachers' Professional Lives in Post-Soviet Tajikistan'. In I. Silova, (ed.), *Globalization on the Margins: Education and Postsocialist Transformations in Central Asia*. Charlotte NC: Information Age Publishing.

Niyozov, S. and **Shamatov D.** (2010). 'Teachers Surviving to Teach: Implications for Post-Soviet Education and Society in Tajikistan and Kyrgyzstan'. In J. Zajda, (ed.), Globalization, Comparative Education and Policy Research. *Globalisation, Ideology and Education Policy Reforms*. Vol. 11. Dordrecht, Heidelberg, London, New York: Springer.

Osipian, A. (2009). '"Feed from the Service": Corruption and Coercion in the State – University Relations in Central Eurasia'. *Research in Comparative and International Education*, 4:2, 182–203.

Shturman, D. (1988). 'The Differentiation of Opportunities in Soviet Secondary Education'. In D. Shturman, *The Soviet Secondary School*. New York: Routledge.

Silova, I. (ed.) (2010). *Post-Socialism is Not Dead: (Re)Reading the Global in Comparative Education*. Bingley: Emerald Publishing.

— (ed.) (2011). *Globalization on the Margins: Education and Postsocialist Transformations in Central Asia*. Charlotte NC: Information Age Publishing.

Tengri News (2012). 'The 30-fold difference between the income of the rich and the poor in Kazakhstan'. Rus. 'V Kazakhstane pochti 30-kratnaya raznitsa v dohodah bogatyh I bednyh'. tengrinews.kz/private_finance/v-kazakhstane-pochti-30-kratnaya-raznitsa-v-dohodah-bogatyih-i-bednyih-213808/ (in Russian, retrieved 15 November 2013).

WHO/UNICEF (2013). 'Progress on Sanitation and Drinking-Water: 2013 Update'. apps. who.int/iris/bitstream/10665/81245/1/9789241505390_eng.pdf (retrieved 15 November 2013).

NOTES:

1   All interviewees are assigned letters A–H according to the order they appear in the article. These letters do not correspond to their initials and are used here to indicate the number of respondents quoted in the chapter. The respondents' career stage (early-, mid-, late-) is also indicated because the involvement of early-career professionals is a significant feature of the post-2010 educational initiatives.

2   In the original paper, Borytko (2005) uses the term 'humanitarian', but we think that 'humanistic' is a more appropriate term.

10 TOWARDS INCLUSIVE EDUCATION: Swimming Against the Tide of Educational Reform

Martyn Rouse (Professor Emeritus, University of Aberdeen)
Natallia Yakavets (University of Cambridge, Faculty of Education)
Anel Kulakhmetova (University of Cambridge, Department of Development Studies)

Introduction

This chapter considers some of the challenges involved in creating a more inclusive educational system in Kazakhstan. It will review some of the reasons why certain children continue to be marginalised from schooling, and will locate this discussion within international attempts to create Education for All (EFA) and current educational reform efforts in the country.

The chapter is informed by local and international reports on educational inclusion and diversity in Kazakhstan and by recent small-scale research projects including interviews conducted as part of 'School reform and internationalisation' (2013), a project described in the introduction to this book. The interviews provide some evidence about levels of understanding and the development of inclusive education across the country. The project was conducted in three different geographical locations in Kazakhstan. Three research teams conducted semi-structured interviews with representatives from regional and district departments of education and interviewed school directors, deputy directors and teachers in six different types of schools in urban, semi-urban and village settings.

In spite of numerous pilot projects and international aid to Kazakhstan to support the development of inclusive education, the concept of educational equity and inclusion only began to gain ground relatively recently. Inclusive education was made a national educational goal in 2008,[1] however the implementation of inclusion has been challenging for several reasons (Rouse and Lapham 2013a).

Efforts to develop inclusion in Kazakhstan have to be understood in the context of two powerful influences on policy and practice. First there are the competing (elitist) policies of the current reforms focused on economic competitiveness and second, there is the institutional inertia associated with a legacy of segregated special provision for children perceived in terms of their disabilities rather than their abilities and located within an approach known as 'defectology'.

Defining inclusion

Inclusive education is difficult to define, but it is a reform that supports and welcomes diversity. It is aimed at the elimination of educational and social exclusionary practices that are a consequence of discriminatory policies, provision and attitudes to diversity in race, social class, language, ethnicity, religion, gender and (dis)ability. An analysis of international research (Ainscow et al. 2004) suggests a typology of five ways of thinking about inclusion. These are: (i) inclusion concerned with disability and 'special educational needs'; (ii) inclusion as a response to disciplinary exclusion; (iii) inclusion as being about all groups vulnerable to exclusion; (iv) inclusion as the promotion of a school for all; and (v) inclusion as EFA (Ainscow et al. 2004).

Inclusion is an important element of a democratic education and, as such, the project of inclusion should address the experiences of all students at school, since the idea itself starts from the belief that education is not only a basic human right, but is the means through which other human rights may be achieved. Therefore, it may be seen as fundamental to a society striving for equity and social justice; the kind of well-being desired for all citizens; and the quality of democracy and social participation people wish to pursue.

However, the idea of inclusive education is often conceptualised in more restricted terms as being only about the education of children with special needs within mainstream education (Slee 2001, 168). This is true in Kazakhstan as well as in the Commonwealth of Independent States (CIS), where inclusive education is predominately understood within a special education framework, albeit a traditional medical approach to 'disability' predominant in the former Soviet Union, which will be discussed later in this chapter.

Education for All and children with disabilities

When the first World Conference on EFA was held in 1990 in Jomtien, Thailand (UNESCO 1990), the challenges associated with the education of children and young people with disabilities and special educational needs were not central to the agenda. Subsequently, however, inclusive education has been seen as the means through which previously marginalised groups, such as children with disabilities, may gain access to education (UNESCO, 1994, 2008, 2010).

Currently too many children continue to be marginalised from education (and consequently from wider society), and according to UNESCO (2010) there are many reasons why this is so. In the former Soviet Union, those most likely to be excluded were children with disabilities and special educational needs (Florian and Becirevic 2011; Miles and Singal 2009; Peters 2004; UNICEF 2012; UNESCO 2005, 2008, 2010). It is claimed that the goal of universal access to schooling and EFA will only be achieved, and the pernicious problems of marginalisation will only be tackled, if inclusive education becomes a central aspect of the broader educational reform agenda (UNESCO, 2009). Although the initial vision of EFA was broad and ambitious, the rhetoric of 'all' has so far failed to reach the poorest and most disadvantaged children, including those with disabilities (Ainscow and Miles 2008, 19). With international attention focused on achieving the Millennium Development Goals (MDGs), EFA has become increasingly focused on ensuring access to, and completion of, five years of universal primary EFA children by 2015 (ibid., 19). Attempts to achieve EFA often focus on reducing barriers to participation for marginalised individuals and groups, and these attempts will vary according to local circumstances.

In most international discussions and declarations on the topic (e.g. UNESCO IBE 2007; UNESCO 2008), the concept of inclusive education has been broadened beyond children with disabilities and relates to:

- the struggle against poverty, cultural and social marginalisation and exclusion
- the consideration of cultural diversity and multiculturalism, as both a right and a learning context within a framework of shared universal values
- the protection of the rights of minorities, aboriginals, migrant and displaced population. (UNESCO IBE 2007, 16)

Indeed, children who belong to such groups as the Roma, refugee and internally displaced children, street children, child workers, children living in remote rural areas, children living in extreme poverty, children from nomadic groups and children from ethnic and language minorities may be particularly vulnerable to exclusion and marginalisation and they are often described as having special educational needs, because it is a convenient way to provide services to them. More negatively, it may be used to justify their segregation into separate institutions, schools or classes. In the worst case, they may be denied access to education altogether. Thus, inclusive education will be defined and enacted in different ways in different places, depending on the purpose and nature of schooling, how it is organised, who has access to it and who is denied access (Ainscow and Miles 2008).

The links between inclusive education and the aspirations of the EFA movement are particularly relevant in Kazakhstan, because the legislative framework in the countries of the former Soviet Union excluded or restricted access to mainstream education for children with disabilities, even when education was supposed to be compulsory and free (UNICEF 2005). Although school participation and literacy rates are reported to be high in many former Soviet countries, the figures may be misleading because not all children are known about and counted by the authorities because their births may not be registered (UNICEF 2005, 2007, 2012). Some children with disabilities continue to be seen as uneducable and may not be the responsibility of education authorities.

Efforts to achieve inclusive education in Kazakhstan have to be understood in the current context of the policies and practices of the Soviet past which still provide the basis for contemporary thinking and practice.

Education in Kazakhstan: the Soviet legacy

Education (particularly special education) in Kazakhstan is influenced by its Soviet legacy, which still affects the ways in which schools are conceptualised and organised today. During the Soviet period and beyond, schooling was not equally available to all children. This was especially true of provision for children with disabilities because the traditional approach — known as defectology — frames disability as a diagnosis for treatment and rehabilitation rather than seeing it as just one aspect of a whole child requiring adaptations in the learning environment (Daniels 2005). In this approach, special education takes place elsewhere, i.e. outside mainstream schools, and is seen as an act of charity and caring for children who are viewed as not having the potential to succeed in schools as they currently exist. In the past, segregation was justified on the grounds of economic and educational efficiency. Children with disabilities were seen as a burden on families, reducing their capacity to be economically active.

Because such children were believed to be qualitatively different, only specially trained professionals were seen as being able to work with them. This belief locates the responsibility for educating the most vulnerable children away from staff in mainstream schools and separates children from the natural systems of support that are to be found in families, local communities and mainstream schools. It also segregates professionals by placing them in separate silos, thus reducing the opportunities for multi-professional support and teamwork.

Historically in the former Soviet Union, institution-based special education was favoured over community-based inclusive education (UNICEF 2012), and these patterns of provision ('correctional schools') continue today. In urban areas there are some special day schools, which permit children with disabilities to live at home. Few children with disabilities attend regular schools, although there are some special classes in mainstream schools. In some cases children with disabilities are educated at home, where home tuition or other forms of support may (or may not) be available. In practice, this option provides little instructional contact between child and teacher and no social contact with other children outside the family. In some rural areas, children with disabilities may be hidden at home because of the shame and stigma associated with disability. Parents see little point in registering their child's birth when the social and cultural costs of acknowledging their child has a disability outweigh any potential benefits.

During the Soviet period children who were assessed and classified by psychological-medical-pedagogical commissions (PMPCs) as having disabilities were likely to be placed in residential institutions, often far from their families and other forms of natural support, where they would have been 'treated' by specialist 'defectologists'. Today, a network of PMPCs still decides who has and does not have a disability and they continue to have considerable power in deciding the type of education a child should receive, although some PMPCs are working in more enlightened ways (Markova and Sultanalieva 2013).

Defectology has its origins in early Soviet attempts to understand and treat mental and physical impairment. It has a long history and continues to be influential in the countries of the former Soviet Union, including Kazakhstan (Daniels 2005). An early pioneer of Soviet psychology, Lev Vygotsky, is considered to be the founding father of defectology, which emerged from debates in the 1920s and 1930s about the nature of disability (Florian and Becirevic 2011) and how it should be dealt with. Over time, defectology as a field of study and a way of organising practice and provision changed from an approach that explained disability as a bio-psycho-social phenomenon, to an approach to assessment and practice that emphasised deficits and segregation. Medical perspectives came to dominate the study and practice of defectology and most of the PMPCs are still dominated by health professionals, although there is some evidence that this may be slowly changing in Kazakhstan (Markova and Sultanalieva 2013).

Most Western commentators are critical of defectology and see it as a barrier to the development of inclusion because it focuses on individual deficits that are thought best dealt with in segregated provision (Power et al. 2004). Although there have been some changes, the training of defectologists and other specialists still takes place in separate faculties in higher education that historically have not been linked with education departments and the training of teachers. Many defectologists still work in separate institutions and are seen as having a higher status and salary than teachers in mainstream schools. It is not surprising therefore that many defectologists see inclusion as a threat to their professionalism and their status.

In Kazakhstan a traditional medical model of disability is still influential in legislation, policies and provision for people with disabilities. It affects the assessment, classification and categorisation of children with disabilities, as well as determining how and where they should be educated. Where available, professional help and provision may still be focused on the *disability* and on rehabilitating, or correcting any perceived deficits (Rouse and Lapham 2013b). The aim of this approach is to make the child 'normal', rather than on working with the child's functional disorder by helping him or her to adapt to the environment or (better) by developing positive attitudes in others and adapting the environment so that it becomes accessible and welcoming to children with disabilities (OECD 2009).

According to Rouse and Lapham (2013a, 12) by changing the framework for responding to disability from defectology to inclusion, we are faced by a new moral imperative. The exclusion of children with disabilities and learning difficulties from education is:

- a human-rights issue, because all children have the right to education, as guaranteed in the Convention on the Rights of the Child and Article 24 of the Convention on the Rights of Persons with Disabilities

- a social-justice issue, because even when children with disabilities attend specialised schools, their segregation from the rest of their peers denies them the opportunity to be active participants in society and to realise their full potential socially and intellectually

- an economic-development issue, because exclusion from education denies children the opportunity to grow into productive members of society and thus denies society the talent and capacity they represent.

In addition it is a political issue because it involves the relocation of power over some aspects of decision making from policymakers and professionals to parents and those who may have been marginalised in the past.

Current developments for children with special educational needs in Kazakhstan

In the first years after independence, Kazakhstan signed the Convention on the Rights of the Child (1994), and later committed to EFA. It also signed UNICEF conventions guaranteeing equal access to education for all children and Article 24 of the UN Convention on the Rights of Persons with Disabilities (2006), which states the right to education in inclusive settings. Further, Article 30 of the Constitution of the Republic of Kazakhstan (1995) guarantees all children equal rights to education.

According to Article 8 of the Law on Education (2007, 2011), every child in Kazakhstan has the right to education and is guaranteed a free pre-school, primary, general secondary and basic vocational education, and free secondary and higher professional education on a competitive basis, regardless of origin, ethnicity, social and property status, gender, language, education, religious affiliation, place of residence, health status or other circumstances.

As signaled by the ratification of the UN Convention on the Rights of Persons with Disabilities in 2008, there has been interest in adopting the worldwide trend of inclusion, although some of the current high-profile education reform efforts in Kazakhstan do not specifically address inclusion and the education of children with disabilities.

Significant changes to education in Kazakhstan, described elsewhere in this book, are underway. The intent of these reforms is to ensure that the country can build on its natural resources and talent with a view to playing a new regional and global leadership role (Rouse and Lapham, 2013a). However, the task of developing inclusion in Kazakhstan may be in tension with the recent reform agenda with its focus on elite educational institutions like the NIS schools and Nazarbayev University.

One aspect of the current reforms involves a large-scale retraining of tens of thousands of teachers across the country through the Centres of Excellence (see Chapter 5). The original brief for this programme focused on planning for the 'gifted and talented', rather than planning for diversity and individual differences, though in practice issues relating to diversity, marginalisation and inclusion have been drawn into this massive staff development initiative. It will be important to observe what impact this has on the capacity of schools to develop inclusive practices in the future.

Alongside the reforms, which could be seen as elitist, a paradoxical call for greater inclusion has been incorporated into a number of strategic policy documents, although there is not the same level of financial and political support for inclusion as there is for the elitist aspects of the reforms. Indeed, according to Makova and Sultanieva (2013), Kazakhstan has consistently overlooked the issues of social justice for vulnerable children by focusing on ambitious educational showcase projects. Although the inclusion of marginalised groups of children in mainstream educational institutions, at all levels, is essential to achieving human rights, social justice and EFA, inclusion is not an obvious feature of the vision for the new system. According to the OECD report:

> despite the law and derived policies promoting the education of children with disabilities, as yet they are not included in the broader discussions of educational reform. It is clear that this omission is incompatible with the concept of inclusive education and with the commitments Kazakhstan has made to the international community and even in its own constitution. (OECD 2009, 52)

Nevertheless, Kazakhstan has made commitments to various international initiatives and conventions which do promote inclusion and these commitments can be used to hold the nation to account in its achievements in educating all children.

The challenge of inclusive education is acknowledged in the 'State Programme of Education Development for 2011–2020', which states that 'inclusive education has not been developed yet' (MoES 2010, 9). According to the Ministry of Education and Science, as of May 2013 (MoES 2013, 151) there were about 151000 children with special educational needs (SEN) in the country, who had been assessed and classified by 56 psychological-medical-pedagogical commissions (PMPCs). These children are predominately served though a system of special educational institutions including: 106 special (*korekcionnie*) boarding schools, 1155 special groups on the premises of mainstream schools, 129 special psychological and special education establishments (*kabineti*), 558 speech therapy and 20 rehabilitation centres (MoES 2013, 151).

According to the United Nations Development Programme report on Kazakhstan:

> attempts of the state to provide the opportunity to children with psychological and physical disorders to study in general educational institutions are highly appreciated, however, the trend of spontaneous integration of children with non-disabled children, and without appropriate conditions for correctional support is observed in practice. (UNDP 2009, 47)

More recently, however, it is claimed that in 1653 mainstream schools, (including one Nazarbayev Intellectual School in Astana), special conditions for inclusive education have been created (MoES 2013). Kazakhstan is very slowly moving from separate (often residential) 'correctional schools' to the relocation of children with special needs to special groups and classes in mainstream schools. It could be argued that such co-location in a mainstream school is better than being placed in a segregated institution or educated at home. It may even be seen as a first step towards inclusion. However, as yet, there are few examples of inclusion in which mainstream schools have developed the capacity to accommodate a broad diversity of learners, so that all children can learn together. It is apparent that many schools are not ready for inclusion.

In addition, there are many children who do not attend any type of school. According to a recent report, over 8000 students study at home on individual programmes (National Report 2011, 30). This type of education typically involves a visit by a teacher for four to six hours a week for primary school children and eight to ten hours a week for secondary and high school students. The government is trying to assist this group of children by providing some learning facilities, although such provision can be very expensive. According to interviews with local officials (research study conducted for this book, 2013):

> In 2011 the city Department of Education allocated 165 215 thousand tenge to purchase educational equipment for 24 students receiving education at home. In 2012 83 more children will receive equipment for distant learning, the cost of the equipment is 36 400 thousand tenge . . .

> . . . there are 383 children who receive education at home. These children really do not have opportunities to go to school for many reasons. These children are provided with computers. . . . it depends on the health of students, for example, if a child has problems with vision, but has good sense of hearing, then the special-ised computers are supplied. (Official, Local Education Department, Location A)

Furthermore, the figures for children not in school, but being educated at home do not include those children not known to the authorities. UNICEF (2012) estimates that there are tens, if not hundreds of thousands of children with no access to schooling or home support in Kazakhstan, although the precise numbers are not known as many births are not registered (Rouse and Lapham 2013a).

In an attempt to address some of these shortcomings, the 'State Programme of Education Development for 2011–2020' has set the target that the propor-tion of schools that offer favourable conditions for inclusive education should increase from 30% in 2015 to 70% in 2020 (MoES 2010). The government's commitment to make 70% of schools inclusive by 2020 seems an ambitious target that requires finding solutions to the many barriers in the current system. The current challenge is to reform schools so that they can accom-modate a greater diversity of learners by adopting a more flexible curriculum and more child-centred approaches to education.

On the one hand, Kazakhstan has committed to follow the example of other countries through a combination of rights-based legislation, training, awareness campaigns and the reform of general education. At the same time, some voices in the educational community warn of the need to create condi-tions for inclusion in mainstream schools rather than focusing on a narrow standards agenda. There are also those who are resistant to change, who sup-port the current system of special education and who think that inclusion is not a good idea as children with disabilities are better educated in segregated facilities.

Another major obstacle is a widespread lack of knowledge among the civil servants, teachers and school administrators about inclusive educa-tion. According to a survey carried out by the Sandzh Centre (2008),[2] the idea of inclusive education provokes mixed reactions. The results of the survey, which included officials of education departments, staff working in child protection, administrators of integrated schools, teachers, professionals working with children with disabilities and representatives of the media, demonstrate that only a third of the respondents supported the idea of inclusive education. A quarter of the respondents expressed their opposition to inclusive education of children with special needs.

It appears as though efforts 'to create favourable conditions for inclusive education' may not be focusing on building capacity in mainstream schools, but rather relying on developing special provision in mainstream schools. For example, in an attempt to reduce the numbers of children out of school there has been an increase in the number of special classes within them. As one regional official explained:

> The most important problem we have is about children with disabilities. We are planning to open special classes for them. This is to ensure that these children are not left out of the general education program. In 2013–2014, we plan to open specialised classes at 9 schools. We already have results for the project in two schools, and it is planned to open 4 such classes. Nowadays three students are enrolled and study at specialised classes, in the school [name] there are 4 classes, in [name] there are 2 classes.

When asked about the conditions that had been created for such special classes, an interviewee replied:

> We have a centre for psychological and medical aspects in [Location C] . . . We submit an application to the regional centre, and then a specialised commission comes to us. After the arrival of the commission, they conduct interviews with students from the specialised classes. These children are treated for psychological aspects, for the medical aspects, followed by the identification of children in levels. The purpose of opening specialised classes is to attract children taught at home because of health problems, to schools to help these children expand their borders. (Official, Raion Department of Education)

Another official indicated a preference for special provision as a means to meet the national target for inclusion:

> As I said before, on this occasion we open specialised classes. According to our plan, by 2020 we should completely, 100% provide these classes for all students with disabilities. By 2015, we should reach 50% according to the plan. (Official, Raion Department of Education, Location C)

This increase in special class provision may build capacity for more children to receive some form of education, but if it remains separate within the mainstream setting, then it may not be the best way to develop inclusion.

With this increase in the provision of special classes, questions also have to be raised about the future roles of specialists such as defectologists and the role of specialist knowledge.

The interviews reveal that a special post has been created at the regional and/or district levels to provide support and co-ordination for inclusive education. The persistence of an expert model of support is apparent. As one respondent explained:

> In our Department of Education of [name] district I am the chief specialist, I'm responsible for the discipline . . . for how disabled children being taught . . . I'm responsible for them as well . . . (District Department of Education, Location C)

The evidence suggests that specialist knowledge continues to be associated with deficit views of children who are thought to need a 'special' provision so that their problems can be 'corrected':

> This is an ungraded school, school of mixed abilities children, we have 281 students, additionally I have been running for about 3 years a special needs group. These children are diagnosed with mental retardation and we have a special class for them to teach them individually. Psychologist, sociologist and teachers work with them individually. In my opinion, such classes need to be operated, so that when these children come to secondary school, they are better prepared; otherwise having been educated in a regular primary school they wouldn't have succeeded much . . . (School Director, School B, Location A)

Barriers to inclusion continue to be found in mainstream schools, and many claim they are not ready for inclusion. Schools are often physically inaccessible because of steps and stairs. Ramps and elevators are rare. Classrooms may lack sufficient space; they may have narrow doors, poor acoustics, and inadequate heat and lighting. Some schools do not have indoor sanitation and accessible toilets. In addition, schools have little flexibility within the curriculum or pedagogy. Children may be expected to keep pace in lessons that are often very didactic (Rouse and Lapham 2013a).

Rouse and Lapham suggest that unsuitable buildings may be used as an excuse for not adopting inclusion, but the real barriers are associated with the attitudes, beliefs, skills and knowledge of teachers and specialists (Sandzh Centre 2008). This problem is associated with the lack of a coherent national strategy for developing training on inclusion, but also because of the separation of the training of defectologists and other specialists from teachers. Many pedagogical universities do not prepare teachers to work in schools that are being asked to become more inclusive, and most departments of defectology are still preparing professionals to work in separate institutional settings. Thus, teachers are not prepared to implement inclusive education, nor are specialists prepared to act as resource persons in supporting teachers from regular schools in their daily tasks, and in involving parents to be an important part of the educational process of their child (OECD 2009).

The interviews reveal a range of other strategies to respond to children's needs. For example, School D accepts and attempts to educate people from all backgrounds, but a major strategy is keeping children back in grades until they are able to achieve a reasonable standard, as explained by the school director:

> . . . [children with very poor grades] do not have to leave the school. We can access external schools but if the child is under fourteen years old, he can spend up to three years in a single grade here. If, particularly after three years, the parents then write a request, explaining that the child can take employment, usually that is when they are fifteen or sixteen years old, then he can leave. (School Director, School D, Location B)

Not all strategies may work in the best interests of the child and there seems to be little understanding of the negative impact of grade retention.

Despite the substantial investments of international donors and successful pilot projects, few teachers have been trained in child-centred pedagogy, activity-based teaching, and collaborative learning. At best, the development of inclusive pedagogies is at an early stage. It is not surprising that many school directors have negative views about inclusion and some mainstream schools are reluctant to accept children with disabilities.

An interesting example of how expectations and the needs of children were addressed was presented in the 'selective' school E:

> When we hold an examination for this school, there are many pupils with their parents. It is like entering university. But we need to have selection; we need to take strong ones. There are pupils who cannot pass the examination because their teachers go to professional development courses and there are no lessons on Mathematics; this is no fault of the children that the school programme stops. In these cases, if there is a request from parents such as to give a chance to their child, we satisfy it, giving a chance to the child, presenting a probation term. Then we watch the changes in the student and if they can manage to learn, we leave it, if not, parents will take him to the school in their village. (School Director, School E, Location B)

There are challenges in developing the capacity of teachers and specialists to work in new ways, but there are examples of individuals and schools that have managed to take the first steps towards becoming more inclusive. For example, the broader social aspects of diversity are apparent in the work of some professionals. Social pedagogues can play an important role in protecting children's rights and in providing support and advice about children with special needs:

> My work is concerned with children's rights protection. We work in accordance with the regulatory legal basis on the protection of children's rights, so we are closely working with school's administration, teachers, parents, state regulatory bodies bearing responsibility for the protection of children's rights – adoption services, marriage services, services responsible for preparing the necessary documents. . . . So first we work to discover the situation in which children are . . . we obtain the information from class teachers. So first we are to uncover children's status – there are parentless children, there are the ones with physical handicaps, then we examine their living conditions . . . and in the third stage, we are doing the correction job . . . there are some families in difficulty, some parents are not fulfilling . . . and we are also holding meetings on how to avoid the children's rights abuse . . . all this makes part of our job. (Social Pedagogue, School B, Location A)

Some schools take a broad view of the types of support that children may need by working with and through the community. Interestingly, some respondents commented on how schools seek to address exclusion by providing access to information and communication technologies:

> Not everyone has a computer. Therefore, sometimes they come and ask to use internet in the classroom, and I allow it, because financial standing of country children's families is significantly lower than financial standing of urban children's families. (Deputy Director, School B, Location A)

There are also examples of schools dealing with some of the negative aspects of poverty by addressing nutritional needs. The importance of support and provision for disabled children and children from low socio-economic status families was further stressed:

> The State provides funds for nutrition for children with disabilities, as well as for children from low-income families. We are in control to ensure that the children receive food in due course . . . Kazakhs have a saying that 'a hungry child will not play with the one who is well-fed or laughing' If children always think about the food, then the studies will remain in the background. (Official, Raion Department of Education, Location C)

There are further examples of positive results arising from the work of social pedagogues in dealing with students' behaviour:

> One of our biggest results is that we had twelve students at risk three years ago ... these are the ones who are inclined to bypass the law and five children had a record at ODN [police department investigating crime committed by the underage]. Some were thieves, some for indecent public behaviour ... and one of our achievements is that ... during the last three years we have not had any student registered with the police ... in the last two years we have not had anyone classified as being in the risk group ... of children inclined to commit a crime. We are trying to fight such kind of behaviour since the early age, since the fifth form. (Social Pedagogue, School B, Location A)

Kauffman and Popova (2013) describe a local initiative in Petropavlovsk in which a disabled person and a small number of committed innovative educators have been able to create a school which takes risks and has been learning about inclusion as they enact it. School 13 has successfully been able to educate children who would have been segregated or excluded in the past. The lessons from such examples do not necessarily provide a template for how inclusion should be developed, but they do provide hope that small groups of committed people can create inclusive schools.

There are other examples of innovative practice in the region, many of which are associated with the growing influence of civic society through parent activism and newly established non-governmental organisations (NGOs). Such initiatives are at an early stage of development and may not yet necessarily meet the standards of international best practice, but they do demonstrate that there are opportunities for innovation, even within the constraints of current policies and practice.

Throughout the world, parents working together through civic society and NGOs play an important role in the development of policies and practices for disability, inclusion and social justice. In the former Soviet Union, the role of civic society and NGOs has developed substantially in recent years, albeit from a low level of activity. According to Makova and Sultanalieva (2013), NGOs and parent groups are likely to be extremely knowledgeable about a particular disability. Indeed, they may be better informed than some professionals and may run training and professional development, not only for parents but also for professionals. They may even participate in shaping state policies and provide feedback on government decisions. In Kazakhstan NGOs have experienced steady growth in the two decades since independence. There has been consolidation of the NGO sector, increased co-operation with the state, and the rise of organisations engaged in service provision and social development. Inevitably these developments challenge the power that professionals once had to make decisions, and new working relationships are beginning to emerge.

In 2006 the registration fee for NGOs was reduced, and tax privileges have greatly improved. In 2007 the government revoked the constitutional prohibition barring NGOs providing social services from receiving state funding (Markova and Sultanalieva 2013). These legislative steps have created favourable conditions for the further development of civic activism. Paradoxically, these reforms also created a way for progressive professional staff with sufficient power within state agencies to register spin-off NGOs with access to grant funding and freedom from the bureaucracy and inertia that can hamstring reform.

Conclusion

This chapter has considered some of the substantial and competing forces that are currently affecting efforts to develop inclusion in Kazakhstan. We conclude with some tentative suggestions that might help the development of inclusion in the future.

In Kazakhstan, knowledge and understanding of inclusion at all levels is limited and there is little public awareness of the negative economic, social and educational consequences of the segregation of disabled children. In spite of this, there are signs at the grass roots level that some progress has been made, but such progress is fragile as it relies on committed individuals and small groups of activists.

It is important to remember that Kazakhstan has signed a number of international conventions on disability and children's rights. It has also enacted its own legislation to support inclusion, even if there has been little progress on the implementation of these policies. The coming years will test the nation's commitment to educate all children as close to home as possible. Local NGOs, the media and the international community can monitor progress and hold the country to account where it fails to meet its commitments. However, attitudes to disability are still negative. There are few positive role models and there have been few media campaigns to raise public awareness. Some NGOs have begun to work with the media, but much needs to be done.

Meeting international commitments to inclusion will depend on a range of professionals adopting new ways of working. This will be particularly true of special educators, such as defectologists, some of whom are resistant to change. They will need reassurance that their skills, knowledge and expertise will still be required, but the focus of their work will have to change, as will their roles and responsibilities. Instead of only providing services directly to children, usually in separate places, they will need to share their skills with colleagues in mainstream schools, with parents and with the broader community in order to build capacity for inclusion. There are already examples of such new ways of working in the country, especially in co-operation with NGOs, but it needs to be spread more widely. In Kazakhstan and in other countries of the region, some defectologists are at the heart of the inclusion movement and are keen to redefine their professional roles and build on the positive elements of the tradition (Florian and Becirevic 2011).

Some examples of inclusive education can be learnt from other countries which have developed a practice of the common school for all – or comprehensive school. In the United Kingdom, for example, the term 'comprehensive school' is used in the context of secondary education and was established as a reaction to a system that had previously allocated children to different types of school on the basis of their attainment at the age of 11, and which reinforced social class-based inequalities. The comprehensive school movement in England is similar to the *Folkeskole* tradition in Denmark, the 'common school' tradition in the USA, and the unified compulsory education system in Portugal. It involves a single type of 'school for all' which serves a socially diverse community (Ainscow and Miles 2008).

Providing incentives for schools by ensuring that funding mechanisms support inclusion would also help. Historically these mechanisms favoured segregation, and in order to receive support children still need to be assessed by the PMPCs. The adoption of a more flexible assessment and classification system is essential and the functions and responsibilities of the PMPCs should be reviewed.

Some of the current forms of provision for children with special needs, such as education at home and long-term residential institutions are very expensive and produce poor outcomes. They are also a violation of many of the country's commitments. The human, material and financial resources that are currently spent on such separate provision could, over time, be reallocated to mainstream schools to support inclusion, but transitional short-term help would also be required. In addition to funding, schools also need reassurance that they will not be 'penalised' if they accept children who may not achieve as well as others. The adoption of a national system of inclusion indicators as proposed by the European Agency for the Development of Special Needs Education (Kyriazopoulou and Weber 2009; EADSNE 2011) might be helpful in this regard as it would enable schools to demonstrate their achievements with inclusion.

The current increase in the numbers of special classes in mainstream schools might enable more excluded children to receive some form of education closer to home, but it should not be seen as a long-term solution. Building capacity in mainstream schools is also required. This would not only benefit children who have been educated separately in the past, but would also benefit children currently in school who find the current inflexible curriculum, rigid approaches to assessment and didactic teaching methods ineffective.

Such changes to the curriculum, to assessment and to pedagogy could be relatively easily incorporated into the current reform and professional development efforts. Refocusing the emphasis within these programmes from 'gifted and talented' to diversity and inclusive pedagogy could improve teachers' ability to cope and bring benefits to many children. Serious consideration should be given to how teachers and specialists are trained and supported in their work for inclusion.

In much of the world, developments in inclusion have not been easy (Florian 2014). This chapter has pointed out many of the barriers to increasing participation for the most vulnerable children in Kazakhstan. Where inclusion has been successful, it has not only been mandated from the top (although a supportive policy framework helps), but it has also been driven from the bottom by committed activists. In many countries the trend to greater inclusion and to disability rights has been achieved when disabled people, parents and committed professionals work together. Although there is not yet a strong tradition of civic activism in the country, there are signs that such grass roots groups are forming. Their efforts to work alongside government and existing agencies should be encouraged, because improving education for marginalised groups brings economic, social and educational benefits for all.

REFERENCES

Ainscow, M., Booth, T. and **Dyson, A.** (2004). 'Understanding and Developing Inclusive Practices in Schools: A Collaborative Action Research Network. *International Journal of Inclusive Education*, 8:2, 125–40.

Ainscow, M. and **Miles, S.** (2008). 'Making Education for All Inclusive: Where Next?' *Prospects* 38, 15–34.

Constitution of the Republic of Kazakhstan (1995). Almaty.

Daniels, H. (ed.) (2005). *An Introduction to Vygotsky* (2nd edition). London: Routledge.

EADSNE (European Agency for Development in Special Needs Education) (2011). *Participation in Inclusive Education – A Framework for Developing Indicators.* Odense: European Agency for Development in Special Needs Education.

Florian, L. (2014). *The Sage Handbook of Special Education* (2nd edition). London: Sage Publishers.

Florian, L. and **M. Becirevic.** (2011). 'Challenges for Teachers' Professional Learning for Inclusive Education in Central and Eastern Europe and the Commonwealth of Independent States'. *Prospects*, 12:3, 371–84.

Kauffman, N. and **Popova, L.** (2013). 'Fools Rush In: A Path to Inclusive Education in Petropavlovsk, Kazakhstan'. In M. Rouse and K. Lapham (eds), *Learning to See Invisible Children: Inclusion of Children with Disabilities in Central Asia.* Budapest: Open Society Foundation/Central European Universities Press.

Kyriazopoulou, M. and **Weber, H.** (eds) (2009). *Development of a Set of Indicators – for Inclusive Education in Europe.* Odense: European Agency for Development in Special Needs Education.

Law of the Republic of Kazakhstan (2007). No. 319–III: On Education, 27 July 2007 (with changes and additions as on 24 October 2011).

Markova, M. and **Sultanalieva, D.** (2013). 'Parent Activism in Kazakhstan: The Promotion of the Right to Education of Children with Autism by the Ashyk Alem Foundation'. In M. Rouse and K. Lapham, (eds), *Learning to See Invisible Children: Inclusion of Children with Disabilities in Central Asia.* Budapest: Open Society Foundation/Central European Universities Press.

Miles, S. and **Singal, N.** (2009). 'The Education for All and Inclusive Education Debate: Conflict, Contradiction or Opportunity?' *International Journal of Inclusive Education*, 14:1, 1–15.

MoES (Ministry of Education and Science) (2010). 'State Programme of Education Development for 2011–2020, Approved by Presidential Order 1118 on 7 December 2010'. Astana: MoES. www.edu.gov.kz/en/legislation/state_program_of_education_development_in_the_republic_of_kazakhstan/state_program_of_education_development_in_the_republic_of_kazakhstan_for_20112020/ (retrieved 10 December 2011).

MoES (Ministry of Education and Science) (2013). *Statistics of the System of Education of the Republic of Kazakhstan: National Collection.* Rus. *Statistika Sistemy Obrazovaniya Respubliki Kazakhstan: Natsionalnyj sbornik.* Astana: MoES.

National Report (2011). *National Report on the Status and Development of Education of the Republic of Kazakhstan.* Astana: MoES.

OECD (Organisation for Economic Cooperation and Development) (2009). *Kazakhstan, Kyrgyz Republic and Tajikistan: Students with Special Needs and Those with Disabilities.* Paris: OECD.

Peters, **S.** (2004). *Inclusive Education: An EFA Strategy for All Children.* Washington, DC: World Bank.

Power, **D.**, **Bartlett**, **B.** and **Blatch**, **P.** (2004). Education in a Recovering Nation: Renewing Special Education in Kosovo. *Exceptional Children*, 17:4, 485–95.

Rouse, **M.** and **Lapham**, **K.** (2013a). *Learning to See Invisible Children: Inclusion of Children with Disabilities in Central Asia.* Budapest: Open Society Foundation/Central European Universities Press.

Rouse, **M.** and **Lapham**, **K.** (2013b). 'The Long Road to Inclusion'. *Journal of Social Policy Studies*, 11: 4, 439–56.

Sandzh Centre (2008). 'Assessment of Needs and Requirements of Vulnerable Groups of Children: Mapping Social Services and Institutions'. UNICEF and Ministry of Labour and Social Welfare. www.sange.kz/index.php/proekty/ (retrieved 11 January 2014).

Slee, **R.** (2001). *The Inclusive School.* London: Falmer Press.

United Nations (2006). *Convention on the Rights of Persons with Disabilities.* United Nations Website: www.un.org/disabilities/convention/conventionfull.shtml (retrieved 1 December 2013).

UNDP (United Nations Development Program) (2009). 'From Exclusion to Equality'. Kazakhstan: UNDP Report. www.undp.org/content/dam/kazakhstan/docs/InclusiveDevelopment/UNDP_KAZ_NHDR_2009.pdf (retrieved 11 December 2013).

UNESCO (United Nations Educational Scientific Cultural Organisation) (1990). *World Declaration on Education for All.* Paris: UNESCO.

— (1994). *The Salamanca Statement and Framework for Action on Special Needs Education.* Paris: UNESCO.

— (2005). *Guidelines for Inclusion: Enshuring Access to Education for All.* Paris: UNESCO.

— (2007). *Preparatory Report for the 48th Session of the International Conference on Education.* Paris: UNESCO. Appendix material available at, www.ibe.unesco.org/en/ice/48th-session-2008/conclusions-and-recommendations.html (retrieved January 2014).

— (2008). *Conclusions and Recommendations of the 48th Session of the International Conference on Education.* www.ibe.unesco.org/en/ice/48th-session-2008/conclusions-and-recommendations.html (retrieved 10 December 2013).

— (2009). *Policy Guidelines on Inclusion in Education.* Paris: UNESCO. UNESCO Website: unesdoc.unesco.org/images/0017/001778/177849e.pdf (retrieved 4 July 2013).

— (2010). *EFA Global Monitoring Report 2010: Reaching the Marginalized.* UNESCO. Paris and Oxford: Oxford University Press.

UNESCO-IBE (2007). 'Preparatory Report for the 48th ICE on Inclusive Education'. *The Third Workshop of the Commonwealth of Independent States (CIS) Community of Practice in Curriculum Development. Inclusive Education: The Way of the Future.* Minsk, Belarus, 29–31 October 2007. IBE/2007/RP/CD/06.

UNICEF (United Nations Children's Fund) (2007). *Education for Some More Than Others? A Regional Study on Education in Central and Eastern Europe and the Commonwealth States (CEE/CIS).* Geneva: UNICEF.

— 2012. *The Right of Children with Disabilities to Education: A Rights-Based Approach to Inclusive Education*. Geneva: UNICEF.
— (2005). *Children and Disability in Transition in CEE/CIS and Baltic States*. Florence: UNICEF Innocenti Centre.
— (2010). *Situation Analysis: Inclusive Education in CEE/CIS and the Baltic States*. Geneva: UNICEF CEE/CIS Regional Office.
— (2012). *The Right of Children with Disabilities to Education: A Rights-Based Approach to Inclusive Education*. Geneva: UNICEF.

NOTES:

1   Kazakhstan ratified the UN Disability Rights Convention in 2008. Furthermore, on 29 December 2008 President N. Nazarbayev signed the Law on Special Social Services. UNDP Report (2009, 39) available online at: www.undp.org/content/dam/kazakhstan/docs/InclusiveDevelopment/UNDP_KAZ_NHDR_2009.pdf (Retrieved 11 January 2014).

2   Sandzh Centre is a research organisation based in Almaty (www.sange.kz/). In 2008 Sandzh was commissioned by UNICEF to conduct research about the needs and requirements of vulnerable groups of children in Kazakhstan. The report was entitled 'Assessment of needs and requirements of vulnerable groups of children. Mapping social services and institutions' (2008), UNICEF and Ministry of Labour and Social Welfare. www.sange.kz/index.php/proekty/ (retrieved 11 January 14).

11 THE ROLE OF THE SCHOOL DIRECTOR in Educational Reform in Kazakhstan

David Frost (University of Cambridge, Faculty of Education)
Olena Fimyar (University of Cambridge, Faculty of Education)
Natallia Yakavets (University of Cambridge, Faculty of Education)
Darkhan Bilyalov (Graduate School of Education, Nazarbayev University)

Introduction

It is an interesting irony that, as education reform becomes more globalised, the focus of attention turns to the school as a unit of analysis. Governments increasingly see the importance of educational reform and are inclined towards interventionism, but whatever the policy aims, it is at the school level that change will occur or not. In most education systems, a school has a director, director or head who plays a pivotal role in not only responding to messages from government, but creating the organisational conditions that make change successful.

The following discussion arises from research conducted between 2011 and 2013. An initial exploration of the views of key policy-makers prepared the ground for interviews and discussions with school directors, their senior leadership teams, members of the teaching staff and a range of officials in local government agencies which support the schools. The research explored the role of school directors in the educational reform process in Kazakhstan and has enabled us to offer suggestions for policy and practice. In this chapter we draw on the leadership literature and available research evidence to illuminate roles, responsibilities and their significance in the reform process.

Support for reform in Kazakhstan is overtly informed by the academic discourse in the West. The increasingly international debate about education reform recognises school leadership as the key factor. A central theme in the professional discourse is that effective management is inadequate for the purposes of reform and improvement. It is argued that it is necessary for school directors to have the strategic vision and the leadership skills to be able to lead change and improvement. This view was supported in a milestone report from the Organisation for Economic Cooperation and Development (OECD) in 2008 which concluded that school leadership had become a policy priority internationally.

> School leadership . . . plays a key role in improving school outcomes by influencing the motivations and capacities of teachers, as well as the school climate and environment. Effective school leadership is essential to improve the efficiency and equity of schooling. (Pont et al. 2008, 2)

In the UK, the realisation that leadership is the key to success was reflected in the government's decision in 2000 to establish the National College for School Leadership. One of its most important programmes was the National Professional Qualification for Headteachers, intended to 'professionalise' school leadership. In the US however, it has taken a little longer for school leadership to move to centre stage as illustrated by this comment, in 2010, by the President of the Wallace Foundation:

> This matter of 'school leadership' was hardly a hot issue 10 years ago. Indeed, it was seen as a distraction, noticeably absent from most major school reform efforts. (de Vita 2010, 2)

It is commonly assumed that the term 'school leadership' refers to the work of the individual who is the most senior administrator in the school, the person typically referred to in the US as 'the school principal', in the UK as 'the headteacher' and in Kazakhstan, 'the school director'. However, this assumption constitutes a key problem in educational reform and can be traced back to the influence of theories derived from the administration science of the 1940s (Greenfield 1986). In order to understand the pivotal role that leadership plays in educational reform and improvement we need to examine the concept alongside, and to distinguish it from, the concepts of management and administration.

The distinguishing features of leadership

In the past, discussions of educational administration and management tended to emphasise technical and operational matters rather than educational vision (Greenfield 1986). This managerialist approach really began to take hold in many developed countries with the spread of decentralisation when headteachers and directors became accountable for budgets, staffing and buildings as well as educational outcomes. For many commentators the effects of excessive managerialism have been extremely negative. Hoyle and Wallace (2005) for example describe the huge financial costs and the diminishing job satisfaction for both teachers and senior staff. More importantly for this discussion is the limitation of management for the purposes of reform and improvement.

In the 1990s it was clear from school effectiveness research that leadership is a key factor in educational success (Sammons et al. 1994), but more recent studies are more sophisticated in their attempts to correlate particular aspects of leadership with measurable learning outcomes (Hallinger and Heck 1996; Silins and Mulford 2003; Leithwood *et al.* 2004). Increasingly studies such as these focus on the way the leadership exercised by the school director cannot be seen in isolation, but instead must be seen as part of a wider pattern of leadership practice. This is illustrated well by a substantial report in 2010 which focuses on the effects of collective or shared leadership (Seashore Louis et al. 2010). These studies have enabled us to see the effects of different leadership strategies and have been used to support recommendations such as this one from the report mentioned above:

> Distribution of leadership to include teachers, parents, and district staff is needed in order to improve student achievement. School and district leaders should, as a matter of policy and practice, extend significant influence to others in the school community as a foundation for their efforts to improve student achievement. Such an expansion of influence to others will in no way diminish their own influence. (Seashore Louis et al. 2010)

However, qualitative studies have helpfully focused on the nature of leadership *practice,* understanding of which is essential for leadership development. A review by Leithwood and Jantzi identified behaviours such as:

- setting direction by building consensus about around vision and strategy
- developing teacher capacity through supervision, support and modelling
- building collective teacher capacity through collaborative processes
- creating organisational structures that favour collaboration
- strategic management of resources. *(Leithwood and Jantzi 2005)*

It is often assumed that the main job of the school leader is to take decisions, but it is clear from lists such as the one above that the practice of leadership hinges on the exercise of influence. This has long been identified as the defining characteristic in the more generic literature on leadership as illustrated by the following extract from a classic book on leadership originally published in 1981 and reprinted many times.

> Most definitions of leadership reflect the assumption that it involves a process whereby intentional influence is exerted over other people to guide, structure, and facilitate activities and relationships in a group or organization.
> (Yukl 2010, 21)

This is echoed in an authoritative report for the American Educational Research Association (AERA) under the heading of 'What we know about successful school leadership'.

> At the core of most definitions of leadership are two functions: providing direction and exercising influence. Leaders mobilize and work with others to achieve shared goals. (Leithwood and Rheil 2003)

Providing direction and exercising influence have to be seen as the central planks of what is known as 'transformational leadership' (Burns, 1978) in which those with executive power use it to create the conditions that enable members of the organisation to work together to create the capacity for continual improvement. In his seminal text, 'Organisational culture and leadership' (1985), Edgar Schein argued that understanding culture is the key to the management of change and that the key task of the executive is to develop the culture of the organisation.

Arguably, schools are quite different from other organisations in that their goals are educational. That is to say that the key aim – to promote learning – can be pursued in part through the architecture and process of the school as an organisation. Resting on the foundations of ideas such as *the learning organisation* (Senge 1990), the concept of the *professional learning community* has emerged as a relatively coherent expression of the need to cultivate a particular set of values and norms which support the learning of the teachers and other members of the school community. Defining such a concept is bound to be challenging.

> There is no universal definition of a professional learning community but there is a consensus that you will know that one exists when you can see a group of teachers sharing and critically interrogating their practice in an ongoing, reflective, collaborative, inclusive, learning-oriented, growth-promoting way. (Stoll and Seashore Louis 2007, 2)

The edited volume from which this extract comes draws on work from the USA, Canada, Australia and the UK over a substantial period of time. It reinforces Schein's general dictum that the most important task for a senior leader is to build a culture conducive to change and development. Without this, educational reform is impossible.

Arguably, capacity building at the school level is essential for long-term educational reform (Gray et al. 1999). An explanation of the term often cited is that it is 'the collective competency of the school as an entity to bring about effective change' (Newmann et al. 2000). In order to build capacity, directors need to exercise leadership which aims to change the professional culture which is as much about values as it is about the norms and routines of practice.

The empirical research

A scoping study in Astana, the capital of Kazakhstan, generated an analytical framework for a more in-depth study conducted through two field visits to the three regional centres. We wanted to explore how the reform translates from the centre to the periphery and the challenges of disseminating key messages throughout the wider educational system. Research teams comprised colleagues from the University of Cambridge Faculty of Education, the Graduate School of Education at Nazarbayev University and Nazarbayev Intellectual Schools.

We visited different types of schools where we interviewed school directors, deputies, teachers and students. We also conducted focus group discussions and administered questionnaires with students and teachers. We interviewed representatives from the regional and local educational authorities, heads of Pedagogical Institutes and the national centres – entitled *Orleu* – which provide CPD programmes. Secondary data was obtained from official school documents such as the school portfolio, as well as some teaching materials developed by the staff and children. In this way we collected solid data on the perceptions of the implementation of educational policies in the three regions in Kazakhstan.

Analysis of the data enabled us to examine, among other things, the role of directors in relation to education reform. Our discussion of this topic is organised under the following thematic headings:

- the appointment and position of school directors
- the director's role in relation to the national reforms
- directors and organisational development
- directors and capacity building

This analysis is best understood as presenting the voices and reflections of school leaders and local actors on their role in relation to educational reforms.

The appointment and position of school directors

The education system in Kazakhstan is highly centralised with strict regulations and guidelines for public servants. Candidates for the post of school director must possess a relevant teaching qualification and a minimum of five years teaching experience. In addition to knowing the basics of pedagogy and psychology, candidates are also obliged to know the Constitution, the legal frameworks for education and children's rights and the anti-corruption laws.

The Ministry of Education and Science (MoES) specifies that a school director must:

- assure compliance with state standards and sanitary norms
- manage the assets and facilities of the educational institution and provide an annual financial report
- select and appoint teachers and support (technical) staff
- promote and monitor the continuing professional development of staff (including the induction of newly qualified teachers)
- supervise the Teachers' Council which carries out appraisals and can reward distinguished teachers and impose penalties within its jurisdiction
- represent the school to the wider community, parents and external authorities

Traditionally a school director's contract would be continuously extended, but an initiative in early 2012 requires that, after each five-year period, there must be competition for the school director's position (MoES 2012). In addition, appointments are subject to approval by the *Oblast* (regional) education department. This signals stricter control over the quality of school director appointments and a shift of authority from district to regional departments of education. Directors' salaries are well below OECD averages and hardly competitive within Kazakhstan, which poses a challenge for the recruitment of high quality professionals able to implement the reform agenda at grass-roots level. The level of directors' salaries varies depending on their qualifications, their classification as a teacher, and the location of the school.

School directors are accountable locally to authorities such as city (urban schools) and district (rural areas) departments of education. These departments report to regional departments of education. In general, Kazakhstan has a decentralised system of school funding that is under the discretionary control of a regional mayor. Performance of directors' work and their schools is assessed on the basis of: students' achievements in the Unified National Test, the participation by students and teachers in various regional, national and international competitions (Olympiads), their achievement of awards and certificates, the director's participation in seminars, workshops, conferences, publications in educational newspapers and journals, and the maintenance of the school's facilities.

Each director must compile a portfolio of evidence – a collection of legal documents, certificates and other artefacts that reflect performance. When the local department of education conducts inspections, the quality and content of the portfolio is a key factor in successful evaluation. The school director is subject to the so-called 'attestation' conducted every five years by the administration of a multiple choice tests and various documents about employee professional and educational activities (MoES 2011).

The Committee of Control in Education and Science, a sub-section of MoES, grants licenses to schools, conducts inspections, ensures compliance with state standards and directs the assessment of teaching personnel. Each region has such a department although some schools such as those for gifted children are assessed at the national level.

The director's role in relation to the national reforms

The school director is linked to the education system as a whole through different routes of communication depending on whether the school is in a rural or urban location (see above). There are considerable variations between City and District Departments in terms of material resources and the number of staff allocated to schools, because expenditure on schools is a function of what can be raised from local taxation.

The national education reforms are communicated to schools and regional authorities through the national programmes for development, presidential addresses and other official documents. Regional departments in their turn develop their plans based on the national agenda, while district and city departments inform their subordinate schools. Directors must then ensure that these plans are operationalised and that the implementation of the plans is monitored daily, weekly, monthly, quarterly, bi-annually and annually. The comments below provide insights into the planning process at different levels of the system.

> The government is preparing an educational programme. In this regard, we are also preparing our plans. We prepare our plans every three to five years, and every three years an adjustment is carried out. Any work starts with a good plan. (Official, Oblast Department of Education, Location B)

> Every quarter we gather all the information in the city and then pass it on to the Department of Education, where it is processed. (Official, City Department of Education, Location B)

A highly centralised and hierarchical communication system puts considerable pressure and responsibility on all involved.

> According to the plan, we meet every month, but in fact, we communicate 24/7. There are 540000 people in the region; including 25000 children in kindergartens; 98000 children in schools; 27000 children in colleges. We are responsible for those who are in educational institutions. That's why I should be available for 24 hours; I have to be aware of everything. (Official, Oblast Department of Education, Location C)

The pace of the reform, which many commentators describe as extremely fast, puts pressure on the schools and directors to be alert, informed and constantly communicating information to their staff. Regular meetings are a normal part of the schools' routines and take up most of the senior leadership team's time.

> Every Monday we have meetings with the director, where he tells us everything. At other times, he makes a telephone call to our cell phones. There is no problem. Any planned events are done by us, without bothering the director, but most of the time we always consult with the director. We bring our plans to the director and show him; ask for any comments and add any. We do monthly plans . . . we (vice directors and lead teachers) discuss it on Friday. On Monday, it is discussed with the director. By Tuesday, everything is already on the board and the information is delivered to the staff. (Vice Director, School D, Location B)

Some interviewees described a slightly different routine in which key messages about reforms appear on a screen.

> We . . . discuss it with teachers during the teacher meetings at six o'clock. For example, if there is a kind of strategy or reform that is sent from the top. ... there is a TV and lots of benches. We watch and see the information there; sitting and, afterwards, discussing. Even students come and sit there and watch the screen and listen to any type of reform that has been sent. (Vice Director, School D, Location B)

Such a scenario leaves the schools in the position of the passive recipient of the reforms, even though the reference to 'discussing', might imply a more participatory approach.

The director of School C explained the difference between planning meetings, staff meetings and urgent (five-minute) meetings, which are summoned by three consecutive school bells.

> We have administrative planning meetings every Friday. This is called the Administrative Council. This is where the planning for the forthcoming week's events takes place. Also every Monday we have a staff meeting, where we summarise the week's results. At times . . . there are urgent meetings of staff which we summon by giving 3 consequent bells. This is for example, when there is an urgent announcement for teachers. The teachers are well aware of this protocol and know that a 5-minute meeting is coming up. (Director, School C, Location A)

The director of School B has a new, more efficient approach for staff meetings. She has daily sessions with groups of subject teachers, class tutors or those responsible for extracurricular activities.

> And this year I have started to introduce 5-minute sessions every day with every group. For example, on Mondays these sessions include only class tutors before classes start; I get them all together and ask which issues they have. Discussions last about 10 minutes, it is enough. The next day I invite all the Heads of the Curriculum and Methodology Department, the other day only those leading extracurricular activities clubs, the fourth day only PE teachers. In such way it takes 5–10 minutes to learn about the overall situation. (Director, School B Location A)

These meetings sometimes feature comments from the school director about the need for teachers to work together as a team and appeals to accept the need for the reforms. As one director explained:

> Not all teachers understand the experiment in our Astana school. We get involved too much in our routine work and very often do not consider whether we need

reforms or not. That is why we are trying to explain to new teachers that reforms are necessary not only in Astana but in the whole of Kazakhstan. (Director N, Focus Group)

The role of school directors in relation to the national reforms tends to be primarily concerned with communicating reform objectives to the teachers. In this context the importance and frequency of various types of meetings is emphasised. The dominant mode of communication remains oral; internet / email communication is so far poorly developed and rarely used at the local level.

School directors and organisational development

The link between organisational structure and school leadership is pivotal. The traditions and mandates regarding organisational structures can inhibit or enable change. Developing the organisational structure of the school can also be a key strategy for directors who want to build the capacity for reform. Our study found organisational structures that differ according to the size of school and age group being taught, but there are some common features. For example, invariably the director has overall responsibility for the school, its staff, its pupils and the quality of teaching and learning. They therefore see themselves as providing strategic management.

Everyday operational control is exercised by deputy directors. The number of deputies varies, but it is common for an administrative team to comprise the director and four deputies, two for each shift. Typically there will be a deputy director for learning or academic affairs, a deputy director for upbringing and 'patriotic education' and a deputy director for maintenance work. In some case there are roles such as the deputy director for learning profiles (mainly for the purpose of 12-year schooling). In one of the case study schools there is a deputy director for innovation and development. In large schools such as a gymnasium, there is likely to be a post of deputy director for international affairs.

There is commonly a middle tier of administration consisting of the heads of methodological units, which are similar to subject leaders and curriculum coordinators found in some other countries. They are responsible for coordinating the work of a cluster of teachers of particular subjects such as Sciences, Humanities and Languages. Usually the head of a methodological unit is a very experienced teacher who is appointed by the director for five years.

Classroom teachers' careers progress through three levels of classification according to assessments of their experience and the results of attestation. There are also teaching assistants especially in subjects such as Biology and Chemistry.

An example of an organisational structure is represented in the diagram below (figure 1).

Figure 1: Organisational Structure: Rural School 1

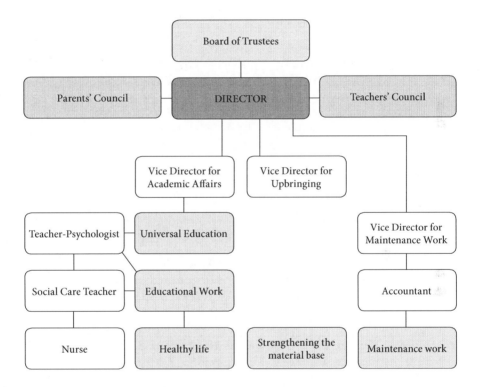

The director, together with deputy directors and heads of methodological units represent the senior leadership team (SLT) of the school. Generally, SLT discuss school-level decisions but if something requires urgent action, the director will make the decision alone.

The representation above is reinforced by the following extract from one of the school's strategy documents.

Administrative leadership is executed by the director and deputies. The main function of the director is to co-ordinate the efforts of all participants in the educational process through the Teachers' Council, Advisory Board, General School Assembly. Deputy directors implement primarily operational management of the educational process and implement motivational, informational, analytical, planning and predictive, organisational, executive, control and adjustment, evaluative and productive functions. (Educational Strategy document, School C, Location A)

Boards of Trustees have recently been introduced in a number of schools as part of the national development plan for education (MoES 2010) which includes the goal to extend school boards to all schools by 2020. Many schools have these boards already, but they are quite different in nature to governing bodies typically found in countries such as the UK. In Kazakhstan, Boards do not have the power to make strategic or financial decisions except for dispensation of the very small amount of sponsorship and 'collected' money. One director commented:

We were told to create the Board at our school. We did so; we have parents involved. But we did not see the value – nobody is willing to make financial contributions. Then, I can be blamed for collecting money from parents – it can be perceived incorrectly . . . So, we had several meetings but there is not much to talk about. (Director, School D, Location B)

It seems that, so far, boards are not intended to support directors or to hold them to account. They do not enable shared responsibility or decision making, nor do they take lift the financial liability from the director's shoulder.

Another important feature of the school organisation is the Teachers' Council. The deputy director of a large urban school explains:

The top level management position in our school is a Teachers' Council, rated even higher than the director of the school because the director should listen to the decision of the teachers' meeting. (Vice Director, School G, Location C)

The overall impression is one in which the director has very little scope for leading organisational development. In general, strict regulations imposed on schools determine organisational structures and limit the scope for initiative:

Unfortunately, we have specific orders, specific law and requirements, under and in accordance with which we have to operate. There are directors who want to introduce something interesting, and they can do this after discussion. We have a specialised council, where we discuss the issue and if such innovation meets our laws and requirements, it can be realised. But . . . directors cannot completely change the school…the nature [structure] of organisation. (Official, Department of Education, Location C)

Directors have to deal with, and are sometimes overwhelmed by, a great deal of routine administration. Numerous checks, inspections, letters and requests from education, cultural and sports units at local municipalities place a significant burden on directors. Their time is also taken up with what are effectively matters of school maintenance:

> . . . we have too many other issues to deal with, such as I have an autonomous boiler room and coal stokers to take care of. Winters are really cold; in December the temperature dropped to minus 40 degrees, so under such conditions we were forced to be on watch round the clock to prevent breakdowns from happening or, God forbid, radiators freeze. One option would be to introduce a new position to the school staff like a Commercial Director/Maintenance Officer who would deal with such issues. (Director, School C, Location A)

It is clear that the lion's share of the director's time is spent on administrative issues and the maintenance of the building, that is to say all that would be covered by the Russian term '*Khozyastvennaya deyatelnost*' (*Хозяйственная деятельность*).

An additional pressure stems from the procurement regulations which make directors vulnerable in their dealings with affairs with commercial suppliers. Directors are commonly obliged to pay fees for essential services in advance, but many are afraid to do so because of cases where the supplier has subsequently failed to supply goods on time. One school director was accused of violating procurement procedures which carries a substantial financial penalty.

> This job [procurement] is placed upon us. There are many problems with it. So, I've placed competition for school tables. A small firm from Almaty (2000 km away) won. So I transfer him the money, but I am very afraid. He might never look at the contract . . . He might just get lost. What he supplied to me was not good. I did not want to take it, but he had submitted the lowest price. Later I placed the competition for a school uniform. What they delivered was four or five different types of poor quality dresses. I did not want to take them. They said go ahead sue us; you've paid us and we've delivered. (Director, School E, Location B)

There is a clear impression at different levels of the system that procurement is a major distraction from the director's leadership:

> I think the work on procurement is not needed for the director . . . this should be done by special economic departments in the schools, but now the directors are like heads of household. The director is also an accountant. I think, if he did not deal with these matters, he would be a real teacher. The director is now responsible for 5–6 things at the same time. (Official, Oblast Department of Education, Location B)

In decentralised systems such as that in the UK, directors have been able to develop their organisations in ways that enable them to delegate responsibilities for the building and associated procurement processes to staff that have that particular expertise.

In Kazakhstan, the centralised state hierarchical organisational structure shapes the role of directors and limits opportunities for them to decide what leadership model or organisational structure to adopt in order to try to implement innovations. Added to this, the burden of administrative work focussed on maintenance, procurement and endless reporting leave little space for directors to focus on the quality of educational experience provided by the school.

School directors and capacity building

It seems clear that directors have little scope for organisational development. However, there are other ways in which they can build the school's capacity for reform.

The schools we visited in this study seemed to have strong professional cultures with directors working hard to cultivate a supportive environment for teachers.

> It is important to have a stable psychological atmosphere, mutual understanding and avoid conflicts. We consult with each other and take collective decisions. (Director, School F, Location C)

> . . . the ability to activate all the levers, such us creating conditions and a favourable working atmosphere, encouragement and incentives for teachers, creating psychologically healthy climate which is of no small importance...(Director, School B, Location A)

The idea of creating a supportive climate for teachers is clearly of concern to directors. However, there is a distinction between a climate for maintaining standards and a climate conducive to innovation and reform. What is perhaps more promising is the extent to which directors involve colleagues in discussion.

> . . . the director does consult with teachers. She considers our advice . . . We listen, may give our remarks and the administration takes them into consideration. (Teacher Biology, School E, Location B)

In some case study schools planning and open discussion meetings are routine.

> Every Monday we have meetings with the director, where he tells us everything. Any planned events are done by us, without bothering the director, but most of the time we always consult with the director...We do monthly plans. For our monthly plan, we (vice directors and lead teachers) discuss it on Friday. On Monday, it is discussed with the director. By Tuesday, everything is already on the board and the information is delivered to the staff. (Vice Director, School D, Location B)

Directors in some case study schools attach importance to teacher's professional development, practitioner research and teacher leadership. The enhancement of teachers' professional competency is prioritised and viewed as a key factor for successful implementation of the nationwide educational reforms.

> . . . I would say, the reforms of the teachers should be organised first of all. As for certification, the skill enhancement, all of them are taking place, but mainly the teachers are not prepared for it. It should be faster . . . the reforms are accepted . . . but it is not entirely clear among the teachers. (Vice Director, School F, Location C)

A respondent from another school commented on the difference between in-house support for professional development and programmes provided by national agencies.

> We conduct various types of seminars here, but usually these are held by the regional professional development centres. There are a lot of programmes from different places . . . and teachers always attend them. (Vice Director 2, School D, Location B)

The provision of professional development programmes is centralised across the country. The *Orleu* – the In-service Teacher Training Institute - is the primary organisation which delivers training according to state requirements. Every five years teachers must go through re-attestation and one of the requirements is to undertake training courses provided by the *Orleu*.

> In our city there are educational centres, and so teachers visit them. Every five years, our teachers are trained. When the teacher is trained, there are seminars, and there in the workshops a discussion is held on how to implement new reforms. (Vice Director, School F, Location C)

An important forum where professional discussions take place is the school's Methodological Council:

> . . . we discuss anything that concerns the quality of education or when teachers return to school after having attended professional development courses, they firstly meet in their methodological groups by subject and share. Once it's been discussed, they present to the Methodological Council. This council is managed by the Head of Curriculum and Methodology. Once they have discussed innovations in the Council meeting, they formulate the problem/question to address and present it at teachers' meeting . . . this is where we scrutinise it. Each teacher's meeting features the problem that has been identified and recommendations are made. (Director, School B, Location A)

Teachers take an active part in their own professional development by creating an individual portfolio which includes a compulsory personal development plan. They also publish collections of student's work and organise events for peer-learning and sharing the best practice.

> . . . we are sharing with each other what students have already learnt, what things we can ask them. And the atmosphere in our school is pretty good, there are no such teachers who go into their shell. (Teacher Biology, School D, Location B)

This sharing of personal and professional experiences with fellow teachers within the school develops collegiality and enhances the professional culture. Our study also includes examples of teacher-leaders who are perceived to be democratic, giving opportunities for their peers to make decisions and lead.

> Yes, they are democratic. They are on the same level. They don't have the attitude of "I know everything! I have more experience" and so on, everything is quite levelled up. Where issues arise between heads of departments and teachers, we bring them into dialogue and join the dialogue with them. Sometimes one fails to understand another or something. We prevent this from happening. (Director, School B, Location A)

The data indicates that directors' support for teachers' professional development, both in and outside the schools, is influenced to some extent by the state requirements of professional attestation. Directors commonly believe that teachers should recognise the necessity for reform and they should seek to acquire new ways of thinking which challenge their views and perceptions. There seems to be some evidence that directors are aware of the need to cultivate particular kinds of professional cultures although this is not necessarily manifest in the form of explicit capacity building strategies.

Implications and recommendations

On the basis of this brief discussion of our data analysis, we can now put forward a number of suggestions for policy and practice. These are presented here as possible starting points, or an agenda for discussion. On the whole, directors see themselves, together with their senior leadership team members, as strategists, but there are a number of key ways in which their strategic interventions could be enhanced.

Extending the level of autonomy for directors

In general, it is clear that, in comparison with their counterparts in Australia, North America and the UK, directors in Kazakhstan are less autonomous. Many important decisions affecting the day-to-day operation of the school and its long-term development are currently taken by agencies and bodies external to the school. To realise fully the goal of reform it may be helpful to pursue a few steps further the trend toward de-centralisation that is already discernable.

Scope for organisational development

Directors might be able to create more effective climates for reform if they had greater scope for organisational development. Currently directors do not feel able or entitled to reconstruct their schools as organisations. This puts a limit on the extent to which they can influence the professional culture and mobilise their staff for maximum effectiveness. To maximise their influence, directors and their senior colleagues need to be able to put in place structures and processes that meet the needs of the individual school.

Relief for the administrative burden

If directors were free to reconstruct their organisations, they might be able to distribute some of the routine administrative tasks which currently act as a constraint on their capacity for strategic intervention. One director from a mainstream school expressed this problem as follows.

> In my experience as a young school director, 99 per cent of our work is spent on routine work and reporting to central and local authorities. (Director T, Focus Group)

There may be more that can be done at national and regional levels to reduce this burden to enable directors to concentrate on leading learning.

Addressing the issue of procurement

This could be seen merely as a sub-set of the preceding point, but it is distinctive in that it is not just about the time taken up by the process of procurement, but also about the anxiety and fear and the sense of powerlessness that the current process generates. Directors should be held to account of course, but it might be more productive for the purposes of reform if such accountability were to be more focused on the school's effectiveness and the level of progress with the reform agenda.

Developing the provision of internal support for professional development

We have noted some good examples within the case study schools of discussion-based activities that support teachers' professional development and we suggest that the reform agenda could be taken forward more effectively if this could be allowed to develop. This is not just a matter of formal seminars and workshops, but could also include such processes as teachers' meetings, coaching, practitioner research circles and other opportunities for reflection and dialogue focused on practice.

Extending shared leadership

There is evidence that some directors see the involvement of teachers and others in decision-making and processes of consultation as key dimensions of successful leadership. This corresponds with experience and research findings documented in the western literature on educational improvement (see above). Authentic reform may depend on the extent to which all teachers, students and ancillary staff feel a sense of ownership, belonging and moral purpose as members of a learning community.

Facilitating the professionalisation of leadership

We have argued that successful school leadership involves strategic planning aimed at influencing the nature and quality of professional practice. By exercising such influence, directors seek to mobilise members of staff so that they are more likely to collaborate in the enterprise of continuous change and improvement. The ability to undertake strategic planning and action has to be nurtured. It cannot be captured adequately by a set of regulations or in a 'manual for school directors'. Rather it depends on the existence of what might be called a *dialogic infrastructure*, that is to say a set of structures and processes which provide directors with opportunities to engage in professional discourse. This should not be equated with prescriptive training, but rather as opportunities for directors and other senior leaders to meet for the purposes of sharing practice and discussing key issues in the practice of leadership. It is encouraging to see the beginning in Kazakhstan of academic courses for leaders such as the one to be provided by the NU Graduate School of Education. This will serve to enrich the discourse by allowing the scholarship of leadership to permeate the system, but because of the problem of scale, such courses cannot be relied upon to provide all directors with the opportunity to engage in a high quality professional discourse about educational leadership.

Conclusion

The evidence on which this account is based is not exhaustive. Nevertheless, when what is known about school leadership in the English-speaking world is used to analyse the data we have obtained, a clear agenda for discussion emerges. We hope that this will be used as a starting point for a robust debate about the role of the school director. It may also help to lay the foundations of a leadership development programme which could play a significant role in taking education reform in Kazakhstan to the next level.

There are, however, legitimate concerns about the pitfalls of policy borrowing (Halpin and Troyna 1995; Steiner-Khamsi 2004), and the appropriateness of applying an analytical framework that might be said to be alien to the particular cultural context in view must be considered. However, we can draw comfort from the fact that we are working within a context where internationalisation is an explicit policy objective. The research can be seen therefore as contributing to the international conversation about school leadership and education reform. We hope that we have helped practitioners, researchers and policy makers to join in this conversation for the long-term benefit of the young people who will be educated in schools in Kazakhstan in the future.

REFERENCES

Agency for Statistic of Republic of Kazakhstan (2013). 'Average monthly salary according to the types of economic activity'. www.stat.kz.

Badalov, U. (2012). 'The Oralmans: Migration of Ethnic Kazakhs from China to Europe'. www.thewashingtonreview.org/articles/the-oralmans-migration-of-ethnic-kazakhs-from-china-to-europe.html (in English, retrieved 6 August 2013).

Bokayev, B., Zharkynbekova, Sh., Nurseitova, Kh., Bokayeva, A., Akzhigitova A. and **Saniya Nurgalieva, S.** (2012). 'Ethnolinguistic Identification and Adaptation of Repatriates in Polycultural Kazakhstan'. *Journal of Language, Identity & Education*, 11:5, 333–43.

Bridges et al. (2012). *Internationalisation and Reform of Secondary Schooling in Kazakhstan.* Unpublished report. Cambridge: University of Cambridge Faculty of Education.

Burns, J.M. (1978). *Leadership.* New York: Harper and Row.

Daly, J.C.K. (2008) 'Kazakhstan's Emerging Middle Class – A Silk Road Paper'. Washington, ML: Central Asia-Caucasus Institute & Silk Road Studies Program / A Joint Transatlantic Research and Policy Center.

De Vita, C. (2010). 'Four Big Lessons from a Decade of Work in Report of the Wallace Foundation's National Conference, Washington, 2009'. *Education Leadership: An agenda for school improvement.* Washington, ML: The Wallace Foundation.

Gray, J., Hopkins, D., Reynolds, D., Wilcox, B., Farrell, S. and **Jesson, D.** (1999). *Improving Schools: Performance and Potential.* Buckingham: Open University Press.

Greenfield, T.B. (1986). 'The Decline and Fall of Science in Educational Administration'. *Interchange*, 17:2, 57–80.

Hallinger, P. and **Heck, R.** (1996). 'Re-assessing the Director's role in School Effectiveness: A Review of Empirical Research, 1980–1995. *Educational Administration Quarterly*, 32:1, 5–44.

Hargreaves, D.H. (2011). 'System Redesign for System Capacity Building'. *Journal of Educational Administration*, 49:6, 685–700.

Hoyle, E. and **Wallace, M.** (2005). *Educational Leadership: Ambiguity, Professionals and Managerialism.* London: Sage Publications.

International Crisis Group. (2011). 'Central Asia: Decay and Decline'. *Asia Report* 201, 47 (3 February). Bishkek/Brussel: International Crisis Group.

Leithwood, K. and **Jantzi, D.** (2005). 'A Review of Transformational School Leadership Research: 1996–2005'. *Leadership and Policy in Schools,* 4:3, 177–99.

— (2006). 'Transformational School Leadership for Large-Scale Reform: Effects on Students, Teachers, and their Classroom Practices'. *School Effectiveness and School Improvement.* 17:2, 201–27.

Leithwood, K. and **Riehl, C.** (2003). 'What We Know about Successful School Leadership'. Philadelphia, PA: Laboratory for Student Success, Temple University.

Leithwood, K., Seashore Louis, K., Anderson, S. and **Wahlstrom, K.** (2004). *How Leadership Influences Student Learning.* Center for Applied Research and Educational

Improvement and Ontario Institute for Studies in Education. www.wallacefoundation. org/wf/KnowledgeCenter/KnowledgeTopics/EducationLeadership/.

MoES (Ministry of Education and Science) (2011). 'Order of the Minister of Education and Science on Establishing Rules for Attestation of Pedagogical Staff'. No. 119, 31 March 2011.

— (2012). 'Rules for Competitive Substitution of Heads of State Institution of Secondary Education'. No. 57, 21 February 2012.

— (2010). 'State Programme of Education Development for the Republic of Kazakhstan for 2011–2020'. Astana: MoES.

Newmann, **F.M.**, **King**, **M.B.** and **Youngs**, **P.** (2000). 'Professional Development that Addresses School Capacity: Lessons from Urban Elementary Schools'. *American Journal of Education*, 108:4, 259–99.

Pont, **B.**, **Nusche**, **D.** and **Morman**, **H.** (2008). *Improving School Leadership, Volume 1: Policy and Practice*. Paris: OECD.

Sammons, **P.**, **Hillman**, **J.** and **Mortimore**, **P.** (1995). *Key Characteristics of Effective Schools: A Review of School Effectiveness Research*. Report by the Institute of Education for the Office or Standards in Education. London: OFSTED.

Seashore Louis, **K.**, **Leithwood**, **K.**, **Wahlstrom**, **K.L.** and **Anderson**, **S.E.** (2010). *Investigating the Links to Improved Student Learning: Final Report of Research Findings*. Washington, ML: The Wallace Foundation.

Schein, **E.** (1985) *Organizational Culture and Leadership*. San Francisco: Jossey-Bass.

Senge, **P.** (1990) *The Fifth Discipline: The Art and Practice of the Learning Organization*. New York: Doubleday.

Silins, **H.** and **Mulford**, **B.** (2003). 'Leadership for Organisational Learning and Improved Student Outcomes – What Do We Know?' *Cambridge Journal of Education*, 33:2, 175–95.

Stoll, **L.** and **Seashore Louis**, **K.** (eds) (2007). *Professional Learning Communities: divergence, depth and dilemmas*. Maidenhead: McGraw Hill / Open Univesity.

WHO/UNICEF (2013). 'Progress on Sanitation and Drinking Water: 2013 Update'. www.apps.who.int/iris/bitstream/10665/81245/1/9789241505390_eng.pdf.

Yukl, **G.** (1994). *Leadership in organizations*. New Jersey: Prentice Hall.

12 THE ROLE OF THE TEACHER IN EDUCATIONAL REFORM IN KAZAKHSTAN: Teacher Enquiry as a Vehicle for Change

Colleen McLaughlin (University of Sussex and University of Cambridge, Faculty of Education), Ros McLellan (University of Cambridge, Faculty of Education), Michael Fordham (University of Cambridge, Faculty of Education), Andrew Chandler-Grevatt (University of Sussex), Alison Daubney (University of Sussex)

Introduction

The earlier chapters in Part One of this book have characterised in detail the process of educational reform. The reforms have been ambitious and recently have been very fast-paced. They have also largely been based on a centre to periphery model of change. The Nazarbayev Intellectual Schools (NIS), which are seen as being at the forefront of innovation or as 'a beta site for innovation, experimentation and evaluation of educational practices' (Ruby and McLaughlin in Chapter 14), have been sites of rapid and large-scale change. This chapter will examine a programme of work which focused on using collaborative learning through action research as a 'bottom up' model of development. The chapter reports on the first year of the work and draws on data from an evaluation conducted by Alison Daubney and Andrew Chandler-Grevatt, as well as the reflections of those involved in the conduct and leadership of this programme – Richard Byers, Kate Evans, Michael Fordham, Colleen McLaughlin, Ros McLellan, Jenny Rankine, Jenny Richards and Jan Schofield.

Rationale for adopting a collaborative enquiry-focused approach

There were many reasons for adopting this approach in the NIS schools: the model of change being used by NIS, a small-scale qualitative study of teachers in Kazakhstan; the international evidence on teacher professional development, and a long tradition of working with enquiry-based approaches by the team and the Faculty of Education at the University of Cambridge. The model of educational reform being adopted in Kazakhstan was built on the twin foundation stones of collaboration and partnership. Both NIS and Nazarbayev University (NU) worked by partnering with international organisations with whom they collaborated very closely. They chose a field and then sought suitable international partners (see Chapter 4), an approach that embodied their attitude to change. In secondary education they chose the University of Cambridge, which involved both Cambridge International Examinations and the Faculty of Education, as their partners.

A second factor was the small-scale qualitative study conducted by the Deputy Director of the NIS schools as part of her doctoral studies (Ayubaeva 2012). She had undertaken a study of reflective practice in NIS schools, since this had been a recently adopted programme. NIS had set out to develop a more student-centred model of learning and to shift the emphasis from teaching to learning, introducing many programmes that aimed to develop the agency and independence of teachers. Ayubaeva's study showed 'that the teacher-participants' experience of engaging in self-analysis, carrying out reflection-in-action, collecting students' feedback and some degree of collaboration with peers helped the teacher-participants to become more confident about their ability to promote student-centred learning and deal with problematic situations that arise in teaching.' (ibid.) Therefore there was a desire to build on the momentum that had developed. The study also identified the central importance of collaboration to the development of practice in NIS schools and the need to create new patterns of interaction and in doing so interrupt a competitive dynamic that had inadvertently grown up. In Soviet times there had been interesting examples of collaboration that had since died out. There was also the desire to evaluate how the teachers were coping with the new curriculum, recently introduced by Cambridge International Examinations (CIE) in concert with NIS. The perspective of the teachers was an aspect that NIS and CIE were keen to understand.

The third key factor in adopting this approach is the body of evidence on the important features of teachers' continuing professional development learning (CPDL) (Cordingley 2013), and in particular the evidence for the use of research and enquiry. Cordingley (2013) summarises the factors identified in research studies as key to effective teacher learning. These are:

- Using specialist external expertise in a sustained way
- The giving and receiving of structured peer support within the school
- A professional dialogue rooted in evidence
- A focus on *why* things do/do not work as well as on *how* they work, involving an integration of theory and practice
- Sustained enquiry-oriented learning undertaken usually over two terms or more
- Learning from observing the practice of others
- The use of tools and protocols to help learning.

These elements are confirmed in the 2013 Royal Society for the Arts (RSA)/ British Educational Research Association (BERA) Inquiry into the impact on teachers of engaging in enquiry-based approaches to teacher learning and practice. The conclusion drawn from examining this body of evidence was that we needed to build an approach based on enquiry-oriented learning and leadership. Therefore the programme aimed to create the conditions for enquiry-rich, collaborative learning and teaching.

The fourth main driver was the tradition of working with teacher learning through an enquiry-based collaborative approach, which was a thread running through practice in the Faculty of Education, the partner in innovation with NIS. Stenhouse's (1975b) view of the teacher as an 'extended professional' who was duty-bound to research their own teaching and to continue to learn about the curriculum and practice throughout their career, was a bedrock of much work in the Faculty. Stenhouse viewed teachers as the prime agents of practice and evaluation. Elliott and Norris summarise the argument well in reviewing Stenhouse's work:

> [Because] it was the teacher who held the keys to the laboratory, it was the teacher who could mount educational experiments in the classroom, it was the teacher who would, maybe with the help of others, marshal and interpret the evidence and it was the teacher who had to learn from the experience of classroom action research if genuine and sustainable education improvement were to be possible. (Elliott and Norris 2012, 3)

Action research as a strategy

The two definitions below identify the main characteristics of action research and they also encapsulate the different emphases of the action research tradition in education.

> The research needed for social practice can best be characterized as research for social management or social engineering. It is a type of action-research, a comparative research on the conditions and effects of various forms of social action, and research leading to social action. Research that produces nothing but books will not suffice. (Lewin 1946, reproduced in Lewin 1948, 202–3)

> Action research is simply a form of self-reflective enquiry undertaken by participants in social situations in order to improve the rationality and justice of their own practices, their understanding of these practices, and the situations in which the practices are carried out. (Carr and Kemmis 1986, 162)

The common elements are the emphasis on reflection on practice, similar to the work of Schön (1983), the undertaking of the research by practitioners and the focus on the practice of teachers. The definition by Carr and Kemmis includes justice as a key purpose. This is reflective of the different emphases of traditions: some have emphasised justice and social change, some have emphasised the understanding and the educational change. Through the use of action research we aimed to develop reflection, to influence the development of practice thorough systematic enquiry, to 'improve the rationality and justice' of the teachers' practices and to generate knowledge about the implementation of the new curriculum.

This use of action research as a curriculum development and innovation strategy is well known and many have argued that it is essential to the development of innovative practice (cf. Altrichter and Posch 2011). The eclectic nature of action research was reflected in a meta-analysis of 46 action research publications carried out by Somekh and Zeichner (2009), who identified five non-exhaustive variations by which action research, as a global phenomenon, has been localised.

1. Action research in times of political upheaval and transition
2. Action research as a state-sponsored means of reforming schooling
3. Co-option of action research by Western governments and school systems to control teachers
4. Action research as a university-led reform movement

5. Action research as locally-sponsored systemic reform sustained over time. (Somekh and Zeichner 2009, 12–18)

Within the context of Kazakhstan, variations 1 and 2 are of particular importance, with the government taking an active role in driving educational reforms that are designed to ease transition and promote national economic progress following the collapse of the Soviet Union (Yakavets 2012; Fimyar and Kurakbayev 2012). The programme drew directly on two partnerships: the School-University Partnership for Educational Research (SUPER), which had been operating in the Faculty of Education for over a decade and the work of HertsCam, a partnership initiated by David Frost which involved Hertfordshire schools. Both of these partnerships focused on the construction of the conditions for teachers to engage in enquiry and research to develop practice.

The programme

The programme for action research was viewed as a long term strategy, extending over three years. The programme had been running for a year when the data presented here was collected. There were three teams involved from Cambridge and they consisted of school-based colleagues from the SUPER partnership, plus colleagues from the Faculty of Education. Pairs or trios of mixed school and Faculty colleagues worked with two NIS schools in each region of Kazakhstan. At the time of starting this programme seven NIS schools were open, and an eighth opened in February 2013. There will be fifteen schools open by the end of 2014. In the first year (2013) there were whole cohort meetings to start the programme followed by regional workshops, and the year culminated in a whole cohort meeting and presentation at a NIS conference. Each school appointed a Teacher Research Coordinator (TRC) who led the in-school development alongside the Senior Leadership Team. This structure has been used successfully in the SUPER schools (McLaughlin et al. 2006). During this time the schools engaged in two cycles of action research. The data were collected through the following methods:

- Interviews from a sample of four schools with:

  - Head teachers
  - TRCs
  - Teachers doing action research projects

- Students involved in action research projects
- Members of the Cambridge team.

- Focus groups/discussions with all involved and observations of those involved.

Aspects involved in development

In our analysis of the data, three key emergent themes were identified as interacting and affecting practice within our programme, and these are shown in Figure 1. We found using these themes helpful as a lens through which to view what was happening, in particular because they were descriptive rather than judgemental or evaluative and because they helped us to develop a more contextually sensitive approach.

Figure 1

Cultural aspects

Reform aspects

Nature of professional
learning and practice

The next sections of this chapter discuss these three key elements, then analyse of a number of factors that appear to facilitate the implementation of the programme. Finally, the perceived benefits of the programme are outlined.

Cultural aspects influencing perceptions of pedagogy and professional practice

In understanding the data and reflecting on the practices it was useful to use Hofstede et al.'s (2010) cultural dimensions theory and to draw on some (but not all) of the dimensions that he identifies. The cultural dimensions theory describes the effects of a society's culture on the values of its members, and how these affect behaviour. The dimensions that Hofstede et al, (2010) delineate as significant are the following:

1. Power Distance Index
2. Individualism Collectivism Index
3. Uncertainty Avoidance Index
4. Quantity of Life versus Quality of Life Index
5. Long Term and Short Term orientation
6. Indulgence versus Restraint

The first three points were the most useful to us and so the theory is described more fully here to illuminate these. The descriptions are clearly broad statements and as such are in danger of being stereotypical, but they also can be helpful in viewing the values or cultural ways of seeing which may inform certain actions or customs. As these are models, they are not necessarily so clearly delineated in reality.

1. Power Distance Index

This dimension relates to the expectation and distribution of power between people. Cultures of low power distance expect that inequalities should be minimised and that there should be interdependence between less and more powerful people. Parents treat children as equals and children often play no role in the old-age security of parents. Teachers expect initiative from students in class and there is an expectation that the quality of learning depends on two-way communication and the excellence of students. According to Hofstede et al. (2010), educational policy tends to focus on secondary schools. Cultures that approve of low power distance expect and accept power relations that are more democratic and consultative.

In cultures where there is large power distance inequalities are expected and desired. Less powerful people are seen as dependent and they are polarised between dependence and counter-dependence. Parents teach children obedience and children are perceived as a source of old-age security to parents. Classroom interaction tends to be teacher dominated with teachers taking the majority of the initiative in class. The quality of learning is seen as relying almost solely on the excellence of the teacher. Educational policy tends to focus on university.

2. Individualism Collectivism Index

Collectivism refers to the degree to which people act predominantly as members of a group or an organisation, as opposed to identifying as an individual. Hofstede et al. (2010) argue that in collectivist cultures students only speak up in class when selected by the group and the purpose of education is for learning how to do. People identify with a group and have large extended families, which are a protection, and loyalty is expected. In individualist societies students are expected to speak up individually in class and the purpose of education is learning how to learn. Management training teaches the honest sharing of feelings and the emphasis is on personal achievement and individual rights.

3. Uncertainty Avoidance Index

This dimension refers to the extent to which society can cope with uncertainty and ambiguity. It relates to coping with anxiety and the minimising of the unknown and the unusual. Cultures with high uncertainty avoidance tend to be more emotional and attempt to minimise the impact of change by the use of rules, laws and regulation. Low uncertainty avoidance cultures are more comfortable with lack of structure or few rules. They are more pragmatic and tolerant of change.

Taking a cultural lens to the behaviour and the data was helpful. Clearly in a programme where the facilitators are from the UK and the teachers working in the programme are from Kazakhstan one cannot ignore culture. Using the Hofstede et al. (2010) framework can prevent the adoption of an evaluative perspective and encourage a cultural dialogue about difference and understanding. Hofstede et al. (ibid.) argue that the forms of manifestation are visible in the elements shown in Figure 2. They use the image of the onion with the core values in the middle and the outer manifestations of these values around the centre. It takes time to engage in direct conversation about the core values but there is a need to engage with values. Without this, a technical engagement with practice is likely to result in rejection of the practice or a superficial dialogue.

Figure 2

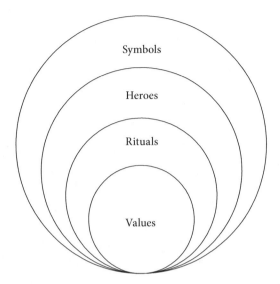

According to Hofstede's model, Kazakhstani culture could be identified as having a large power distance, collectivist and uncertainty-avoidant characteristics. These influence professional practice in predictable ways. To start with, the dominant view about teaching and learning appeared to be premised on a transmission view of teaching and learning. In other words the teacher is the source of knowledge and therefore the authority figure in the classroom: students passively receive the knowledge which the teacher transmits:

> The first formal . . . the important one that most teachers, almost [all] of the teachers, they just give facts and knowledge and students they do not work they don't get involved in the process of learning and teaching. Students just sit in a passive way and accept everything from teacher. Students they don't interact with each other during lessons. (Director, School 1)

> We are used to following a certain model [of teaching]. (TRC, School 3)

In this model students are not seen as active agents in their learning. However this passive and hierarchical model does not just apply to the situation of learners in the classroom but also to teachers as professionals going about their daily practice. This is implicit in the second excerpt above, when the Teacher Research Coordinator (TRC) comments that teachers essentially do as they are told, but it is more explicit in the description of a mechanistic approach to teaching in the following:

> I'd like to say that we are used to having very repetitive, routine work, every day we would teach the same thing. (Teacher, School 4)

> Like on schedule, but because in the ninth grade we do, we have six nine grades, and we should do it [teach a particular topic] according to our school policy, we should do all of the same thing in every group to prepare properly for the examination.(Teacher, School 3)

Such cultural differences around understandings of pedagogy and professional practice posed a challenge to our enquiry-based programme, which assumes teachers have agency to develop their practice and is antithetical to a transmission-based view of learning.

Younger and more junior teachers are expected to defer to older staff and those in more senior positions, which as the quotation below demonstrates, presented another challenge for a programme such as the one described in this paper, which is premised on the need for teachers to work together:

> At the beginning I also thought like: 'Ah, I am younger than them! How can I tell them what they should do?' (TRC, School 2)

Our field notes and reflections made during workshops have many references to the operation of this hierarchy, with the following extract being typical:

> [The teachers] are very respectful of the managers' group – one of who tended to speak at length and obvious authority. The higher status people were more likely to speak more often. . . . By the end of the week the senior managers had disappeared and the teachers were coming out of their shells as a result. By the final day lots of teachers were putting up their hands and getting involved, asking questions and even being critical. (Faculty Team A, Reflections)

However, as this last quotation reveals, cultural values can be challenged in a different environment such as that provided by the workshops we ran as part of the programme. Nevertheless the context of workshops facilitated by overseas 'experts' also created its own problems of hierarchy:

> Another challenge potentially was developing the teachers as critical friends to each other when the Cambridge 'experts' were present. After each presentation there was usually quite a bit of discussion between the teachers and the presenter before turning to 'Cambridge' for comment. Undoubtedly they were expecting us to pronounce judgement and I was very conscious I didn't want to undermine the value of the preceding discussion. (Faculty Team B, Reflections)

> I think that they [Cambridge facilitators] analysed everything we have already done, and they said that we are going in the 'right way'. (TRC, School 1)

We were therefore mindful of the need to work collaboratively with the participating teachers, and not to adopt a superior and evaluative discourse, however difficult that seemed at times when we were trying to explain socio-cultural and constructivist notions of pedagogy and collaborative learning.

The final aspect of culture that is most obviously an issue for us as international facilitators implementing a reform programme is the language barrier. Teachers we were working with spoke Kazakh or Russian as their first language, and generally also spoke the other as a second language but not in all cases. Teachers in NIS schools are also expected to learn English as part of the trilingual policy which has been implemented in these schools, but in many cases they were at a relatively early stage of English language acquisition. This meant that materials developed by the Cambridge team had to be translated into two different languages and we were reliant on NIS colleagues who spoke good English (usually the English teachers) to help us communicate with the group during sessions. Issues associated with translation are discussed elsewhere in this volume, however one of the more immediate practical problems for us was understanding what sense our Kazakhstani colleagues were making of the ideas being presented in the workshops, and this created a certain amount of frustration:

> It was primarily the language barrier which seemed to stop even more people becoming involved. The language barrier made it difficult to follow what they were writing, even when this was translated. (Faculty Team A, Reflections)

Characteristics of the wider reform process

The sheer pace of the change and the pressures this placed on the NIS schools to adapt their practice appeared to be overwhelming, as this director clearly states:

> At the beginning yeah. The beginning I was against. To tell the truth of the [last] three years of function of this, [the] first school we have changed three course plans, changed three times, subject programs changed several times. When we moved to [an] integrated new curriculum additionally action research truly I was against [it]. First reaction was . . . why do we need this project? There are scientists and scholars people who can deal with it but not teachers? . . . Every year there

was a kind of experiments new change not one change but several changes and we were tired of them. (Director, School 1)

As NIS is seen as a model for the country and a test bed for innovation, it is not surprising that teachers have experienced a constant stream of change. However, teachers need time to implement new ideas so it is understandable that they felt there was a lack of time to get things done and that they were overloaded.

In addition to the sheer number of changes, there is also pressure to succeed as leaders of the reform, and this has led to teachers feeling they need to perform to the highest standards. The combination of the cultural context and the pressure to perform appears to have led to competition between teachers to be seen as the best performers, with a notable lack of sharing of their best practice, as the following excerpts demonstrate:

> There is always some sort of competition among teachers. (Teacher, School 3)

> The teachers think that their lessons must be the best one, the excellent and the kind of selfish, arrogant they were not for sharing their lessons or their method or their experience. (Director, School 1)

> There is a teacher, she was very, very serious always, and I never had an opportunity to come and ask, and I, for me, I thought that she's very selfish. I know that she's an excellent teacher, but I thought that she didn't like to share her experience, her ideas with someone. (TRC, School 1)

This lack of sharing and competition was also evident during workshops with teachers:

> There were still occasions when the group work broke down, however, and discussions threatened to descend into confrontation. As workshop facilitators we had to intervene regularly in order to repair group processes and get tasks back on track. (Faculty Team C, Reflections)

The reform process also requires that NIS schools adopt what is perceived by the Government of Kazakhstan as best practice internationally. In terms of conceptions of pedagogy for the Action Research Programme, this meant adopting socio-cultural and constructivist views about learning and positioning the teacher as a learner reflecting on his or her practice through conducting action research. As discussed above, cultural values lead to the widely held view that the teacher has unquestionable expert knowledge to transmit, which clashes with the beliefs and values required for the programme, thus creating difficulties for the teachers working with us in this programme. The following extract highlights the emotional response this created for at least some of the teachers. The director of School 1 described how other teachers were 'shocked that we were researcher[s]' and how the other teachers were at first unco-operative with this 'kind of project because they don't know the idea of the project.'

> Maybe there are teachers who are still afraid of being involved with it. (TRC, School 2)

Overall it appears that teachers were weary of and in some ways feared the reforms, which, given the high-stakes nature of the situation, is hardly surprising. However, this did pose something of a challenge to us as we attempted to introduce the Action Research Programme.

The nature of professional learning in the NIS school context

Teacher learning seemed to be premised on the view that something was either right or wrong, and that if the teacher was doing something wrong they needed to be told so that they could fix the problem and perform better:

> Before the project so we observed lessons from the critical viewpoint always with the aim of how to criticise how to find out some drawbacks of the lesson. (Director, School 1)

Teacher performance in the Kazakhstan education system is very public with teachers being expected to compete in Olympiads to demonstrate their abilities. Teachers are also graded at different levels and have to demonstrate their competence through various tests as well as maintaining a portfolio to show that they are worthy of promotion to a higher level. Given this view of teacher learning and professionalism, the dominant perception of the teacher as expert and the high stakes nature of the reform process, it was not surprising to see that teachers who were involved in the programme were initially reluctant to take risks as they feared failure:

> Some of them stopped or just did not start to do, because it was risky or they were not quite sure what they wanted to do. (TRC, School 2)

> There was a lot of fear and uncertainty – concerns with getting it right. (Faculty Team Meeting Notes, February)

> There was some fear from the teachers that their action research would be graded or marked and that they were going to struggle to get their work completed in the time available. (Faculty Team A reflections)

By not taking risks, it could be argued that teachers were not initially prepared to be learners, and it is interesting that in our first workshop in October 2012, there were many occasions when we were asked by the participating NIS colleagues to increase the pace as they felt they already knew what was being discussed, which appears to lend weight to this interpretation.

As has already been noted in several of the excerpts above, teachers also did not see themselves as researchers, viewing research as something that was carried out by academics at a university. This view was at least attributable to the fact that their view of research was generally limited to research in the form of large-scale experiments.

> In our case people think that research is something very difficult, that you have to collect .. thousands and thousands of different data and then make do .. some statistical research, that it should be very scientifically oriented. (TRC, School 1)

> Because we had to .. have evidence, we chose two groups and we compared their results. For example, [we used] strategies which we thought useful in focus group and we did the usual lessons with another group, and we compared the results. (Teacher, School 3)

Teachers working on the project did not on the whole know about other types of research, such as action research or what value different types of research might have to them as practitioners. Thus the views of professional learning and what constitutes research did pose some challenges for us in implementing the Action Research Programme.

Overall, therefore, cultural values, perceptions of the reform process and notions of professional learning were to some extent misaligned with the underlying beliefs and values associated with the Action Research Programme. Discussion within the Cambridge team helped to identify and explore some of these issues, which sensitised us to our Kazakhstani colleagues' situation and allowed us to think of ways of working that would respect their value system, while also allowing us to introduce new ideas about pedagogy and professional learning. A number of factors were helpful in this process, and these are outlined further in the next section.

Factors facilitating the implementation of the Action Research Programme

Undoubtedly NIS schools are well resourced compared to other schools in the country, however in the specific context of the Action Research Programme, the online resources developed during the first year of the project and shared between the Cambridge team and participating teachers through the Moodle open-source learning platform were seen as key facilitating factors. Two types of resource were seen as particularly helpful: the materials developed by the Cambridge team for the workshops, which could be downloaded and referred to after face to face workshops and the presentations prepared by participating teachers to share their ongoing research and emerging findings. The latter were particularly helpful as other workshops had been held regionally, so this mechanism enabled teachers from different regions to hear what all their programme colleagues were doing:

> The useful thing is that the materials from all the seminars are uploaded there, There are also some books and methodological materials. We have access to all these, We can always download and read something useful. Also, the projects from other schools and other cities are presented there, so we can learn about their work. We had seminars with only two schools involved; all the other ones took place in Astana, so it was interesting to learn about the research of others and what they do. (Teacher, School 4)

The second main factor that appeared to be important was the nature of the support from Cambridge. The workshops were seen as crucial for developing their understanding of action research:

> They show us how to do action research, how to focus your topic, how to make it more specific, what questions should you write at the beginning, what will help you during and again after. (Teacher, School 1)

> If it weren't for them (workshops) I would never have understood what Action Research is. (Teacher, School 3)

But perhaps more importantly, the ongoing support between workshops provided through the Moodle site, and regular email and Skype conversations between the Cambridge team and TRCs and sometimes groups of teachers to discuss emerging issues and problems were also seen as vital:

> I can answer them [teachers] and support them somehow and if I can't I just contact with the Cambridge coordinators. (TRC, School 3)

> We find their help very useful and we always keep in touch with them. Whenever we have questions we can address them. There is also [Cambridge colleague]. We contacted her as well and she sent us certain information we required. (Teacher, School 4)

Another facilitating factor was the support provided within the school. Directors in particular recognised the need for the Senior Leadership Team to support the work:

> Every project can be very successful if the schools principals, schools leaders also support the project. . . . But it not only depends on school principal's co-ordination of the project but the vice principal who also co-ordinates the process, because school principal does not always does not have time to check the progress of the process, and that is why much responsibility lies on the shoulders of vice principal as well. If vice principal cannot support in an appropriate way the project also fails. (Director, School 1)

Informal conversations between participating teachers and the Cambridge team and some preliminary data suggested that support from Senior Leadership Teams had grown over the course of the year as teachers became trusted to do the work. As this director notes, 'I'm not really the person who is involved one hundred per cent in this research here because I know that [TRC] is doing this work and I trust her' (Director, School 2). Support from the TRC was also seen as vital:

> [The TRC] helps me out a lot. Usually before we get together [the TRC] asks us personally if we have any questions or issues to be discussed and then when we meet we discuss them and other questions that arise. (Teacher, School 3)

> If we have some problems with and have questions, we ask [TRC], our co-ordinator. She helps us, she tells us, because she was in Cambridge University, she has some experience. (Teacher, School 2)

Finally support from other teachers involved in the Action Research Programme in their school, either working collaboratively on a joint project or as a critical friend, was also extremely important, both in terms of moral support and with helping with the workload:

> Here I like the idea of a critical friend, who never blames you, never says you are wrong but just supports with advice. I enjoy this different format of work. I like it. (Teacher, School 3)

> We have a team of three people. I am a member of this team. And I'm doing the entire analysis of what was learnt during the lessons, like questioning, etc. And

afterwards we prepare the posters and reports. This is all with the help of X and Y. The key person in our team is Y. Actually we are working with her classes. . . . The work itself was divided into three of us. (Teacher, School 2)

Changing practice is difficult and requires a high level of support. The teachers working with us have made considerable progress in implementing a wide range of action research projects that are beginning to meet some of the aims of the programme, and a major contributory factor has been the support provided for this process. Our data suggests that support is required at different levels including from outside the organisation, from senior leadership, and from colleagues who are participating in the same programme on an ongoing basis. Furthermore the nature of this support needs not only to be informational in terms of developing knowledge and skills but also emotional and non-judgemental to develop trust and relationships.

Benefits of the Action Research Programme

Although the Action Research Programme has only been running for a year, a number of benefits are beginning to emerge for teachers and, more generally, for the schools involved. Perceptions of some of the teachers involved suggested that students may also be beginning to benefit from the work.

For teachers, one of the main benefits appears to be the fact that working collaboratively in the project gave them the opportunity to share problems and get advice from colleagues with whom they were working:

Earlier we have never worked together on the same project or in the same team, because we teach different subjects. We knew each other but never collaborated. When we started to participate in this project, we started to work as a group and naturally we would ask each other for advice, and this influenced us in a very good way. We started to share experience, we have learned a lot from each other. If you do not know something there is always someone to ask and there will always be someone to help you out. (Teacher, School 4)

Thus teachers involved were more prepared to try out new ideas based on advice given by colleagues:

I've taken some of their ideas and tried to use them at my lessons. So if I had some difficulties, I went to them and asked what should be done in this or that case, or how should I behave for example if my student is underachieving. (TRC, School 3)

Sharing ideas and practice extended beyond the immediate project teams to the action research group in school (of between 9 and 15 colleagues) and to other colleagues in school more widely:

> Twice a month so they gather together. It is voluntarily, nobody pushes you to go there but if someone want just they come to the hall and they share ideas so people who are involved in action research projects they are sharing their experience and other teachers just can come and listen to the colleagues twice a month. (Director, School 1)

Thus other teachers appeared to be benefitting from the work done by teachers in the Action Research Project, although this claim has to be tested further in the evaluation. This process of working together and sharing experience also had a notable impact on how teachers regarded each other:

> Next year I think that we will continue, and our teachers, when we meet, when we discuss, they also I think that they change in their opinion about me, now they just come, collaborate, now they don't think that I am a Vice Director, as there is no other gap between us. (TRC, School 1)

> The most important thing is that despite the fact that the [teacher] is so young; we learnt a lot from her. And[the teacher] learnt a lot from us. We had a mutual exchange of experiences. (Teacher, School 2)

Thus there is some evidence that power hierarchies based on age and position were being broken down, which is likely to have a wider impact on school culture. It could also be argued that the staff was a more cohesive body, as they had got to know each other much better:

> We began to speak to other teachers and we . . . discovered . . . that they're very different. My opinion changed: they're very helpful. (TRC, School 1)

> We tried to find the time for exchanging our experience. For example, after lesson I want to tell my colleagues about how it was – successful or not – maybe talk about some problems I had. It makes us closer. (Teacher, School 2)

Engaging in action research has also enabled teachers to start to develop their practice:

> Action Research on this topic gave me many insights, I learned a lot as a teacher. What I learned is that the problem comes not only from the students but from the teacher as well. So I changed my approach to teaching and to homework giving accordingly. (Teacher, School 3)

> After engaging with the Action Research, we started to develop some new prac-
> tice and actually apply this practice within the class taught. And also we were
> figuring out some minuses and positive things which should be applied further
> on or which should not be applied at a particular stage. (Teacher, School 4)

However, changing practice is a process and it was apparent that the teachers
involved were on a learning journey:

> We are still doing it, and practising. I tried reciprocal reading in two different
> grades and it didn't work in one of those. So, that's when I decided not to have
> it in the 7th grade but in the 8th grade. (TRC, School 3) This excerpt demon-
> strates that although the teacher had acted upon the findings of their action re-
> search project, there is perhaps a lack of reflection as to why the strategy deployed
> was unsuccessful with one age group, which might have led to a further cycle of
> action research rather than an acceptance of the outcome. Indeed there were a
> number of misconceptions about action research evident in what teachers said,
> though space precludes a further discussion here. Interestingly a few teachers
> recognised that they still had much to learn:

> I have already told you but I will repeat that in the long term it is overall change
> in my teaching practice. We gradually start to understand that we need to change
> something in the teaching process and international experience shows us this.
> (Teacher, School 3)

This is particularly interesting, as it shows that at least some of these teachers
explicitly positioned themselves as learners, which is contrary to the traditional beliefs about teachers discussed previously. Overall this seems to suggest that the Action Research Programme is not only ameliorating certain
cultural beliefs, which will have a wider impact on school culture, but also
it could be argued that teachers are developing as professionals. Learning is
beginning to be seen as part of the professional role:

> I think that our teachers perhaps understand that every teacher should learn, but
> he can only learn if he researches his work [to find out] what works, what doesn't
> work. Only when he or she can study, can he start to change something in his
> teaching. (TRC, School 1)

> So, I definitely know that Action Research is a part of my teaching, because first
> of all any teacher should be reflective during his practice and he, he or she should
> find what the main issues are in his work and what he or she is doing right or
> wrong and how to improve his teaching practice. (TRC, School 3)

As the second excerpt outlines, action research is perhaps unsurprisingly seen as a vehicle for reflection and learning, given the focus of the work we have been doing together. An outcome of this shift in professional identity to enable the teacher to be seen as a learner is that teachers are becoming more confident in taking risks:

> As I have noticed, during the Action Research our teachers change. Transform. If at the very beginning they were more reserved and shy at times, then now they are more confident. (TRC, School 4)

Being able to try things and see oneself as a learner represents a real change in perception about professional learning. It is heartening from the perspective of the Cambridge team as we had worked hard to work with and develop notions of professional identity that were respectful of Kazakh culture but which did not accept assumptions about teaching and learning unquestioningly. Although beyond the scope of this chapter, it should be noted that learning was reciprocal between Kazakhstan and Cambridge colleagues, and there has been a positive impact in the UK schools that have been involved and that have contributed members of the team going to Kazakhstan.

Finally, turning to the students: there was a small amount of evidence that the programme is beginning to have an effect on how they learn. In some cases students were being given more responsibility for their learning:

> It was interesting not only for teachers; [it was interesting] for our students. We see that they like this work. And they can check them[selves] with [the help of] laptop, and they say: 'I need to improve my speech'. (Teacher, School 1)

And in other cases strategies such as group-work appeared to have enhanced the socio-emotional climate of the classroom:

> What I have noticed is that at least the students' interpersonal relationship is improving. I can't say that this has an immediate and positive affect on their attainment in Maths, but as to their interpersonal relationship, I think there are some improvements. I have noticed improvements. [Laughs]. (Teacher, School 2)

Given that change takes time as beliefs and values have to be re-examined, we would not expect great changes in practice after one year of the Action Research Programme. However, the fact that there is some evidence of changing beliefs, values and practice, even if these changes are small, represents real progress.

Conclusion

The preliminary reflections on this early data suggest that the bottom-up approach is useful and is affecting notions and practice of collaboration and enquiry, the primary aims of this programme. We would argue that the three areas of the framework – reform, professional practice and cultural values – all need to be kept in mind when trying to understand and facilitate cross-national action research in Kazakhstan. We need to work in all the three areas. The work is mutual: both facilitators and Kazakh colleagues need to work explicitly on deep values and an explicit cultural dialogue needs to be established, which is respectful and sensitive, for this is delicate work. This is slow cooking and the programme is intended to be progressive but slow, something that is not too common in Kazakhstan. As facilitators we feel there is a need to protect experimental and developmental practice in a climate of quick reform and high pressure to demonstrate impact. Working in these three arenas makes a complex set of demands on facilitators and in negotiation. It is highly valued already and reports suggest that it is proving worthwhile for all involved including the pupils and it is exciting to see that such a teacher-led and teacher-focused initiative is showing some green shoots.

REFERENCES

Altrichter, H. and **Posch**, P. (2011). *Action Research as a Precondition for Innovation*. Paper presented at the CARN Conference, Vienna, Austria, 4–6 November 2011.

Ayubaeva, N. (2012). *Teacher Engagement with Reflective Practice and its Implications for Teacher Learning: A Case Study*. Unpublished MPhil Thesis, University of Cambridge Faculty of Education.

BERA/RSA (2013). *Research and Teacher Education: The BERA-RSA Inquiry*. British Educational Research Association and the Royal Society for the Arts. Paper presented at the British Educational Research Association Conference, Brighton, Sussex, UK, 5–7 September 2013.

Carr, W. and **Kemmis**, S. (1986). *Becoming Critical: Education, Knowledge and Action Research*. Lewes: Falmer.

Cordingley, P. (2013). 'The Role of Professional Learning'. In C. McLaughlin (ed.), *Teachers Learning: Professional Development and Education*. Cambridge: Cambridge University Press.

Elliott, J. and **Norris**, N. (2012). *Curriculum, Pedagogy and Educational Research: The Work of Lawrence Stenhouse*. Abingdon: Routledge.

Fimyar, O. and **Kurakbayev, K.** (2012). '"Soviet" in the Memories and Teachers' Professional Beliefs in Kazakhstan'. In *Internationalisation and Reform of Secondary Schooling in Kazakhstan*. Unpublished report, University of Cambridge Faculty of Education, Nazarbayev University, Penn Graduate School of Education.

Hofstede, G., Hofstede, G.J. and **Minkov, M.** (2010). *Cultures and Organizations: Software of the Mind*. New York: McGraw-Hill.

Lewin, K. (1948). *Resolving Social Conflicts: Selected Papers on Group Dynamics*. Gertrude W. Lewin (ed.). New York: Harper and Row.

McLaughlin, C. (2012). 'Bullets or Butterflies? Teaching, Research and Knowledge Creation'. *Zeitschrift für Erziehungswissenschaft*, 3, Special edition on Didactics in Europe.

McLaughlin, C., Black-Hawkins, K., Brindley, S., McIntyre, D. and **Taber, K.** (2006). *Researching Schools: Stories from a Schools–University Partnership for Educational Research*. London: Routledge.

Schön, D. (1983). *The Reflective Practitioner: How Professionals Think in Action*. London: Temple Smith.

Somekh, B. and **Zeichner, K.** (2009). *Action Research for Educational Reform: Remodelling Action Research Theories and Practices in Local Contexts*. Educational Action Research, 17:1, 5–21.

Stenhouse, L. (1975a). 'Research as a Basis for Teaching'. In J. Elliott and N. Norris, (eds), *Curriculum, Pedagogy and Educational Research: The Work of Lawrence Stenhouse*. London: Routledge.

Stenhouse, L. (1975b). *An Introduction to Curriculum Research and Development*. London: Heinemann.

Yakavets, N. (2012). 'The Recent History of Educational Reform in Kazakhstan'. In *Internationalisation and Reform of Secondary Schooling in Kazakhstan*. Unpublished report, University of Cambridge Faculty of Education, Nazarbayev University, Penn Graduate School of Education.

PART THREE:

The International and Intranational Translation of Educational Policy and Practice

13 LOST – AND FOUND – IN TRANSLATION? Interpreting the Processes of the International and Intranational Translation of Educational Policy and Practice in Kazakhstan[1]

David Bridges (University of Cambridge, Faculty of Education)
Kairat Kurakbayev (Nazarbayev University, Graduate School of Education)
Assel Kambatyrova (Nazarbayev University, Graduate School of Education)

Introduction

In Kazakhstan, as in many parts of the world, educational reform takes the form of (i) a certain amount of what is sometimes called 'policy borrowing' (Phillips and Ochs 2004) from international policy and practice to national policy (which of course has many local sources as well as international ones) and, then, (ii) a centre to periphery model through which this conjoined policy and its attendant practices are 'cascaded'/'disseminated'/ 'transferred' by a variety of processes to schools. In Kazakhstan (as in Egypt and Mongolia among other countries) there is an intermediate stage by which new curriculum and educational practices are first implemented in selected (and in all these cases selective) schools before being 'translated' to the mainstream sector.

This much can be fairly simply stated, but it conceals some very complex interactions. 'Education policy, even when centrally mandated,' argue Singh et al., 'is interpreted, translated, adjusted and worked differently by diverse sets of policy actors, in processes of enactment in specific contexts' (Singh et al. 2013, 466). In Kazakhstan as anywhere else a variety of different players from international consultants, through national advisors and ministry officers, curriculum designers, textbook writers and test developers, teacher trainers, regional and local officials, school directors to, in the end, classroom teachers and pupils are selecting, interpreting (and re-interpreting), resisting, embracing, promoting, sharing, diverting, subverting or 'hijacking' policies and practices at every stage in the process.

The following flowchart offers a picture of this process, although it is an over-simplified one (see Figure 1).

Figure 1: Transferring policy: from the international or the national to the local

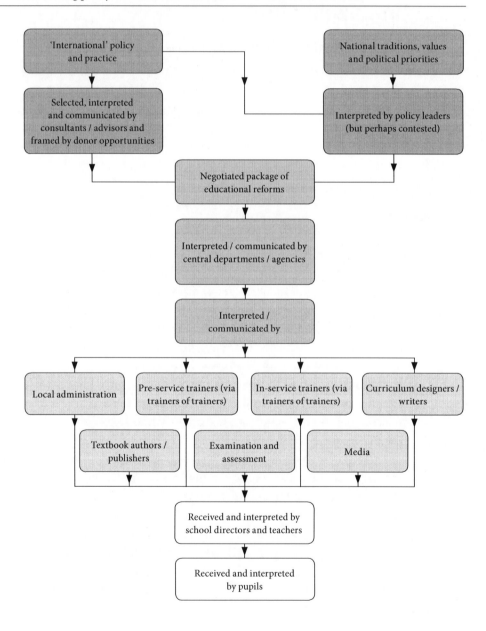

Kazakhstan's own historical location on the Silk Road offers perhaps a richer metaphor. For the Silk Road was of course not a single road: 'The term is a misnomer: the Silk Road was not really a road at all – it was a vast network of land-based and maritime trade routes, and the merchants who used it carried far, far more than silk . . . Along with trade goods came new ideas – religions, medical knowledge, scientific and technological innovations passed in both directions and the Silk Road became a complex network of veins and arteries, carrying the lifeblood of nations across the then known world' (Tucker 2011, 1). The Silk Road had not one starting point nor one destination but several. Nor did goods necessarily travel all the way from one end to another; rather they were traded at different points, carried on through a kind of relay, sometimes worked on and processed to add value and thus transformed as they were transported. This, rather than the flowchart, is a richer, more complex and more accurate picture of the process of the translation of educational policies and practices, not least because it points towards the changes that might take place through the series of exchanges in their journey from source to destination.

In the UK there is a children's game known as 'Chinese whispers' in which a message is whispered from one person to another around a room. The fun is in comparing the message that is announced at the end of this process with the original – to which it rarely bears any resemblance. This is also the common experience of the dissemination of educational ideas and practice. Robert Cowen makes the point with admirable succinctness: 'When it moves it morphs' (Cowen 2009). The flowchart illustrates layer upon layer of screening and interpretation by different agencies and individuals as policies and practices are translated from international arena to national arena and/or national arena to local institutions and finally classrooms.

Given these plentiful requirements for selection and interpretation, it should not surprise anyone to find that the messages for policy and practice that start life outside Kazakhstan and even those generated from central bodies in the country get lost, or, more neutrally for the moment, changed in translation. Such changes are sometimes treated as frustrations or betrayals of the true reforming agenda – even 'subversions' or 'hijacking'. In this paper we shall treat them more sympathetically, acknowledging the polyphony of voices outside and inside Kazakhstan that are speaking to the reform agenda; the instability of many of the key concepts in 'the global educational space'; and the necessity of processes of assimilation as well as accommodation to the internalisation of new ideas and practices within different conceptual frameworks and socio-cultural contexts. Finally, we draw on the theory of literary translation to re-evaluate the role of translators and, eventually, the receivers of policy and practice 'texts' in reconstructing or co-constructing meaning in their own terms. These are the themes that are developed in the sections that follow.

1. The multiplicity of agencies seeking to drive or influence reform

In the wake of the collapse of the Soviet Union and with Kazakhstan's independence in 1991 a plethora of international agencies flooded into Kazakhstan to fill the vacuum of power and, inadvertently or otherwise, impose their ideology. Some of the most powerful (like the World Bank and the Asian Development Bank) brought with them a neo-liberal economic and social agenda, including the opening up of educational provision to the private sector, the reduction of the personnel in the Ministry and elements of de-centralisation (which has the continuing consequence of inhibiting the Ministry of Education and Science's capacity to manage change), cost sharing and so on. In parallel came NGOs like the Soros Foundation with their own agendas for change and eventually, as Kazakhstan's independent sources of wealth became apparent, more commercially orientated organisations have entered the field to meet the demand, such as Haileybury School, which offers an elite education for the newly prosperous; the plethora of English language schools offering English language competence; the US Education Testing Service, and Pearson's technical educational services, all of which might be regarded as *pushing* the international agenda. Indeed, the multiplicity of agencies involved in educational reform in Kazakhstan and the polyphony of voices risks creating what Steiner-Khamsi describes in other contexts as 'a mismatch between standards, curriculum framework, teacher education, textbooks and student assessment,' which is, she argues, 'a tragedy that reflects the harmful effects of uncoordinated aid' (Steiner-Khamsi 2012b, 29). In Kazakhstan, however, this is something that is being explicitly addressed under the 2015–20 strategic planning process.

At the same time, of course, Kazakhstan has been developing its own national agenda for change, and it has actively sought to engage with international sources for policies and practices that might serve these ends – *pulling* in international policies and practices. MoES has had its own programme of international visits and its own carnival of international consultants. It has, for example, looked to Finnish consultants on school textbooks and to the UK's Office for Standards in Education for practice in school inspection and continues to draw on Estonian expertise in trilingual education. And so it is at all sorts of different levels in the system. The deputy director of a regional *Orleu* explained:

> I have carefully studied many standards from the international experience. I like Singapore's education program. They have primary education lasting for 6 years. I like the idea that upon graduating from school, they prepare for several years to enter the university, and it's great. In Kazakhstan, if a child fails UNT then there is no guarantee that next year he will try to pass it again. That's why I think that we need to have Singapore's standards. (Orleu Deputy Director)

The picture is further complicated by the development of the well-resourced Autonomous Education Organisation[2] Nazarbayev Intellectual Schools (NIS), which in many ways represents a parallel system for the introduction of educational reform (see chapter 4). Senior NIS officers have been active in seeking out 'best practice' from across the world: drawing on the International Baccalaureate from Switzerland; new curriculum and assessment from Cambridge International Examinations and from the Central Institute for Test Development (CITO) in the Netherlands; approaches to talented and gifted education from Johns Hopkins Centre for Talented Youth in the US; approaches to trilingualism from Estonia and Quebec; and approaches to pre-school education from New Zealand and Italy – to name but a few.

Nor is it just people from MoES or NIS who are setting out to learn from international experience. The director of one school explained:

> And what are also common are the visits to other cities and sometimes countries. For example, last year in May a number of Heads from this entire region and two people from Pavlodar went to Turkey to learn about the system of education there. Upon their return a seminar was organized for other teachers to share their experience. (School C Director)

A teacher in one of the focus groups gave another example:

> For example [name] . . . in her times as a Head, she focused entirely on the teaching and educational process. They went to Russia, brought course books from there, introduced some novelties, they dedicated time to doing this. (School C, Teachers' focus group)

Another teacher presented an even wider perspective:

> Nowadays, we have more opportunities to learn a lot in comparison with then [the Soviet era]. We can travel, we have *Bolashak* students . . . and they can study

round the world. They can come back here, which helps us to widen our view and outlook. . . . We know the world and we are people of the world. (School D Teacher 8)

It is clear that the sources of the 'international' in Kazakhstan – both those pushing their own agenda and those who are being sought out – are very diverse. It is a very different picture from the experiences of countries under colonial or neo-colonial regimes (including the USSR) when there was essentially a single external source for the received policies and practices and little or no choice as to whether to adopt them or not. In the context of international policy transfer, Kazakhstan can and does – at many different levels – choose its sources and make its own decisions as to what to adopt, adapt or reject.[3] This has consequences for the heterogeneity of the policies and practices being adopted – and their hybridisation.

2. The heterogeneity of the policies and practices that are being drawn upon: education in the marketplace of ideas?

The literature on comparative and international education gives extensive attention to the discourses not just of 'policy borrowing' (see, for example, Phillips and Ochs 2004); 'policy transfer' and 'policy travelling' (Silova 2005); but also of the 'internationalisation' and 'globalisation' of educational policy (see e.g. Sayed 2006, 12; Giddens 1990, 64 on these key terms); and of 'international socialisation' (Sayed 2006) and of the creation of a 'global educational space'. Donn and Manthri describe how as a consequence:

> By the end of the first decade of the twenty-first century, we have become accustomed to seeing, across the continents, similarities in education policies: almost identical education policies exist in relation to curriculum development, higher education institutional development, administrative practices and financial management systems – for all levels of education. (Donn and Manthri 2010, 7)

Lingard et al. write of the construction of 'a global educational policy field' (Lingard et al. 2005) which increasingly shapes and defines education policy at national level. But Mukhopadhyay and Sriprakash argue on the basis of their study of the Kamataka School Quality Assessment Organisation in India that: 'global neo-liberal frameworks are not homogenising as they are often assumed. They are re-worked, reinterpreted and re-enacted contextually, the outcomes of which would vary from one context to another, one country to the other' (Mukhopadhyay and Sriprakash 2011, 323).

What we have already described with reference to Kazakhstan supports the idea of an ongoing and increasingly internationalised marketplace of educational policies and practices – a marketplace in which the trade, as on the Silk Routes, is multi-directional[4]. It is a trade in which Kazakhstan has aspirations to be a leader in terms of educational practice, at least in regional terms. Already, the Ayb Foundation in Armenia is among those showing interest in the Centres of Excellence (CoE) in-service training programme. Nazarbayev University has been founded on precisely these terms and its annual conference for higher education leaders is designed to disseminate its own thinking to a regional and international as well as national audience. The proposed educational research journal of the newly established Kazakhstan Educational Research Association will have the title *Eurasian Journal of Educational Studies* and will be published in English.

At a high rhetorical level certain themes do indeed seem to dominate international exchange, but the level of commonality of educational policies and practices can easily be overstated: the reality is better reflected in Steiner-Khamsi's description of the polyphony of 'myriad international donors pulling in different directions, each advocating for their own "best practices" and funding their own "international standards"' (Steiner-Khamsi 2012b, 29) than in terms of a univocal global educational programme. The World Bank and others may welcome competition from the private sector in educational provision, for which the USA may serve as an example, but the country which is especially admired for leading the PISA tables of achievement, Finland, abolished private education in the 1970s and has seen steady educational improvement ever since. In social democratic parts of Europe there is an emphasis on collaboration as an instrument of educational progress in contra-distinction to the more purist attachment to neo-liberal ideals of competition as a driver of educational standards espoused in the USA and by recent administrations in the UK. In short, it is still possible to draw some rather different messages about educational policy and practice from the global educational marketplace. The significance of this observation for our discussion of 'translation' is that the translators, whether these be international consultants or national leaders, will inevitably have some choices to make from within the variety of models of practice available in the international educational market, informed perhaps by evidence of their effectiveness, judgements about their appropriateness and an assessment of their cost.

To make things more complicated, and to throw a further burden of interpretive responsibility on the translators, many of the key ideas that are identified as part of a global or at least international policy discourse

– outcomes-based education, active learning, student centred learning, evidence based policy, etc – are themselves contested within that discourse. As a consequence the 'message' available to any newcomer to the discourse is itself inherently ambivalent and unstable and, independently of any further re-interpretation that might take place, any 'translation' has to involve a selection from possible versions and interpretations of the policy or practice and a weighing of the critical discourses that surround them. Reference to 'international practice' or 'the global educational policy field' will not in itself answer the question 'what needs to be done?'

3. Assimilation and accommodation: individual conceptual unreadiness for new ideas and practices

So far we have argued that the international transfer of educational policies and practices is rendered problematic because of (i) the multiplicity of sources for such policies, (ii) the heterogeneity of available examples in international experience and (iii) the unstable and contested nature of many key policies and practices. These observations all relate to the *sources* of policy transfer; there is another set of problems to do with the nature of the *destinations* for policy transfer, i.e. those receiving and being expected to act upon new policy imperatives. Put simply, new ideas, new practices can only be taken in and incorporated in the practice of someone who has the conceptual apparatus to be able to grasp what is meant and/or the mental flexibility to accommodate new ideas.

The transfer of policy and practice is a process of learning (Perry and Tor 2009) and it is in classical learning theory that we can find some useful pointers to its requirements. The Swiss psychologist, Jean Piaget wrote of a 'cognitive equilibrium' which is achieved through two processes:

1. the assimilation or incorporation of an outside element (object, event and so forth) with the subject's sensori-motor or conceptual scheme; and
2. the accommodation that is the result of the necessity to consider the particularities characteristic of the elements that are to be assimilated. (Piaget 1978, 6–7)

Piaget points, then, to two sides of the coin of the absorption of new ideas or practices. On one side the ideas themselves get re-shaped in order for the receiver to be able to accommodate them to their existing conceptual apparatus. In the extreme case, where they are too far removed from what the subject can make sense of, they may simply be totally rejected. On the other side, the understanding, the thinking, the conceptual apparatus of the learner gets changed to a greater or lesser degree in order to accommodate the new ideas. Either way a new balance or 'equilibrium' is struck between previously held beliefs and the new ways of thinking.

This is a model that resonates very easily in the context of the classroom or of policy transfer. We can recognise that what gets taken in is not necessarily identical with what was put forward in the first place; it has been adapted to the thinking of the recipient (the process of assimilation). Equally, we may hope or expect that the recipient has himself/herself been changed as a result of the engagement with the new ideas. The point of this reference to learning theory is, however, to *normalise* these responses. We should not be surprised if in the process of transfer of policy or practice these get transformed to a greater or lesser degree in order that they can be accommodated by people who might find these ideas strange, even incomprehensible. This is normal. It does not necessarily betoken a refusal to take on new ideas, subversion or rebellion; merely perhaps an incapacity to do so on the basis of the individual's intellectual resources (though anger and frustration at not understanding can easily turn into revolt against the ideas).

The theory also points, however, to an important practical consideration: that in order to introduce new ideas to people for whom they are unfamiliar, it is important to prepare them for the novelty by first establishing a framework of understanding, a nest of related concepts that will render them intelligible. A notion like 'teacher action research' for example, (which NIS are keen to introduce into the professional practice of their teachers) presupposes perhaps a different concept of small scale applied research from those that teachers are mainly familiar with; it presupposes a higher level of self-actualisation and professional autonomy than teachers in a country like Kazakhstan may be accustomed to; it presupposes (in most of its forms) a professional collaborative culture which may be non-existent in schools in which teachers are encouraged to compete with each other for credit for innovative practice. Without at least some elements of this interconnected conceptual apparatus in place it will not be surprising if, as one Kazakh colleague bewailed after a difficult meeting, 'They just don't get it!'

4. Assimilation and accommodation: cultural non-alignment

What is true for individual learners can also be applied to communities or whole societies. It may be a matter of principled or politically expedient choice to seek to adapt imported ideas to local culture, practice or tradition, but in terms of learning theory it might also be a matter of collective psycho-logical necessity.

Educational policies and practices are deeply embedded in the cultures and traditions of the countries in which they are embedded. The laicism of French schools owes as much to the French Revolution and its inheritance as the identity and affiliation of many English 'church' schools owe to the religious inspiration behind the expansion of public education in the 19th century. Education is after all the practice through which a society 'initiates' (Peters 1966) new members into the values, ways of life, forms of knowing, understanding and being that it holds to be most worthwhile; it is the prac-tice through which it sustains itself and seeks to improve itself (as judged by its own assessment of what is best). 'It is a value-laden activity, inextricably connected to our broader aspirations for society' (Levin 2004, 2).

> Education is at least partly about the overall aims that society has for itself and how these aims are realised in practice. It cannot, therefore, be a neutral tech-nical exercise, but is invariably a deeply ethical, political and cultural one bound up with ideas about the good society and how life can be worthwhile. (Winch and Gingell 2004, Preface)

Therefore you cannot detach education from its cultural context – and this carries warnings about the shallowness of 'borrowing' policies and practices which are uprooted from their native soil and the naivety of expecting such policies and practices easily to establish roots in a very different climate and environment.

The 'indigenisation' of imported educational policies and practices is not on this account a failure of will or intent by the translators, nor a victory for the forces of conservatism, but a necessary part of the process of assimilating new ideas and practices to an established environment.

What 'indigenisation' means in Kazakhstan is, however, not straightfor-ward. One senior government officer explained:

> We are Kazakhs, nomads, and many cultures crossed our steppes. Even dur-ing the USSR, Kazakhstan became a refuge for many repressed nations. Many nations found a second motherland – Germans, Koreans, Chechens, Turks and various Caucasus nations. We have more than 137 nationalities and we have rich experience in tolerance and multiculturalism.[5] (Respondent A, MoES)

Kazakhstan is a country shaped by what was, until Stalin's systematic de-struction of this way of life, the nomadic character of its farming population; shaped by successive invasions from the East, most notably that of Chinggis

Khan in the 13th century; shaped by its strategic positioning on the old Silk Roads; shaped by its links with Turkic language and culture (evidenced by its costly refusal to join with Russia against Germany and Turkey in the First World War and by the influential presence today in Kazakhstan of the elite Turkish Lyceum schools); shaped by Stalin's dumping of whole communities in the country during his years of oppression; and shaped by the presence and inward movement until independence of a large Russian population. So what is the 'indigenous' to which imported ideas need to be assimilated? Its history has given Kazakhstan not only a multi-ethnic, multilingual, multi-cultural society, but also natural cultural affinities stretching out across central Asia and into Eastern Europe. As Bhabha has argued in a different context, 'the "locality" of national culture is neither unified nor unitary in relation to itself, nor must it be seen simply as "other" in relation to what is outside or beyond it' (Bhabha 1990, 4).

Many features of contemporary educational policy are clearly aimed at reconstructing Kazakh identity, language and culture, all of which were subordinated to Russian in the Soviet era.[6] All children have to learn Kazakh in school:

> ... everything that has Kazakhsha [i.e. that has 'Kazakh in it'] is studied in Kazakh [laughing], for example, History of Kazakhstan, Geography of Kazakhstan, Kazakh Language, Kazakh Literature, i.e. everything that has word Kazakh is in Kazakh language. (Vice Director, School G)

All civil servants have to pass a Kazakh language proficiency test (the Kaztest); and the personal and social values that feature prominently in statements of educational aims and form a central part of the 'upbringing' element of the school curriculum and in 'patriotic education' are recognisably embedded in Kazakh tradition, albeit that these sit alongside a strong commitment to respect for the diversity of cultures to be found in Kazakhstan.

At the same time, however, the Russian and Soviet inheritance remains a powerful, perhaps the most powerful, influence on educational thought and practice. 'We all are a bit conservative, we are still members of the Soviet school, it also brought us a lot of good results in good time,' acknowledged one school vice director in a predominantly Kazakh region (School F case study). The director of one of the CoE observed: 'We can't say that all we had previously was bad. We should keep the best traditions and add new skills and qualifications to teaching, to improve the student, making him more free, more liberated' (Director, CoE Location 2, School G). Olena Fimyar's chapter explores the residual power of the 'Soviet' in teachers' professional imagination and beliefs – a power that owes something to the undoubted legacy of educational advance in the Soviet period but which many reformers see as the major obstacle to continuing and contemporary reform.

So, again, what does 'indigenisation' mean in this context? Reflecting on our own experience of school level educational reform over the last few years, a number of examples come to mind.

One of the key people involved in the process of developing teacher training programmes with Cambridge University for the Centres of Excellence described the process in the following terms:

> We receive a new document, a new programme from Cambridge. We are the customer, we order a programme. We tell them that we need a new programme which would meet all the requirements of the world education space. We want to have this programme so that our children that study and teachers that work by that programme could be competitive. So teachers and students could be embedded in the world mainstream. All right, we then receive such a programme. Of course, we contribute to the design of such programmes. They offer a lot of such approaches but we select what could be well-embedded in our context. So we have a professional gut feeling, intuition and our experience that tells us that 'yeah, this is new and it will harmonize with our local educational context.' (Centre of Excellence Location 1 Respondent A, 25 July 2013)

When the CoE in-service education programme was introduced in 2012 the Cambridge programme developers were committed to a form of assessment based on portfolios of teachers' work showing how they had implemented new approaches in the classroom. Colleagues in NIS were eventually persuaded to accept this approach, but insisted, against all advice from the international team, that this must be accompanied by a more traditional unseen multiple choice test. This insistence grew partly out of a desire to maintain a familiar and well established form of 'objective' assessment, but also out of a desire to have a form of assessment that could be more visibly protected from corrupt practices. So the old and the new forms of assessment went forward in parallel, though in practice it was the old system that played the larger role in determining who passed and who failed the assessment. 'Indigenisation' in this case is an uncomfortable and incomplete process in which the old and the new sit alongside each other without real assimilation or accommodation of one to the other.

5. Translation: viewed from the periphery

It is tempting for external observers to view educational systems through the eyes of those perceived to be (or under the illusion of being) in control of them, in other words to take a top-down view of the processes of translation. From such a perspective adaptations or diversions from the transmitted message tend to be seen as failures or acts of policy vandalism. In the first year of our research in Kazakhstan (2012) we focused on the view of educational reform that we could gather from the centre, including the translation of selected pieces of international policy and practice. This is what Bernstein (1990) refers to as the Official Recontextualising Field (ORF). In 2013 we turned our perspective around and looked at the system through the eyes of school directors and teachers – what Bernstein calls the Pedagogic Recontextualising Field (PRF).

Mukhopadhyay and Sriprakash (2011) are among those who have found value in following the translation of educational reform to the point that it encounters 'complex local particularities that arise to challenge the homogenising effects of dominant policy prescriptions and regimes' (ibid., 314) and the 'displacements and transformations that are inevitable in the movement of policy across contexts' (ibid., 312). They explain that:

> [the] outcomes of school programmes are often cast as the 'failure' of teachers or other local actors, in ways that isolate their practices from other social relations. By tracing the 'translations' of a programme, we can acknowledge the multiple relationships that reconstitute the programme and how it is taken up in local contexts. (ibid., 315)

This captures something of the longer-term ambition of our own research in Kazakhstan. What follows draws from some of our preliminary data.

Some schools certainly see themselves as being at the bottom of a chain of command:

> We are immersed into these educational reforms. We have to use all innovations. In any case, whether you want it or not – you have to use them, after some time you understand that such use is necessary. . . . There are some issues that are down-streamed to us from the Ministry or from the Department of Education – if they order us to send them something – we cannot discuss this decision. We have to perform immediately. (School C: two Vice Directors)

The director of one of the CoEs explained that 'All new innovations and decisions come to us through the central office of the Ministry' (Director, CoE

– S). Notwithstanding these claims, one of the things we quickly learned from the first year's work was that 'the centre' was something of a fiction.

While strategic direction was clearly given through Presidential pronouncements and subsequently enshrined in law (including but not limited to the 'State Programme'), these pronouncements were themselves sourced from a number of quarters before being given Presidential authority, and tended to be fairly high-level statements that still needed a good deal of interpretation, as teachers who sometimes observed these speeches together on the school television explained (Case study schools F and C).

In terms of educational reform, then, 'the centre' in Kazakhstan is in fact a multiplicity of different agencies with weak co-ordination and somewhat intermittent communication. These include: the National Academy for Education (responsible for curriculum, standards and textbooks); the National Testing Centre (responsible for major tests including the UNT); the Committee for Control (responsible for school inspections); and the *Orleu* (responsible for in-service teacher training).[7]

The 'centre' seems at time to be wherever you are situated. Officials locate it in MoES, the *Oblast* or the *Rayon*, but the vice director of a local *Orleu* was also able to claim: 'We are the centre of all educational reforms.' It does not stop there: one deputy head explained: 'time has shown that we have already anticipated all the reforms that later have come from education authorities' (Deputy Head 2, School F). And finally, and perhaps most compellingly: 'Everything depends on the teacher. . . . Speaking frankly . . . everything depends on the teacher' (Biology teacher School F).

Both the weakness of central co-ordination and the key agency of the school and the teacher are clearly evidenced when one starts to look at the experience of reform at school level. One school we studied was among those selected to participate voluntarily in the experimental introduction of the trilingual policy, which they entered into with some enthusiasm. This meant (amongst other things) that Science and Maths would be taught through the medium of English at senior grades. The school embraced this challenge, but quickly encountered problems that might have been foreseen and prepared for if there had been a more considered and co-ordinated approach to change from 'the centre'. To begin with, there were no available English language textbooks, so the Physics teacher explained that she had to stay up late at night to translate the Russian textbook into English for her students' use the next day. In some subject areas including Maths, there was no one who could combine the subject knowledge with the English language competence, so Maths was taught through the medium of English by an English teacher during the day and then the school director taught it through Russian after school. Further, though students were studying Science (and all its technical terminology) through the medium of English, they would have to face an examination which was offered in either Russian or Kazakh, so another teacher put on a supplementary course in technical translation to help the students cope with the assessment (Source: Case study School G).

This experience illustrates two points of relevance here. First, and most obviously, it illustrates the lack of co-ordination between those responsible for the trilingual policy, for school textbooks, for national testing and for the preparation and supply of teachers.[8] What it also illustrates, more encouragingly, is the remarkable resilience of schools in the face of such poor management and their readiness to help to make things work in spite of the shortcomings of 'the centre'. In so doing of course they are playing their part in the process of translation, in the co-construction of the reform process.

Some see this creative engagement with innovation – what Ball et al. refer to as 'the creative processes of interpretation and re-contextualisation' (Ball, Maguire and Braun 2012, 3) as a strength of the process rather than a failing (in so far as it involves potentially a departure from the original blueprint for change). For example, Hayes, writing about a major cascade programme in Sri Lanka, argues that for cascade training to be successful the training must (among other things) 'be open to reinterpretation; rigid adherence to prescribed ways of working should not be expected' (Hayes 2000, 138). Darling Hammond reminds us that:

> In devising new policies for educational change, policy makers need to understand that policy is not so much implemented as it is re-invented at each level of the system. What ultimately happens in schools and classrooms is less related to the intentions of policymakers than it is to the knowledge, beliefs, resources, leadership and motivations that operate in local contexts. (Darling Hammond 2005, 366–7)

This is perhaps especially the case in a vast country like Kazakhstan where 'the centre' conceived of as government, can seem a very long way away. 'Our teachers are not at a high level and our students do not strive to learn . . . the reason is that we are a distant, the outermost, region, we are the last to get the news' (Pedagogical Institute Director, Location 3). 'For example, representatives from "Daryn" (network) school did not participate in the seminar which was held in Semey. This happened because the trip takes 3 days to get there but the seminar lasts for 1 day and this is not reasonable. That's why directors do not have sufficient information' (CoE representative, Location 3).

Perhaps evidence of a willingness to develop new initiatives locally points to the potential for a more grassroots approach to educational development,[9] under which the problem of translation becomes not 'how do we take educational reform from the centre to the periphery?' but 'how do we take educational reform initiatives from the local to the national?' – and, who knows, into 'the global educational space?'

If this teacher's observation is anything to go by, however, this will require some significant changes of attitude not just by teachers but by administrators:

> Often [teachers'] ideas and innovations do not find approval of the educational authorities. That is why teachers cannot share their new ideas. Quite often they lose the desire to attend seminars, attend conferences because they cannot implement their ideas. (Deputy Head 1, School F)

6. Language and concepts in translation

So far, the notion of translation has been used in a kind of metaphorical way, or at least out of what is perhaps its natural habitat in the context of language and literature. But many of the issues that have been touched on so far, particularly those to do with the problems in translating innovative concepts into new settings, are reflected in problems we have also encountered in translating the contemporary and dominantly English language educational discourses into Russian and Kazakh, not to mention a plethora of minority languages including Uzbek, Ukrainian, Korean, Kyrgyz and so on.

In this section, we will provide a couple of examples of the problem of inter-linguistic translation of educational concepts travelling to Kazakhstan as a consequence of policy borrowing. As messengers of change, teachers have been at the frontline of educational reform (Fullan 2007). They play a crucial role in the success or failure of understanding borrowed concepts. In a way, teachers play a dual role of recipient and translator of the educational practices and concepts. They receive the educational concepts during their training experiences and make meaning of it based on their cultural and learning experiences. Next, they forward this new concept through their educational practices and word of mouth to their peers and students. As practitioners, teachers develop their own ways of knowing and hence attach their own cultural meaning to everything they learn on their international teacher training courses. So, processes of international policy borrowing amplify the role of the pedagogue as the translator (Dobson 2012).

The largest in-service teacher training programme in Kazakhstan is that mediated through the CoEs (see Chapter 5). We interviewed teacher educators and teachers on this programme in order to elicit difficulties and challenges that they experience when it comes to translation of new terms from English to Kazakh and Russian. One respondent from the CoE offered the following example:

> We're experiencing a situation when a new academic programme, a new reform always brings new concepts, a new conceptual apparatus. The conceptual apparatus, in its turn, is not static as it is always changing. It is going either through transformations or renewal. For instance, we are dealing with these two new concepts – 'Action Research' and 'Lesson Study'. We have a guest from Japan. He hasn't coined the term of Lesson Study on his own but must have learnt to use that concept as a consequence of his communication with colleagues abroad whilst our local pedagogues falsely recognise features of *otkritiy urok* (lit. translation: 'open lesson') in that concept. (Centre of Excellence Respondent B, Location 1)

The 'open lesson' is widely used in Kazakhstan as a way of demonstrating 'good practice'. Such demonstration lessons would be typically performed in front of the school director or deputy director who would evaluate the teacher's teaching based on that lesson. This is rather different from having other teachers observe one's lessons as a basis for collegial discussion. Open lessons do not take place frequently (a teacher is supposed to teach a demonstration lesson once or twice a year) and are not likely to constitute teachers' day-to-day practices of collegial collaboration compared to the widespread professional development practice of Lesson Study. The respondent goes on suggest:

> We should juxtapose these two concepts [*otkritiy urok* and Lesson Study] rather than trying to find something common between them. They definitely should be contrasted. They look similar only on the surface, but within the former, I come to the class in the role of evaluator – I am an outsider and I've come just to watch; whilst within the concept of the Lesson Study, I am part of the classroom and a member of the teaching-and-learning process. I am more embedded in that context. (Centre of Excellence Respondent B, Location 1)

This example illustrates the risk of placing wrong meanings on a borrowed concept as a result of differences of perceptions of education practices and more generally language, culture and traditions. As Anderson-Levitt points out, 'beyond language differences and the cultural concepts they encode, distinct disciplinary traditions can hinder easy circulation' (Anderson-Levitt 2011, 13).

The risk carries wider consequences if an act of conceptual misunderstanding happens on the level of an intermediary institution like the CoE, as this conceptual misunderstanding will then be cascaded to mainstream schools across towns and villages. One of the administrators of the centre points out a sense of responsibility when dealing with inter-linguistic translation:

> So far, discussing and analysing the existing literature on how this or that English word is used in neighboring countries we haven't still decided how to translate the word precisely (translation at the level of a single word). But so far, we are inclined to use the descriptive type. We cannot translate it right away. We have difficulties. We cannot translate it literally, we always follow a type of descriptive translation. When we introduce a new concept, we explain what it means. We cannot just translate it and go further since we understand that it is a new concept to Kazakhstan and requires the explanation. Now we are trying to develop the glossary of all the terms, which we use within all the programmes that we are developing in order to facilitate course participants' understanding. (Centre of Excellence Respondent C, Location 1)

Another example of inter-linguistic translation is linked to the level of development of educational discourse in the original and target languages. The Kazakh language, due to its cultural history, suffered slow development during Soviet times and educators find it challenging to find the right equivalents in Kazakh.

> The first difficulty in the Kazakh language in terms of translation is that the Kazakh terminology is not completely developed. Firstly it's not only in our sphere but across the Republic as well. Secondly, Kazakh is yet to gain a wider use and that's why the terminology is still being developed. When at first I had to deal with the term 'critical thinking' I started checking the way it is used in Kazakh. I looked through the several books, went to the library, did searching in the Internet and found three versions: *synioilau, syniturgydanoilau, synturgysynanoilau*. Then I checked the correctness of use of all the three versions and it turned out that all of them were used equally. First time I used the version 'syniturgydanoilau' since it was used in all the ministerial documents. As we are subject to the Ministry I used that version. (Centre of Excellence Respondent D, Location 1)

At a very practical level we quickly discovered that we had to allow for the fact that a Russian translation from English required 30% more space.

Along with the adaptation of new policies and practices, the education system adopts new terms and concepts into the established pedagogical discourse, and in particular, at the national/international interface, inter-linguistic translation appears to be a major challenge for the introduction of new education practices.

7. What we might learn from literary translation theory

A variety of different terms are used to refer to the processes by which policies and practices are taken from one source (perhaps an international one, perhaps a national institution) to its destination in a school or classroom: 'transmit', 'transfer', 'roll out', 'cascade', 'disseminate' and so on. Our preference for the notion of 'translation' is informed partly by the insights into the process of translation from the theoretical literature on literary translation (for example, Benjamin 1997; Derrida 2001; Wang 2002; Brisset 2010 and see also Chapter 9), and these insights inform some of the analysis provided above.[10] This body of literature points to a number of features of literary translation which have application to the translation of educational policy and practice but also provokes thought about differences between the two. There are two ways in which the translation of policy is *unlike* literary translation:

(i) One of the ethical obligations of the translator of the literary text is, as far as possible, to be *faithful* to the text, to be *true* to the original work. The translator of policy or practice – at least in the context of the international translation – really has no such obligation. Indeed it is almost the opposite: the policy translator has a responsibility to adapt international practice to local requirements and to the functions they are expected to perform in that context. Derrida allows room for a slightly pragmatic function of translation even in his discussion of literary translation:

> A relevant translation would therefore be, quite simply . . . a translation that does what one expects of it, in short, a version that performs its mission, honours its debt and does its job or its duty while inscribing in the receiving language the more relevant equivalent for an original. (Derrida 2001, 177)

But does this freedom/responsibility of translators to adapt (for example at regional level or at school level) apply equally to the intranational translation of policy and practice, or does the centre here have an entitlement to require conformity rather than adaptability?

(ii) The translator/interpreter of a given text does not assume responsibility for the truth or value of what that text has to say. His/her task is to translate, not to pass any judgements or enter into any debates about the truth or falsity of what is being said or written. It is not obvious, however, in the context of policy or practice translation that the translator can avoid some such responsibility. The position is analogous to the contrast that the philosopher G.E.M. Anscombe draws between the interpreter and the teacher:

> Consider the belief reposed in what an interpreter says – I mean the belief reposed in the sentences he comes out with. If you believe those communications, probably – i.e. in the normal case – you are believing his director: your reliance on the interpreter is only the belief that he has reproduced what his director said. A teacher, on the other hand, even in no way an original authority, is wrong if what he says is untrue, and that hangs together with the fact that his pupils believe (or disbelieve) him. (Anscombe 1979, 147)

Neither government officials nor external consultants are simply in the business of describing how things are done elsewhere; by deciding to translate practice or policy from one place rather than another they are giving it their own approval and authority, and they have to take some responsibility for the validity of what they are putting forward.

But there are also important ways in which the theory of literary translation *does* apply to, and illuminates the translation of, policy and practice:

(i) The active role of the translator in interpreting the source material:

> Translation ultimately depends on dynamic, contextual reading, understanding and sometimes creative reception of a source text. In the process of translation, the mediator's own understanding or "misunderstanding" of the source text will be realised in the translated text. (Wang 2002, 284)

(ii) The importance of understanding the possibilities and limitations of the destination language and culture if the meaning of the original text is to be successfully conveyed:

According to Brisset (2010) 'the cultural turn' that revolutionised translation studies came in the wake of post-colonialism, though the need to problematise the cultural context of translation came from as far back as the anthropological work of Malinowski. 'The problem for anthropologists,' writes Brisset, 'is that the translation of other cultures is always set by the dangers of distortion posed by interpreting indigenous concepts in a conceptual system that is foreign to them' (Brisset 2010, 71). Such is the problem of translating educational policies and practices.

(iii) The charge of neo-colonialism when there is a one-way traffic in translation:
Wang (2002), for example, discusses this in the context of the rather unbalanced traffic of translation between China and the English speaking world. The UNESCO *Index Translationum* suggests that only a trickle of books get translated from English compared with the flood that get translated from other languages into English. In education policy terms, Kazakhstan is clearly a major receiver rather than a transmitter of texts, though the sources are very diverse.

(iv) The role of the reader and not just the author or translator in constructing meaning from text:
Dobson writes of the translator as pedagogue and of the pedagogue as translator, and he highlights 'the teacher's need to teach the pupil to be active and collaborative with the pedagogue in order to co-author meaning through acts of translation in the classroom' (Dobson 2012, 283). We see the translator of educational policy and practice as emphatically in this pedagogic role and those at the destination of translation as actively engaged in redefining and co-constructing the locally applicable meaning of what is received.

(v) The scope for creativity and the bringing of new meaning through translation.
This is a rather crude way of expressing something that, for example, Walter Benjamin conveys rather more subtly in his classic *L'essai sur la traduction* (1997). Benjamin points out that translation proceeds not so much from the life of an original, which are rarely translated in the age in which they are produced, but from its 'afterlife' or 'survival' [*Überleben*] and perhaps because of their continuing life [*Fortleben*]. 'Translations that are more than transmissions of a message are produced when a work, in its continuing life, has reached the age of its fame. . . . In them the original's life receives its constantly renewed, latest and most comprehensive unfolding' (Benjamin 1997, 154). Further, 'in its continuing life, which could not be so called if it were not the transformation and renewal of a living thing, the original is changed. Established words also have their after-ripening' (ibid., 155).

Educational policies and practices tend similarly to receive the attention of 'translators' some time after their original development and in forms that have already – by the time they have achieved 'fame' – departed perhaps from their original sources. Translators serve their 'readers' and their text poorly if they fail to contribute to the continuing renewal of the original, to its 'after-ripening'. The real risk is not just about what might be *lost* in translation but what the translator fails to create, to discover, to *find*.

REFERENCES

Anderson-Levitt, K. (2011). 'Translating Anthropologies of Education'. *Anthopology News*, 52:2, 13.

Anscombe, G.E.M. (1979). 'What is it to Believe Someone?' In C.F. Delaney, (ed.), *Rationality and Religious Belief*. Notre Dame IN: Notre Dame University Press.

Ball, S.J., Maguire, M. and **Braun, A.** (2012). *How Schools do Policy: Policy Enactments in Secondary Schools*. London: Routledge.

Benjamin, W. (1997). 'L'essai sur la traduction'. *Traduction, Terminologies, Redaction*, 10:2, 151–65. Trans. S. Rendall as 'The Translator's Task', downloaded at www.erudite.org/iderudit/037302ar, 4 August 2013.

Bhabha, H.K. (1990). *Nation and Narration*. London: Routledge.

Bloom, B.S. (ed.) (1956). *Taxonomy of Educational Objectives I. Cognitive Domain*. London: Longman.

Botha, R.J. (2002). 'Outcomes-Based Education and Educational Reform in South Africa'. *International Journal of Leadership in Education*, 5:4, 361–71.

Bridges, D. (2008). 'Evidence-Based Reform in Education: A Response to Robert Slavin'. *European Educational Research Journal*, 7:1, 129–33.

Bridges, D., Smeyers, P. and **Smith, R.D.** (eds) (2009). *Evidence-Based Education Policy: What Evidence? What Basis? Whose Policy?* Chichester: Wiley Blackwell – first published (2008) as volume 42 supplement 1 of the *Journal of Philosophy of Education*.

Brisset, A. (2010). *Cultural Perspectives on Translation*. Oxford: Blackwell/UNESCO.

Cowen, R. (2009). 'The Transfer, Translation and Transformation of Educational Processes: And their Shape Shifting?' *Comparative Education*, 45:3, 315–27.

Derrida, J. (2001). 'What is a "Relevant" Translation?' *Critical Inquiry*, 27, 174–200.

Dobson, S. (2012). 'The "Pedagogue as Translator" in the Classroom'. *Journal of Philosophy of Education*, 46:2, 271–86.

Donn, G. and **Al Manthri, Y.** (2010). *Globalisation and Higher Education in the Arab Gulf States*. Oxford: Symposium.

Fierman, W. (1998). 'Language and Identity in Kazakhstan: Formulations in Policy Documents 1987–97'. *Communist and Post-Communist Studies*, 31:2, 171–86.

Fullan, M. (2007). *The New Meaning of Educational Change*. New York: Teachers College Press.

Giddens, A. (1990). *The Consequences of Modernity*. Cambridge: Polity Press.

Gleeson, J. (2013). 'The European Credit Transfer System and Curriculum Design: Product Before Process?' *Studies in Higher Education*, 38:6, 921–38.

Hayes, D. (2000). 'Cascade Training and Teachers' Professional Development'. *English Language Teaching Journal*, 34:2, 135–45.

International Crisis Group (2011). *Central Asia: Decay and Decline*. Asia Report No. 201, 11 February 2011.

Johnson, M.S. (2009). 'The Legacy of Russian and Soviet Education and the Shaping of Ethnic, Religious and National Identities in Central Asia'. In S.P. Heyneman and A.J. DeYoung, (eds), *The Challenge of Education in Central Asia*. Greenwich, CON: Information Age Publishing Inc.

Koyama, J.P. and **Varenne, H.** (2012). 'Assembling and Dissembling: Policy as Productive Play'. *Educational Researcher*, 41:5, 157–62.

Levin, B. (2004). 'Making Research Matter More'. *Education Policy Analysis Archives*, 12:56, 1–20.

Lingard, B., Rawolle, S. and **Taylor, S.** (2005). 'Globalising Policy Sociology in Education: Working with Bourdieu'. *Journal of Education Policy*, 20:6, 759–77.

Mukhopadhyay, R. and **Sriprakash, A.** (2011). 'Global Frameworks, Local Contingencies: Policy Translations and Education Development in India'. *Compare: A Journal of Comparative and International Education*, 41:3, 311–26.

Perry, L. and **Tor, G.H.** (2009). 'Understanding Educational Transfer: Theoretical Perspectives and Conceptual Frameworks'. *Prospects*, 38, 509–26.

Peters, R.S. (1966). *Ethics and Education*. London: Allen and Unwin.

Phillips, D. and **Ochs, K.** (2004). *Educational Policy Borrowing: Historical Perspectives*. Oxford: Symposium.

Piaget, J. (1978). *The Development of Thought: Equilibration of Cognitive Structures*, trans. A. Rosin. Oxford: Basil Blackwell.

Pring, R. (1971). Bloom's Taxonomy: A Philosophical Critique II. *Cambridge Journal of Education*, 1:2, 83–91.

Sayed, F. (2006). *Transforming Education in Egypt: Western Influence and Domestic Policy Reform*. Cairo: The American University in Cairo Press.

Silova, I. (2005). 'Travelling Policies: Hijacked in Central Asia'. *European Educational Research Journal*, 4:1, 50–59.

Singh, P., Thomas, S. and **Harris, J.** (2013). 'Re-contextualising Policy Discourses: A Bernsteinian Perspective on Policy Interpretation, Translation, Enactment'. *Journal of Educational Policy*, 28:4, 465–80.

Slavin, R.E. (2008). 'Evidence-Based Educational Reform in Education: What Will It Take?' *European Educational Research Journal*, 7:1, 129–33.

Sockett, H. (1971). 'Bloom's Taxonomy: A Philosophical Critique I'. *Cambridge Journal of Education*, 1:1, 16–25.

Spreen, C.A. (2006). 'Appropriating Borrowed Policies: Outcomes Based Education in South Africa'. In G. Steiner-Khamsi, (ed.), *The Global Politics of Educational Borrowing and Lending*. New York: Teachers College Press.

Steiner-Khamsi, G. and **Stolpe, I.** (2006). *Educational Import: Local Encounters with Global Forces in Mongolia*. New York: Palgrave Macmillan.

Steiner-Khamsi, G. (ed.) (2006). *The Global Politics of Educational Borrowing and Lending*. New York: Teachers College Press.

— (2012a). 'The Global/Local Nexus in Comparative Policy Studies: Analysing the Triple Bonus System in Mongolia Over Time'. *Comparative Education*, 48:4, 455–71.

— (2012b). 'What is Wrong with the "What Went Right" Approach in Educational Policy?' *European Educational Research Journal*, 12:1, 20–33.

Stenhouse, L. (1975). *An Introduction to Curriculum Research and Development*. London: Heinemann.

Tucker, J. (2011). *The Ancient Silk Road: An Illustrated Silk Road Map*. Hong Kong: Odyssey.

Wang, N. (2002). 'Translation as Cultural "(De)colonisation".' *Perspectives: Studies in Translatology*, 10:4, 283–91.

Winch, C. and **Gingell J.** (2004). *Philosophy and Educational Policy: A Critical Introduction*. London: Routledge.

NOTES

1   This extended chapter brings together material from what might have been two separate chapters, but the interplay of the material was such that it was judged that they were better presented as a single consecutive piece. We hope this will not prove too daunting to the reader.

2   Its 'autonomous' status means that it sits outside the laws that govern other schools in the state sector, so that it can reinvent the way in which schools work. The NIS Supreme Board of Trustees is chaired by President Nazarbayev and includes the Deputy Prime Minister and the Minister of Education, so that the schools are still ultimately under centralised political control.

3   Some NGOs have been heard to complain that with the government independent of external funding for its reform programme they lack leverage in terms of their own reform agenda.

4   UK political leaders, for example, seem increasingly to refer (selectively) to Finnish educational practice, to the teaching of Mathematics in Taiwan, the approach to vocational education in Germany and to assessment in Singapore. (This last case is somewhat ironical, since the Singaporean exams are the result of a long-standing partnership with Cambridge Assessment.)

5   The same officer saw this diversity as an advantage when it comes to the internalisation of international policies and practices: 'This helps us import best practices from all over the world in different (social sectors). For example, what kind of pension scheme should we have? Experts in 1990s analysed different models and chose the Chilean model as the best and we added a mixture of elements from other countries . . . The same can be said about education' (Respondent A, MoES).

6   A study conducted in 1998 indicated that 60% of Kazakhs spoke native or near native Russian but only 1% of Russians and 40% of Kazakhs claimed fluency in Kazakh (Fierman 1998, 174), but today an increasing number of parents are choosing to send their children to Kazakh medium schools and the language is expanding rapidly.

7   In both these last cases, functions that were until recently distributed to the regions have now been brought under centralised control.

8   Alarmingly (in terms of the capacity of teachers to deliver on this promise), the government plans to introduce trilingual education in schools nationwide in 2015 without yet (2013) taking any serious steps to secure the supply of adequately prepared teachers.

9   Not that school improvement needs to be either top-down or bottom-up: Darling Hammond endorses Michael Fullan's position that neither centralisation nor decentralisation works. 'Just as systems cannot change schools by mandate' she argues, 'widespread school change cannot occur by school invention alone, without supports and leadership from the policy system' (Darling Hammond 2005, 366).

10 The authors gratefully acknowledge advice from Lynne Parmenter of Nazarbayev University on this section.

14 TRANSFERABILITY AND THE NAZARBAYEV INTELLECTUAL SCHOOLS: Exploring Models of Practice Transfer

Alan Ruby (University of Pennsylvania, USA)
Colleen McLaughlin (University of Sussex, UK)

Introduction

The Nazarbayev Intellectual Schools (NIS) is a network of publicly funded schools across Kazakhstan that act as a beta site for innovation, experimentation and evaluation of educational practices (see Chapter 4). In the tradition of Dewey's laboratory school they are to identify and model good practice. Once efficacy of a practice has been established it is to be transferred to the public schools of the nation. The purpose of this chapter is to examine ways in which other educational innovations have been purposefully shared with large numbers of schools in order to offer a framework to categorise different forms of dissemination or transfer, and to suggest which form is most suitable for NIS.

Context

The NIS schools share some common design principles. They are aspirant organisations that seek to have outcomes comparable to those of the best schools in the world. They are elite institutions that enroll less than 1% of the age cohort. The schools are intellectually selective and have a competitive entry process while aiming to be accessible to all segments of society. The entrance tests are available in both Russian and Kazakh, the schools are spread across the nation, many have boarding facilities and the schools are tuition free with meals, uniforms and lodging also free of charge.

In less than ten years from the opening of the first school, much progress has been made: an integrated academic programme has been developed in partnership with Cambridge International Examinations (CIE), an integrated trilingual strategy has been defined, and professional development courses have been designed and delivered by CIE and the University of Cambridge Faculty of Education. These and other new policies and programmes are at different stages of implementation. The next and immediate strategic question facing the NIS leadership and the Ministry of Education and Science (MoES) is how to transfer successful practice from an elite and well-resourced network of twenty schools to public schools nationwide.

Spreading innovation

The current literature on policy reform and innovation, despite being written from a variety of perspectives – be it a 'developmental paradigm' (e.g. OECD and World Bank), 'neo-liberal imaginary' (e.g. Ball 2012) or 'policy borrowing' model (e.g. Silova 2005 and Steiner-Khamsi 2004) – lacks a clear, articulated strategy for transferring policy into practice. This is in part due to a history of unsuccessful, partial or contested education policy transfers in national or regional settings and in part to conceptual ambiguity. This ambiguity is illustrated by the array of terms used to discuss the spread of innovation: the adoption or implementation of innovation, 'going to scale' and the metaphors from science and medicine such as 'laboratory schools' and 'demonstration schools'. We summarise some of both the history and the diversity of language and use that as a basis for categorising six different strategies of educational change.

Lighthouses, laboratory and demonstration schools

The NIS model has begun by developing and testing policies and practices in a new school environment before looking for a means or a method of transfer. This makes the NIS more akin to an older tradition of educational innovation and experimentation, the laboratory school.

The conventional image of laboratory or model schools was that they would act as agents of change by demonstrating good practice. They would be 'lighthouses' illuminating other public schools, and ideas would diffuse across the system.

The idea of demonstration schools persisted from the 1850s onwards, and even recently found new expression in the US Charter Schools which grew quickly from the 1990s, and in the shortlived (1998–2005) Beacon Schools in the UK. While they all share the general idea that change can be promoted and spread by demonstration sites, the different types of model schools usually differ in the ways in which they approach innovation and reform. One approach is to focus on teaching practice, to demonstrate the art and craft of good teaching. These 'demonstration schools' were often connected with formal teacher education programmes. An early example is University High School at the University of Illinois. Founded in 1857 its mission was, and is still stated to be, to 'promote effective high quality education throughout the teaching profession and to aid other educators in the process of improving the quality of education in their schools.' It aims to continue the tradition of serving as a 'clinical experience and practice site for pre-service teachers and experimental teaching activities' (uhigh.ilstu.edu/aboutus.htm accessed July 2012).

The Parker School established at the University of Chicago in the 1900s was in the same tradition. Colonel Parker was interested in 'what would help children learn . . . not why' (DePencier 1967, 18) and saw part of the mission of the school to be a practice school for novice teachers. The demonstration schools persisted even as teacher preparation became more discipline based. The Falk School, 'a progressive . . . school for demonstration purposes' was established in 1930 at the University of Pittsburgh. And demonstration schools spread. They were operating in Australian public schools into the 1970s (Fletcher and Burnswoods 1980) and the North Sydney Demonstration School still operates today. The model or demonstration school concept has also been recast or re-labelled. For example model schools were created in the USSR in the 1930s to showcase the standard curriculum (Holmes 1999, 7). One recent version is the Professional Development Schools (PDS) in the USA, which were 'envisioned as institutional settings that would be both models of the best P-12 practice and optimum sites for clinical preparation of novice teachers. In addition they would be schools where new knowledge and organizational structures would be generated, tested and refined. The practices that emerged . . . could then be disseminated to the larger educational community' (Abdal-Haqq 1998, 2). In the UK the most recent policy establishes the notion of 'teaching schools' and has two forms of arrangement. One borrows from the Scandinavian model of schools attached to universities to generate innovative and good practice informed by research. These are called 'University Training Schools' and would be run by universities.

The other, which has developed much faster, is the 'Teaching School'. These are 'on the model of teaching hospitals to lead the training and professional development of teachers and head teachers, and increase the number of National and Local Leaders of Education – head teachers of excellent schools who commit to working to support other schools' (DfE 2010, 9). They are also born of a desire to link the generation of knowledge by researchers or academics and the knowledge of practice in the schools. This mode of learning is to be found in the hospital and this is the analogy often invoked for all forms of demonstration schools: the teaching hospital, where best medical practice was displayed and new entrants to the profession trained systematically and under expert supervision. The weakness of the analogy is that the teaching hospital has a regime of individual diagnostic cases focused on individuals with specific conditions. The school usually deals with groups of students and more broadly defined ends. The strength and weakness of the demonstration school model is how, if at all, knowledge is shared, transferred to others and then applied. The first assumption is that display and, presumably, observation by novices will lead to learning or changed behaviour. This assumption is often elaborated to include recording, analysing and codifying the observed practice, with the resulting artefact distributed to the target audience. What happens when the observation takes place or the artefact reaches the school or classroom is unknown.

The same problem of lack of transferability and application was embedded in the concept of laboratory schools. The most famous is the laboratory school at the University of Chicago established in the 1896. John Dewey's intention in founding the school was 'to attempt a systematic organization of the school curriculum, testing and developing methods both from the psychological and practical sides' (Durst 2010, 21). As adjunct to the university and its education department it would be a laboratory with 'two main purposes: (1) to exhibit, test, verify and criticise theoretical statements and principles; and (2) to add to the sum of facts in its special line' (Mayhew and Edwards 1936, 3). But Dewey had no plan for dissemination or diffusion and only a secondary interest in teacher preparation. His interest was essentially scientific 'to "demonstrate the feasibility" of the sorts of schooling he envisaged' (Cohen 1998, 442). Even after his departure while his successors, like Judd, encouraged faculty publication the 'key principle was "concerted analysis of the learning process under laboratory conditions"' (DePencier 1967, 72).

In summary the notion of an exemplary site of practice or experimentation as a means of spreading innovation falls short of the goal because there is no explicit means of transferring practice and no motivation for teachers to take up new ideas or methods other than a desire to emulate or copy 'good' behaviour. The laboratory or demonstration school places greater value on experimentation and display than on the distribution of knowledge and the diffusion and adoption of effective practice. They lack a theory of action or a model of change.

Money, volunteers and mandates

The theory of change underlying the US federal government's educational interventions in the early 1970s worked on the assumption that 'seed money' would introduce and sustain change and if successful the changes would be taken up by others voluntarily. In reality additional money alone 'had little if any influence on the motivation' to innovate. Money alone does not shape commitment to change nor create motivations to reform or a 'concern for innovation'" in school authorities. Other elements were important. Leadership and an institutional culture that welcomed innovation were 'necessary but not sufficient for effective implementation'. To be effective there also needed to be a well-structured implementation strategy with staff training and local material development (Berman and McLaughlin 1975, v–xi and 23).

The need for a range of measures to support innovation and programme adoption can be found in a recent study of two large scale interventions in US elementary schools. Both interventions, 'Success for All' and 'America's Choice' are well established school improvement networks serving hundreds of schools. These organisations were strongly affected by the operating environment: 'networks are prone to a high degree of uncertainty and unpredictability.' To survive this turbulence they need strong community infrastructure including curriculum and assessment materials, training, information systems and leadership development (Glazer and Peurach 2013). The main method of diffusion or adoption in both interventions was for schools or schools districts to 'opt in', to volunteer to adopt the particular practice or programme. Diffusion of innovation by volunteerism or 'mimicry' is a well-established strategy. Examples include the long standing International Baccalaureate (IB) and the more recent Khan Academy, an online educational resource. These programmes offer a set of policies, materials, professional development and suggested practices to schools. These become criteria or standards for 'membership' of the community. Some organisations, like the IB with its phases of candidature and stress on teacher development, have rigorous processes and requirements to join and to maintain membership. Others are more open, with fewer process requirements. But the distinctive feature is that schools elect to pursue a pre-designed path or model of improvement.

At the other end of the spectrum to volunteerism are centrally mandated, national or systemwide attempts to improve or change the ways schools work. Adoption relies on the authority or power of an agency to compel or enforce adoption. Policy statements, edicts or ukases specify what the school or teacher should do.

In some cases the policy or programme is designed by experts within ministries, or under contract to ministries, and rolled out uniformly. In recent times, this approach owes much to the public service nature of the school systems that operate within requirements of equality of treatment for individuals. It also avoids debates about the risks of 'experimenting' on groups of children that may harm them or give them an advantage over their age peers.

One example of a government mandated reform is the English National Literacy and Numeracy Strategy (NLNS). Initiated in 1997, NLNS set specific goals and communicated them widely. Implementation was backed by clear accountability, professional development and data mechanisms to monitor progress, distribute rewards and allocate support services. The initiative was 'heavily directed from the centre' and highly scripted, with little room for professional reflection and 'local creativity' (Fullan and Earl 2002, 4).

Some argue that assessment protocols can be ways governments transmit or promote teaching regimen or time allocations. Referring to the international programme of assessment (PISA) Meyer and Benavot, (2013, 17) argue that 'centralization, standardization, uniformity, training (in the sense of "drilling") technocratic elitism – have increasingly become part of the western institutional practice.'

There is variation within this centrally directed, 'sit up and listen', approach. In London the 'City Challenge' has the same drivers as most national and provincial government policies. 'It was designed to improve educational outcomes for young people and "to crack the associated cycle of disadvantage and underachievement" in the Black Country, Greater Manchester and London' (DfES 2007, 1). This initiative was occurring within a context of centralised mandated reform which many would argue was driven by an authoritarian transfer model of enforcement of policy through a rigorous national inspection model, known locally as Ofsted.

The City Challenge used a different set of strategies: school-to-school collaboration, a belief that the educational problems facing urban areas should be addressed at area level, for all schools in that area, with an emphasis on leadership and with support from external informed professionals either local or national (Hutchings et al. 2012).

There was also a very specific set of structures and procedures for knowledge transfer such as conferences, schools working together in small groups, a stronger school supporting a weaker one (which may also include soft federations); groups of three, led by the head teacher of a more successful school; and the setting up of knowledge centres or hubs in schools that had specific areas of outstanding practice that others could visit and learn from (Hutchings et al. 2012, viii, ix). The evaluation of the work (ibid.) concludes that the improvement of educational outcomes (attainment measured on inspection criteria, as well as the impact on disadvantage) was consistently above the national average for attainment and rates of progress. The factors that were seen as key included general points of planning such as having clear objectives at area and school level and having a clear focus on school leadership, especially through coaching, mentoring and other development opportunities. Other factors distinguished it from the centralised, mandated approaches, for example, avoiding target setting, offering additional support; working at an area level; offering bespoke solutions to tackle specific issues; an emphasis on observation of teachers by teachers, opportunities to reflect with colleagues, and coaching in the teacher's own classroom (Hutchings et al. 2012, xi). The three-year time scale for improvement proved to be too short. Hutchings et al. (2012) concluded that 'Perhaps the most effective aspect of City Challenge was that it recognised that people, and schools, tend to thrive when they feel trusted, supported and encouraged. The ethos of the programme, in which successes were celebrated and it was recognised that if teachers are to inspire pupils they themselves need to be motivated and inspired, was a key factor in its success' (2012, xi).

These large-scale efforts at initiating change in public education in the USA and London all struggled with the concept of adoption and scale. They attempted to have large numbers of existing schools apply sets of policies and procedures, designed and codified by a central agency. Some offered incentives; others depended on authority or a means of compliance like inspection and some relied on external leadership and support.

Going to scale, franchises and fidelity

Elmore (1996) made 'getting to scale' a key variable in the design and imple-mentation of educational reforms that were beyond the current competence of the main actors, be they teachers or administrators. His conclusion was that money and exhortation were not enough to change well established cul-tural institutions. The idea has been taken up by Coburn (2003) who argues that scale in educational reform is 'under theorized' and usually expressed solely in terms of numbers of schools. This overlooks the complexity of im-plementation and the extent to which a reform is adopted in practice, the 'depth' or quality of changed behaviour. Simply counting school sites also overlooks issues of sustainability and the extent to which norms, values and principles associated with the desired behaviours change. Coburn prefers to assess the pervasiveness of change; does it 'spread' throughout the institution and is it adopted or 'owned' and championed by people in the workplace?

The importance of sustainability is underscored by Datnow's (2002) quali-tative research which showed that comprehensive reform efforts were often modified, adapted and abandoned as leadership and other contextual vari-ables changed. She questions whether educational reform can realistically be 'transplanted,' adding further to the metaphors used to delineate the transfer of educational innovation.

Another approach is to conceive of the take-up of innovation in terms of 'replication'. This evokes notions of franchising where outlets are created by following a specified set of norms and practices, where signage, product array, pricing and location are all regulated by a central body. Compliance is checked by inspection and penalties for deviance are specified in fran-chise agreements. An alternative view of replication comes from Winter and Szulanski (2001) who use empirical evidence to support the idea that an effective replication strategy includes a phase of 'exploration' where the programme or intervention is developed, tried and 'refined' before it is 'sta-bilized and leveraged' (730). Winter's work has influenced Peurach (2012) in his comprehensive study of Success for All (SfA) which led him to conclude that rather than operating as a compliance franchise model SfA was largely a collaborative exercise that used knowledge of best practices to build effective professional relationships between teachers and the external agency (See also Glazer and Peurach 2013).

All four approaches informed Levin's (2013) study of three well known US educational interventions: Teach for America; the Harlem Children's Zone and Knowledge is Power Program; the KIPP academies. Levin's primary interest was to 'develop a set of criteria for assessing (the) scalability' of innovations especially those 'intended to have a national impact'. From an analysis of the generic literature on innovation and implementing change Levin argues that five factors are 'essential' when considering the scalability of an innovation: cost, capacity, infrastructure, political support and external environment. He applies these factors to the three innovations in order to assess the challenges each faces to reach 25% of the target population. While Levin's work is a valuable tool for analysing innovations, by his own admission the five factors do not capture the key questions of 'fidelity [and] efficacy' (2013, 10).

The tension between a franchise model with a strong emphasis on fidelity or compliance to ensure efficacy and the reality that organisations or teams need to learn and adapt processes to local circumstances is accentuated by going to scale. The increased number of sites or delivery points brings an increase in the diversity of those served and an increase in the number of environmental factors that can and will shape implementation. As scale increases so does the likelihood of variation.

The other source of variation is the professional practice of teachers. This is well-illustrated in a study for the Department of Education in the UK (Fielding et al., 2005) on the transfer of practice between schools, which concluded that four elements had special significance. Firstly and most importantly, 'that this kind of teacher learning is a social process that is sustained by relationships and trust; secondly, that it is a personal and inter-personal process that has to engage with our sense of who we are, with teacher and institutional identity; thirdly, that it requires conditions that provide support for learner engagement fostering the willingness to try something out; and, lastly, that the work of transfer has to be sustained over time. It is not a quick fix. It requires a more sophisticated and more patient understanding of time than is customarily acknowledged or allowed' (2005, 6). The team concluded that joint practice development better describes what happens when teachers collaborate to develop practice. It is not a notion of transfer or travel but rather a collaborative process in which one teacher develops their existing practice in the light of the collaboration. The teacher employs judgment about what to discard and what to adapt or adopt. This model sees the teacher who is learning as an active and engaged learner rather than a passive vessel.

Conclusion

The cross-national, national and school site models of reform reviewed briefly above lack a clear, articulated transfer strategy (with the possible exception of the NLNS). They assume that observation of practice or access to information about why a practice is effective will lead to changed behaviour and that this change will become 'routinised' – the sign of successful innovation (Berman and McLaughlin 1975, vii). Looking at these examples and other education reforms of the last forty years of 'school reform' in the industrialised democracies we see six basic strategies for knowledge transfer or take-up of reform. The first two characterise the demonstration sites. They are:

1. Observation of a desired practice will cause teachers to imitate or emulate that behaviour (transfer by mimicry)
2. Understanding why a practice is desirable or effective, or both, teachers will initiate and sustain changed behaviour because it will attain 'some socially desirable end' (epistemological transfer). (Bennis 1963, 134)

The third, fourth and fifth strategies have different approaches to motivation ranging from compulsion, to incentives to volunteerism. They are:

3. Change can be mandated or required (authoritarian transfer)
4. Fiscal incentives will stimulate and reward new behaviour (market transfer)
5. Change can be voluntary as school staff or individuals opt in (unguided transfer).

The sixth strategy is grounded in a model of collegiality and a community of professional practice:

6. Change can be constructed by school-to-school collaborations and local leadership supported by external informed professionals (collegial transfer).

The arguments put forward by David Hargreaves embody this, the sixth, model of change. Hargreaves' (2012) thinking underpins the teaching schools model in the UK. He argues that there are three core elements to a self-improving school system:

- a partnership dimension
- a professional development dimension and
- a collaborative capital dimension.

Similarly, Mourshed et al. (2010) argue that collaborative practice is a key feature of the most improved school systems and that 'collaborative practice is the method by which a school system "hardwires" the values and beliefs implicit in its system into a form manifest in day-to–day teaching' (2010, 74).

Our argument is that for NIS and Kazakhstan this sixth strategy is the most apposite. It incorporates the elements that contributed to the effectiveness of other reform strategies more comprehensively than the other five approaches. It includes the external support and guidance that were important to the London City Challenge and SfA. It explicitly includes the school to school transfer and networking found to be important by Fielding et al. The emphasis on school-to-school transfer allows for ready observation of the practices of other teachers and departments which is a powerful process of learning in many reforms. It allows for the easy exchange of ideas, techniques and 'recognizable experiences' (Bruner 1966, 44). The collegial strategy also underscores the professionalism of many of the actors and encourages them to accept responsibility for improvement and for sharing knowledge.

The collegial strategy is also compatible with the proposition that knowledge transfer and the dissemination of reform or change in a social institution, like a school or system of schools, are best pursued through 'communities of practice'. These communities 'share cultural practices reflecting their mutual learning'. The members of these groups do things jointly and hold each other accountable. They share some norms of mutual respect and create and use a common 'repertoire of communal resources' (Wenger 2000, 229). These groupings of people within and across schools and involving actors from outside schools are effective ways of transferring, initiating and implementing change. This strategy is especially salient when a new system of schools is emerging, when the actors are coming together for the first time, bringing a variety of experiences drawn from different national and linguistic settings.

Communities of practice are not delimited by school boundaries, nor should they be. The experience of the London City Challenge and other reforms shows that networks that cross school boundaries can be very powerful ways of bringing people together to achieve practical results. This is reinforced by evidence on the benefits of teacher networks as change agents. Niesz (2007, 609), discussing voluntary teacher professional development networks, sees these as a focus on 'sound improvement informed by big ideas' about learning and change, flexibility and acting as a 'foil . . . to the myriad other factors' competing for teachers' time and attention.

Networks can also be a way for a central agency to support and guide development collegially. While many of the US examples of effective networks are voluntary networks it is important to note that many of them were external to schools, hosted by universities or non-profit agencies. Lieberman (1995, 74) concludes her review of them for the US National Science Foundation by arguing that in bringing teachers together 'whether in regard to particular subject areas, [or] articulated principles for reforming schools, new . . . techniques . . . provided them with access to new ideas and a supportive community.'

In short we argue that the collegial approach to the transfer of innovation, reform and practical knowledge is appropriate for NIS and Kazakhstan. It is an approach grounded in international experience. It also sits well with the realities of the nation where the challenges of distance and a relatively weak infrastructure are balanced by the presence of a well-educated, highly motivated teaching force. In practical terms for a post-Soviet nation with nascent institutions after twenty years of independence, it means placing a premium on the growth of voluntary professional associations, be they subject specific like Mathematics teachers, or thematic, such as trilingualism, or cross-curricular, like student leadership. These associations could operate at the regional and national level and act as self-sustaining networks for professional dialogue and the exchange of ideas and best practices. Support for these networks or communities of practice could be fiscal and technical or, in the form of infrastructure, they could be spaces and forums for meeting. It could extend to creating electronic bulletin boards, in Kazakh, Russian and English, to promote action research and discussion on educational issues, and the exchange of good practice. Whatever form this support takes, it should be based on the principles of collegial learning, emphasise the importance of learning from the observation and systematic discussion of practice and be supported by informed and trained professionals.

REFERENCES

Abdal-Haqq, I. (1998). *Professional Development Schools: Weighing the Evidence*. Thousand Oaks CA: Corwin Press.

Ball, S.J. (2012). *Global Education Inc.: New Policy Networks and the Neoliberal Imaginary*. London: Routledge.

Bennis, W.G. (1963). 'A New Role for the Behavioural Sciences: Effecting Organizational Change'. *Administrative Science Quarterly*, 8:2, 125–165.

Berman, P. and **McLaughlin, M.W.** (1975). 'Federal Programs Supporting Educational Change: Vol. IV The Findings in Review'. R-1589/4-HEW. Santa Monica CA: Rand.

Bruner, J. (1966). *Towards a Theory of Instruction*. Cambridge MA: Harvard University Press.

Cartwright, D. (1951). *Field Theory in Social Sciences: Selected Theoretical Papers*. New York: Harper.

Coburn, C.E. (2003). 'Rethinking Scale: Moving Beyond Numbers to Deep and Lasting Change'. *Educational Researcher*, 32:6, 3–12.

Correnti, R. and **Rowan, B.** (2007). 'Opening up the Black Box: Literacy Instruction in Schools Participating in Three Comprehensive School Reform Programs'. *American Educational Research Journal*, 44:2, 298–338.

Datnow, A. (2002). 'Can We Transplant Educational Reform, and Does It Last?' *Journal of Educational Change*, 3:3-4, 215–39.

DfE (Department for Education) (2010). *The Importance of Teaching*. London: The Stationery Office and online www.education.gov.uk.

DfES (Department for Education and Science) (2007). *City Challenge for World Class Education*. London: DfES.

DePencier, I.B. (1967). *The History of the Laboratory Schools: The University of Chicago 1896–1965*. Chicago: Quadrangle.

Durst, A. (2010). *Women Educators in the Progressive Era: The Women Behind Dewey's Laboratory School*. New York: Palgrave, MacMillan.

Fielding, M., Bragg, S., Craig, J., Cunningham, C., Eraut, M., Gillinson, S., Horne, M., Robinson, C. and **Thorp, J.** (2005). 'Factors Influencing the Transfer of Good Practice'. DfE Research Report RR615. London: Department for Education.

Fletcher, J.J. and **Burnswoods, J.** (1980). *Sydney and the Bush: A Pictorial History of Education in New South Wales*. Sydney: NSW Department of Education.

Fullan, M. and **Earl, L.** (2002). 'United Kingdom National Literacy and Numeracy Strategy, Large Scale Reform'. *Journal of Educational Change*, 3, 1–5.

Glazer, J.L. and **Peurach, D.J.** (2013). 'School Improvement Networks as a Strategy for Large-Scale Education Reform: The Role of Educational Environments'. *Educational Policy*, 27:4, 676–710.

Hargreaves, D.H. (2012). *A Self-Improving School System: Towards Maturity*. Nottingham: National College of School Leadership. www.dera.ioe.ac.uk/15912/1.

Holmes, L.E. (1999). *Stalin's School. Moscow State School #25, 1931–37*. Pittsburg: University of Pittsburgh Press.

Hutchings, M., Greenwood, C., Hollingsworth, S., Mansaray, A. and **Rose, A.** with **Minty, S.** and **Glass, K.** (2012). 'Evaluation of the City Challenge Programme'. Department for

Education Research Report RR215 (Ref: DFE-RR215). www.education.gov.uk/publications/standard/publicationDetail/Page1/DFE-RR215 / London: The Stationery Office.

Levin, B. (2013). 'What Does It Take To Scale Up Innovations?' Boulder CO: National Education Policy Center. www.greatlakescenter.org/docs/Policy_Briefs/Levin_Scalability.pdf.

Lieberman, A. (1995). 'Practices that Support Teachers' Development: Transforming Conceptions of Professional Learning'. In *Innovations and Evaluating Science Education: New Evaluation Forums 1992–94*. www.nsf.gov.pubs.

Mayhew, K.C. and Edwards, A.C. (1936). *The Dewey School: The Laboratory School of the University of Chicago 1896–1903*. New York: Appleton-Century.

Meyer, D.M. and Benavot, A. (2013). *PISA, Power and Policy: The Emergence of Global Educational Governance*. Oxford: Symposium Books.

Mourshed, M., Chijioke, C. and Barber, M. (2010). *How the World's Most Improved School Systems Keep Getting Better*. London: McKinsey.

Niesz, T. (2007). 'Why Teacher Networks (Can) Work'. *Phi Delta Kappan*, 88:8, 605–10.

ORS (2004). *Theory of Change: A Practical Tool for Action, Results and Learning*. New York: Annie E. Casey Foundation. www.aecf.org/upload/publicationfiles/cc2977k440.pdf.

Picciotto, R. and Anderson, J.R. (1997). 'Reconsidering Agricultural Extension'. *The World Bank Research Observer*, 12:2, 249–59.

Resnick, L.B. and Williams Hall, M. (1998). 'Learning Organizations for Sustainable Education Reform'. *Daedalus*, 127:4, *Education Yesterday, Education Tomorrow*, 89–118.

Rowan, B. (2002). 'The Ecology of School Improvement: Notes on the School Improvement Industry in the United States'. *Journal of Educational Change*, 3, 283–314.

Ruby, A. (1991). 'Real Change or Traditional Advice'. In C. Fasano and B. Winder (eds), *Education Policy in Australia*. Wollongong: University of Wollongong Press.

Wenger, E. (2000). 'Communities of Practice and Social Learning Systems'. *Organization*, 1:1, 225–46.

Winter, S.G. and Szulanski, G. (2001). 'Replication as Strategy'. *Organization Science*, 12:6, 730–43.

15 TRANSLATING PEDAGOGICAL 'EXCELLENCE' INTO THREE LANGUAGES or How Kazakhstani Teachers 'Change'

Olena Fimyar (University of Cambridge, Faculty of Education)

Introduction

Drawing on the works in policy sociology and comparative education, this chapter addresses the question of how discourse of teacher professionalism advanced by Kazakhstan's large-scale teacher professional development initiative, the Centre of Excellence (CoE), is enacted by the trainers going through the programme. Celebrated as a professional development programme of the 'new format', the initiative brings together representatives of the three language (and practice) communities including English-speaking trainers, Kazakh-speaking teachers, Russian-speaking teachers and English-Russian and English-Kazakh translators. The presence of English-speaking trainers and the areas of expertise upon which they draw makes the act of translation an indispensable part of the process of educational 'change' in Kazakhstan. The lack of attention to the question of how linguistic translation impacts the conceptualisation of educational 'change' and behaviour of different language and practice communities involved in the process of 'change' is surprising amidst the proliferation of interest in teacher education programmes around the globe. Thus, keeping a simultaneous focus on discourse of teacher professionalism and its enactment, this chapter points to the increasing pressure to perform 'change' in the Kazakhstan context, which raises questions about the degree of internalisation and understanding of 'change' by teacher trainers and teacher educators in Kazakhstan.

Translation between languages: a blind spot in policy sociology and comparative education

Despite their attempts to better understand the effects and manifestations of globalisation in education and society, works in policy sociology and comparative education rarely reflect on the issues of translation between languages and translation of policy between different language communities (see Srivastava 2006). Similarly left unaddressed are the questions of how professional discourses in the field of education are translated into languages other than English and the effects the act of translation has on the (re)definition of the teaching profession in local settings. What is also surprising is that both comparative education and policy sociology use the term 'translation', but with a meaning that is detached from the linguistic context. This section provides a brief outline of how the term 'translation' is used in the fields of policy sociology and comparative education, and argues for bringing the issues surrounding the act of translation back under the spotlight of analysis.

In the field of comparative education the concept of *translation* is used in relation to the 'reception' of global policy in local contexts. Such broad framing of the object of analysis, however, does not include the question of translation between languages and its effects on the national projects of professionalisation. Even though some of the works in comparative education are particularly interested in the gaps and 'subversions' (cf. Silova's 'hijacking', 2005) of meaning at the point when 'travelling' policies hit the local grounds, there is an implicit assumption that the 'local speak', although different from the 'global talk', is still conducted in English. Nor is the question of translatability between languages and professional discourses raised in such otherwise insightful studies as those collected in the 2005 European Educational Research Association Special Issue on 'Travelling Policy in Post-Socialist Education' (see Silova's 2005 paper in particular), *Globalisation on the Margins: Education and Post-Socialist Transformations in Central Asia* (Silova 2011), and the *World Yearbook of Education 2012* on *Policy Borrowing and Lending in Education*. An important exception to this general tendency is Steiner-Khamsi's (2012) work on policy bilinguism, to which we will return later in the section.

In the field of policy sociology, the meaning of the term 'translation' is detached from its linguistic origin. The term 'translation' is used interchangeably with 'policy implementation', 'policy interpretation' and 'policy enactment' (e.g. in Braun, Maguire and Ball 2010; Singh, Thomas and Harris 2013; Mukhopadhyay and Sriprakash 2013). Yet again, the main preoccupation of these studies is not translation in linguistic terms, but rather a movement of policy within and across different domains (political, educational, mass media), and the process of coding, decoding and re-coding (hence, translation) of policy in different textual media (education laws, curriculum documents, textbooks, newspaper articles and so on). In these studies translation is understood as the process of 'putting those texts into action, literally "enacting" policy using tactics, talks, meeting, plans, events, "learning walks"' and so on (Ball et al. 2011, 620). Hence, these studies deal with the translation of policy text into action, which takes place predominantly in monolingual settings.

However, policy making in many countries, including a growing number of the former Soviet countries, takes place in a multilingual environment, where the national languages are spoken (with the help of translators) on par with English as the language of 'Western' expertise (Silova and Brehm 2013). English is also spoken in these countries by a growing number of academic returnees, who, upon their return, join the ranks of the national academic, business and policy elites (as is required by many government-sponsored scholarships, including the Kazakhstani *Bolashak* – 'Future' – programme). Rizvi refers to this group of professionals as a 'new global generation', who, due to their newly acquired dispositions and symbolic capital, have 'multiple cultural defining points' (Rizvi 2000, 223). The presence of 'Western' expertise and the role of Western-educated professionals in redefining the boundaries of professional knowledge, including education, raises questions about the balance of power between the national and foreign experts in the field of policy as well as the distribution of power and knowledge between the national and regional levels (Bacevic 2005, 2010; Silova and Brehm 2013; Fimyar 2010, 2011).

Either celebrated or resisted by the local actors, the presence of foreign experts in the national policy field changes power dynamics within it. The observations of Codd (1988) and Steiner-Khamsi (2006) about the harmonising and conflicting effects of policy are important in this respect: on the one hand, policies 'work to mask social conflict' (Codd 1988, 237), yet, on the other hand, 'the very act of borrowing [produces] a salutary effect on domestic policy conflict' (Steiner-Khamsi 2006, 671). Being attentive to the issues of power, this chapter attends to the question of how a trilingual policy environment and selective borrowing of Western educational discourses shapes the process of establishment and operation of the CoE teacher development programme (see Chapter 5 for a general introduction). Related to this is the question of how the process of policy enactment and the redrawing of the boundaries of teacher professionalism is further complicated by the fact that many concepts translated from the original language (in this case English) do not have direct equivalents in the pedagogical and social practices of the target languages (that is, Kazakh and Russian). Examples of concepts that are difficult to translate and, consequently, difficult to enact are 'inclusion', 'action research', 'feedback for learning', 'assessment for learning' and others.

Useful conceptual tools for addressing these questions can be found in Steiner-Khamsi's (2012, 468) discussion of policy bilingualism (not to be confused with bilingual policy), which she uses to account for the process whereby the same policy issue, in this case the triple bonus system for teachers in Mongolia, is presented differently to the Western and national audiences. By bringing our attention to the notions of 'positionality' and 'audience', Steiner-Khamsi analyses examples of governmental officials engaging in, what she calls, 'double-talk': one aimed at donor organisations and another addressed to the Mongolian audience. Both of these talks have their own vocabularies and rationalisation techniques and are best understood as two distinct scales or 'spaces' from which one and the same policy actor or state institution speaks or operates (Steiner-Khamsi 2012, 468). In the case of the Kazakhstani nationwide in-service teacher training programme, jointly developed by the CoE, Cambridge International Examinations (CIE) and the University of Cambridge Faculty of Education (FoE), it is more appropriate to talk about 'policy trilingualism' and the effects it produces on the definition of teacher professionalism in the country.

In situating the analysis presented in this chapter within a broader field of policy sociology, it is important to mention the studies which provided important guidelines for analysis attempted here. In its focus on the most recent developments in the system of in-service teacher training in Kazakhstan the chapter contributes to the analysis of the national projects of the construction of 'teacher professionalism' in 'neoliberal times'. The importance of this question is emphasised in the *World Yearbook of Education 2013 on Educators, Professionalism and Politics: Global Transitions, National Spaces and Professional Projects* (Sheddon and Levin 2013). In its critical treatment of the questions under analysis, this contribution is inspired by Maguire's works on 'The Modern Teacher' (2004) and 'Towards a Sociology of The Global Teacher' (2009). In its critical take on the global advance of neo-liberalism in education, the chapter draws on Ball's studies on 'The Teacher's Soul and the Terrors of Performativity' (2003), on 'Performativity, Commodification and

Commitment: An I-Spy Guide to the Neoliberal University' (Ball 2012a), as well as his other works critiquing the advance of neoliberal governance in education (Ball 2012b; Ball 2012c; Ball and Junemann 2012).

The main part of this analysis will focus on the 'trilingualism' inherent in the professional development discourse of the CoE programme. Before that, however, the next section presents a brief introduction to discourse analysis itself, which assists readers in understanding the differences between discourse analysis methodology and more traditional ways of analysing policy through the content analysis method, which dominates the fields of policy consultancy and international development.

A brief introduction to discourse analysis methodology

The procedures involved in discourse analytic research are elaborated in what can be considered classic works on discourse analysis methodology (e.g. Codd 1988; Gale 2001; Scheurich 1994; MacLure 2003; Wetherell et al. 2001a, 2001b, Jorgensen and Phillips 2002). In familiarising the reader with the key analytical strategies this chapter will turn to Dreyfus and Rabinow's (1982) most complete account of Foucault's methodology. As Dreyfus and Rabinow explain, discourse analysis method as it is proposed by Foucault unfolds around two main tasks. The first task is formulated as the problem of the positioning of a researcher. More specifically, anyone interested in the study of discourse needs 'to avoid becoming involved in arguments about whether what they [the discourses] say is true, or even whether their statements make sense', but instead study discourses as 'objects' (Dreyfus and Rabinow 1982).

Treating discourses as 'objects' is important because any policies, and education policies in particular, work by establishing themselves as a 'common sense', and the only possible, solution. The policies do this by citing the latest research, seeking alliances with 'world-class' experts and by weaving the web of 'responsibilisation' around the actors involved in the reform. The most commonly utilised responsibilisation techniques one can find include the appeals to morality and humanity, which may be cited in the text as concerns for 'the future of the country', 'the benefits to all children', 'responsibility for the whole of humanity' and the like. In order not to be caught on either side of the policy debate, and make a moral choice between those advancing the reform agenda and those ostensibly *resisting* it, a researcher requires some distance from the object of analysis and be particularly attentive to the passages in the text which appeal to morality, national values and humanity.

This is because through these passages the policies seek to silence the alternatives and pursue their own agendas which, under a close scrutiny, can have highly detrimental consequences to these very values.

However, achieving a desired analytical distance is not an easy task because moral responsibilisation sits deeply inside all of us as individuals and as researchers. Useful suggestions on how to seek detachment can be found in Codd (1988) and Derrida (1996). Codd, for example, advises to treat policy texts as 'cultural and ideological artefacts' (Codd 1988, 243). This advice can be extended to research interviews, which as situational products of the interaction between the researcher, the participants, institutional ethos and dominant discourses reflect the development of a discourse at a particular moment in time. Derrida describes the detachment from the object of analysis in an even more striking manner: 'to relate to an object as such means to relate to it as if you were dead' (Derrida 1996, 216). This powerful insight captures the difficulty of detachment, because to resist siding with the virtuous, 'right' side of the debate, makes the work of the researcher a highly political exercise given the stakes involved in the reform and the efforts put into advancing a particular reform agenda.

Upon achieving detachment from the object of analysis, the second task in discourse analytic methodology involves, as Dreyfus and Rabinow put it, a 'purely descriptive enterprise' (1982, 56). Such an enterprise revolves around four descriptive categories; *objects, subjects, concepts* and *strategies of discourse*, the elements of which constitute the discourse morphology (Dreyfus and Rabinow 1982, 61; cf. Scheurich 1994, 300). In this chapter, which explores the process of 'change' from the point of view of both official discourses and interviewees' perceptions of 'change', the four analytical categories employed are *the time of 'change', the model of 'change', the agents of 'change'* and *the experiences of 'change'*, which to some extent correspond to the four categories of *concepts, objects, strategies* and the *subjects* of discourse.

There is a third important requirement that is particularly relevant for research in cross-cultural settings. This task can be formulated as the need to resist comparison, especially the sort summarised in a rather trivial phrase: 'we have the same here/there'. Summarised in this way, comparison turns from a useful research instrument into a hindrance to thought, a limit to one's ability to keep the focus on the actual practices and, by extension, to one's capacity to understand the logic behind the practices. Pronounced with the best intentions, the apparently harmless yet very powerful 'same here' aims to amplify the imagined relatedness between cultures and to orient the cultures, the target culture in particular, 'towards a new social future' (Gouanvic 2005, 147). The act of comparison, similarly to the act of translation, produces social effects, which the researchers should seek to grasp in their analyses. At the same time, while resisting comparison as such, the researcher needs to be attentive to the aspects of social practice that are the object of analysis for others, because more often than not, comparison indicates areas of social practice where the actual meaning has become detached from the linguistic meaning. Examples of the practices often sidelined by the 'we have the same' comment include complaints about the pressure of reporting on schools and teachers in Kazakhstan, the amount of paperwork, the long hours at work, dissatisfaction with the pressure to teach to the test (UNT), and so on.

To sum up, by applying analytical strategies of detachment, systematic description and resistance to comparison, discourse analytic research departs from more traditional accounts, which offer an important but rather uninspiring chronology of education reform. Discourse analysis breaks with the tradition of working on the level of policy text and providing 'commentary and critique' rather than analysis (Ball 1990, 9; Taylor 1997, 23). It is less interested in the chronology of the events, but in how the 'truth' about the reform is being constructed in the discourse. It is interested in how discourse weaves the web of intelligibility and thus inescapability from the imagined version of development and the model of the individual required for the reform. The resultant narrative produced by discourse analytic research is far from being an easy text to 'digest' (cf. Lemke 2007), for it takes the readers out of their comfort zone by demonstrating that any masterfully drafted policy 'masks the contradictions and incoherence of the ideology' and contains an 'implicit critique of its own values' (Codd 1988, 245). In short, discourse analysis makes one think, think critically, think outside one's comfort zone and think 'otherwise' (Ball 1994, 23).

Understanding the morphology of educational 'change'

So how do we think 'otherwise'? In Foucault's understanding this involves:

> [A] readiness to find what surrounds us strange and odd; a certain determination to throw off familiar ways of thought and to look at the same things in a different way; a passion for seizing what is happening now and what is disappearing. (Foucault 2000, 325)

Tracing structures, metaphors and definitions of 'change'

There have been numerous attempts to capture 'what is happening now' in education policy in Kazakhstan (for a comprehensive overview see Bridges et. al., Chapter 3 in this volume). The post-2010 educational initiatives, in particular, have become an object of close observation for all who are interested in understanding the new model of reform in Kazakhstan. In their attempt to grasp the nature of the recent initiatives, national and international observers have suggested the following metaphors and definitions: a 'radical reform package' (governmental official); 'reform by example' (governmental official, cited in Yakavets 2012, 71); 'policy cherry picking' (international observer); 'globalisation on the margins' (Silova 2011); 'sites of beta testing' (Ruby and McLaughlin, Chapter 14 in this volume); 'points of growth' (the logos of the NIS and the CoE), and, more expressively, 'viruses' which are believed to transform the current system (a metaphor often used by both local and international observers). Despite some obvious differences in the above views of educational change in the country, all these definitions capture the idea of a 'radical' and 'rapid' change. This sense of urgency is fuelled by political rationalities of 'catching up' modernisation, which in the case of Kazakhstan are epitomised in the ambitious goals of its political leadership to see the country enter the list of the 50[1] (or, most recently suggested 30[2]) most competitive world economies (cf. the 'catching up Europeanisation' argument in the analysis of educational policy rationalities in Ukraine in Fimyar 2010).

Each of the Commonwealth of Independent States (CIS) countries, depending on the availability of natural resources, professionalism and long-term vision of political leadership, and emerging and historically established political alliances, have at their disposal different methods for achieving their ambitious and at times ambiguous development goals. Kazakhstan, recently enriched by the oil revenues, the presence of multinational corporations such as Chevron, Shell and others, and the growing number of early- and mid-career professionals educated abroad, chose to reform its education through building the sites of best international practices 'at home'. These sites, which are entrusted with the mission to transform the current system, are the highly selective and well-resourced Nazarbayev University (NU) and the network of 20 Nazarbayev Intellectual Schools (NIS), both working through the model of international partnerships with world-class universities including the University of Cambridge FoE, which is directly involved in several education support programmes with both NIS and NU.

Directly serving less than one per cent of the student cohort in the country,[3] NIS has been increasingly under pressure to share its practices, standards, curriculum and pedagogy with the mainstream schools. For this purpose two projects for *curriculum transfer* and *the transfer of pedagogy* have been set up under the auspices of NIS. Each of these projects has a complex implementation structure, which is subject to change depending on the feedback from the implementation process and the advice of international partners. Currently the first project is being implemented in 35 NIS partner schools, while the curriculum transfer in the mainstream sector is scheduled to begin in 2015 in Grades 1 and 2 and to be completed in 2027 when the NIS-based curriculum will be implemented in Grade 12 throughout the country.

The second project, which is the object of analysis in this chapter, is established under the auspices of the CoE, a daughter organisation of NIS, and is aimed directly at teacher trainers and teachers from the mainstream sector. In its second round of implementation, which takes the form of cascade training, responsibilities for the implementation of the project have been transferred to the *Orleu*, a nationwide network of in-service teacher training centres, while the CoE continues to oversee the programme as a whole. This chapter is concerned with the first phase of the roll-out, that of cascade training, the so-called 'training of trainers' programme jointly developed by the Faculty of Education (FoE), the CoE and Cambridge International Examinations (CIE) and which has been delivered by staff of the FoE in Astana since February 2012. The content of the programme, advanced through three levels, encompasses seven areas specified by Kazakhstan, which may seem to signal the sites of intervention in the discourse of teacher professionalism in the country. These areas are:

- New approaches to teaching and learning
- Learning to think critically
- Assessment for and of learning
- Using ICT in teaching and learning
- Teaching talented and gifted children
- Responding to age-related differences in teaching and learning
- Management and leadership of learning.
  (NIS/CoE brochure, unnumbered, En.)[4]

At level three, the emphasis is on teachers bringing about change in their own classrooms; at level two it is additionally on supporting the professional development of colleagues through coaching and mentoring, and at level one it is on bringing about whole school change through their school development planning. Each level of the programme is being delivered by FoE trainers to Kazakhstani trainers through two two-week face-to-face periods with school-based work conducted by the trainees in between. In 2013 the programme was supplemented by a mentoring component whereby FoE trainers observe the sessions of some of their former trainees who are now training teachers in different regions in Kazakhstan. In the same year the leadership programme for school directors was developed and is currently in operation. The completion of each level of the programme by teachers is assessed through the completion of a portfolio containing reflective accounts of the work carried out in schools and through presentations about this work. In addition, the Kazakhstani state requires teachers to take a multiple choice test which, if passed successfully, entails a salary increase of 30%, 70% or 100%. The appropriateness of the multiple choice test for assessment of reflective practices, which is a major component of the CoE programme, has been a subject of disagreement between the national and international actors involved in the reform.

Understanding the pressure to perform 'change'

The brief outline of the CoE initiatives above suggests that the CoE programme is being implemented through the model of cascade training with an ambitious goal of re-training '120 000 teachers throughout the country in the next five years' (*Kazakhstanskaya Pravda*, 4 April 2012, cited in the CoE brochure, unnumbered, En.). According to the same source:

> This programme does not have analogues in the territory of the former Soviet Union; the programme approved by the Government is an investment in human capital of the country, in this case – teacher professionalism. This way the Government solves the issue of increasing the quality of pedagogical staff, the task set by the Head of the State in his Address to the People of Kazakhstan. (ibid.)[5]

What this report does not say is that the underlying mission of the CoE programme is to re-orient established didactic approaches from teacher-centred to child-centred ones. With its focus on economic competitiveness and the aim to be a distinct leader in the region, the educational component of the message gets lost in the official rhetoric, which is then echoed in the mass media, as in the above quotation. Viewed as an example of policy trilingualism, the extract from *Kazakhstanskaya Pravda* demonstrates how 'neo-liberal imaginary', to use Appadurai's term (2001, 15), triumphing around the globe, is being played out at the level of the text and thought in Kazakhstan. What authors like Appadurai remind us is that explicit to the researcher's eyes, but often left unnoticed (and thus uncritically accepted) by the practitioners' economic colonisation of the social advances a narrow view of education – education *as a means* to economic competitiveness, thus silencing the view of *education as a right* and means of *personal fulfilment*.

Another interesting case for analysis presents an official video of the CoE programme uploaded on the youtube website on 9 February 2012 (referenced as 'Web 1' hereafter). The 4.55-minute long video narrated in three languages, which provide further examples of policy trilingualism, tells the official story of the establishment and operation of the CoE. The video opens with quotes by Kazakh, Soviet and English thinkers on education: Al-Farabi (872–951), Vasily Sukhomlinsky (1918–70) and John Locke (1632–1704). The quote in Kazakh reads: 'To be educated means to have a skill to discover the un-known. Al-Farabi' (Web 1, Kz., 0:00–7). The quote in Russian reads: 'To give a child the spark of knowledge, the teacher needs to absorb the sea of light. Vasily Sukhomlinksky' (Web 1, Rus., 0:08). The quote in English reads: 'The improvement of understanding is for two ends: first, our own increase of knowledge; secondly, to enable us to deliver that knowledge to others. John Locke' (Web 1, En., 0:16).

The use of black and white colours in the portraits of the thinkers and the white letters gradually disappearing in the darkness of the screen, as one quote emerges in the background of the other, creates a mysterious yet authoritative atmosphere epitomising the sacred nature of the knowledge of the past. This tapestry of languages and historical epochs sets the scene for the second part of the video which features Nursultan Nazarbayev addressing the Kazakhstani Parliament with the words:

> We need to continue the modernisation of education. Today we have completed the [state programme of] computerisation of schools. The schools are being equipped with multimedia classrooms and interactive technology. Lifelong learning should become a personal credo of every Kazakhstani citizen. (Web 1, Rus., 0:31–0:49)

From the Kazakhstani Parliament the viewer is transported inside a highly equipped science classroom in Astana Nazarbayev Intellectual School (NIS). The camera provides a close-up view of the male teacher, an interactive white-board, a group of students in the same classroom and President Nazarbayev seated as one of the students in one of the front desks. The voice of the narrator states:

> It is difficult to overestimate the role of quality education in the life of every individual. And today in the age of information, when everything changes very rapidly, the role of the teacher who is able to use modern technologies is especially valuable. (Web 1, Rus., 0:50–1:1:03)

The previous image of an open-space school interior and a highly equipped science classroom is contrasted with the image of a traditional Soviet classroom, showing a male teacher in front of a traditional blackboard. The voice of the narrator explains:

> Until just recently it seemed that the use of the previous teaching methods was entirely justifiable. School teachers could for decades teach outdated subjects without taking the trouble to update their resource of knowledge [Rus. 'baggage of knowledge']. But today this approach does not meet the current demands. (Web 1, Rus., 1:04–1:17)

The viewer is then presented with a variety of images from the already familiar NIS classroom, the CoE programme and the façade of the Ministry of Education. The narrator presents the rationale for the creation of the CoE programme:

> That is why innovative technologies, multimedia classrooms and many other IT resources are being introduced in modern schools. Students now have more opportunities for independent study under the supervision of an experienced and intellectual mentor. That is why it is particularly important to create such an educational environment, which will help, first and foremost, teachers to continuously upgrade their professional competencies. [. . .] For this purpose a new institute – The Centre of Pedagogical Excellence – which will work according to international experience, has been created. At the heart of its activities lies the idea of continuous professional development. (Web 1, Rus., 1:17–2: 16)

Having explained the reach and the scope of the CoE programme, which is a focus of the following two minutes of the narration, the video ends with the quote by a famous Kazakh thinker Abai Kunanbayev (1845–1904). The narrator's voice reads: 'Let the words uttered by the wise, be heard by the talented. Let the talented see the light and master the mysteries of the unknown, through the eyes of their soul (Abai)' (Web 1, Kz., 4:36–4:41).

To conclude the analysis of the CoE video, it is important to note that the use of the images in the video is reminiscent of Phillips and Ochs' (2003) observation that the 'eternal politically motivated quest for something to fix the real and imagined problems, preferably quickly and visibly' remains the key driver for policy borrowing in all observed settings (Phillips and Ochs 2003, cited in Schweisfurth 2013, 173). Through the use of text, images and colours the official video about the establishment of the CoE programme seeks to achieve its core objective – i.e. to place the CoE initiative at the crossroads of historical and philosophical epochs, languages and teaching traditions. By presenting the CoE programme as such, the text, the images and colours work towards constructing a distinct (yet imaginative) break between the traditional (in this case Soviet), and modern approaches to teaching, which are contrasted by using the images from the Soviet classroom alongside the images of technologically equipped NIS classrooms.

However, the imaginative break between past and present, and between traditional and modern, approaches to education associated with these two epochs gets rather blurred when we refer to other sources of data. For example, one interviewee affirms: 'We have about 80% of teachers who are still domineering over pupils' (Interviewee A, CoE, Rus.); while another documentary source emotively appeals: 'That is enough! We need to change something very radically in our often rigid and at times very cruel in relation to our children school' (CoE essays, 197, Rus.), or in the same source: 'Our frozen-in-time modes of teaching have been overthrown in the first days of participation in the programme' (ibid., 152).

The discussion above demonstrates that the break between past and present in describing educational 'change' in Kazakhstan works as a rhetorical device rather than as a conceptual category or a category of description. As a rhetorical device, references to the temporality of 'change', and the vocabulary associated with it ('now' and 'then', 'old' and 'new', 'traditional' and 'modern'), are mobilised by the actors to demonstrate, and act out, the 'change', rather than to describe or reflect on it. This highlights a performative aspect of the discourse of teacher professionalism in Kazakhstan and suggests that the stakes involved in the reform agenda put pressure on the actors to perform 'change' rather than to reflect on it. An observation from the international consultant involved in the reform supports this tentative conclusion. With reference to the most recent educational initiatives, the consultant explains:

> Due to the pace of the change they haven't necessarily had the kind of background information and awareness, and reflection; an opportunity to reflect on what they have been doing to be able to absorb the new ideas quickly. (Interviewee B, International Organisation)

Conceptualisations of educational 'change' in three language communities

The remainder of the section presents a summary of the key findings which demonstrate how differently educational 'change' is conceptualised and experienced by the actors representing three language communities in Kazakhstan. Table 1 was compiled as a result of the application of four categories of analysis – the *times of 'change'*, the *model of 'change'*, the *agents of 'change'* and the *experiences of 'change'*, to the data collected in three languages.

Table 1: Data summary – Examples of policy trilingualism across four categories of analysis

Categories of analysis	Kz.	Rus.	En.
Times of 'change'	[The wisdom from the past carries important messages for the changing present] (Web 1)	'Age of information', 'everything changes very rapidly'; 'previous teaching methods do not meet the demands of today.' (Web 1) 'Globalised society'; 'highly mobile human resources'; 'dynamically changing labour market'; 'constantly changing demands'; 'increasing demands for qualified professionals'; 'the nature of work is changing'. (Web 2)	[Tradition rather than change] 'centuries-old practice' (Web 1)
Model of 'change'	[Allusions to the wisdom from the past] e.g. 'To be educated means to have a skill to discover the unknown.' (Al-Farabi quoted in Web 1); 'Let the words uttered by the wise, be heard by the talented. Let the talented see the light and master the mysteries of the unknown, through the eyes of their soul.' (Abai Kunanbayev quoted in ibid.)	'Modernisation and computerisation of schools'; 'interactive technology'; 'multimedia classrooms'; 'opportunities for independent study [for students]'. (Web 1)	'International experience'; 'strong link between policy and practice'; 'the best achievements of professorial and teaching staff'. (Web 1)

Categories of analysis	Kz.	Rus.	En.
Agents of 'change'	'The wise', 'the talented', 'the master' [from the quotes], alongside the image of an early-career teacher. (Web 1)	'Experienced and intellectual mentor', 'new cohort of critically thinking teachers, teacher-researchers', 'life-long learners' [in relation to all citizens]. (Web 1) 'Critical and creative thinking, the ability to think and take decisions under pressure and in the shortest possible timeframes.' (Web 2) 'Teacher-facilitator' (Web 3); 'modern teacher should be a facilitator, a process engine'. (Web 4); 'successful teacher' (CoE essays, 134); 'reflective teacher'; 'professional community of teachers'. (CoE brochure: unnumbered)	'Strategic partners'; 'University of Cambridge Faculty of Education and the Centre of Excellence staff' (Web 1) 'Cambridge trainers' (CoE essays, multiple references)
Experiences of 'change'	'We are pleased.' (Web 1) 'Their faces were bright and enthusiastic, their appearance was relaxed, and they started to use a different lexicon.' (Interviewee B, CoE 8) 'More relaxed; more confident even in front of very experienced teachers.' (Interviewee C, Teachers Focus Group) 'I am glad that I cooperate creatively with my colleagues.' (CoE essays, 30) 'Difficult for me to express in words my excitement about the course.' (ibid., 34) 'My approaches to teaching have been revolutionised.' (ibid., 36) 'Changed my understanding about teaching and my whole world.' (ibid., 66)	'Need to concentrate efforts at implementing the task; continuously upgrade [our] professional competencies.' (Web 1) 'The teacher needs to absorb the sea of light.' (Vasily Sukhomlinsky quoted in ibid.) 'Received the charge of positive emotions.' (CoE essays, 154) 'The course has energised my mind and inspired my soul.' (ibid., 35) 'See the changes in my consciousness.' (ibid., 110) 'I had a mini-revolution in my mind about the constructive teaching.' (ibid.,132 9) 'We have been delegated an immense responsibility – to bring the Cambridge model of education to the awareness of every teacher.' (ibid., 37) 'I am very proud to be part of this wonderful beginning.' (ibid., 50)	'We are happy.' 'We are pleased.' 'I hope it will help [to raise teachers 'professionalism].' (Web 1) 'I felt very nervous and worried that our ideas would not translate well and would not be workable in Kazakhstan. However, our fears were unfounded.' (CoE brochure, unnumbered, En.) 'Some of the most uplifting moments [. . .]'. (ibid.) 'I could not have felt more welcomed.' (CoE essays, 14) 'People [. . .] have welcomed me into their country and into their hearts.' (ibid., 18)

To summarise the key attitudes towards educational 'change' articulated by the representatives of the three language communities in Kazakhstan, is to suggest that the continuous appeals to the wisdom of the past in the Kazakh-language data contain the view of educational 'change' in the country as one's 'destiny'. The Russian-language data, with a view of educational 'change' heavily colonised by economic imperative, encapsulates an attitude towards educational 'change' as one's *'task'*, which they are diligently performing. The English-language data meanwhile places an emphasis on both the values of tradition and the excellence of the present, suggesting that for international actors 'educational 'change' is the 'job', which they hope will contribute to educational development in Kazakhstan.

Conclusion: Dilemmas of inevitability and possibility of 'change' in the Kazakhstani context

This chapter has attempted to conceptualise and reflect on the process of educational change in light of recent discussions within the disciplines of policy sociology and comparative education. By focusing on examples of policy trilingualism, it has revealed some new approaches to capturing the complexity of educational change in a multilingual environment. One of the key conclusions is that the economic imperatives embedded in the way in which educational objectives are presented in the official rhetoric of the Russian-language data overshadow an extended view of education *as a right*, and instead promote a curtailed view of education *as a means* to economic competitiveness. The advance of neo-liberalism in education and educational governance, the far-reaching and irreversible consequences of which we are warned about in the policy sociology and comparative education studies (e.g. *Journal of Educational Policy, Comparative Education Review, The World Yearbook of Education 2012* and *2013*), is celebrated and takes unprecedented forms in the way in which education is conceptualised in Kazakhstan. Taking the views of the opponents of neo-liberalism in education seriously, the situation calls for a more balanced way of describing the goals of economic development and education as well as an open dialogue about the relationship between education and the economy.

The most visible examples of how deeply 'neo-liberal imaginary' has affected the way education is discussed in Kazakhstan are collected under the *times of 'change'* category of analysis. In Kazakhstan, as in other parts of the world, a 'pseudo-concept' of *'globalisation'* (Bourdieu 2003 cited in

Lingard et al. 2005, 765; Bourdieu 2004, 34) and its attributes of 'mobile human capital', 'changing demands of labour market', and so on, works at once to describe and prescribe the model and the direction of 'change' alongside the model of the actors called upon to bring this change about. The data collected under the category of the *model of 'change'* demonstrates that the international expertise from the strategic partner institutions involved in the reform is highly regarded in Kazakhstan. It is believed that the adaptation of 'the best international experience' to the 'national circumstances' will raise the competitive advantage of Kazakhstani students, teachers and the economy – a dynamic that will be ultimately reflected in international ratings. This model and vision of 'change' is then cascaded through the system via a series of in-service training and curriculum transfer initiatives which are called on to transform the current standards and approaches to teaching. This new model of reform calls for a 'new' *agent of 'change'*, a 'new' teacher: a 'teacher-researcher', 'teacher-facilitator', 'teacher-mentor', the new categories in the discourse of teacher professionalism in Kazakhstan.

The data collected under the category of *experiences of 'change'* reflects the immense degree of responsibility the actors feel in implementing the 'change'. The participants report highly positive feelings after the completion of the CoE training and some concerns and uncertainty before embarking on the programme. Yet what is striking when reading the participants' statements in Kazakh and Russian, are phrases such as 'mini-revolution in my mind', 'changes in my consciousness', '[it has] changed my whole world', 'my approaches to teaching have been revolutionised', which indicate the 'radical' and 'revolutionary' nature of the reported 'change'. While the participants admit that the content of the course is not entirely new to them, because the ideas of critical thinking and student-centred learning were in circulation in Kazakhstan before the start of the CoE programme, such insistence on the 'revolutionary' nature of the 'change' highlights the performative aspect of 'change' whereby actors feel pressure to 'perform' change rather than be provided with a space and the language to reflect on it. This situation demonstrates the need to closely follow trainees' experiences and reflections on change, its depth, meaning and consequences for their professional lives and in their classrooms, for an extended period of time after the completion of the programme.

The understanding of the performative aspect of the process of change leads to a question about the dilemmas of educational change in the Kazakhstani context. On the one hand, the processes already set in motion by the sheer amount of financial and human resources invested in the reform make the change in Kazakhstani education inevitable and irreversible. On the other hand, the pace of the reform and the pressure on the actors to 'perform' change means the task of making this incremental change long-lasting (often referred to in the field as 'the change of mind-sets') is a difficult one, if not impossible.

The allusion to the magnitude of the challenge of making this change is implicit in the oft-cited quote by Kanysh Satpayev, the first president of the Kazakh Academy of Sciences (years of Presidency 1947–51), which directly addresses the recent graduates of the regional CoE programme:

> Knowledge and labour turn the person into a hero, a giant, who can move mountains . . . The union of labour and science is our force. Remember it [these words], be diligent and persistent, brave and daring. Only then will you be able to change the life for the better; [only then will you] be a worthy member of society. Only then will the Universe open its inmost secrets to you. (Orleu 2013, regional bilingual publication, 1: 63, 1, Rus.)

REFERENCES:

Primary sources:

CoE Brochure: NIS/CoE (2012). Centre of Excellence. Astana: NIS/CoE (CoE brochure, Kz., Rus., En.)

CoE Essays: NIS/CoE (2012). We are Changing in the Changing World. Astana: NIS/CoE. (CoE essays, Kz., Rus., En.).

Orleu (2013). *Congratulations!* [to the graduates of the level courses] Orleu regional bilingual publication, 1:63, 1. (Rus.)

Web 1: Centre of Pedagogical Excellence official video (2012) (Web 1, Kz., Rus., En.). www.youtube.com/watch?v=CkDLzWLmqT8 (retrieved 29 October 2013).

Web 2: Speech by the Chairperson of the AEO 'Nazarbayev Intellectual Schools' Kulyash Shamshidinova at the Republican Pedagogical Teacher Congress 23 August 2013. nis.edu.kz/ru/press-center/perform/?id=2590 (retrieved 29 October 2013).

Web 3: The in-service courses of the new format (2012). orleupvl.kz/ru/innovaczii-eksperiment/obuchenie-uchitelej-3-bazovogo-urovnya/153-kursy-povysheniya-kvalifikaczii-novogo-formata (Web 3, Rus.) (retrieved 29 October 2013).

Web 4: News Briefing from the European Education Research Conference – ECER 2013. nis.edu.kz/ru/press-center/news/?id=2614 – (Web 4, Rus.) (retrieved 29 October 2013).

Web 5: 24.08.12 'Day Panorama' News STV Channel. www.youtube.com/watch?v=OuF_ZxZvTuI – (Web 5, Rus.) (retrieved 29 October 2013).

Secondary sources:

Appadurai, **A.** (ed.) (2001). *Globalization*. A Millennial Quartet Book. Durham, NC: Duke University Press.

Bacevic, **J.** (2005). 'Educational Policy Between Nationalist and Euro-Integrationist Politics: A Case Study of Serbian Educational Reform'. www.academia.edu/828646/Educational_Policy_Between_Nationalist_and_Euro-Integrationist_Politics_a_Case_Study_of_Serbian_Educational_Reform (retrieved 29 October 2013).

Bacevic, **J.** (2010). 'Masters or Servants? Power and Discourse in Serbian Higher Education Reform'. *Social Anthropology*, 18:1, 43–56.

Ball, **S.J.** (1990). *Politics and Policy Making in Education: Explorations in Policy Sociology*. London: Routledge.

— (2003). 'The Teacher's Soul and the Terrors of Performativity'. *Journal of Education Policy*, 18:2, 215–28.

— (2012a). 'Performativity, Commodification and Commitment: An I-Spy Guide to the Neoliberal University'. *British Journal of Educational Studies*, 60:1, 17–28.

— (2012b). *Global Education Inc.: New Policy Networks and the Neo-Liberal Imaginary*. London: Routledge.

— (2012c). *Foucault, Power and Education*. New York: Routledge.

Ball, **S.J.** and **Junemann**, **C.** (2012). *Networks, New Governance and Education*. Bristol: Policy Press.

Ball, **S.J.**, **Maguire**, **M.**, **Braun**, **A.** and **Hoskins**, **K.** (2011). 'Policy Actors: Doing Policy Work in Schools'. *Discourse: Studies in the Cultural Politics of Education*, 32:4, 625–63.

Bourdieu, **P.** (2003) [2001]. *Firing Back: Against the Tyranny of the Market 2*, trans. L. Wacquant. London: Verso.

— (2004) [1998]. *Acts of Resistance: Against the New Myths of Our Time*, trans. R. Nice. Cambridge: Polity.

Braun, **A.**, **Maguire M.** and **Ball**, **S.** (2010). 'Policy Enactments in the UK Secondary School: Examining Policy, Practice and School Positioning'. *Journal of Education Policy*, 25:4, 547–60.

Codd, **J.A.** (1988). 'The Construction and Deconstruction of Educational Policy Documents'. *Journal of Education Policy*, 3:3, 235–47.

Derrida, **J.** (1996). *Archive Fever: A Freudian Impression*. Chicago: University of Chicago Press.

Dreyfus, **H.L.** and **Rabinow**, **P.** (1982). *Michel Foucault: Beyond Structuralism and Hermeneutics*. Brighton: Harvester.

Fimyar, **O.** (2011). 'A Manifesto of a Post-Communist Post-Structuralist Researcher: Post-Viva Voce Reflections'. *European Education: Issues and Studies*, 43:2, 74–97.

— (2010). 'Policy Why(s): Policy Rationalities and the Changing Logic of Educational Reform in Post-Communist Ukraine (1991–2008)'. In I. Silova (ed.), *Post-Socialism is not Dead: (Re)reading the Global in Comparative Education*. Bingley: Emerald Publishing.

Foucault, **M.** (2000). *Ethics: Subjectivity and Truth: Essential Works of Michel Foucault 1954–1984*, vol. 1 (new ed.). London: Penguin.

Gale, T. (2001). 'Critical Policy Sociology: Historiography, Archaeology and Genealogy as Methods of Policy Analysis'. *Journal of Education Policy*, 16:5, 379–93.

Gouanvic, J. (2005). 'A Bourdieusian Theory of Translation, or the Coincidence of Practical Instances: Field, "Habitus", Capital and "Illusio"'. *The Translator*, 11:2, 147–66.

Jorgensen, M. and Phillips, L.J. (2002). *Discourse Analysis as Theory and Method*. London: Sage Publications.

Lemke, T. (2007). 'An Indigestible Meal? Foucault, Governmentality and State Theory'. *Distinktion: Scandinavian Journal of Social Theory*, 8:2, 43–64.

Lingard, B., Rawolle, S. and Taylor, S. (2005). 'Globalising Policy Sociology in Education: Working with Bourdieu'. *Journal of Education Policy*, 20:6, 759–77.

MacLure, M. (2003). *Discourse in Educational and Social Research. Conducting Educational Research*. Buckingham: Open University Press.

Maguire, M. (2004). 'The Modern Teacher: A Textual Analysis of Educational Restructuration'. In S. Lindblad and T. Popkewitz (eds), *Educational Restructuring: International Perspectives on Traveling Policies*. Connecticut: Information Age Publishing.

— (2009). 'Towards a Sociology of The Global Teacher'. In M. W. Apple, S. J. Ball and L. A. Gandin (eds), *The Routledge International Handbook of Sociology of Education*. Abingdon: Routledge.

Mukhopadhyay, R. and Sriprakash, A. (2013). 'Target-Driven Reforms: Education for All and the Translations of Equity and Inclusion in India'. *Journal of Education Policy*, 28:3, 306–21.

Rizvi, F. (2000). 'International Education and the Production of Global Imagination'. In N.C. Burbles and C.A. Torres (eds) *Globalization and Education: Critical Perspectives*. London: Routledge.

Scheurich, J.J. (1994). 'Policy Archaeology: A New Policy Studies Methodology'. *Journal of Education Policy*, 9(4), 297–316.

Schweisfurth, M. (2013). 'Learner-Centred Education and Teacher Professionalism at the Local-Global Nexus'. In T. Sheddon and J. A. Levin (eds), *World Yearbook of Education 2013: Educators, Professionalism and Politics: Global Transitions, National Spaces and Professional Projects*. London and New York: Routledge.

Singh, P., Thomas, S. and Harris, J. (2013). 'Recontextualising Policy Discourses: A Bernsteinian Perspective on Policy Interpretation, Translation, Enactment'. *Journal of Education Policy*, 28:4, 465–80.

Sheddon, T. and Levin, J.A. (eds) (2013). *World Yearbook of Education 2013: Educators, Professionalism and Politics: Global Transitions, National Spaces and Professional Projects*. London and New York: Routledge.

Silova, I. (2005). *Traveling Policies: Hijacked in Central Asia. European Educational Research Journal*, 4(1), 50–59.

— (ed.) (2011). *Globalization on the Margins: Education and Post-Socialist Transformations in Central Asia*. Charlotte, NC: Information Age Publishing.

Silova, I. and Brehm, W.C. (2013). 'The Shifting Boundaries of Teacher Professionalism: Education Privatization(s) in the Post-Socialist Education Space'. In T. Seddon, J. Ozga and J. Levin (eds), *World Yearbook of Education 2013: Educators, Professionalism and Politics: Global Transitions, National Spaces, and Professional Projects*. New York: Routledge.

Srivastava, P. (2006). *Reconciling Multiple Researcher Positionalities and Languages in International Research. Research in Comparative and International Education*, 1:3, 210–22.

Steiner-Khamsi, G. and Stolpe, I. (2006). *Educational Import in Mongolia: Local Encounters with Global Forces.* New York: Palgrave Macmillan.

Steiner-Khamsi, G. (2012). 'The Global/Local Nexus in Comparative Policy Studies: Analysing the Triple Bonus System in Mongolia Over Time'. *Comparative Education*, 48:4, 455–71

Steiner-Khamsi, G. and Waldow F. (eds) (2012). *World Yearbook of Education 2012: Policy Borrowing and Lending in Education.* London and New York: Routledge.

Taylor, S. (1997). 'Critical Policy Analysis: Exploring Contexts, Texts and Consequences'. *Discourse: Studies in the Cultural Politics of Education*, 18:1, 23–35.

Wetherell, M., Taylor, S. and Yates, S., (eds) (2001a). *Discourse as Data: A Guide to Analysis.* London: Sage Publications Ltd.

— (2001b). *Discourse as Data: A Reader.* London: Sage Publications Ltd.

Yakavets, N. (2012). *The Recent History of Educational Reform in Kazakhstan. In Internationalisation and Reform of Secondary Schooling in Kazakhstan.* Study report: Cambridge.

Web resources:

www.eurasianet.org/node/65035 – Kazakhstan: Elite Schools May Limit Opportunities (2012) (Rus.) (retrieved 29 October 2013).

nis.edu.kz/ru/about/subsid/center-teach-sk/ – Centre of Pedagogical Excellence AEO 'Nazarbayev Intellectual Schools' (2012) (Rus.) (retrieved 29 October 2013).

www.cpm.kz/index.php?lang=en – Centre of Pedagogical Excellence website. (2013) (Kz., Rus., En.) (retrieved 29 October 2013).

www.zakon.kz/4453639-v-jetom-godu-100-uchitelejj-nazarbaev.html This year 100 teachers will go through the 'Nazarbayev Intellectual Schools' training. News article (2011) (Rus.). (retrieved 29 October 2013).

www.youtube.com/watch?v=nDL7i2lw6eE – Courses of the new format. Youtube materials uploaded by the trainees about their experiences of the course (Rus.) (retrieved 29 October 2013).

www.akorda.kz/en/page/page_poslanie-prezidenta-respubliki-kazakhstan-lidera-natsii-nursultana-nazarbaeva-narodu-kazakhstana – Address by N. Nazarbayev, President of the Republic of Kazakhstan. 'Kazakhstan 2050 Strategy: New political course of the established state" (En.) (retrieved 29 October 2013).

www.zakon.kz/top_news/4581331-polnaja-videoversija-zhestkogo.html – The video briefing of Nazarbayev's hard conversation with the government (2013) (Rus.) (retrieved 29 October 2013).

NOTES

1 www.akorda.kz/en/page/page_poslanie-prezidenta-respubliki-kazakhstan-lidera-natsii-nursultana-nazarbaeva-narodu-kazakhstana-.

2 www.zakon.kz/top_news/4581331-polnaja-videoversija-zhestkogo.html.

3 According to 2013 figures, 6591 NIS students enrolled in 20 NIS schools (data March 2013, informal communication), which is 0.26% of the 2.5 million student cohort enrolled in 7576 schools throughout the country (www.eurasianet.org/node/65035).

4 To keep the focus on the trilingualism of policy, the original language of data will be indicated in all quotes as Kz., Rus. or En.

5 The list of sources analysed in the chapter is presented in the reference list under the 'primary sources' heading.

6 www.youtube.com/watch?v=ckdLzwlmqt8.

7 The time is sequenced with the beginning of each sentence.

8 Russian-language data, but describes experiences of Kazakh-speaking trainees.

9 English in the original.

THE WAY FORWARD

16 TOWARDS THE NEXT STAGES OF REFORM in Kazakhstan

Alan Ruby (University of Pennsylvania, USA) and Aslan Sarinzhipov
(Nazarbayev University and Minister of Education, Republic of Kazakhstan)

The future direction of education in Kazakhstan is shaped by its past, guided by the aspirations of its people and constrained only by the limits of imagination. The policy steps and resource allocation decisions for the next five to ten years are products of the interactions of these factors. As such it is important to note some of the most salient and more powerful forces as we sketch out what might, and what should, lie ahead for school education in Kazakhstan.

Looking back

Kazakhstan benefited a lot from the Soviet era. Literacy rates were very high. Small and remote villages had schools and teachers. The participation of girls equalled that of boys in the first stages of schooling. But central control and regulation from Moscow limited responsiveness to local needs and strengths and impeded the development of local capacity for policy development and governance. And little attention was paid to the Kazakh language or Kazakh history. The schools were teacher-centred, assessment valued memorisation rather than application, the Sciences dominated the curriculum and there was little place for critical thinking or appreciation of the wider world. It was a school system of a failed political ideology that depended on command and control and valued conformity over entrepreneurship and independence.

Independence brought changes in all aspects of society and especially in education. It has been a volatile twenty years. The first ten years were times of rapid transition, with periods of economic hardship and recession. There were real reductions in public expenditure on education. School facilities eroded and many well-educated and experienced teachers resigned. Yet this was also a time when there was a pressing need to adapt the school system to support and respond to new social and economic structures and a new form of government.

From the mid-1990s onwards the school system slowly began to adapt to and shape a market economy. Legislative frameworks were established which acknowledged the importance of provincial and local authorities and the role of the private sector. New textbooks were produced and by the year 2000 a national programme on education was established. In 2004 a Unified National Test was introduced to promote fairness in university admissions, with significant consequences for what was taught and valued in the final years of schooling.

Rapid change continued after 2004 and innovation and experimentation accelerated through the creation of the network of Nazarbayev Intellectual Schools (NIS) and the subsequent development of a large-scale professional development programme for schoolteachers through the Centres of Excellence. These were augmented by the aggressive implementation of a programme to increase access to preschool education (*Balapan*).

Looking back, Kazakhstan inherited the skeleton of a good school system from the Soviet era with basic services reaching most of the nation but with little local capacity for self-governance and self-determination in an area as complex as human capital policy. Kazakh language and history were undervalued and largely missing from its schools. Political and economic transitions were not always smooth but after twenty years the framework of an effective school system has been established.

Where we are today

Kazakhstan's school education policy has reached a point where major changes can be firmly embedded in the national system. The NIS and associated centres are producing teaching and learning materials aligned with a globally recognised curriculum. Thousands of teachers have been trained in the importance of student-centred pedagogy. The *Balapan* preschool programme has reached over 70% of the 3–6 years age group. Fiscally the nation is in a strong position and the economy is beginning to diversify in order to reduce its dependence on energy, minerals and agriculture.

The combination of these elements provides a platform for a sustained period of implementation and reform. The nation's leaders share a clear vision of the direction of education policy and priorities. President Nazarbayev articulated the overarching goal of the nation's education system as developing the 'human capital [that] will allow us to build a solid foundation for future economy, which will be competitive and highly integrated with Science' (Nazarbayev 2013). To reach that goal the Ministry of Education and Science aims to make Kazakhstan's school education system as effective and productive as those of the developed industrialised countries. It has taken the average performance of the OECD nations on student achievement and resource standards as a benchmark. There is political determination and the necessary resources to reach this goal. The challenge for the nation's educators and leaders at every educational level is to identify major systematic issues that will be obstacles for further development and find ways to overcome them.

In secondary education one systematic challenge is the increase in demand from an increased population base. The size of the school-age population (ages 6–18 years) in 2030 will be one and a half times the size of the current population. This will put further pressure on the strained school infrastructure and challenge the pedagogical institutes to produce more and better prepared teachers.

The impact of an increased demand is falling first on the preschool sector. Currently, preschool participation in Kazakhstan approaches the level of developed countries (in Eastern Europe it is 80%, in Germany it is 92%, and in Russia it is 62%). But there is still much to be done. There will need to be a significant growth in the number of places to meet increased demand and to move closer to universal preschool education with equal access to high quality programmes.

While additional places are important, a more pressing challenge is raising the quality of programmes and strengthening the professional development of teachers. There are virtually no experts in early childhood development and childcare, and barely 20% of those working in the sector as teachers have a degree in education that specialises in preschool programmes.

More problematic is the nature of preschool education. The content of most preschool education programmes is not oriented towards the child as an active, responsible learner. Good preschool education helps young people learn from a variety of experiences, and to develop capabilities for team work and co-operation while encouraging inventiveness and creativity. These are very large changes in the scope and direction of practice in early childhood classrooms. There are lessons to be learnt from programmes in New Zealand and Italy as well from Finland and Japan, especially in the use of child-centred teaching and learning strategies and the willingness to let children take responsibility for parts of their learning experiences.

An important step in reorientation is adjusting and redesigning the training and professional development system of preschool teachers to focus on the idea of early childhood development rather than 'schooling'. This is a fundamental and sweeping change in initial teacher education and in the professional development of existing teachers in the sector. After initial training and intensive professional development both the new and experienced cadres of teachers will need on-the-job support through networks of peers and experts working together, sharing resources and solving problems. Ideally these communities of practitioners will be supported by resource centres and visiting specialists and mentors who can also assist with quality assurance.

The demographic challenge will soon flow through to the secondary schools. The effect of the increase in student numbers on the day-to-day life of the school will be amplified by the vastly different skill set *Balapan* graduates will bring. The graduates of early childhood development programmes will be more independent, more used to learning by doing, with a greater familiarity with self-directed inquiry methods and able and ready to take significant levels of responsibility for organising learning. They will have begun to acquire the skills needed for effective participation in a globally connected society and an economically interdependent nation. These students will need and demand, and can benefit from, a demanding and intellectually rigorous curriculum, and teaching and learning practices that value the students' capacity for experimentation, investigation and co-operative project work. One important step in meeting these demands is to ensure that from the first years of formal schooling children should be able to learn how to shape and realise their vision of the future, be able to work in and lead a team and use modern technology. This is a very different learning environment from the ones most commonly found in the public schools of Kazakhstan, but it is an educational setting that is found in the high-achieving public schools and colleges of Finland and Singapore and across the leading independent schools of the USA and the UK.

Kazakhstan has been exploring new approaches to learning and instruction and to school organisation and leadership in these environments through NIS. The Intellectual Schools are important beacons of innovation and good practice that can serve as models to the wider public school system of Kazakhstan. The Ministry of Education and Science (MoES) has begun reviewing the policies and practice of the Intellectual Schools to discern what elements can and should be transferred to the nation's schools. The first outcomes of that review are likely to be:

- The introduction of a new educational programme across all subjects from Year 1 starting from 2015.
- The implementation of new subjects such as 'Projects in the Natural Sciences' and critical thinking in addition to the current model of an 11-year secondary schooling programme.
- The strengthening of the teaching of languages (Kazakh, Russian and English) and Computer Science.

These changes should be supported by changes in the assessment regime especially in national testing. MoES is revising the contents of the testing materials to shift from knowledge-based assessment to competency-based assessment and is moving to computer-based testing to increase the integrity and reliability of assessments. All of these changes should support the use of students' assessments as a key element in guiding student learning as well selection and recruitment decisions by higher education institutions and employers.

Another area of pressing concern is the Kazakh language. President Nazarbayev has set MoES a goal of facilitating Kazakh language competence for school students who will finish their studies in 2020. This is an important step in the continued development of Kazakhstan's national identity and national culture. It also touches all parts of the school system: the assessment system; the inclusion of Kazakh language materials in libraries and resource centres; the preparation and professional development of teachers of the Kazakh language and history; and simple things like the artwork and signs that decorate classrooms and hallways. These developments also need to be designed and implemented in an environment which respects the ethnic, linguistic and cultural diversity of the nation and ensures that the tolerance and inclusiveness that has distinguished modern Kazakhstan is maintained and enhanced.

One of the realities of Kazakhstan is the spread of its peoples across vast distances. Many communities are small and relatively isolated. Providing high-quality education to young citizens in these areas is difficult and costly, and yet vital to the nation.

Kazakhstan's best and most experienced teachers are concentrated in urban areas. The physical infrastructure of schools in rural areas needs urgent attention to reduce reliance on emergency accommodation and triple-shift schooling.

The problems of rural schools have serious consequences. The gap in the quality of education, confirmed by an analysis of the Unified National Test and the views of international experts, reduces educational achievements for many in the nation's rural schools and colleges. These low attainments have a direct correlation with high unemployment rates, low youth incomes and increased numbers of marginalised young people in rural areas and on the margins of the larger cities and towns. All this will have a negative impact on community engagement and stability and on economic productivity, industrial innovation and regional development.

To offset the imbalances between urban and rural areas many provinces operate 'ungraded schools' in communities with small populations in order to provide access to education. Of the 7600 schools across the country, 75% (5700) are located in the countryside. Of these, 4100 are ungraded schools where students are often in multi-age class groups or taught by part-time teachers or teachers ill-prepared for specialist subject teaching. Supporting these schools and the teachers who work in them is vital if all young people are to have access to a high-quality education that will open them up to a range of career choices in their immediate community and in the wider world. Currently educational resource centres do offer support to some 200 'ungraded schools' by holding short-term training sessions and helping with the evaluation of students. The role of these centres could be widened and the services expanded to increase the number of schools and teachers served. In the short term information technology could expand the service areas of resource centres as it will allow teachers to conduct online classes, systematise distance learning and provide methodological support to teachers in ungraded schools.

Expanding the number of support centres and services does not take the place of dealing with the basic problems of infrastructure: the dependence on emergency or temporary accommodation and the use of the shift model of schooling. Many of the worst infrastructure problems are in provinces with weak revenue bases and it may be prudent and justified to use the republican budget to resolve these basic problems in these regions.

In short there are four immediate challenges for the future of education in Kazakhstan: an increase in demand for early childhood education and schooling as the population increases; the need to introduce a modern student-centred inquiry-based curriculum; the need to strengthen the Kazakh language and culture in school; and the need to meet the aspirations and broaden the opportunities for young people in rural Kazakhstan.

Looking further ahead

The immediate issues of implementation and marshalling and delivering resources can often distract attention from the strategic, from those long term issues that underpin systematic sustained reform. Three large and fundamental issues that need more policy attention in Kazakhstan are: the way teachers are compensated; the different tax bases of the provinces; and the lack of innovation in teacher education.

Teachers in Kazakhstan are compensated through the *stavka* system which bases a teacher's pay on the time spent in a class room teaching and then supplements it with additional payments for additional hours, specific tasks, bonuses and allowances and in some cases by parental contributions. This is in contrast to the practice in most OECD nations where a teacher's salary acknowledges that work includes professional meetings, lesson planning, grading and extra curricula and leadership roles that benefit student learning. The *stavka* system was designed to allow people to work for part of the time, increasing work place flexibility. In practice it created the perception that school teaching is a low paid, part-time, low status job. This discourages young talented people from entering the profession, atomizes the work of teachers which means they do not focus on the whole student but on the task that gets compensated. This impedes student learning which is the main task of the system. It also discourages co-operation between teachers because sharing lesson plans and materials is seen to be equal to giving away an opportunity to earn more (Harris-Van Keuren, 2010).

It is hard to change the way teachers are paid. It worries every schoolteacher, as well as their partner and immediate family. There are probably some 2 million people who would be directly affected by a change in Kazakhstan's public schoolteachers' pay. Even those who benefit worry that their colleagues will resent them for the salary increase.

In addition, any increase in schoolteacher salaries will flow into other sectors as an increase in teacher salaries will flow to the other mass professions such as nursing and may lead to increased inflation. But it may also increase tax revenue and reduce untaxed payments. Nonetheless the impact on domestic salaries of an increase in secondary school salaries is a real issue.

A decision to move away from the *stavka* system would be bold. It should be combined with a requirement for certain specified reforms in teacher practice, such as training for the new trilingual curriculum and its implementation. Whatever reforms it is linked to, getting away from the *stavka* pay system is vitally important because it would transform the daily life of a school and free teachers to focus on what is best for the student, rather than on what discrete, limited tasks or actions will bring more pay. But it is a change that would need to be linked to significant reforms and improvements in schooling and which would increase teacher productivity.

The second powerful constraint on systematic reform in education that has been identified by many local and international experts is that there are marked differences in the capacities of provinces to meet the costs of high-quality service delivery and educational reform. This comes in part from the differences in regional and local economies. Some regions have weak tax bases and are unable to raise the funds necessary for good social services.

This difference in fiscal capacity is accentuated by funding mechanisms in all sectors of education that are not always suitable for the purpose of promoting equality of opportunity. Generally these funding mechanisms are not needs based. They favour the wealthier and they are skewed to the urban population and are not market led. The funding arrangements do not align with the desired end of an inclusive and cohesive nation of citizens who are well equipped for the 21st century.

One solution is a system of fiscal equalisation. Fiscal equalisation moves money from richer provinces or states to poorer ones through the national government. Tax or revenue redistribution systems operate in various federal nations such as Australia and Canada. They rely on high integrity data and accountability systems and are often complex and hard for the wider population to understand and support. Internationally, equalisation systems that work well cover a sector, something wider than school education, such as all activities and programmes in the field of human development, to avoid substitution; such as *Oblasts* minimising local expenditures on local schools to maximise national transfers.

There are two other options: (i) centralisation of particular educational activities or functions, and (ii) targeted or categorical programmes. In centralisation, MoES pays for the production and delivery of all things such as learning materials and the training for teachers to use them. It could extend to centralising the payment of teachers through the creation of a national teaching service. In categorical programmes, money for a specific purpose such as a new curriculum or the learning of a priority language or to serve as specific student population is transferred to the province, with tight expenditure and accountability controls.

The three modes of fiscal administration, regionalised, centralised and categorical, are not mutually exclusive. All three have weaknesses. This is not an area where education authorities can act independently of the whole array of government-financial relationships, but it is an area which needs policy attention. Most federal nations where schooling is largely a matter for the states or provinces have some form of fiscal equalisation to even out the capacity to pay for high-quality services and to promote equality of access and opportunity. Learning from the experience of these nations in the design of financial transfers and the associated accountability mechanisms that maximise the use of the funds for specified purposes would be a good first step.

The other area that needs policy attention and reform is the initial training for teachers. There is a widespread view that the Pedagogical Institutes are dominated by theory and have too little contact with practice. The US response to this problem was, and still is, to create alternative pathways to enter the profession, for example Teach for America. The UK has followed this idea through Teach First. The Teach for America programme graduates tend to leave teaching after two or three years, making it a short-term solution. The Nordic nations such as Finland have a different response. They have professionalised teaching by making entry to the role highly selective and competitive.

Initial teacher education in Kazakhstan has not had the benefit of the sustained periods of innovation and experimentation that NIS and Nazarbayev University have given the school and university sectors and that Kasipkor is providing for vocational education. The right place to initiate such a phase is open to debate but there is no doubt that innovation and the development of new and better ways of preparing teachers is necessary if Kazakhstan's public schools are to reach the performance benchmark of the industrialised democracies.

Three strategic issues represent large and seemingly intractable problems: reforming teacher compensation to increase the productivity of learning; grappling with the different tax bases of the provinces that limit innovation and improvement and increase inequities; and the lack of innovation in teacher education. All three are amenable to sustained and systematic inquiry and analysis. Kazakhstan has come a long way in the last twenty years, and especially in recent years, by studying the successes and failures of other nations, by innovating and building local expertise and capacity, and by testing, evaluating and adapting practices from high performing institutions and systems. These paths are likely to be just as fruitful in dealing with these fundamental barriers to an outstanding highly productive school system in Kazakhstan.

REFERENCES

Harris-Van Keuren, C. (2010). 'Influencing the Status of Teaching in Central Asia'. In I. Silova, (ed.), *Globalization on the Margins: Education and Postsocialist Transformations in Central Asia*. Charlotte, NC: Information Age Publishing.

Nazarbayev, N. (2013). 'The Concept of the Republic of Kazakhstan's Entry into the Top 30 Developed Countries'. www.akorda.kz/ru/page/page_214714_doklad-glavy-gos-udarstva-n-a-nazarbaeva-na-evraziiskom-forume-razvivayushchikhsya-rynkov-(retrieved on 20 December 2013).

INDEX

Fatima Shirviglo
← 05 MAR 2015
University of Sussex, Brighton.

From Brussels With Love

With inky blots, and rotten parchment bonds;
That England, that was wont to conquer others,
Hath made a shameful conquest of itself.

John of Gaunt
Richard II

First Published in 2016 by
Duckworth New Academia
an imprint of
Duckworth
Literary Entertainments Limited

From Brussels With Love

ISBN 978-0-9564346-6-1

A catalogue record for this book is available
from the British Library

Typeset and printed by CPI Books

CONTENTS

PROLOGUE

This book is written in the context of the referendum in the United Kingdom on whether to remain in the European Union. This is the biggest democratic decision for the British people for generations. Much has been and will be said about the policy issues permeating the campaign – but the deeper political, economic and historical landscape against which this Referendum is being conducted is lacking, including the evolving roles of the United States and Germany on our own parliamentary democracy.

In historic terms, this referendum compares to other great watersheds in British history: to the conflict between the Crown and Parliament in the Civil War and the Restoration; with Britain's development in the eighteenth century into a world power; our defeat of Napoleon in 1815; the repeal of the Corn Laws in 1846; the 1867 Reform Act that gave the vote to the working class; and with the development of our modern parliamentary democracy. The issue of Home Rule, the First World War, then appeasement and the Second World War, dominated the first half of the twentieth century. It was at this time that the evolution of integrated Europe impinged directly on the British people, leading to our joining the European Community in 1972. These are the historic landmarks against which this referendum takes place. The decision of the British people will define our relationship within Europe, and the life of our United Kingdom itself, for generations. But what is at the heart of this referendum is simple: who governs us, and how, just as it was with these previous landmarks. There is one major difference – the European question has been self-induced.

From this question of freedom and democracy everything else flows: our borders and immigration, energy, trade, innovation, economic policies and our relationship with the rest of Europe and the world. On our democracy, all else depends.

The debate has so far has failed to take proper account of the forces that have influenced our journey since the 1940s: from within the United States and the countries of Europe, and from Germany in particular, which under the cover of the European Union is now pursuing a policy of assertive economic nationalism. Our diminished democracy and our place in the second tier of an undemocratic European Union – which is itself unstable and does not work – are the consequence of these forces.

It was said that the British Empire was created 'in a fit of absence of mind'. This is not the case with the European Union, a carefully constructed framework for supranationalism at the expense of democratic decision-making. Those who inspired it did so to avoid a repeat of the world wars that violated Europe successively. No one can doubt the devastation they wrought, the consequent dangers of the Soviet occupation, and dreadful fascist movement which led to the Second World War. But the European project has gradually transformed into a new threat in and of itself.

Tragically, the apparent benefits have not materialised; the dysfunctional state of Europe is now profoundly counterproductive, and is creating its own calamitous self-destruction, deeply distrusted by the people ruled within it.

There is much irony in the United States, for reasons that were understandable in 1945, being such a central force for the present European Union – indeed that the President of the United States should come to the United Kingdom in April 2016 with the specific purpose of telling us how we should be governed. It was the principle of taxation without representation, and the very spirit of democracy, which led to the rebellion of the colonies against King George III and his ministers, and the creation of the United States itself. Candour is needed between friends, and the very benefits of our parliamentary democracy have been forgotten.

The consequence is our subordination into a European Union dominated by Germany, which will increasingly dominate the member states, as Chapter 10 demonstrates. Those who argue that we should remain will soon have to face a simple fact: the European Union does not work. The ideology of European integration is leading to greater disintegration and implosion across Europe, with the very objective of containing Germany now clearly unachievable.

The alternative is to take the decision to leave the European Union, bringing the other member states the understanding that this island has for so long provided, in democracy, liberty and democratic self-government, peaceful trading and cooperation on the basis of an association of nation-states, not an undemocratic, authoritarian and unstable European control.

So this is the story of the European Union from its true beginnings. We think this is a story worth telling, simply because there are some things the British people have not been told – how it began, and how it is actually run.

When the verdict of the referendum is given, we trust that it will be said, as did William Pitt the Younger in 1805, 'England has saved herself by her exertions, and will, I trust, save Europe by her example'.

INTRODUCTION

This is the *status quo*.

Our leaders have taken Britain into a vast organisation called the European Union, at whose apex sits the *European Commission*. The Commission is the main centre of power, deciding what the EU actually does. It is a group of 27 people, each overseeing a particular area. It is unelected and meets in secret: taking minutes is banned. No one is allowed in the Commission Room without the Commissioners' permission. This is the most powerful body in all Europe.

The Commission takes one person from each member state, all appointed for five years at a time. Below this group of 27 men and women are 35 *Directorates-General* (or *DGs*), like *DG4* (the *Directorate-General of Competition*), *DG6* (Agriculture) and *DG7* (Transport), which act as supranational government departments, each overseeing its own area of policy. Their number is rising. These DGs are run by sub-bosses called Directors General. The Commission often consults them before it issues directions.

The Commission drafts most of its policies privately however, then discusses them with the *Council of Ministers*. Next, the Commission tells a huge gathering called the *European Parliament*, followed by anyone else it likes. The *Council* is more fluid than the Commission, and who sits on it depends on the policy being discussed at the time. When agricultural policy is discussed, the Council summons Britain's relevant secretary of state and his continental counterparts. The Council passes EU legislation, often by the appearance of majority voting, having come to a consensus in private beforehand, which means vetoes are impossible. It also meets in secret, and Britain has only 8.4 percent of the votes. The Council sometimes consults the European Parliament, but not always.

The European Parliament is not strictly a parliament, because it cannot draft laws: only the Commission can do that. Sometimes it can delay or block legislation, but often it is not consulted, and can be ignored by the Commission most of the time. It consists of 785 MEPs elected every five years. Britain has 78 of them, and they mainly make comments on the Commission's proposals. In theory it can dismiss Commissioners with a two-thirds majority, but this has never happened.

A supplementary special council called the *European Council* is meeting more and more often. The public don't hear much about it, but this meeting of heads of government sets the grand direction of Europe. The European Council sometimes sets up an *Intergovernmental Conference* (*IGC*) to analyse big challenges. These IGCs organise *Summits*, and from these come Treaties: Rome, Maastricht, Amsterdam, Nice, and Lisbon.

Next, *Coreper* is the *Committee of Permanent Representatives*, where bureaucrats bargain over Commission proposals. Made up of top civil servants from member states, it also meets secretly. Sometimes proposals are altered, and new versions go to the *Council of Ministers* and the *European Parliament* for final consultation. The Commission, Council, Parliament and Coreper form a Tetrarchy. The Commission directs the lot.

The Commission's laws are imposed in the form of *Regulations*, *Decisions* and *Directives*. A Regulation is a general edict, applying identically in each member state. Decisions are case-specific and binding upon a particular state, company, or individual. Directives operate through national parliaments, which must tailor their new laws to fit their will. In the event of any conflict with previous national law, the latter is changed.

The *Court of Auditors* officially monitors how the taxes the EU takes to pay for itself are used, but this Court is EU-funded and has no independent power; even so, it has refused to sign off the EU's accounts for two decades.

The *European Court of Justice* (or ECJ) enforces the EU's laws. It has the final say on all EU legal matters, is also paid for by the EU, and its judgements are binding everywhere. Any member state or institution can be taken before the court by another member state or institution, or by any person for breaking any of the EU's over 30,000 legal acts (numbers are rising). Its word is final, and there is no right of appeal.

What follows is the story of how we got here.

PART ONE
THE ABDUCTION OF EUROPA

Europe's nations should be led towards a superstate,
without their people understanding what is happening.
This can be accomplished by successive steps, each disguised
as having an economic purpose, but which will eventually
and irreversibly lead to federation.

Jean Monnet, 30th April 1952

1.

THE AMERICAN SETTLEMENT
1942-1974

TWO MEN IN ALGIERS

> **War is the father and king of all:**
> **some he has made Gods, and some men;**
> **some slaves and some free.**

Heraclitus, Fr. 53

In December 1942 Winston Churchill summoned a man named Harold Macmillan, MP for Stockton-on-Tees in County Durham and Permanent Secretary to the Ministry of Supply. Tasked with briefing the PM on developments in French North Africa since Allied landings there on 8th November, Macmillan was told that rivalries between the French representatives meant that a Minister Resident of Cabinet rank would have to represent Britain at Allied Force HQ[i] in Algiers.

After France had collapsed, Britain gave staunch backing to London-based Charles de Gaulle and his Free French, while Washington had decided to recognise a panoply of French quasi-governors, reflecting Roosevelt's distrust of de Gaulle. These were the collaborationist Marshall Pétain in Vichy, the pretender Admiral Robert across the Atlantic in Martinique, and de Gaulle himself in London.

From the beginning, Macmillan stressed the need for a different attitude. Acknowledging that while a 'difficult person'[ii] de Gaulle might be, he asked both London and Washington to recall his steadfastness against the Nazis at Britain's bleakest hour, and in North Africa, Macmillan soon became de Gaulle's most steadfast advocate. Persuading Churchill to be more indulgent of his manners, Macmillan asked him to pretend that:

> 'Hitler and Sea Lion had succeeded and the King had fallen, but supposing we had got to America and made a government in exile there, what would you have thought it your duty to do to the Americans? To insult them at every point, and stand up for the past... We would have felt it necessary to stand up and be *ultra* rigorous about the rights of the British Empire...' He said, 'Yes, I see that...'

Still other considerations towards de Gaulle were taking shape. In January, Foreign Office man Pierson Dixon (whose writing at the time we can assume matched Macmillan's views) reminded London that any French regime put together in Algiers would likely be the template for post-war government in Paris.[iii] De Gaulle's rival in Algiers was the ultra-conservative General Henri Giraud. Perceiving Gaullism as 'broadly a movement of the Left', Macmillan knew de Gaulle was at the least a necessary counterweight in a post-war configuration, and must cooperate with Giraud, who retained the loyalty of many French troops.

Both Churchill and Roosevelt put this project into immediate doubt. Meeting in Casablanca, the two leaders summoned de Gaulle from London to meet Giraud, against Macmillan's advice that he would baulk at an invitation to French territory by two foreigners. As de Gaulle became 'very haughty' and refused numerous times, Churchill informed him:

> 'The fact that you have refused to come to the meeting proposed will in my opinion be almost universally censured by public opinion... The position of His Majesty's Government towards your movement while you remain at its head will also require to be reviewed...'

The Prime Minister then told Foreign Secretary Anthony Eden:

> 'If in his fantasy of egotism he rejects the chance now offered, I shall feel that his removal from the headship of the Free French

Movement is essential to the further support of the movement by HMG. I have doubted very much whether we should go so far to give him a further chance, but this really must be the last... I think for his own sake you ought to knock him about pretty hard'[iv].

On the 22nd January Charles de Gaulle finally arrived at Casablanca. He was at his petulant best, taunting Churchill into shaking a finger in his face and growling in *Franglais: 'Mon Général, il ne faut pas obstacler la guerre!'* For what was left of the conference Macmillan had to fight to persuade Churchill and Roosevelt to let de Gaulle off the hook; by the next day Macmillan was in virtual desperation, concluding that only some kind of public gesture would force de Gaulle to keep cooperating once the Conference ended.

Having discovered that the meeting was underway, the Anglo-American press corps were by then gathering nearby. With crowds of photographers forming, Macmillan and Bob Murphy (an American diplomat monitoring the situation for Washington) shoved the two French generals out towards the press-pack. Macmillan recalled de Gaulle joining Giraud 'in a picture that went out around the world... shaking hands with the best approach to a smile that they could manage'[v]. With such buttonholing and cajoling ended Casablanca, Macmillan's first taste of top-table diplomacy. He reflected on de Gaulle that

> 'Although, in certain moods, the PM talked big about breaking him, I knew well that in his heart he was very anxious not to be forced to do so... So he was really relieved when he came, and I think pleased at the modest degree of cooperation between the two French generals which was reached...'[vi]

The Minister Resident had now to convince Bob Murphy that this approach was right (who had left Casablanca describing de Gaulle as a 'Frankenstein Monster of which we ought to welcome the opportunity to rid ourselves'). But the repercussions of the Casablanca meeting were not over. Barely returned to Algiers, Macmillan stumbled upon an intrigue which he called in his diary 'the Anfa mystery'[vii], after the Casablanca suburb that hosted the conference.

Not long after the departure of Churchill and Roosevelt, Macmillan overheard a conversation between Murphy and American diplomat Harry Hopkins, about private negotiations on the sidelines between Roosevelt and Giraud.

These had been organised by Jacques Lemaigre-Dubreuil, a businessman with interests in the North African vegetable oil industry. Lemaigre-Dubreuil had arrived in Casablanca in time to convince Giraud to take a memo he had drafted to Roosevelt on the final day of the meeting. This memorandum stated that America – *and Britain* – committed that the French Commander-in-Chief based in Algiers would have the 'right and duty of preserving all French interests'. This single commander would by implication be Giraud, not de Gaulle.

On his initiative, Macmillan wheedled two documents from Murphy that showed Presidential approval of Lemaigre-Dubreuil's memo. One even stated: 'it was agreed between the President of the United States, the Prime Minister of Great Britain and General Giraud that it was their common interest for all the French fighting Germany to be reunited under one authority, and that every facility would be given to General Giraud in order to bring about this reunion'.[viii] Back in London this information was rebuffed in 'emotion and even anger', but Downing Street avoided a row by rephrasing the statement to make de Gaulle equal, again, to Giraud[ix]. Macmillan would later describe the episode as a 'reprehensible action on Roosevelt's part... the use of Churchill's name was unpardonable', and one that justified Churchill's perception of Roosevelt's 'deviousness'. De Gaulle of course also found out about the meeting.

Macmillan would keep pressing de Gaulle's case, and the importance of a single French government in exile. This was not easy. After meeting Churchill and Eden on 9th Feb, 1943, Moscow's ambassador in London Ivan Maiski committed to his recently discovered diary: 'Churchill mentioned de Gaulle and Giraud in the course of our conversation. The prime minister is highly irritated with de Gaulle and perhaps that is why he leans toward Giraud. I'm not surprised. Churchill has never liked de Gaulle, and that episode concerning his trip to Casablanca inflamed the prime minister even more. 'I'm fed up with that Jeanne d'Arc in trousers', Churchill snarled. Eden made an attempt to mollify Churchill and calm him down, but without much success'.[x] Come late February, the FO's William Strang described Macmillan's thinking in a note to Eden: 'The French Empire should be an ally in every sense of the word; French armies should participate in the re-conquest of France; and France should be present at the victory. For the future, we should hope that France would be a strong and independent power, acting with Russia and ourselves for the containment of Germany.' Strang concluded that 'Eisenhower agrees generally with our views, and it now appears that Mr Macmillan is bringing Mr Murphy round'.[xi] Eden scribbled on the memo: 'I agree'.

Macmillan himself would be lucky to see out the year, his plane crashing in flames on take-off from Algiers to a meeting in Cairo. Roosevelt's Assistant Secretary of War John McCloy, whose own plane was landing at the same moment, ran over to try to help. He saw 'a fellow going back into the plane... It was Macmillan going back... to get out a Frenchman. It was the most gallant thing I've ever seen, and I'd been in the first war'. Macmillan suffered serious burns, and it seems his sight was only saved by his spectacles.

In spring 1943, his political challenges were captured in a letter from his wife Dorothy, who wondered 'if it will ever be possible for these two generals to agree about anything... It would surely be possible to get many of the things de Gaulle wants if he was a little more tactful. In point of fact, I suppose he wants everything, but should he have it?'[xii] By May, Roosevelt even suggested jokingly to Churchill that de Gaulle should be packed off to govern Madagascar as some latter-day St Helena. Macmillan recalled later that London had given de Gaulle a codename: Ramrod, for a man with 'all the rigidity of a poker without its occasional warmth'[xiii].

In his struggle to rescue de Gaulle – the only plausible French leader – from his own arrogance, Macmillan now needed allies. He stumbled upon one in Jean Monnet. This urbane Frenchman from a family of Cognac merchants, posted in Washington with the Allied Purchasing Council, had won American praise for his diplomatic skill, and was sent to Algiers by Roosevelt in the first half of 1943. Charged with overseeing munitions shipments to the French, he had considerable power, and used it to win the confidence of de Gaulle *and* Giraud, possibly the only man to do so. Macmillan knew he was 'the lubricant, or even catalyst, between the two bitterly opposing factions'.

Macmillan and Monnet became close, agreeing on the need to forge a provisional French government as a political instead of simply military entity, to speak as an equal to the US and British governments. The two men knew this had to mean an alliance between de Gaulle and Giraud. They also saw beyond the war, to the role a strong France could play in the new Europe, agreeing that this must be central to British war policy.

More was to come from de Gaulle. In London on 4th May, he launched a new attack on Giraud so savage as to remind Monnet of speeches by Hitler himself. Macmillan now had to placate Giraud, convincing the politically naive general that breaking off negotiations simply because a politician 'made an offensive remark about another' was not done. Drafting for Giraud a message to de Gaulle, Macmillan penned the outlines of the future French Committee for National Liberation (FCNL) he had sketched out with Monnet previously. This meant Cabinet instead of 'personal government',[xiv] and the despatch forced de Gaulle into a public undertaking that he would not launch a post-war dictatorship. The safeguards on which Macmillan insisted may have saved France from Communist civil war after VE Day.

In Tunisia on 13th May 1943, Britain's General Alexander received the surrender of all enemy troops in North Africa. Britain's esteem had perhaps never been higher, with Eisenhower particularly fulsome in his praise for Britain's forces[1] (from Ambassador Maiski's diary, 21st January, 1943: in an 'interesting conversation' with Eden on 18th they discussed North Africa: 'the US Army is still 'too green' to wage serious military operations', said Eden. Tunisia had to be completed before the Allies could launch 'a military operation in Sicily').[xv]

This was the pinnacle in the Atlantic relationship, and de Gaulle understood he had no choice but to acquiesce to Macmillan and Monnet's request. A week later Macmillan flew to London, lent a B-17 Flying Fortress by a man who had learned his value. 'Come back as soon as you can. I don't want to be without you,' General Eisenhower told him[xvi]

From Washington, Roosevelt was still pressuring Churchill to cut de Gaulle out. A lengthy note arrived from Eden, 'bearing the unmistakeable imprint of Macmillan'. This urged the Prime Minister to ignore Roosevelt, 'on the grounds that the union was nearer than it had been at any time'[xvii]. Even in war, Macmillan seemed to understand that were de Gaulle pushed to the sidelines, Britain would be accused of encroaching on the sovereign affairs of France. He was heeded. On 29th May de Gaulle departed London, to be received on equal terms with Giraud in Algiers. Bidding farewell to his British hosts, he would later recall:

> 'Mr Eden good-humouredly said: 'Do you know that you have caused us more difficulties than all our other European allies put together?' 'I don't doubt it,' I replied... 'France is a great power.'[xviii]

De Gaulle landed in Algiers to a welcome choreographed by Macmillan. Stepping out of his French plane, he was greeted by a French guard of honour

---

[1]As his biographer Alistair Horne informs us, Macmillan himself received Tunisia's *Medal to be Proud Of, First Class*. Its colours matched the MCC's. Swiftly rebuked by an FO official (ministers were forbidden from accepting decorations from foreign countries), Macmillan hid it in his children's dressing-up cupboard.

and band playing the *Marseillaise*. French officials stood in front of their British and American counterparts, and de Gaulle was ferried away in a French car. In conversation later that day, de Gaulle would observe casually to his Anglo-Saxon hosts that their 'domination of Europe'[xix] was a mounting threat, and should it continue, France would have to move closer to Germany and Russia after the war. There would be other omens of de Gaulle's feelings about the Brits: to show his independence from the Anglo-Saxons, in December 1944 he flew to Moscow to sign his own theatrical anti-German alliance with Stalin. The next May Britain had to stop a scrap between the French and Syrian armies: this left de Gaulle so humiliated that a month after VE Day he declared that, given the resources, France would have gone to war with Britain.[xx]

After lunch the next day, Macmillan joined de Gaulle, this time alone. Keen to avoid any more unforeseen obstacles to a working alliance between de Gaulle and Giraud, he gave de Gaulle the most obvious hint.

> 'I felt sure that as the weeks and months went by he could, without straining the law, or acting in any way unconstitutionally, obtain for himself and those who were with him the reality of power.'

De Gaulle listened attentively. When Macmillan had finished he told him that he had always believed it was he who really understood him. The French Committee of National Liberation was finally begun, for the formal direction of the French war effort, on 3rd June, under the joint leadership of de Gaulle and Giraud. On 5th June Macmillan received a letter from de Gaulle: 'your sympathy is precious to me, which permits me also to call it our friendship'.[xxi] Yet Macmillan's work was not done.

Six days later, Macmillan received a letter from the PM, still apparently under Roosevelt's influence. Churchill, doubting the wisdom of recognising the Committee, referred Macmillan to the Bible, Matthew vii, verse 16: 'Ye shall know them by their fruits. Do men gather grapes of thorns, or figs of thistles?' Macmillan advised Churchill to refer to: 'Revelations, chapter ii, verses 2-4 inclusive... 'I know thy works, and thy labour, and thy patience and how thou canst not bear them which are evil... Nevertheless I have somewhat against thee, because thou hast left thy first love..."[xxii]

Before the fortnight was out King George VI arrived in Algiers. He told Macmillan that the PM had suggested he should not lunch with the French should they misbehave. Macmillan informed the King that they were not currently, and joining them 'may do good, and it can do no harm.'[xxiii] The King was amused by the suggestion, and entertained by the company. Afterwards Macmillan mentioned to de Gaulle that he would take an afternoon's drive to the coastal resort of Tipasa for a swim. The Frenchman came too. At the coast the two future leaders wandered the Roman ruins, talking of 'every conceivable subject – politics, religion, philosophy, the Classics, history (ancient and modern) and so on'. As Macmillan swam naked, 'de Gaulle sat in a dignified manner on a rock, with his military cap, his uniform and belt'.[xxiv]

On 2nd July, Roosevelt threw yet another stick in the spokes. Feeling a White House party would lend Giraud gravitas back in North Africa, the President invited him to Washington. This was a serious error of judgement which the FCNL took to be an intrusion on French sovereignty.[xxv] On 26th August 1943 Roosevelt grudgingly recognised the joint-led Committee. The obstructions to its recognition had been broadly American, but de Gaulle would not forgive what he took to be combined Anglo-Saxon perfidy. For his part, Macmillan had not only saved de Gaulle, but placed him firmly on the path to power. In fact he had saved de Gaulle's career five times.

THIS MASTER PROGRAMME

Educated Germans and French found much in common at war's end. In Germany, the *Declaration of Guilt* drafted by Pastor Niemoller framed a moral purging through honesty that could not have been further from Japan's face-saving denial. In France, Marc Sangnier led the Gratry Society, a Catholic spiritual movement for nothing less than a 'new international state of mind'.

But the sacrifice had not created security. The Soviet Union loomed over Europe, with half a continent in the grip of Communism. If togetherness is a feeling usually generated by a shared threat, it was at this moment that a sense of community began to arise in Western Europe. The threat came also from within: France and Italy had large communist parties of their own, and closer association with western neighbours would make a point to their own citizens.

No one was more supportive of this young movement than Winston Churchill. Out of office and with time for a grander view, Churchill knew that the USSR sought to expand its reach, and described 'a kind of United States of Europe' as the 'timely action' needed, instead of the appeasement of a decade before. Yet as Mark Twain tells us, history does not repeat itself, but sometimes it rhymes. In a passage curiously like attempts to see the best in Hitler because he gave Germans jobs,[xxvi] *The Times* suggested that 'Western Democracy and Communism have much to learn from each other'. Churchill's belief that new forces would push for European unity was 'outrageous', with 'little to suggest that the unity so much spoken of is on the way'.[xxvii] But in a speech at the Royal Albert Hall in May 1947, Churchill suggested that in future:

> 'United Europe would form one major regional entity. There is the United States with all its dependencies; there is the Soviet Union; there is the British Empire and the Commonwealth; and there is Europe, with which Great Britain is profoundly blended. Here are the four main pillars of the world Temple of Peace.'[xxviii]

Churchill told his constituency chairman in Woodford however that, 'we have another role which we cannot abdicate, that of leader of the British Commonwealth. In my conception of a unified Europe I could never contemplate the diminution of the Commonwealth', and 'nor do we intend to be merged into a Federal European System'[xxix]. It was not something he always clarified away from home. The next year, Churchill visited The Hague to chair the Congress of Europe, and before 800 dignitaries described his vision of a Europe of nations:

> 'We must proclaim the mission and design of a United Europe whose moral conception will win the respect and gratitude of mankind... I hope to see a Europe where men and women of every country will think of being European as of belonging to their native land, and wherever they go in this wide domain will truly feel 'Here I am at home'.'

At the time, Prime Minister Clement Attlee was at home in Number 10, struggling with the fallout from a winter so cold it had closed coal mines, causing power cuts and food shortages. The winter was harsher still in continental Europe. In February 1948, communists took power in Prague by force, with Foreign Minister Jan Masaryk found dead beneath his office window. Central Europe's liveliest democracy was trampled again without anyone coming to its aid. History rhymed and Europe looked on.

***

As the war ended, Charles de Gaulle, zealous protector of French sovereignty, returned as premier for two years from 1944. In the years immediately after the war he remained against the integration of Europe, but in the coming two decades de Gaulle as a man, and France as a nation, would shape Europe as we know it today.

The idea of a modern federal Europe was first seriously suggested by a Frenchman, foreign minister Aristide Briand, in 1929. After an attempt to occupy the Ruhr failed in 1924, France accepted reduced reparations and attempted to cooperate with Germany. In 1926, under Briand's tutelage, a steel cartel was created between the industrialists of France, Germany and Belgium-Luxembourg. While British ministers preferred liberal trade policy and links to the Commonwealth, French security was to be guaranteed by building a European framework with Germany. Briand's cooperative German counterpart Stresemann died in 1929, and Briand thereafter produced little. Come 1946, Britain rejected a French scheme to remove the Ruhr and Rhineland from Germany, preventing Paris fuelling German nationalism yet again.

Britain calmly dismantled her empire largely voluntarily after the war, but France hung on, guaranteeing brutal conflict in Indochina and Algeria. The Fourth Republic was eventually paralysed by the death agonies of the French Empire, while political skirmishes with communists and far-right *Poujadistes* sprung up at home. With a new prime minister every six months, the Fourth Republic was brought to its knees by events in Algeria, where in 1958 a revolt of army officers nearly metastasised into a military coup in Paris. De Gaulle was compelled to return from retirement to crush the revolt, and he changed everything. Gone were the revolving-door prime ministers, the *immobilisme*. De Gaulle had always believed in strength at the centre, and he would make it his, with a new presidency independent of the National Assembly and able to form governments of its own. French dynamism was harnessed. The centre had taken power and the Fifth Republic was born.

That Germany is propelled into Europe by its past is certain, but the Fourth Republic's instability also made dedicated European federalists of much of the French elite. Haunted by their own ghosts, all de Gaulle's successors – Pompidou, Giscard d'Estaing, Mitterrand, Chirac, Sarkozy and Hollande[2] – have revered the tradition at the heart of their Fifth Republic, that the stability

---

[2] Georges Pompidou was President from 1969-74, Valery Giscard d'Estaing 1974-81, Francois Mitterrand 1981-95, Jacques Chirac 1995-2007, Nicholas Sarkozy 2007-2012, and François Hollande since 2012.

of the state is preserved by tying France deep into European integration. In a country that had been wracked by divisions more extreme than any in Britain, Europe provided a way of discerning all reasonable political opinion. Federal Europe would begin because France allowed it.

Prime Minister Clement Attlee was joined in the 1945 Labour government by Chancellor Hugh Dalton, Foreign Secretary Ernest Bevin, President of the Board of Trade Stafford Cripps, and Herbert Morrison as Deputy Prime Minister. Much has been written of the 'natural' transition of the Anglo-American special relationship into the post-war world, but only with the arrival of George Marshall as President Truman's Secretary of State in 1947 – and obvious Communist activity in Berlin and Prague – did something like the wartime special relationship begin to be rebuilt. Britain's bespectacled Foreign Secretary did much to tease America from its new isolationism, but this was no time of Anglo-American friendship.

Churchill was out of office but not out of worries. In the final two years of war, Churchill's aides described a virtual obsession with the threat of nuclear holocaust, and the friction it created with the Americans. By the 1950s, Churchill saw the danger of an American 'showdown', either with Russia or a China supporting the Viet Minh's war against France. The British people might know little of war in Southeast Asia, he said, 'but they did know that there was a powerful American base in East Anglia'. Nuclear weapons dropped in East Asia could soon lead to 'an assault by hydrogen bombs on these islands... and of all the nations involved, the United States would suffer least.'[xxx] British governments would soon understand that Washington was equally concerned with the role of continental Europe in anti-Communist strategy.

Many European politicians who had been in exile in London, like Norway's Trygve Lie, Holland's Echo van Kleffens, and Belgium's Paul-Henri Spaak, wanted British-led European cooperation. Eden however preferred an American 'one world' scheme, in particular a United Nations, while the Foreign Office even worried that any western bloc would harm relations with Moscow[xxxi] (although in September 1945 Russian foreign minister Vyacheslav Molotov said he had no objections to an Anglo-French alliance). Restoring French power in Europe had after all been one Britain's core war aims, and London helped France gain its permanent Security Council membership.[xxxii]

The position Britain would take in Washington's European strategy should have been clear in the Anglo-American Financial Agreement of December 1945. Its terms were harsh, attacking the Commonwealth and sterling, and requiring free convertibility of the pound within a year. They demanded Britain ensure countries with sterling balances reduce or refund them, banned quantitative discrimination against American imports, blocked credit from Britain to Commonwealth countries on terms more favourable than those in the agreement (two percent annually). They also brought Britain into the Bretton Woods structure which created the IMF, fixed exchange rates, and made the dollar the reserve currency instead of the gold standard.

Before the Anglo-Soviet alliance of 1942, Britain's traditional approach to Europe had been in essence to maintain a balance of power. In the new order however, the Soviets seemed likely to forge a continent under a single hegemon. Both Churchill and Attlee looked to America to restore a balance, while seeking a world role for a Britain paramount in a loose concert of European nations, underpinned by the Atlantic alliance. As Ernest Bevin put it, 'No one disputes the idea of European unity. That is not the issue. The issue is whether European unity cannot be achieved without the domination and control of one great power'[xxxiii].

Bevin's interest went beyond bilateral arrangements, and he urged the British government to study a Western European customs union as an option for European trade and security. The view of the Treasury and Board of Trade was poor, given that the British interest seemed to be in freer world trade in general. Britain clarified its position in a document distributed in Washington in 1947: 'US opinion is thinking of a continental rather than a country approach to the present trade and production problem of Europe... [however] the position of Great Britain, which is not merely a European country but an international trader, presents difficulties'[xxxiv].

The Americans however had all but decided on a so-called 'dumb-bell' structure spanning the Atlantic. Its mechanisms would appear rapidly. In July 1947, under the auspices of Marshall Plan aid (after American Secretary of State George Marshall, but officially the *European Recovery Program* or ERP) Attlee joined French Premier Paul Ramadier to create the *Committee for European Economic Cooperation* (CEEC), given the job of assessing Europe's reconstruction needs. CEEC's findings were sent to Washington by September. Despite Congressional reductions to the aid figure recommended by the White House, 1948 saw the launch of the *Economic Cooperation Administration* (ECA) for American aid.

The same year, the CEEC was renamed the Organisation for European Economic Cooperation (OEEC), taking responsibility for executing the

European Recovery Programme. As a link between the ECA and OEEC, President Truman created the post of United States Special Representative in Europe for then Ambassador to London W. Averell Harriman (infamous during the war for conducting an affair with Winston Churchill's daughter-in-law Pamela while his son Randolph was on military service in North Africa). The programme was launched in April 1948, soon becoming Truman's personal focus in Western Europe. Both Truman and Marshall advocated European integration – indeed this was at the core of Marshall's work, bolstered by American interest in overcoming 'excessive fragmentation... of a large consumers' market'[xxxv]. Integration would provide for the safe reconstitution of West Germany, form a barrier to Communism, and build political stability in Western Europe. Western European unity would be a manifestation of America's growing confrontation with the USSR.

US aid to European federalists had begun on a small scale during the war, facilitated by an Austrian Count named Richard Coudenhove-Kalergi, in exile in the US from 1943. But it was in March 1947, just before the Marshall Plan address, that Coudenhove-Kalergi successfully lobbied Senator J.W. Fulbright to support European unity, with the Senator passing motions in the Senate in favour of a 'United States of Europe'. Coudenhove-Kalergi proceeded that year to found the short-lived Committee for a Free and United Europe,[xxxvi] but it took the arrival in New York the following summer of the representatives of another group, the International Executive of the European Movement, to secure real American backing. Arriving in America to urge the formation of an American support committee,[xxxvii] the European Movement would become the central focus of American efforts – and funds.

On 21ˢᵗ March 1947, Congress passed a resolution sponsored by Senators Fulbright, Thomas and Boggs for 'the creation of a United States of Europe', an idea to which Secretary Marshall felt 'deeply sympathetic'. A US delegate to the UN General Assembly named John Foster Dulles had been talking up European unity since the new year, and in November recommended to Congress that the Marshall Plan be used as a 'positive instrument for a United Western Europe'. Celebrated journalist Walter Lippmann described the need for 'no less than economic union'[3]. Meanwhile William Clayton, Assistant Secretary for Economic Affairs, wrote in a 1947 memorandum to Marshall:

---

[3]Lippmann believed the modern world was becoming too complex for ordinary citizens to comprehend, and as such they should be governed by 'a specialised class whose interests reach beyond the locality' (in his book *Public Opinion*, 1922).

'Europe cannot recover from this war and again become independent if her economy continues to be divided into many small watertight compartments as it is today.' Indeed, in the Economic Cooperation Act of 1948, Congress would even state: 'It is further declared to be the policy of the people of the United States to encourage the unification of Europe'.[xxxviii]

On Capitol Hill, 'Europeanists' like Senator Fulbright now saw European unity as America's primary aim in Western Europe, and vital to lasting economic recovery. These politicians soon proposed regularly that American aid be contingent on progress to political union, and the White House saw this as a longer-term aim: the ECA's Deputy Administrator Howard Bruce argued that 'the economic recovery which is being made possible by Marshall Plan aid is the most important factor readying Europe for actual economic and political union.'

***

Britain and France were also busy remoulding their relationship to post-war realities. Instead of the Western European customs union that had interested Bevin, a new Anglo-French treaty was signed by France's Anglophile leader Leon Blum at Dunkirk in March 1947. This treaty was very limited however, being a 50-year alliance against German aggression. The Treaty of Dunkirk preceded the Treaty of Brussels. In that city the following year, Britain and France were joined by the Low Countries, impressed by Britain's attitude, to expand the promise of mutual defence. Britain foresaw a military alliance, but the 'Brussels Pact' included commitments to social, cultural and financial cooperation, plus regular ministerial meetings in 'Consultative Councils'.[xxxix] Aware a European parliament was a step too far at the time, France and Belgium proposed that one should at least be studied, pressuring Bevin into agreeing a *Brussels Pact Committee of Inquiry into the European Assembly* by assuring him its conclusions would be non-binding.

It was during these debates that the French emerged as leaders of a federalist group. Talks in May 1949 would also create the Council of Europe, a broad parallel association which included the Scandinavians, who shared Britain's fears about losing sovereignty. When France first proposed discussing a European parliament, adding the possibility of economic union, an FO official wrote back to base at Charles Street: 'It is hoped that this item will not take up too much time'.[xl]

In January 1948, after discussions with Marshall and French foreign minister Georges Bidault, Bevin penned a Cabinet paper stating that the 'First Aim of British Foreign Policy' should be a Washington-backed 'western union' between Europe's nations. Attlee's personal take was far from anti-Soviet, and resembled the view of the *Keep Left* group, a collection of Soviet-apologist Labour MPs:

> 'At [one] end of the scale are the Communist countries; at the other end the United States... Great Britain... is placed geographically and from the point of view of economic and political theory between these two great continental states... Our task is to work out a system... which combines individual freedom with a planned economy.'[xli]

Discussed at the Congress in The Hague in 1948 and begun in London in 1949, the Council of Europe member states, guided by a Consultative Assembly, began the practice of coordinating law through 'Conventions'. The most famous of these would be the European Convention on Human Rights (ECHR) in 1950. Although officially separate from the European Union that would take shape, the Council of Europe combined the traditional intergovernmental approach with a parliamentary assembly. This would soon be copied, creating the European parliament in the same city – Strasbourg.

As President of the Council's Consultative Assembly, despite a British preference for the less radical Dirk Stikker, liberal foreign minister of the Netherlands, the Americans backed Belgium's Socialist Prime Minister Paul-Henri Spaak. During autumn 1948, Ambassador Harriman even urged Spaak to resign as Belgian PM to 'give greater vitality to movement for increased unity' in both organisations, at the expense of more moderate members. He quit a year later, to head the Council until 1952.

For now, the Marshall Plan guided European unity. Having created the Committee for European Economic Cooperation in 1947 to advise Washington's Economic Cooperation Administration in the dispersal of American aid, the Committee became the Organisation for European Economic Cooperation (OEEC), and Congress backed the Truman White House to begin using these organisations for integration. In summer 1948, the ECA's chief administrator Paul Hoffman described the situation facing Europe:

'While there has been a growing conviction that it is in the deepest interests of the United States that Europe should again become a living, workable and independent economic and political organization, there has at the same time been a growing conviction that this goal cannot be set in the frame of an old picture or traced on an old design. It cannot be brought about by old ways of doing business or through old concepts of how a nation's interests are best served... readjustments cannot be made in the course of national action along the old separatist lines. They can only be accomplished if each nation seeks its new goal in terms of the economic capacity and the economic strength of Europe as a whole... What seems to me to be called for and quickly is such a master plan of action based upon the full recovery of the European economy by June 30th, 1952, when American aid terminates. This master program would, of course, be a composite of programs developed by [the] participating nations.'[xlii]

Washington, said Republican Senator Henry Cabot Lodge Jr., saw the OEEC as 'the practical symbol' of economic unity, with a purpose of recovery and integration:

'I think there are a great many Americans whose enthusiasm for this whole concept will be governed by the extent to which the OEEC increases its influence and authority. I think there are many people in this country who regard that as the plus, as distinguished from the minus aspect of this thing which is vitally important. Of course, the minus is the dropping of communism. The plus is the extent to which Europe integrates itself, and the OEEC is the symbol of that unification...'[xliii]

Hoffman and the ECA began to push for faster reform, urging Washington to use trade liberalisation as the lever for unity. First, OEEC countries agreed to a steady lowering of quantitative restrictions, resolving in November 1949 on the initial goal of a fifty percent reduction of their quotas.[xliv] Hoffman pushed for eighty percent liberalisation in a year, followed by complete disappearance of quotas by mid-1951. Under pressure, in October 1950 the OEEC adopted the goal of seventy-five per cent liberalisation for all imports.

Despite an open row with President of the Board of Trade Stafford Cripps, Hoffman told OEEC members that if they failed to move towards liberalisation by 1st May 1949 he would be unable to report to Congress on a 'satisfactory degree of European self-help and mutual cooperation'.[xlv] Aid would be on the line. (Hoffman said later he 'had never argued harder with any man than Cripps apart from Soviet foreign minister Molotov'.[xlvi]) London buckled, and on 3rd June the OEEC favourably received Cripps's proposal for progressively removing quotas on intra-European trade.[4]

Ceaseless pressure for British participation demonstrated America's conception of Britain's new role.[xlvii] Washington also made clear its poor view of the Commonwealth and sterling.[5] London saw the Commonwealth, colonies, and sterling area as its pillars of strength: Washington wanted them opened up for American trade. In a statement to the House Committee on Foreign Affairs on 8th February 1949, Ambassador Harriman was

> '...increasingly impressed by the long-range importance of the development of the dependent overseas territories of the participating countries and of the vigorous resumption of American private investment abroad. As American industry continues to expand and its productivity continues to increase, the volume of raw materials needed from foreign sources will grow larger... This seems to me one of the most promising ways to assist in reaching a balance of payments... These are common problems which call for a common program among the European countries involved.'[xlviii]

---

[4] Ambassador Maiski sheds some light on Cripps's attitude. From his entry for 4th March, 1942: 'Cripps dined at mine. [Cripps:] 'Unfortunately, about a year ago, when England was fighting alone and wanted to involve the USA in the war, the British government promised the Americans not to recognise changes in the European borders without prior consultation. England became wholly dependent on the Americans. It's awkward, but what can be done?'

[5] Meanwhile a curious article in the *Wall Street Journal* revealed a counter-current of Anglo-Americanism in the State Department: 'An economic union of the United States and Britain. That startling idea is being seriously discussed privately by a growing group of key State Department officials as 'the only way out' of Britain's 'permanent' dollar shortage. These officials think Britain could but won't solve her own problems. For political-military reasons, they figure, the United States must solve them for her permanently... Yet the two nations would keep their political independence. How this could work out is a question the State Department men have not quite cleared up.' The leading architect of this idea was a diplomat named George Kennan, later Ambassador to Moscow. Kennan in fact had the idea of a *US-UK-Canada* economic union as early as the start of the Marshall Plan, but still saw it as complementary to the 'dumb-bell' combination of 'a unit at the European end based on the Brussels Pact, and another unit at the North American end.'

Hoffman summarised his own view of OEEC progress in a valedictory message to President Truman in September 1950:[xlix]

> '...now that the nations are facing the urgent need of expanding sharply their armed forces and increasing their production of war material the further strengthening and the integration of their economies have become essential... What remains to be done will be harder and far more significant for the permanent strength of free Europe... We can now say with assurance that Europe is through the first phase of its economic recovery. In the months ahead Europe must tackle the more difficult problem of making major readjustments which break away from its traditional – and now inadequate – ways of paying its way in the world.'

Britain would keep trying to impress upon the Americans that its economic relationships were focused elsewhere. But it was precisely these 'traditional – and now inadequate – ways' that America was determined to change.

THE COMMITTEE

**We do not draw the moral lessons we might from history.
On the contrary, without care it may be used to vitiate
our minds and destroy our happiness.**

Edmund Burke, *Reflections on the Revolution in France*, **1790**

Back in 1948, Churchill closed the Congress of Europe by announcing that the new European Movement would take as honorary presidents French Prime Minister Robert Schuman, Alcide de Gasperi from Italy and Paul-Henri Spaak. In August the following year, the new 'Council of Europe' opened for business in Strasbourg on the Franco-German border. Membership soon grew to eighteen countries. As a member, Britain insisted that the Council would have no executive powers. The new Council presided over a European Court, and commissions on legal cooperation, culture, crime, and human rights, yet to the new integrationists it had insufficient vision. In the belief that Britain was suffocating Council ambitions, in 1950 a group led by Robert Schuman hatched a new plan.

This *Schuman Plan* was prepared entirely in secret and without consultation with London, and it was extraordinary. The Plan was designed to terminate the British belief that Franco-German ill feeling permitted only London to mediate between them. It proposed political, economic and military integration. It proposed a European army, and explicitly proposed a United States of Europe.

Schuman wrote his plan with Franco-German reconciliation in mind, so as the most politically acceptable area its first creations were two proposals for a coal and steel body. The European Coal and Steel Community (ECSC) was founded in May 1951 by France, Germany, Italy and the Benelux countries ('the Six'), pooling coal and steel policies to prevent a new military-industrial complex. Paul-Henri Spaak became the first President of the new Assembly of the European Coal and Steel Community. Commentators often describe the ECSC as having begun European integration, but this is not true. The ECSC was just one article, indeed the least radical one, in the greater Schuman plan. None could oppose the ECSC, a small act of trust between France and Germany. But the train was moving.

Despite the Schuman Plan, the real Father of Europe was Jean Monnet. A civil servant and economist never once elected to office, Monnet had been born in Cognac in 1888, beginning his career in the family brandy business.[1] In 1940 he suggested to Churchill a Franco-British national union, a notion Churchill flirted with briefly. Leaving this idea behind, it was during the war that Monnet became fascinated by pan-European integration.

Developing his country's National Economic Plan in the late 1940s, Monnet, an operative who thought real influence was gained and held in the shadows, gained leverage over a host of ministries. During this time he crafted the philosophy he called *Fonctionalisme*. This envisaged the slow transfer of 'spheres of activity' from nation states to supranational control,[li] an environment in which former nation states would be unable to fight again even if they wanted to. Monnet believed nations were already irreparably damaged, and only their political elites could create a stable higher order. Functionalism underpinned a belief in a union of Europe that had never been limited to economics, but encompassed military and political life.

Jean Monnet knew that memories of bloodletting meant union would be a gradualist enterprise, and that the economic cooperation with which it would start was only a means to political union. Schuman himself acknowledged that his plan's purpose was 'not economic but eminently political', and would 'enable each country [especially France] to detect the first signs of rearmament'. This would rest on the skill of the willing, of the national politicians he had at hand. In May 1951 the Coal and Steel Community's founding treaty made Monnet its President. This was his Trojan horse.

The American use of covert operations to promote European unity is still little understood, but at its centre lay the European Movement, the prestigious umbrella group which led the calls for the unification of Europe. As the intelligence historian Richard J. Aldrich has shown, as the Movement arrived in New York in 1948, its first problem was a lack of funds. The secret provision of millions of dollars by the US secret services between 1949 and 1960 were vital to forging the necessary support for the Schuman Plan, and the Europe that sprang from it. American funding was never less than half European Movement funds, and after 1952 likely constituted two thirds. The origins of this US-European cooperation were found in the informal networks between US intelligence and European resistance movements in the war.[lii]

One of the central aims of American funding through this period was to undermine opposition in Britain.[liii] In early summer 1948, a small group of senior American intelligence figures organised a coordination centre named the American Committee on United Europe (ACUE).[liv] ACUE's founder was Allen Welsh Dulles (younger brother of John Foster Dulles, who would become Secretary of State under President Eisenhower). His assistant and co-founder was General William J. Donovan, who during the war had been head of the Office of Strategic Services (OSS), and who in the mid-1940s persuaded President Truman to begin creating the Central Intelligence Agency. Dulles also used his role as chairman of a committee organising the new CIA to provide ACUE with resources.

From June 1948, US covert activities were, in theory, overseen by the Office of Policy Coordination (OPC), which required covert operations which 'if uncovered the United States Government can plausibly disclaim any responsibility for them'.[lv] The OPC was placed officially under the administrative oversight of the new CIA, but took its orders from the National Security Council (NSC) and the State Department.

This reorganisation coincided with the creation of a new CIA department, the International Organizations Division, proposed by Allen Dulles's Special Assistant Thomas W. Braden. Its task was to carry out 'cultural activities'.[lvi] Dulles had begun looking at the possible use of 'private organisations' for foreign policy work the previous year, using another of his roles, as Chairman of the Council of Foreign Relations, to gain the help of American foundations, including proposing initiatives like a European university for former exiles. But when Dulles began work with the CIA in 1950, he found that its work with youth groups, cultural movements and trade unions were still highly fragmented: another CIA official called it an 'operational junk heap'. The reorganisation and leadership of the CIA, by its Director from 1950 to 1953 Walter Bedell Smith, and Allen Dulles, who became Director from 1953 to 1961, was carried out in tandem with their work as the founding Directors of ACUE.[lvii]

For the crucial first three years, William J. Donovan was ACUE's chairman (he also worked for the CIA until 1955).[lviii] Allen Dulles became vice-chairman, with executive director Thomas W. Braden, also formerly of OSS, carrying out everyday administration (Braden formally joined the CIA in late 1950, as Special Assistant to Allen Dulles).[lix] Although in operation since 1948, ACUE was only formally established in February 1950, and its Board of Directors came from four main groups. These were senior government figures, including Secretary of State for War Robert T. Paterson and Director of the Budget James E. Webb; officials from the Economic Cooperation Administration (ECA) responsible for US aid to Europe, including Paul Hoffman and his deputies Howard Bruce and William C. Foster; prominent business figures such as Herbert H. Lehman and Conrad N. Hilton; and labour movement figures including union leaders David Dubinsky and Jay Lovestone.

From the beginning, ACUE's main purpose was to fund groups working for European unity, many of which drew their members from the wartime resistance groups with whom Dulles and Donovan had worked.[lx] ACUE established strict criteria for receiving funds, including that groups had to work for rapid, not gradual, European integration, which had to include strengthening the Council of Europe; they also needed the capacity to influence a substantial swathe of European public opinion. ACUE's other objectives were to publicise the cause of European unity within the US, lobby Congress, and sponsor scholarship, allowing the group to keep an office known to the public at 537 Fifth Avenue, New York.[lxi] Indeed a full year into ACUE's operations, the British Foreign Office still knew only of its American publicity work.[lxii]

The European Movement was soon the main recipient of the 'moral support and money' they told ACUE they needed. Private correspondence between Donovan and Winston Churchill also shows that Dulles and Donovan believed ACUE's promotion of European unity was the little-known 'unofficial counterpart' to the Marshall Plan.[lxiii] In the early stages of partnership, control over this money was given to Duncan Sandys, Winston Churchill's son-in-law and president of the European Movement's International Executive, with Paul-Henri Spaak among its senior European statesmen members. To survive 1949, the almost bankrupt Movement needed an initial grant of £80,000. But while Sandys pleaded for 'a really large contribution from America', he was also 'very anxious that American financial support for the European Movement should not be known'.[lxiv]

While ACUE support reached its height after 1952, its greatest impact was in the preceding three years. After saving the European Movement from financial collapse in 1949 and 1950, sponsoring the conference in Brussels in February 1949 that created the Council of Europe in Strasbourg, and paying a good deal of the Movement's administration costs.[lxv]

By 1950 however, the obstacle to progress was increasingly clear: British resistance to a federal Europe, especially within the Labour Party, which was still in government. The Labour Party of the time was vociferously against any movement which would threaten British sovereignty, preferring cooperation between nation states. Indeed, British resistance had begun to spread, as Duncan Sandys, and more importantly his father-in-law, began to see how the European Movement was turning towards federalism to an extent neither man had foreseen.[lxvi] The disagreements that followed within the European Movement saw its near-collapse by early 1950. Braden flew to Europe to take control.[lxvii]

Braden returned from his 1950 trip to report once more that 'the Movement is very low on funds', as ACUE stepped in financially yet again. While financial needs could be met straightforwardly, Braden also reported back on the growing anti-federalism of the British and Scandinavian members. Spaak had informed him that the lack of British support left him unable to pursue any federal plans, but American backing would allow him to press on regardless, as 'Britain would be forced sooner or later and in a greater or lesser degree to come along'. In June, Braden promised him ACUE's support, as Spaak told the Americans he was willing to take over the European Movement leadership. Sandys abandoned the leadership in July 1950, and with American backing Spaak and the federalists took control.[lxviii] Braden would later send a secret report to CIA Director Walter Bedell Smith, condemning Duncan Sandys, and outlining how in early 1950 Sandys 'attempted to disband the

European Movement', but 'Spaak and Retinger together have handled the Sandys situation… and kept the whole fracas from reaching the public'.[lxix] Given that Sandys would have been working closely with his father-in-law, this implies that, shortly before he became Prime Minister for the second time, the United States was working secretly to undermine Churchill's wishes for the future of Europe.

With financing from ACUE, the European Movement's international secretariat now moved from London (and Paris) to Brussels. At American suggestion, its objective now became to generate support for federalism with the 'initiation of major propaganda campaigns in all countries'. With Donovan especially favouring the Schuman Plan,[lxx] the American administration now agreed that the goal was a federal Europe.[lxxi]

Britain remained a serious obstacle to American plans. On 19th January 1950, Spaak complained to Secretary of State Dean Acheson about British obstruction of the Council of Europe. On behalf of the American embassy in Paris, diplomat Charles Bohlen complained to ACUE that Washington was still hesitating to apply serious pressure on London because of the residual wartime special relationship, and argued that the Commonwealth should be broken up, and Britain merged with a federal Europe.[lxxii] Still, in autumn 1950, Acheson suggested only that 'the British themselves must be the judge of whether a step as far as genuine federation with Western Europe would be… in the best interests of their people'.[lxxiii]

This dismayed the Americans working in Europe, including ECA special representative Averell Harriman, and ambassador in London Lewis Douglas. Harriman was particularly angry, and meeting US ambassador to Paris David K. Bruce and US High Commissioner in West Germany John J. McCloy, told them he found British Chancellor Sir Stafford Cripps 'petulant and arrogant', and that 'the US should no longer tolerate interference and sabotage of Western European integration by the United Kingdom'.[lxxiv] Should Labour win the 1950 election they would 'be even more cocky', and the US 'would not stand for this much longer'. At a meeting in March 1950, senior US officials requested a study of the degree and timing of the pressure to bring on Britain, although Ambassador Douglas requested this not be done before the election, as this would allow Labour to pose as defender of the Commonwealth. Since January 1950 however, ACUE had already been funding federalist MPs within the Labour Party, much to the resentment of Clement Atlee and the leadership. One was R.W. Mackay,

Member for Hull North-West (although his proposed path to federalism, nicknamed the 'Mackay Plan', was blocked by the British and Scandinavians the following year).[lxxv] Labour won the election, before losing in 1951 to Churchill's Conservatives.

When Churchill returned to power in 1951, despite having helped launch the European Movement, he set himself against the federalism the United States had pushed within it. ACUE now changed tactics, deciding that the best route to federalism was via 'mass agitation' through 'publicity and propaganda',[lxxvi] instead of making open political arguments to Britain's leaders. In the US, ACUE paid for lecture tours by numerous European figures; Spaak visited for a six-week coast to coast tour in January to February 1951, with much press coverage. ACUE also set about forming 'respectable' opinion in America, ensuring it was the first port of call for television and radio producers, and universities who sought speakers on European questions[lxxvii] like the Schuman Plan, and paid for Americans to visit the Council of Europe. ACUE publications in 1950 included *Britain's Problem in European Union* and *Why the United States Needs a United Europe*.[lxxviii]

ACUE sponsored numerous academics, including Carl Friedrich at Harvard, a historian, propaganda expert and committed federalist. An ACUE cultural section was launched in 1950 by Harvard's William L. Langer and Frederick H. Burkhardt, president of Bennington College in Vermont.[lxxix] In 1951, ACUE began providing scholarships for American students to attend the College of Europe in Bruges, the training-ground of a future European political class;[lxxx] its principal Dr H. Brugman, among others, had promoted federalist ideas among clandestine wartime publications such as *Résistance* in France[lxxxi] – in 1959 ACUE would pay the *Economist Intelligence Unit* $11,200 for a report on Britain's economic relations with Europe, to generate among Britons a 'more realistic view'.[lxxxii] Allen Dulles also held a press conference in New York to release a letter to Schuman in support of the Schuman Plan, signed by '118 big names', including former Secretary of State George Marshall. By 1951 ACUE was publishing a fortnightly newsletter for US circulation, as well as the European Movement's own bulletin, *Europe Today and Tomorrow*. General Donovan made his own radio programmes and had his articles published in the *Atlantic Monthly* and *San Francisco Chronicle*. An April 1952 advert in *The New York Times*, 'The Survival of Europe' advocated a European union.[lxxxiii]

After 1950 ACUE sponsored federalist action in the city of Strasbourg itself, launching in a building next-door to the Council of Europe the 'European

Council of Vigilance', led by French resistance leader Henri Frenay. With an initial ACUE grant of $42,000, the organisation provided the Council of Europe with a constant stream of federalist petitions, as ACUE helped Spaak and Frenay generate support for the Schuman Plan.[lxxxiv]

In spring 1951, a wide-ranging discussion between Donovan and Eisenhower, now Supreme Commander of NATO and preparing his successful presidential run, led to ACUE dedicating more resources to integrating Germany into Western Europe, to create, in Donovan's words, 'a pattern of specialised authorities [to] create the unified military force and free economic trade area in Europe that are necessary if Europe is to obtain maximum strength and assure the success of General Eisenhower's mission'.[lxxxv] The US Mutual Security Act that year stated that resources must be used to 'further encourage the economic and political federation of Europe'.

Later that year, the ACUE directors decided to fund a new project, a federalist campaign for young Europeans. In the next five years, ACUE sponsored over 2,000 European Movement rallies, creating the appearance of popular demand for European integration. Financing the rallies through the European Movement also helped disguise the extent they depended on American funds (an especially large number were held in Germany with the US Army's help, including a German-Europe conference in Hamburg in November 1951). In 1952, Spaak requested another layer of secrecy, with American funding diverted to European Movement 'Special Budgets' which would not appear in the overall budget of the Movement.[lxxxvi]

By 1952, the Movement had a youth newspaper in five languages and a European Parliament of Youth whose aim was to 'inform the masses of European youth of their obligations to themselves and the free world'.[lxxxvii] In a letter to William J. Donovan in October 1952, Jean Monnet wrote: 'Your continued support, now more crucial than ever, will help us greatly toward the full realisation of our plans'.[lxxxviii]

As Allen Dulles replaced Walter Bedell Smith as Director of the CIA, ACUE's position within the US government became even more central.[lxxxix] At this point ACUE began to revive its use of elite politics, adopting alongside the European Movement Jean Monnet's Action Committee for a United States of Europe, with its emphasis on small gatherings.[xc] Monnet was even more careful than the European Movement to disguise his links with ACUE, and the only recorded American funds to Monnet came to his secretariat through the Ford Foundation. By 1949 however, at Allen Dulles's request, the Ford

Foundation was working with the CIA on various European programmes, and was already coordinating its federalist efforts with ACUE; by 1953, John J. McCloy and Shephard Stone, who had channelled US government funds to the European Youth Campaign, were board members of the Ford Foundation, with McCloy its Chairman by 1955.[xci] In a letter to Richard J. Aldrich, Monnet's principal private secretary François Duchêne wrote that: 'He made it plain on many occasions that CIA or quasi-CIA funds must be avoided because of the political risks to his prestige'.[xcii] But it is hard to imagine that the Foundation would not coordinate direct gifts of money to Jean Monnet himself with ACUE generally, and with Allen Dulles in particular.

In an interview in the 1980s, Thomas W. Braden admitted that ACUE was financed by the CIA, while the European Movement's founding Secretary General Józef Retinger acknowledged in his memoir, published after his death, that their funds came from the US government. Its second Secretary General George Rebattet stated in an interview:

> 'There were no less than four members of the CIA among the Officers and Directors of ACUE... The vast majority of the American funds devoted to the campaign for European unity, and practically all the money received for the European Youth Campaign came from State Department secret funds. This was of course kept very secret. ACUE thus played the part of a legal covering organisation. Donations from business made up a maximum of one sixth of the total sums...'[xciii]

While ACUE had employed a professional fundraiser to raise funds from private individuals, after US government funds were tripled in 1951 his services were no longer required.[xciv] Richard J. Aldrich found that from 1953 to 1960, ACUE funds probably constituted two-thirds of the European Movement budget.[xcv] Aldrich finds that the European Movement created enough appearance of support to wear down its opponents, with the Labour Party leadership perceiving 'a lot of pressure from European and US public opinion' by April 1950.[xcvi]

NOW IS THE TIME

In Paris in 1950, the Schuman Plan also signalled the emergence of new French tactics. Launching the Plan without warning, France then did nothing for two weeks, until suddenly issuing invitations to discuss it, making London decide at speed whether to join in. Although Stafford Cripps thought Britain should sign up to 'steer' proceedings in an acceptable direction,[xcvii] a British Cabinet committee recommended rejection due to French demands for an *open-ended* commitment to supranationalism.

The Schuman Plan gave America an opportunity. President Truman saw the Plan as an instrument for his German policy in particular, allowing America to launch its own conception of European unity. The first foreign statesman Schuman told of the plan was Secretary of State Dean Acheson. This was on 8th May, during Acheson's brief stop in Paris *en route* to London, when he saw Schuman and Monnet together, privately. According to historian R.B. Manderson-Jones, 'Acheson gave his complete and unequivocal support for the proposal, and forthwith wired President Truman informing him of the revolution about to occur and bidding him do nothing until further notice'.

When the Schuman Plan was announced the following evening, the French knew it had crucial American support. German Chancellor Adenauer was informed on 9th May, accepting the proposal wholeheartedly; Britain would not. Foreign Secretary Bevin was only informed by the French Ambassador later on 9th May, between sessions of discussions with Acheson, who even then had failed to tell him. A rift began to develop between the two men.

The Plan served to fortify the French position as the only willing leader of Europe. Britain's statesmen still saw the Atlantic relationship as paramount, but Washington had begun looking beyond Britain, to European unity, as the great bulwark in the fight against Communism. Indeed Dean Acheson had urged Schuman in October 1949: 'Now is the time for French initiative to integrate the German Federal Republic [into] Western Europe'.[xcviii] As we will see, the Americans did not anticipate just what implicit powers Europe would give to Germany.

Despite its American backing, the Plan provoked British opposition through its evident supranational intent, and because of French insistence that it would become the pre-condition to participation in European negotiations. Bevin thought the Schuman Plan was ill-thought out, and that its inevitable failure would give Britain the chance to sculpt a leadership scheme of its own.[xcix] But in this new and sudden appearance of Franco-German agreement as sanctioned by the United States, Britain faced a huge diplomatic coup.

Schuman and Monnet were not after all the only men with Europeanist ideas. In opposition in March 1949, Macmillan gave a speech to the

Commons in which he described French fears about Germany's future. 'The only guarantee,' he suggested, would be 'if the soul of the German people is won for the West. If Germany enters a West European system, as a free and equal member, then indeed German industry can be subjected to control'.[c] Within a year Konrad Adenauer's West Germany received a formal invitation into this very system.

Once more, a British statesman thinking out loud was taken more seriously on the Continent than at home. The Schuman Plan's proposed combination of French and German coal and steel production[ci] precisely matched the points Macmillan had made in the Commons.[6] In June 1950, Churchill told the Commons from the Opposition benches that he would accept the principle of abrogating national sovereignty without hesitation – provided the conditions and safeguards were satisfactory. He announced: 'The Conservative and Liberal Parties declare that national sovereignty is not inviolable, and that it may be resolutely diminished for the sake of all the men in all the lands finding their way home together.'[cii] This came from a preoccupation Macmillan already recognised: '[Churchill] thinks about one thing all the time... his chance of saving the world – till it has become an obsession'[ciii]. Macmillan knew Churchill's entreaty was no considered programme for government, but 'an old man trying to give a new lead to the world... It was for others to find detailed solutions'.

Until Britain's refusal in June 1950 to take part in the Schuman Plan negotiations, Truman assumed that, seeing the disappearance of her world leadership, Britain would fit smoothly into the European scheme as seen, and to a considerable extent driven, from the White House. Truman's Planning Staff briefly suggested developing a continental European union, linked to a US-UK-Canadian maritime trading bloc, but the President saw the difficulty of persuading an Anglophobe Republican Congress to give Britain special treatment. The wartime climax of the Anglo-American special relationship was by now much diminished, and American criticism of Britain's rejection of the Schuman Plan was tremendous. Britain's economic position was considered the central problem. At the Senate Foreign Relations Committee Hoffman described London's move as 'torpedoing our efforts toward achieving an

---

[6]However Macmillan made a more despairing remark in the earshot of Labour MP Hugh Dalton after a meeting in 1950: 'I think Europe is finished; it is sinking. It is like Greece after the second Peloponnesian War. Athens and Sparta are quarrelling and Philip of Macedon is watching and waiting to strike. I have been reading Thucydides lately and it is just like our times. If I were a younger man, I should emigrate from Europe to the United States'.

integrated economy in Western Europe'[civ]. Asking Congress for a new tranche of $600 million in aid, he made sure to remind them:

> 'If in the first instance some nations say they cannot join for some particular reason, it simply means they do not get their proportionate share of the $600,000,000.'

Soon afterwards, seeing his opportunity to move to a more pro-European position than the Labour government, Macmillan joined his colleague David Eccles MP to launch a plan for a non-supranational coal and steel association; it was not taken up by the leadership. Although Monnet told Schuman: 'the British are waging a skilful campaign to sabotage our plan', Britain simply waited for the Europeans to establish their community, aiming to form an association with it[cv]. As Churchill returned to the premiership in October 1951, the White House believed Britain would stay cautious towards European unity but happy for the continent to pursue it. This attitude appeared in a sarcastic note after Churchill's visit to Truman in January 1951:

> 'United States officials do not suggest that Britain should join in the Schuman plan, the European army, or any other project looking to a European federation. They accept the often-reiterated British refusal to participate in any form of European unity that entails supranational institutions. But they contend that [they] might facilitate the success of these projects by approving and encouraging them.'[cvi]

The mood in Washington was hardening. One senior State Department official recorded that 'the Conservatives were even worse than Labour, and [new Foreign Secretary] Eden thought he was a Palmerston'. On Capitol Hill, Senator Fulbright of the Foreign Relations Committee repeated Hoffman's threat to withdraw aid unless Britain join European integration, noting:

> 'I sincerely hope [Britain's] government will consider most seriously the possible consequences of rebuffing this courageous and far-sighted leadership on the part of the French Government. Many of us, including myself, have been losing our enthusiasm for the Marshall Plan because of the apparent impossibility of making

any progress towards European federation. If none is made, I believe the British must assume much of the responsibility, and I believe the consequences will be very serious indeed.'[cvii]

The ECSC treaty was signed in April 1951 by West Germany, France, Italy and the Benelux countries. But cooperation by 'the Six' was never the final objective of American policy. The outbreak of war in Korea in June made the American desire for Western European consolidation stronger still. A second French proposal, from Premier René Pleven in October 1950, seemed to provide the means to secure a German role: the European Defence Community, or EDC.[cviii] For the first half of the 1950s Washington's policy was thus almost entirely preoccupied in driving two French proposals.

In 1951 France invited the other countries to discuss this European army. Britain sent only an observer. Eden's remark in November 1951 that Britain would never join a European army drew criticism from Macmillan, but Eden always denied that he was 'anti-European', and none of his critics of the time openly advocated losing any sovereignty[cix]. Indeed Eden persuaded the Cabinet that the EDC was the only method with which Britain could both sustain NATO and let Germany re-arm, adding 'our Commonwealth connections and the Sterling area inhibit us from subordinating ourselves... to any European supranational authority; nevertheless we have assured [the Six] of our goodwill and our wish to be associated with their work, short of actual membership.'[cx] The ECSC was followed in just one year by both the Bonn Agreements that restored German sovereignty, and the European Defence Community treaty the next day.

Just a month before this proposal, during talks in New York, the subject of German rearmament had been emphasised by Secretary of State Dean Acheson to both the French and British foreign ministers, clearly signalling support. That Germany's resurrection as a nation and its binding into the European project happened within 36 hours of each other was also a Franco-American decision. Churchill had once described a 'European Army' in which 'we would all bear a worthy and honourable part'[cxi]. This may have been whimsical, but was taken more seriously by the French. When actually presented with the plans for EDC, in which German units would be amalgamated into a single supranational command, Churchill described 'this vast Foreign Legion' as more 'sludgy amalgam'[cxii] than workable plan.

Acheson is known to have written to Schuman however: 'if the French government, in the spirit which spoke so distinctly from the Schuman Plan, worked out the main outlines of a plan to promote the further rapprochement of the free peoples of Europe in close contact with the Governments of Germany and the other European countries prepared to participate in the common work, one was justified in the hopes that long-term solutions for many of the present political, economic and military problems might be found'. He went on to highlight that 'the United States Administration [gave] its full and wholehearted support to European integration'[cxiii]. The treaty beginning the European Defence Community was signed by the Six (but not Britain) on 27th May 1952. But Churchill was right. The EDC would fail.

By the end of his time in office, President Truman was under growing criticism, not only for appeasing Communism, but for being pro-British and too gentle on European unity through a 'support it, don't push it'[cxiv] approach. That before his election in January 1953, Churchill and Eden showed considerable interest in Dwight D. Eisenhower's choice of Secretary of State was no coincidence. Eden even suggested to Eisenhower himself that he appoint anyone but a man named John Foster Dulles; he did appoint Dulles, and gave him free rein over foreign policy. Dulles soon began pushing the Europeans as quickly as possible towards a European army, and to the regional consolidation that would allow the United States to devote its attention to Asia. Beijing had fallen to the Chinese Communists in 1949 (and Communists led by a man under Stalin's tutelage). In London, Washington's behaviour amounted to 'perfidy', but Dulles believed Stalin was pursuing an 'Asia first' strategy that Washington had no choice but to match (it was told of Dulles that 'his nose followed Chiang Kai-shek, while in Europe his ear was set on Adenauer'). Eden wrote to Ambassador Sir Roger Makins in Washington:

> 'Americans may think the time past when they need consider the feelings or difficulties of their allies. It is the conviction that this tendency becomes more pronounced every week and is creating mounting difficulties for anyone in this country who wants to maintain close Anglo-American relations.'[cxv]

Dulles did not mince his words when it came to the roles of democratically elected governments in Western Europe. Eden tells us:

'Mr Dulles [said] that it might be necessary to work for a French government which could take office solely for the purpose of putting through EDC... [he] then told me that he thought we, by which he apparently meant the United States and Britain, were approaching a parting of the ways with regard to American policy. If things went wrong, the United States might swing over to a policy of western hemispheric defence, with the emphasis on the Far East... Mr Dulles pointed out that the consequences of a swing of American policy towards hemispheric defence were of obvious concern to Great Britain. He hoped, therefore, that I might find occasion to underline the warnings which he had issued in his statement, and make some appeal to France.'[cxvi]

But on 30th August 1954, seeing threats to their own sovereignty, Gaullists in the French parliament voted down the EDC. Monnet resigned his ECSC presidency, to support integration in a private capacity, and Dulles faced the German question once more. After the EDC's failure, Dulles believed the 'disunity of the Brussels Pact Powers' would require them 'to seek the weakness and disunity of Germany'[cxvii]. Dulles now sought an alternative.

Britain's reprieve was brief. Indeed the only lasting result of the EDC's failure was that the Foreign Office failed to foresee the 'relaunch of Europe' that was about to arrive. The EDC had failed, but the ECSC had not, and it would allow integration to continue. The US remained unwilling to be identified overtly with federalist schemes, but behind the scenes, Dulles began to apply pressure.

It was after a London meeting with the Secretary of State on 17th September 1954 that Anthony Eden first began to buckle under American weight. At this point Eden records Dulles informing him that future aid was 'highly doubtful', and that Britain 'must assume that continued American participation in Europe, on the present scale and in the present form, was impossible'. This threat meant America would cease to guarantee British and European security unless Britain accepted European unity through supranationalism. Having been a staunch critic of the supranationalist idea for years, the Foreign Secretary now concluded that it was 'wise to have something in reserve'.

Bevin had believed Britain would never go further into Europe than the United States, but Eden now understood that if America was to remain in Europe at all, Britain must go much deeper into Europe than they had ever foreseen. This was brutal timing: Churchill was still Prime Minister, but just beginning to lose his touch. He received this in a memo from Eden:

> 'I realise that this would be an unprecedented commitment for the United Kingdom, but the hard fact is that it is impossible to organise an effective defence system in Western Europe, which in turn is essential for the security of the United Kingdom, without a major British contribution. This situation will persist for many years to come. By recognising this fact and giving the new commitment, we may succeed in bringing the Germans and French together, and keeping the Americans in Europe.'[cxviii]

A hasty conference in London was followed immediately by the Paris Agreement of 23rd October 1954 that created the Western European Union. The WEU strengthened the original structure of the Brussels Treaty through the replacement of the Consultative Council by the Council of the WEU. This was granted powers of decision. The activities of the WEU went beyond the Brussels terms, including an agency to control armaments through majority voting. This was Britain's first submission to supranationalism. Eden described it as 'a practical move on our part, to show our friends in Europe that we are in earnest', as the tone with which British leaders described European policy suddenly changed. While Eden stressed that this was not a European army in the making, Dulles told Eisenhower they had succeeded in saving

> '...most of the values inherent in EDC. The Brussels Council will have many supranational responsibilities, and while the present arrangements do not go as far as EDC in creating parliamentary controls, this disadvantage is to an extent offset by the British commitment to continental Europe...'[cxix]

Dulles perceived that 'Now, Britain, recognizing that modern developments had largely obliterated the Channel, was ready to identify itself irrevocably with Continental Europe'. America had pushed Britain in. But for the fundamental change of heart towards European unity, Washington would have to wait, not for Churchill's return, but for Prime Minister Harold Macmillan.

2.

AT THE BAR OF HISTORY
1950-1974

ON THE CAPITOLINE HILL

**Of course, Britain must decide for herself whether
it is in her interest to enter a USE [United States of Europe].
Maybe ultimately your choice is either to become the 49th state
or to join the USE.**

**General Eisenhower, 19th December 1951,
in the diary of Hugh Dalton, Chancellor of the Exchequer 1945-1947**

When Prime Minister Clement Attlee had announced that Britain would not join Europe's Six to discuss their Plan in summer 1950, Macmillan had been appalled that we would be aloof from discussing Europe's future. He cannot have known how Atlee's decision was made.

With the Prime Minister and his Chancellor Stafford Cripps out of the country (and Bevin in poor health), the question was never discussed in a full Cabinet session. Instead, it was decided by Deputy Premier Herbert Morrison during dinner at Covent Garden's Ivy restaurant after a trip to the theatre: 'We can't do it, the Durham miners won't wear it',[cxx] said Morrison. Macmillan would tell his constituency that 'without British participation, Franco-German unity may be a source not of security but danger'.

By then Macmillan was moving emotionally in a European direction. A commentator of the time recalled how, when speaking of Europe, 'Macmillan put an arm on my shoulder and spoke with a fervour which I thought embarrassing about his belief in the European idea'. On 17th August 1949, he even suggested that Europe's 'Committee of Ministers shall be an executive authority with supranational powers. The Committee shall have its own permanent secretariat of European officials',[cxxi] an early description of the structure that would be adopted twenty years later.

Despite refusing to join Schuman Plan discussions, and having won an election with a four-seat majority but sure another was on its way, in early 1951 Attlee's government quickly ratified the Council of Europe's *European Convention on Human Rights*, despite opposition from British legal opinion. Lord Chancellor Lord Jowitt knew the Convention was contrary to British legal custom:

> 'Most [British] lawyers hated it, because they didn't like foreigners interfering, because they thought human rights were perfectly secure in Britain anyway (they had, after all, been invented there), because they felt that such rights shouldn't be defined (British judges knew what they were instinctively), and because they believed that if they were defined they would be exploited by Communists, crooks and cranks.'[cxxii]

Churchill returned to the premiership in 1951, and within a year joined his new Foreign Secretary Anthony Eden on a visit to President Eisenhower in Washington. On Eden's return his impressions shocked the Cabinet. Macmillan wrote in his diary that Eden had been 'forcibly struck – indeed horrified at the way we are treated by the Americans today'. On the journey from Washington on the *Queen Elizabeth*, against Eden's advice, Churchill sent what Macmillan called 'rather a fulsome message' to Moscow's former foreign minister Vyacheslav Molotov, suggesting a personal meeting with one of Stalin's closest advisors, Georgy Malenkov. Despite Churchill stating Eisenhower had made no commitment, the President was 'amazed' and Dulles 'appalled'.

On Tuesday 23rd June 1953, after a dinner at Number 10 in honour of Italian Prime Minister de Gasperi, Churchill had a stroke. When he presided over the Cabinet the next day, his speech was slurred, his mouth drooping, and on Thursday he returned home to Chartwell, where his condition worsened. Yet as Churchill recovered, his Personal Private Secretary Jock Colville achieved the 'in peace-time unique success of gagging Fleet Street', as

Rab Butler 'took charge of the Cabinet with tact and competence'.[cxxiii] But Churchill was fading. The next year Macmillan even committed to his diary: 'It breaks my heart to see the lion-hearted Churchill begin to sink into a sort of Pétain'. Macmillan visited the Prime Minister at his house at Chartwell in the summer, desperate to persuade him to retire. For hours Macmillan was kept outside in the hallway, as Churchill played bezique with his Private Secretary Jock Colville. Teatime came and went. Churchill's wife Clemmie offered Macmillan a whisky, and the old man stayed at his card table. After Macmillan had finally left, Churchill asked Colville, 'What did he come for?'[cxxiv]

***

With EDC shelved, the Schuman planners busied themselves with economic integration, their chance to bring Britain in. In April 1955 Anthony Eden finally became Prime Minister. And in summer, the coal and steel countries' foreign ministers met in Messina, where Gaetano Martino hosted in his native Sicilian fortress city the following men: Antoine Pinay of France, Paul-Henri Spaak (then Belgian foreign minister), Dutchman Johan Willem Beyen, Luxembourg's Joseph Bech and Walter Hallstein of Germany.[7] Despite many claims to the contrary, Britain did not even send an emissary to Messina, and despite the imminent arrival of the Common Market our Ambassador to Paris Gladwyn Jebb suggested 'no very spectacular developments are to be expected'.[cxxv] But the US was concentrating its efforts on integrating the Six, who five years after creating the ECSC would force supranationalism forward in Rome, in March 1957, to establish the EEC. Eden snubbed the offer of joining his counterparts in Messina, at the meeting that would lead to the Community. On 14th December 1955, about to become Chancellor, Macmillan told his diary: 'The French will never go into the 'common market' – the German industrialists and economists equally dislike it...'[cxxvi] At this point even our Ambassador to Paris Gladwyn Jebb (the founding UN Secretary General after the war) scribbled on a government memorandum on the emerging Common Market: 'embrace destructively'.[cxxvii]

Chancellor Macmillan remained concerned by the Six and their supranationalism, and in New Year 1956 decided the time was right for a new

---

[7] Jean Monnet had also stayed busy. As they gathered he published his book, *Les États Unis d'Europe ont Commencé.*

approach, ordering the Treasury in February to draft an alternative European plan. Swiftly rebuked by the mandarins, who claimed they lacked the time for this 'huge task', Macmillan cajoled Eden into going around the Treasury with an investigative group of his own.

Among the list of possibilities Eden gathered, 'Option (e)' was a Partial Free Trade Area with Europe, 'by which tariffs would be removed on imports from the Six to the UK'. In July Macmillan gave it his backing, and Option (e) was renamed 'Plan G'[cxxviii]. This suggested British association with the Messina Plan through a free-trade area to allow continued free entry of Commonwealth produce into Britain.

Plan G soon became EFTA (the European Free Trade Association), otherwise known as the 'Seven', of Britain, Denmark, Norway, Sweden, Austria, Portugal and Switzerland. The timing was not auspicious. Macmillan recommended Plan G the day Egypt's General Nasser nationalised the Suez Canal. He recalled later that 'since the House of Commons finds it difficult to deal with more than one great issue at a time, there was a certain unreality about the discussions'. On 16th October he sent Spaak a message asking the Six for 'a little more time before final decisions are made'.[cxxix]

Nasser also renewed ties with the Soviets and recognised Mao's China. Washington, which feared turning the Arab world towards Communism, refused to support the ensuing Anglo-French-Israeli attack on Suez. The Labour Party organised an anti-war rally in Trafalgar Square, and *The Guardian* urged its readers to write to their MPs in protest. The attack failed. In Bonn, Chancellor Konrad Adenauer, a staunch supporter of the strike, was furious at Washington, but this only brought him closer to Paris. Having backed Nasser, Soviet prestige among Arabs soared anyway. Nasser, emboldened, soon began purging Egypt's Jews. Anthony Eden resigned, and on 10th January 1957 Harold Macmillan replaced him. Eisenhower would later tell friends that he regretted opposing the Suez intervention.[8]

In Number 10, Macmillan decided that Plan G should be built in stages: and that it should be run via Washington's OEEC. The Six were welcome to join as one entity (which itself suggested they would probably keep together).

---

[8] The seeds of the Eden-Eisenhower dénouement may have been sown two decades before. Ambassador Maiski on 17th Feb, 1943, before then Foreign Secretary Eden flew to Washington: 'Eden has no luck with America! In 1938… He met all the notables there, starting with Roosevelt, but he failed to make a good impression on the Americans. He failed to win their hearts… We shall see what Eden's visit to America will bring. Will he be able to impress the Americans? Or, on the contrary, will the Americans succeed in influencing Eden? I don't know. The latter, I fear, is more likely: for all his merits, Eden is not a very strong person.'

Under pressure from Paris, Macmillan soon promised to delay. The leaders of the Six next stated that unanimous agreement among them would be needed before decisions on a free trade agreement with the Seven could be made, meaning France could veto any plan. Macmillan complained: 'The French are determined to exclude the UK. De Gaulle is bidding high for the hegemony of Europe'.[cxxx]

French information minister Jacques Soustelle now told Macmillan that EFTA was impossible without an external tariff, while de Gaulle visited Adenauer and talked him into avoiding any British plan. France then put the ECSC's first tariff reductions into effect. The free trade agreement was dead. The Scandinavians in particular urged action, and Britain needed a response. Although Macmillan saw EFTA as a potential settlement, Britain's association had a smaller population than its rival and still offered relatively few economic advantages to world-trading Britain. Worse, precisely because it lacked a vision of political integration, Washington looked down on the new body.

The United States now strove to prevent agreement between the Seven and the Six, a fact exploited by the supranationalists, who believed any accord would undermine them. In February 1956 Dulles had insisted to Eden that he not hinder the Six in their creation of a customs union (and turned the OEEC into a better-funded new Organisation for Economic Cooperation and Development, or OECD, to strengthen his hand). On arrival in Europe just before Christmas, Under-Secretary of State Douglas Dillon complained that EFTA was liable to be divisive, even bad for US exporters, and Washington expressed even more disdain for any trade deal with EFTA for the same reason.

The minutes from Messina became Spaak's own *Spaak Report*, which would start the Common Market, at first in atomic energy and transport, with more areas to follow. To this end his report suggested another meeting, to take place in 1957 atop Rome's Capitoline Hill, where in 44 BC Brutus and his band of conspirators had sought refuge after the death of Caesar.

The Rome summit was held in an atmosphere of profound and unsettling change. More than any other event, Suez symbolised the waning might of Europe's great nations. In March, Britain's colonies of Gold Coast and British Togoland combined to create Ghana, the first of many independent African states. In the same month, the US Congress approved the Eisenhower Doctrine, a new mandate for a global role that stated America's right and duty to intervene on behalf of any government threatened with Soviet-backed aggression. Soviet premier Khrushchev ended hopes that real liberalisation would follow the reforms begun on Stalin's death in 1953, crushing democratic uprisings in Hungary and Poland.

After Suez, many French, including de Gaulle, believed Albion had left the French high and dry, deserting them at Washington's behest. Perceived betrayal at the highest levels saw them speed talks on further integrating the Six. Britain meanwhile focussed on restoring its relationship with America, but with Washington now pushing European supranationalism Macmillan gravely misunderstood the situation.

At the very moment of the ceasefire in Suez, Adenauer was to be found in French Premier Guy Mollet's office, discussing the European alternative to the dangers of association with the Anglo-Saxons. Suez also sealed the fate of the Fourth Republic, bringing de Gaulle back to power a year and a half later. He would be willing to play for time while French influence could grow.

***

The Treaty of Rome, whose signatories on 25th March included Paul-Henri Spaak and Konrad Adenauer, set the course to which Europe has stuck ever since, to integration. As the European Economic Community (or EEC) was born, the treaty made its aims plain: to eliminate 'national barriers to free competition', harmonise agriculture, transport and taxation, eliminate all internal tariffs, forge one common policy on non-European trade, and create the free flow of capital and people. Not for the last time, the ultimate intention was to be found in the small-print, specifically the preamble. This announced to Europe the forging of 'ever closer union'.

The treaty described the 'four freedoms', the free movement of capital, goods, services and labour, but also created institutions not normally seen in free trade areas. The European Court of Justice, with no right of appeal, would be supreme over all courts in the nation states. A European Parliament would supersede the Council of Europe in Strasbourg; a Council of Ministers would sign all new policies and 'oversee' an executive Commission in Spaak's hometown of Brussels. The Commission would run numerous policy directorates, each sending ideas upwards for consideration. And deep in the text, Article 189 pronounced: 'a regulation shall be binding in its entirety and directly applicable in all member states'. All this became effective at the stroke of New Year 1958.

Back in Britain, people learned that the Americans' first attempt to launch their version of *Sputnik* had failed, and that communist rebellions were shaking Malaya and Cuba. But quietly, through a treaty of six countries signed by twelve men, the bland-sounding new EEC became the highest power in Europe. Except for one thing: the document that created European power over nations was, in fact, blank. Because of a delay at the Italian printers, the Treaty did not arrive on time for the signing ceremony. Instead, dignitaries ceremonially signed a blank piece of paper.[cxxxi] Perhaps Brutus, Cassius and Casca wished their own coup on the Capitoline Hill never to be upstaged.

MACMILLAN

That year Britain led Norway, Denmark, Sweden, Switzerland, Portugal and Austria to form the European Free Trade Association. EFTA, which Iceland joined in 1970, took its first chairman in the shape of a canny civil servant called Sir Frank Figgures. A man of some awareness, in an interview with an American journalist, Sir Frank left us this:

> 'Most of the European states... had been occupied militarily; in effect, in one form or another, they had suffered military defeat, and had had their societies under very considerable strain if not destroyed. They were not in a position where they had great confidence in the capacity of 'the state' to safeguard the welfare of the citizens. In one way or another they had all failed.'[cxxxii]

But our experience, said Sir Frank,

> '...had been different. On the contrary, our society had survived. It had been under the most tremendous stress, but a democratic society had survived. It had thrown up one of its greatest leaders, and the House of Commons had certainly had one of its greatest experiences. It had fought a great war under cover of a House of Commons leader. It was in no position to say, 'We have no confidence in the state to serve the purposes of this country.' Elsewhere it was reasonable to say, 'We're not strong enough to do these things on our own, let's do them with other people' ...I must say I do think on the other hand that I wasn't really conscious at

the time that there were many governments in Europe who were terribly anxious to abdicate their political responsibilities and hand the thing over to somebody else. And this is after all in the end what matters.'

Sir Frank's EFTA eliminated the duties on manufactured products, but didn't intervene in agriculture or maritime affairs. It is often said that EFTA was established just to create a partial free trade bloc, but EFTA also gave funds for countries in need. In 1975, after the Carnation Revolution in Portugal toppled António Salazar's half-century regime and returned Britain's oldest ally to democracy, EFTA launched the Portugal Fund, a $100m reconstruction loan that would continue after Portugal left EFTA to join the EEC in 1985. But in the 1950s the supranationalist countries were still a minority, and the 'intergovernmentalists' included Britain, the Scandinavians, and Greece.

EFTA members were also free to determine their own terms of trade with non-EFTA countries. The fruits of the initiative were rich, with the volume of foreign trade among members rising from $3,522m to $8,172m in eight years. Britain could still help its colonies and former colonies, giving preferential trade access, allowing Britain to punch above its weight while assuring the Commonwealth that London still cared about their interests, and giving better access to the markets of the rich world. Sir Frank was replaced by Sir John Coulson, then a Swede, then a Swiss, but EFTA slid gradually into irrelevance. The truth is that, given Washington's plans, it was doomed from the beginning.

On entry to Number 10 in 1957, Macmillan knew the effects of Suez on the Anglo-American relationship. In *The Rise and Fall of Anthony Eden*, Churchill's son Randolph sees 'one of Harold Macmillan's greatest acts of statesmanship' being 'that he was able to heal the break so very soon after he became Prime Minister'.[cxxiii] This was achieved with little American assistance: Chancellor Adenauer said to new foreign secretary Selwyn Lloyd how Dulles had told him the British had no foreign policy and were finished. Macmillan wondered that 'it may be that people are right in dubbing him the 'double-crosser''. He responded by writing to our Ambassador to Washington Sir Harold Caccia, 'instructing him to marshal Eisenhower's active support over EFTA' (Macmillan would tell Eisenhower early in his Premiership that 'the most favourable economic climate for us to meet the communist threat is that of a steadily expanding level of world trade, in which the underdeveloped countries would feel that the future would hold increasing opportunity for them'[cxxxiv]). His entreaty was no trifle: 'while the Americans want nothing of the French and can afford to lecture them, we want a great deal from them. The French have it in their power to wreck the European Free Trade Movement'.

But the Americans wanted a great deal of the French. In 1958 the State Department, relieved that West Germany was joining the European path and moving away from the USSR, sought to push unity with France harder. John McCarthy, a US delegate to the OEEC/OECD in Brussels, informed our Deputy Under-Secretary for Economic Affairs Paul Gore-Booth, that his instructions from the White House were to lavish 'fulsome praise' on the Six, and he was having 'an uphill battle with his own people who moan about British threats... the United Kingdom had not got through to either Dulles or [Under-Secretary of State] Dillon'[cxxxv]. This was confirmed when Dulles declined Selwyn Lloyd's request for help preventing the Six starting discriminatory tariffs from new year 1959 (the year would see the European Convention on Human Rights become the European Court of Human Rights, allowing any citizen to take his own country to court in Strasbourg). But still Britain tried to persuade Washington to support EFTA. Ambassador Sir Harold Caccia met Dillon, who informed him that Washington would not risk slowing the process of Franco-German reconciliation, and would promise 'nothing'.

An alternative plan for Britain to join a North Atlantic free trade group had gathered support in Canada and the City, but Dillon turned this down flat. In February 1959, Paymaster General Reggie Maudling and Chancellor Derrick Heathcoat-Amory became concerned that Macmillan was beginning to doubt the future of EFTA, and even considering joining the EEC instead. Maudling reminded Macmillan that 'at the moment it is American policy to urge us to maintain the military expenditure and to increase the aid. The acceleration of the Treaty of Rome will mean a serious damage to our trade'.[cxxxvi] Macmillan resolved that he would raise it in Cabinet on 23rd March 1960, then with Washington; it appears he did neither. Heathcoat-Amory now tried telling Dillon that London could offer EFTA tariff reductions for the Six if they would reciprocate. Dillon batted this away: 'we are faced with a situation for which there are no perfect solutions'.

Wondering why the US was pushing the abandonment of the Special Relationship for the Six, Macmillan wrote to Selwyn Lloyd, 'Why is it difficult to make the United States realise that the Six which they support for the sake of European political unity is in fact (because of the economic threat to the

United Kingdom and others) a threat to European unity?'[cxxxvii] For Washington, nothing in Europe was more important than integration, protecting France and Germany from the influence of Moscow and, they believed, creating a larger European market while extending American economic reach into Britain's commonwealth. This meant supporting the Six. Britain would spend the next two years trying also to convince France to allow a free trade area that would include the Six (and all the OECD). The 1950s would end with any prospect of an EEC-EFTA free trade agreement consigned to history. Macmillan wrote in his diary:

> '...pondered a lot... Shall we be caught between a hostile (or at least less and less friendly) America and a boastful, powerful 'Empire of Charlemagne' – now under French but later bound to come under German control? Is this the real reason for 'joining the Common Market' (if we are acceptable) and for abandoning a) the Seven b) British agriculture c) the Commonwealth? It's a grim choice...'[cxxxviii]

The choice was soon made for him. According to one minister, in February 1960 Eisenhower himself warned the PM that the Special Relationship would decline if London did not sign up to the EEC. In June, *The Economist* joined *The Guardian* in supporting EEC membership.

By the end of 1960 at the latest, Macmillan decided Britain must apply to join the Six, completely against British public opinion at the time. And in May 1960, the American Committee for a United Europe suddenly dissolved itself. Although much work remained on the greater project of European integration, at this point, around the time Macmillan resolved to join the EEC, ACUE's directors appear to have judged that its strategic task was done.

By April 1961 Macmillan had become defeatist, saying Europe would no longer simply accept Anglo-Saxon leadership, had regained its strength, and could undermine Britain, which meant we should join the EEC if reasonable terms could be won. His Press Secretary Harold Evans said Conservative whips believed the Tories could stay unified on Europe; Macmillan hoped his influence could create an 'outward-looking' EEC.

Macmillan now fast-tracked pro-EEC ministers into Cabinet. Edward Heath took special responsibility for Europe, and Lord Home became Foreign Secretary. Sir Frank Lee, Chairman of the Economic Steering (Europe)

Committee released a paper which has been called 'the definitive document that was to set Britain on a new course' in Europe. It suggested membership could attract American investment and stabilise Europe. The government had accepted the American view.

With a few objections (from Home Secretary Rab Butler for example), on 22nd July 1961 the Cabinet joined Macmillan in a 'unanimous decision in principal' to apply to join the EEC. Lord Beaverbrook told the Cabinet what they could expect from his newspapers (including the *Mail*) about 'that blasted Common Market', which he understood was an 'American device to put us alongside Germany".[cxxxix] In late September, as an opinion poll showed that two-thirds of Britons still did not know whether they were in the EEC or EFTA, the Six accepted Britain's request for talks.

In January 1961, John F. Kennedy became President. With the young Commander in Chief, Macmillan would try to uphold the Atlantic alliance, and find support for the British (and Commonwealth) trade position in Europe. To incorporate de Gaulle into the strategy he wanted Kennedy to respond to de Gaulle's suggestion of closer 'tripartite cooperation' on NATO[cxl]. Yet Kennedy brought with him Robert McNamara as Defence Secretary, and a number of advisors later called 'Europeanists', in particular Secretary of State Dean Rusk, a quiet, uncharismatic southern academic, although 'never one of the inner circle'[cxli] (despite falling in love with Oxford while a Rhodes Scholar, bad experiences with the Brits during the war in the Far East had led to a preoccupation with 'British arrogance'). Former officer Sir Solly Zuckerman, who knew a number of the new president's advisers well, advised Macmillan before his visit:

> 'President Kennedy hates and despises President Eisenhower; your visit will be our last chance to influence the policy of the new administration before it crystallises; the new administration will not respect you if you pull your punches with them... President Kennedy is very anxious to get a position in which the free world can start building up its economic strength. He realises that America cannot do this alone. He wants ideas.'[cxlii]

Britain's new ambassador in Washington was one David Ormsby-Gore. Of identical age to JFK, and having made his friendship in London in 1938, they had grown closer still when the president's sister Kathleen 'Kick' Kennedy married Ormsby-Gore's cousin Lord Hartington. After her husband was killed in action in the war, Kick became godmother to one of David's children. This relationship with the Commander-in-Chief would provoke considerable envy in the reserved Rusk.[cxliii]

It is widely accepted that President and Prime Minister enjoyed a warm relationship in the 'Jack and Mac' years: But this picture is incomplete, and more recent sources point to recurring strategic disagreement, catalysed by Kennedy's advisors pushing him towards a pro-EEC stance. Dean Rusk was followed into *State* by 'a powerful lobby of 'Conceptualists' or 'Europeanists'', in particular Francophiles such as George Ball, William Tyler, Walt Rostow, Robert Bowie and McGeorge Bundy, another academic and Kennedy's Special Adviser on Security. These advisors pursued a 'downgrading of the Special Relationship [to] place France and West Germany on a more equal footing with Britain', while Bundy in particular argued that Britain's standing would be greater in America were she to join the Six. This would have serious ramifications in the final year of Kennedy's life.

On his first foreign visit, to Paris in May 1961, Kennedy 'played up loyally'[cxliv] from Macmillan's point of view, making the case for British entry for the sake of western stability. The next year, Kennedy proclaimed his 'Grand Design', describing a 'Declaration of Interdependence'[cxlv] whereby North America and Europe would uphold the security of the West together. The 'Grand Design' was originally a memo Macmillan drafted at New Year 1961, which he began with the working title of 'Problems of 1961'. It concluded that, for Britain, 'exclusion from the strongest economic group in the civilised world must injure us'. Macmillan spent '7 or 8 hours' working on it on New Year's Eve.[cxlvi]

Britain's first ministerial-level meeting with the Six came on 10th October. Heath announced Britain would accept the Treaty of Rome in full, but in return asked for a special deal for Commonwealth imports to the EEC, and protection for EFTA's 'legitimate interests'. He also hoped to guide the Common Agricultural Policy.

The CAP, a French-led scheme to restrict agricultural imports and establish a common 'target price' for produce to protect farmers' incomes, would only come into force in 1970, and funds were yet to be found (in the end they would be, through British entry). The scheme presented London with major problems. CAP would cut the cheap imports of Commonwealth food that helped Britons keep down their living costs, forcing them to buy more expensive European produce. As well as harming Commonwealth trade, given Britain's smaller farming sector it would damage competition in real terms.

Macmillan hoped for cooperation with de Gaulle on a non-supranational Europe, not seeing that this was liable to alienate those members who *did* wish British to join (the PM noted in his diary that de Gaulle 'talks of Europe, and means France',[cxlvii] but that he actually 'does *not* want political integration'[cxlviii]). As negotiations progressed, on 1st December 1962 Heath reported to Macmillan from Brussels that the French were 'opposing us by every means fair and foul. They are absolutely ruthless. For some reason they *terrify* the Six – by their intellectual superiority, spiritual arrogance, and shameful disregard of truth and honour'.[cxlix] Macmillan's low mood fell lower after a speech by ex-Secretary of State Dean Acheson, who told his audience that 'Great Britain has lost an empire and has not yet found a role.' The Premier wrote in his journal that Acheson had always been 'a conceited ass, but I don't really think he meant to be offensive'.[cl]

For the men still in office, political life became yet more fraught. The Europeanists now convinced Kennedy of the need for an anti-nuclear proliferation policy. Britain had been a partner of the US and Canada in developing the bomb, but at Christmas, rumours made their way to Macmillan that the missile promised to the UK, Skybolt, had hit technical trouble. 'The failure of Skybolt might be welcomed in some quarters as a means of fencing Britain out of the nuclear club',[cli] one minister warned. Macmillan told de Gaulle that he would inform Kennedy that should Skybolt fail, he expected a replacement such as Polaris. Otherwise, 'Britain would have to develop her own system... at any cost'.[clii] Like Churchill, Macmillan knew where the first line of conflict was likely to fall. 'If there was an attack against Europe at some future date', he wrote, 'the United States might perhaps hesitate to use her nuclear forces. Some European deterrent was therefore perhaps necessary'.

McNamara had other ideas. In Washington, the Europeanists' vision of foreign relations included preventing Britain gaining its own nuclear weapons, making the subject difficult, though peripheral, for Kennedy. For Macmillan the question was pivotal to British defence. McNamara claimed that 'independent national nuclear forces within NATO' would be 'dangerous, expensive, prone to obsolescence and lacking in credibility as a deterrent', and in a comment historian Richard Lamb believes was also a swipe at French ambitions, that 'the creation of a single new nuclear force would encourage the proliferation of nuclear power with all the attendant dangers'. But Ormsby-

Gore observed to Macmillan: 'The more McNamara or any other American attacks the French deterrent the more it [also] makes the General and those around him determined to carry on with [their] nuclear policy'.[cliii]

A growing sense of betrayal in London poisoned the start of the Anglo-American summit in the Bahamas on 19th December 1962. As Kennedy stepped off Air Force One, George Ball noticed the tune being played by the Bahamas band: 'Oh, Don't Deceive Me'.[cliv] Soon Macmillan met Kennedy privately, and they walked together discussing the Skybolt crisis without their staff.[clv] The Europeanists had told Kennedy that giving Polaris to Britain could provide de Gaulle an excuse to block Britain's path into Europe, but Macmillan informed him de Gaulle was in the picture. The deal was struck.

In giving Polaris to Britain, Kennedy saw the need to help maintain the Conservative Government in office, given the Labour opposition both opposing EEC entry and likely to 'spend more on social welfare and less on defence'. As the diplomatic correspondent at *The Express* René McColl suggested that the price of nuclear defence was joining Europe, in the final weeks of Macmillan's premiership, the Government brought together a high-level Anglo-American symposium at Ditchley in Oxfordshire. Historian Michael Howard told the delegates:

> 'An independent force under British control provides in the eyes of a substantial section of public opinion – a section particularly well represented in Whitehall – a certain sense of assurance even if the defence analyst can prove rationally that this assurance has no valid foundation. This assurance is not for the eventuality of our being abandoned by our allies in face of the existing threat. It is for the possibility of the whole pattern of world politics changing in the future as radically as it has changed in the past... What the future holds in store no one can tell.'[clvi]

A Deputy Under-Secretary at the FO named Sir Bernard Burrows briefed Edward Heath about the meeting:

> 'The whole American team and practically the whole of the non-official British team expressed strong disapproval of the retention of an independent deterrent by the UK. They argued that its military value was slight and that in spite of its assignment to NATO. Its

existence played an important part in encouraging the French to continue with their plans to have an independent deterrent... The Americans emphatically stated their view that it would be far better for the alliance if the UK nuclear deterrent were scrapped and resources devoted instead to increasing conventional forces both in Europe and Asia.'[clvii]

Following Suez and the atom bomb, a British White Paper described plans to rely on nuclear weapons for defence, and reduce our Army of the Rhine. It was criticised throughout Western Europe. In London, the Cabinet were about to receive another jolt. Britain's second National Economic Development Council report, *Conditions Favourable to Faster Growth*, was published early in 1963. 'The effect of non-entry [to the EEC] is negligible',[clviii] it said, because while 75 percent of the trade of the Six was within Europe, at least 75 percent of our trade was outside.

***

Between 1955 and 1963, when the report was published – and almost parallel to Macmillan's premiership – the Labour Party was led by Hugh Gaitskell. A Londoner, Gaitskell had lectured on economics to Nottinghamshire miners at the Workers' Educational Association before returning in the 1930s to University College London. In Vienna in 1933 Gaitskell witnessed the short-lived Austrofascist dictatorship of Engelbert Dollfuss, an experience that would make him a dedicated democrat, but as suspicious of leftist utopianism as of the far right. Gaitskell's leadership would be characterised by constant infighting between the Left and his own moderates. Gaitskell would try in vain to scrap his party's unilateralist position on nuclear weapons and abandon Clause Four, thirty-five years before Tony Blair managed the same. In autumn 1961, Gaitskell addressed his party in Brighton. Tearing into Macmillan's failure to explain what the EEC would really mean, he warned that:

'Britain would be no more than a state, in the United States of Europe, like Texas or California... in a supranational system with a federal parliament, and Britain as no more than a province. ... We must be clear about this; it does mean, if this is the idea, the end of Britain as an independent European state... it means the end of a thousand years of history. You may say 'let it end'. But my goodness, it is a decision which needs a little care.'[clix]

A stormy ovation followed: Gaitskell had told the British people they were being deceived. Aware he could not persuade Britain of the value of membership, Macmillan was keeping Britain in the dark. Or as Gaitskell put it:

'The people are being told they are not capable of judging this issue. The government knows best, the top people are the only people who can really understand it. The classic argument of every tyranny in history.'[9]

Macmillan would respond a week later, but some of Labour's own big men were already getting nervous. Denis Healey thought Gaitskell was guilty of:

'Romantic chauvinism… It's inconceivable that the Common Market would acquire supranational powers in any major area, still less become a federation.'[10]

Home Secretary Rab Butler rebuked Gaitskell: 'For them a thousand years of history. For us the future.' When Macmillan spoke to his Conference, he made no attempt to argue with Gaitskell. Instead, he mocked him:

'Mr Gaitskell now prattles on about our being reduced to the status of Texas or California. What nonsense! Certainly if I believed that I wouldn't touch it on any terms. There can be no question of Britain being outvoted into some arrangement which we found incompatible with our needs and responsibilities and traditions.'

---

[9] Gaitskell and Monnet meanwhile were introduced by the MP Roy Jenkins in 1962, who recalled: 'In April 1962 [I] organised one of the least successful meetings with which I have ever been concerned. I arranged for Jean Monnet to address a meeting of the XYZ dining club and made sure that Gaitskell would attend. I think I fondly imagined that Monnet would lucidly meet all Gaitskell's points and dissolve his doubts. I have never seen less of a meeting of minds. They were both at their worst. Monnet would not answer Gaitskell's detail and swept it aside as trivial against the grand historical view which the issue merited. Gaitskell was uncomprehending of Monnet's faith and got more and more stubbornly pedestrian. I drove Monnet back to the Hyde Park Hotel in a deep depression'.

[10] *"Inconceivable… any major area'* makes more sense when we remember that inconceivable does not mean impossible, it means *'I cannot currently understand'.*

He then chided Gaitskell with a music hall number:

> 'She wouldn't say yes, she wouldn't say no; she wouldn't say stay, she wouldn't say go; she wanted to climb but she dreaded to fall. So she bided her time, and clung to the wall.'

In 1961 Conservatives sat in Conference wearing 'Yes' badges and found it all very funny indeed. Lampooning Gaitskell was the only option for Macmillan, who knew he could not begin to describe the EEC's real political implications to his Conference – or to Parliament.

In November, Macmillan invited de Gaulle to Birch Grove, his Sussex country home. He was briefed beforehand by Ambassador to Paris Pierson Dixon, who told him: 'It is fairly certain that [de Gaulle] considers our presence among the Six to be a risk which is worth taking only if he can get us in on his conditions that might make it difficult for us to resist the general direction in which he would like to steer the formation of Europe'.[clx]

Through the first half of 1962, British diplomats were also warning Edward Heath that Commonwealth nations would receive no 'comparable outlets' for food exports after EEC membership denied them British trade preference. These were ignored. On 16th May, Dixon sent the FO a lengthy memo detailing the French attitude to Britain's application, which provided ample evidence that de Gaulle wanted it to fail:[clxi] 'Interesting, but unbelievable', Macmillan responded. Beleaguered EFTA Secretary General Sir Frank Figgures stated on 28th February:

> 'We should not underestimate the feeling of hatred against the UK which was being put out at all levels by both the European Commission and the French administration. This is very real and a factor to be reckoned with. It is reflected in the mass of information which comes to EFTA from all sorts of sources (including American businessmen and bankers visiting here) and indicating a highly organised and well put over operation.'[clxii]

Heath admitted to the Cabinet on 25th June that on the most serious obstacle, imports of temperate Commonwealth food, negotiations had seen little progress (meaning after 1970 Commonwealth nations would be treated like any other third countries; American diplomat George Ball had written on 25th April 1962 of the need 'to resist any increase in the number of nations that have preferential access to the Common Market as against US producers'[clxiii]). The Cabinet are recorded as having been 'not unduly alarmed'. Heath informed them on 5th July that the French had refused to substantively discuss their views on British accession in the presence of any Brits, pushing them with the Six instead. Two weeks later formal negotiations resumed in Brussels, and immediately the Six rejected a proposal for 'comparable outlets'. The EEC also threw out a twelve-year transitional period for British agriculture, and Britain agreed that all special provisions for British farmers would cease by 1970.

In the evening of 29th July, the Commercial Counsellor at the British Embassy at The Hague had a visit from a senior Dutch diplomat called Dr Hoogwater, who informed him: 'the French are determined to block [Britain], and will succeed unless they can be faced with firm opposition inside the Six'. Furthermore, 'the Italians will not fight the French, so that the only chance would be for the Dutch and Germans acting together to try to move the French from their present insistence on absolute preference for Community agriculture'. The diplomat suggested that Heath should have lunch with Dutch and German ministers, and the Germans, disgusted by 'French intransigence', might accept a 'final assessment of what [Britain] could get through Parliament and would join the Dutch in standing out for this inside the Six'.[clxiv]

Before Heath could dine with the ministers however, deadlock returned. On 4th August a new crisis appeared in the form of the regulations being devised for income through tariffs on food imports. As the biggest food importer Britain would be by far the greatest contributor to this levy, and in preparing the new regulations the French had not informed the British delegation in Brussels. Archival evidence demonstrates that once informed, Heath and his negotiating team in Brussels simply ignored this looming threat. The Commonwealth did not ignore the situation. On a visit to London that summer, Australia's Deputy Prime Minister John McEwen told Heath:

> 'A price basis as you suggested would mean that Britain would be paying for Australian wheat substantially less than would be paid from a supplier in the Community. She would be collecting on Australian wheat levies at least part of which could very well be used to subsidise exports of Community wheat to our disadvantage in other markets. This is a situation to which we would have strong objection.'[clxv]

Macmillan would write in his memoirs: 'We were encouraged by Mr McEwen's general attitude to the Common Market'.[clxvi]

Issuing a statement in June with New Zealand's deputy premier Jack Marshall, warning of the drastic economic consequences for their countries without adequate safeguards,[clxvii] Australian PM Robert Menzies now considered appealing directly to the British people instead of Macmillan and his government, 'with the (perfectly justified) allegation that Macmillan was betraying Australia and not admitting the fact'. As historian Andrew Roberts suggests, Macmillan would have been in serious trouble had he done it: he was already accused of sinking a free trade agreement with the Canadians, and Menzies was very popular in Britain. Macmillan told him over dinner on 5th September 1962 that 'I thought he had the power to prevent Britain joining Europe. But I thought it a terrible responsibility before history...'[clxviii] In the event, Menzies was too proper to do it. Canada's Prime Minister John Diefenbaker now informed London that should Britain join the EEC, Commonwealth countries would move closer to Washington. As American writer James C. Bennett later put it:

> 'The severing of Britain's economic ties with its Commonwealth partners as a price of European entry further strained [relationships]. Today, Germans arriving at London's Heathrow airport breeze through the domestic arrivals line, while Australians who fought against the Germans at El Alamein for Britain's sake wait in the foreigners' line with the Japanese. As many Australians noted... 'There were no bloody queues at Gallipoli; no bloody queues at Alamein'.'[clxix]

Macmillan admitted to Menzies that he could not 'chuck' the Commonwealth, partly because 'our Canadian friends would not agree'. (Macmillan also gave a little-known reason Britain, unlike Australia, opened the gates to mass immigration: 'both the Communists and the Free World must try to attract the unaligned nations to their side by any means'.)[clxx]

In the evening of 4th August, a French diplomat named Bernard Clappier paid a visit to Pierson Dixon. Clappier informed him that Foreign Minister Maurice Couve de Murville had told the other five nations that Paris was about to 'wreck' negotiations, by blocking any concessions whatsoever on the food imports regulation. At 3am on Monday 5th August, Couve de Murville produced a document giving their new interpretation of what the Six had agreed about the regulation. Not even an outline of this news had been presented to the British delegation beforehand. The document made clear that the worst fears of the Commonwealth were correct: tariffs on their food imports to Britain would subsidise continental food exports, while the British budget contribution would rise hugely with no refunds allowed. The British people were still being allowed no idea what European harmonisation would really mean.

A preferable price system for British farmers was only one objection. The more serious one was that the British system gave British consumers lower food prices than their continental counterparts, giving our manufacturers wage advantages over their continental competition: quite simply, France needed Britons to pay more to eat. As Anthony Rumbold, a British diplomat in Paris surmised correctly, the French

> '...felt it would be in their interests for the negotiations to drag on into the winter as our position would become weaker and [they] thought we were in a 'hurry' because a British General Election had to be held shortly, and the Government wanted to negotiate entry beforehand so as to be able to point to it as a great achievement accomplished'.[clxxi]

Heath now turned to Dean Rusk, asking him on 6th September what US help would be available should negotiations break down. Rusk replied that specific issues would have to be looked at on their merits. A fortnight later, over lunch at Buck's on 21st September, Rab Butler delivered another warning to Macmillan. According to the Prime Minister's memoirs, Butler told him that he had decided to support Britain's joining the Six, despite '(a) the farmers; (b) the Commonwealth; (c) the probable break-up of the Conservative Party'.[11]

---

[11] Sir Frank Figgures was right that Britain's wartime experience had not created the same collapse of national belief as Nazi Germany had created in continental Europe; but in private conversations leading Conservatives made clear a collapse in their own confidence in free market nation states. On 2nd June, 1943, Ambassador Maiski wrote in his diary that he and a lunch guest 'spoke a great deal about England's post-war prospects... [he] anticipates that England's post-war development will take the following paths: 1) A mixed type of economy, i.e. some sectors (electricity, the railways, possibly coal) will be nationalised, some (road and sea transport, civil aviation, etc.) will come under public control... 2) The 'constitutional factory' will gradually emerge, i.e. factories in which workers' representatives will participate in the management of the business... 3) The education system should be democratised, i.e. almost all *public schools* should be abolished (though [he] would like to keep two or three of them)'. He asked his guest, 'So you want England to develop along Fabian lines?' He replied: 'Call it what you will. We English, you know, can do revolutionary things, so long as they are done under the old names.' Maiski felt he 'undoubtedly reflects the mood of the ruling Tory elite'. The guest was Rab Butler. He was not alone. In November 1938, Maiski told another guest that capitalism was a 'spent force': 'Yes, you are right. Capitalism in its present form has had its day. What will replace it? I can't say exactly, but it will certainly be a different system. State socialism? Semi-socialism? Three-quarter socialism? Complete socialism? I don't know. Maybe it will be a particularly pure British form of conservative socialism', replied Anthony Eden.

Butler, who had mocked Gaitskell's fears, said the same to the Cabinet the next day. While Butler and Macmillan were dining at Buck's, Heath was entertaining Dutch Foreign Minister Dr Joseph Luns, and told Luns that he knew Britain would apply 'the Common Market agriculture system without restriction',[clxxii] undermining Britain's negotiators and the government's official wish to protect the British people and Commonwealth.

By October, British negotiators knew de Gaulle had gained enough confidence to push Britain into a situation from which she would have no choice but to withdraw. De Gaulle now called a referendum on his presidency. Had he lost, the mood of the other five governments would almost certainly have seen an accession treaty rapidly signed. He won, with 61 percent.

The Prime Minister met de Gaulle at Rambouillet on 15th and 16th December. Macmillan's memoirs describe a 'wrangle', in which he told de Gaulle that for Europe to refuse admission to the £2.5bn of food coming into the Continent, much of it from poor countries, would be 'immoral'. De Gaulle seems to have been unimpressed, and his message was certainly brazen. De Gaulle informed Macmillan that he knew the French position in the Six, and that France could, in this crucial period, say no to anything that was against her interests, a situation likely to change after Britain (and the Scandinavians) joined. Macmillan replied that this 'most serious statement' implied a basic objection to Britain's very entry into the EEC, and 'if this was really the French view it should have been put forward at the very start'.

One British diplomat recalled that Macmillan was almost in tears after the meeting,[clxxiii] but it seems he soon convinced himself he had a way out. De Gaulle had told him in the past that although he had no personal interest in nuclear forces, they may be needed for French prestige. Macmillan decided that he was in a position to persuade Kennedy to allow a French nuclear force, and so help de Gaulle see British entry in a new light. It was this belief that led him, in the Bahamas on 19th December, to persuade Kennedy to give Polaris not only to Britain, but to France.

This was a grave error. According to Jacques de Beaumarchais, Charles de Gaulle's *Directeur d'Europe* and later Ambassador to London, de Gaulle had indeed hinted at Rambouillet that Anglo-French nuclear cooperation might change his attitude to British entry. But this appears to have been a deceit, and de Gaulle cut any mention of it from the French transcript to avoid looking like a *demandeur* (beggar).[clxxiv] Heath saw Couve de Murville one more time on 11th January 1963. Couve promised there would be no veto from de Gaulle. Three days later, there was.[clxxv] De Gaulle tricked Macmillan into getting France the bomb.

'WHAT IT'S ALL ABOUT'

> **Thou hast it now: King, Cawdor, Glamis, all,**
> **As the weird women promised, and I fear**
> **Thou play'dst most foully for't**

Macbeth

At the end of the negotiations in Brussels, Macmillan wrote in his diary: 'The Brussels negotiations came finally to an end in a brutal way – Couve de Murville (who is a pretty cold fish, anyway) behaved with a rudeness which was unbelievable. The 'Five' rallied round, but in the end were powerless… French duplicity has defeated us all… There is the fear of immediate political and economic injury to us, as the French plans unfold. (They began an attack on Sterling, by selling heavily in Paris, but I think this has been staved off)… The Italians are angry and alarmed. They hate the French, esp. de Gaulle… But the Italians are also weak… I rather fear that the French calculation is right. All this indignation, they believe, will blow over…'[clxxvi]

Macmillan had once accused Heath of being 'bitterly anti-French', but that summer Heath took his holiday in the south of France, and lunched at Couve's house in the spirit of friendship.[clxxvii] Although we cannot know what terms Macmillan's government could ever have got for Britain, what is certain is that by the time the Treaty of Rome was signed, Europe was supranationalist and largely designed for French economic interests (the treaty gave good terms for their overseas territories for example). In this light, Macmillan's mockery of Gaitskell's 'hesitation' seems especially ironic.

Macmillan was out of ideas. He wrote in his diary: 'All our policies at home and abroad are in ruins'. Yet still he believed it would be wrong to respond by organising 'even more strongly a combination with EFTA and the Commonwealth countries'.[clxxviii] Macmillan had thought Britain's entry was so important to the Six that concessions would flow his way, but de Gaulle had played for time, and the PM succeeded only in harming Britain's alliances. On 30th January 1963, he said in a broadcast to the nation: 'When in the last few weeks it became clear that the remaining points could be settled then the French brought the negotiations to an end',[clxxix] neglecting to mention how obvious this outcome had become long before. Spaak, like most others, blamed France, but none told de Gaulle, while Macmillan complained to JFK that de Gaulle wanted 'a Napoleonic or Louis XIV hegemony' in Europe. In October 1963, wounded by the Profumo affair,[12] Macmillan became ill, resigned as Prime Minister, and was replaced by Alec Douglas-Home.

De Gaulle knew that Adenauer was now virtually senile, and proceeded to charm the enfeebled Chancellor with the promise of Franco-German amity. Although Adenauer's government were eager to have Britain in the EEC to restrain the French, Adenauer joined de Gaulle in opposition to British entry. Just one week after his veto, de Gaulle met a near-geriatric German Chancellor to sign the historic Franco-German friendship treaty against the wishes of the government in Bonn.[clxxx] Adenauer's pro-British foreign minister quoted Milton: 'the desire for posthumous fame is the last infirmity of noble minds'.[clxxxi] It is to be recalled that on 16th December 1962, Macmillan, deeply depressed about negotiations with the French, wrote 'they underrate the German danger in the future'.[clxxxii]

Tradition accepts that the reason de Gaulle blocked Britain's entry was some kind of ill-feeling left over from the war, or jealousy at the Atlantic relationship enjoyed by Jack and Mac (JFK would meet his death in Dallas just a year later). Britain's later entry appears logical if the Frenchman was truly this irrational. But these reasons feel discountable. When Macmillan announced Britain's wish to begin negotiations, de Gaulle noted in his diary: 'the English attack again... having failed to prevent the birth of the Community they now plan to paralyse it from within'. Seeing his counterparts in the Six as lacking the necessary guts, the General knew he must accept the challenge or pull France out of the venture.[clxxxiii] Far more than Britain's government at the time or since, de Gaulle grasped precisely the different situations faced by Britain and France. He said:

> 'If Britain and the Commonwealth enter, it would be as if the
> Common Market had dissolved... Always the question is posed,
> but the British don't answer. To please the British, should we

---

[12] The revelation that Cabinet minister John Profumo was sharing a call girl with a Soviet spy.

call into question the Common Market [and] the agricultural regulations that benefit us? Britain continues to supply itself cheaply in Canada, New Zealand, Australia. If we have to spend 500 billion a year on agricultural subsidies, what will happen if the Common Market can no longer assist us? These eminently practical questions should not be resolved on the basis of sentiments.'[clxxxiv]

De Gaulle meant that he simply could not believe Britain would pay the huge agricultural subsidies France would depend on, or accept the harm it would do to the Commonwealth. So de Gaulle's speech can be read in reverse: I would never dream of accepting terms like this for France, so we shouldn't expect Britain to do so either. But he was wrong.

***

In 1963, Hugh Gaitskell died suddenly from a bout of *Lupus erythematosus*, a disease that provokes the immune system to attack the organs. He was just 56, and left the chair empty for Harold Wilson to succeed him (with George Brown competing for the leadership, Labour's Anthony Crosland MP described the choice as being between 'a crook and a drunk'). Wilson would win the following year's general election, and lead Britain until 1970, then again from 1974 until 1976.

When Harold Wilson became Prime Minister in October 1964, narrowly beating Alec Douglas-Home, one of his first moves was to annoy all Britain's EFTA partners by slapping a surcharge on imports to reduce Britain's balance of payments gap. Yet according to his biographer Philip Ziegler, Wilson's 'prime concern' was simply that Europe 'should not be allowed to breach party unity', and having become more pro-Europe by 1966, he now realised 'Britain was of secondary importance in US thinking'.[clxxxv]

Labour's new leader would prove utterly unlike Gaitskell – like much else that was changing. In November 1963, John F. Kennedy was assassinated in Dallas. Winston Churchill died in January 1965. The dismantling of Empire continued apace. In Washington, the State Department's policy was described by Henry Kissinger thus: 'The reasons that America welcomed closer European integration were several: it was believed to provide a bulwark against communism, it was hoped to become a richer outlet for American exports and it was thought to guarantee internal peace, with no more European wars into which American soldiers might be drawn'. Even if this meant America 'urged European unity while recoiling before its probable consequences', British membership of the Common Market, he said, was 'a direct objective of American policy'.

The decade until 1966 saw Britain's economy lag badly behind the big continental countries. Per capita income grew 26.2 percent from 1958 to 1966, compared with 47.5 percent in France and 58.2 percent in West Germany. Now even this growth was threatened, with sterling under attack and Wilson forced to slap a surcharge on imports. With the economy in trouble, the pro-Europeans in cabinet became assertive, especially Home Secretary Roy Jenkins. Wilson saw only one way to bolster his support, and gave his Cabinet a vote on EEC membership. It was in favour by thirteen votes to eight.

Labour MP George Wigg[13] thought Wilson only took up the European issue in 1966 because he needed 'a device that looked and sounded like business' to deal with Britain's economic problems.[clxxxvi] But Europe was firmly a party political issue by this time: the Tories under their new leader Edward Heath favoured membership, and Wilson sought simply to outplay them.

In mid-1966 France warned Britain publicly that a devaluation of the pound might be needed before Britain could ever become a member. Paris resented the link between sterling and the Dollar and disliked the pound's role as a reserve currency, suggesting a return to the gold standard. Nonetheless, London applied for entry once more in July 1967. Germany supported British entry, but de Gaulle remained reluctant, noting that if Britain obeyed the rules our balance of payments would be 'crushed'. The only way Britain could avoid this would be to make special provisions to stay outside the agricultural subsidy structures, undermining the entire French strategy. In December 1967, de Gaulle vetoed again, delivering 'Le Grand Non'. Wilson's gambit was quickly finished.

In early 1969 Anglo-French relations would reach a new nadir. On 4th February, Charles de Gaulle joined new British Ambassador (and former Tory minister) Christopher Soames for lunch. The conversation that followed would begin the 'Soames Affair'. De Gaulle described to Soames his vision that instead of remaining so close to Washington, Britain should join France to build a new European free trade area, as Britain had suggested in the 1950s,

---

[13] A Labour MP known for relaying gossip to Harold Wilson, and who placed on Parliamentary record questions into the affair which led to the downfall of John Profumo.

but including agriculture. Franco-British talks would be a tentative first stage. The dramatic proposals seemed to be an attempt to combine his preoccupation with independence from NATO with Britain's wish for a European role, free trade, and less supranationalism. But they troubled the FO, where suspicions grew of a plan to corrode Anglo-American relations. The plan also put Wilson, about to visit German Chancellor Kurt Kiesinger, in a difficult position. Not telling Kiesinger about the proposals would risk the Chancellor finding out at a later date and suspecting deceit. So the Germans got a 'sanitised' summary of de Gaulle and Soames' lunch conversation.

The FO then circulated a brief on the conversation to the Low Countries, Italy, and America. The French were livid, and cancelled the proposals entirely. New President Richard Nixon made no criticism of de Gaulle for his suggestions. Nixon soon travelled to Europe on his first official visit, and called on de Gaulle first. Wilson's Press Secretary believed the FO had sought to humiliate de Gaulle in an act of revenge for his vetoes; if so, this achieved nothing, and only harmed Britain's interests. No one came to Britain's defence, and de Gaulle removed all French representation from the Western European Union, which had remained the diplomatic link between Britain and the EEC.

***

The name Edward Heath will always be associated with Europe, but the manifesto on which Heath won a surprise general election victory over Wilson in June 1970 said only of Europe: 'to negotiate, no more, no less'. The authors Christopher Booker and Richard North found that in his election campaign Heath devoted just 3 percent of his speeches to the Common Market, hardly a democratic mandate for membership. But Heath never intended to try to get one, and his 'negotiations' were always intended to mean more, not less.

Like Macmillan before him, Heath selected his Cabinet to ensure support for Community membership (Norman Tebbit would observe that the Community was the one area where Heath maintained his early determined manner). But as historian John W. Young noted, 'Heath's greatest strength probably lay in the fact that Britain had retreated from earlier hopes of changing EEC policies fundamentally in entry talks. He was ready to accept the EEC as it stood, CAP and all.'[clxxxvii]

In 1970 the European Commission published its *Werner Report*, which set out the path towards monetary union. This foresaw a 'transfer of powers to the Community level from the national centres of decision', acknowledging that it would raise a 'certain number of political problems'. Heath later admitted that he knew of its publication and was personally committed to its aims, but when he began 'negotiations' this was unknown to all but a tiny number of close associates.[clxxxviii] Even the Foreign Office produced a memorandum for the PM advising that the Werner Report 'could imply the ultimate creation of a European federal state with a single currency... the basic instruments of national economic [management] would ultimately be handed over to the central federal authorities'.[clxxxix] Heath is not believed to have disagreed with the FO's conclusions. The PM meanwhile continued to refer to the project simply as 'the Common Market', denying the British people any way of understanding what 'joining Europe' was going to mean.

De Gaulle left office on 29th June 1969, replaced by Georges Pompidou, who led France until his death in 1974.[14] On 20th May 1971 Heath met a president keen to balance growing German influence in the EEC,[cxc] with much talk about reaffirming the 'world vocation' of Britain and France. Its real point was missed by almost everyone, being to get Heath's support for a common currency.[cxci] But the French need not have worried – Heath was already on side. The official communiqué stated:

> '[The President and Prime Minister] also discussed the progress of the European Community towards economic and monetary union... The Prime Minister reaffirmed the readiness of Britain to participate fully...'

When asked about this on his return, Heath claimed simply: 'On the subject of Sterling, there was no discussion of parities or items of that kind'.[cxcii] In the 1995 documentary *The Poisoned Chalice*, a senior civil servant recalled a conversation between Heath and his Foreign Secretary Alec Douglas-Home. 'The House isn't going to like this', Douglas-Home told the PM. 'But that', Heath replied, 'is what it's all about'.[cxciii] The stage was set for referendum.

The 'negotiations' that followed the summit came to some basic conclusions. Britain's budget contribution, by proportion and amount, would be able to

---

[14] One of Pompidou's more memorable Cabinet ministers was André Malraux, a writer of postmodern and communist leanings who served as Minister of Culture. The Historian Anthony Beevor describes him as 'a mythomaniac in his claims of martial heroism — in Spain and later in the French Resistance'. Malraux leaves us with various soporifics: from his *Anti-Memoirs*, published, naturally, in 1968: 'What is man? A miserable little pile of secrets'.

rise without limit. Agricultural policy would make Britain the highest net contributor after Germany. A 'regional policy' touted as a redistributive boon for Britain's poorer areas seems simply to have been Heath's attempt to gain a small amount of compensation.

Britain had had no role in the creation of Europe's then 13,000 pages of legislation. Negotiations could not change them now, and Britain would have to pass all past and future European legislation as a matter of course. Our courts would be subservient to the European Court of Justice, without the right of appeal that had been a fundamental part of British law since *Magna Carta*. This went unmentioned when the government pushed a pamphlet through taxpayers' doors (at their expense) called *The United Kingdom and the EC*, a tactic it would repeat in 2016. Based on a White Paper of the same name, the pamphlet claimed negotiations had been 'successful' [cxciv] (indeed the whole pamphlet was equally vague, a template for the British government's pro-EU communications ever since).

It also contained three outright untruths. The first was that the legal system would continue 'as before'; the second was that 'there is no question of Britain losing essential national sovereignty', offering instead the 'sharing' and 'enlargement' of 'individual national sovereignties'. Finally the prospect of losing control of the country's fisheries was already troubling enough Britons for their government to need the third: 'the Community has recognised the need to change its fisheries policy'.[cxcv] This was a fiction.

Billed as 'the great debate', what followed was in reality a PR campaign to sell the EEC to the British people – but first to their MPs, because a Bill on the Treaty of Accession needed steering through Parliament. This would be achieved by persuading members of parliament that public opinion was becoming pro-EEC. The great debate was engineered by a PR executive, Geoffrey Tucker,[cxcvi] handpicked by Heath (a 2003 obituary in the *Independent* described his 'guile, street wisdom... exquisite stealth') and was coordinated by the Brussels-funded European Movement. It was typified by a level of inter-organisational coordination unknown since the War.

As this war for British minds began, it became clear the campaign had tremendous artillery. The Conservative Political Centre joined forces with the Labour Committee for Europe and the TUC Committee for Europe; the CBI brought its own funding and prestige; the National Farmers Union was brought in, and the Associated Chambers of Commerce. Divinity was even represented in the form of the British Council of Churches.

The campaign brought to bear forms of subterfuge more commonly associated with black ops, one in particular having been used by agents to prepare the ground for *coups d'état* in countries including Iran. Employees of the European Movement ghost-wrote salvoes of letters to *The Times*, having them signed by leading businessmen, industrialists and politicians as if they were their own work.[cxcvii] The government broke protocol to co-opt taxpayer-funded information services to coordinate these groups, and with the European Movement funded by both the government and the European Commission, British taxpayers were paying twice over. Taxpayers were made to pay to persuade them that joining the EEC was a good idea.

After their debate lasting six days, the Commons was due to vote on 28th October. But MPs had still not been allowed to examine Britain's entry terms, the very words to which they were asked to commit their country's future. Labour leader Harold Wilson now argued that the issues were still simply economic and not political, and made the impossible commitment that party leaders have made ever since. 'What we should do', he said,

> 'Would be to immediately give notice that we do not accept the terms negotiated by the Conservatives... If the Community refused to negotiate, we should sit down amicably with them and discuss the situation.'[cxcviii]

Like many since, Wilson believed he could halt the integration engine after getting into power. The Commons fell about with laughter, as if they already realised the European engine had no reverse gear. Indeed from the heart of Europe, some were warning of what was afoot. Ralf Dahrendorf, a German-born Briton who would later become a Commissioner, wrote at the time (under a pseudonym):

> 'Europe becomes increasingly bureaucratic [with] a craze for harmonisation... Whoever regards harmonisation as a value in itself very rapidly loses the ability to distinguish between important and unimportant, necessary and superfluous matters. More than that, he interferes with the principle of *differentiating* between regions and countries, and runs into the danger of creating a uniform Europe.'[cxcix]

Edward Heath had in his possession a letter from Lord Chancellor Lord Kilmuir, whom he had asked to report on 'the constitutional implications of our becoming party to the Treaty of Rome', which said 'in my view the surrenders of sovereignty involved are serious ones'.[cc] But with the support of pro-European Labour MPs the Treaty of Accession passed by 22 votes. Heath not only ignored his Lord Chancellor, but managed to prevent MPs reading the full text, claiming 'constitutionally, there could be no final and authentic text of the Treaty until it has been signed'[cci]. Our Parliament never read the Treaty that began the gradual suffocation of its own power.

Heath's government still faced a legislative hurdle. With Britain joining at this stage, accession should have meant splicing over 13,000 pages of EEC law into our own, an enormous task that would have given the Commons an opportunity to examine what membership really meant. Quite apart from what was in store for British democracy, the documents detailed what was coming for our fishing industry (to take one example), and this alone could have sunk the project. The Prime Minister gave his Solicitor General Geoffrey Howe the task of finding an alternative. Howe, born in the Welsh town of Port Talbot and a product of Winchester College, was a QC who had been knighted on joining the Cabinet. Heath would not be disappointed in his new recruit, whose ploy was one of considerable legal stealth, and worked as follows.

In a long-established tool of British law known as the 'Enabling Act',[ccii] Howe found a device allowing Parliament to delegate power to ministers to enact law directly. This had been designed to allow swift action during national crises, but would now be used to effectively staple every item of European law onto our own. After a millennium in which his country had pioneered freedom under law, the 'European Communities Bill' Howe created constituted perhaps the biggest movement of power away from accountable representatives that the country had ever seen.

By now some MPs were waking up to Gaitskell's warnings. Britain was about to lose its seat on the WTO, an organisation it had co-founded, relinquishing it to Europe.[cciii] Wilson revised his opinion, telling the Commons the Bill was an attempt to impose a foreign system of law 'literally at a stroke'.[cciv] But many recall the atmosphere of collaboration between Labour MPs and Tory whips; Labour Europeanist John Roper kept a little red book of Labour names, plus engagements to which they could be sent to guarantee enough absences to pass the bill. When the vote arrived, only nine Labour and Liberal MPs voted in favour, but only fifteen Tories voted against, and Heath and Howe's move became law. Heath's political secretary Douglas Hurd described the entry terms as the 'greatest single feat'[ccv] of Heath's premiership. Benjamin Disraeli had said that the purpose of the Tory Party was to protect the constitution of the country. Heath, Howe and Hurd thought differently.

Labour's Tony Benn told the press what he thought the bill really was: 'a *coup d'état* by a political class who did not believe in popular sovereignty'; Enoch Powell agreed. Yet there was the problem, as Europe's opponents had now become the unfashionable. Having gained the approval of an uninformed Parliament, Heath wasted no time pursuing what had become the project of his political life, talking regularly with Jean Monnet about 'the difficult transition from national to collective sovereignty'.[ccvi]

In September 1973, Monnet joined the PM at Chequers, where he told Heath about a new plan he had drafted to create in structure a 'Provisional European Government'. Despite having a sort of European parliament, this government would meet in secret. For the new structure Monnet favoured the name 'European Union'. While he wanted to make the proposal public, Heath wouldn't hear of it, telling him 'Let's just do it'.[ccvii] So it was that the EU began in the Prime Minister's residence, snug in the Buckinghamshire Chilterns.

We will see exactly how the budget of Europe, especially in agriculture and fishing, was tailored by intent and accident against British interests. For now, with 91 percent of the EEC's budget consisting of CAP financing for more agricultural economies, our contribution was already set far out of proportion to the size of our economy. To offset public anger, Britain was allowed a five year hiatus before it began paying over a fifth of the EEC's budget, rising from 11.5 percent in the first year. Food prices would rise as we swapped our imports from developing Commonwealth countries for wealthy European ones, creating much poverty in the process.

The next autumn, the provisional European government was approved by a leaders' conference in Paris, taking the name 'European Council', and it set to work quickly. States tend to arise organically from a common identity; Europe, a state without an identity, was the wrong way round, so within two months the Council set up a group to devise a new passport[ccviii] for all 'Community citizens' (today's 'little red books'), within a project to begin forging the symbols of nationhood.

And then, quietly, Jean Monnet stopped work altogether. Barely three years earlier the British people had been told that there was 'no question' of a loss of sovereignty, which in a sense was true: there was no question of it. The process underway was now far beyond the public gaze, and a new pattern had formed, as that which went unnoticed would be most profound.

REFERENDUM

By 1974 European discontent in the Labour Party had grown so severe that in February, Harold Wilson led Labour back to power on a manifesto promising the renegotiation of our membership terms, a document that even described the 'draconian curtailment of the power of the British Parliament to settle questions affecting vital British interests'.[ccix]

Returning to Downing Street, Wilson sent his Foreign Secretary James Callaghan to lead the 'renegotiation'. Attempts to get the CAP reformed went nowhere (and Roy Jenkins felt Callaghan was hampered by being 'a bully'[ccx]), but the negotiations dragged on until on 10th March 1975, when, in an attempt to bring back a deal he could call a success, Wilson flew over. What he brought back was a complex budgetary correction formula concerning trade but limited mainly to imports of butter and cheese from New Zealand (Belgian PM Leo Tindemans complained that heads of government were now reduced to 'supermarket auditors'[ccxi]).

Wilson returned home proclaiming his 'success', telling Britain that its membership now had the approval of the Commonwealth, and recommending to the British electorate that in the first referendum in their history they should vote to remain in Europe. Wilson had been more concerned however with preventing a leadership bid from the left of the party, fearing Callaghan in particular, hence entangling him in Brussels at the earliest possible moment. Now all the main parties proclaimed renegotiation success, and opinion polls showed the majority against membership was eroding. Edward Heath admitted privately that the negotiations had been 'a sham',[ccxii] then joined the launch of the Britain in Europe (BiE) referendum campaign, supported by the European Movement. 'What we need', said Cabinet minister Shirley Williams, 'is a major re-education campaign'.[ccxiii] The BiE would be just that.

The campaign was well named (being against a simple geographic statement would seem deluded), and from the outset was so strong as to make Heath an auxiliary, including every living former prime minister and foreign secretary, Labour's former Home Secretary Roy Jenkins, former Liberal leader Jo Grimond, a former general-secretary of the TUC, National Farmers Union president Sir Henry Plumb (later President of the European Parliament and a founder of leading EU lobbying firm Albert and Geiger), former Archbishop of Canterbury Michael Ramsay and virtually every Anglican bishop in the country; even Margaret Thatcher played her part.

The 'No' campaign was somewhat different. Wilson had been faced during 'renegotiation' by dissent from Tony Benn, Michael Foot and Barbara Castle, the rebels issuing an early statement of opposition to their government's referendum bill which gave Wilson no choice but to allow his MPs a free vote (the last time Labour MPs were allowed one on Europe). The antis stood little chance in the referendum, getting just 7 percent of the funds available to their opponents. Their drearily named National Referendum Campaign was formed of people who hated each other, as hard-Leftists Benn and Foot found themselves alongside Enoch Powell. Benn led from the front by refusing to share a platform with any Conservative.[ccxiv]

In the 'Yes' camp, Roy Jenkins recalled how the sight of 'politicians in different parties sitting and working together was a pleasant shock for most of the public'. The campaign was officially independent, but again used government resources, with a nerve-centre in a Foreign Office coordination room.[ccxv] From big business came big support. The less involved the senior∞management of a firm in its British affairs, the more likely they were to join the campaign, as the biggest arguably knew they would be the ones in the loop in Brussels. Households received one 'No' leaflet and two communications urging them to vote 'Yes', one from BiE and one from the government.

The leafleting campaign marked a new development in intellectual subterfuge – and double-think – in marketing. The government's leaflet *A New Deal in Europe* played on Britons' fears of national isolation in a post-imperial nuclear age. '

We cannot go it alone in the modern world',[ccxvi] it implored vaguely, comparing the EEC to organisations with very limited remits: 'groupings like the United Nations, NATO and the IMF have not deprived the British of their national identity'. Public opinion seemed to be shifting because so many believed the Wilson government's *new deal in Europe* meant the Common Market would remain just that. To this end, the government's leaflet contained another straightforward untruth:

'There was a threat to employment in Britain from the movement in the Common Market towards Economic and Monetary Union. This could have forced us to accept fixed exchange rates for the pound, restricting industrial growth and putting jobs at risk. This threat has been removed.'

BiE's leaflet meanwhile was more advanced. The directly titled *Why You Should Vote Yes* employed a reassuring delivery, using the same fear of isolation while providing the psychological redoubt of a Europe that 'made good sense... for world peace' and classically, 'for our children's future'. It threatened 'the dusty wings of history', then the alternative 'centre stage where we belong'.[ccxvii] BiE then listed all the major public fears about the EEC and told its readers that the opposite was the case: the EEC would strengthen our relationship with the Commonwealth, help retain the Monarchy, be good news for Common Law. Having begun life in the BiE campaign, this method of political advertising (the pretence that all positions are reconcilable[ccxviii]) would later be employed by another brilliantly effective PR campaign: New Labour.

On 5th June, never having been given an honest description what the EEC really was or where it was going to take them, 67.2 percent of the British electorate voted for entry.

3.

VOWS MADE IN WINE: THE EU
AND OUR FOOD SUPPLY

**How oft the sight of means to do ill deeds
Make deeds ill done!**

King John

THEFT

In 1970, in the months before Britain, Ireland, Denmark and Norway applied to join (the Norwegians soon pulled out), someone in the EEC realised that between them the new entrants had the continent's richest, best conserved fishing waters.

Here the Community had a problem. A proposal was in the works at the UN to extend national control of fisheries to 200 miles offshore, meaning new members would have over 90 percent of the fish in Western Europe, 80 percent of which would be Britain's:[ccxix] France, Germany, and the Low Countries had already overfished their waters. The Council of Ministers' lawyers were asked to find out whether under the Treaty of Rome a way could be found to transfer the new members' fishing grounds to European control as a 'common resource' to grant 'equal access' to all members.

It couldn't be done, said the lawyers. Article 38 in the treaty referred to a common market in fisheries *products*, but not the fisheries themselves. Articles 39-43 referred to agricultural policy. Articles 52-66 produced only references to services.[ccxx] The treaty offered no legal justification whatsoever for taking the new members' fish. But a momentum had gathered.

Time was running out before the new applicants were to begin negotiations. At the last moment, the Community's lawyers simply penned a new ad hoc regulation to define the 'equal access' principal that would become part of the accord. Early in the morning of 30th June, the principle of equal access to 'Community fishing waters *up to the beaches*'ccxxi was agreed without legal precedent. This would become the Common Fisheries Policy, or CFP. Just after lunch the same day Britain entered its application to join the Community. From the beginning, the Norwegians seemed to understand what was really afoot. Not so our own Ministry of Agriculture and Fisheries, which told one minister they 'could not believe the equal access proposals are serious', assuming they 'must be a basis for bargaining'.ccxxii

Patrick Wolridge-Gordon, an Aberdeenshire MP who realised that his constituents' livelihoods were at stake, wrote to Geoffrey Rippon MP, Chancellor of the Duchy of Lancaster and the man Heath had made responsible for negotiating entry. 'There is not a fisherman who does not think that if territorial limits are to be abandoned, it means the end of an extremely successful and worthwhile industry'. Rippon replied that 'there is as yet no common fisheries policy'.ccxxiii The Scottish fisheries department released a memo admitting that Britain's fisheries faced serious damage, adding that we had 'limited negotiating capital'. The department also allowed a moment of clarity:

> 'The more one is drawn into such explanations, the more difficult it
> is to avoid exposing the weaknesses of the inshore fisheries position,
> the only answer to which may be that in the wider context they
> must be regarded as expendable.'ccxxiv

The Commission's tactics were brilliant. France stalled negotiations through spring 1971, insisting on fishing access, as promised, right up to the new members' beaches. The only concession Britain could get was a temporary six mile 'concession' zone, to be 'reviewed' after five years. Britain was out of time, its government outplayed, and one option was left: to mislead the public. The government claimed in July that 'the Community has recognised the need to change its fisheries policy'.ccxxv The review would require unanimous agreement to allow even the concession zone to remain, and Heath must have known this was impossible.

As Edward Heath prepared to fly to Brussels to sign Britain up, Norway and Ireland informed the Community they could not accept their proposals.

Cabinet ministers told the Norwegians they were being 'stubborn', and Heath wrote immediately to his Norwegian counterpart Trygve Bratteli, telling him that should he accept the concession zone, the Community would understand Norway's concerns, in due course giving them 'the essential concession which you expect'. The letter was leaked – many believe by Bratteli himself – and read in the Norwegian press by an astonished public [ccxxvi].

Britain's fishermen hoped that after the equal access policy was imposed on them they would at least still be able to fish the deep waters off Norway and Iceland, who didn't become members. This wasn't to be. In January 1977 the UN introduced its Law of the Sea, which included a new 200 mile fisheries limit. As nationals of a European Community member state, British fishermen were excluded from these rich Nordic waters. The ensuing Cod Wars off Iceland have since been depicted by much of our own press as an outburst of British aggression. Fishermen only continued venturing into Icelandic waters because of desperate competition with the fleets now in their own waters. Caught in a pincer, Britain could not benefit from the new UN law. The deep-water fishing fleet was being forced out of business, but for the existing EEC members, it was a jackpot.

After much pressure, at the end of the 1970s Brussels slowly began a 'conservation policy' of 'national quotas', informing fishermen what they could catch. But these were more disadvantageous to Britain. The quotas' reference points spanned from 1973 to 1978, when Brits had been concentrating on the international north Atlantic, and French boats were already fishing our own then rich waters. The rules were also agreed centrally, but the job of enforcing them fell to each member, meaning an advantage for turning a blind eye to overfishing. Britain's monitoring was soon seen to be the most responsible, perversely helping do our fishermen out of their livelihoods.

In summer 1980, over lunch at the *Sunday Times*, Mrs Thatcher mused, 'fishing is the next big thing… it was what kept us out in the first place… Fishermen are not going to like it'. [ccxxvii] Indeed telling fishermen how much fish they can land has no connection to the realities of fishing. When a fisherman hauls in the nets, he will see a wide range of species, but for many of them he will have no quota, so it becomes a criminal offence to land them. Then his only option is to throw them, dead, back into the sea. In many areas, more fish are dumped than landed: in the Bay of Biscay in 1985, 130 million hake were discarded with 110 million landed. In Norway meanwhile, fish dumping remains as it has always been: illegal.

The Commission's next so-called conservationist gambit was called 'decommissioning' to 'reduce fishing effort'. The British government never announced it. Decommissioning required the British fishing fleet to be cut by 19 percent, while Spain's would be cut by just 4 percent (as a poorer country much of this loss was to be compensated by the EU's 'structural fund' money that would be channelled back to Spain). Britain was allocated £25m for the cut, but of this, £20m had to come from our Treasury.

In 1995 the Commission proposed a fresh cut in British quotas. What happened next helped sculpt the methods the government used to present negotiations in Brussels to the British people. First, government spokesman Michael Forsyth told the press that there were simply 'too many people chasing too few fish'.[ccxxviii] Ministers then returned from Brussels, where they had been informed that our quota had just been cut by 23 percent for sole, 27 percent for plaice and 33 percent for mackerel. The government next announced that a 'famous victory' had secured 'the best possible deal for British fishermen'. What had happened was considerably less impressive. When our ministers had departed for Brussels, unfeasibly high cuts had been proposed, allowing Europe to provide the subsequent mirage of 'concessions'. Lacking real power over the outcome, our politicians were left to celebrate a pretend 'famous victory' instead.

Under European government, responsibility is divided between Commissioners, who each oversee a Directorate General (DG). Fishing is the domain of the fisheries commissioner, and the environment commissioner has no real influence over the oceans. As such, our seas are now legally European 'fisheries' before they are anything else, and any suggestions from elsewhere in the Commission can be ignored by the relevant Commissioner, often with the various interest groups to whom each is invariably connected.

EU policy has ruined the livelihoods of our fishermen and destroyed our marine environment, once Europe's richest, as control over our fishing waters was given away almost totally. In 2001, the Doha Round of the World Trade Organisation in 2001 stated that fishing subsidies should be phased out everywhere. The EU ignores this. Of Europe's major fish stocks, two thirds are now on the verge of collapse (including cod, plaice, sole and hake). In the Atlantic and the Indian Ocean, subsidised southern European fishermen are destroying the remaining populations of endangered big-eye tuna. Fines do not nearly match the gains that come from cheating what system the EU has: illegal catches now make up 60 percent of Spain's annual trawl of hake.[ccxxix] Many believe that all developed countries are beset by similar fishing crises, but this is not true. In New Zealand, any skipper found to be under-reporting his catch, or lying about where he caught his fish (on which checks are made against satellite records) is put out of business, for good.

A SYSTEM DESIGNED TO FAIL

For losing its fisheries, Britain would be made to pay in cash. In the mid-1980s Spanish fishermen developed a new practice. By registering their boats as British they were allowed a share in the British quota itself, despite sailing from Spanish ports. The British parliament tried to respond, and in 1988 passed the *Merchant Shipping Act*, which stated that in order to qualify for a British quota a ship had to be owned and manned in Britain. Parliament was about to learn the new limits of its control.

Shortly after the Act was passed, a firm called Factortame and a number of other Spanish companies brought a case against the British parliament to the High Court. They stated that under Article 7 of the Treaty of Rome, by passing the Merchant Shipping Act to protect their own fishermen, Parliament had committed the crime of 'national discrimination'.[ccxxx] The case went to the House of Lords, who were reminded by Lord Bridge that the United Kingdom Parliament had voluntarily agreed in the European Communities Act 1972 to accept all European treaties and legal obligations, as well as the final jurisdiction in these matters of the European Court of Justice. They referred the case to the European Court, which had no trouble reaching a judgment. In 1991 Britain was informed that its Act was 'not compatible with Community law',[ccxxxi] and a British Act of Parliament was struck down. The Spanish companies lost no time suing the British government (and taxpayers) for compensation for each of the 18 months they had been deprived of their rights to our waters. Britain was ordered to pay £100 million for trying to protect its own fish.

In 2007 alone for example, 6,000 tonnes of whiting and 31,048 tonnes of haddock were thrown overboard, as well as 23,600 tonnes of cod, over three times British fishermen's landing limit.[ccxxxii] For British boats alone, the equivalent of 6.08 billion fish fingers are dumped every year; total Common Fisheries Policy discards are now 880,000 tonnes annually. The world's average discarding rate is 8 percent; around Ireland and Scotland it is now 90 percent. In 2004, our government banned British vessels from a type of trawling for sea bass that killed dolphins and porpoises, but was not allowed to ban foreign vessels from doing the same in our waters. Sand eels, used for feed in Danish pig farms, are now dredged intensively, a species which is a bedrock of the marine food chain. Money is now being pumped into researching cod farming, reliant on intensive fishing of already overfished stocks of other fish to make fish-feed for cod fry.[ccxxxiii] By 2020, fish farming giant Nutreco plans to export over 400,000 tonnes of cod annually to the European Union, whose own cod population has now been almost completely exterminated.

In a non-serious attempt to cushion the collapse of the North Sea cod, Brussels made British fishermen from fishing towns like Fraserburgh in north eastern Scotland stay in the dock for 15 days a month in the early 2000s,[ccxxxiv] a policy to which London had no choice but to acquiesce. The fishermen meanwhile – from a town with one of Britain's highest rates of heroin addiction – had no alternative but to steam to the south west of England to fish (including for sea bass). At the time, Tony Blair made a maudlin personal call to the Commission to beg for British fishermen to be allowed to increase their catch in their own waters. He was not heeded.

On any day in the shining new halls that line Iberia's fishing ports – often paid for with 75 percent subsidy direct from Brussels – the floors are covered not just with fish from European waters, but exotics that local fishermen now trawl in the most distant seas. One of them is swordfish, whose North Atlantic stocks, having nearly collapsed, have recovered in part thanks to an American boycott. Now having almost completely rid the Mediterranean of swordfish, European fishermen are now allowed within 100 miles of the coasts of the Azores, one of its last refuges and previously open only to the Portuguese.[ccxxxv] As journalist Charles Clover puts it, 'the wheel-house of this great trawler bent on destruction of Europe's fisheries [is] in Brussels'.[ccxxxvi] He adds:

> 'If there were a prize for the most disgraceful country or group of countries on Earth for pillaging the sea, the European Union would be the most favoured recipient.'

The British public were told that the CFP was there to 'preserve Europe's fish stocks', but nothing of the sort has happened. Nearly half of all British jobs at sea have been lost, then the livelihoods of those on land who sold and maintained fishermen's boats, nets and bait. It is believed the CFP has cost British fishing communities 115,000 jobs, more than the population of Exeter.

By 2008, Britain had more vessels dating from before EEC membership than had been built in the last decade.

For every £1 our fishermen get from Europe, Portuguese fishermen get £1.43, French £1.54, and Spanish fishermen get £7.72. At least £150 million of our money has gone to support foreign fishermen in the EU, while British fish landings are now only slightly above the catches of 1915, when our seas were a warzone. Britain is doubly penalised however, because unemployment from the industry adds around £138 million in social security bills (in 1997 there were already only 18,600 working fishermen in the UK, but in 2005 there were merely 12,600[ccxxxvii]). Among the EU's policies, the CFP alone makes the average household pay £186 extra each year in shopping bills.

Seas managed in this way as a 'commons' do not work because no one is ultimately responsible for their sustainability. Reforms to the system that would increase transparency have been rejected precisely because they would reduce the opportunity for various groups of fishermen to absorb funds. But Britons are also made to pay another £12 million to Brussels, to pay poor countries' governments to allow European vessels to fish their waters.

By the mid-1990s, without knowing it, taxpayers across Europe had paid £739 million in seven years for Spanish fishermen alone to modernise their fleets. Even less understood was that they had also paid £894 million, through Brussels, to the governments of developing countries for fishing rights for Spain and Portugal (the British contribution was £228 million). The EU is still paying for the practice on a huge scale, but little has been said about what these 'fishing rights' actually mean.

This began as southern European fishing nations have reminded Brussels that the terms of their entry stipulated that because their access to common European waters would only be phased in between 1995 and 2002, these countries' fishing industries were needed help from the Community's Structural Fund. This has provided huge sums to enable them to buy up industrial-scale fishing rights, allowing their fleets to fish the waters of developing countries, especially in Africa.

It appears that Spanish and Portuguese trawlermen have a particular disregard for conservation. Since the 1990s, industrial freezer-trawlers, many from Spain and Portugal, have been a common sight along West African coasts, and are now moving along Africa's eastern seaboard. Around Africa's western tip at Senegal, in the blue waters of Angola, the great fertile upwellings off Mauritania and the Ivory Coast, and past Kenya and Madagascar, they plunder endangered species of tuna and many other fish. Now that North Sea stocks have plummeted, the EU spends £127 million each year buying fishing rights from the governments of countries like these.[ccxxxviii]

In Angola, where hundreds of thousands are malnourished, Brussels paid £18 million to allow Spanish, French, Greek and Italian fleets to trawl tuna, prawns and bottom-dwelling fish. Spain keeps a fleet of 200 trawlers off West Africa; Senegal, one of the countries in whose waters they fish, has a tradition of fishing with *pirogues*, wooden sea canoes that carry a crew of just a dozen men.[ccxxxix] They must now compete with industrial European vessels equipped with the most powerful sonar, satellite navigation and fish-finding systems, technologies that help skippers move their nets with an agility that was recently unimaginable, curling them around sea-mounts, crevices, canyons and rock formations, creating 3D pictures that let them sweep shoals from what were once safe havens.

A recent Canadian study showed that once industrial fishing moves in on new marine territory, it takes just 10-15 years to reduce a fish community by 90 percent. In China, party cadres are promoted if they demonstrate increases in fishing output that are totally unsustainable,[ccxl] a fact British observers have wryly pointed out. We have not noticed that the EU operates along comparable lines.

MONEY FOR NOTHING

Yet it is on farming that the EU spends the largest proportion of our money. For the Europeans of the 1950s, one of the most frightening memories or war had been of food, or rather the lack of it. War meant the ever present threat of famine, and food was one of the Nazi weapons of choice. Even as the Second World War drew to its end, the Low Countries among others lived in the shadow of shortage. The Treaty of Rome enshrined the need for European self-sufficiency in food, promising both 'food at reasonable prices' and a 'fair' standard of living for farmers. But it was in 1968 (before Britain joined) that the Common Agricultural Policy, Brussels' huge system of agricultural subsidies, was unveiled. Even in the early days it was obvious that Europe's new policy would be a problem. As Labour MP Stuart Holland put it:

> 'One of the clearest examples [of] unjust return was to be the terms
> imposed on Britain, through accepting the CAP as a condition

of EEC membership. The switch from low cost producers, and generally low prices for food products, to higher costs and higher prices through the CAP, represented a real welfare loss for British consumers, which was not compensated...'

The EU spends 48 percent of its money on the CAP, and although Brussels claims this will fall by about 15 percent, but the bill still rises by about €1 billion every year. The CAP gives a direct subsidy for land and crops, minimum prices for European produce, plus strict import tariffs and quotas for produce from outside the Union. As economists Larry Elliott and Dan Atkinson point out in their book *Fantasy Island*, it was fear about what the CAP would do to food prices that lead the government, in 1975 referendum leaflets, to tell us that

'...food prices in the rest of the world have shot up, and our food prices are now no higher because Britain is in the European Common Market than if we were outside.'

This was a false claim even at the time. As Elliott and Atkinson note, 'even the most passionate British pro-Europeans condemn the nonsense of CAP', but it usually remains the elephant in the room.

In 1988, Europe would introduce a new way of making more national wealth its 'own resources',[ccxli] with every member state required to make an extra payment based on a proportion of their GDP. This sleight of hand arrived as Britain's economy grew, making Britain contribute to financing its own rebate (the Commission claimed this would involve 'very small amounts', but the cumulative effects would be huge). Whenever the UK applied for CAP funds above a level agreed in 1984, the Commission would take back a large proportion through its 'correction mechanism'.

On joining the EEC Britons were told that Commonwealth trade would not be harmed. Time has proven otherwise. In 2010, butter from New Zealand was hit with a £25m import tax, putting up the price of every pound bought at the checkout by 25p. The CAP keeps Britain's spend on food £5 billion higher every year, which for a two-child family means £398. We also have to spend an extra £300 million more on welfare bills, because people on benefits have to spend more on food too. We then pay another £5 billion subsidising farmers across Europe, while the civil servants running the CAP cost £72 million (including, for example, an annual furniture allowance of

£5.4 million). £5.6 million is spent on promotion (even if we have little choice but to eat food), while £12 million has been stashed by the Commission in case it is sued, meaning we will pay their fines too (although all CAP fraud before 2008 is now untraceable, having been 'regularised' by a new accounting system).[ccxlii] The total bill to Britain is over £10 billion every year.[ccxliii]

The CAP's staunchest backer has historically been France. Many point out that France is now a net contributor to the EU (with an *official* net spend of just under €1000 per capita per year, still behind Britain, Germany and the Nordic countries), but this misses the point. For French farmers, the EU is above all a mechanism for bringing in cash, not just from other countries but other French people (or city-dwellers who are not organised into lobby groups). But Eastern European farmers now get the most support. Romania takes home €1500 per capita, while Estonians get a notch under €2500 each.

In 2008, the famous mountains and lakes of unused produce included 30,000 tonnes of butter, 109,000 tonnes of skimmed milk powder and 230 million litres of wine.[ccxliv] At the end of 2008, despite a growing national spend on the EU, France presented a paper to the Commission demanding the maintenance of the core principles of the CAP, possibly until 2050. If anything, with its days as a net benefactor over, France needs more than ever to get what it can from Brussels, and the CAP isn't going anywhere.

When auditors recently tested payments they found 40 percent of the fields for which farmers' claimed subsidies were impossibly large. In Greece, farmers' unions control all the data input into the systems that determine payouts. In Italy, over one in five subsidised special beef cows didn't exist; in Slovenia 50 percent of subsidised suckler cows didn't exist (or weren't suckler cows). An aid scheme in Bavaria (one of Germany's wealthiest regions, but taking nearly half its farm subsidies) allowing farmers to share machines was intended to help spread the cost of seasonal equipment. Farmers were using it to build landscape businesses, waste treatment plants, roads, sports facilities and golf courses. Campaigning journalist Jack Thurston has also revealed that in 2008 in Germany alone, 194 recipients took home over €1 million in subsidies, including the conglomerate Südzucker AG, which bagged over €34 million.

In 2004, with silk production rising in China, India, Uzbekistan and Vietnam, the EU authorised aid to European silkworms, €86 for every 100 eggs.[ccxlv] In 2008, Brussels trumpeted revising its oft-lampooned rule against curvy cucumbers and other vegetable deviants. On closer inspection it turned out that those which accounted for 70 percent of consumption would still be regulated in size and shape, including tomatoes, lettuces, citrus fruits and apples, hitting smaller producers of lesser known varieties.

The way the subsidies are shared out even in Britain means the CAP donates most of the money to richer landowners, regardless of whether their main business is even farming. Between 2002 and 2007, handouts included £88,000 to a chain of hotels, £28,000 for a gypsum mining conglomerate, £27,000 for British Telecom, £16,000 for a water company and £5,000 to Eton College. Recent changes to the (already highly complex) system meant that, having anticipated 10,000 notifications of 'changes to land' to arrange subsidies, the Department for the Environment, Farming and Rural Affairs (DEFRA) received 100,000 of them, seeing thousands of new 'customers' registering any piece of land larger than 0.3 hectares, or one thirteenth the size of a polo field (the administrative cost of each claim was over £450).

CAP's primary objective was to raise farm income levels to those of other sectors, but this has failed, while in acting as a food tax it has transferred income from poorer consumers. Agricultural protection also harms manufacturing because it means huge dumping on poor countries, harming their economies to the point of reducing demand for EU-manufactured products.

The farm lobby's privileged access in Brussels prevents any real change. Money is poured into projects which would have happened anyway, among many other frauds. CAP recipients tick every box they can to obtain grants, inventing uses for 'pallet boxes', 'forklift trucks', and 'delivering water', while only Britain even tries to set measurable targets for farmers. A €3 million programme in Spain was supposed to go on things like irrigation and greenhouses; 98 percent was spent on cardboard boxes.[ccxlvi] Agribusiness free-riding is now a vast and permanent problem.

VULTURES

Without the CAP, many of Britain's southern chalk downs and northern moors would still be intact. But moors don't get handouts. Large tracts have gone needlessly under the plough, destroying rare plants, birds and mammals, a phenomenon reproduced all over Europe. Commission officials use the misleading tagline 'Green Europe' for the farming industry,[ccxlvii] legitimising agricultural subsidy on the grounds that it 'preserves the rural landscape'. The intensification of agriculture and the standardisation of the countryside have been encouraged through CAP financial incentives.

In 1995 the RSPB described the CAP as 'the engine of destruction in the countryside'.[ccxlviii] Environmentalists see bird species as indicators of the countryside's health, the canaries in the coal mine. Since the 1960s, numbers of British skylarks and song thrushes have plummeted. Between 1969 and 1994, as CAP took hold, the ornithological emblems of our countryside were decimated: bullfinches fell 76 percent, turtle doves 77 percent, corn buntings by 80 percent and grey partridges by 82 percent.[ccxlix] Draining wetlands for CAP cash has hit our wader populations like curlews, pintails and garganeys.

But in Spain, by subsidising farmers on a per animal basis, the CAP is encouraging mass livestock rearing in the parched badlands of the Spanish south, with disastrous results. There native raptors that depend on smaller animals are dying out, the red kite, golden eagle, Bonelli's eagle, kestrels, peregrines and harriers all in decline.[cd]

Modern farming methods and the environment need no longer be in conflict. New Zealand abolished price supports for farming in 1989. Since then its countryside has been 'de-intensified', with tremendous environmental results.[cdi] In Britain, millions of man hours of research have shown that the CAP funds types of farming that harm our wildlife and landscape. The hidden costs of the intensive farming it promotes, like polluted water, are picked up by local budgets and populations.

Brussels sends out a range of Directives to attempt to compensate. The *Directive on the Conservation of Natural Habitats (92/43/EEC)* instructed member states to put up environmental protection areas. Most were already doing that anyway, so they were given a new EU name, 'Special Protection Areas'.[cdii] The EU has also created *Regional Indicative Forest Strategies*, but in Britain this has led to planting swathes of North American conifers instead of native woodlands. Meanwhile, we can protect our national parks from over-building, but not from CAP-fuelled intensive farming. The first British government *Countryside Survey* in the early 1980s showed that 28,000km of hedgerows were being removed annually, and noted the 'general impoverishment of the landscape'.

What lets this destruction go unnoticed is its very ubiquity. Milk and livestock production is far higher than what Europe actually needs, and the CAP incentivises battery farming, making substantial improvements to animal welfare impossible. EU countries with poor welfare standards have the advantage: imports of pork from Denmark easily undercut more humanely reared British pork, stunting the free range market. French battery chicken giant *Doux* is its country's second most subsidised agribusiness, netting €4.69m a year, and it is suspected of dumping cheap chicken on world markets. These benefit-absorbing giants run the factory system that defines farming today.

WE WILL NOT SURVIVE IN THIS GAME

In the US at the turn of the millennium, the proportion of farmers' income from subsidies was 25 percent; in the EU it was half their pay.[ccliii] As the global food crisis continues, the EU's agricultural subsidies may have a greater affect on poor countries' ability to feed themselves than the effects of climate change. The EU pays millions in aid to African countries in agricultural training programmes, field instruction and courses on sustainable farming methods, then floods these countries with European dumped food that is often cheaper than what local producers can charge to make a living.

Studies have found that most of the EU's development programmes are small-scale, or 'one-offs', and do not follow sound development templates. Mali is one example in West Africa. European money is spent through various aid programmes to help Mali develop an indigenous beef industry, while Europe dumps subsidised surplus beef at 50 percent below the cost of Mali's own.[ccliv] Analysts now find that the EU is a major contributor to famine, actively undermining the agriculture of developing countries, especially Africa's poorest.

The rules of the relationship between Brussels and the developing world's food system were established in Paris. When France signed up to the European project it secured grants for its colonies and ex-colonies, formalised in an agreement in 1963 in Cameroonian capital Yaoundé. When Britain joined, Whitehall agreed with Brussels a division of the Commonwealth into *associables* and *non-associables*, the latter being countries deemed too developed to merit easier trade terms, and were restricted to negotiating their own agreements with Brussels later on. They included India, which then had a per capita income of $144.

Since then, the Commission has set out four central objectives for development policy. Number one is reducing poverty, two supporting economic growth through 'enhancing competitiveness in the rural sector', three is promoting good governance, democracy and human rights, and four improving environmental and institutional sustainability. These rules made a test case of South Africa's transition to democracy and return to the Commonwealth in 1994.

From the outset, Brussels considered South Africa a 'developed country', and began negotiations lasting four years, during which a number of member states objected to South Africa using any of the terms *port, sherry, ouzo, grappa, grand cru* and even *ruby* in products being shipped Europe's way. At the end of this wrangling, South African negotiators trawled the text to notice that Brussels's negotiators had slipped new clauses into the agreement at the last minute. After the South Africans refused to sign, Austrian Commissioner Franz Fischler assured them they could negotiate changes after the agreement came into force, exactly the same tactic used with Britain when it joined the Community all those years before.

The final agreement gave little scope for easier exports to Europe, and was far from what the new government in Pretoria had imagined, and sowed widespread suspicion that it was not above bullying much poorer countries into dubious trade deals. This grew when Brussels began pushing South Africa to allow European vessels to fish their seas (this time the South Africans did not give way). A 2007 report on European negotiating methods by the charity *Tradecraft* called Brussels simply 'a bully'. An official from newly democratic Ghana declared: 'we will not survive in this game'.[cdv]

In Britain, we are told by every incoming government that change to the CAP is just around the corner. In the few cases where the so-called 'major reforms' are effective, they target only selected budget tranches or price adjustments. Many of the organisations who should be protesting have become strangely silent. In the four years up to 2011, Christian Aid received €27,109,352.12 from Brussels, and it has since campaigned for more power to be ceded to the EU to help fight climate change.

The CAP is Europe's elephant in the room. The system creates huge fraud and dumping that cannot be compensated by aid, and like the Common Fisheries Policy it creates poverty, hunger and immigration into Europe by people trying to escape its effects. The only people who benefit are the big farmers who have been turned into benefit-businesses. But Brussels would probably be unable to fund it without us.

PART TWO
NONE DARE CALL IT TREASON

**Joining Europe was a coup d'état by a political class
who did not believe in popular sovereignty.**

Tony Benn

4.

THE INITIATIVE 1975-1987

ROI JEAN QUINZE

To the extent that they were engaged in it at all, Europe by the mid-1970s was an unpredictable business for the British people. In March 1974, Harold Wilson returned as premier, replacing Edward Heath despite taking fewer votes than the Conservatives (as the Liberals refused to join Heath in coalition). And on the Continent, an idea was resurfacing. Picking up the plan Monnet had described to Heath at Chequers in 1973, a December 1975 report from Belgian PM Leo Tindemans proposed replacing the Council of Ministers and Commission with a new supranational government of Europe, elected by a powerful European parliament. The plan was named simply, 'European Union'. This would mean one chamber elected by the 'peoples of Europe' and a new 'Chamber of States', a labyrinthine construction made necessary by the inability of intergovernmental cooperation to 'help solve European problems'. Although the plan was too ambitious for the time, it would reappear.

In March 1976, two years into his second premiership, Harold Wilson suddenly resigned. James Callaghan easily saw off Roy Jenkins' leadership bid, and Jenkins accepted an invitation to become European Commission President. Jenkins was President from August 1977 to January 1981, succeeding the Corsican Gaullist François-Xavier Ortoli.[15] Jenkins is usually thought to have been Callaghan's choice, but this isn't strictly true: he was

---

[15]Who followed Walter Hallstein (1958-67), Jean Rey (1967-1970), Franco Maria Malfatti (1970-73) and Sicco Mansholt (1972-73). Jenkins was succeeded by Gaston Thorn (1981-85), Jacques Delors (1985-95), Jacques Santer (1995-1999), Manuel Marín (1999), Romano Prodi (1999-2004), José Manuel Barroso (2004-14), and Jean-Claude Juncker (2014 to present).

French President Valéry Giscard d'Estaing's, who blocked Callaghan's first choice, Christopher Soames.

As Commission President, Jenkins would later recall Monnet's influence from younger days: 'the lesson that he taught me was to always advance along the line of least resistance'.[cclvi] He would put his mentor's advice to use in his support for monetary union, the beginning of which he oversaw with the 1979 launch of the European Monetary System (EMS), a proto-Single Currency.[16]

Jenkins brought back the single currency idea in Florence in October 1977, and the next February Chancellor Helmut Schmidt would take up the theme. But Britain when the EMS began in 1979 Britain refused to join, so an angry President Giscard retaliated by demanding France be given the same increase to the Regional Fund as Britain, preventing a real funding increase to compensate for the disparity in agriculture. 'It still seems to me impossible to explain what had come over Giscard', Jenkins said at the time. Britain's high contribution was referred to as the BBQ (British Budgetary Question), although Jenkins and the other mandarins were soon calling it the 'Bloody British Question'.

Britain's new Premier James Callaghan however was facing immediate economic crisis, forcing him to take out an IMF loan conditional on spending cuts. A majority of Britons now believed the Community was making Britain's economic problems worse, but with no majority Callaghan was forced into a 1977 voting pact with the pro-EEC Liberals. In 1977, EEC food prices rose significantly above world levels, as did Britain's financial contribution to Europe. Callaghan complained to Brussels, and was reminded that Britain had agreed the rules. By 1979 our net contribution was £780 million, and rose the next year when Britain became a full member. At the time the third poorest nation in the club, Britain was the second biggest donor. In London, the winter of discontent cost Callaghan his job, through a vote of no confidence in the Commons that he lost by one vote. The resulting election brought the Conservatives to power with a 44 seat majority, and on 4th May 1979 Margaret Thatcher walked into Number 10.

---

[16] Jenkins provoked particular reactions. On returning from meeting him in the early 1980s, the Queen was asked her impression: 'Far too grand for me', she is said to have replied. During his time in Brussels he was known unofficially as King John XV (the French pronunciation of his name is *Roi Jean Quinze*). Jenkins was educated at Balliol, which has produced more leading Europhiles than any other British institution. Jenkins is joined by Harold Macmillan, Edward Heath, Chris Patten, James Purnell, Tony Wright, Yvette Cooper, Stephen Twigg, Kitty Usher (former chief economist of the Britain in Europe campaign), the SNP's Neil MacCormick MEP, Jo Grimond, Denis Healey, Alan Beith, and Jo Johnson.

Margaret Thatcher had been elected to Parliament as Member for Finchley under Macmillan in 1959. Despite backing membership, Thatcher had since the mid-1960s grown increasingly close to the think tank the Institute for Economic Affairs, where economists inspired by Friedrich von Hayek argued that statism was gradually sapping Britain's strength.[17] Eager to deal with Britain's disproportionate contribution to Europe, she flew to her first European Council meeting in Dublin, of which she recalled:

> 'I had the strong feeling that they had decided to test whether I was able and willing to stand up to them. It was quite shameless: they were determined to keep as much money as they could.' [cclvii]

It worked. Britain was offered a £350 million rebate, with a net loss of £650 million. Even Europhile journalist Hugo Young noted that her fellow leaders were

> '...rude and derisive, and determined not to meet her anywhere near half way. Roy Jenkins [says] that Schmidt feigned sleep during one of her harangues [and] Giscard had his motorcade drawn up at the door, engines revving, to signal he would delay no longer.'

Such tactics that secured the deal. Little news of it got back to London, but a European conflict had begun that would define Thatcher's premiership. In June 1982, after victory in the Falklands and economic recovery since the 1981 recession, Thatcher and the Tories won a landslide, beating a Labour party that had veered left, and a Liberal-SDP alliance led by Roi Jean Quinze.

Her confidence renewed, Thatcher now proposed the Community live within its means by cutting waste and corruption. Wholehearted reform was needed, and she would soon tell the Community that it was 'on the edge of bankruptcy'.[ccclviii] A funding limit of 1 percent of national VAT imposed a sort of control, but was soon ignored.

German Chancellor Helmut Kohl chaired the next meeting, in Stuttgart in June 1983. France's new President François Mitterrand, in power since

---

[17]The think tank was founded by Antony Fisher, a former RAF pilot and entrepreneur who lost his father in World War One, then his brother in the Battle of Britain. He founded the IEA as part of a lifelong fight against totalitarianism after reading von Hayek's He was knighted in 1988.

1981, began by supporting Thatcher's suggestions for fair payments from Britain, then suddenly and completely changed position, telling her he could support only a one-off payment to compensate the country. Thatcher responded by telling her counterpart she would only accept an increase in Community funding if agricultural spending was reined in (reported as the 'anti-European' Thatcher stance).

Now came the turn of Mitterrand, who wanted the Community's VAT takings to rise to 1.6 percent to increase CAP funds and benefit France in particular. Thatcher and Kohl suggested a compromise increase of 1.4 percent, before Kohl suddenly offered Thatcher a rebate for a five year period (now believed to have been a secret agreement with Mitterrand). Thatcher's aim had been turned on itself. The Council broke up, and to make a point France (with Italy) blocked Britain's agreed refund for 1983.

The next gathering, in June 1984, was at Fontainebleau, a chateau just outside Paris to which Thatcher left hoping once more for a rebate (of 70 percent). Having lost the 1975 Conservative leadership election to Thatcher, Geoffrey Howe had become her first Chancellor, but was now Foreign Secretary. He soon informed the PM that the other ministers would settle for 50-60 percent, and attempted to persuade her to accept the offer, with the proviso that Britain's rebate would rise, but for only two years. Thatcher would later write:

> 'How Geoffrey, who had been splendidly staunch in the negotiations
> so far, had allowed the foreign ministers to reach such a conclusion
> I could not understand.'[cclix]

She stuck to her 70 percent, Mitterrand stuck to his 60, and Kohl told them both he would accept 65. Thatcher had to accept the apparent compromise. Mitterrand also gave way, but now Kohl played another card. With all parties exhausted, he declared that in addition to the already incomprehensible small-print, his own farmers should get extra payouts. This was totally against the rules, and for Thatcher circumvented the whole object of the talks, but at this late stage everyone wanted to go home to show off a deal. None demurred, and the British press hailed Thatcher's victory at Fontainebleau.

ENTER DELORS

> **Governmental elites would be involved in the**
> **central decision-making process and increasingly identify**
> **with it... The process is not, in itself, democratic.**

> *Stuart Holland MP, former adviser to Jacques Delors*

Just after Leo Tindemans's *European Union* report was published in the late 1970s, a cluster of EEC insiders began working on the next step forward: a *Treaty on European Union*. This was so ambitious that it was discussed only in secret, and the group resolved to cut it into two treaties, five years apart: the first would be called the *Single European Act*, the second would become the *Treaty of Maastricht*. The man responsible was an Italian former communist MEP named Alterio Spinelli.

Spinelli collected a small group who supported a move towards integration which held its dinner meetings at Strasbourg's *Crocodile* restaurant,[cclx] included a British Tory named Stanley Johnson, father of Boris (Johnson *fils*, 17-years-old at the time of the *Crocodile* meetings, would become Brussels correspondent for the *Daily Telegraph*, and from 1989 to 1994 was one of the first to report on 'straight cucumber edicts' and enforced metrification. He would later reflect: 'The longer I stayed in Brussels – and I served five happy years – the more obvious it was that it would never work. The Germans had German dinner parties, the French had French dinner parties. The British sent their children to play cricket at the British School in Tervuren'.[cclxi])

On 9th July 1981, the European parliament founded a 'standing committee for the institutional problems charged to work out a modification of the existing treaties', the kind of jargon known to go unnoticed. Spinelli however knew that they had 'the initiative fully to give new momentum to the establishment of the European Union',[cclxii] and that the Committee's task as it worked through the early 1980s was to devise a completely new treaty for Europe (although Commission chief Roy Jenkins's autobiography suggests he knew of none of this).

Spinelli's blueprint proposed expanding the parliament's powers, giving it the right to oversee and veto the Commission, while the Community would 'coordinate' the laws of nations, with an eye to 'constituting a homogenous judicial area'. There would be complete coordination of economic policy, plus the outline of 'procedures and stages for attaining monetary union', including a central bank. Brussels would take 'concurrent competence' with the nations over social policy, regional policy, health, consumer protection, environment, education and research, and culture and 'information' policy.[cclxiii] Despite the different interests of Community countries, this 'competence' would extend to parts of nations' foreign policies, beginning with the exclusive right to decide trade deals with third countries – so the EU's total negotiation of trade with the US over British heads in the EU-US trade talks of 2013 began with just a sentence in this report. His committee's *Solemn Declaration on European Union*, presented at the Stuttgart meeting in June 1983, informed Thatcher and the assembled that, quite simply,

> 'The Heads of Government, on the basis of an awareness of a common destiny and the wish to affirm the European identity, confirm their commitment to progress towards an ever closer union among the peoples and Member States of the European Communities.'[cclxiv]

On Valentine's Day 1984, the European parliament accepted Spinelli's draft. With France in recession, Mitterrand hungered for European quarry to bring home to Paris, and in May declared that he supported the proposals.[cclxv] This was part of a pattern: such decisions on the French side were being taken with a clear eye to domestic expediency as much as for the nobler pan-European aims many British Europhiles by then believed. Another pattern was about to emerge, as Brussels became bogged down in technicalities it lacked the capacity to handle, demanding more integration (and access to national civil servants' expertise) to cope.

Just after one of the authors entered Parliament in a by-election in May 1984 (becoming a member of the European Select Committee within a year, where he has remained, and become chairman), the European parliament elections in June produced a low turnout across Europe, and at 31.8 percent Britain's was lowest of all. The European peoples appeared not to see the value of Brussels, a state of apathy that spurred a new initiative. President Mitterrand had already urged 'stronger institutions'. At the Fontainebleau summit in June 1984 he submitted for the meeting schedule the establishment of another expert committee for new reforms. It would be chaired by an Irish ex-foreign minister named James Dooge. Come December, the Dooge

Committee proposed a conference to prepare yet another treaty. Britain, Greece and Denmark, opposed the idea. The Dooge Committee would deliver its report at the end of March 1985. At the same moment, with Mitterrand's support, French civil servant Jacques Delors became the new President of the Commission, and Italian foreign minister Giulio Andreotti leader of the Council of Europe.

Jacques Delors, a Parisian, and also a background functionary, had come to prominence as a social affairs advisor to Georges Pompidou's government in the late 1960s. One anecdote recounts that at an early press conference with Delors, Thatcher found herself doing more of the talking while the Frenchman appeared to have 'switched off'. As he sat oblivious to an invitation for him to speak, she bantered: 'I had no idea you were the strong silent type.'[cclxvi] Thatcher had amused the press, but the Westminster knockabout style rubbed Delors up the wrong way. Delors believed Thatcher had tried to humiliate him, and would not forget it.

The hard political difficulties would soon become apparent too. Dooge's proposals were radical indeed, and included the mark of supranationalism: scrapping national vetoes to begin majority voting on new measures. In theory this would prevent big states overriding the interests of small ones, but it also meant Britain would be left with a shade over one seventh of the voting power. The Dooge committee would also 'give a European dimension to all aspects of collective life in our countries'; Dooge went further, promoting an 'external identity' with 'common cultural values',[cclxvii] in other words a federation with a common foreign policy. Sources state that Malcolm Rifkind saw no reason to make a single comment on these matters at the meetings of the committee,[cclxviii] but over lunch at the Garrick would confide in Hugo Young: 'there is no effective opposition to the EEC any longer in Parliament'.

Having harvested ideas from his discussion group, Spinelli now put Tindemans's European Union idea into action, moving a resolution to the European Parliament which stated that British, Danish and Greek objections must not prevent the discussion of a new treaty,[cclxix] a motion that in late April 1985 was heartily approved – it was just a discussion after all. With that, the road show continued, and for a meeting (to agree to have a discussion) the leaders made for the next jamboree, in Milan.

In Milan, the European Movement had bussed over 50,000 activists onto the medieval streets, who stomped merrily through the city, banners and placards urging 'down with frontiers'.[cclxx] Thatcher described the 'highly partisan' atmosphere, with Italian Bettino Craxi in the chair (now known to have been deep in Mafia corruption). Craxi heralded the desire of all Europe to 'overcome the obstacles before us and achieve the necessary consensus to go forward together towards the objectives of the European Union.'[cclxxi]

At the time, having become a member of the European Select Committee, Bill Cash arranged to meet Henri Mattieson, legal advisor to the European Commission. This was when he discovered Mattieson and his colleagues' deep-rooted determination to achieve a European federal system. He reported this, as we will see, to Margaret Thatcher.

'European Union' was now out of the closet, and the meeting led to the Single European Act (the first stage of Leo Tindemans's European Union blueprint), which would create the Single Market. During the 1985 meeting, Delors took it upon himself to attend the foreign ministers' gatherings, a new feature and a canny move. Delors dictated the pace by pressing his own proposals, using up time and kicking others' into the long grass. Majority voting now became a required part of the Single Market, which as a member Britain would simply have to accept. Thatcher had been persuaded into this by her advisors, including Lord Cockfield (who would become a European Commissioner) which she later came to regret. Despite lacking the authority to do so under the Treaty of Rome, Delors created strange new paragraphs about 'cohesion', something called 'subsidiarity', and 'space without frontiers'.[cclxxii] This was a territory-grab at immigration policy.

Delors also insisted that the single currency should get a chapter in the new treaty. Thatcher opposed him, and thought she had German support, but one Franco-German meeting later and it became clear she did not. Delors inserted a commitment to the 'progressive realisation of economic and monetary union'[cclxxiii] into the treaty's preamble. Our Foreign Office zealously assured the PM that its legal status was zero. The Act went well beyond anyone's idea of a 'Common Market': social and regional aid, environmental standards, research and development, and monetary cooperation were all brought to Brussels's table. Bill Cash was so deeply worried in the light of his experiences with Mattieson that he put down his own amendment to this Single European Act, expressly to preserve the sovereignty of the United Kingdom Parliament in relation to this legislation – which remained on the Order Paper in his name alone. During the Committee stage, he was refused the right to debate this issue despite his remonstrating with the Clerks of the House, with the

Speaker himself, and then on the floor of the House with the Deputy Speaker Sir Paul Dean, who told him that his amendment went beyond the boundaries of the Bill, and he was ruled out of order.[18]

As she left, Thatcher claimed the mention of the single currency was irrelevant and meaningless.[cclxxiv] Such claims were becoming common for British premiers reporting back. With the BBC reporting that 'all that emerged were a few modest reforms of the Treaty of Rome', the Bill to approve these 'modest reforms' was passed, but most of our MPs were not even there.

Economics was also becoming a political – and integrationist – ruse. Despite all the concessions, on one economic matter Thatcher was certain: under Europe's Exchange Rate Mechanism (ERM), first proposed in 1979, exchange rates would be placed at levels which would expose sterling to dangerous speculative attacks. Lawson disagreed, and fired up by an economic boom that bore his name he began a secret project of his own. Thatcher forbade taking sterling into the ERM, so the Chancellor quietly began fixing the pound to follow the *Deutschmark* by controlling interest rates and reserves. It would take months for Thatcher to discover the gambit – she would describe it as 'a personal economic policy without reference to the rest of the government'[cclxxv] – before which there was another election to win, on 9th June 1987.

A European Council meeting followed on 29th June, in Brussels, where Jacques Delors proclaimed that 'new rules' were needed to control the gigantic sums now being spent on agriculture, although these were vague. His other response to Europe's straining budgets involved throwing more money at Brussels, with regional funding to be doubled over five years from an original contribution of 1.4 percent of member states' GNP. Delors sewed together the agriculture 'reforms', the growth of 'own resources', and doubling regional funding into one seamless package,[cclxxvi] and the governments backed the package 11 to 1: only an aghast Thatcher was against. This time, against the most audacious Brussels power grab yet, Thatcher would not budge. European leaders returned home to tell their peoples the failure was hers.

Diplomatic and Cabinet pressure later became so intense that Thatcher gave way. A limit of 1.2 percent GNP for Brussels' own resources was agreed, but so was a rise in regional funding that would add up to 25 percent of Brussels' budget. Brussels began its own direct 'partnership'[cclxxvii] with local governments to decide how regional funds were spent, bypassing national capitals.

---

[18]Following his campaigns it would no longer be possible to rule this out of order.

5.

PLAYING SOLDIERS

THE PHONEY WAR

Reflections on the Revolution in France was written by Edmund Burke in 1790. 'Make the revolution a parent of settlement', wrote Burke, 'and not a nursery of future revolutions'.

Jean Monnet and his friends lived after a period of terror. When it was over they sought stability, above all peace, and believed they had found the grail with which to secure it. But the spirit of the affair was caught by the French poet Paul Valéry: 'Politics is the art of preventing people from getting involved in affairs which concern them', and the fear of one evil often leads us into another. So it is fitting that with Europhile journalist Will Hutton as our guide, we begin this chapter with a nod of sympathy to the men who forged a new plan.

> 'If it seems that contemporary Europe could never again repeat the mistakes of the past, it is the fact that the post-war generation and its visionary leaders – men like France's Jean Monnet and Robert Schuman, Belgium's Paul-Henri Spaak, Italy's Alcide de Gasperi and Germany's Konrad Adenauer – had the courage and foresight to lay the cornerstones of what has become the contemporary European Union that makes it probable if not certain that Europe will never again go to war with itself. It is an achievement that, given Europe's tormented past – and the ethnic conflicts that overwhelmed the former Yugoslavia in the 1990s – is worth consolidating and protecting to the last'. [cclxxviii]

We shall turn soon to Yugoslavia, but while the EU has probably not saved Europe from war, it does use World War II to justify its continued existence. It is commonplace to say that the EU is one of the results of the peace, not the creator of it. More than this, to claim that without the Union, Europe could plunge itself again into war is above all a misunderstanding of the nation at its heart: modern Germany.

At the heart of this historical misreading is that independent democracies are dangerous, because democracies went to war in 1914. Germany, however, was not a democracy then. In Germany, Russia and Austro-Hungary, all kinds of political structures survived well beyond their use-by dates. The German Reichstag had universal suffrage, but very little power indeed. German democracy was largely cosmetic and the Reichstag's main task was to pass an Army Law every seven years to fund the huge armed forces. To do so, every seven years there had to be a militaristic panic. As the historian Arno Mayer describes in *The Persistence of the Old Regime*, the First World War was a 'pre-emptive counter revolution' against democracy by Germany's aristocracy.

Hutton is not above deploying similar stratagems that perpetuate this understanding of history. His book *The World We're In* was released in 2002, at the very height of Europeanist enthusiasm among the British political class. On early German zeal for the EU, he suggests:

> 'For Germans, terrified of their past, this was a European coalition that locked their country into a commitment to liberal democracy and market capitalism while offering it a legitimate means to exercise non-threatening influence on the development of Europe.'

And in southern Europe meanwhile:

> 'The dictatorship of the Iberian fascists and the Greek junta could not be repeated if Spain, Portugal and Greece were to sustain their membership. The EEC was becoming the guarantor of democracy, liberty, prosperity and markets in a continent that had been plagued by authoritarianism, fascism, communism and every variant of command and control economics. This alone justified its presence.'

But the premise is untrue: the dictatorships of Iberia and Greece *could* be repeated, just as any army in any country could simply carry out a swift coup and revoke their country's EU membership. The EU has not created postwar democracy, it just came along at the right time. *Species virtutibus similes*: appearances resembling virtues. Thus the EU and peace have been bled together. But the idea that to protect democracy we should turn a blind eye to the bureaucratic destruction of that democracy just doesn't stand.

ETHICAL FOREIGN POLICY

Beyond the encomium, sooner or later the supposed guarantor of peace will need hardware to look convincing. This can be in the form of technical collaborations with countries that have invested in their own defence (although the amount of money we lavish on Brussels every year would *double* the British defence budget).[cclxxix] Yugoslavia's civil war was something Europe did try to deal with, and a European partnership Britain joined with enthusiasm.

As Communism collapsed, Croats and Bosnians watched Slovenia break decisively from Belgrade with only limited skirmishes, and their own leaders began manoeuvring for independence. By early 1992, after the removal of over 400,000 Croats and other non-Serbs from their homes, and the murders of Bosnian prisoners of war at the hands of Serbian troops, Bruce Jackson, the former President of the US Committee on NATO remembered:

> 'Our point was that the Europeans should do it themselves, because this was a small bush fire that was clearly within their ambit of responsibilities and if they let it burn out of control it's going to suck us in.'[cclxxx]

Indeed, President of the Council of Europe, a Luxembourger named Jacques Poos, hailed 'the hour of Europe'. And so the Americans waited. 'We were quite happy to let the Europeans have a go at it', said former Defence Secretary Richard Perle (the US occupied with a simmering Iraq and the break-up of the USSR).

The Americans would be waiting some time. By mid-1992, Secretary of State James Baker heavily criticised his European counterparts for having failed to contain the fighting. What is little known is that having lost faith in the EU's ability to deal with the Yugoslav problem, military planner Lt. Gen. Karl Lowe and Supreme Allied Commander Europe Gen. John Galvin had already joined Baker to prepare the US military for intervention. Historian Brendan Simms tells us that in London meanwhile, with the support of Heseltine and Foreign Secretary Douglas Hurd (a politician Hugo Young described as possessing 'the effortless superiority of Etonian man'), John Major was keen to keep in step with Paris to build a post-Cold War defence relationship. So sanctions were imposed on Belgrade in May at the behest of the US, but with the 'misgivings'[cclxxxi] of Britain and France. General Galvin suggested sweeping 'those Serb [guns] out of there, taking care of the artillery as well'.[cclxxxii] But the Brits, with Paris and Brussels, had become firmly opposed to intervention. Through spokesman Lawrence Eagleburger, outgoing President Bush Sr. delivered a parting shot to Serbian strongman Slobodan Milosevic, denouncing him publicly for war crimes. By now, according to a well-placed British source in NATO,

> 'Many people in the United States really saw the Brits as Chamberlain-style appeasers. I remember one meeting I went to in the State Department... where the anti-British feeling, again Chamberlain/appeasement/Munich, was very strong. I am talking about [people] who had a long tradition of working with the Europeans and with the UK, no natural animus'.[cclxxxiii]

For the many Anglophiles in the American mission at NATO HQ, Britain's behaviour was 'a shocking new phenomenon', but come August 1994 Hurd still insisted that 'we don't have the power to impose a solution' on the Bosnian Serbs. As new President Clinton's Secretary of State Warren Christopher reminded him, the west had plenty of power, it just wasn't using it. Satellite pictures made clear that most of the Serb artillery massed around the Bosnian capital Sarajevo could be destroyed in one day. Keeping close to EU opinion, Britain opposed the effective use of air power.

Hurd kept his meetings with the beleaguered Bosnian government to a minimum, but claimed that 'what is being done on the ground is being done by Europeans'. This was little. European soldiers were indeed there, but their ineffectual activities seemed a token presence to keep Americans off Europe's turf, even as a corner of it collapsed into slaughter.

As Serbian leaders stepped up the killing of civilians, Britain and France – backed by Russia and China – demanded the arms embargo on Bosnia, extended from the old Yugoslavia to its successor states, stayed in force. Soon after moving into the White House, Clinton pointed out to the Europeans that light arms could be distributed within just 72 hours, while the European support of the embargo 'unfairly penalised the victim of the conflict'. Hurd and Major put about various reasons for holding the course, with much of the establishment happy to toe the Europeanist line. One employee of the BBC's Croatian Service noted that FCO briefings were seeping 'in an undiluted form'[cdxxxiv] into World Service programming.

Even so, Defence Secretary Malcolm Rifkind admitted that as the European Union looked languidly on, the worst crimes Europe had seen since the Holocaust and the Second World War were now being committed. Showing signs of growing discomfort, in April 1993 Rifkind told Parliament that he was 'not aware of any ethical distinction between a war in Bosnia and a war [in] Cambodia'.[cdxxxv] The newly ennobled Lady Thatcher went on the attack: Bosnia, she said, was 'a killing field', and warned that there could be 'a holocaust', which 'should be in Europe's sphere of conscience... we are little more than an accomplice to the massacre'.[cdxxxvi]

In Cabinet however, Britain's Foreign Secretary and leading Europhile was now in control. The FCO briefings would not be enough for Douglas Hurd, who now went on the offensive, saying 'most of those who work for the BBC, *The Times, The Independent, The Guardian*... they are the founder members of the *Something Must be Done* school'. He had reason to be agitated. By mid-1993, MORI polls showed over two-thirds of Britons wanted their troops dispatched to stop the fighting. But to Hurd the subject was fast becoming unmentionable. Even in September 1992, when asked to name the greatest challenge facing the EU, he refused to talk about Bosnia.

Europeanists certainly had other things on their minds. Although Europe offered no real response to the killing, some were attempting to use the conflict to justify an EU military in the long-term. Indeed, the prolonged bloodshed may now have been serving this very purpose. At Christmas 1994, US officials claimed to be in possession of evidence (obtained by eavesdropping) suggesting that 'Paris might be purposely inflaming tensions over Bosnia to drive a wedge between Britain and the US'. With the Europeanists running British foreign policy, such tactics seemed to be working. French Foreign Minister Alain Juppé told his people at the time, 'the conflict in Bosnia has shown the necessity to move beyond NATO and American guarantees', in other words to an EU military, whereas, given the will, the British and French armed forces could have dealt with the Serbs in days. One Europhile civil servant claimed the conflict proved 'just how much Europe needs to be autonomous where intelligence gathering [and] satellite reconnaissance are concerned.'[cclxxxvii] Hurd was an enthusiast too: 'defence in Europe is not an opt-out subject for us'.

As the conflict ground on, in 1994 a joint RAF and French *Armée de l'Air* planning group began: Hurd claimed that 'the experience in Bosnia brought service cooperation between the British and the French to a new post-war high', seeing no irony in adding: 'Suez didn't count because it was short and it was a disaster'. In October 1994, the French attended their first NATO summit in 30 years, but while Major and Hurd trumpeted a new Anglo-French *entente*, France exploited the division Bosnia had created between Britain and the US. Says Brendan Simms:

> '...anything that involved the French was likely to be militarily backward and politically frivolous... the French had no intention of allowing NATO any kind of veto over European initiatives.'[cclxxxviii]

The Anglo-American rift that allowed the bloodshed to continue was in the first place a result of Britain's Europeanist policy. As Jean Monnet's former private secretary Georges Berthoin told Hugo Young, 'what do you suppose [Milosevic] thinks when he keeps getting the American, the Russian and the Franco-Brit people waiting on him? There is no one voice. Holbrooke [US Representative to the UN, 1999-2001] was effective because he just said, 'stuff the others, this is what I am demanding', and Milosevic bent to him. The Euros cannot do that'.[cclxxxix]

This was well beyond British Europeanist understanding. Major's government pursued its French *entente* right through the mid-1990s, which was picked up by Tony Blair when he came to office, formalised in the Anglo-French defence summit of 1998 in St Malo. Hurd himself said that Bosnia: 'was a prelude to St Malo. There is now a much closer relationship between our armed forces than there used to be, and that is the result of Bosnia'.

After World War Two, this was the source of modern European defence cooperation. Once more, Britain's establishment never really got a grip of what cooperation would mean. Having seen the EU's methods of 'guaranteeing the peace', Czech President and former prisoner of conscience Vaclav Havel made a personal request to President Clinton for NATO enlargement. As

Bruce Jackson put it: 'in order to [ensure] the never again in Europe, you can't [have] a holocaust break out in Europe. It makes you look like a fool'.[ccxc] Or as Edmund Burke wrote:

> 'Wise men will apply their remedies to vices, not to names; to the causes of evil which are permanent, not to the occasional organs by which they act, and the transitory modes in which they appear. Otherwise you will be wise historically, a fool in practice.'

POWER

**The political class are interested in power.
If power is moved elsewhere, they naturally become obsessed[ccxci].**

Michael Portillo, Defence Secretary, 1994

In 2003, through the European *Common Security and Defence Policy*, two military operations were carried out under the EU flag for the first time. One was *Artemis*, a limited and cosmetic intervention in the Democratic Republic of the Congo, while the other, *Concordia*, was a longer military-lite presence in Macedonia, plus the despatch of 7,000 peacekeepers to Bosnia. In 2005, Brussels set up its own military planning unit separate from NATO, the European Union Military Staff (EUMS).[ccxcii] Numerous collaborations have landed British troops with bargain basement kit at Harrods prices, such as the Horizon frigate project, Eurologistics, Euromissile, and Galileo (a multibillion euro duplication of the American GPS system without a legal basis in any treaty, one of whose functions has been to help the Chinese navy play intimidating war exercises off Taiwan). Characterised by inability to carry out proper operations, Artemis and Concordia are typical of taxpayer-funded EU military projects. Others are worth recounting.

In Afghanistan, under their own deployment rules, German and French soldiers refused to fly their helicopters when it gets dark, even if the British, Canadian and American troops doing the actual fighting needed help. Article 4.7 of the EU Forces Agreement with Gabon allowed EU-flagged submarines to sail to the central African country to help peacekeeping in the nearby Democratic Republic of Congo's elections, even though the DRC has only

20 miles of coastline (the EU also sent a Rear Admiral to run its peacekeeping in Bosnia, with 12 miles of coastline and no ports[ccxcii]). By comparison, at the end of the 1990s Britain's on-the-hoof intervention in Sierra Leone ended a ghastly civil war and reinstated democracy, but did require some actual fighting. After an interview with Foreign Secretary Peter Hain in 2000, Hugo Young noted:

> 'MOD: Hoon and Guthrie[19] have both told Hain that the boys like going to Sierra Leone, because it is real action... Our Rapid-Reaction Force got its first outing there, and did it in forty-eight hours, which even the US said nobody else in the world could have done...'

Despite this, one of the premises on which the entire EU ideal sits is that should we throw our armed forces (or our country), into a European bloc, we would become more powerful ourselves as a result. Like much pro-European thought, this pays limited attention to how the EU actually works. As we have seen, our European neighbours frequently have very different goals, a fact that EU integration has helped hide. However the idea that we will have more influence in the world through Europe is itself little questioned.

Sadly it does not add up. The EU as an armed entity in the world could have more power than Britain on an *absolute* basis. However, to establish what this means for *the British people as individuals* we have to divide that total power by the European population, at 500 million and growing. Just as Britain is a disproportionately high contributor to the EU in cash terms, we would also be a very disproportionate contributor to the EU in military capacity. In fact, despite recent governments' cuts to our military, Britain remains almost the only country in Europe with a seriously capable army, the other being France.

So the EU may get more powerful, but *we*, the British people, won't. In fact, in placing our army under EU direction or influence – let alone overall control – Britons as individuals will become *less* powerful. When a stream feeds into a huge river, the stream does not become greater. It disappears.

As the historian Sir Michael Howard has pointed out, a question mark now hangs over the sovereign state itself. Interventions under the command of a combined EU military force would also give the EU more credibility as an

---

[19] Geoff Hoon, Defence Secretary 1999-2005, and General Charles Guthrie, Chief of the Defence Staff 1997-2001.

upholder of rights in general. But if we use the EU to exercise *droit de regard* over the affairs of other states, we should take care that it does not take the same attitude to our own. The former MP Sir Richard Body has described five 'critical powers' that define a nation state. The first four, the power to make law (which Brussels clearly has), the power to tax (such as the EU's VAT rules and other indirect taxes), the power to interpret law (the European courts overrule our own and fine the British government), and the power to make treaties with other countries (when the WTO replaced GATT, Britain lost its place to the Commission) are now completely or largely in the hands of Brussels. Only one power remains: the power to declare war. As Machiavelli had it, 'hence it comes about that all armed prophets have been victorious, and all unarmed prophets have been destroyed'. Brussels would use British expertise to arm the EU.

After all this, has Brussels really ensured peace in our time? Britain's world role has been downplayed by pro-Europeans of all political stripes, and to diminish it is a point of view so fashionable it is almost political gospel. But this view of Britain as a third rate power is rarely shared abroad. If we continue to integrate into the EU militarily, the 'third rate power' propaganda will become reality, and the Europhile prophecy of Britain's continual decline self-fulfilling.

6.

CENTRE OF GRAVITY 1988-1997

O, he sits high in all the people's hearts;
And that which would appear offence in us
His countenance, like richest alchemy,
Will change to virtue and to worthiness.

Casca
Julius Caesar

HOW THE LEFT WAS WON

In the early 1980s, anti-European feeling was firmly associated with the Left. The last time a Labour manifesto proposed leaving the Community was in 1983's 'longest suicide note in history' (700 pages of dreck that also promised unilateral nuclear disarmament and the nationalisation of swathes of the City). By 1988 however, two great European disruptions to British politics would occur on either side of the channel, in Bournemouth and Bruges. But by 1983 the Labour MP Stuart Holland, who would soon work for Jacques Delors in Brussels, had foreseen that

> 'Because several major parties in Western Europe wish to see it gain enlarged powers, the European [Parliament] is set to increasingly negate the nominal sovereignty of national parliaments. Without positive policies for the defence of its interests at Community level, national labour would tend to find its national base eclipsed by negative policies... such an outcome is not inevitable. However, it is likely so long as Community integration remains capitalist

integration, which itself is probable so long as the Right remains in office and the Left remains divided on Community policies.'

In 1988, Thatcher remained determined not to concede central bank control. Knowing Brussels's plans, she flew to Hanover for the next Council meeting, insisting a document could be produced that made no references to any European central bank, and that any group established to discuss the matter should consist only of (reliably self-interested) national central bank chiefs.[ccxciv] All seemed well, until an unknown party entered the suggestion that this new committee's chairman should be Delors. Thatcher, who presumably realised she had been outplayed, was left to insist on her return to the Commons that any moves to 'monetary union' need not 'involve a single currency or a European central bank'.[ccxcv] This was unconvincing, and she must have known it.

Delors would tell the European Parliament that summer that most member states were yet to understand how these decisions 'would involve a seepage of their sovereignty to the Community',[ccxcvi] and that in the name of 'efficiency' the beginnings of real European government would be needed by 1995.[ccxcvii] Thatcher was stunned. Things were about to get worse.

In July 1988, sensing the urgency of European developments, Bill Cash wrote a memorandum to Margaret Thatcher, warning her in explicit terms of the dangers of 'creeping federalism', as he put it, which he had encountered in visits to Europe as a member of the European Select Committee. He warned that, based on his visits, there was 'ample evidence of the strength of federalist feeling in key places in the Community. I thought it would be helpful to indicate to you some of the evidence of this'.

He referred to European Commission documents, as well as meetings with, for example, the advocate general of the European Court Sir Gordon Slynn, and that a legal adviser to the Council of Ministers, referred to their desire for 'legal-political power play'. That in the Council of Ministers, some refused to use the word 'scrutiny', and wanted to ignore the scrutiny reserve of the UK, and that the use of the veto was dead. He referred to further immediate emphasis on 'political unification' on which he had challenged European Commissioner Lord Cockfield in the context of 'creeping federalism'. He added that all this added weight to the claims of Mr Delors, and mentioned that the European Select Committee had encountered bitter criticism of Britain from the *Bundestag* European Affairs

Committee, adding 'I think there is a growing desire by West Germany to achieve permanent pre-eminence in the EEC'. He referred to the increasing demands by members of the European Parliament 'for more power to be devolved from the national parliaments to the European Parliament and indeed to the European Commission itself', and criticised the European Parliament, which needed 'proper democratic scrutiny and accountability to be maintained because without it contact is lost with the people.' Concerned about the expression 'European Union' and its real meaning, which 'would be followed by autocratic government at worst or benevolent despotism and breakup', he went on to state that 'if those who continue to pursue the course of federalism persist in their objectives it will be they and no one else who destroy the mutual benefits of the European Community'.

Bill warned that 'supranationalism would create disruptive internal tensions and could possibly even provoke external aggression. The scale and kind of changes now being successfully sought in Europe today are the stuff of which world wars were made – they require careful cultivation with full and open consent and commitment, not stealth and centrism by pan-Europeans.' He stated that 'at bottom, the only way in which in the long term a European Government could be avoided, given the basic structure of the EEC and trends, is by a considered re-emphasis of influence to Westminster and other national parliaments...', and noted that Article 24 of the West German constitution included as part of the basic law 'European unity', but that the British Parliament 'because of the doctrine of the supremacy of parliament is not used to working within a context in which it is not able to make changes in legislation after the event'.

Although Margaret Thatcher replied to this letter on 12th August, it is curious that despite all her correspondence being lodged in the archives in Cambridge University, this memorandum cannot be found there, although of course the author had a copy of his own. In the meantime, and in the light of these developments, preparations were made for a major speech to be made by the Prime Minister later that year, at Bruges. This was against the background of vigorous and undisguised disagreements between Margaret Thatcher and Geoffrey Howe, as the 'Bruges Speech' evolved.

In 1988, Jacques Delors arranged to speak at the TUC's annual conference in Bournemouth, and addressed a packed gathering on 8th September. Apparently there to sell Europe's 'social dimension', this would be Delors' next move in what had become his *danse macabre* with Thatcher.

Christopher Booker and Richard North describe a broadside against everything Thatcher stood for, as an impassioned Delors told the assembled TUC's delegates:

> 'The internal market should be designed to benefit each and every citizen of the Community. It is therefore necessary to improve workers' living and working conditions, and to provide better protection for their health and safety... Europe needs you!'[ccxcviii]

To the union members, this must have been an oasis in the desert. Delors shared their fears, and the reception was rapturous. A Catholic socialist of long standing, no doubt Delors believed what he was saying. The unions overestimated what influence they would have in Brussels, but Delors now gave the Left a method to circumvent their domestic unpopularity at the time: simply bypassing national democracy. 'Europe is not just about material results', he told them, 'it is about spirit. Europe is a state of mind'.

But if Delors made the decisive move, Labour's embrace of Europhilia was now possible because the baby boom new Left, inculcated in cultural relativism through education in the social science departments of the 1960s – the friends of every country but their own – had reached maturity. Having transferred their grievances from the working class to immigrants in particular, the tectonic shift in the culture of the Left in general and the Labour Party in particular was a product of Labour's own demographic shift. Labour now ceased to be a vehicle of representation of the British poor, and became instead a movement of the metropolitan tax-farming middle class, the political cadre of a public sector originally swelled, by the Labour Party itself, to serve working class interests.

***

Shortly after Bill Cash's election as Member of Parliament for Stafford in 1984, he was appointed to the Select Committee on European Legislation (thus a member of the European Scrutiny Committee and its forerunner, the European Legislation Committee, for over thirty years). It was clear even that the then Single European Act would affect the sovereignty of the United Kingdom, hence voting for the Act but tabling an amendment, to the effect that nothing in this measure would derogate from the sovereignty of the United Kingdom Parliament – given his reservations about how the

EC was moving to majority voting. The amendment was not accepted. 'The notion of sovereignty embraces effective control', he explained to the House of Commons back on 10th July 1986. If that amendment had been allowed for debate, which it was not, it would have changed the whole nature of our EU relationship. He was strongly supported by those who understood that if we were to have an association that did not work, the only way to retrieve the situation would be through some form of overriding clause. Real power and sovereignty lay with the British people.

So at the suggestion of George Brock of *The Times*, he wrote an article on the Single European Act, explaining in an article in *The Times* on 16th June 1986 – 'Warding off the EEC steamroller' – of the dangerous decision-making under the Single European Act and arguing that 'the real decisions remained with Westminster and not with the semi-autonomous working groups of civil servants who have flown over to Brussels for the day'. 'It is vital', Bill Cash argued, 'to ensure that the legislation that flows from it is in the interests of this country.'

It was then that he realised what was really at stake: the European Community was in danger of rapidly becoming a political federation, although this was always denied. The issue of Europe at this time did not figure highly in the minds of many. His interest was spurred by a Select Committee visit to Brussels at the end of 1985, just before the Single European Act, when they met a disturbing number of officials from the European Commission whose federalism was beyond doubt.

In more articles in *The Times* between June 1988 and 1990, he warned of the 'insufficient control by elected representatives over decisions vital to our commercial and industrial future', 'a growing tendency for powers to be delegated by the Council of Ministers to the Commission', 'an increase in the use of regulations' and 'the bypassing of national parliaments', attributing the increase of this 'democratic deficit' to the 'more frequent majority voting introduced under the Single European Act.' This was 'creeping federalism'.

Not a fortnight after Delors spoke in Bournemouth, on 18th September 1988 Thatcher was herself in Bruges, at the Great Hall of the College of Europe, the training academy for the emerging European bureaucratic class. Europe, she urged her audience to remember,

> '...is not the creation of the Treaty of Rome. Nor is the European idea the property of any group or institution... We have not

successfully rolled back the frontiers of the state in Britain only
to see them re-imposed at a European level, with a European
super-state exercising a new dominance from Brussels.... Willing
and active cooperation between independent sovereign states is the
best way to build a successful European Community.'[ccxcix]

Her reception was dire – 'stunned outrage', Thatcher described it.[ccc] One
man who took it badly was her Foreign Secretary Geoffrey Howe, who had
already been extremely critical of the developing text of her speech. Thatcher's
position on the European issue now crystallised, and Brussels assumed the
central role in her downfall. After all, the EU was beginning to determine the
texture of British political life.

Immediately following Thatcher's Bruges speech however, Bill Cash founded
the Friends of Bruges, an informal grouping in the House to promote the
anti-federalist message of the speech inside Parliament, and at the end of 1989
the group were elected officers of the Conservative Backbench Committee
on European Affairs, with Bill as Chairman. While Labour was now sliding
into Europeanism with relatively little internal protest, concern was growing
throughout the Conservative Party about the direction in which the EC
was heading. This was borne out by their re-election after Mrs Thatcher's
resignation in November 1990. After being appointed to Douglas Hurd's
Manifesto Committee, he invited Bill to write the paper on the future of
Britain and Europe.

In one of many meetings with Margaret Thatcher on the European issue,
in mid-summer 1990, just before her resignation, Bill was invited to lunch
at Number 10, to what he thought would be beer and sandwiches. She
met him on his own in the drawing room – with her Private Secretary
Charles Powell sitting at the far end of the room, on a window seat. No beer.
No sandwiches. 'Let us go in for lunch', she said. Following her through
corridors as she bustled along in a business-like manner, she opened a door
and to Bill's astonishment, there around the lunch table were many if not
most of the Cabinet. She had not said that this was about to happen. They
walked into the room, and she said 'Bill, you will sit next to me'. They
sat down. Geoffrey Howe was immediately opposite. Looking at him and
turning to Bill, she said, 'today we are speaking about Europe'. 'Bill', she
said, 'what do you feel about Europe?' (not 'think'). His immediate reply
was 'Prime Minister, I think your task is more difficult than Churchill's'. She

responded: 'Bill you will have to explain that. Geoffrey did you hear what he said?' 'Prime Minister', Bill said, 'Churchill was faced with bombs and aircraft – you are faced with pieces of paper'. The conversation continued, with Margaret Thatcher occasionally and robustly responding to Geoffrey Howe's increasingly vain attempts to hold his own. This was part of a series of events which ultimately led to Geoffrey Howe's resignation speech.

In the European elections of summer 1989, Labour gained their first national victory of any kind over the Tories since 1974, as the electorate voted largely on domestic concerns, unsure of what their votes would mean in Brussels. But in this momentous year there had quietly crystallised a new British politics.

**

Chancellor Nigel Lawson was now growing more agitated about the ERM. It is clear from his speeches that by 1989 he had decided the mechanism was simply an agreement between nations, unlike a single currency which meant losing sovereignty. On 25th January 1989, Lawson told an audience at Chatham House that while monetary union meant handing over control over key economic decisions to a European central bank, ERM was 'an agreement between sovereign states', not the first step towards monetary union his European colleagues knew it to be.[ccci] The disagreement in Downing Street was now becoming public knowledge.

In April 1989, Jacques Delors presented a new report on monetary union, suggesting this would eventually become the irrevocable commitment of the Community,[cccii] and recommended proceeding in three main stages towards its achievement. The first would see all Community countries signing up to the ERM. The second would involve the creation of the institutions necessary to build the currency, including a central bank. The third stage required fixing exchange rates, as this central bank took over monetary policy.

Dutch PM and federalist Ruud Lubbers now gave Lawson and Howe a new argument, that by joining the ERM Britain would actually strengthen its case against the aims of Delors' report.[ccciii] Geoffrey Howe's Foreign Office soon concurred with Lubbers, and at dinner at Chequers, Chancellor Lawson informed the PM that unless she gave way and agreed to join the ERM, he would resign with Geoffrey Howe's support.

On 26th June 1989, the very day after Lawson and Howe told the premier of their demands, Thatcher flew to Madrid for another European Council.

Here, buoyed by his visit to Bournemouth, Delors was rallying support for his social charter on workers' rights and health and safety at work. To the surprise of the gathering, Thatcher did as she had been forced to by Lawson and Howe, and announced to the Council 'the United Kingdom's intention to join the ERM'.[cciv] The Prime Minister must have known she was trapped, and made no commitment on the timing of the deal.

Much else was moving that autumn. As Mitterrand tried to set a date for an Inter-Governmental Conference on economic and monetary union, the grip of Communism in Eastern Europe, which had driven European integration in the days of Jack and Mac, began to shake.

In London, Thatcher attempted to deal with Howe by demoting him to Leader of the House, replacing him with a little-known social security minister named John Major. British interest rates reached 15 percent, a record high, as the pound tracked a *Bundesbank* rate rise.[ccv] Under fire from both the press and Number 10 advisers, Lawson resigned on 26th October, meaning another promotion for Major, who moved to Number 11. He was replaced as Foreign Secretary by the patrician Europhile Douglas Hurd.

As the Soviet reformist Mikhail Gorbachev visited Bonn in June 1989, two of Helmut Kohl's senior advisors, Michael Mertes and Norbert Prill, described the European 'centre of gravity', which will replace the 'confusing diversity of Europe's overlapping structures… with a single consistent structure': in other words a 'European federal state' with 'the United States of Europe' as the 'centrepiece'. The document added that 'Anyone who questions this consensus that has existed for decades is striking at the very foundations of democracy and the rule of law in Europe'.[ccvi]

As the 1990s began, Kohl and Mitterrand called for 'political union' in tandem with monetary union. They suggested this should take effect from 1st January 1993, as well as a common foreign policy. To make a point, their first such act was a joint letter to the new President of Lithuania, urging him to suspend his country's declaration of independence and ease Community talks with Moscow for 'the good of Europe'.[ccvii]

By now all the mainstream broadsheets were pushing for ERM, and Thatcher was isolated. An official rate had to be set, and Britain would join at DM2.95 to the pound. Perversely, Delors was furious.[ccviii] He wanted Thatcher out of power as soon as practicable, and joining the ERM risked giving her a reprieve.

At the next European Council in Rome in October 1990, Delors proposed that the Community act in unison to block independence from the Soviets for the Baltic States and eleven other countries. Thatcher insisted this be ignored. France and Germany next proposed that monetary union 'stage two' should begin at the turn of 1994: supposedly a compromise, as this was a year later than formerly suggested.[cccix] The others agreed, but Thatcher could not. Yet again, with the leaders of Europe against her and the Left of the British press denouncing her 'xenophobic' attitude, the premier stood alone. A French civil servant debriefed his staff on the outcome of the meeting. One asked whether he regarded it as a failure. Not at all, he replied,

> '…an outstanding success, since [it] re-established an eleven-to-one situation in the Community and destabilised Thatcher at home.' [cccx]

He was right. On 13th November 1990, Howe resigned as Leader of the House, and before his Prime Minister and a packed Commons declared:

> 'I have done what I believe to be right for my party and my country. The time has now come for others to consider their own response to the tragic conflict of loyalties with which I myself wrestled for perhaps too long.'

He added a metaphor which has remained embedded in the national memory: 'It is rather like sending your opening batsmen to the crease, only for them to find, as the first balls are being bowled, that their bats have been broken before the game by the team captain'. But closer examination of the unusually long resignation statement shows the inaccuracy, in retrospect, of his European predictions. As the BBC settled happily on a story of 'Tory disunity', Michael Heseltine (the former defence secretary who had left the cabinet three years before to wait in the wings) took his cue, launching a leadership bid almost immediately. Thatcher beat him by 204 votes to 185 in the first round. But as Major would write in his memoirs, an empress was falling. On 22nd November 1990, Margaret Thatcher resigned. Boris Johnson, then 26-years-old, would recall:

> 'There is no need to rehearse the steps of matricide. Howe pounced, Heseltine did his stuff. After it was all over, my wife, Marina, claimed she came upon me, stumbling down a street in Brussels, tears in my eyes, and claiming that it was as if someone had shot Nanny.'

Not someone, as much as something. Through its supporters in Britain's cabinet, an emerging foreign super-state had toppled Britain's most successful post-war Premier. The Tories could not bring themselves to elect Heseltine, the Casca who had struck the first blow, and chose John Major instead. Major took Norman Lamont as his Chancellor.[20] As John Major entered Number 10, so arrived the moment Jacques Delors, still president of the Commission, had waited for.

By the time the new PM arrived in the Dutch city of Maastricht in 1991 for his first Inter-Governmental Conference as leader, Delors had made sure to have a new draft treaty ready. Putting forth proposals to introduce a single currency, we can assume Jacques Delors was not completely surprised at Major's irritation – the new PM also being occupied with British preparations for war in the Gulf. But Delors had no intention of seeing his plans halted by the Brits, and informed the new premier darkly: 'If we have to provoke another crisis, we will'.[cccxi]

The gathering in Maastricht would transform the Community into a *European Union*, the second phase of Spinelli's EU plan. Major knew he was in trouble even before Maastricht got underway. He also understood that giving away too little on the continent would make his working life as a member of the new European elite unbearable.

The meeting began, as predicted, with various speeches of high sentiment for a single currency. Belgian PM Wilfred Martens then launched a more ambitious tactical offensive, speaking of a union defence policy that would ban national vetoes, in other words potentially rid nations of their own independent military. Major spoke against it of course, but he also knew that to the Europeanist tacticians like Martens, by taking a 'negative' position he would now be expected to make 'concessions'. These would include large extensions of so-called 'cooperation' in the area now called Justice and 'Home' Affairs, and extensions to majority voting. This meant more transfers of power.

Brussels' counter-attack constituted little less than an attempt to amalgamate Europe. With Major wrong-footed, the Commission succeeded in taking still more 'competences' under its growing wingspan. These included social policy, economic guidelines, consumer protection, telecommunications, energy, transport, education, public health, vocational training and culture. A new *Committee of the Regions* would consist of a representative from

---

[20]Although a Cambridge contemporary of Michael Howard and Kenneth Clarke, Lamont had been born in the Shetlands, then raised in the fishing port of Grimsby.

each of the new 111 'regions of the Community', which would have to be consulted on new legislation, promoting regional identity and further emasculating national capitals. Although none had been consulted, every individual in every member state was about to become a 'citizen' of Europe, allowed to vote or stand in European or local elections even outside their own country. The power of the European Court of Justice would now loom even larger over the member states, with the power to impose hefty fines on any government that failed to impose its rulings on their people.

The Draft Treaty that explained the thinking of the Intergovernmental Conferences in May 1991 was only made available to the House of Commons at 1.30pm on 26th June, the very day it was to be debated. Mrs Thatcher was given no copy of this document beforehand (although it was made available to Ministers well in advance.)[cccxii]

All this would soon create the largest and quickest increase in regulation that history has ever seen, and by the end of the decade Europe's budget would rise to £64 billion. Major and Hurd seem to have made no effort to inform the British people what they had agreed to in their name, and it would be some months before Delors even released the full treaty in print.

When Brussels released the Maastricht Treaty it would be made almost totally incomprehensible to all but the most seasoned Brussels-hands. Paragraph upon paragraph were marked only as 'amendments' to the old treaties,[cccxii] making no sense unless constantly checked against earlier texts in full. Maastricht gave Europe a single currency schedule. It massively expanded the EU's reach, allowing it to intervene in huge areas that had once been the birthright of each nation state, and build or block transport systems and energy networks that crossed national borders, the very arteries of national economies. The EU gave itself a guiding role in developing foreign policy, justice and home affairs.[cccxiv] Major now signed us up and flew home.

A REBELLION LIKE NO OTHER

Bill Cash received a copy of the Maastricht Treaty as he was boarding a flight to meet Vaclav Klaus, first Prime Minister of the Czech Republic. Understanding the Treaty was essentially the provision for European Government, he decided he would rebel against it.

The HQ of the rebellion would be 17 Great College Street, a beautiful 18th century house, once the home of the poet Shelley. This was the nearest house to the House of Commons, near The Green and overlooking the Abbey Gardens. Bill knew the allies would need a Headquarters, so rang Alistair McAlpine as he was about to board a plane for Italy. 'You can move in at once' he said. Indeed, Margaret Thatcher had just left No 17, where she had lived for some time after her political assassination.

Within a few days, banks of photocopiers, computers, telephones and other equipment were being carried into the oak panelled rooms and placed among the antique furniture and comfortable sofas. Bevvies of keen volunteers occupied all corners of the four floor house, as work began on opposing the Maastricht Treaty.

They moved in on November 26th 1992; with the committee proceedings on the Bill beginning on 1st December, work had to begin at once. Bill had drafted hundreds of amendments in his own name and had solid support for them from other colleagues. The objective was to force the Government to reply to their reasoned arguments as to why the Maastricht Treaty should not go through. The vast number of amendments meant they had to be grouped into subject matter, the objective being steadily to put the Government to the sword, continuing day in day out, and often into the deep recesses of the night.

Every Member of Parliament was given a briefing paper on every amendment, so that piles of these briefing papers were taken over to the House of Commons every day. The moment the Whips saw the efficiency of the operation they realised that there was nothing they could do to stop this relentless campaign, argued clause by clause, page by page, and obstructing the Treaty at every turn. The Government simply could not cope. The Labour Party commissioned Geoff Hoon, then a newly elected MP, to shadow Bill Cash's amendments almost word for word, but not precisely, then pretended they were voting on their own amendments to justify their being in the same lobbies as the Maastricht rebels (even though the amendments were in Bill's name). On the first vote in the Committee Stage, Leader of the Opposition John Smith approached Bill, telling him 'We'll see by the end of all this whether you're a man or a mouse'. In the last vote, before the Confidence Motion, having voted against the Government more than anyone else except Nick Winterton – 47 times on a 3-line Whip – he said to Bill as they went through the Lobby that night, 'Now I know you're not a mouse.'

All this was accompanied by perpetual streams of interviews and soundbytes (Tony Benn had even recovered from his aversion to sharing platforms with Conservatives, describing Bill Cash as 'my very dear friend'). Keen for the number of rebels not to grow, the Whips soon began putting pressure on MPs' constituency chairmen, threatening deselection. Teresa Gorman later gave several accounts of this:

> 'At lunchtime I bumped into Walter Sweeney, who was almost in tears after his run-in with the Chief Whip the day before... He has been subjected to considerable pressure from some people in his constituency which he had resisted. Then this morning he received a fax from the chairman of his association ordering him – ordering, mind – to vote with the Government. 'They are hinting that they will de-select me if I don't vote for the Government in the lobby tonight', he said. He was visibly shaken. 'Apparently someone from Central Office has been down there to organize this.'

> 'You mean Central Office is leaning on party chairmen?' I was astounded. 'I believe so, yes', he said, in his quiet, measured way. 'Other members have received similar 'advice' in phone calls from their constituency offices.'[cccxv] ...As tension built up, nowhere was safe: the Whips were everywhere – even in the lavatories. A story was sweeping Westminster that when it came time for the vote, heavy-weight David Lightbown who has a walk like a bull elephant – his head and body roll into the room ahead of the rest of him – trapped a luckless Euro-rebel in the lavatory.'[cccxvi]

Much of the press were intrigued. This was a rebellion like no other before it, and Major's 'House of Horror' was becoming a new focal point of political life, with journalists, friends, businessmen, ambassadors, MPS and Lords all coming to see what was happening. Bill would meet them in the sumptuous sitting room upstairs, where countless bottles of wine were consumed. The atmosphere was electric, and entertaining. William Sitwell was the Chief of Staff, Ian Milne was Head of Research with legal assistance from Martin Howe, David Carlisle and others. William Sitwell had left a beach in Corfu at a moment's notice and provided the back up as a young aide-de-camp. With numerous parties, unlike the fear that typified the government operation, and days full of laughter, Bill's wife Biddy Cash kept a watchful eye on the media and MPs flowing in and out all day long.

The Maastricht Pie Parties became a regular feature (both pie and party featuring on *Newsnight*). A butcher from Eccleshall in Staffordshire named Brian Seddon made huge meat pies embossed with a massive 'M' on their pastry lids, brought down for the delighted guests to become pivotal to the enjoyment of the evening. At one party Bill noticed a dishevelled individual carrying a backpack into the room, only to discover he was one of the major donors.

Bill soon realised the absolute necessity of having a Referendum Campaign to petition Parliament. Time was short, and this was planned like the military operation it indeed became: Bill put a General in charge, indeed the former Commandant General of the Marines, Sir Martin Garrod. He worked with the highly experienced Russell Lewis, former editor of the *Daily Mail* and director of the IEA, and the young Ashley Grey in charge of media operations. This had to be all-party, from the Lords and Commons, so apart from Margaret Thatcher and Lord Stoddart in the Lords, Bill persuaded the Duke of Devonshire as a cross-bencher to join them as joint Patrons. From the Commons Bill persuaded Labour's Bryan Gould and the Liberal's Nick Harvey to join. The campaign became highly efficient, with mass advertising in the press, a national poster campaign and activities in every part of the population. Bill soon spoke to a massive rally of Sikhs in West Bromwich, attended by thousands. In London, the taxi drivers were on side, as were bikers throughout the UK. An organisation called Dial for Democracy was established, with a dipping headlight campaign for people to encourage each other throughout the country.

The Prime Minister and Government were getting more and more angry, with a great deal of bullying and intimidation. Some were in tears even before some votes took place. David Lightbown, also a Staffordshire MP, dared to tell Bill that it was his intention to encase him in concrete and drop him from the very end of a very long pier. He didn't reckon with the furious response he received, at the end of which he never dared confront him again.

Come the vital vote on the Social Chapter – which was tied – there was a huge row. The team had calculated through their whips, Christopher Gill, Roger Knapman and James Cran, how tight the vote would be. Bill Walker, the Scots Conservative MP for Tayside North, who was extremely ill at the time, insisted on taking the train from Scotland despite being offered a helicopter, arriving at 17 Great College Street where he was received by Biddy Cash, who kept him hidden until the vote was called. He was then helped over to the House, to John Wilkinson, who with a protective arm around him walked him through the lobbies.

The House procedure required two votes at the end of the debate, so the rebels would be asked to vote yes or no on Labour's amendment 'that this House rejects the Government's proposal to omit the Social Chapter from the Maastricht Treaty'. The second vote was on the main motion, the Government's proposal to accept Maastricht bar the social chapter. Some Conservative MPs would not vote for the Labour amendment – afraid it would look like they supported the social chapter – the core rebels on the other hand knew it was their opportunity to stop Maastricht altogether. They knew the vote on the amendment would be extremely close.

As the division bell rang Bill Walker hurried through the Central Lobby, where Whip Greg Knight, at six feet three, blocked his path. After claiming that he was 'paired' with an opposing MP, so shouldn't vote, Knight eventually moved away (the rebels never found out how he had known Bill Walker would be in the Central Lobby at that moment). Other members rushed in through the exit door before it was closed. Rebel Members Christopher Gill and Teresa Gorman covered the Aye and No lobbies to count their votes. One Labour MP taunted Teresa Gorman – 'It isn't easy for a right-winger to vote for the social chapter'. She replied, 'I'm voting to dump this wretched Bill. And if your party had any sense they would too... It was a bad day for the Labour Party when Neil Kinnock did his U-turn'.[cccvii]

As the counting continued there was still no sign of Bill Walker. As Nick Budgen told Teresa: 'It looks good. I think we've won'. Bob Hughes, another Government Whip who was often reprimanded by the Speaker for shouting abuse at the Labour benches, grabbed her arm. 'You ****s', he said, 'You ****ing little ****'. After Speaker Betty Boothroyd eventually calmed the House, the vote was read. 'The Ayes to the right, 317, the Noes to the left, 317'. When the huge cheer died down, Boothroyd spoke once more. 'The numbers being equal, it is my duty to cast my vote. It is not the function of the chair to create a majority on a policy issue where no majority exists amongst the rest of the House. In accordance with precedent I therefore cast my vote with the Noes'. Only the Speaker had saved Major. But the second vote was decisive. 'Ayes to the right, 316, Noes to the left, 324.'[cccxviii] The Government had lost. John Major had failed to ratify the treaty he thought would be his epitaph.

But as the rebels began to go home for the night, Major convened an emergency meeting in his Westminster room. The next morning, with his Foreign Secretary Douglas Hurd and Chancellor Kenneth Clarke, he would tell the Commons he would fight to impose the treaty all over again. That evening, Number 10 announced that a new vote on the treaty would also be a confidence motion in the Government. Losing would see Major resign and call a general election. Many rebel MPs knew they would lose their seats. Major was prepared to push the treaty through at any price.^{ccxix}

At the end of this extraordinary saga and historical rebellion – indeed what lies at the heart of the present referendum – is that it was the Maastricht Treaty which created the government of Europe through the EU. This is still embedded in the same Treaties on which the question today depends – remain or leave? The subsequent treaties up to Lisbon were all passed by Labour under Tony Blair and Gordon Brown, building the vast legal edifice, taking Britain further and deeper into European integration. But the essential foundation of 'European Government', with all its trappings, was the Maastricht Treaty.

In his book *Against a Federal Europe*, published at the time of the Maastricht rebellion, Bill predicted that this would culminate in protests and riots on the continent, massive unemployment and waves of immigration from central and Eastern Europe. This was ridiculed by much of the mainstream press at the time. In 1993, he wrote that 'this *Brave New Europe*, this undemocratic, authoritarian and social European Community' would, under Maastricht, undermine the Community, 'and therefore, more dangerously, Europe as a whole'. When monetary union collapsed, there would be 'massive political and commercial instability throughout Europe', and that 'EMU will bring massive unemployment. With this will come the increased likelihood of strikes and civil disorder, but with less and less political accountability – as the leaders of Europe, especially those of the European Economic Area, withdraw from their responsibilities and hand over more decisions to unelected bankers and officials… the neutering, under Maastricht, gathers pace, so the paralysis of the real Europe will give way to the prospect of the collapse of the rule of law, compounded by waves of immigration… recession and lawlessness.'^{ccxx}

In 1995, Margaret Thatcher was invited to the Stafford constituency, and told the crowd – 'The question is often asked, 'Can one member in Parliament make a difference?' Oh, yes, he can. It has happened through history. There have been some famous names and it all seems to me that Bill is very much like Hampden of the Ship Money, who made a tremendous difference to our whole future. Bill has made tremendous difference to the whole future debate on Europe by relentlessly analysing the real issues, not merely the propaganda, not merely the false, shallow assessments – assertions – that are put about, but in fact steadily analysing the things, analysing what we have done for Europe, analysing what it would mean to us, and he has made a tremendous difference and I am one of his greatest fans.'

BRUSSELS DISMANTLES A PRIME MINISTER

Thatcher at the time described the treaty as a 'recipe for national suicide'. But Major and Hurd may never have known what they were pushing on Parliament. On 7th February 1992, after signing the Treaty of Maastricht that created the European Union, our own Foreign Secretary Douglas Hurd said simply 'now we've signed it, we'd better read it'.ccxxi This was how Britain's leaders signed their country into the European state.

The Maastricht Treaty had another, almost unknown result. After a German newspaper began a campaign to 'save the D-Mark', a German former EC employee, afraid that the EC was encroaching on Germany's affairs, took the German government to Germany's constitutional court on the grounds that the treaty infringed German sovereignty. The court ruled that it did not – but it also proclaimed itself responsible for the interpretation of basic rights in Germany, and for interpreting the terms in which the treaty was binding. This was contrary to the rules that Maastricht sets for every other country, that European law is supreme. Germany had given itself a safety valve, in effect demonstrating that it had the power to exempt itself from the finality of Brussels' rule. But Brussels did not protest.ccxxii

In the spring, Labour leader Neil Kinnock lost a second general election, and was replaced by John Smith. Across the North Sea in Denmark, the treaty was not done yet. In a referendum on 2nd June 1992, against the advice of all their major parties and the far better funded 'Yes' campaign, 50.7 percent of the Danes rejected Maastricht. Like Hurd, the Danish Foreign Minister had helped the 'No' cause by admitting that even he couldn't understand what he had signed. Denmark's five million people just said no, and sent shock waves across Europe. Soon the threats began.

Mitterrand, unpopular at home, saw a high-risk opportunity, a referendum that, in France, he could win. But having rejected Maastricht once, the Danes were given another chance to give Brussels the correct answer. To achieve this, it was arranged for their new Prime Minister Poul Nyrup Rasmussen to 'declare to his people' that despite their dark suspicions their new union citizenship did not 'in any way take the place of national citizenship', and that Danes need not be involved in any future common defence policy.[cccxxiii] Yet Nyrup Rasmussen had not been PM when the treaty was being negotiated: that had been his predecessor Poul Schlüter. The treaty did not guarantee these things (although Denmark was given the right to notify Brussels should it not wish to join the single currency). Many Danes reminded their government that the constitution forbade double voting on one referendum. They were ignored, and on 18th May a 57 percent vote in favour was followed by the worst peacetime riots the country has ever seen.[cccxxiv]

At the end of all this, the lead German negotiator at Maastricht said simply: 'there is no alternative to European integration. Any other choice could cause the other countries of the continent, one day, to unite against us'.[cccxxv] This is perhaps the simplest insight into why German European policy has purpose, while Britain's has remained on the back foot. Shortly afterwards, Germany put up its interest rates to cool the post-unification boom, trapping Major and his Chancellor Norman Lamont. Their response could have been to raise Britain's interest rates to strengthen the pound, but with Britain's economy in recession and fearing another rise in mortgage rates which would infuriate homeowners, Lamont had no choice but to drop rates, producing an instant shock in the markets. Skies darkened.

As they met, French, British and Italian finance ministers put the representatives of Germany's Bundesbank under pressure, pleading for a cut in German interest rates. The request was sternly refused. Public knowledge of this would have hinted to the French that their President had lost prestige on the continent, at which point another country might have given Maastricht the wrong answer. For the leaders this was unthinkable, so they simply declared that it was the Bundesbank that had agreed it would not raise its rates. Granted a huge free PR blitz by Brussels, Mitterrand won the referendum with just 51.05 percent of the vote. It is widely suspected that the balance was tipped with a blatant bribe in the form of promising the citizens of French overseas territories subsidised flights to France,[cccxxvi] and that French colonies voted France in.

Helmut Kohl had another hand to play. On 11th September 1992, a Friday, Kohl travelled secretly to the Bundesbank. Against all the rules he had agreed for the ERM, in a move to protect the Franc he struck a deal that left the other currencies exposed.[cccxxvii] Now Britain was isolated. On the following Tuesday, the pound crashed almost beneath the ERM floor, finishing at its lowest point since Lawson and Howe had forced Thatcher to sign sterling up. Traders in New York smelled blood, and as London markets closed and night fell over Britain, the pound plummeted below its permitted limit.

Sticking to the ERM's rules, Lamont had only one option left, and he now put interest rates up to 12 percent. This had no effect. At two o'clock the next afternoon he raised them again to 15 percent, and at that point it became obvious to world markets that the government had no more shots in the locker (selling duly surged, and much has been made since of the money speculators made out of the collapse, but by undermining the irrational parities they reversed the decline of the British economy, which would have been impossible under a single currency)[cccxxviii]. Lamont was left with no choice but to remove the pound from the ERM, and he was pilloried. Labour grabbed a lead in the polls and, save for a three week blip, they would keep it until 1997. Labour rejoiced and Lamont fell, but few understood the bind Europe's new economic rules had put him in. In 1990, just after Britain joined the ERM, *The Financial Times* economics correspondent Samuel Brittan wrote: 'Will British monetary policy be made in Frankfurt – and eventually perhaps in Berlin? I very much hope so.'[cccxxix] But Brussels was now taking apart another British government.

On 12th May 1994, Labour party leader John Smith died. The Euro-election campaigns being delayed, but when they came the Conservative share of the vote crashed to 27.8 percent, the Tories' worst in any nationwide election in the entire century. Britain once again saw Europe's lowest turnout at 36.1 percent. With Jacques Delors due to retire at the end of 1994, Major would spend a good deal of energy in June embroiled in negotiations over his successor, eventually being manoeuvred into agreeing on another federalist Jacques, this time Luxembourg's PM Jacques Santer.

Meanwhile two other leading federalists, German Karl Lamers (a *Bundestag* member from south Germany and Kohl's foreign affairs spokesman) and Wolfgang Schäuble (then assumed to be Kohl's likely successor), were making plans for the autumn. The two men – from the CDU mainstream – released a policy paper named *Reflections on European Policy* warning that despite all the events of the decade, the new EU was still at risk of being watered down to an economic association. The two Germans put forward a solution to this threat: a 'constitution-like document which delimits the competences of the European Union... based on the model of a federal state structure'. It recommended: 'the European Parliament would progressively develop into a legislature with the same rights as the Council; the Council, in addition to other tasks primarily in the inter-governmental sphere, would take on the duties of a second chamber, i.e. of a chamber of states; and the Commission would assume the characteristics of a European government'. It added the Germany and her allies 'should not be blocked by the vetoes of other members'. 'Monetary Union', wrote Lamers and Schäuble, 'is the hard core of Political Union'.

Two years later, frustrated at the speed of integration, the Commission would respond in kind. A constitution could build the appropriate identity, it believed, ridding Europe of national vetoes once and for all, so the Union could avoid 'stagnation'. Almost unnoticed in Britain, the constitution idea was rolling again.

John Major's position was now almost untenable. On 11ᵗʰ June 1995, telling his backbenchers to 'put up or shut up', he resigned as leader of the Conservative Party. Only one stood against him: John Redwood. Many Tories knew they had been misled about Maastricht, but on 4ᵗʰ July Redwood took just a quarter of the vote. With an extended lease on Number 10, Major trotted off to meet the new French president Jacques Chirac at the European Council meeting in Cannes. The big agreement to emerge from the Cote d'Azure would be a French initiative to create 'Europol', a Euro-FBI which had begun life as a small office called the European Drugs Intelligence Unit. In two years it had been pumped with a £2.8 million budget and dozens of staff.ᶜᶜˣˣˣ By 2010 a Union plan would exist for European monitoring of a list of national terror targets (which may require a European anti-terror force). Cannes saw the start of a federal *gendarmerie*.

For Major however, beating Redwood hadn't silenced the rebels. Indeed the PM was now beset on all sides. Major had taken to calling the Eurosceptic rebels 'bastards', suggesting he was 'going to flipping crucify them'. But as Major launched a new white paper in the Commons in the spring of 1996, the green benches' Foreign Affairs Committee told the PM his optimistic, limited view of the EU's ambitions was simply 'not valid'ᶜᶜᶜˣˣˣⁱ. The white paper meekly urged Europe to contribute more to the costs of security, but also stated that British membership of the EU was now 'irrevocable'. Given three hours' Commons debating time, and noting the paper's claim that it was crucial 'that national parliaments remain the central focus of democratic legitimacy', even Edward Heath would ask, 'three hours in which to discuss a White Paper containing ten vital subjects... is 'democratic legitimacy' what we have this evening?'[cccxxxii]

The general election approached, and another government would be taken apart by Brussels. Chancellor Ken Clarke informed the Eurosceptic Home Secretary Michael Howard that his views amounted to 'paranoid nonsense'. On Radio 4's *Today* programme early in 1997, Malcolm Rifkind declared himself against a single currency, a comment which was followed by a rebuke from Heseltine, another from Ken Clarke and a clarification from Major.[cccxxxiii]

The election too was to be quite extraordinary. The British economy now seemed healthier than almost any EU counterpart, but Major's government had never been able to scrub out the stain of the ERM. But instead it was 'Tory sleaze' that became a watchword Fleet Street knew was guaranteed to shift copy. On election day, after a turn in the garden in his Cambridgeshire constituency of Huntingdon with his friend Jeffrey Archer, Major reflected:

> 'I looked at where we could plant more fruit trees by taking out the venerable old unpruned apples. A rambling rose was needed up against the wall, and there was space around the edge of the garden for more trees and new beds. The lime trees were in leaf, the Virginia creeper was opening, the wisteria was in bloom... The sun had gone down. I was refreshed and ready for the slaughter.'

Slaughter it was. In an election worthy of Hieronymus Bosch, the quirks of our electoral system gave Labour 63 percent of the seats on 43 percent of the vote, a landslide. On 2nd May 1997, Tony Blair kissed hands, became prime minister, and entered the European garden of earthly delights.

PART THREE
GERMAN HEGEMONY

The Federal Republic will ultimately be the country
which profits most from European unity,
even if this is not immediately visible.

Johann Wilhelm Gaddun,
Vice President of the Bundesbank, 25th June 1998

7.

POST-DEMOCRATIC AGE 1997 -

ZEAL OF THE CONVERTS: NEW LABOUR IN BRUSSELS

Today's ministers are a bit like actors in a huge, dark theatre, initially delighted at the absence of heckling or booing, but beginning uneasily to ask themselves whether anyone is still watching.

Andrew Marr, 1999

Shock and awe. Blair came to power in 1997 with an army of 418 MPs, a majority of 179. His new MPs would soon turn out to have trouble discerning the difference between loyalty and gulled subservience, as the parliamentary Labour party became the most politically correct cohort of MPs in British history.

New chancellor Gordon Brown's very first pronouncement was on the future of the Bank of England, which would be overtly politically independent, free to set interest rates without deferring to government. Few in our press noted that although he had set the Bank free of Whitehall, he had pushed it closer to Brussels.[cccxxxiv] This was a treaty obligation set out in Article 109e(5) of Maastricht, which stated:

> 'Each Member State shall, as appropriate, start the process leading to the independence of its central bank.'

As Brown took control of the domestic agenda, Blair paraded abroad, and at the Amsterdam summit Blair told them he wanted to retain frontier controls, opposed European control of defence, and stressed that enhanced cooperation should only happen given unanimous agreement between the member states. Blair also wanted a limit to the number of foreign boats fishing British waters.

What Blair got in Amsterdam was the splicing of the Social Chapter into Britain's obligations (imposing myriad employment 'rights' for employers to keep up with, and limits to legal working time), the abolition of the national veto in a full sixteen further areas of policy (including employment, social exclusion and equal opportunities[cccxxxv]) then gave concessions on defence integration into the EU. He managed an opt-out of the Schengen agreement that abolished intra-EU border controls, but secured no treaty change on fishing (although he did get a small concession on landing 50 percent of a boat's catch locally, which he hyped).[cccxxxvi] Amsterdam also created the position of *High Representative for the Common Foreign and Security Policy*, a foreign minister in all but name, designed to take responsibility gradually from national foreign ministers. The EU also took over members' asylum policies and discrimination laws.[cccxxxvii] Most Britons believed they had been given an opt-out from the Working Time Directive, which mandated a maximum 48-hour working week, but the ECJ soon started imposing it anyway (many doctors now start work with less than half the hours of real life experience they once had).

Demonstrators huddled in front of Amsterdam's Royal Palace in the cold early hours of 2nd October 1997. None noticed when security men rushed through a door at the back of the palace, carrying a number of sealed aluminium canisters which they threw into a security van. These contained the Treaty of Amsterdam. Escorted by police, the van careered through the backstreets in the direction of Brussels[cccxxxviii]. Thus was the treaty, the quintessence of the Union, given to Europe. But Tony Blair had won a nice bicycle race, and so was Amsterdam remembered. Back home on 27th October, Brown would announce to MPs his own Famous Five, the economic tests that must be met before Britain would join the single currency (although Ed Balls would later admit that Brown 'never really was a Eurosceptic – this was a game'[cccxxxix]).

As Britain's Tories began to reawaken, their new leader William Hague, whose leadership was secured by virtue of Margaret Thatcher's support following his last minute article in Bill Cash's *European Journal* opposing the single currency in principle, announced that he also opposed the Amsterdam Treaty. So a new group of rebels emerged. Just like the Eurosceptics they had once berated for disloyalty, Ken Clarke, Michael Heseltine, and the new father of the house Edward Heath began agitating in the shadows.

In the twilight of the millennium, as overseer of 'the Regions', the Deputy Prime Minister John Prescott now pushed through a huge mass of legislation to devolve Britain's government. With the return of local government to London (which had been the only non-self-governing capital in the free world), Labour created a tranche of assemblies for Northern Ireland, Wales and Scotland. But for its eight 'Regions' – as described by Brussels – England got quangos called *regional development agencies*. Prescott said grandly:

> 'If you look at Newcastle or Gateshead, even over twenty years, even with the previous administration, it has moved quite remarkably in transforming itself... In a sense, what we do with the regional development agencies is to give them resources to look at the deficiencies in the economy in the regional areas, so they can address themselves to that... In the north east, there, they have had quite a bit of government offices moving in.'

What Prescott didn't mention was that the programme was designed to move Britain further away from Britain's city and county-based local government that once thrived because it matched local identities. Instead the European model 'regions', to which people had little attachment, were being strengthened. In the 'North West' for example, the shared identity of Cumbrians with the people of Cheshire is negligible. When Prescott made the mistake of holding a pilot referendum, the people of 'North East' made the point clear. As Gordon Brown would fail to mention in his lament to 'the Balkanisation of Britain', while one union in Europe was growing in strength, his own government was putting British identity through a blender.

One reaction the Europeanising process has provoked in our central government in Britain is to suck power upwards from local government. The people who have lost power are us. In Britain, this is the logic of European integration. This has been underway since the 1970s, under governments of Left and Right.

In 1969, staff at the Royal Commission on Local Government came up with something called the 'Marbella test'.[cccd] On a beach in the Med, one Brit meets another and asks where he's from. If he is from Wales, Scotland, or Northern Ireland, that will be his reply. If he is from England, he will say a city or county: if this is Manchester, Leeds or Birmingham, that's enough. But if he's from somewhere smaller he'll give two answers at once: 'Sidmouth in Devon', or 'Wigton in Cumbria'. So people owe a double allegiance, to their locality, but also to their county.[cccxli] In Germany, Italy and France, the local object of identity is the region. This is because these countries arose by confederating their dukedoms. But in England the local units of identity were always the cities and shires. The English 'regions' recognised by Europe have no real affiliation, but still Cornwall is lumped together with Gloucestershire in the imaginary region of 'South West'.

British governments have slashed and merged rural counties into 'unitary authorities', creating 'metropolitan counties' of the big cities: Berkshire has been abolished, divided into three unitary authorities.[cccxlii] It is joined by creations like *Bath and North East Somerset Unitary Authority*, the *Metropolitan Borough of Barnsley* and the *Metropolitan County of West Midlands*. So Prescott's attempts to push Regional Assemblies were rejected by the citizens of 'North West'; if it doesn't match identity, democracy doesn't work.

For his part, Gordon Brown gave economic independence to the Bank of England as he took it from local councils. Britain's local governments are now financially emasculated, ruled by a Whitehall civil servant army 60,000-strong. [cccxliii] This coordinated force is run from the centre and works with a reserve of management consultants, all operated through the centre's offices in cities like Newcastle, Sheffield and Reading. Local governments have also been denied their traditional role in planning. John Prescott took responsibility for planning, rural conservation and local economic development for Whitehall, giving limited local accountability only to 'Regional Planning Boards' appointed by Whitehall itself. But since most services have to be administered locally, the enormous target burden set by the hyperactive state falls on the local councils. Like some provincial android, a council chief executive can watch on his monitor screen the hundreds of 'performance indicators'[cccxliv] to which the government, since Blair, holds him accountable.

Despite its Orwellian government units with no popular affiliation, government has still not succeeded in breaking the psychological ties between people and place (presumably William Hague, raised in the town of Wath-upon-Dearne, considers himself to come from Yorkshire, not the Metropolitan Borough of Rotherham). But electronic communication is creating ever more distance from the greater central power in Brussels as news of mismanagement spreads faster. Mega-government, not the nation state, is now the real anathema. The same obsession with centralising power has driven Brussels and Whitehall.

The year 1998 brought new leadership to Europe's biggest member state, with a German Chancellor in the shape of Gerhard Schröder. Schröder got to the Chancellery on a flurry of Euroscepticism, calling the euro a 'sickly premature infant',[cccxlv] but once in office he manoeuvred fast to reinforce the Franco-German alliance. In his shadow, Blair met Jacques Chirac in St Malo to propose what Germany couldn't: serious participation at the heart of a European armed force. But Chirac's hostility to US-UK cooperation in Yugoslavia and Iraq continued, so he turned instead to Berlin, launching their *Eurocorps* force, separate from NATO, to begin a new 'European Defence Identity'. The next year Brussels poached Spanish head of NATO Javier Solana as the first 'High Representative'.

Another crisis was now growing in the nerve centre of Europe. Dutch MEP Paul van Buitenen was suspended after blowing the whistle on massive fraud at the highest levels, and the report that followed said it was 'becoming difficult to find anyone who has even the slightest sense of responsibility'. On 16th March 1999, the European Commission resigned.

Then they had lunch, and under the guise of a caretaker Commission, went back to work. For Commission boss Jacques Santer however, this was the end of the road. He was replaced by Romano Prodi later that year, who had faced repeated corruption allegations back in Italy. The Commission hailed him as 'Mr Clean'.[cccxlvi]

BLACKBERRY POLITICS

Make him a Bishop and you will silence him at once.

Lord Chesterfield, 1694-1773

The EU's reach was now visible everywhere. As the ties of national parties beyond their borders had consolidated, between the Single European Act in 1987 and Maastricht in 1992, Labour and the Tories had reversed their positions on Europe. The Tories had expected Brussels to help them create a free market. Now Labour supported what they thought was its social role, after Delors had signed them up as comrades. But the approach was the same: working through Europe was the way to change the national game in your favour while circumventing the electorate. This way the EU is considerably responsible for falling public interest in political parties. In reducing drastically national governments' freedom of movement, Brussels placed a stranglehold on the parties that vie to form them, and the policies they may propose. With policies already fixed in Brussels, little point remains in discussing the alternatives at home; where once was wide-ranging debate, now there are gimmicks. In the 2010 general election, Tory central office emailed its members to tell them they had the backing of the actor who plays Ken Barlow on Coronation Street. Labour fired back with Cheryl Cole. Drained of real authority, gravitas has slipped away from national politics.

The side-effect for Labour in particular was to find they had more in common with their brothers and sisters in Europe than with the parties on the green benches back home. To the Lib Dems Europe is – or perhaps was – something else again. More than simply being pro-Europeans, and lacking until 2010 the national attention that would force them into a more honest political conversation, the Lib Dems spun Europe, constituency by constituency, into whatever it needed to be. In Nick Clegg's constituency of Sheffield Hallam (the city's *Guardianista* academic ghetto), Europe remains the social democratic New Jerusalem. To then MP Andrew George's Cornish constituents in St Ives, many of whom have been relieved of their fishing grounds, Lib Dems tried not to draw too much attention to Brussels. For the Scottish National Party and Plaid Cymru, European partnership helps them pursue the fracture of Britain (Plaid never having advocated an independent Wales until 2000). This is ironic given what 'independence' as small states within the EU would actually mean.

In this gimmick-laden political supermarket a variety of shiny brands disguises a lack of real choice, the product of a deal between Brussels and the parties, or more exactly their leadership. Brussels has given them an elite circle where they can fraternise, but the leaders' networking has emasculated the grassroots party activists whom previous leaders needed constantly to consult. For Labour, this dislocation from its moderate working class activists has allowed a takeover by a new militant tendency from outside the party.

From 1999, the Labour government 'delegated' administration to numerous British quangos administering the laws of powerful European Regulatory Agencies, which for Brussels was a way of increasing Commission governing capacity. This was also a way to preserve the 'credibility of integration',[cccxlvii] keeping governance away from the 'irrational short-termism' of the political sphere, but the widening democratic deficit seems not to have occurred to Blair and his pliant ministers. Part of the Commission's drive in building these agencies was in the name of another intra-Brussels game, its wish to limit the grasp of the European parliament. The European Policy Forum (a Brussels-sponsored think tank on Whitehall) claimed: 'the depoliticisation of many government decisions [is] one of the most promising developments since the last war'.

Britain's condition as a result has been described as 'walking without order'.[cccxlviii] Blair allowed an already weakened democracy to be further 'improved' by this technocratic (and elite) reform. Gaitskell's warning of his country becoming a federal entity like California or Texas was wrong only in so far as the actual process was being done by stealth, and power was not moving to democratic central institutions. This 'depoliticisation' was at the very core of New Labour statecraft, as Secretary of State for Constitutional Affairs Lord Falconer[21] outlined:

> 'What governs our approach is a clear desire to place power where it should be: increasingly not with politicians, but with those best fitted in different ways to deploy it. Interest rates are not set by politicians in the Treasury but by the Bank of England. Minimum wages are not determined by the DTI, but by the Low Pay Commission... This depoliticising of key decision-making is a vital element in bringing power closer to the people.'[cccxlix]

Labour's response to public disengagement was to shrink further the role of democracy, and promote quangos answerable ultimately to Brussels policy. Tony Blair was complicit in creating a European Union patronage system of huge funds and arbitrary powers. The apparent shift in democracy downwards through devolution disguised the real movement of power upwards, and overseas.

In the last summer of the millennium, Britons passed judgement on their new supranational institutions. On 10th June, Labour and the Tories lost seats, UKIP won 12 (up from two), while a new pro-euro Tory faction took not even 1 percent. At 23 percent, the turnout was the lowest ever recorded in a British

---

[21] Charlie Falconer, Blair's flatmate when they were doing barrister pupillage. Falconer supported the abolition of the 1000-year-old position of Lord Chancellor on the grounds that the position of judge and head of the judiciary could not be supported by European convention.

national election. Across the EU, turnout dropped below 50 percent for the first time, but Britain's was lowest of all. In Brussels, the returned Parliament moved into a new £1.05bn complex, and disgraced Jacques Santer sauntered back into the Commission, presented by Prodi as 'Europe's government'.

The Commission now launched proposals to become more governmental yet. Seeking a stronger president and 'majority voting the rule and unanimity the exception', Prodi continued to push a European army, while emphasising the pivotal role of a Commission that 'has always been the driving force for European integration'. The Commission would now bind the nations tighter. At the dawn of 1999, 30,000 people clapped the beginning of economic union in the cold outside the European Central Bank, borrowing the tune to *Land of Hope and Glory* as a backing track.[ccl] From the beginning of 2002, the Euro would reign. And at the end of the millennium, British leaders readied for a new European jamboree in Nice.

The *Charter of Fundamental Rights* prepared for the summit was a re-vamp of the European Convention on Human Rights of 1950. But using human rights nomenclature was also a canny PR move, shifting attention from the new Charter's real content. This promised further 'harmonisation' of the nations, equality between men and women in *all* areas, the universal right of workers to go on strike (including in the armed forces), and a requirement to consult workers on any matter affecting them in the workplace. The EU also wished to grant itself the Mugabe-like ability to suspend *any right of any citizen at any time* if needed, for the 'objectives of general interest being pursued by the union'. While Blair's government played down the aims of the treaty, France, Germany and the Commission heralded the Charter more honestly, as 'the final transformation of European integration from its essentially economic origins to a fully-fledged political union'[cccli].

Treaties were now coming thick and fast, with only four years since the last one in Amsterdam. But after 53 percent of Danes rejected the single currency in a referendum on 28th September, when the Nice summit began on 7th December 2000, Blair was in a shaky position. He began by misinforming his own people, telling them that the Charter of Fundamental Rights would have no legal status, constituting merely a 'declaration'. The European Select Committee disagreed, on the evidence of Richard Plender QC; astonishingly, Blair's Minister for Europe Keith Vaz even described the charter as having no more significance than the *Beano*. As the Nice summit began, he was already preparing to abandon his commitment to twelve British decision-making vetoes, insisting on keeping them in only six areas: tax, borders, social security, EU revenue raising, treaty changes and defence.ccclii

Even this didn't work: news of a 'furious confrontation' between Blair and his host Jacques Chirac was soon coming out of the summit. The French president had produced a draft treaty scrapping national vetoes on social security, tax and asylum. Denmark backed down, agreeing to lose the social security veto. Sweden did so on tax, and Germany on asylum.

In place of equality, the EU would now introduce 'positive' gender discrimination in employment, while the Charter of Fundamental Rights would soon lead to schoolchildren suing their own governments on the grounds that it was their right to wear religious appendages to school, while convicted murderers would sue governments to reduce their sentences. Asylum was reinforced as an 'area of common concern'. The Charter of Fundamental Rights was originally opposed by Blair in 2007, sending Peter Goldsmith to negotiate a protocol to keep us out of the charter. This did not succeed. The European Court is now applying it to the UK, despite Blair having claimed we have a complete opt out. The consequence of this is that it is not just the repeal of the Human Rights Act which is necessary (which Bill Cash introduced as Conservative Party policy as Shadow Attorney General in 2002). The implementation of the Charter is causing severe problems for counter-terrorism, for the prevention of jihadists from returning to the United Kingdom and in myriad other ways.[22]

Britain avoided conceding on tax and social security, but when William Hague later pointed out that the PM had signed away still more British vetoes, Blair described him as an 'idiot'.cccliii These laws arguably devalued human rights in Europe, with a flood of faux-rights sweeping over nation states' judiciaries. The BBC's online news provided the usual take on 'bread and butter issues', claiming vaguely (without even using quotation marks) that:

> 'EU leaders agreed to extend qualified majority voting to at least 23 more decision-making areas, but Mr Blair said many were uncontentious issues – like decisions on the pension

---

[22]The European Scrutiny Committee recommended that the Charter should be excluded from UK law, notwithstanding the European Communities Act 1972, but the coalition government refused to accept this. It was not even part of Cameron's renegotiation package, because it would undermine our subservience to the sovereignty of European law under the European Communities Act itself (Cameron meanwhile still claims we would be more secure by remaining in the European Union).

rights of certain high-ranking Eurocrats. Others were directly in the UK's interests, he said, such as trade in financial services, where majority voting would stop protectionism holding back British business.'

In other words Britain had lost another swathe of democratic control over its own destiny.

BRAVE NEW WORLD: THE CONSTITUTION BEGINS

Of course this is the end of British democracy as we have known it, but if it is properly handled the people won't know what's happened until the end of the century. With any luck, old boy, by then I'll be dead.

Senior British civil servant, 1971[cccliv]

As 2000 began, Chirac proclaimed that across Europe, people 'would be called upon to give their verdict on a text which will then be able to establish the first European Constitution'. Blair told Britain no such thing, because Europe now needed a new depth of political subterfuge. Brussels had driven a wedge between Major and his electorate and threatened to do the same to Blair. Pollster Philip Gould said privately of Blair at the time that 'the Third Way plus Europe are his two big things', and if he didn't hold a referendum on the euro 'he would be a historic failure'.[ccclv]

Europe was also dominating the Prime Minister's time, as even Chris Patten mused: 'he totally neglects places where trade could be big, notably Latin America (especially Brazil). Also... India. This is all inexplicable.'[ccclvi] July 2000 saw the leak of a private memo from Blair, the third in a month, in which he pondered whether his government was seen as 'somehow out of touch with British gut instincts'. A journalist called it:

'...terribly depressing... Some new images of Blair begin to rise in my mind: of a man who is lightweight as a butterfly, skimming along the surface. Suddenly you begin to remember that Blair has not a great deal of weight.'[ccclvii]

Psychologists theorised on radio programmes that without political profundity of his own, he craved the acceptance of other power centres, although they suggested Washington instead of Brussels. Blair would slide out of Downing Street before his electoral chickens could come home to roost, but it seems that by then he had been schooled in the underhand aggression with which Europe was being integrated. Though he didn't tell his country, he presumably knew that decisions over the new constitution for the EU would be taken in a year's time, at Laeken in Belgium.

In the real world outside the leaders' heads, the political tremors were growing. Again the Danes were ordered to the polls, this time in their second referendum on the single currency, and now they faced down their political class to vote No. Apart from a vociferous band of consistent Eurosceptics, Britain's Tories however stayed all but mute on the rapidly developing constitution. Still languishing after their crushing defeat in 1997, on 7th June 2001 the Conservatives lost again, and William Hague resigned. The next day the Irish, who unlike Britain had a referendum on the Nice Treaty, voted No at 53.9 percent, and Irish PM Bertie Ahern announced another referendum immediately, and took extreme measures to ensure that this vote would be reversed. The next month provided an early sign that the peoples of Europe were beginning to think again about the EU, as a *Eurobarometer* opinion poll revealed that just 45 percent of people across the continent believed they had benefited *in any way* from EU membership.[ccdviii]

Back in Brussels, a new white paper would deliver the response to the 'No' votes. This paper began by describing a 'democratic deficit' that could no longer be ignored. At its root, felt Romano Prodi, the problem was the lack of a European 'demos' (an odd conclusion, given that part of the rationale for the EU's establishment was that one already existed). So a demos there would have to be. The white paper sought to build a 'European Identity' that could exist in a 'transnational political space', as the 'representative democracy' of the nations became the new 'consultative democracy'[ccclix] of Europe.

Next, the white paper looked at areas where the Commission could 'extend' its role. These would include spreading still further its network. New offices would include the European Food Standards Authority, the Food and Veterinary Office, the Medicines Evaluation Agency, the Air Safety Agency and the Maritime Safety Agency, among others, all of which are characterised by their undemocratic nature. These would let the Commission coordinate the work of national civil servants, with the bill picked up by nation states' taxpayers. Another aim was to take from nations the role of enforcing EU legislation. This would now happen through various methods, including a European Fisheries Agency with the authority to direct Royal Navy vessels.[cccx] Picking up the tone of the white paper, France and Germany pre-empted the next summit, at Laeken in Belgium, by declaring the need for a constitutional convention to discuss these bold new moves (which was only supposed to be decided at Laeken itself).[cccxi] By this stage it must have been clear to Blair, and to the FCO, that Laeken was going to be just another exercise in stage management for a destination that was already known.

Brussels kept holding referenda and losing, so this had to be Europe's big reforming moment. At Laeken on 14th December it was announced that the Convention's Presidium (to prepare a new treaty draft) would be headed by a French federalist. 75 year old Giscard d'Estaing was back.

In 1985, 81 percent of the EU edicts for new laws already came in the form of *Regulations* (tighter than *Directives*, whose goals member states themselves may work out how to meet). By 2009 this was 94 percent (and Germany's president estimated that up to 84 percent of his country's laws now originated in Brussels). Laeken decided that Brussels had been 'behaving too bureaucratically', but the new draft Constitution it produced did not touch the then 102,000 pages of *acquis*, and launched a new instrument, the Non Legislative Act, by which the Commission could pass sweeping, binding laws.

Laeken said the 'division of competences must be made more transparent', then gave no reassurance on how power could be shared in future, and informed member states they were forbidden to legislate in any area where Brussels decided to act. The meeting pronounced that 'the Union must be brought closer to its peoples'. It did so by transferring more decision-making power from member states to the Union, including on criminal justice at its discretion. It created the European Arrest Warrant (EAW) which would soon see British police arresting their own people at the behest of other countries' magistrates: yet again, this sprang from innocent-sounding 'harmonisation', in this case of extradition rules by the Maastricht Treaty. Laeken stressed that 'the European institutions needed to be less unwieldy and rigid', and launched a Constitution that promised to give more power to the EU institutions, create a new European Presidency, more jobs for politicians and less influence for individual citizens. Delegates proclaimed the importance of 'national parliaments' and 'more transparency and efficiency', then gave more political and budgetary power to the Commission and European parliament at their expense (leaving them a 'right of request' which the Commission could ignore at will). Laeken stressed that 'if we are to have greater transparency, simplification is essential'. Its draft constitution was 200 pages long.[ccclxii]

Pursuing rule by committee, Brussels simply closed ranks. One independent-minded Spanish economist described the events as 'in the spirit of Robespierre',[ccclxiii] and bureaucrats left talking openly of a Constitution by 2003. For Blair, the only option was masquerade, and he left insisting that despite what the white paper actually said, none of it really meant a superstate.[ccclxiv] The euro had come to continental Europe, and the European Constitution, or 'Lisbon Treaty' as it would be renamed, would soon be upon Britain. Blair was isolated, but could rely on the BBC to report the Laeken shindig thus:

> 'European leaders have launched a major review of the future shape of the European Union in the hope of increasing efficiency and bringing the EU closer to the people... 'There are weaknesses in the EU that must be eliminated,' Belgian Prime Minister Guy Verhofstadt said at a summit in the royal palace of Laeken outside Brussels... The leaders adopted a declaration that sets up a 105-member convention to analyse the EU's shortcomings, and to propose structural changes.'

While the constitution was being crafted, the EU expanded eastwards. Most of the new eastern and central European members were small countries, and their experiences at the hands of greater powers – the Austro-Hungarians, the Ottoman Empire, Germany, the Soviets – gave them little cause to trust large political entities, or ideological grand designs. While the Commission cast itself as the protector of smaller states' interests (against the European parliament where each has little voting power), a perverse situation arose. Regardless of their scepticism, the new members were soon manoeuvred into approving the new constitution.

In 2003 the new Europeans got a foretaste of what they could expect. Amid the political fracas before the war in Iraq, in a fit of what one Czech scholar called 'Euromachismo', President Chirac informed the new Europeans whose governments supported the war that they were 'infantile', suggesting they 'shut up', while the German weekly *Der Spiegel* called Poland a 'Trojan donkey',[ccclxv] and that Warsaw's different opinion represented an American fifth column, although Czech President Václav Havel (a former dissident incarcerated under Communism and no man's donkey himself) described his own government's position as 'precisely halfway' between America and the 'European neighbours'. This treatment was the price of independent thoughts.

The diplomatic autism towards countries wishing to be treated as equals fed Eastern European concern over the EU's behaviour towards Russia. This grew in 2007 when, after Russian Foreign Minister Sergei Lavrov[ccclxvi] applied pressure on Brussels, Chancellor Schröder sided with Moscow in a row with tiny Estonia (after the Estonians moved a Stalin-era war memorial most Estonians saw as a symbol of Soviet repression, Schröder informed Estonia this contradicted 'every form of civilised behaviour'). Europe's new Eastern democrats were yet to develop the unity fetish, but their conditioning was underway.

The EU itself would not meet the democratic standards it requires of new entrants, and the democratic deficit is now being exported eastwards, a sad homecoming for democracies with an emotional need to 'return to Europe'.[ccclxvii]

It was little reported in our media that even in the 1990s 'new' Europe's opinion of Brussels was not high. Between 1990 and 1996, according to the Commission's own polls, the proportion of Bulgarians with a 'positive view' of the EU fell from 47 percent to 42 percent; among Hungarians from 51 to 33 percent, Czechs 49 to 33 percent and Estonians 38 to 24 percent. What support there was for EU membership was largely vague, based on an assumption, which Brussels encouraged, that it would bring 'security' (riding on the real security guarantee from NATO[ccclxviii]). Signs of discontent are now widespread; in the last European elections continent-wide turnout dropped to 43 percent, while a *Eurobarometer* poll has registered trust in the EU at minus 60 percent. Estonians and others have realised that, after leaving the USSR, they were forced to resurrect trade barriers in joining the CAP.[ccclxix] Schröder's outburst also raised questions about what kind of security their new friends would promise them.

ON THE RIVER TAGUS

In the late autumn of 2002, Blair went to Cardiff to make a speech on Europe. It was classic doublethink. Blair decided he had heard enough of 'this far and no further'.[ccclxx] His 'Europe of sovereign nations' would work 'together for the mutual good', but the EU 'should and will' integrate even further. Unhappy at what he had found in Europe, Blair appears to have replaced the reality at large with a new one: supranationalism and sovereign states, he had decided, were no longer 'in opposition to each other', and a strong Commission was in 'our interests'. So to fortify Europe 'at every level' we needed 'a proper Constitution'.[23]

Somewhere in the Commission building, Delors' former deputy chief of staff François Lamoureaux was already hard at work on this constitution. With a new Commission-appointed group at his disposal, his task was a project under the code name 'Penelope'. In early December, he put his name to a lengthy document engineered for the integrationist cause, outlining possible new European taxes, a European army, the virtual scrapping of national vetoes, and bringing justice, home affairs, and foreign policy under EU control. It also included a clause forcing any country wishing to stay in the EU to adopt whatever constitution was agreed.[ccclxxi] The document that would become the Constitution was developed within Brussels over the following six months, and in June 2003, Giscard d'Estaing passed the heads of member state governments the draft, with his own additions. Blair spun this immediately as a 'victory for Britain'.

The Constitution was described by German Minister for Europe Hans-Martin Bury as 'the birth certificate of a new United States of Europe',[ccclxxii] and was drafted by numerous European civil servants, none known to the British people. These bureaucrats, who presumably wished for a secure career in Brussels, decided the people of Europe wanted, in the new Constitution's words, to be 'united ever more closely'. The Constitution would underpin democracy by giving

> '...citizens the right to invite the Commission to introduce proposals on appropriate issues, if they can gather one million signatures in a significant number of member states.'[ccclxxiii]

A group of MEPs actually managed to do this by collecting a million names against Commission fraud, so the Commission ignored them.[ccclxxiv] The Constitution also stated that:

> 'The member states shall facilitate the achievement of the Union's tasks and refrain from any measure which could jeopardise the attainment of the Union's objectives.'

---

[23]David Miliband would soon cite Oxfam as a supporter of Europe's new constitution, without mentioning it was receiving over €37m a year from Brussels.

It then informed member states that:

> 'When the Constitution confers on the Union exclusive competence
> in a specific area, only the Union may legislate and adopt legally
> binding acts.'

It also made clear that the EU had exclusive access to agriculture, trade
agreements, tariff levels, fisheries, industrial support, competition policy, the
movement of capital, and of course the movement of people.[ccclxxv] In those
areas of 'shared competence', countries could make their own laws only if
the EU had not *yet* decided to take them over. Brussels made clear there was
another area it meant in due course to make its own:

> 'The Union shall have competence to define and implement a
> common foreign and security policy, including the progressive
> framing of a common defence policy... Member states shall make
> civilian and military capabilities available to the Union for the
> implementation of the common security and defence policy.'[ccclxxvi]

An article on permanent structured cooperation created a legal basis for
army battle groups under EU command. In the 1990s, German Defence
Minister Volke Ruhe explained:

> 'Today, the Security Council does not reflect the shifts in political
> influence and the new realities within the global community. It is
> part of the logic of the unification of the European processes that the
> European Union should in the future also speak with one voice in the
> United Nations Security Council. We need a reform at the UN.'[ccclxxvii]

The Treaty appears to have begun to put this into action. A future independent
voice for Britain at the Security Council would be inappropriate because:

> 'When the Union has defined a position on a subject which is
> on the United Nations Security Council agenda, those member
> states which sit on the Security Council shall request that the
> Union minister for foreign affairs be asked to present the Union's
> position.'[ccclxxviii]

At this point Blair was still promising Britain a referendum. In May and June 2005 the French (many of whom had also grown alarmed at Brussels' erosion of French global influence), then the Dutch, rejected the Constitution in their own national referenda. Italy's foreign minister contrived that the No vote was a request 'for more Europe, not less', while Giscard d'Estaing decided that 'it was a mistake to use the referendum process, but when you make a mistake you can correct it'. All the national leaders then signed a document stating that 'the results do not call into question citizens' attachment to the constitution of Europe'. Then they got on with setting up the Constitution's foreign policy service that the French and Dutch people had just said they didn't want.

But the Union needed to appear to listen, so at the Lisbon summit of December 2007, the Constitution had to be rearranged. It was rearranged, literally, by cutting and pasting. Of the Constitution's 250 proposals, only 10 were altered even slightly, and the Lisbon Treaty remained 96 percent the same, being shortened only by changing the font size. One change involved rewording the position of EU Foreign Minister, to become the *High Representative of the Union for Foreign Affairs and Security*ccdxxix. Indeed, Lisbon gave Brussels a grandiose new foreign policy edifice. The High Representative holds monthly meetings of member states' foreign ministers and replaces the foreign minister of the country with the EU's rotating presidency. The EU also gave itself a diplomatic corps named the European External Action Service (EEAS). Member states are now lobbying vigorously to have their people accepted to its key positions. Cutting Foreign Office costs by 40% is leading to a bleeding of responsibilities to the EU's new network of 136 embassies, whose 7,000 staff already have a price tag of €9.5m for salaries aloneccdxxx.

When Blair and Brown said the document was different to the Treaty, they were right – it was even more strongly integrationist, the new preamble adding 'advance European integration'. Said German Chancellor Angela Merkel: 'the substance of the Constitution is preserved. That is a fact'. With jaw-dropping cynicism Belgium's foreign minister Karel de Gucht explained how Brussels would get it past the peoples of Europe: 'the aim of the Constitution Treaty was to be more readable. The aim of this treaty is to be unreadable... It is a success'.

In the United Kingdom parliament, the Treaty was vigorously opposed by the Conservative Party as a whole, under its new leader David Cameron, with amendments tabled to every part of it by Bill Cash and his colleagues, as well as the official opposition, who together presented a united front; except on one crucial issue, where Bill Cash's amendment to preserve the sovereignty of the United Kingdom, harking back to the Single European Act, was not supported by the front bench, but by fifty-five other members of parliament.

Finality, then, is not the language of politics in Brussels. Lisbon is 'self-amending', a new Orwellian legal method which means it is as changeable as the EU wishes. When Brussels wants new powers, it will thus need no new treaties.[ccclxxxi] Lisbon is also irreversible. Leading Eurocrats hinted they have national taxes (among other things) in their plans, one saying 'differences in national tax law remain a serious obstacle to the completion of the Single Market'. This has a ring of constant revolution since the Single Market was meant to have been completed in the 1980s.

On his visit to the EU parliament in February 2005, President George W. Bush removed from his speech a paragraph applauding Europe's proposed Constitution – comparing it with America's – only moments before his address. This was wise. The whole US Constitution fits onto twelve sides of A4 paper, while the Brussels Constitution comprised 265 sides of impenetrable jargon. But the relative willingness on the Continent to adopt it may also be explained by the fact that many European countries' constitutions are very young compared to Britain's constitutional monarchy of 1688-9, built upon *Magna Carta* of 1215. The French Fifth Republic's constitution was only enshrined in 1958, Germany's in 1949, Italy's in 1949 and Portugal's in 1976.

When given Lisbon instead of the Constitution, Blair refused a referendum and forced the treaty through Parliament with just a fortnight's debate.[ccclxxxii] This was just as German president and legal expert Roman Herzog warned publicly that the European Court of Justice 'pulls judgments out of a hat... systematically ignores fundamental principles of the Western interpretation of law [and] invents legal principles serving as grounds for later judgments'.[ccclxxxiii] Only 29 Labour MPs voted against the Lisbon treaty, as Ed Miliband, Ed Balls, David Miliband, Andy Burnham, Yvette Cooper, Douglas Alexander, Sadiq Khan, Diane Abbott and hundreds of others broke their promise to hold a referendum, and voted Britain in.

The Dutch and French had rejected the Constitution. Then the Irish rejected Lisbon, and had it pushed on them again. Having lavished the Yes campaign with tranches of taxpayers' cash to 'better educate' the Irish about Europe, through an organisation called COMECE (the Commission of the

Bishops' Conferences of the European Community), Brussels employed Catholic Bishops to develop campaign ploys.[ccclxxxiv] This was one of many avenues for the much wealthier campaign. The No campaign, depending in a recession on ordinary citizens' donations, had little left over from the last campaign, and was exhausted and bankrupt.

Having promised an ethical – and pro-democratic – foreign policy, the British government's approach the government of Britain had become more opaque, as Blair gave the British people their new European Constitution, and a new term crept into EU parlance: post-democratic age.

8.

THE CLOSING OF THE
EUROPEAN MIND

NO ONE EXPECTS THE EUROPEAN UNION

The man of system seems to imagine that he
can arrange the different members of a great society
with as much ease as the hand arranges the
different pieces upon a chess-board... But, in the
great chess-board of human society, every single piece
has a principal of motion of its own.

Adam Smith, The Theory of Moral Sentiments, 1759

When argument over the single currency was at its height, in nine weeks
in 2000 the *Today Programme* featured 121 speakers on the topic. Some 87
were pro-euro, just 34 anti. As Rod Liddle (then editor of Radio 4's *Today*
programme) recalled, 'the whole ethos of the BBC [was] that Eurosceptics
were xenophobes',[ccclxxxv] and this is how respectable opinion has been made.
Numerous liberals have also put to use the seniority and status of pro-European
figures. Andrew Rawnsley in *The Observer* on January 31ˢᵗ, 1999 had: 'on the
pro-euro side, a grand coalition of business, the unions and the substantial,
sane, front rank political figures. On the other side, a menagerie of has-beens,
never-have-beens and loony tunes.'

The EU happened because a group of experts had decided that European
political integration was inevitable, so the public had to be helped towards
the right decisions – and we ended up seeing it as inevitable. But this was not

inevitable. Historians often claim events are or were inevitable, but they become inevitable only after the fact. Many big events are highly unpredictable, but their impact changes their environment so much that it becomes impossible to imagine the world without them.

The concept of historical inevitability of a unified Europe being used to demoralise, who are wasting their time before they succumb to historical forces that a political class can better understand. But if the EU is not inevitable, continued integration is not inevitable either. There are plenty of instances that demonstrate the failure of the 'experts' of any era to know what's going to happen. Nassim Taleb has described how things are made to look inevitable using the trick of hindsight, and how the diaries of expert correspondents in Berlin in the 1930s make clear one of the most important facts about that era, or any era: 'experts' didn't know what was going to happen next either. 'One would suppose that people living through the beginning of World War Two had an inkling that something momentous was taking place', writes Taleb, 'Not at all'. In July 2001, *The New York Times* published a piece about 'The Declining Terrorist Threat'. Americans were 'bedevilled by fantasies about terrorism', and believed it was 'becoming more widespread and lethal... None of these beliefs are based in fact'. Two months later some were carping about the clear chain of events that led to 9/11, and the experts at the CIA who should have warned them.

Whenever something big happens, like planes flown into skyscrapers or the hurricane of a financial crisis, we turn to the experts and ask why they didn't warn us, as if they were an oracle. Each time, we fail to grasp the bigger message: we should stop trusting expertise about the future of things altogether.

OUR THING

Only puny secrets need protection.
Big discoveries are protected by public incredulity.

Marshall McLuhan

It is highly inconvenient for British Eurosceptics that an accurate description of the way the European Union works is liable to sound faintly silly. But Edmund Burke was onto something when he said that when a community is subordinately connected with another, the great danger of is the self-complacency of the superior, because in all matters of controversy it will decide in its own favour. In this way, for example, Brussels has hit whistleblowers hard: Paul van Buitenen, Hans-Martin Tillack, Dorte Schmidt-Brown, Bernard Connolly and Marta Andreassen among them.

The EU doesn't release the number of people on its payroll, but the figure *directly* employed by the EU appears to be around 85,000 (some say more like double this). This is about the same as the entire British army.[ccclxxxvi] But EU perks would make our soldiers more than slightly envious. Officials who go on regular trips get their own MasterCard with a memo informing them, 'this card is totally free and may also be used for private purposes'. There is no annual charge, all cash withdrawals outside the EU are paid by the European Parliament, there is accompanying travel insurance up to €260,000 on tickets paid for with the card, and the monthly limit is €5,000, but all these limits can be reviewed on request and the parliament is never allowed to look at transactions made.[ccclxxxvii]

MEPs meanwhile have their basic salaries fixed at the level of their home countries' MPs, so British MEPs (currently) take home £78,444, while Italians (the best paid) get over £127,000. What gives the job its real appeal though is its luxuriant expenses, as MEPs can claim £48,721 a year tax and receipt-free as a 'subsistence allowance' (British MEPs have nicknamed this SOSO: Sign On and Sod Off). If an MEP's spouse helps out at the office (or claims to), another £60,000 a year goes into what we can reasonably call the family business. A receipt-free constituency office allowance is also provided, at £41,556 a year. MEPs who stay in for three elections can now reasonably expect to become millionaires,[ccclxxxviii] and can even be jailed for up to a year and still keep their seat. In the middle of a deep recession in summer 2009, two countries' MEPs took a pay cut, but everyone else picked up a rise, from 6 percent for French MEPs, 32 percent for the Brits, 100 percent for the Spanish and 214 percent for the Czechs.[ccclxxxix] The Westminster expense scandal of recent years was completely insignificant by comparison, but British MEP and journalist Daniel Hannan describes a gangrene that is:

> '...not confined to Brussels: it is contaminating our own body
> politic, carried by cash handouts through our veins and arteries.'

In 2008 a report uncovered 'widespread abuse' of the allowance system for MEPs' assistants, but MEPs voted to prevent taxpayers ever being allowed to see it. The report (which only a few MEPs have even been allowed to read) was put in a room protected by biometric locks and security guards. A British MEP who told a journalist about this report was informed by a colleague that 'passing information to the press is a misuse of information'.[cccxc]

One senior official left Brussels' employ for a new job, bought a house, then got his job back with a pay hike, still collecting an accommodation allowance for the house he started letting out.[cccxci] Another employee was given invalidity benefit after she started taking naps on her office floor, despite being fit enough to work in an election team. Another was caught stealing, then had a seizure and was kept on. One department uses a temping agency run by the daughter of the head of the typing pool; there are reports of numerous individuals being ostracised for refusing to sign off doctored accounts. Petty fraud in the offices of senior personnel is rife, car rental procedures are routinely abused, and building contracts have been awarded to relatives of senior officials. One official was accused of committing a crime simply by saying that fraud is rife in EU institutions, while whistleblowers have been accused of being mentally ill, an old Soviet trick.

Independent studies claim EU fraud is 10 percent of its budget at the very least.[cccxcii] Even without this the acknowledged burden of EU administration on Britain tops £6.3 billion.[cccxciii] The agencies are so profligate that they appear actually corrupt by design – the following is a far from exhaustive list, but it gives a hint of what we are funding.

The European Aviation Safety Agency lacks proper internal audit and awarded one £74,000 contract 'by direct agreement and without justification'. The European Medicines Agency ignored best practice in giving IT contracts; the European Agency for Reconstruction failed to control its spending in Kosovo; the European Agency for Health and Safety at Work signed off bids without evidence of their quality; payment files at the European Maritime Agency were 'incomplete or confused'; the European Food Safety Authority paid excessive staff mission expenses (plus £3m annually for temporary buildings because it botched moving into its own offices); the European Centre for Disease Prevention and Control gave out *all* its payments without due authorisation; the European Centre for the Development of Vocational Training used dubious accounting software, ran seventeen costly websites, handed out allowances that weren't even covered by its regulations, and gave out two contracts against its own rules worth £428,000; the European Training Foundation had two items worth 10 percent of its budget missing from its books.[cccxciv]

The European Foundation for the Improvement of Living and Working Conditions doled out money on projects that had nothing to do with its mission; the European Monitoring Centre for Drugs and Drug Addiction had no asset inventory, and also had unsound recruitment procedures (sending one member of staff on a two-year mission at a cost of £60,000, with no serious workload and no clear aims, and after he was seconded to the Commission the Centre continued to pay his salary). This Centre also accepted bids even before officially starting procurement, with apparent favouritism in tendering. Employees of the European Monitoring Centre on Racism and Xenophobia recruited their own seniors; the Community Plant Variety Office lacked a computer system that could handle account audits; the Office for Harmonisation of the Internal Market had hundreds of payments signed for and signed off by the same employee and awarded questionable contracts; rural development agencies spend money on areas that are 'not predominantly rural' (including a six-year set of projects for £21bn).[cccxcv]

The Commission and European parliament together got through £139m in 2003 alone on interpreters, and at the parliament 8 percent (£5.1m) was wasted on off-days or hours when they weren't needed. Eurojust (meant to fight corporate and organised crime) has an improperly drawn up asset list, while some assets have disappeared. One discrepancy in the Structural Funds for just two countries weighs in at £9.8 billion, – unsurprising, because most eligible states lack proper management systems. This plethora of agencies has helped give Brussels pension liabilities that, even by New Year 2005, stood at £22bn, but was up by £2.6bn within the year and with an influx of Eastern European staff[cccxcvi] is climbing. Our own much-maligned Health and Safety Executive (HSE) is in fact viewed in Brussels as simply the 'UK Focal Point' for the European Agency for Health and Safety at Work.[cccxcvii] Our own government admits it can no longer work out which of the UK's own quangos are simply replicating work already done by EU agencies.

Every year EU staff cost around £6bn. They then spend £50bn on the CAP and £59bn on regional aid. This comes from GNP-linked payments from member states, the EU's cut of VAT income and hefty duties on imports. These alone cost every person in the EU £231 every year, but this is not a comprehensive figure, as the CAP forces people across Europe to pay over £43bn more for food than they would at market prices.

In 2010 British taxpayers contributed £92bn to the EU. Fraudsters siphon off between £51bn and £102bn every year. When we then add the costs of national civil servants administering edicts from Brussels, then the economically detrimental effects of EU trade policies, then the enormous volume of EU fraud, recent studies (by the World Bank, the Treasury and the consumer magazine *Which?*) have shown that the cost of the EU to you, me and each person inside it may be as high as £1,708 every single year.[cccxcviii] As Westminster debated spending cuts in the aftermath of the financial crisis of 2008, not one mainstream politician mentioned the elephantine potential saving worth tens of billions. It doesn't take a genius to work out that at the heart of the European Union there is a racket.

As Chancellor, Helmut Kohl provided DM 1.5m to Harvard, Georgetown and Berkeley for 'German and European Studies',[cccxcix] and *DG Education and Culture* gives £820m a year to nearly 500 universities and schools; another £116m goes to 'Youth in Action', a programme to 'foster the idea of belonging to the European Union'.[cd] A huge number of academics have been receptive, perhaps not unrelated to the fact that Europhilia also allows academics to strike a sceptical pose to their own nation state, the *sine qua non* of all fashionable baby-boom thought.

The 2010 culture programme also found some interesting ways to spend £366m in a recession, giving £900,000 to the *European Laboratory for Hip Hop Dance* to improve its 'recognition and visibility', encouraging 'connectivity between hip hop artists' in 'an often under-represented side of European culture'. £143,000 went to TRANS-Mission, a project to 'improve assistance to the contemporary circus sector'. £180,000 was dished out to the Project of Generosity, whose mission is to 'spread the movement of reaching out and sharing'. £162,000 went to the Flying Gorillas dance group, originators of 'the brilliant smelly foot dance'. £410,000 was spent on teaching teenagers in Burkina Faso 'therapeutic dance' on the grounds that Africans find that 'expression of feelings through the spoken word is often difficult and complicated'. A European House of History, will cost £90m. In 2011 the EU launched a £2.6m project to promote the eating of insects.[cdi]

Recently Brussels also found another tchotchke worth £939,000, in the establishment of CHERPA, the Consortium for Higher Education and Research Performance Assessment, established by the Commission to draw up new league tables of world universities. This may seem strange, since we already have *The Times* Higher Education World Rankings, the Shanghai Jiaotong University rankings, the QS rankings and Taiwan's HEEACT table. But the Commission feels these do not 'represent the diverse and multifunctional nature of universities', which may not be unconnected to the fact that only British and American universities rank in the top tens, with continental EU universities rarely even in the top twenty.

In early 2010, lecturers across Britain were receiving a Tintin-style picture book named 'Hidden Disaster', in which a powerful earthquake has struck the fictional land of Borduvia. In the 'European Commission Crisis Room', although it's late at night a group of serious Sean Connery-ish characters in open necked shirts are getting stuck in ('any reports from the field, Max?'). The quake has caused floods to strike Borduvia, but without feedback from the Borduvian government 'it's difficult to start work on follow-up measures'. One replies: 'I think we'll probably need extra funding' – and that's just two pages in. Soon our liquid-lipped heroine Zana, EU badge on her khaki-clad breast, is helicoptering Angelina Jolie-style into the quake zone. We follow Zana saving numerous Borduvians. By the last page, below the image of her Latin features against the Borduvian dusk, we read, 'the European Commission has a longstanding commitment to help the victims of such crises. Its humanitarian aid department provides relief that goes directly to people in distress...'

Shortly after *Hidden Disaster* hit people's desks, a real earthquake hit Haiti. As the death toll climbed (it would eventually reach a quarter of a million), the US sent 3,500 troops, hundreds of medics, and committed $100m in initial aid. In Brussels, the EU's High Representative Baroness Ashton held a press conference. Rambling through her statement, she pledged €3m and sent her condolences – to UN Secretary General Ban Ki Moon. But help was on its way: an official *European Union Representative* travelled across the border from the Dominican Republic, stayed a few hours and reported back.[cdii] An official report into the Commission's response to the 2004 Indian Ocean tsunami uncovered chaos. Too many charities were allowed to join in and were poorly coordinated, creating a logjam in some areas and neglect in others. So many new fishing boats were sent to Sri Lanka that the UN warned fisheries would not cope, but a year later some 67,000 people were still living in tents.[cdiii]

If we are rarely told about this chaos, it is because Brussels has largely bought the academic study of itself. When journalists and broadcasters want serious information (not the 'populist' kind), they usually get it from the 'independent' institutions that turn out to be funded by the Brussels saturation strategy. So is mainstream opinion made.

While the EU is a political sphere that is incomprehensible for the people of its member states, for the lobbying industry it means an economy of scale. Brussels swarms with lobbyists, an industry that exploded in the 1980s when the Union went into overdrive drafting the hundreds of directives that would become the single market, decisions thrashed out in closed committees beyond the public reach.

The Commission in this era became populated by major business leaders, such as Étienne Davignon of Société Générale de Belgique, while groups like the European Roundtable of Industrialists, the European Centre for Infrastructure Studies and the EU Committee of the American Chamber of Commerce (AmCham) emerged. Like its European counterparts, AmCham was strongly for European unification. Said its former manager for European affairs:

> 'We may disagree with the Commission or the Parliament on certain issues... but this strategic direction of where Europe is going – as far as greater integration and companies preferring to deal with Brussels rather than with fifteen member states' administrations and political systems – is quite straightforward.' [cdiv]

The Maastricht and Amsterdam treaties of 1992 and 1997 increased the European parliament's 'competences', seeing it converged upon by hordes of lobbyists, now five for every MEP. [cdv] But in the parliament chamber itself there is virtually no real debate. With 751 MEPs, anyone seeking to speak must apply for a slot in advance, to receive usually one minute of speaking time. This means policy amendments are made in the 20 standing committees behind closed doors. Every MEP has to join at least one committee, but most rarely turn up. Every four weeks the parliament meets in Strasbourg for a monthly voting frenzy, where MEPs sometimes spend entire days pressing YES/NO/ABSTAIN buttons every few seconds. Party leaders sit at the front, instructing their MEPs how to vote with a *thumb up* or *thumb down* motion.[cdvi]

In the US, where the modern lobbying industry was born, lobbyists' insidious power is a major concern. But much of what Brussels' lobbyists get up to would be out of the question across the pond. Unlike their American counterparts, lobbyists in Brussels are not required to record for whom they work. This is the real power lobbyists have over Britain, yet being in Brussels means being much better hidden (*A Quiet Word*, a recent exposé of the lobbying industry by two *Guardian* journalists, had no direct criticism of Brussels, and just one, complimentary, comment).[cdvii]

As accountability has slid from national capitals and the EU takes on more and more responsibility, the privilege of access to the top decision makers stays open to top executives. A 1998 fraud investigation into the Commission found it was 'difficult to find a responsible civil servant' [cdviii], and Brussels has since become more complex. The decisions our own ministers claim to have taken are frequently decided for them in advance by hidden bureaucratic committees – a typical example was the pre-emptive decision by Franz Fischler, agricultural and fisheries commissioner from landlocked Austria, to ignore recommendations for species-specific fishing bans, against scientific advice. Journalist Charles Clover suspects that

> 'Mr Fischler clearly enjoyed his position, his comfortable office and his even more comfortable EU salary and expenses too much to take a stand'.

Before 1987 there had been eleven directives on health and safety (despite the absence of any treaty basis). In the first decade after the introduction of QMV, at least 40 new labour regulations were introduced, in almost all cases more restrictive than previous national laws – so the loss of the veto created a tactical game whereby even heavier regulation tended to win through. One German scholar has shed light on why this is. [cdix]

After Blair abandoned the British opt-out in the Treaty of Amsterdam in 1997, the advent of qualified majority voting meant that when Britain could not assemble a blocking minority (which it usually could not), the other countries would now be more eager to regulate because they would no longer be afraid of losing national competitiveness to the UK, which could now simply be outvoted. Thus supranational government immediately began to lead to more law, and less freedom.

From 2017, according to Lisbon, the upper voting threshold in the Council will fall from 73.9 to 65 percent, while country weights will be replaced by population weights. This means the combined vote of the countries who typically oppose heavier regulation (the UK, Ireland and the Scandinavian countries) will drop from 21.2 to 20 percent, giving them little hope of blocking regulation, with two large and two small states combined able to form a majority. This costs the EU itself little, the costs being borne by the member states.

Although the idea that integrating markets could decrease the weight of regulation dates back to Immanuel Kant (who said in his *Idea of a Universal History from a Cosmopolitan Point of View* 'If the citizen is hindered in seeking his prosperity in any way suitable to himself that is consistent with the liberty of others, the activity of business is checked generally and, thereby... the powers of the whole state are again weakened'), if a large group of countries agrees on regulation the cost in loss of competitiveness will be smaller for each country – except those who also trade more outside the bloc, like the UK.

But there may be another strategy at work: nations seeking to strategically raise rivals' costs (which economists call SRRC and which Roland Vauble of Mannheim University refers to as 'regulatory collusion'). Again, this simply requires a qualified majority. In Germany after 1871, a majority coalition of states led by Prussia imposed their higher regulations on the more liberal states in the Northwest (the coastal states who traded a great deal with Britain). The game theoretic situation was, and is, simple: if government 1 prefers a higher level of regulation to government 2, and if it commands a majority in the union legislature (if necessary with its economic allies), it can impose its level of regulation on country 2. But why does country 1 raise its own level of regulation as well under SRRC? Because being able to dictate the common level of regulation, it is relieved of competitive pressure from government 2. SRRC raises regulation in both states but much more in state 2. Thus state 1 improves its competitive position, and its share of world capital stock, even as the increase in regulation reduces world capital stock overall (this allows national labour ministers to collude against their parliaments, while being more likely to escape censure than if they tried to enact the legislation through national parliaments at home). Scholars have found that all the main European labour regulations (including the Working Time Directive) qualify as SRRC manoeuvers, not least because EU workplace protection now extends even the previous level of the most harshly regulated member countries,[cdx] harming both freedom and employment. Politics, they say, is ethics done in public. This is how our politics is done.

FOOD CHAIN

At the top of the European food chain the lobbyists feed Brussels. At the other end live the leeches, the organised criminals. In the early morning hours before dawn breaks over Bucharest, a dingy bar nestled in a side street is the scene of a business deal. It is one that will be repeated all over Eastern Europe that day.

The subject of the deal is a Romanian girl. She is 19. A €2,000 price, for a sale in which the girl naturally has no say, is agreed with the man who would be her third owner. The men selling her assure the foreign buyer, who says he intends to take her to work in his club in London, that he can take all her income until she has earned her price back. Then he can keep the money for rent. Her traffickers were unlucky this time: the buyer was British journalist David Harrison.

Up to 6,000 such girls are transported to Britain every year as prostitutes. 'We stop one gang and another one moves in straight away', says a Scotland Yard detective. In autumn 2005 three people from the new EU countries were convicted of auctioning two teenage Lithuanian girls in a cafe in Gatwick airport. Under threat of death and torture, the girls were forced to work in brothels in London and Sheffield [cdxi] (where the Lib-Lab council allows a 'zone of tolerance' in Attercliffe, now a red light district in the city's east end). Two others brought nearly 600 women into Britain, forced them to work as prostitutes, pay £300 a day rent and repay the £20,000 they told the girls it cost to get them into the country. This is standard practice. The most popular recruitment area in Romania is in the villages of the south, where girls of 15 to 19 are poor and pliable. Initial recruiters, usually women who gain the trust of girls more easily, promise good jobs, but passports are seized by the gangs on arrival, and girls are often kept locked alone in dank, dark rooms. Girls have told the Romanian police that traffickers have killed other girls in front of them to 'break their spirit'.

The Commission is in the process of creating a Common European Asylum System under its control (the reason it uses to justify this is simply 'common values shared by member states', a sweeper tactic the Commission employs when treaty grounds don't actually allow it to take an action [cdxii]). Britain's Labour government underestimated immigration from the new Eastern European member states by a factor of 1000 percent: [cdxiii] over two million people have come from the new member states to Britain since 2004.

Labour, the unions, and the Left in general have been totally hamstrung by political correctness about immigration. In the meantime, immigration by deluge has permitted the industrial-scale degradation of trafficked human beings and hurt the most vulnerable of our own citizens by driving down their wages. At the beginning of 2010 the government claimed only 700,000 Eastern Europeans remain in Britain, a claim swiftly rebuffed by Warsaw's Centre for

International Affairs: 'this is not true', stated Professor Krystyna Iglicka, who estimated there were a million Poles in Britain.

Britain is very often the final destination for traffickers. Although the EU has created a border-lite traffickers' paradise, our government has pretended for years that reinforced action through the EU will make 'a significant impact on the trafficking of people, reducing the horror and suffering it produces'. [cdxiv] Yet while it has increased inequality and overcrowding, immigration has not done for national identity what many federalists supposed, and hoped, it would. If anything, immigration from the Continent has increased our sense of independent national identity. If Brits who prefer France go to live there, and the French who like Britain settle here, each nation gets people who like it for its particular characteristics: they are not seeking homogenised Europe.

So the people traffickers pass through Heathrow freely. Britain is the most favoured destination for the modern European slave trade, as controls for those from Eastern Europe are especially relaxed, Tony Blair's government having refused to apply possible immigration exemptions.

The much eulogised free movement of people around the EU is not always on these people's own terms. Some of the prostitutes moving 'freely' around Europe make it to Strasbourg, where they tend to live in the German half of the city, where, unlike on the French side, using them is legal (they are summoned by clients on both sides of course). The use of these prostitutes by MEPs and civil servants is known to be rife. One explained: 'parliamentarians are not interested in street prostitutes. They prefer... girls of a slightly higher level. They find little adverts and make telephone calls. That's how they take care of business'. [cdxv] MEPs' use of Eastern European prostitutes is now so widespread that a group of northern European MEPs tried - unsuccessfully - to propose that EU staff stay only at hotels that do not allow prostitution. Of course, as taxpayers, it's all on us.

9.
The Euro

The single currency, far from being an agent of continental style corporatism, is probably the greatest export vehicle of Anglo-Saxon economics. The euro has done more to enforce budgetary discipline, to promote privatisation and force through labour and product market liberalisation in the rest of Europe than any number of exhortations from the IMF, the OECD, or the editors of *The Economist*.

Nick Clegg, 2002

JEWEL IN THE CROWN

Few events in our recent history are as notorious as Black Wednesday, 16th September, 1992. On this dark autumn day, under sustained attack by speculators the pound was pulled out of the ERM by Chancellor Norman Lamont. In June, the people of Denmark had voted against the Maastricht Treaty, a result that currency dealers and foreign exchange markets found profoundly worrying: after all, this was meant to have been the next step to single currency, but little of this was explained to the British people as their currency began its long trip down the plughole that summer.

The ERM was sold as a way to create strong currencies through fixed exchange rate solidarity, or, more accurately, for other currencies to take advantage of the strength of the Deutschmark. Yet this was only the proximate, not ultimate goal, because the ERM was just part of a long-term strategy for the single currency about which the electorate were not informed. Black Wednesday happened because the currency markets noticed what politicians didn't want to know: that binding together the currencies of

Europe involved binding together countries whose economic fortunes were going to be very different. In other words Black Wednesday blew apart the idea that the economies of member states were similar enough for a single currency to be possible. Or it should have done.

At the northern and southern ends of Europe lie two very different groups of countries. In the north are those like the Netherlands, Germany, Finland: the Northern countries that do most of the right economic things and usually run trade surpluses. In the south there are the PIGS: Portugal, Italy, Greece and Spain, the Southern countries that (mainly) ran massive budget deficits (although there are slight differences in the Spanish case, as we will discuss). Had these countries kept their own currencies, the results of irresponsibility would discipline them because there would be nowhere to pass the buck. Under the euro, their reckless politicians would be able to put off the day of economic reckoning – because Northern surpluses cancel out Southern deficits. As single currency supporter and former Commissioner Chris Patten once wondered aloud though, 'how can Italy measure up?' [cdxvi]

Indeed back in 1956, the Spaak Report that led to the Community's establishment reminded Europe that it should be careful about economic union, claiming it was 'wrong to suggest that when areas which have not attained the same stage of economic development are suddenly joined together, the lower cost of manpower and the higher return on investment automatically assure faster progress of the initially less developed region, leading ultimately to the alignment of economic levels. On the contrary, as shown by [the] United States after the [civil] war, the gap may widen cumulatively if the basic conditions are not met by public means'. So poorer regions would not necessarily catch up – and they might need a lot of money if they didn't. Meanwhile Europe also has much less mobile labour than America, partly because of linguistic diversity, but has clear investment winners and losers.

No inconvenient facts however were going to stop the euro; as Helmut Kohl put it, 'economic and political union... is the next step towards a United States of Europe'. Because a single currency is impossible without parallel control over taxation and spending, EMU creates, steadily, a single European state with a single government. As the Bundesbank described in the early 1990s, it 'entails the necessity of dispensing with autonomous national domestic and external monetary policies, and of transferring the responsibility for such policies to Community institutions. In this way, the participating economies will be inextricably linked to one another, come what may… In the final analysis, a Monetary Union is thus an irrevocable [joint] community which, in light of past experience, requires a more far reaching association, in the form of a comprehensive political union, if it is to prove durable.'[cdxvii] And among Europhiles, a belief that southern Europe had 'found its way' emerged, whether to northern European governance standards generally, or economic standards specifically. This was Will Hutton in 2002:

> 'The state – in all cases a post-1945 creation – has much less legitimacy than in the north, and the traditions of social citizenship and political participation which inform northern Europe are much less firmly embedded, but southern Europe has found its way to a capitalism and social contract that perform in similar ways.'[cdxviii]

Alas, southern economies were nothing like their northern counterparts, and whether Europhiles ever really believed it themselves is by no means certain, because the economics were invented to fit the need.

The year 1987 saw the creation of a little known group called AMUE (or the Association for the Monetary Union of Europe). Usually thought to have been founded by Helmut Schmidt and Valerie Giscard d'Estaing, AMUE was actually begun by five continental corporates: French oil giant Total, Rhône-Poulenc, Solvay chemicals, Fiat, and Philips. Its first chairman was Wisse Dekker, who was instrumental in creating the Single Market.[cdxix] In 1991, AMUE's publicity told Europe: 'Japan has one currency. The US has one currency. How can the community live with twelve?' AMUE organised over 1000 events and conferences, most between 1996 and 1998, involving Commission officials and member states' civil servants. The tactical focus was on the core European countries where public support for the euro was weak, with 90 meetings in Germany in 1997 alone (AMUE employed a firm specifically to bulletin the German and Austrian press with weekly 'briefings'). This was so successful that when the Commission needed expert monetary opinion AMUE was often its first port of call. In 1994, when the Commission launched an 'independent' committee to analyse a transition to monetary union, fully a quarter of its members were from the AMUE board, and when in 1995 the Commission's Green Paper introduced monetary union into summit discussions, the paper was based on committee work.

Jacques Santer would later thank AMUE for keeping monetary union on track, telling AMUE's directors in 1998, a year before the currency began:

> 'Tonight, I really feel at home among friends. When I became President of the Commission in 1995, the association was about the only body which supported us in our firm belief that the single currency would become a reality. So it feels like playing a home game.'[cdxx]

Joining the currency is now mandatory for all new EU entrants as soon as they meet its requirements. Quite apart from anti-democratic coercion, the new members have to meet the same requirements the PIGS countries once did.

P.I.G.S.

As the new century began, Blair gave up much of our £1bn budget rebate, stepping in to stave off an EU budget crisis – a budget crisis that stemmed largely from the huge sums being pumped out in pre-accession aid to new members.

In the corrupt former Communist economies of the EU's eastern frontier, the damage this aid will do is likely to be more permanent than western observers have envisaged. The EU panicked at the last moment before letting in Bulgaria and Romania, and laid down sensible but vague conditions (regarding not too much 'maladministration') they had to meet before getting any EU cash. They didn't meet them, but got the money all the same. A 2007 EU report on Romania admitted: 'instead of progress in the fight against high-level corruption, Romania is regressing on all fronts', caused partly by 'the intense resistance of practically the whole political class of Romania'.[cdxxi] Of the flood of aid that went to Romania and Bulgaria, fully half was spent partly or not at all on where it was meant to go, and many aid projects have the mark of kickbacks. A bridge connecting Romania and Moldova over the River Prut cost €3.1m but was unusable, lacking border checkpoints or even a road on the Moldovan side. Software sent to the Bulgarian public prosecutor's office turned out to be useless, and in one storeroom 37 brand new computers were found gathering dust (similar cases were found in Romania).[cdxxii] This has helped cause chaos, as a pilfering elite has created a net outflow of funds from Bulgaria and Romania which these countries cannot afford.

Something will have to give, and it won't be their deep-rooted corruption. A Bulgarian MP and former chief of counter-intelligence made it plain: 'other countries have the mafia. In Bulgaria the mafia has the country'. The deep negative effects of economic integration as led by Brussels may only be appreciated when it is too late to stop the havoc it is quietly wreaking, and the aid given to get these countries in good enough shape to join the euro has become a lesson in how to make corrupt countries worse. Because like Greece, where EU aid made up 4 percent of national income for decades, in these countries the euro, like oil, has become a resource curse. Governments can only develop economies by allowing enterprise to flourish and taking (reasonable) taxes. Massive sums of aid work like huge pipes spewing rivers of cash onto the presidential palace floor. A government never really has to help its country flourish. It can just throw the money at its people, until it runs out.

So let's put the wishful thinking to one side and look at some proper economics. Clearly plenty of economists have helped get us into a dreadful mess over the last few years, but there were always some who tried to warn us what was likely to happen. The Canadian economist Robert Mundell came up with the idea of 'optimal currency areas' to define which groups of currencies could and could not safely be merged into a single currency. First, one thing you don't want for your single currency is the risk of 'asymmetric shocks'. Let us say for example that Norway and Sweden created a single currency for just the two of them. One big difference between these two Scandinavian neighbours is that Norway has oil, and Sweden doesn't. This means if Norway's oil price needs to go up, so too does its currency, because its economy will simply be stronger. But in response to Norway, Sweden – an oil importer – would need to send its currency down. So a currency partnership would be ill-advised.

The Eurozone doesn't have oil, but it does have big differences in kinds of economy, and strengths of economy. Germany has a lot of medium to high-tech industries, Greece doesn't: it has tourism and various bargain-basement industries, and it's the same story across most of the Med, as the economies of southern Europe are much weaker than the north.

Now let's add something new to the mix: China. For Germany (which essentially manufactures high-end everything), China hasn't posed too big a threat. Most of what gets made along the Chinese seaboard is actually still quite low tech. In fact for Germany, China's growing middle class, hungry for new mod-cons, has provided a new market. Actually it's even better: Germany now hardly produces any low tech goods, and the Germans are glad to import them from China instead of the more expensive producers it had to rely on in the past. For southern Europe it's a very different story. The PIGS are trying to compete with China in medium to low-tech manufactures, things like furniture and fabrics that China (and increasingly other Asian countries) can make much more cheaply. It should have been obvious for years that they were going to be in enormous trouble.

Now according to the optimal currency areas thesis, there are three main ways that a country can adjust to circumstances like those faced by Germany on the one hand and Greece on the other. First, an economy which has hit the rocks can *cut prices and wages*. In a single currency area, this is the nearest thing allowed to a devaluation, and Ireland has been doing it since the start of the financial crisis. But it's pretty ham-fisted, not as elegant as devaluation, and it isn't usually politically feasible: Greeks aren't queuing up to take a wage cut. Furthermore, the euro disincentivised politicians from doing this, by providing an alternative way out (more on that later).

The next option (*pace* Norman Tebbit) we can call 'on your bike' (he didn't actually say this, but the phrase has stuck anyway). This option is not easy however. In the US, where a common language unites the population, workers can flee a downturn in one area by packing and pitching up elsewhere (quite a lot of them can anyway). In Europe, linguistic barriers (not to mention a few cultural ones) make this a lot harder. A large number of Poles have moved to Britain, but they have done this to quadruple their wages, and this is a far from typical case. There is also the problem of increasing population density in these dynamic regions that attract economic migrants; for instance, how many more people does the South East of England or the *Île-de-France* really want?

The only option that remains is *federal government help*. When a nation state's economy hits trouble, the centre will need to bail them out. For Europhiles this is the key, because with the other two options all but closed, more and more money will need to be committed to Brussels so that it can rescue struggling member states. But this rescue money can ultimately come from only one place: northern Europe.

The gulf between the southern and northern economies has kept growing. Inflation has been higher in the Mediterranean, and while productivity has grown in Germany and the northern nations, on the whole it has barely risen at all in the south. But this didn't stop the Greeks and others awarding themselves wage increases that, not being based on anything tangible, they couldn't really afford. The Germans however would have been behaving in more or less the same way had they still had the Deutschmark: a productive economy, affordable wage rises based on productivity, and a currency fluctuating freely according to their own needs. With the arrival of China on the global scene, it would have been revalued. The southern European economies meanwhile would have had to devalue, but that would have kept their economies in line too. Yet the euro suits neither party.

Into this dangerous cocktail let us throw still another ingredient: the great financial over-optimism of 2000 to 2008, during which the EU made no attempts to tackle the divergence between the north and the PIGS (for its part, the Greek government lied about many of its economy's problems, but in the end couldn't lie about its worsening budget deficit). The EU was just as blind as the Anglo-Saxon economies to the gathering storm that struck in 2008, and the euro gave a significant boost to the wave of mergers and acquisitions throughout Europe, especially in banking and insurance, helping to create the 'too-big-to-fail' financial giants well known since the crisis.

Indeed, concentrating money and power in a few hands is rarely a good idea. Bigger and bigger political and financial entities do not encourage responsible behaviour, be they Lehman brothers or the French and German banks which loaned money to the Greek government which they could not seriously have believed they could repay. German anger at the ensuing Greek bail-out has shown that the EU is not bringing the peoples of Europe together. On the contrary, it is creating resentment that would not otherwise exist. There is another side to this story, however – the leaders of EU member states are now seeking to shackle London's capabilities so their own financial centres will profit from the crisis. The EU is proposing a system of financial control that will see Britain, the EU's financial powerhouse (but the country some European leaders have told their people is mainly to blame for the crisis), given the same voting power as Malta.[cdxxiii] The EU failed completely either to predict the financial crisis, or act to pre-empt it. But this did not stop European leaders turning on the US, Britain and the English-speaking world as its 'originator'. German Chancellor Angela Merkel told her European allies imbalances were simply an 'ersatz' issue (meaning blaming the crisis on Anglo-Saxon greed was a narrative so convenient that she didn't want to talk about awkward problems[cdxxiv]). This is a trend: when the crisis struck, the response was nationalistic and uncoordinated. During a boom we are 'partners', but when the European economy nosedives it is time to turn to national electorates for political survival.

In reports from at latest 2009, before the Greek budget deficit became headline news, the Commission quietly expressed its worries about the rising short-term external debt in Greece and Portugal created by current account deficits. In its report on the euro's first decade however, the Commission gave current account imbalances just three paragraphs of 328 pages (as the economist David Marsh put it, this report was 'largely laudatory'). Economic gravity is now reasserting itself, and the results are dire. The PIGS have spent themselves into enormous trouble, and are now being forced to tighten up, but the process is still barely underway.

In terms of ease of doing business, Greece is ranked lower than Jamaica or Colombia. This is the country for which Brussels ignored debt rules, allowing it to join. The single currency then allowed Athens to borrow at a low cost, funding its huge, economically disincentivising state. The most recent manifestation of the Greek malaise set in with the 1981 election victory of George Papandreou Sr. and his *Pasok* socialist party. Journalist Tony Barber has described a cancer of patronage, metastasising as 'deep Pasok' spread its state sector network throughout the economy, a network which now sabotages attempts at reform, around a government that evolved 'into a beehive of clientelism'.[24] One reformer tells of a government department in Athens where the chief of staff discovered that all his employees but one were on the take. His expectations were so low that he asked why the other staff had let him stay clean. As eurozone finance ministers inform the Greeks that 'national unity' is a 'prerequisite for success', their demands are now ridding them of their one last asset: democracy.

Greece has slowly put together an austerity package that will wrack the country with prolonged economic strife, so it seems a reasonable time to recall that in order to allow countries that were in no condition to meet the rules to join, these rules were bent out of all recognition. To prevent unsustainable economic bubbles, countries like Greece and Spain also needed to have higher interest rates than economies like Germany, so not getting them made their crises much worse. They now desperately need to devalue. They can't. The PIGS are trapped.

The results of the southern squeeze in the PIGS countries themselves will be prolonged and painful. But what will this do to northern Eurozone countries?

---

[24]The disease is an old one. Memoirist Yannis Makriyannis (1797-1864) lamented: 'Misfortune spread throughout the land. There were many cases of corruption. Out creditors asked for a settlement; and the ambassadors were very pressing.'

The PIGS buy a lot from the northerners, so demand for their exports is going to keeping falling hard. Thus the PIGS are trapped by an overvalued currency and the northerners are trapped by the PIGS. And when – not if – some or all of the PIGS default, the losses will have to be borne by northern European taxpayers. This is because they will be expected to bail out the main creditors: their own countries' banks.[25]

All undemocratic governments attempt to bend economic reality to their will, and Brussels is now trying to get away with violating another basic economic principle: moral hazard. After the collapse of Lehman, the Fed propped up major investment banks. Similarities between Greece and the investment banks are manifold. Investors paid too little interest in the risks both were running, and gave both too much money too cheaply. Both used off-balance sheet structures to hide debts, and Greek leaders also had every short-term incentive to keep borrowing. While keeping Greece afloat keeps a default from happening (for a time), it also gives Greece, whose government also knows it is too big to fail, the incentive to get back to scrounging later on.

National regulators can make new laws for banks, but what mechanism exists for Greece (or any other nation) to be turfed out of the single currency? The answer is none. Worse, EU policymakers have an incentive to cover only the short-term: future loans will have to be made by future generations. Furthermore, refusal to give Greece any more money would involve terminating in due course the rescues of the other PIGS, bringing down the whole system. Still worse news is that IMF research has shown how rescues lead to unsustainable borrowing further down the line: Uganda was the first country to have debt cancelled under the initiative for heavily indebted poor countries, with more cancelled later by multilateral institutions. Since 2007, its debt has been rising again. A country receiving debt relief becomes 20 percent poorer than it would otherwise.

Should Greece now have to leave the eurozone, the country is liable to find itself in a little-appreciated nightmare scenario of Brussels' creation. It would be very hard for a Greek government to impose a new drachma upon its people. As printing money would be the only way of priming a new banking system and financing a budget deficit, a new currency would fall fast against the euro. Greek firms and families would attempt to insure themselves

---

[25] Amid the huge deficits run by the southern Eurozone members, another fact gives the lie to claims that the euro helped them keep their houses in order. One piece of the European apparatus yet to be imposed on the old Eastern bloc is the euro. The reason for this is simple: their fiscal deficits, which the EU long considered unacceptable.

by denominating all their contracts in euros, so of a currency's three core functions – as a medium of exchange, store of value, and unit of account – a new drachma would probably fulfil only the first. As financial writer Lorenzo Bini Smaghi reminds us, by leaving the euro of its own accord Greece would violate the Lisbon treaty, which obliged the irreversible renunciation of the old currencies. The Commission could therefore sue Greece at the ECJ if they felt 'materially damaged'. Non-compliance could also lead to European sanctions, which could be avoided only by leaving the EU entirely. The only alternative to this would be for Athens to negotiate jointly with all the other EU nations a treaty under which Greece adopted a new drachma, at which point Greeks, as discussed, would likely start a bank run to withdraw euros for transfer abroad. Capital controls would then be enacted, and all loans to Greece and the Greeks be put on hold, creating the spectacle of a modern state unable to pay its most basic expenditures. At this point the government may likely conclude that leaving the euro was impossible.

The point of all this is that the eurozone is a political union by stealth. Greece has taken most of the attention, but other southern countries deserve just as much. In autumn 2011, Portuguese non-financial companies (NFCs) had debts of 16 times their pre-interest profit, a figure of 12 times in Spain. Interest rates of 6 percent and 8 percent respectively would wipe their profits out; a ratio of about 10 renders NFC sectors junk. Spain's situation is exactly where Japan was in 1995 (Japan saw no real growth again until 2003), but Japan did at least have a currency, which devalued in real terms by 20 percent over the next six years, helping adjustment. Because it had a currency, Japan could also craft a monetary policy, the 'ZIRP' (or zero interest rate policy). Third, Japan had a fiscal policy, and chose to use it by employing budget deficits to offset private sector debt repayment through financial surpluses. German finance minister Wolfgang Schäuble informed his Spanish partners that their deficits must be cut 'no matter how politically painful'. Being in the Euro, Spain cannot devalue or employ monetary policy tools, and recent fiscal tightening by the ECB in Frankfurt is exactly what Spain cannot handle. The country is now in extended depression.

Although Spaniards have not been told how much of their crisis has been caused by Brussels, they have more reason to be angry than anyone in the Med. While Ireland, Portugal and Greece together make up under 5 percent of the EU's economy, Spain is a much bigger fish, and a Spanish banking collapse could sink the Continent's financial system. Spain was running a budget surplus before the crisis, and can thank the euro for its depression. Indeed, as Daniel Hannan has put it, Prime Minister José Luis Zapatero 'never went in for anything like Gordon Brown's demented financial incontinence'. With its economy overheating, what Spain needed was to raise interest rates. What Spain got were rates designed for Europe as a whole, giving it real interest rates at *minus 2 percent* in the decade before the crash. This is like giving amphetamines to someone having an epileptic fit. With the rubble of an insane construction boom now to be seen around the country, Brussels' solution is to give Spanish banks more cheap credit: the Spanish government has recently been borrowing at 7 percent to bolster banks which can borrow from the ECB at 1 percent, then lend money back to their own government at 7 percent so it can bail them out – through Brussels. Instead of the madness of treating debt with more debt, Spain should do the only thing a country in its situation can: default on its debts, leave the single currency, and work out how to make or do something useful from which it can make real money.

Britain could easily have been stuck in the same long-term situation: indeed, when the financial crisis hit, Britain had a little local difficulty of its own. With an economy particularly dependent on financial services, we felt the full force of the crisis. Had Britain been in the Euro, we couldn't have let our currency fall. With the pound, we did. A recession – the eurozone's first serious test – has made apparent the realities of the currency's model, and has made the obvious, well, obvious. The PIGS got pretend monetary credibility when they joined, but needed to set higher interest rates than Germany to deter unsustainable booms. They could not, and their bubbles grew huge. They have now burst, and their crises are much worse. The PIGS need to devalue, but cannot.

We may tut that it was silly of the Germans to have gone in at all: but not so fast. On the eve of the euro's birth, opinion polls showed *most* Germans were against joining the single currency, as were a large number of their economists. There too, the euro was the project of a political class, who encouraged the perception of overlapping German and Brussels interest, no matter the reality. So the Germans never wanted their national politicians to become Brussels's tax farming *douaniers*. Stuck in a failing project, most Germans are now in favour of Greece being thrown out 'if necessary', and over two thirds oppose bailing that or any other country out.

Even Karl-Otto Pöhl, Germany's chief negotiator for the ECB treaty in 1998, said that the 'alleged huge savings in transaction costs... are not in the least convincing'.[cdxxv] But when Josef Joffe, foreign editor of German daily

Süddeutsche Zeitung penned an essay a year earlier against the coming single currency, he was forced to publish it in the *New York Review of Books* (his own paper carried it discretely in a supplement a month later).

Having imposed their own terms of civilised debate, Europhiles are now trying to rewrite history. In 2006, Otmar Issing, former Bundesbank chief economist and latterly of the ECB, said the euro 'could work and survive... without fully fledged political union'. Now he informs his people: 'in the 1990s many economists – I was among them – warned that starting monetary union without having established a political union was putting the cart before the horse'. Come September 2011, Roger Altman, former US deputy treasury secretary, told Europe that it risked dragging America and the world into depression unless it resolved the sovereign debt crisis that the euro had helped create. But the solutions he suggested, pumping more money into the European Financial Stability Facility (EFSF), and fiscal union, demonstrated that extremely hazardous economic tactics would be the only ones Brussels would allow.

Against this background, we may bear in mind that the instability that the European system has created is reflected not only in the fact that there are approximately five countries in the EU which have recently had either no government or barely any (Belgium, Slovakia, Greece, Ireland and Portugal).

IF THE EURO FAILS, EUROPE FAILS

We have a Treaty under which there is no possibility of paying to bail out states in difficulty.

Chancellor Angela Merkel, 1st March 2010

The European Financial Stability Facility (EFSF) was originally intended to provide Greece with a loan of €30b. This soon climbed to €60bn, then €110bn. The total lending capacity of the EFSF became €440bn in July 2011, and on 27th October 2011 it was given a lending capacity of €1 trillion. As Eurosceptic Slovak politician Richard Sulík has pointed out, loans granted by the EFSF must be 'compatible with debt sustainability', but this is a vague hope for the nations to which it is lending (Sulík also describes the EFSF as an attempt to solve 'the debt crisis by creating new debts'). For his part, Greek former PM George Papandreou claimed his country was being used as a 'laboratory animal', and that 'the EU's own credibility is being tested... so it will be especially strict with us'. Yet not so strict, it seems, with itself. Article 125 of the Lisbon Treaty – the 'no bail-out clause' – was meant to underpin proper economic management. The EU has quietly forgotten its own rules.

Other dangerous tactics are inherent to the eurozone. By keeping sterling, Britain has avoided sharing Europe's enormous hidden liability of unfunded pensions that will now tempt the ECB into creating inflation over the long-term (we should note however that inflation, though unpleasant during peace, remains an essential weapon in wartime: the ability of independent nations to control it protects them against aggressors). There is a greater question at stake however, and that is how we deal with economic globalisation as a country. There is an oft-heard claim that by joining a single currency Britain would have reduced exchange rate risk. This is a myth.

This becomes obvious once we consider volatility against the dollar as well as with Europe. Getting rid of competing currencies stops citizens choosing the economic regime under which they live, the alternative being an enormous economic zone from which firms and people cannot escape. This is no kind of defence against the effects of globalisation – indeed it is one of the nightmare outcomes of globalisation. When currencies compete against each other, central bankers are made to protect the quality of their currencies (and the level of currency competition has a direct effect on other areas such as regulation). As the single currency will hang on for a while, sterling will force the ECB to face institutional competition. The idea that exchange rate volatility will be reduced by fixing a currency to the euro is dubious, and so too is the belief that flexible exchange rates harm trade growth. As about half of Britain's trade is with the dollar area, sterling's real exchange rate volatility will be lower than the euro (by substituting the Deutschmark for the euro before 1999, we can see that this has indeed been the case since 1980).

Nor have flexible exchange rates harmed the immense growth of world trade in the last thirty years. From 1972, when the Bretton Woods fixed exchange rates system collapsed, to 2001, trade rose 6.43 times (when corrected for GDP growth). Between 1950 and 1971, when exchange rates were fixed, world trade grew 1.79 times. Britain and Ireland ended their 150-year monetary union in 1979 (when a fall in trade until 1982 coincided with an economic contraction in Ireland and a rise in sterling). But trade soon bounced back. A report by HM Treasury in 2003 found that 'the estimated impact of the Anglo-Irish currency regime on trade between the two countries appears insignificantly different from zero'.

Another area is responsibility. Commission President Romano Prodi is reported to have said that the euro's *Stability and Growth Pact* which was supposed to secure its future was a 'silly rule' – indeed when it did not suit Germany in 2004 they simply ignored it, but Germany has insisted on rigorous application of the rule in Italy and the southern countries. While the northern European countries argued for a serious position, the south had its way, and it is well known that entry terms were fudged. Aware that the eurozone won't let any member go bankrupt, its rogue states know they will be bailed out. The moral hazard problem should always have been clear. Only currency competition can ensure that poor economic policy results in falling demand for that currency. Again, this means the world needs more currency competition, not less.

But members hid their debt, and their irresponsibility. In reality, only Britain and the Netherlands have engineered near-manageable pension liabilities (and the public debt of most developed nations is astonishing). Implicit debt from pension, health and environmental liabilities is equivalent to nearly 300 percent for Spain and 150 percent for France and Germany (Britain's is a touch above 100 percent of GDP). Even the eurozone's deficit rule as it was did not account for the hidden debt of pensions and the medical need of an ageing population. Apart from the British and Dutch exceptions, Europe's welfare systems are programmed to create disaster unless changed radically. These changes would hurt, but they become more urgent as the population ages.

They come in five possible forms, which are as follows: 1) to reduce pension rights; 2) increase taxes and social insurance contributions without scaring off wealth generating investors; 3) increase the age of retirement; 4) issue bonds to finance the debt while privatising pensions; and 5) create inflation. Knowing what we do about the power of unions in continental economies, the most likely option is depressingly clear: recall also that sovereign issuers of money will be tempted by the fact that their money is legal tender across the eurozone. Another irresponsible tactic governments have pursued is to allow immigrants to flood the labour force, creating a cash surplus. But this is temporary: most of these immigrants have been low skilled low earners, who ultimately take more than they contribute in the cost of falling productivity, overcrowding, crime, policing and welfare. In future there will also be constant pressure on the ECB to keep interest rates low: member states' elections happen constantly, so pressure to irresponsibly loosen monetary policy will be continual,[cdxxvi] as monetary expansion generally happens before an election for obvious vote-winning reasons. These demands are likely to be veiled as suggestions to help growth.

Finally, there is the question of freedom. Dutch economist Wim Vanthoor saw two kinds of monetary union: supra-regional and inter-European. The former were Switzerland in 1848, Italy in 1861, and Germany in 1871. Here, different regions accepted the same currency only *after* political union. Without political unity the inter-European unions however, like the Latin Monetary Union, have all failed. And because monetary expansion is carried out intentionally by states with severe deficits caused by partly by corrupt tax systems (like the PIGS), the union requires methods of transfer from rich to poor regions. As Vanthoor put it: 'EMU is the most suitable instrument to deepen European integration, as it may potentially develop its own dynamics from which the need for political union may arise'.[cdxxvii] Quite so: it is now clear that if the single currency is going to stick around for a while (at least until the inflation-wracked demise we have described above), political union will have to be forced upon Europe.

Vanthoor's surmise was of course the game all along. Economic reforms are being used to further political integration, whatever the disasters along the way. The irony of the ECB being called a 'central bank without political pressures' is that it has always been a tool for European political unity. While a variety of currencies imposes discipline on respective central bankers by giving people different havens against inflation and central bankers' bad behaviour, under a unified Europe this becomes much harder. A politico-economic union will also tend to conceive of free trade agreements as 'concessions', or defeats, not the aids to competitiveness they really are. So Europe is becoming a politico-economic cartel: as Spanish economist Pedro Schwarz puts it, 'the pound can still do sterling work for individual freedom', and in keeping it, 'Britain will once again be battling for the freedom of Europe'.

Asked whether he had any concerns about the erosion of democracy required to create the euro, former Commissioner Étienne Davignon was withering: 'I find it total rubbish',[cdxxviii] he said. AMUE was not disbanded with the birth of the single currency at the dawn of 1999. Flushed with success, the group's ambitions could only broaden, because there was unfinished business: us. In Britain, Denmark, Sweden and even Norway, away from their peoples' eyes, AMUE stayed busy, campaigning quietly for the euro.

The creation of the single currency however was a pyrrhic victory. The euro can now only survive if the Germans and their fellow northerners continue agreeing to guarantee Greek debts (if their constitutions let them). How can we expect the German people to feel about this? One German worker in Aachen recently asked a pollster why he should pay for a teacher in Athens who fancies retiring at 55. It is a good question, and he shouldn't. What is more, in the end he probably won't have to, because the whole thing must fall apart.

HOW TO CREATE A GLOBAL DEPRESSION

As the crisis deepened, analysts suggested that 'a game of brinkmanship' was being played by the EU's central institutions. At the beginning of March 2011, the ECB shocked observers by pre-announcing the rate rises that Portugal would have to pay on its debt, making it inevitable that Portugal will need a bailout. The intention by 2011 appeared to be to push the leaders for a huge fiscal and monetary solution at the summits that were about to begin. Spanish household and company debt stood at €2.5 trillion. Now the other PIGS were on the brink: Greece was undergoing the toughest fiscal crunch ever experienced by a western country, and unemployment had jumped to 14.8 percent by December 2010, before austerity had even begun. Greek newspaper *Aviana* despaired, 'we should default and return to the Drachma'.

As the euro began to shake, it became apparent how the client states of southern Europe – and their own client regions – had flourished on northern largesse for decades. *The New York Times* reported from Madeira, the hugely subsidised Portuguese archipelago where every single election since the 1978 return to democracy had been won by social democrat Alberto João Jardim. In September 2011, Portugal's finance ministry reported a 'grave irregularity' of over €1.1bn in Madeira's accounts, a sum which alone equalled 0.3 percent of Portugal's GDP and followed a €78bn bailout of the country's economy. After its bailout had been agreed, Portugal admitted that Madeira's debt totalled €6.3bn and rising, not the €5.8bn originally claimed. European Commissioner for Monetary Affairs Olli Rehn called this a 'surprise', and Portugal's own finance minister Vítor Gaspar described Madeira as an 'isolated case', but this is not true either in Portugal or southern Europe generally. In Spain's Castilla la Mancha region for instance, the local government has been accused of failing to account for €2bn in 'unpaid bills'.

Meanwhile with Europe's economies in recession, budget Commissioner

Janusz Lewandowski announced plans for a 4.3 percent EU budget increase, opining that 'despite the climate of austerity, we have to grow'. In their 2011 report, the Court of Auditors' figures revealed that serious questions remained about €4.5bn in payments made by the EU in 2010, a figure which had increased from 2009. The official EU response was simply untrue: 'for the fourth year in a row, the EU's accounts have received a clean bill of health from its external auditors'.[cdxxix] Britain's net contribution to the EU budget rose by 74 percent that year.[26]

A euro 'no bail-out clause' was supposed to stop the 'negative effects of national misbehaviour' from spilling over elsewhere, but Germans will have to pay for Greece regardless. Emergency government loans are the method usually discussed, but they will have to pay indirectly too, though support for German banks lumbered with Greek debt. As public support for throwing more money into the euro sank further, in October 2011 Angela Merkel carved out a *Bundestag* majority for continuing a rescue fund. She did this by raising the possibility of war, telling MPs:

> 'Nobody should take for granted another 50 years of peace and prosperity in Europe... that's why I say: if the euro fails, Europe fails. We have a historical obligation: to protect by all means Europe's unification process begun by our forefathers after centuries of hatred and blood spill. None of us can foresee what the consequences would be if we were to fail'.

Actually, Merkel (with Nicholas Sarkozy) was making the situation worse, as they suggested Greece could be expelled to preserve the euro. Markets reacted by selling the bonds of any eurozone nation that seemed vulnerable, making the funding situation even tougher. They also suggested Greek default could be 'voluntary', rendering credit default swaps (a type of insurance against default) worthless. The implication for investors was that the eurozone would find ways of reneging on its contracts whenever necessary.[cdxxx]

By then the failures were everywhere. In mid-November 2011, German

---

[26]Guy Vorhofstadt, former Belgian PM and leader of the European Parliament's so-called 'Alliance of Liberals and Democrats', which includes Britain's Liberal Democrats, informed Britain in June 2011 that this should rise further as Brussels increased its budget during a recession: 'Her Majesty's Government is very disappointed by the [draft] report. That means that we have a very good [draft] report today I think dear colleagues'. There followed applause and desk banging. He went on: 'Another suggestion that we can make to Her Majesty's Government is that if they want to make savings in the British public sector then it's by increasing the role of the European Union'.

sovereign bond yields rose above Britain's, as investors started betting that Germany would be unable to hold the currency together (and that whatever her dire prophecies, Merkel would not in the end manage to force Germans to bail out the PIGS). Investors started fleeing euro denominated assets of any kind, including German bunds, as sterling became Europe's choice default asset. As journalist Ambrose Evans-Pritchard declared, 'this is no longer a serious currency'. Britain has begun preparing for the 'biggest mass default in history', and the Financial Services Authority has asked British banks to be ready for the euro's disorderly collapse.

As the eurozone crisis has grown, it has become clear that Brussels's proudest creation can only be saved in the long run with the help of Britain, the US, and the international community. France's former Finance Minister Christine Lagarde warned that the problem had to be dealt with 'as collectively as possible'. Lagarde described the euro as 'the Gordian knot of the crisis', and raised the prospect of developing countries such as Brazil and India loaning money, via the IMF, to some of the wealthiest countries in Europe to preserve the Eurozone. By mid-December 2011 Moscow had committed $10 billion to an IMF whip-round to bailout the euro, in return for Brussels lifting visa controls. Head of the ECB Mario Draghi said in a speech in Berlin that the eurozone countries were thus 'on the right track'.[27]

Although the Left has always been convinced that the EU is a counterweight to America, it was to Washington that Brussels now turned again. By winter 2011, the Federal Reserve had begun to act as a global lender of last resort to the eurozone. Unable to roll over $2 trillion in dollar-denominated debts, eurozone banks had become effectively shut out of the dollar market, able only to raise funds on a week-by-week basis. Indeed the 'stress alarm' – the euro/dollar three month cross currency basis swap – hit minus 166 points by late November, very similar to events before Lehman collapsed in 2008. As China cutting reserves to boost liquidity in case Europe's banking system went into meltdown, an offer to cut currency swap rates (made by the central banks of the US, Britain, Canada, Japan and Switzerland) was described as intended to 'ease strains in financial markets and thereby mitigate the effects of such strains on the supply of credit'. The reality was that the Fed and the other Anglo-Saxons had stepped in to stop a huge European credit crunch.

---

[27]Draghi was a member of Goldman Sachs' management committee between 2002-2005. He has been accused of involvement in the swaps for Greece and other European governments that helped disguise their real economic condition, which he denies.

Another way of putting this is that the countries whose economic policy remains under democratic control stepped in to save a post-democratic state. But the elephant in the room was this: whatever gambit the leaders were going to produce at financial summits, the PIGS economies do not produce enough of value, so they need to devalue. A currency can only ever be a reflection of an economy, and you can't bail it out forever.

10.

A European Germany or A German Europe

I have always found the word Europe on the lips of those who wanted something from other powers which they dared not demand in their own name.

Bismarck

PRUSSIA

In order to understand the European question, it is essential to understand the German question. It is equally essential to understand Germany in the context of its history without interpreting Germany exclusively by its past aggression. By the same token, it is important to be aware that Germany, whilst now a peaceful and democratic country, still retains its intrinsic character, which is bound up with much of its present assertiveness and dominance of the European Union.

This is not a new phenomenon, and does not derive exclusively from reunification. It traces its origins in modern times to the post-war reconstruction of Europe, and as has already been seen, was already on the minds of those, like Macmillan, who were trying to build the post-war settlement.

The idea of unifying Germany by unifying Europe is at least 300 years old. Made famous in the 1700s by the romantic poet Novalis, the idea appeared even earlier in philosopher Gottfried Leibniz's *Caesarinus Furstenerius (De Supremium Principium Germaniae)* in 1677. Leibniz called for Germany to be unified through the unification of Christendom, to solve Germany's myriad religious and political divisions and messy borders, for good. Today many – though not all – Germans equate their country's interests with those of Europe, and the story of Germany's unification bears profound similarity to the creation of the European Union of today.

The dominant German power of the 19th century was Prussia, and the historian Heinrich von Treitschke described Prussia's early empire as the 'Prussian-German unitary state'. The creation of this hegemony – and the 'Zollverein' economic union that began it – never required any secret agenda or conspiracy, just a Prussian pre-eminence that was allowed to go unchecked. From the creation of the Zollverein in 1834 (following a process of centralisation that had begun at least thrity years earlier under French pressure) to the declaration of the Empire in 1871 took almost forty years, but the roots of unification can be found in 1818, when Prussia unified her tariff system (that Prussia was divided between East and West actually forced her to apply pressure to the states in between).

Although Austria opposed the actions of its major German competitor, Prussian Finance Minister von Motz explained in 1829 that the German economic union for which Prussia was striving was just the first stage of political union 'under the protection of Prussia'. But he understood that a union would be created with the application of economic pressure. In 1834 this pressure created the Zollverein, an economic union unlike its military predecessors. The economist Friedrich List, born in Württemberg, suggested that this new state would be no mere unit, but one whose concept of trade would mean not trade overseas, but trade internally, to guard its industries from the ravages of the British and their free trade. This state would transform trade between the old German states into a single internal market. To compensate the smaller states for their inferiority to Prussia, they would receive a place at the top table by agreeing to confederation. The Zollverein turned customs union to economic union.

Article 14 saw member states commit only to 'discuss' monetary union. When they began to in 1837, Hessen, suspicious of threats to its sovereignty, suggested a parallel currency scheme (much like an idea of Nigel Lawson and John Major's, 'competing currencies'). Prussia agreed reluctantly to this in 1838, buying time before the adoption of its Thaler. Parities with the Thaler were fixed however, allowing a common currency to circulate with the others. Full monetary union was implemented thirty-seven years later, after the foundation of the German Empire in 1871 with its Reichsmark in 1875.

Prussia never moved too fast. Having defeated Austria in 1866, the Prussians may have been able to enforce their own terms for federation, drawing up an outline for union 'with Prussian characteristics' the same year. But Otto von Bismarck (Minister President of Prussia, 1862-1890, and first Chancellor of Germany, 1871-1890) understood that, given a Council of Ministers and a directly elected assembly, the other German states would confederate of their own accord. He talked passionately of the federal, decentralised nature of new constitution, assuring the lesser states that there was no risk of their separate identities being subsumed. The southern states soon joined the union, which was then renamed the German Empire (and to placate Saxony, the Imperial Court of Justice was located in not in Prussia, but Leipzig).

Agreement was cemented with various concessions to material questions of sovereignty about which they felt particularly strongly (Bavaria was given concessions on beer duties). But the German Empire, Bismarck said, 'has its firm basis in the princes' loyalty to the federation, in which its future also lies', its constitution describing an empire of princes and free towns in 'eternal union'. But the empire's desire, Bismarck told its smaller states, was to see a German Prussia, not a Prussian Germany. Far from being a Prussian empire, Bismarck explained that the empire would contain and restrict Prussia, giving the other states the security from potential Prussian aggression which they craved but once lacked.[28]

It is hard to claim that the German empire contained Prussia, in the end. Even in the forty years immediately after its foundation, the federal empire saw massive centralisation, its constitution's unitary elements winning out over federal promises. Centralisation almost invariably meant convergence with the most powerful state, Prussia. Upon its creation the imperial authorities released a flood of harmonisation, overstepping even their own powers. One German historian wrote how 'the codifications in this half century exceed in scope, significance and long term effect any comparable period in German legislative history'. The advantage of codification was simple: it lasted. There were new imperial standards, legal directives, industrial and business codes and legislation, competition legislation, civil legislation, foreign exchange,

---

[28]This was a classic hegemonic relationship under the usual definition (from Murray Forsyth's *Unions of States*): 'I will use my strength to guarantee you and, in return, you must follow my lead with regard to other powers, and give me support and assistance when I call upon it... an unequal relationship established between a great power and one or more smaller powers which is nevertheless based on the juridicial and formal equality of all the states concerned. It is not an empire.'

banking, tax and economic regulations, imperial foreign policy, naval policy, and embryonic social policy.

Imposing all these new rules meant more power was needed for the imperial bureaucracy, which had to grow to oversee them. Power accrued in the central organs of the new state, all without Prussia ever possessing a majority in the Federal Council. Prussia could have been outvoted, but her decision became '*de facto* decisive for the most difficult political negotiations'.[cdxxxi] Smaller states had the right of veto, but also had dependence: 'Prussian ministers took the lead in the Federal Council, Prussian initiatives dominated in legislation. Prussian authorities partly took over the function of imperial authorities.'[cdxxxii]

Prussia allowed some of her own of sovereignty to seep to the imperial institutions, but refused to be moved on what really mattered. Separate passports gradually fell out of use due to freedom of movement within the empire, and in 1914 imperial taxes were imposed for the first time. Looking back on the first forty years, constitutionalist Heinrich Tiepel found that the original promises that the empire would remain decentralised disappeared with the deluge of new laws, mainly conforming to Prussian practice. He proposed his own definition of hegemony: 'the totality of all laws and other arrangements by means of which the leading power of a union of states can give the community the desired direction and the stamp of its own spirit'.

FICHTE: ONE OF THESE FEW

In the century preceding the creation of the Zollverein, then the Prussian hegemony, the whole question of what one even meant by freedom – and when one should obey a power – had become, as the great philosopher Sir Isaiah Berlin put it, 'a scandal'.

Thinking men knew that in the physical world the sciences had begun to create order – in astronomy, chemistry, physics. But in Germany in the decades after the Thirty Years War, human affairs continued to be a frightening and cacophonous chaos of intellectual conflict. None could institute the order that Newton had found in nature, and the minds of men began to seek a simple order to establish an irrefutable structure for an unpredictable world. More than anyone else, the philosopher Johann Gottlieb Fichte did so by launching a concept of freedom profoundly different to that of the English-speakers of the late eighteenth century, so although the contemporary German began talking of freedom with as much passion, what they meant was very different to the people of the Atlantic coast of Europe – where freedom meant guarding individual liberty from encroachment by others.

Fichte himself said freedom was the only thing that concerned him, and 'no other ingredient' entered into his ideas. But he had a warning. Ordinary men should not expect to understand them, and only the select really interested him:

> 'To men as they are in their ordinary education, our philosophical theory must be absolutely unintelligible, for the object of which it speaks does not exist for them; they do not possess that special faculty for which, and by which, alone this object has any being. It is as if one were talking to men blind from birth...'

In each generation only a small vanguard could carry the torch of freedom. Fichte was among these, his grasp of freedom possible through his penetration of the true nature of the universe. For the thinkers of Western Europe, the problem was how the arbitrary rules of some individuals might make them unfair authorities over the majority, and this was where the threats to men's freedom lay – in other words they were not just 'in the nature of things'. This meant that just because there were things one could not do – like flying – that did not make us slaves, because to be a slave means being *prevented* from doing something by other people. But not for Germans like Fichte, who worried not about the ill will of other men, but sought freedom from the very nature of the universe.

Naturally, much of this was informed by their experience of German life in the eighteenth century. Amid brutal humiliation by the martial French state of Louis XIV (1638-1715), economic waywardness and political strife typified the life of the German after the Thirty Years War, which ended in 1648. In this insecure world, the average German depended entirely on the personal will of his Prince: in short, he was nothing like the conquering Frenchman or the free and defiant English.[cdxxxiii]

To the German, freedom was a distant thing indeed, and he knew there were few things he could really do. If his Prince was a tyrant, and abused him, and took what was his, this was no less a natural misfortune than the rain and the wind in his face. The things one could prevent were few, and the very idea of freedom became at once impossible and wonderful, a distant utopia.

Isaiah Berlin suggests that at such times men have often turned inwards. With no hope of getting what they really want, they begin trying to deprive themselves of the want itself, to find 'that calm and that serenity which is as good a substitute for owning the things which I want as can be found in this vale of tears'. Unable to change what seem the rigid realities of the universe, he has one escape route left: through 'a very grand, very sublime form of the doctrine of sour grapes'. He makes instead a 'strategic retreat' to 'inward serenity... inner thoughts... inner ideals': in other words the place the tyrant cannot reach. Through the work of Immanuel Kant (1724-1804), Fichte and other German romantics discovered that the only truly valuable thing in the universe was the true state of the spiritual inner self. Ideals and strivings, it turned out, did not rest on external circumstances, or negotiation, or compromise, but on living up to the inner ideal.

Kant had assumed his enlightened followers would find in their ideals enlightened and rational personal conduct. But now Fichte turned from his mentor. Morality was not a discoverable, factual state of affairs, but meant honestly heeding one's 'inner voice', whatever its commands may be. Morality was now like a work of art, made, not found, and just as Marx wrote a few decades later, failure to see this was to risk being an unwitting slave in another's system. This was a profound moment in the history of European thought.[cdxxxiv]

Western European thinkers had usually seen man as naturally autonomous – acting, having will, not just being acted upon – but Fichte insisted he was in fact heteronomous, always liable to be overwhelmed by passions, fears, hopes, desires, which may force him to do what he might regret, and which at his best he might not do. Man was in great part a slave, through things over which he had no control. This meant that to be moral meant retreating to a place where he could be totally free from outside molestation, where what counted was not the achievement, but the attempt, of personal virtue. This meant a kind of political 'quietism'.

All that mattered now was an inner integrity, dedication through self-control to the personal cause. This was the fundamental dogmatic position, but it is also a kind of self-protection. The outside world could hurl hurricanes in his face, but that was outside his moral realm now. Nature no longer meant observable facts in the world outside, but was 'dead matter on which you impose your will'. Morality became one's own project, and so became a question of projecting oneself. So political activity became a type of self-projection.

Now Isaiah Berlin describes a leap in Fichte's thought. Only if this 'inner self' is active can one be free. But this self, this spirit, is not isolated, and Fichte starts to draw strange conclusions about a self that does not represent individual human beings at all, but has something to do with society instead – a 'super-self'. So the individual who must impose his moral will against nature is not a human being, but a collectivity, a race, a nation, or even mankind. With Napoleon having occupied Berlin in 1808 – the Frenchman himself a triumphant example of self-assertion – Fichte delivered his famous speech from the city. All Germans, he said, must rise:

'Either you believe in an original principle in man – in a freedom, a perfectibility and infinite progress of our species – or you believe in none of this. You may even have a feeling or intuition of the opposite. All those who have within them a creative quickening of life, or else, assuming that such a gift has been withheld from them, at least reject what is but vanity and await the moment when they are caught up by the torrent of original life, or even if they are not yet at this point, at any rate have some confused presentiment of freedom, those who have towards it not hatred, nor fear, but a feeling of love – all these are part of the primal humanity, and considered as a people they constitute the primal people. I mean the German people. All those, on the other hand, who have resigned themselves to represent only derivative, second-hand products, who think of themselves in this way, these become in effect such and shall pay the price of their belief. They are only an annexe to life. Not for them those pure springs which flowed before them, which still flow around them; they are but the echo coming back from a rock of a voice which is silent. Considered as a people, they are excluded from the primal people, they are strangers, outsiders. A nation which to this day bears the name of German (or simply the people) has not ceased to give evidence of a creative and original activity in most diverse fields. The hour has come at last when philosophy, penetrated through and through by self-awareness, will hold to this nation a mirror wherein it will recognise itself with a clear perception, and at the same time will become quite clearly aware of the mission of which it has hitherto had but a confused premonition, but which nature herself has imposed upon that nation; an unmistakeable call has been addressed to it today to labour in freedom calmly and clearly and to perfect itself according to the notions which it has framed of itself, to accomplish the duty which has been outlined to it. And everyone who believes this kind of thing will join with these people whose function, whose mission, is to create.'

From the person wishing not to be intruded upon in his 'inner world', we have come to an absolute freedom subject only to the ideals of inner conscience. And as I can conquer the things that are low and unnecessary in me, the leader will also suppress the base, unnecessary, and compromised things in the group. But what has become of freedom in all this – the individual freedom of the British thinkers, whereby, within some limits, a man can be frivolous or profound or good or bad – just because that freedom is sacred? Fichte finds that some über-self can decide about that. And acquiescence to it is in fact the root to freedom. So freedom has become submission.

In 1834, the same year the Zollverein came into existence, the Jewish German poet Heinrich Heine, then living in Paris, tried to warn the French of what was coming. The ideals upon which democrats were building Western Europe would soon need desperate defence from the consolidating power to the east. The Fichteans will arm. They will see compromise with the external world as nothing better than defeat:

> 'Thought precedes action as lightning precedes thunder. German thunder too is a German, and not in a hurry, and it comes rolling slowly onward; but come it will, and once you hear it crashing, as nothing ever crashed before in the history of the world, then know that the German thunder has finally hit the mark. At that sound the eagles will fall dead from the air and the lions in the remotest deserts of Africa will… creep to their royal lairs. A drama will be performed in Germany in contrast with which the French Revolution will seem a mere peaceful idyll.'

Because its aims are total, any pretext will do. Heine pleads with his French hosts not to disarm. Because on Mount Olympus:

> 'Amidst the nude deities who feast upon nectar and ambrosia, there is one goddess who amidst all this merriment and peace keeps her

armour and her helmet and a spear in her hand – the goddess of wisdom.'

The British and French found that freedom gave 'each man his own circle, that small but indispensable vacuum within which he can do as he pleases, go to the bad or to the good, choose for the sake of choosing, in which the value of choice as such is regarded as sacred'. But to the new Fichtean Germans it was no such thing. Freedom was transcendental, and the German nation had a special destiny to find it, to march towards it, to impose its will. These concepts – the liberal and the authoritarian – vied for the minds of Europeans as the German union came into existence in the nineteenth century.

By 1914, when British and French academics called on their German peers to distance themselves from Prussian militarism and the bid for European hegemony, they failed to understand that Berlin's actions fitted the worldview of much of the German-speaking cultural class.[cdxxxv] Releasing the 'Manifesto of the 93', these German scholars and artists stated: 'It is not true that the struggle against our so-called militarism is not also a struggle against our civilisation, as our enemies hypocritically pretend it is. Were it not for German militarism, German civilisation would have long since been extirpated from the earth.' The signatories included Siegfried Wagner, the physicist Max Planck, philosopher Alois Riehl and historian Friedrich Meinecke. As historian Peter Watson says, this 'did reflect the views of educated people in Germany at the time'. In Berlin the *Bund Deutsche Gelehrter und Kunstler* recruited 200 leading intellectuals including Thomas Mann to present the case for war. Their themes included the superiority of authoritarianism to British parliamentary democracy.

Karl Lamprecht, advisor to wartime Chancellor Theovald von Bethmann-Hollweg put it bluntly: 'It is subjectively recognised and objectively proven that we are capable of the highest achievements in the world...' A generation of German historians – among them Hans Delbrück and Otto Hintze – suggested that the system of smaller nation states would now be replaced by a smaller number of 'world states', of which an area of German hegemony would be one. To force Britain to accept this was the point of the war. Delbrück explained that 'This nation is invincible... against that island nation... men of commerce who merely hand out money... it is [these] men we need to be fighting against... with the certainty of our eternal inner superiority'. Oswald Spengler described a fight against English liberalism, 'with its emphasis on individual freedom and self-determination' and superior 'Prussian' socialism, 'with its emphasis on order and authority', while Friedrich Meinecke dwelt on the German nation's 'mission from God to organise the divine essence of man in a separate, unique [and] irreplaceable form... Only the Germans had managed to find the combination of *Innerlichkeit*, individual freedom, and willingness to sacrifice selfish interests to the good of the whole.' The democratic national governments of Britain, France and America were not German, thought Thomas Mann: 'This most introspective of people, this people of metaphysics, of pedagogy and of music, is not a politically oriented but a morally oriented people... and less interested in political progress towards democracy'.

By arguing – especially in the United States through their publication *Deutschland und der Weltkreig* – for a 'balance-of-power' with Britain, Delbrück and many other German historians became accepted as the 'moderate' view, against those intellectuals who sought straightforward annexation. But even as the war turned against Germany – amid battles so ferocious they could be heard from Hampstead Heath – the philosophical rage went on. Philosopher Adolf Lasson wrote that 'the whole of European culture... has gathered itself together like a focal point on German soil and in the hearts of the German people. It would be quite wrong to express ourselves on this point with modesty...'[cdxxxvi]

Inspired by the economist Friedrich List, the economic element of Germany's dash for hegemony in 1914 was called *Mitteleuropa*.[cdxxxvii] After Germany had lost the competition with Britain for naval supremacy around the turn of the century, in 1913, Gustav Stresemann, Secretary General of the Alliance of German Industrialists (and Foreign Minister after the war who became famous for *rapprochement* with the French) described Germany's demand for a 'closed economic area to secure our need for raw materials and our exports'. Chancellor Theovald von Bethmann-Hollveg himself wrote the 'September economic programme' of 1914, whose aim was to forge a customs union with France, the Low Countries, Austria-Hungary, Poland, Italy, Denmark, and if possible the other Scandinavian countries, a similar area to Napoleon's economic bloc (and later an inspiration for the Nazis and their collaborators in France). Bethmann-Hollveg believed this economic union was the only means of assuring German security.[cdxxxviii]

This union would impose a protectionist regime known as a *Großraumwirtschaft*, or 'Great Space Economy'. It was supported by a large swathe of German industrial interests, especially growing chemical and electrical concerns. Walther Rathenau, chairman of AEG, said this would be 'civilisation's greatest conquest' and would merge 'Europe together through practical common interest'[cdxxxix]. But a policy which was described as being defensive became offensive soon enough.[cdxl]

As historian John Laughland points out, when modern Germans say they will never again 'go it alone', but will always cooperate with European allies, this is the most traditional German policy imaginable; so is claiming they are acting in those allies' interests (Henry Kissinger also suggests that a clearer coalition of states against Germany in 1914 could have prevented war).[cdxli] A more sustained attempt at European unity would come after 1918.

After the German drive to hegemony in World War One induced the collapse of the old European system of states, Germans now took the lead in proposing new forms of union to protect the peace. With the founding of the European Customs Union, Germany's SPD committed to 'the creation of a European economic unity, which has become urgent for economic reasons, and the creation of a United States of Europe'. The Pan-European Union was then set up by Count Coudenhouve-Kalergi in 1923. Gustav Stresemann then acquiesced to his French counterpart Aristide Briand's proposal of a European Federal Union in 1929 to 'domesticate' Germany. Stresemann, says Dutch historian WH Roobol,

> '…was inclined to embrace Briand's plan because he foresaw that in the not-too-distance future it might give Germany an outstanding opportunity to establish at least an economic predominance in East-Central Europe. He may also have calculated, as some German diplomats did, that the desired customs union with Austria, which had been forbidden by the Treaty of Versailles, could be attained under the cover of Briand's plan for European unity.'

Kissinger describes Stresemann as a 'ruthless practitioner of realpolitik who pursued traditional national Germany interests with ruthless persistence' (in 1925 he began a trade war with Poland, arguing in a letter to the German ambassador in London against any settlement until Poland's 'economic and financial distress has reached an extreme stage and reduced the entire Polish body politic to a state of powerlessness'[cdxlii]). Recalling AJP Taylor's description of a 'fundamental continuity' between Stresemann and Hitler's foreign policy, Laughland suggests that had Stresemann not died suddenly in 1929 at the age of 51, he might have attained by diplomacy what the man who took power in 1933 in his 'hectic impatience' destroyed.[cdxliii]

THIS TIME IT'S DIFFERENT

Probably feeling that he had wasted enough time already with the company assembled in the room, and at the same time unwilling to give too much away to someone he did not know, Guggenbühl returned... to the model theatre. Ostentatiously, he continued to play about with its accessories. We drank our beer... His uncompromising behaviour no doubt expressed to perfection the role to which he was assigned in her mind: the scourge of frivolous persons of the sort he knew so well.

Anthony Powell, *A Dance to the Music of Time*, **1955**

The German idealism – that passion Immanuel Kant helped ignite – was by Kant's own admission born from conscious rejection of the British empirical view. Its two fundamental tenets were that an individual's freedom had to be seen in the context of 'metaphysical necessity', and that reality is determined, at least partly, by the perceiver.[cdxliv] As we have seen, this meant ideals could be defined first in the mind, then imposed on reality. Any individual might object to this, but he was anyway destined to play a subservient role to grand historical processes – processes known to that class of men who could impose their will.

Kant took it upon himself to build a plan for nothing less than eternal world peace, which he based on a romantic ideal of classical Greece. His follower Friedrich Schelling described a pan-European, or perhaps worldwide, federation that would create it – and here the German thinkers were not alone. In 1814, with Napoleon yet to be defeated, the French philosopher Henri Comte de Saint-Simon (who considered himself a liberal) published *On the Reorganisation of European Society, Or One the Necessity of Grouping Together the Peoples of Europe into One Body Politic, While Conserving the National Independence of Each*. This proposal for European federal union urged homogeneity to overcome Europe's 'disorganisation'. Although each nation could keep its own parliament, they would 'recognise the supremacy of a general parliament placed above all national governments, and invested with the power to judge their differences'.[cdxlv] Saint-Simon, who would have a considerable influence on Marx, had begun his intellectual life as a liberal, but now decided that politics was simply the 'science of production, a state being 'nothing but a large industrial company'. Instead of individual freedom, which was 'vague and metaphysical', this meant a power that could 'choose the direction to which the national forces are applied'.[cdxlvi] In his *Industrial System* of 1820, he proposed that under this European system of production, the liberty of individuals would be 'contrary to the development of civilisation and to the organisation of a well-ordered system'. This was technocracy. When he dismissed those who disagreed as being 'like quadrupeds',[cdxlvii] his transition from liberal to authoritarian was complete.

But if Germany in particular lacked any serious alternative model to Anglosphere liberalism and mercantilism, this has only fuelled a passion that somehow, through some different way, Germany has a great future ahead. As Nietzsche put it, 'the Germans are a people of the day before yesterday and the day after tomorrow'.

One of the Nazis' leading intellectual inspirations as they rose to power was the political scientist Karl Haushofer (1869-1946), who in 1924 had visited Hitler in prison in Landsberg as he wrote *Mein Kampf* after the Beer Hall Putsch, before associating in the highest German wartime circles, and eventually killing himself in 1946. Haushofer believed in a *Raum* – living space – and that Europe had to unite to defend itself against other spaces. If Versailles had made Germany incapable of defending itself, Germans like Haushofer decided that Germany's return to a position of strength constituted a European act: in Haushofer's words, for Europe to be 'a part of the world which counts for itself'.[cdxlviii] Like the leaders of the Germanic Holy Roman Empire before him, Haushofer was sure it was the division of Europe into states – the principle of 'power politics itself' – which was the real enemy. In place of national 'order' there would be a 'common European idea and meaning'.[cdxlix] Haushofer understood who the prime cultural enemy would be: in 1930 his follower Erich Obst coined the phrase '*Anglosaxia contra mundum*'.[cdl]

The middle of this Europe was naturally Germany. What the British historian (and arguable founder of 'international relations') Halford Mackinder feared in 1887 was that: 'expansion over the marginal lands of Euro-Asia [would] permit the use of the vast continental resources for fleet-building, and the empire of the world would then be in sight. This might happen if Germany were to ally herself with Russia.'[cdli] Historians have tended to see the German-Soviet non-aggression pact of 1939 as an act of ideological debauch on the Nazis' part, but for Haushofer this was the natural step.[cdlii] In winter 1941, Karl C. von Lösch (a planner of SS activities in Operation Barbarossa whose books included *The Breakdown of the German National Border*, 1937, and *Bohemia and Moravia in the German Countryside*, 1943) wrote:

> 'If we Germans call ourselves the actual people of Europe, that means we take a heavy duty upon ourselves. It is now clear what Germany lacked in the last century: the European task, to find justice, and to be a pace-maker for better conditions in this part of the world, which is still so fateful for humanity. A struggle for justice, that is what it must be, not any attempt to trick people. A struggle for justice is a German task, it is a European task, it is a task for humanity... Let us unfurl the banner of the struggle for true peace in Europe.'[cdliii]

In 1942 Karl-Richard Ganzer looked back to the Holy Roman Empire, writing that 'there is simply nothing else in the 300-year history of the medieval empire than a powerful striving to organise unformed Europe from the German core space', and that 'the Reich is, ethically considered, carried by a special force, which allows the *Reichsvolk* to become the protectors of Europe'.[cdliv] Territorial clarity and national sovereignty, as parts of liberal thinking, were explicitly dismissed, for 'community':[cdlv] 'the greater Germany army has achieved its calling to lead Europe to unity with greatest possible circumspection, in the knowledge of the common greater home for all Europeans. For it is not a matter of an imperial dream or a German hubris, but rather of the fulfilment of an epochal task.'[cdlvi] Other German scholars claimed that the Reich was the moderate and respectable force, and Britain represented the real extremism. British imperialism had 'sabotaged and defamed' that 'spatially defined idea of order, the concept of a certain *Lebensraum*, that honest, limited and modest great-space-idea'.[cdlvii] German writer Frank Ebeling, who with his *Geopolitik: Karl Haushofer und seine Raum Wissenschaft 1919-1945* in 1994 succeeded in partially rehabilitating Haushofer and his work in Germany, finds that 'All the concepts of '*Reich*', despite the intrinsic vagueness of their content, longed for the supranational union of the peoples of Europe'.[cdlviii]

The leading philosopher of law in the Nazi court however was Carl Schmitt. His 1941 work, *Constitutional Great-Space-Order, Forbidding the Intervention of Powers Exterior to the Space*, crystallised the theoretical basis for Hitler's leadership. The world consisted of *Reiche*, or *Großräum*, meaning a nation with enough strength to organise beyond its borders. Just as there was an 'America for the Americans', so the world should be divided into other *Großräume*, into which others would be forbidden from interfering. Schmitt, described as the theoretical father of European integration by modern German scholars,[cdlix] thought individual states could not remain independent in the modern world, and zones of 'regional influence' would now go beyond borders. Carl Schmitt would also transmogrify after the war, into a close friend and advisor of Kurt Kiesinger, German Chancellor from 1966-69.[cdlx]

Leading Nazi Europeanist Friedrich Stieve described the German middle – '*die Deutsche mitte*' – that since Charlemagne had 'never lost its longing for European unity'. Hitler however had replaced Bismarck as the 'source of energy', allowing the 'resurgence of the middle'. As the Reich grew from Prussian core, through the German states, through Austria-Hungary and outwards, Stieve was breath-taken: 'What a resurgence of the middle! What a European reversal!' 'This part of the earth', he wrote, 'was not only more firmly welded together than ever before, but thanks to the magnetic force of its new construction, it began to draw towards it deliberately separated parts and thus ineluctably to increase its size.' This was possible because the 'middle' was asserting the 'freedom and autonomous development of the whole'. Dr Hans Pflug, also a Nazi theorist, saw Germany at 'the heart of Europe', always aware of its 'over-national duty'. And Martin Heidegger, required reading in many social science faculties today (and member of the Nazi party from 1933 to 1945), believed Europe was a 'great area... in the great pincer between Russia on one side and America on the other'.[cdlxi]

In September 1941, Foreign Minister Joachim von Ribbentrop's staff drafted a set of guidelines for the German press on the theme 'Europe'. A 'federal Europe' was the Nazis' goal: 'the fight against England is a fight for European unity', an aim that would be secured 'by the elimination of Britain, destruction of Bolshevism, and the voluntary adherence of France to the policy of European solidarity'.[cdlxii] In a speech the same year, von Ribbentrop found that, under attrition, 'Even France is beginning to develop a European conscience on this subject'.[cdlxiii] In conferences organised in France by the *Groupe Collaboration*, Friedrich Grimm attacked 'the eternal treaty of Westphalia',[cdlxiv] in other words nation states themselves. The Nazis' magazine *The New Europe: A Magazine of Struggle Against the English-American World and Historical View*, edited by Walther Körber, attacked the British 'enmity towards Europe', with articles entitled, 'Europe is Fighting for Unity', 'The Co-operation of European Science', 'The Enemies of the European Construction',

'European Economic Community', 'The Economic Unity of Europe', and 'The New Europe: A victory Over Anglo-Saxon Hostility to the Reich and to Europe'. The magazine sought, among academics and journalists, 'Voices of the New Europe'.[cdlxv] The outsiders to this cause were, in particular, 'England, Victim of its Own European Policy', and 'The World Lodge of Jewry Against Europe's New Order', both of whom acted against 'the European interest'. [cdlxvi]

The Nazis were certainly the most violent example of this dogmatic romanticism, but also just one manifestation of Germany's older psychodrama. Often called nationalists, more exactly the Nazis were 'ethnicists'. That a Swede was as Aryan as a German meant the Nazis could present themselves as pan-European, fighting for a new European order against peripheral, impure, and compromised powers. With Germans uneasy about their security as a more straightforward nation state, Nazism promised that Germany was the core state that could guide the true European people, in this manifestation 'Aryans'. Germany, wrote Arnulf Baring in 1989, 'did not get a grip on a timely, feasible concept of the state. Instead, people either reached for the medieval Holy Roman Empire as a model, which had been constituted quite differently and which was, as a result, very misleading in a number of different ways, or, hardly less disastrously, for the murky concept of the Volk'.[cdlxvii]

This meant 'Europe' was also the calling of Nazism's opponents, which created a sort of surrogate nationalism which could also unite Leftists after the war. As Klaus Mann said in 1942: 'I try to give a name to my longing, to name my inheritance and my duty. Europa!' Come 1953, the writer Thomas Mann called for 'a European Germany'. Germans had quickly discovered the new, old ideal.

This German philosophical tendency – to take a dogmatic position, informed by a belief that compromising one's ideals against the political realities of the day constitutes moral failure – is one that British governments perpetually underestimate, approaching negotiations with German leaders with the virtue of compromise in mind. Thomas Mann called this refusal to compromise 'unpolitical': 'there is in the political thought of the Germans an old tradition which allows consciousness to escape from complicated political circumstances into the promise of the pure idea'.

While Germans usually claim to believe in a democratic, bordered, nation state, Germans continue to judge political maturity by the extent to which they believe in the going German ideal – designed to redeem them from the last one (this is always liable to release destabilising shockwaves onto the rest of Europe, Merkel's invitation to any Middle Eastern 'refugee' to enter Germany being one example). Campaigning for the European elections, a leading German politician advocated federal Europe in emotional terms: 'My heart rages with passion at the thought of a Single Government and a Single Parliament'.[cdlxviii]

If, as the German philosopher Karl Löwith argued as he returned from exile in 1952, the disasters of the twentieth century were created in Germany in the middle of the nineteenth,[cdlxix] the philosophy of the same country has also created much of the west's political discourse since: that British Europhiles express similar passions demonstrates a ubiquitous German influence on the English-speaking world's new political class.

Hamburg-born peer Ralf Dahrendorff (son of a Weimar Social Democrat politician, a naturalised Briton and director of the LSE), asked in *Society and Democracy in Germany* in 1965 what he called the 'German question': why so few Germans had embraced the principles of liberal democracy – a nation state featuring democracy and free speech. Apart from the size of German firms having led them to swallow up liberal democracy, he felt a German 'nostalgia for synthesis', a belief in truths separate from and not 'battered about' by public debate, as well as a 'certain knowledge' available to the 'chosen few'[cdlxx] distinguished Germany from Britain (where a belief in empirics and experiment underwrote our freedoms).

This meant the respected 'intellectual upper class' allowed the emergence of the Third Reich through choosing 'inner emigration' over real opposition, but also that the democratic institutions that had emerged by the early 1960s were still not deeply embedded, but 'external, distant, ultimately irrelevant'. The German was therefore still liable to authoritarianism because 'he would prefer not to be drawn out of the 'freedom' of his four walls' (Alexander and Margarete Mitscherlich suggested this *innerlichkeit*[cdlxxi] manifested itself in seeing 'true' literature and art as being concerned with inner conditions). In other words, the modern German was still a Fichtean.

Even as late as the 1960s, in his *The Structural Transformation of the Public Sphere,*[cdlxxii] Jürgen Habermas felt the need to explain to Germans that open debate was 'a crucial precondition for civic freedom' – not news to the Anglosphere since *Magna Carta* in 1256 at the latest. By 1952 Yale professor of French Henri Peyre suggested in a lecture on the 'cultural migration' that the German contribution to American intellectual life was now well ahead of the British.[cdlxxiii] Yet the same influence was increasingly apparent in Britain itself. Having also moved to the LSE after Hitler took power, Karl Mannheim's *Diagnosis of Our Time* in 1943 took the 'planned society' of Karl Marx totally for granted:[cdlxxiv] 'war', he thought, was 'the maker of a silent revolution by preparing the road to a new type of planned order' (a thesis that later led Cardinal Joseph Ratzinger to note his countrymen's tendency to make 'partial points of view absolute guides',[cdlxxv] and to use scientific reasoning to control rather than observe and enjoy the world).

By the early 1940s, the social theory group the Frankfurt Institute had moved to California, where in 1950 its director Max Horkheimer penned *The Authoritarian Personality*,[cdlxxvi] a lodestar of the 1960s counter-culture. The work was attempted to demonstrate quantitatively that the attitudes of conventional Americans were actually symptoms of anti-Semitism, 'submissive', and that middle class American suburbs constituted 'the dark heart of modern civilisation'. In other words his book found nationalism and reaction wherever it looked. German anti-national anxiety had become a major export. To say the European Left now finds the same is trite – the point is that this began as an extreme reaction to the last (nationalist) extreme reaction, as the German psychodrama continued. And as the counter-culture became the New Establishment, patriotism certainly found itself suppressed as suspect: even as an anti-patriotic EU state becomes steadily more authoritarian. (In the last five years this tendency has begun its acceleration into something like a new totalitarianism: a German music festival that prides itself on its 'liberalism' hands out flyers informing revellers that if they hear any 'sexism, racism, or homophobia', they should inform the 'concert police' and transgressors will be expelled.)

The parallel to the new spirit of non-nationalism[cdlxxvii] is the cultural Marxist idea that all worldviews are equal. This coda to Marx's attack on the dominant culture of the West in general, but Britain especially, has disabled patriotism such that the metropolitan media's only permissible commentary on Britishness is now by means of self-deprecation. But the contemporary 'carnival' of post-modernism[cdlxxviii] that emerged in Germany did so as the reaction against a specifically German authoritarianism – the authors who encouraged it included Günther Grass, now known to have been a member of the SS. This was where Orwell felt that simply walking through devastated Cologne in 1945 was 'to feel an actual doubt about the continuity of civilisation'; Walter Gropius found Berlin two years later to be little more than 'a corpse'.[cdlxxix] The uniquely anti-nationalist 'normalisation' that Green foreign minister Joschka Fischer hailed in 2002 also appears, at the extreme, in the barely-disguised celebration of attacks on countries which still possess a capacity for patriotism: a week after 9/11, composer Karlheinz Stockhausen (whose mother was euthanised by the Nazis) described the events in New York as 'the greatest possible work of art which ever existed'.[cdlxxx]

Marx was not the first German thinker to urge his followers to think 'beyond nations', supposing national borders to be ruling-class tricks. But Marxism itself is now so ubiquitous that we have almost ceased to notice it. We accept economics as the driving force of societies' development,[cdlxxxi] even though the Euro has demonstrated again that culture creates the economic superstructure, not vice-versa.

Though Sigmund Freud has had a less catastrophic impact than Marx, he is no less ubiquitous, with his influence permeating the lives of 'even people who have never heard of him' (according to the American writer Alfred Kazin in 1956). In Britain, Frank Furedi's *Therapy Culture: Cultivating Vulnerability in an Uncertain Age* diagnosed the rise of cultural *innerlichkeit*: 'an inward turn… the self acquires meaning through the experience of the inner, emotional life'.[cdlxxxii]

But in Freud, it is Fichte who is also present at every turn. In *The Freudian Ethic* of 1960, Richard Lapierre noted how, to Freud, 'man is not born free with the right to pursue life, liberty, and happiness; he is shackled by biological urges that can never be freely expressed and that set him in constant and grievous conflict with his society.' In the 1960s Lapierre foresaw this inwardness leading to the 'maternalisation of politics', as American historian Kit Lasch suggested 'rugged individualism' and its commensurate freedoms were increasingly discussed cynically, replaced by a narcissistic grievance culture of 'therapeutic sensibility'.[cdlxxxiii] This, then, is the identity politics weakening nation states alongside EU law: the SNP is not the only grievance movement to work out that the coolest thing to be in our society is a sensitised minority.

But if this *innerlichkeit* makes it difficult for Germans to 'act politically, like Englishmen' (as German writer Martin Walser suggested in *The Inner Man*, 1986)[cdlxxxiv], one of the results of 'inward migration' was the failure of a reliably sceptical cultural elite to emerge and balance what T.S. Eliot called the 'power elite'.[cdlxxxv] Hannah Arendt detected a 'pre-totalitarian atmosphere' in Germany, as the difference between 'truth and falsehood ceases to be objective and becomes a mere matter of power and cleverness'.[cdlxxxvi] But the EU has also merged these two elites, through projects like Jean Monnet Professorships in our universities plus a noticeable lack of scepticism in the metropolitan media class. Former Commissioner Christopher Tugendhat described the dreamlike sensation in Brussels, where the daily drama of Community life goes almost entirely unreported in the national newspapers on sale in the city[29].[cdlxxxvii] As Peter Watson concluded, 'the climate of opinion under which we live our differing lives is, much more than we like to think, German'.[cdlxxxviii]

RESURGENCE: GERMANY SINCE REUNIFICATION

It belongs to German nature to present oneself as un-German: a tendency to cosmopolitanism, to undermine the sense of nationhood are inseparable from the essence of German nationality; the idea that one must lose one's Germanness as much as possible in order to find it, that any restriction to the purely German is felt to be barbaric.

Thomas Mann, *Reflections of the Unpolitical Man,* **1919.**

In spring 1945, as American troops approached Munich, the local Nazi leaders of the 'capital city of the movement' realised they were in possession of what German historian Malte Herwig calls 'an embarrassing legacy' – the central membership index of the National Socialist party, more than eight million members. On 18th April, a heavily armed SS convoy of twenty trucks left the city for Hans Huber's paper mill, where they told Huber under threat of the severest punishments to destroy the hundreds of tonnes of documents, before they left. But Hans Huber did not wish to take orders from the SS – his brother and Jewish sister-in-law had been forced into exile just before the war, and he soon realised he was being asked to destroy the records of the people who had persecuted his family. Knowing the Americans would soon arrive, Huber simply kept the mountain of files. But by April 1945, the Americans had drawn up a list of tasks for high-ranking officials, and on realising the importance of their discovery set about cataloguing its contents.[cdlxxxix]

Despite German protests, the Americans did not make the records public

---

[29] This is true across much of the continent, where the continental Europhilia much lauded by the British Left is in fact no such thing, simply an even greater inability to hold the political class to account. In France for example, radio and TV programmes of even the calibre of Today or The World at One do not exist to anything like the same extent. During the Maastricht negotiations, Britain saw saturation coverage of John Major's first appearance at a European summit as Prime Minister, the BBC calling it 'this historic summit'. The summit was not even mentioned on the main TV news programme in France.

until 1994, meaning Germans were prevented from knowing which of their senior politicians and other leading figures were actually transmogrified Nazis. It cannot have escaped the Americans that possession of these files gave them tremendous potential power over those whose names were contained in the Berlin Documentation Center (BDC) that they ran. Alas, denying large numbers of people information is also invariably about power. An internal US embassy memo on 9th September 1986 read: 'While we support the legitimate pursuit of Nazi war criminals, in our view it cannot be justified in anyone's interest or with regard to the private sphere of the individuals in question for us to grant access to journalists and others so that they can go fishing... We don't want to encourage sensationalist reporting, which would be very likely in the case of open access...'cdxc In other words, the reputations of new allies needed protecting.

For almost twenty years, Hans-Dietrich Genscher, as foreign minister, led the department responsible for restitution discussions with the Americans, who sorted the names of Nazis who had become senior ministers in the post-war government out of any publically available files to avoid embarrassment. When a *Bundestag* vote in 1989 demanded the Americans grant Germany control over the centre, allies of Genscher asked the Americans to refuse to do so for 'technical reasons'. The Americans delayed until 1994, when the German public finally found out that one of their leading politicians had once been a Nazi: party member 10123636. His membership card had been removed from the Berlin Documentation Centre, to be kept with files of other especially prominent Germans in a safe owned by the American director – the State Department even tried to have these files destroyed before returning the centre to German control. In Günther Guillaume, Genscher shared a close advisor with his Chancellor Willy Brandt. Guillaume, who while advisor to cabinet ministers was also spying for the Stasi, had joined the Nazi party on 20th April 1944, Hitler's 55th birthday. Kurt Kiesenger, Chancellor from 1966-69 was a member (although this had been known since a leak in the 1960s). Willy Brandt himself is supposed to have said that should the full contents of the BDC become known, 'we would lose all our best people'.cdxci

In July 1979, the director of the BDC received a letter from the State Department containing a list of names to be investigated, and the request that the letter be burned. It wasn't. The letter was later found with a bundle of other papers including a list of the members of Chancellor

Helmut Schmidt's cabinet. The names of two men now known to have been Nazis, Hans-Dietrich Genscher and agriculture minister Josef Ertl were crossed out. So was the name of Helmut Schmidt. No membership card has ever been found, and Schmidt denied knowing why his name was crossed off the list. Had Schmidt been a Nazi, this would mean former Nazis inhabited the Chancellery through the crucial years 1966-69, then 1974-82, and in Hans-Dietrich Genscher occupied both Vice-Chancellor and Foreign Ministership from 1982 to 1992 (in other words the two most powerful positions in Germany for all except four years between 1966 and 1992).[cdxcii]

Most contemporary German Europhiles would tell us that modern German behaviour in Europe is nothing like Prussia's creation, then dominance, of the German Empire, because Germany is now democratic. Alas, this misses the point.

Bismarck forged the empire – with the acquiescence of Europe's other powers – through brilliant diplomacy, and in particular by persuading the concerned British that Germany would be restrained by becoming parliamentary. The British, failing to foresee how power would be kept from an elected German parliament (and seeking a bulwark against Russia), became broadly favourable to the foundation of the empire that would, among much else, terminate our status as a superpower.

Europhiles have tended to take as a given that Germany began with a blank slate in 1945, the EU emerging as a rational response to Europe's security situation. In fact the preamble of the German Basic Law of 1949 includes a policy leading to a United States of Europe as one of the constitutional foreign policy goals of Germany.

Chancellor Adenauer's simultaneous Europeanism and alliance with the United States soon became a challenge. In 1949, social democrat leader Kurt Schuhmacher taunted him in the *Bundestag* as 'the Allies' Chancellor', telling him he was working for the enemy. Yet Adenauer knew Germany's unique geographic position – hemmed in at the centre of Europe, with few naturally agreed borders – gave Germans a sense of feeling both threatened by the entire continent and responsible for it. 'Now more than ever', Adenauer said, 'we need the help of our friends'. This meant the US especially: 'we Europeans must be clear about one thing: without the help and protection of the United States, Europe [is] powerless against the pressure of the Soviet Union'. Adenauer's policy had the side-effect of renewing a sense of moral purpose for West Germans. As Adenauer said,

'The people which only a few years previously had committed brutal genocide and waged a terrible war of destruction suddenly found themselves in the role of the great advocate of justice, peace, and the protection of the West from the communist danger. Looking eastwards, the feeling of being in every respect a superior people with a concomitant missionary task found the desired confirmation.'

In joining the western alliance that had defeated the most violent form of German romanticism (Naziism) Germany now held the fort for Europe, facing down a Soviet bloc that had fallen to another romantic German philosophy (Communism) and through its geographic position found itself uniquely able to look beyond its own divided nationhood and respond to the greater promise of a new romantic German cause (Europe)[30].

If the socialist opposition agreed on Germany's centrality, they continued to disagree with the Atlanticist orientation, resurrecting the 'third way' principle of the Kaiser's Germany: the Continent, with great powers on both sides, must unify, just as Karl Georg Pfleiderer described Germany's 'middle way' in the 1950s, a 'centre of balance between East and West'. Bonn also attached to the Treaty of Rome the *Protokoll über den innerdeutschen Handel*, making trade between West and East Germany 'internal' and therefore not subject to the usual EEC tariff barriers.[cdxciii]

To achieve this the 1972 treaty codifying relations between West and East Germany accepted *Ostpolitik*, accepting moral equivalence over the East German regime and stating that accommodation with this other German state was the key to peace in Europe (Foreign Minister Hans-Dietrich Genscher would add, 'There is not a capitalist Germany and a communist Germany, there is only one German nation'). But the 1970s saw a resurgence of anti-Americanism in Germany more generally, in parallel with renewed confidence among German intellectuals, as 1968 drew a line under the tainted 'Brown generation'. Although anti-Nazi, the new German intellectuals' totem of Anti-Americanism bore considerable resemblance to 'Englandhass',

---

[30]However Adenauer's cabinet had contained at least one man whose view of Germans as a superior people to the countries to the east had taken a different shape not long before. Peter Watson has shown that in the years before World War Two, the Nazis turned the Kiel Institute of World Economic Studies into their *de facto* think-tank, from whom they commissioned no less than 1,600 reports. One particularly well-received study developed the idea of Poland as a 'population problem', and the Kiel academics reasoned that between 4.5m and 5.83m Poles 'represented nothing but dead ballast'. The original 'population problem' study that created a respectable academic basis for genocide was written by Nazi officer Dr Theodor Oberländer. Between 1953 and 1960 he served in Adenauer's cabinet as Federal Minister for Displaced Persons, Refugees, and Victims of War.

the dislike of British free-trade that permeated the justifications of Prussian, then united German, expansionists before the First World War.

With the fall of the Soviet Union, our former Ambassador to Bonn Sir Julian Bullard noted that, 'some Germans argue, in a single confident jump, from the reduced military threat from the East to the possibility of a world without alliances or without nuclear weapons', as they moved quickly to a new idealistic position. Beyond pacifism, Genscher's remarks about 'one German nation' gave a clearer picture about the German outlook post-reunification. Genscher's suggestion that Germany transcended the difference between capitalism and communism, between liberty and its suppression, hinted at a re-emerging romantic calling: German policy-makers for years had described the need to 'overcome the division in Europe'.

Thus as scepticism about the EU project grows among the German public, the Prussian dynamic in fact grows stronger. German politicians keep their own people on board by persuading them that Europe will be made in the German image. This typically makes German denials of the country's growing hegemony quite confused. The Bundesbank's chief economist insisted that 'The economic weight of Germany and its political role have nothing to do with a 'bid for hegemony'. Rather the size and position of Germany give us the task of fashioning the growing together of the entire continent in an orderly political way and fitting ourselves into this order'.[cdxciv] Many German academics have been even clearer about the geopolitical cause behind European integration. In his article 'World power political ambitions based on economics', respected pro-EU political scientist Werner Weidenfeld of the University of Munich described where the EU would lead Germany:

> 'The euro-space [der Euro-Raum] will catapult Europe into the status of a world power. A new world monetary system dominated by Europe and America will replace the old dollar-based arrangements. The Atlantic relationship will have to be re-evaluated. But what the Europeans still lack is the ability to think in world political categories.'[cdxcv]

Weidenfeld suggested a 'power-political vacuum' existed in the world, and while the EU did not yet fill it, it was emerging as 'a central field of gravity'. He noted that 'soon every seventh state in the world will be a member of the EU', and concluded: 'the dreams of the war generation are about to be fulfilled'. Germany's political advisors are often quite honest about their intentions.

One argument between France and Germany over the presidency of the ECB in spring 1998 demonstrated Berlin's strategy clearly. In their approach to monetary union Germany had assumed they would be able to count on the support of a small core of EMU members: Belgium, the Netherlands, Luxembourg, Austria and France. Berlin assumed they would have a natural majority within this group, of which they would comprise nearly 50% of the population. But the Mediterranean countries instead had to be admitted to monetary union, and in this new scenario Germany insisted its man was nominated as ECB president. The Franco-German row that followed demonstrated the extent to which the ECB was really independent of political control: behind the rhetoric of the post-national era, both knew the true importance of the Bank's president. The victory of Germany's chosen candidate, Dutchman Wim Duisenberg, showed how the 'independence' of the ECB had been subverted in spirit and in law before monetary union had even begun (he was chosen on the strange condition that he resign at some point in the course of his 8-year term, despite a rule against splitting terms). The episode also showed the importance Berlin attached to dominating the institution, which it was resolved would be built in the capital of the Holy Roman Empire, Frankfurt. Germany's victory here demonstrated the influence of Bundesbank president Karl-Otto Pöhl, and the choice of Frankfurt meant that, in Helmut Kohl's words, 'European Monetary Policy will be German monetary policy'.[cdxcvi]

In one sense however, the new situation is different to the story of Prussia. The economically productive regions of Germany can sustain the parts of the old German Empire that lie within Germany's own borders, but lack the economic strength and political will to maintain a construction likes the EU. In the long run, as we have seen, as any sensible economist recognises, monetary union means either constantly funding poorer areas – not sustainable when they do not share an identity – or accepting workers continual movement to wealthier countries to find work. But just as Berlin has overstretched in Europe before, it is likely to keep trying for some time, even if the results of German exertions will once more be increasingly severe. Without cultural and political cohesion, Brussels will need undemocratic means to hold the union together.

In Germany, a united German identity has never been about a polity and its law as much as it has been economic or cultural, and the leaders of the German movement for national unity like Fichte identified statehood with a structure of command more than with freedom under law.[cdxcvii] In classic German thinking there is space – *Raum* – which needs a structure. Hence Edgar Meister of the ECB: 'Germany has now returned to the middle of the whole European economic *Raum*'.[cdxcviii] In his study *Diplomacy*, Henry Kissinger said of Bismarck's empire that 'the reason German statesmen were obsessed with naked power was that, in contrast to other nation-states, Germany did not possess any integrating philosophical framework. Bismarck's Reich was not a nation-state, it was an artifice, being foremost a Greater Prussia whose principal purpose was to increase its own power... It was as if Germany had expended so much energy on achieving nationhood that it had not had time to think through what purpose the new state should serve.' When Bismarck described 'the nightmare of coalitions', he meant the German position in the heart of Europe, surrounded by neighbours who could at any time become hostile. The first purpose of German power was to keep them neutralised. Germany's lead negotiator at Maastricht, Horst Köhler, explained this frankly to a French newspaper: 'There is no alternative to European integration. Any other choice would push the other nations of the continent to unite against us'.[cdxcix] As Genscher told us, Germany was 'assuming new responsibilities'. This is *realpolitik*, hard and cold.

Some Germans are open about the pursuit of national interest through Brussels, but Germany's political taboos mean most find it impossible to be frank about their national interests, which usually come out sideways as actions 'in the European interest'. Others are less hidebound. In his 1998 article entitled 'The option of restraint no longer exists', CSU politician Michael Glos explained in large measure why Germany is so keen to create a European army: assigning military operations a European or international cause is what makes it possible for Germany to carry them out.

Since reunification, Germany has grown increasingly aware of the need to reassert control over its traditional periphery using European initiatives. A CDU policy paper in September 1994 warned that 'Without this further development of [Western] European integration, Germany might be tempted or challenged, on the grounds of its own security needs, to bring about stabilisation in Eastern Europe alone and in the traditional manner'.[d] Policy papers from Helmut Schmidt's office used the phrase 'the Federal Republic/ Europe' twice as if they were the same thing, including 'more autonomy for the Federal Republic/Europe'.[di]

In December 1957, Prime Minister Harold Macmillan wrote in his diary after a private talk with Adenauer, 'he knows how far his people (since Bismarck) hanker after eastern dreams. When he is dead, he fears that his people will fall for the bait.'[dii] The growing tension between Germany and its eastern neighbours has passed almost unnoticed by the British press. In 1998, German 'Homeland Day', organised by the German Expellees' Association, was marked by a demand from its President (a CDU *Bundestag* deputy), that Czech and Polish EU membership be conditional upon Germans being allowed to resettle areas from which they were expelled in 1945, and upon Germany being paid compensation by both countries[diii] (German politicians also frequently demand the return of German 'cultural goods'). Polish suspicion of Brussels's motives is also growing. Warsaw was 'humiliated' (according to the Polish press) when the Commission cancelled a large swathe of grants shortly after the Polish Minister for Europe declared his support for 'a Europe of Nations'. After his election, Hungary's Prime Minister Viktor Orban told the *Frankfurter Allgemeine Zeitung* that he was not interested in EU membership at any price, a position judged 'arrogant' by much of Germany's media.[div]

Both the Christian Democrats and the Left court support from the Expellees, and re-creating Germany's 'leading role' in Central Europe through Brussels is central to German foreign policy regardless of party. Two Europhile commentators have written that 'the breakdown of the Soviet bloc created a power vacuum in Eastern Europe. Germany's economic strength and its historical connections with countries such as Poland, the Czech Republic, Slovakia and so on present opportunities for expanding its influence eastwards, at the same time giving it a claim to a greater prominence on the world stage'.[dv] But the unavoidable implication is that whether through Brussels or 'in the traditional manner', Germany intends to be the dominant power in Central and Eastern Europe.

Despite this, British Europhile Margaret Blunden writes that 'Much hangs on the maturity and understanding of Germany's European partners if a historic opportunity is not to be lost and Germany is not to be driven to look for unilateral solutions to the problems on its eastern frontier',[dvi] suggesting the problem is Britain and France's attitude, not Germany's. Even so, Margaret Blunden adds, 'to many Germans, Europeanisation is not about losing national power but regaining it'.[dvii] European policy has not replaced German national interest, it is simply a vehicle for it. As Hans-Dietrich Genscher said, 'The more European our foreign policy is, the more national it is'.[dviii]

The British press rarely discusses the dangers of German domination, but its French counterparts are less cautious. Margaret Thatcher is still mocked by Europhiles for her concern about German reunification, but President Mitterrand visited Gorbachev in Kiev in December 1989 to try to stop it. The persistent trade deficit with Germany is also increasingly sensitive in many countries, including Poland and France. Edith Cresson resigned as French Minister for European Affairs in October 1990 after German resistance to French investment in East Germany, telling the Cabinet: 'Our companies often encounter resistance from West German companies in gaining access to the best parts of this market... I am very European, but it is quite unacceptable to build Europe on the basis of an imbalance with Germany'. In 1983 the French even considered leaving the European Monetary System (the Italians later joined the French in attacking the deflationary effect of Germany's dominant position on their own economy, saying this prevented other countries catching up with her).[dix] German scholar Hans-Eckart Scherrer noted at the time,

> '...the French are convinced that the Germans want to preserve their monetary hegemony as EMU approaches: the more dominant the Mark is, the more Germany will be able to dictate conditions and draw up plans for a European Central Bank based on the Bundesbank. A senior French official [explains] 'What is disturbing in the German attitude is that it betrays a very hegemonial mentality. Germany wants all the European currencies at her feet, and she is on the point of abusing her dominant position.'[dx]

During the April 1990 meeting at Ashford Castle in Ireland, it even appears the Germans suggested the Deutschemark actually become the single currency. Delors became very angry during this meeting, saying, 'this [German] hostility to the ecu is dangerous. For political reasons the ecu must be developed.' The apparent German idea was rejected, but Pöhl could still declare the next month that 'the German concept regarding the principles of a common European central bank has been accepted by most European governments'. After all, he had made clear that the Germans would never give up their currency unless what they got in return was just as good.

German influence remained dominant. The Commission gave Pöhl a decisive say in drawing up the draft statutes of the proposed European Central Bank. In June 1990, the *Bundestag* decided the ECB would be located in Frankfurt.

After the statutes were submitted to the European Council, in an article entitled 'Karl-Otto Bismarck', *The Economist* wrote, 'Mr Pöhl's influence over the 46 pages is not hard to spot... where they had previously wanted 'binding rules' for budget deficits, now they called for sanctions to be available... as a means of enforcing the Bank's decisions on recalcitrant member states' (although having indirectly ended Mrs Thatcher's premiership for her failure to sign up to their timetable for EMU, with a growing budget deficit of their own the Germans suddenly seemed happy to let the timetable slip).[dxi] But French fears had not gone away, as one French newspaper made clear:

> 'The French see their dreams of European domination being shattered as the 'centre of Europe' shifts from Paris to Berlin. Many fear that France could be relegated to a secondary role. Hence the importance of anchoring Germany within Western Europe by speeding up European integration.'

To achieve this Paris allowed Frankfurt the European Central Bank and a majority voting system that would become reliant on German-dependent voting alliances. 'Before Prussia had actually beaten France', wrote Jacques Bainville in his biography of Bismarck in 1932, 'Bismarck treated her carefully, made a fuss of her – and tricked her'.[dxii] The French had made a profound strategic mistake.

Before the signing of the Maastricht Treaty on 7th February 1992, John Major asked Bill Cash to see him privately in his room behind the Speaker's chair. He asked what he would do in relation to Maastricht if he were in the Prime Minister's situation. 'You will have to veto the Treaty', he replied. 'Why?' asked Major. 'It will be a German Europe... Just look at what's going on in relation to interest rates and who is setting them'. 'Well if that's the case', Major said, 'I will have to enter into an alliance with the French'. The conversation went no further.

THE NATIONAL INTEREST VS. THE NEW PRUSSIA

Today Europhile politicians often claim that the principle of 'subsidiarity' in the emerging federation will allow states to retain independence on the grounds that federalism means decentralisation.

Subsidiarity is a doctrine of German Catholicism and is never mentioned in the federal constitutions of the Anglosphere. The *Oxford English Dictionary* called it: 'a meaningless or even misleading phrase in English'. Even its advocates are confused. Sir Christopher Prout (leader of Conservative MEPs in the late 1980s) said that it means that 'the higher levels' of government (i.e. Brussels) should be 'subsidiary' to 'lower levels' (national governments), but elsewhere that 'all that the concept of subsidiarity boils down to is an expression of the national interest of member states. In other words, if a majority of member states want to adopt a piece of legislation which has the effect of transferring sovereign powers from national governments to the European Community institutions, that is at one and the same time an expression of national interest'.

The assumptions of continental advocates of subsidiarity also differ from Britain's liberal tradition. The great theorist of federalism, Denis de Rougemont (whose work has been called 'anti-parliamentary, anti-capitalist, anti-individualist, anti-liberal') suggested, 'C'est pour obérir que nous somme libres': it is to obey that we are free. He also rejects the nation state and parliamentarianism, saying these systems take into account people's 'interests' but not 'needs', and that a class of politicians can know these needs better than an individual himself.

Having been designed for use in types of government with undivided power, subsidiarity is therefore applied and removed at will. Germany has made it plain that 'in the field of monetary policy the principle of subsidiarity does not apply', in other words no one should expect it to account for the needs of different countries. In other fields subsidiarity is being quietly dropped for 'parallelism', the centralisation of power. According to the Commission, 'Coherence within the economic union requires a decision making capacity such that the determination of policy at Community level avoids inefficient overlapping and contradictions in various aspects of economic policy', and that 'the list of policies which qualify on the grounds of being more efficiently discharged at Community level than at national level is likely to evolve gradually over time'.

Constitutional experts have found distinguishing between federal and unitary states themselves notoriously hard, and some reject the distinction altogether. Although the definition of a federal state appears straightforward enough, 'one in which the several units and their respective powers are constitutionally or otherwise legally united under the ultimate power of a central state or government',[dxiii] it could apply as easily to Richmond-upon-

Thames Borough Council as to Bavaria. Moreover there is scant evidence for the claim that federal states are decentralised, with some so centralised it is doubtful they are federal at all: Austrian federalism, for example, is 'banished to insignificant social roles [and] has taken on something of a folklore quality'.[dxiv] When we compare the ratio of central to regional or local expenditure in federal against unitary states, there is no evidence federal states are less centralised. Indeed, 'for the past several decades the majority of modern federations have shown a trend towards centralisation in connection with economic development and social problems' [dxv]. Thus the 'subsidiarity' principle has nothing to do with decentralised power, more to do with the traditional structure of the Catholic Church.

For its part, Germany associates federalism with the opposite of centralised power, because German federalism was adopted with the Allies' approval to prevent a return to totalitarianism. But this federalism is enigmatic. German Basic Law divides legislation into 'exclusive' and 'concurrent', the former giving German states (*Länder*) no rights except those granted by the Federation. In concurrent legislation the *Länder* must agree, but do so through the *Bundesrat*, a forty-member Council of *Länder* Ministers. In other words the power to legislate and tax lies overwhelmingly at the federal level, as it has since 1914, where individual *Länder* can be outvoted in a federal body that must pass laws and raise taxes for all Germany. When the modern constitution was written, the idea was suggested of making the *Bundesrat* more powerful, like its namesake under Bismarck. This was rejected for a more unitary state in which not only is *Bundesrat* consent not required for all laws, but the *Bundestag* has both the power to overrule it and virtual free reign to extend its 'areas of competence'. This is through Article 72, a perfect example of 'subsidiarity':

> '...in the field of concurrent legislation, the *Länder* shall have powers of legislation as long as, and to the extent that, the Federation does not exercise its right to legislate. The Federation shall have the right to legislate in these matters to the extent that a need for federal legislation exists because a matter cannot be effectively regulated by the legislation of the individual *Länder*.'[dxvi]

The criterion for deciding whether to extend those powers is whether 'such responsibilities are important to safety as a whole', or the 'maintenance of legal and economic unity'. With the constitutional requirement to foster comparable living standards between the *Länder*, this has created a mighty centralising force. The reality of subsidiarity has been clear for some time:

> 'The Federal Republic has become more unitary since 1949. Legislation has shifted more and more into the federal domain, which was not what the authors of the constitution intended... The legal authority of the *Länder* has been reduced to legal administrative authority by the federal administration. Defence and foreign policy, the necessity of employing the latest technology in areas such as transport, modern economic and cooperation policy and the associated taxation and planning requirements, above all defence and social policy... These tasks are concentrated at the federal level, far more than was foreseen in 1949, and with them naturally expenditure, bureaucracy and political power.'[dxvii]

But concentration of power in the centre has not, in Germany for instance, meant that here the citizen can hold the mighty to account. In the *Bundestag*, oral questions are often answered by the *Staatssekretär*, not the minister himself, and answers are typically uninformative with the length of the questions limited. A highly consensual relationship exists between the parties. Parliamentary questions exist, but individual *Bundestag* members may ask only *Kleine Anfragen* (small questions), with a quorum of 26 needed to ask a *Grosse Anfrage* (major question).[dxviii]

For individual citizens it is increasingly hard to understand who is responsible for what, in housing, education, or any other task a federal government has become involved with. This fragmentation makes targeted criticisms of the system increasingly hard. In Britain and other EU countries, even ministers no longer know how to affect change, and complain that the levers don't seem to work. These divisions lead to the accretion of power by the civil service, allowing interconnected metropolitan elites to mediate within – and between – countries, as power becomes more confusing to the populace, creating policies advantageous to their clients and themselves.[dxix]

This growing technocracy is a threat to parliamentary democracy. As French scholar Michel Winock noted by 1990: 'the modern state in all advanced countries has become a formidable machine of which the control lies less in the hands of elected representatives of the people than of technicians, specialists, experts. The era [of] technocracy has a corollary in the decline of the powers of a parliamentary democracy in the true sense'.[dxx] A 2014 study by Christine Reh of the steady growth of the technocracy showed that 'political decisions are taken under conditions of increasing complexity', which 'stems from a variety of sources... the plethora of (non-state) actors and... the overlap of national, supranational and international governance in the 'de-bordering space'.[dxxi] This means that 'informal decision-making' away from elected national parliaments 'is a growing trend [typified by] restriction and seclusion.'[dxxii] (While Saint-Simon imagined a technocracy in the early 1800s, Winock describes the modern French version as the *technoénarchie*, referring to the *énarchs*, graduates of the École Nationale d'Administration (ENA) who dominate the French political class.)

In 1964, Ernst Frankel had also observed in Germany the phenomenon of federalism as it would soon appear in Britain:

> 'If the belief becomes current in public opinion that in the arguments between governments and opposition it is not really a matter of opposing opinions being presented, then the impression will increasingly gain currency that parliamentary discussions are just a game. If political groups and parties atrophy into a façade behind which there hides nothing but the power struggles of bureaucrats in the party apparatus, then a pluralist, democratic society will be transformed into a mass of isolated individuals.'[dxxiii]

Hans-Dietrich Genscher has said straightforwardly that a strong Germany is good for Europe. But this ignores the unsustainable relationship between the core of this Continental System and the periphery. Germany's strength is reinforced by saturating Eastern, Central and Mediterranean Europe with its exports, but as Berlin consolidates this position through the single currency and single market, its dominance, through interest rates, industrial standards, and the panoply of economic policy, is ruining its European satellites. Many are now essentially under German tutelage – fiscally, for instance. Asked about the hard facts of Germany's overwhelming economic power, Genscher suggested: 'I think our neighbours should overcome the tendency to think in terms of nation-states'.[31] But as Triepel described, 'Hegemony is always a means of 'integration'. All hegemony presupposes a certain measure of federalism... The fact that Prussia exercised hegemony... did not undermine [German] unity, it strengthened it.'[dxxiv] Thus the CDU's policy paper in the mid-1990s criticising France for its belief that 'the 'nation state' still carries weight, even though that sovereignty has long ago become an empty shell.'[dxxv]

In industrial standards, Germany has promoted its own interests effectively. Standards institutes invariably represent the interests of their own manufacturers, and the German Institute for Standards (DIN) has written more European standards than any other, heading 40% of EU standards committees, as many as Britain and France combined.

The industrialist Sir James Dyson has described how having failed to create products that match his own, German competitors use the closed system of European standard setting to block his products, saying: 'it's a European Union dominated by Germany... in our particular field we have these very large German companies which dominate standards setting and energy reduction committees [so] the old guard and old technology are supported, and not new technology'.[dxxvi] The impact on innovation is increasingly serious; since the 1950s at the latest, we have known that the most important single factor for economic growth among developed countries is technological change – in other words a technocracy that suppresses innovation will create an atrophying civilisation.

Chancellor Kohl said at Louvain in February 1996 that the only alternative to monetary union was war. But Berlin's desire for political union misunderstands that this would not contain them, instead would do the opposite. While European integration is overwhelming post-war Germany's democratic achievements, the same integration through the German direction of commerce and industry is increasingly expanding the German elite's influence over the continent. Former President of the Bundesbank Hans Tietmeyer for example (at the time also Kohl's personal financial advisor[dxxvii]) warned that it was an illusion for states to think

---

[31] As Bill Cash put it: '...one could well imagine a scenario in which a strong Germany was bad for Europe. If industries in other countries were... depleted by German domination, and if the single currency removed the competitiveness of weaker economies while the Social Charter, with its minimum wage, insulated German workers from competitively low wages abroad, then one could well imagine economic decline and rising unemployment on the periphery of the EC financing the German stranglehold... the idea that in the 'new Europe', envy, rancour and resentment can be abolished by a [directive] is optimistic to say the least. As Hobbes observed, men are not like bees, 'Men are continually in competition for honour and dignity...and consequently there ariseth among men on that ground envy, hatred, and finally war...'. Who is to say that the poorer countries of Europe are to be happy with a dominant Germany just because it is said to be good for 'Europe'?'

they would keep their independent tax raising powers under monetary union. The surrender of monetary policy and the power to tax and spend (the latter now requiring annual EU approval) means surrendering the fundamental powers of independent government. Instead of a democratic association of sovereign nations trading freely, it was clear well before Tony Blair signed the Lisbon Treaty that this was an undemocratic proto-state dominated by Berlin.

Even by the mid-1990s, former Chancellor Helmut Schmidt told Bill Cash in a meeting in his Hamburg office why he wanted to meet: his group of friends were 'the only ones, apart from Russia', from where he had just returned, 'who are not afraid of Germany.' He suggested this was an admirable stand but that nothing would stop, he regretted, 'the emergence of German predominance.' Our Prime Ministers had given him every reason to believe this. John Major signed a treaty at Maastricht giving Berlin a majority voting system through which it could use voting alliances with much smaller nations dependent on a German economic relationship. The White Paper of 1971 – the basis of Britain accepting membership – promised that the veto would never be abandoned for majority voting and called it vital to our national interest. When our Parliament's European Scrutiny Committee recommended its reintroduction, this was rejected by the government.

Whereas without the Euro, natural currency adjustments would restrict Germany's ability to export cheaply, through the single currency Germany floods the southern nations with artificially cheap exports at their expense, deflating their economies and drawing jobs and migrants north. Long before the Euro, Eurosceptics on the Right predicted consequent huge waves of immigration and the re-emergence of nationalist parties. While Berlin now strictly enforces budgetary control in the Mediterranean, both Germany and France have broken the Stability and Growth Pact when it suited them, and Germany continually breaks the Macroeconomic Imbalance Procedure without punishment, but its trade surpluses at 6% provoke little protest. In Germany's own hard times, through the 1953 London Debt Agreement the Allies forgave 50% of her debts, around £90bn in today's money. The Germans (and French) broke the original Stability and Growth Pact in 2004-5, because they had high unemployment which they addressed with an excessive budget deficit; whereupon (naturally) the Stability and Growth Pact was loosened. When the crackdown on the southern economies got going in 2010-11, the Pact was tightened again (the Germans having now through their export surge and huge current account surplus got their unemployment under control). Others complained in 2010-11 that the Germans had their own 'macro-economic imbalances', which were contributing to the problem. Thus the Macroeconomic Imbalance Procedure. But the Procedure has 14 indicators, of which just one relates to the current account – and only above 6 percent (i.e. very large indeed) does a current account surplus count as an 'imbalance' (the trigger point for a deficit is 4 percent). So Germany doesn't break the Procedure (it has imbalances, but not 'excessive' ones), presumably because it wrote the Procedure rules.

It is the very architecture of the supranational institutions of the EU which is the portal to German hegemony. Whether or not it was deliberate is yet to be discovered. But drafting treaties is not a game of snakes and ladders but a game of chess. The majority voting system, which has grown inexorably and by design, has, because of the intrinsic power of German foreign direct investment in the countries surrounding her, and in the Eurozone, has led to such economic influence over jobs and growth in those countries, as to determine their economic dependency on Germany, and of course the very substantial revenues that flow from the German subsidiaries and partners in those countries, back to Germany itself. Thus Germany has a surplus of £67bn a year at least in its trading within the single market with the other member states. This creates a German economic hegemony. Moreover it creates a political hegemony, because the institutional architecture of the EU as a whole includes political decision making over an ever-increasing vast encroachment on national sovereign decision making, now whittled down to mere appearances. These now involve spheres of activity which were never originally contemplated in the early days of the community, and the turning point for which was the Maastricht Treaty, hence the rebellion by Eurosceptics in the United Kingdom.

This European government went beyond the single market. To take but one example, any independent examination of the trade balances between Germany and the other 27 member states, with the exception of very few countries, shows that only five countries in Europe do not have a trade deficit, but that the trade deficit of the United Kingdom, in goods and services, imports and exports, is no less than £58bn a year. This is not a beneficial single market for the United Kingdom, particularly as we would continue to trade with the EU and with Germany whether we remain or leave.

None of this, of course, means that modern Europhilia is a Prussian, let alone fascistic cause. It means more straightforwardly that since the twelfth century at the latest, German location and surrounding by others has led Germans to craft the same 'defensive'-inspired *core* programme of 'European' policy, whose internal logic sees it turn both anti-democratic and on the offensive, and against both philosophic and geographic 'enemies'. This cyclical phenomenon alternates between diplomatic and military means. Despite being willing, at times, to fight its most egregious side-effects, it is also a phenomenon that Britain's political class cyclically fails to notice. But if Thomas Mann diagnosed German thinking as 'unpolitical', the one thing that has traditionally impeded the growth of German hegemony has been politics – the politics of other nation states.[dxxviii]

The southern European experience of German economic tutelage had an antecedent in the East German experience of unification. Despite East German unit costs being around three times more than West Germany's, the East's *OstMark* was converted to the Deutschemark on a 1.18:1 basis, a monetary union that gave East German products little chance of competing. East Germany was ravaged within six months of unification, her industrial production halved, GDP falling 15% in 1990, with another 31% fall the next year. By 1993 over 35% of East Germans jobs were gone and little over half of East Germans were working full-time. While Britain had a brief and unpleasant taste of German economic hegemony in the ERM, the imposition of the euro in the Mediterranean and transfer of economic decision-making northward has replicated this outcome closely.

Just as the economic superstructure does not create the necessary shared culture, nor will it create freedom and democracy. Germany's saturation of Europe with her exports, control of the Single Market with her industrial standards, maintenance of trade surpluses, tutelage over other countries' budgets, and *de facto* control of the single currency have created a situation in which a strong Germany is bad for Europe. German dominance is now eroding the industries of other European countries, while the social charter insulates Germany's workers from competitively low wages abroad. This is not a European Germany – it is a German Europe. There is no serious doubt that it was German influence, and the need, as they saw it, to restrain a Greek-type situation developing with a government which wished to pursue austerity that led to the President of Portugal, under German influence, declining to allow the Portuguese government to take office.

In a speech in Berlin on 13th November 2014, John Major resurrected the pretend solution of subsidiarity, saying on the Andrew Marr Show that 'subsidiarity is the answer and we must nail it down as a matter of EU law'. But it is already a matter of EU law, and the European Scrutiny Committee has never come across a single example of its direct application. In the 1990s John Major himself reported its failure. The same month, in a formal conference under the Lisbon Treaty, the chairmen of national parliamentary committees of all the member states and of the European Parliament gathered in Rome. They heard the German delegation formally propose a Defence Commissioner, a Defence Council of Ministers, and reintroduce the idea of a Military Headquarters for an EU army, all with the support of EU Commission President Jean-Claude Juncker. The British delegation defeated the proposal, but their German counterparts insisted that, through majority voting, 'it will have to be put back on the agenda...' Britain, they warned, 'will simply not be able to maintain their line'.

In the twelfth century, the political thinker John of Salisbury asked, '*Quis Teutonicos constituit iudices nationum?*' – 'Who appointed the Germans to be the judges of nations?' In John's day, the German fraction of the old Frankish empire under Emperor Frederick Barbarossa was named Holy Roman Empire and behaved accordingly, dominating smaller states like those in northern Italy – including the great political centre of a previous age, Rome. Eventually, the Empire was beaten back by a coalition of these smaller states, and out of the local autonomy and trade that followed sprang the Renaissance. In this new world the Lollards of England inspired the religious liberation of Bohemia, leading to the Reformation; and from this came forth the flowering of the Low Countries and the innovations of the scientific Enlightenment, and onwards.

Just as the collapse of this German hegemony had to happen for the European Renaissance that followed, so today the politico-economic constraints of hegemony imposed through Brussels ensure that European nations are losing the 'global race': to innovate, to grow, and to prosper. It is precisely this hegemony that means ours is a continent in decline – for now. In the end, Germany must learn to contain itself.

As the Victorian *Pax Britannica* demonstrated, Europe grows and innovates when it is free and has a system of freely trading nation states, and it atrophies when it does not. After Pearl Harbor, America strained every sinew to defeat Germany's armed attempt at hegemony. After the war, with a view to preventing any repetition of the carnage, in the light of Soviet aggression, and in its own commercial interest in the reconstruction of Europe, America became the midwife for the European Community, which gave birth to the new German predominance on the Continent – and which only Germany itself can restrain.

11.

FREEDOM AND DEMOCRACY

The fault, dear Brutus, is not in our stars,
But in ourselves, that we are underlings.

Julius Caesar

IN CONCLAVE

A report released on 8th March 2016 by the House of Commons Library detailed the European Union's 'Consensual nature of voting arrangements', in other words how law is actually made.

The concept of a 'Trilogue' is not mentioned in any EU Treaty, and the word does not yet appear in any dictionary. However Article 295 of the Lisbon Treaty states the general principle that 'the European Parliament, the Council and the Commission shall consult each other and make arrangements for their cooperation by common agreement.' According to these institutions' 'Joint Declaration' made in 1999 and updated in 2007, 'the institutions shall cooperate throughout the procedure with a view to reconciling their positions as far as possible and thereby clearing the way, where appropriate, for the adoption of the act concerned at an early stage'. This means closed meetings to pre-emptively agree law before it ever sees debate.

To speed legislation the use of trilogues has grown dramatically in recent years, and as a result around 85% of legislative proposals are now adopted after first reading.[dxxix] Finnish legal scholar Päivi Leino of the University of Helsinki found in 2016 that trilogues largely escape public scrutiny, and that 'national parliaments often experience difficulties following decision-making in trilogies, especially since amendments are made at great speed, which hinders their effective scrutiny at national level".[dxxx] Leino finds that although the Lisbon Treaty promised to 'make EU law-making much more transparent', so far 'this has remained an unfulfilled promise. Access to documents relating to the EU legislative procedure, in particular trilogues, the informal three-party meetings between the European Parliament, the Council and the Commission used at every stage of the EU legislative procedure, has become particularly topical during the past months... following legislative procedures requires a serious amount of detective work... exercising your democratic rights should not be this difficult.'

Trilogues are steadily becoming the main forum where the three EU institutions make legislation. The EU has glorified 'informal decision-making' for its efficiency,[dxxxi] but the reality is that law-making is now highly opaque, meaning Europe is regressing from formal democratic institutions to closed, elite, courts. In the Trilogues, power is in the hands of the very few: *Rapporteurs* from the European Parliament, representatives of the Council, and a few officials from the Commission. They largely escape public scrutiny, and in the Joint Declaration above there is no mention of access to information during the process.[dxxxii] If information is power, the trilogues give both to a small group, with deals effectively concluded before they ever reach a minister; according to a House of Lords paper, national parliaments also find it hard to understand their decision-making.[dxxxiii] In the European Commission's opinion, trilogues however are:

> 'A preparatory step in negotiations of a purely legislative nature and it is hard to see how any aspect of their conduct, such as whether or when to hold trilogue meetings, the choice of representatives by each institution to attend trilogue meetings, whether or which supporting documents to produce etc., can give rise to maladministration, except as regards questions related to public access to the documents used during trilogue meetings.'

Using Kafkaesque logic, the European Council agrees:

> 'The organisation of the legislative process cannot be considered an administrative activity – and therefore cannot give rise to possible instances of maladministration.'

Even the EU's own European Movement admits that over 80 percent of EU laws are now drawn up in these conclaves,[dxxxiv] described by others as 'a dangerous cascade' which 'can be compared to another one: legislation'.[dxxxv] The frequency of trilogues, campaigners believe, not less than once or twice a week, is probably meant to keep up the pressure for deals, and the European Parliament and Council now frequently merely rubber-stamp the trilogue compromise, which then becomes legislation.[dxxxvi] Carl Dolan, director of anti-corruption NGO Transparency International's EU Office says that trilogies are now 'the norm for thrashing out agreements on most EU legislation', and that no minutes come out afterwards, making it impossible to really know how decisions are made. The 10,000 known lobbyists in Brussels do much of their work around trilogues, but there is no way of knowing which parts of law they have influenced.[dxxxvii] The Trade Secrets Directive for instance was debated only by a select few in these secretive meetings, creating a law to help industry keep secrets and make more information confidential.[dxxxviii] Their impact can be seen in the percentage of 'files' (i.e. bills) concluded at first reading in the European Parliament – this implies agreement has already been reached between Commission and Council. Between 1999 and 2004 this was 28 percent; in 2004-2009 it jumped to 72 percent; from 2009-2011 it was 78 percent.[dxxxix] Trilogues have gone from a method of occasionally pr-g major disagreement between the EU's three main power bodies, to the way most of our own laws are made.

A study in 2014 showed that trilogues differ from the legislative process the EU claims it uses in four ways. First, membership in trilogues is 'restricted and non-codified', involving a 'limited group of actors [who are not] publicly known.' Second, trilogues are 'secluded, and their seclusion has neither been formally decided nor publicly justified... documentation on the decision-process is not publicly available'; third, the rules specifying what is 'requested, prohibited, or permitted' in trilogues are informal; and fourth, 'MEPs in plenary face considerable political pressure not to re-open the compromise.'[dxl] Meanwhile, the *rapporteurs* sent to these meetings are selected in a process 'that is largely consensual',[dxli] uses an 'unclear and complex set of rules',[dxlii] 'takes place behind closed doors', and is characterized by 'general informality'.[dxliii]

The European Parliament is arguably the world's only elected chamber which cannot initiate legislation, as the right to propose new legislation lies with the appointed bureaucrats of the Commission. However the EU's founding treaties require the European Parliament to adopt its position before the Council does: because the EU is breaking its own law to create new laws, and therefore now sees itself as above the law, the implications for the rule of law itself in Europe are serious. As we have seen, there is no mention of trilogue meetings in the EU treaties, so in legal terms trilogues simply do not exist.[dxliv] This is legislation in a black box.[dxlv] Even MEPs now complain that they have almost no idea what they are voting for.[dxlvi]

Shortly before German reunification, Bill Cash was invited to Number 10 for his view on its impact: he said that 'we would need to reappraise our approach to the EC and the voting system'. It is easy to speculate why the explosion of trilogues followed the introduction of qualified majority voting. There is now relatively little that is put to qualified majority vote. The more powerful Germany has become, the more that the imposition of its demands through overt voting alliances, requiring very few other countries, risks becoming a scandal. Instead decision-making has been moved away from view.

STOCKHOLM SYNDROME

Controversial proposals, once accepted, soon become hallowed.

Dean Acheson, 1962

Stockholm syndrome, the psychological phenomenon whereby people fall in love with their kidnappers, has been explained in evolutionary terms. Bride kidnapping used to be a fairly common practice, and women who fought back, the theory goes, did not increase their life expectancy, and were less likely to pass on their genes. But those women who eventually submitted to, and even bonded with, their captors were more likely to have children, thus pass on the genes that caused passive behaviour towards captors. Over many generations, this made the human population more prone to submission, then bonding, if kidnapped.

We are told the British people chose Europe, but Britain consented to join the Common Market, through voluntary acceptance by its own parliament, and endorsed by a referendum in 1975. However, political union was at that time merely an aspiration for its advocates, and the accretion of European powers within the framework of the European Communities Act by successive treaties signed by successive governments was not accompanied by a referendum until this year. The political union which was originally an aspiration has now morphed into a greater reality with the Five Presidents' Reports of 2015, but particularly focused on the Eurozone dominated by Germany. This has not however altered the fact that although outside the Eurozone the United Kingdom is profoundly affected by being within the framework of the European Union as a whole, both politically and economically, and that under the evolving arrangements we would be in the second tier of a two tier Europe dominated by Germany, which is what the British government sought to avoid in the post-war settlement, but is now becoming a reality. This in itself is a reason for leaving the project. The fundamental question therefore is who governs the United Kingdom, and how. The people may be made to follow a course of action but they may not be made to understand it, said Confucius.

So what is the point of it all? It's asked rarely, what the point of the EU actually is, as it creates slowly but steadily a vast, protectionist state. And how will this make anyone happier? This last question is never explained. Because what indeed is the point of any country? The point is surely to exist just because its people want it to exist. Indeed, when you last visited another European country, what was it that made you happy? Was it the things that were just the same as the next country? Was it the same currency as its neighbour, and its neighbour's neighbour, the same credit card signs in the restaurant window, the same brands in the same supermarket with the same products of the same size? Was it really the things that had been unified, that had been... integrated?

Or was it the differences? The unique appeal of a different country, town, village, the things that you have not seen since your return. What really made you happy were probably those things that were not even tangibly better than what you have back home. The things that were different, small, novel, strange, quaint, human. With the destruction of variety, so passes the beauty of the world.

The tragedy is that we have come to think of Europe – the world's most outrageously brilliant continent – and the European Union as being the same. Jean Monnet thought that the economic binds his comrades put in place would create a political union: 'the day of the nation state is over', declared the German president in 1996. Even though the entire economic and political argument is flawed, we have been told that if you don't see that integration must continue, you just don't get it.

Well, human beings are not profit maximisation machines, and our national life cannot be distilled into a debate about the supply of goods. We do not want a world, or a continent, that has been harmonised in the name of someone else's idea of utility. Suppose that we continue to fashion this new European society, to shape people and their new attachments; who writes the blueprint for *Homo Europaeus*?

We are told that the nation states to which we feel attachment make war possible. They also make peace possible. The nation state remains the only effective way in which citizens can make their own laws and govern themselves. When we cannot act without our elected politicians checking with the EU first, as increasingly they must, we will also become incapable of fulfilling the international obligations on which security depends. A community of electors must be united by identity, because that is the only thing that creates democratic engagement. If there is no demos, there will soon be no democracy. As Machiavelli told us, 'the historians on the one hand admire what Hannibal achieved, and on the other condemn what made his achievements possible'.

Thirty years of intense Eurofication have not altered the primary object of loyalty of the British people. In the age of electronic media, the political class in western democracies no longer have the monopoly on opinion they once enjoyed. Democracy involves making mistakes, and letting people have the responsibility to make them. Yet as Brussels has taken political responsibility from individuals, another of the EU's strengths has been revealed. As much as any creation of Franz Kafka's imagination, the EU is both confusing and boring. One of boredom's best outlets is nationalism. Rather than protecting us from the past, the EU is now the primary cause of its resurgence. The peoples of Europe, ignored by their national governments, become nationalists to get attention, a glandular reaction against other parties' inept self-suppression and political correctness. The EU is creating the nationalism that was supposed to have created it.

IN EXILE

In England we have come to rely upon a comfortable time-lag of fifty years or a century intervening between the perception something ought to be done and a serious attempt to do it.

HG Wells

Andrew Symeou is a young Briton who spent two years being shuttled between Greek jails. In July 2009, he was extradited from Britain to Athens under a

European Arrest Warrant (EAW) for alleged manslaughter, taken from his own home by policemen from Scotland Yard and flown in handcuffs to Greece.

Accused of punching another Briton while on holiday on the Greek island of Zakynthos, causing him to fall off a nightclub stage and suffer fatal head injuries, Andrew always maintained he could prove he arrived at the club long after the incident took place. Greek magistrates however accepted the prosecution case as fact, declaring even before trial that there was sufficient proof that he 'committed the indictable act of manslaughter'. This is a breach of presumed innocence, and evidence in the case appears to have been fabricated or obtained through intimidation and violence against key witnesses, including beating Symeou's friends. It took three years after his arrest for Symeou to be acquitted, during which time he spent months in one of the worst jails in Europe. At his acquittal, the father of the murdered man walked across the courtroom to hug him. Greek police never bothered to question Symeou himself. 'The statements from the supposed eyewitnesses didn't just contradict each other, they proved I wasn't the person', he said, adding that the trial became 'some kind of sick war'.

The NGO Fair Trials International (founded to help Britons being unfairly tried in the developing world) took up Andrew's case, and has found that others have been arrested – by the British police – and deported to other EU nations following apparently spurious accusations. Some warrants have been issued many years after the supposed offences. Even if warrants are refused they remain in force, putting the 'suspect' at risk of arrest should they travel to other European countries. British citizens are being extradited even when it is known that their trials have been, or will be, unfair.

Deborah Dark is a British grandmother who is unable to leave the country because of her conviction by a French court, in her absence, of possession of cannabis. Sentenced to six years in jail, she was arrested in Turkey in 2007, and again the next year in Spain. Fair Trials International calls this an unfair trial. Gary Mann is another victim of the EAW. The Kent fireman was arrested, tried and convicted *in under 48 hours* of taking part in a football riot in Portugal in 2004. He vigorously denies playing any part in the riot, but was unable to instruct a lawyer or understand the court proceedings unfolding around him. Sentenced to two years in jail, he was told he would not have to serve the sentence if he confessed and accepted immediate deportation back to the UK. In March 2009 British police arrested him at his home, acting on an EAW issued by the Portuguese authorities who said they want him back to serve his two years. NGOs have declared his trial a travesty.

Early 2011 saw a strange twist to the EAW story, as Britain's General Medical Council revealed that it had become seriously concerned by European rules banning them testing foreign GPs' language skills. One doctor, German cosmetic surgeon Daniel Ubani, killed a patient with a lethal dose of painkillers during his very first shift as a Cambridgeshire GP. The Crown Prosecution Service tried to get hold of Ubani, who returned to Germany, through issuing a European Arrest Warrant. German authorities informed their British counterparts that legal proceedings were underway, then that they had been 'finalised'. Doctors from other EU nations cannot be prevented from registering in Britain, but the British authorities are banned from even testing their competence, giving every incentive for those found to be incompetent elsewhere to migrate.

If any judge or magistrate anywhere from Tallinn to Transylvania wants to get hold of a British citizen, he has simply to fill out a form, and our police are compelled to arrest the suspect. A system of extradition without trial to EU countries without *prima facie* evidence is in place. Our police have been subverted to act against the people they were established to protect. Our government will not and cannot protect us.

Usually considered the first human rights document, *Magna Carta* gained the signature of King John in 1215. A document David Cameron claimed on an American talk show to know nothing about, it has been the very foundation of our nation ever since. Clause 30 reads as follows:

> 'In future no official shall place a man on trial upon his own unsupported statement, without producing credible witnesses to the truth of it.'

Clause 38 guarantees us that:

> 'No freeman shall be taken, or imprisoned, or outlawed, or exiled, or in any way harmed, nor will we go upon him nor will we send upon him, except by the legal judgement of his peers or by the law of the land.'

Given what we know of young Andrew Symeou, has *Magna Carta* been broken by the British government and British courts in their submission to EU regulations? Andrew was placed on trial, abroad, *without credible witnesses to the truth of it*; he was *taken, imprisoned, outlawed, exiled,* and he was *in any way harmed,* and the police did *go upon him and send upon him* without *the legal judgement of his peers or the law of the land.* His own country failed to protect him because the police and magistrates who once protected our rights having become nawabs to Brussels. We, his peers, failed to protect him. Clause 41 spells out our duty to ensure the laws of the land are upheld:

> 'To any man whom we have deprived or dispossessed of lands, castles, liberties, or rights, without the lawful judgement of his equals, we will at once restore these.'

The freedom of the individual under law was a philosophical triumph, and most of all a British one. Brussels has subverted it, pushing more and more cheapened 'rights' in our workplaces, schools, homes and lives. All the while our real rights are withered, and the nation state that secured them made anathema. The EU has rendered us unprotected by our own country, our ancient freedoms rubbished. There is no such thing as part-freedom. If a country does not protect its own citizens within its own borders, it is no longer a country, indeed it is not anything. This is the easy step from politics to silence.

PRETEND PARTIES

Nobody who is unelected has a right to govern a civilised country

Martin Wolf

If the Whig reformer and poet Thomas Babington Macaulay was right, and our history really is 'emphatically the history of progress', then our country's path is supposed to involve the gradual distillation of good ideas. An increasingly informed public is growing tired of having fear for the integrity of their country, their security, and their rights belittled. While the Left condemns the power of a multinational class in finance, the rise of a *dirigiste*, statist pan-European equivalent in politics is at least as unpopular. A Dutch friend who arrived to work on his first day at *The Guardian* was surprised when his taxi driver told him he was working 'for the enemy – that's them and Brussels'. Fashionable dinner party conversation about the EU has been dominated by pro-European platitudes.

While the Left is trapped by anti-patriotism, the Tories have come up with a selection of gimmicks. A European immigration policy that no country owns has helped give Britain, especially south-eastern England, a flood of cheap labour, overcrowding, and semi-functional public services. Labour ministers never explained how they would deal with immigration, one that would soon be someone else's anyway. While the Europeanist liberal press has enforced silence on the subject, the Tories promised a 'border police' for borders we aren't allowed to police in the first place. Furthermore, in the Conservative manifesto of 2015, the British people were promised that the number of immigrants would be reduced to the tens of thousands; it is now acknowledged that we have received 2.1m, and immigration is completely out of control.

David Cameron has promised to halt the slide of power from Westminster to Brussels, but when the Polish, then the Czech leadership, were trying to hold out against Brussels' pressure to ratify the Lisbon constitution, he gave them little support. With the end of New Labour on the horizon, Cameron could have publicly supported Czech President Vaclav Klaus, who, had he held out just another six months, would have allowed Cameron to hold his promised referendum on Lisbon, changing the game with the forceful prospect of a British No vote.[dxlvii] He didn't, promising instead a 'this far and no further' bill for Parliament.

Come the signing of the 32-page agreement that forged Conservative-Lib Dem coalition government, Cameron and his team dropped any commitment to a 'Sovereignty Act' designed to curb EU power. And soon after the coalition got to work, European institutions made their power over British national life plain once more.

At the time Muslim extremists Babar Ahmad and Abu Hamza were both in jail, pending extradition to the US where they were wanted on terror charges. The two men appealed separately to the European Court of Human Rights, claiming that possible 'inhumane or degrading treatment' made extradition a breach of their rights (on the grounds that they could be held in a 'supermax' prison). HMG was informed the Court had 'decided to prolong, until further notice, the interim measures it had adopted indicating to the UK Government that it was in the interests of the proper conduct of the proceedings that the applicants should not be extradited'. Come September 2011, and the prolonged human rights-focused legal battle over the eviction of travelers from Dale Farm in Essex, Strasbourg was calling for 'traveler site legalisation' (even when they breach national planning law). In the meantime, Strasbourg's activist judges urged Britain and other countries signed up to the European Convention on Human Rights that they should waive the rules on these sites 'once the situation has been tolerated for a long period of time by the public authorities'.[32]

British judges are now more frequently using the European Convention to prevent their country deporting convicted criminals. Nigerian Philip Olawale Omotunde is still in Britain, despite being convicted of fraud. Claiming he had to care for a six year-old son, his 'right to family life' thus risked being violated (although he could have taken his son with him). Just a week before, Nick Clegg had written in passionate defence of the same European rules that guided the judges to this decision. Within a year, Strasbourg prevented the Home Office deporting 200 Somali migrants, mostly criminals, citing the European Convention Article 3 prevention of 'inhumane treatment'. The European courts meanwhile are becoming more, not less, aggressive. In February 2011, ECJ advocate-general Juliane Kokott (of whom no one in Britain had ever heard), banned insurers from differentiating between men and women drivers, even though their different risks were backed up by solid data. Estimates suggest that from the age of 17 to 25, British women would pay an extra £4,300 on average.

This time, discontent on Tory back benches appeared early. At the 2010 general election it was revealed, if little reported, that the European Commission was sitting illegally even by its own terms. According to Lisbon itself, the old Commissioners should have retired by 31st October 2009, but in January 2010 were still there. The BBC reported 'Brussels bashing 'back in fashion' with new Tory MPs'.

In the short term, Brussels-bashers' eyes were on the upcoming EU budget negotiations. By spring 2011 it was clear Brussels had ignored British pleas for budget cuts. In place of cuts, or even a budget freeze, the EU demanded an extra 4.9 percent for 2012, bloating its budget by £5.5bn to £117bn. Britain's own official figures finally acknowledged that Britons paid the EU £5.3bn in

---

[32] At another traveller site a few days later, police discovered a modern slave camp – in Bedfordshire. Raiding the Greenacres travellers' site, they found 24 men from Britain and Eastern Europe who had been held for up to 15 years, made to live in horse boxes, and work for no pay.

2009 and £9.2bn in 2010. The Brussels plan meant that in 2012 Britons started paying over £10bn to the EU (rising costs include the post-Lisbon EU 'foreign service'). Auditors found £9.5bn of 'quantifiable errors' in Brussels' project funding: equal to almost all Britain's contribution, this is likely to consist mainly of fraud. With Clegg beside him, at PMQs each Wednesday Cameron was now under sustained questioning from his own MPs over his inability to prevent the increase.

In fact while Cameron had been in talks with the Lib Dems in May 2010, all 27 EU finance ministers were summoned to Brussels to approve the Eurozone's European stabilisation mechanism. Already declared a 'done deal' by 16 eurozone leaders, who approved the mechanism at French and German behest while there was no clear government in London, the mechanism employed Lisbon's Article 122, enabling collective response to 'natural disasters or exceptional circumstances beyond [a] member state's control', overriding the need for unanimous agreement given that all 27 finance ministers including Alistair Darling were summoned. The move made Britons potentially liable for the debts of governments over whom they had no democratic control, beginning EU borrowing on a huge scale, and setting the course for fiscal union. It also ensured a confrontation with the new Tory Prime Minister.

With Gordon Brown out of Downing Street (and rarely visiting Parliament), his replacement Ed Miliband admitted that 'economic migration' had 'increased the pressure felt by those in lower skill work' and that 'we underestimated significantly the number of people who were going to come in from Eastern Europe'. He did not acknowledge that the government in which he served had been warned about it in advance, or that this was a sacred part of the European system. With polls showing a majority in favour of British exit from the EU, Cameron's suggestion of returning 'some powers' failed to quell discontent.

While David Cameron opposed the Lisbon Treaty, despite his 'cast iron guarantee' he did not ensure a Referendum. Having opposed it at the time he implemented its provisions year after year (and now is implicitly in favour of a Britain and Europe run according to its rules, despite the 'concessions' he claims to have obtained). It was this failure of the guarantee which meant that Conservative MPs felt they had to insist on a referendum on all the existing Treaties. They secured this in October 2011 against a three-line whip, on a Motion in the name of newly elected David Nuttall MP and co-drafted by Bill Cash. This ultimately forced the referendum commitment into the

Conservative manifesto. As a report from think tank Civitas called on Britain to prepare 'an exit strategy from a failing EU', Tory MPs called a Commons vote to give Britons a referendum. Cameron ordered them to vote down Nuttall's motion, even threatening MPs tempted to defy him that they would never be promoted while he was premier. Cameron got his majority, but 111 MPs defied party whips, including 81 of his own. Major's Maastricht rebellion had doubled.

The stalwarts were joined by swathes of the new intake, including Priti Patel, Zac Goldsmith representing south west London's *kulturni* suburbs, and York Outer's Julian Sturdy, farmer son of an MEP. Twenty MPs on the Labour benches supported the referendum motion, while it even gained the support of a Lib Dem, Torbay's Adrian Sanders. Shaken by the rebellion's scale, Cameron now cajoled those he had threatened, inviting groups of his MPs to 'lasagne suppers' at Downing Street. According to journalist Benedict Brogan, before his departure to the summit in Brussels on 8th December, Hague gave the PM his advice: 'if it's a choice between keeping the euro together or keeping the Conservative Party together,' the Foreign Secretary told Cameron, 'it's in the national interest to keep the Conservative Party together'.

In Brussels Cameron faced demands to approve fiscal union, and for new rules for the City. The proposed changes to the Lisbon treaty would have moved more power from democratic control to Brussels, involving Britain in a gigantic moral hazard experiment. In Eastern Europe, whose people were being told to fund richer countries that had lived beyond their means, the Hungarian and Czech premiers Viktor Orbán and Petr Nečas agreed to sign up only after parliamentary votes. After the usual gruelling style of overnight talks, the other EU leaders also agreed to an EU demand for 'balanced budgets' (defined by Brussels as a maximum deficit of 0.5 percent GDP) to be written into their national constitutions, and sanctions for any country whose deficit exceeds 3 percent. They also agreed to give national budgetary oversight to the Commission, granting it the right to revise budgets as it chooses. This included in theory non-eurozone countries, and in Denmark's case was agreed by new PM Helle Thorning-Schmidt, Neil Kinnock's daughter in law.

Nick Clegg did not mention the Commission's insistence on budgetary control when, having failed to appear in Parliament himself for the debate, he declared instead on the BBC that he regretted no deal had been reached. The French government prepared for Christmas by attacking its European partner, and against diplomatic norms suggested Britain take a credit rating downgrade instead of France. Apparently ignorant of EU history, Ed Miliband squeaked that Cameron had 'failed to build alliances before the summit'. Cameron had refused to sign up his country to a catastrophe for democratic control over economics, but Britain was further outside the law-writing Brussels mainstream than ever.

Like Saint-Simon before them, the Liberal Democrats, inheritors of British liberalism, decided in the mid-twentieth century that the fruits of a liberal society were best sought through an illiberal 'planning-state', and one run by a post-national 'expert' class. Their ensuing collapse was not coincidental. Cameron's forthcoming promise that victory in the 2015 general election would mean a referendum on EU membership did nothing to stop the Eurosceptic tide, taking shape in a historic pummeling at the hands of UKIP in the May 2013 local elections, where the party took 25 percent of the vote. The electorate was taking out its mid-term frustrations on the governing party, but not through the main opposition.

***

Following a Conservative victory in 2015 over Ed Miliband's dedicatedly Europhile Labour Party, against the predictions of almost every metropolitan political commentator, Cameron flew to Brussels in early 2016 to 'battle for Britain'. On the 24th February 2016, the Prime Minister claimed that the 'deal' he had reached in Brussels was 'legally binding'. A fair assessment of the reality of Cameron's deal was provided soon afterwards in a detailed briefing paper, published on 8th March, by the House of Commons Library.[dxlviii] The paper stated that the deal:

> 'Does not bind the EU institutions, and is not necessarily legally enforceable under either EU or domestic law. It could be very problematic if either the Court of Justice of the EU or a domestic court found an inconsistency between the Decision and the EU Treaties. The Decision… cannot guarantee all of the outcomes envisaged in it.'

The House of Commons Library's analysis was thorough, and we quote it here at length. The first section of the report is entitled 'European Council Conclusions', and it states:

'At the December 2015 meeting of the European Council, Member
States agreed to work together closely to find 'mutually satisfactory
solutions' in the four areas set out in the Prime Minister's letter to
European Council President Donald Tusk on 10th November 2015.

On 17-19th February 2016, the Heads of State or Government
of the EU Member States, meeting within the European Council,
considered – among pressing issues such as the situation in Syria
and the migration crisis at the EU's borders – draft texts submitted
by the European Council President Donald Tusk on 2nd February
2016 to address the UK's EU membership concerns.

Agreement was reached on 19th February and David Cameron,
satisfied with the outcome, announced that 'the Government's
position will be to recommend that Britain remains in a
reformed European Union'. The texts agreed are in Annexes to
the European Council Conclusions, 19th February 2016, and the
package is called the 'New Settlement for the United Kingdom
within the European Union"

The second section is entitled '2. Legally binding and irreversible?' The report
dissects this question as follows:

'It is not a Decision of the European Council as an EU institution,
so it is not EU law. Nor is it an EU Treaty. The Decision omits
most of the final clauses that are customarily included in treaties,
as well as the 'testimonium' (the final, formal wording of a treaty
beneath which the diplomatic representatives sign). The Decision
itself does not state anywhere that it is legally binding.'

The report reinforces this point by going into more detail here. On 'EU
practice', it analyses a 1996 survey of the then 15 EU Member States, which
'identified what for them would distinguish a legally-binding instrument
from a non-legally binding one'. It concluded that 'if an instrument was not
intended to be binding it would be worded to reflect that intention and avoid

mandatory language; it would omit treaty-type final clauses; and there would be no parliamentary procedure.' That is the case here.

Following the registration of the Decision with the UN, it was in a tweet on 24th February that the Prime Minister said: 'I welcome the registration of our legally binding EU agreement @UN today. Shows its strength and importance.' However, the report finds that Article 102 of the UN Charter requires that UN Member States 'register with the Secretariat every treaty and every international agreement entered into by them', and that 'registration with the UN Secretariat is not intended to give an agreement any status it would not otherwise have.' In the EU however, the closest thing to binding is the fact that it must be 'taken into account', which means that although it 'is therefore likely to carry considerable weight,' this 'is not the same thing as saying that it must be enforced.'

However the Decision is likely to carry different weight in different places. This second section asks whether it is 'for governments not EU institutions', and quotes legal expert Professor Steve Peers, who states that in the event of any conflict with pre-existing EU law – which has not yet been tested – the primacy of EU law 'means that the latter takes precedence over the renegotiation Decision. But is there any conflict? This is a substantive question'. In other words we cannot know until it is tested in the European Court of Justice. According to German scholar Roland Vaubel however, the ECJ 'has a clear history of expanding rather than limiting the EU's powers', and after Lisbon, 'the EU's democratic deficit is not narrowing but widening.'[dxlix]

But enforceability, says the report, is limited. Although Peers says: 'It follows from the above that the renegotiation deal is binding – and anyone who says otherwise (without clarification) is just not telling the truth', he adds: 'But there are two significant caveats to that: (a) parts of the deal, concerning the details of the changes to free movement law and Treaty amendments, still have to be implemented separately; and (b) there are limits to the enforceability of the deal.' The report clarifies therefore just how strong the bind actually is:

> 'None of the EU institutions – the European Commission, European Parliament or Court of Justice of the EU – are parties to the Decision [only member states], so they are not bound by it as a matter of international law.'

Crucially, 'The Court of Justice... is not a party to the decision [so] this does not necessarily mean that the Court of Justice will actually enforce the Decision, if it considered the Decision inapplicable to the case before it or contrary to the EU Treaties.' And on past precedence: 'In the Rottmann case, it is not at all clear the extent to which the Court of Justice gave effect to the Edinburgh Decision: its judgment applied EU law to an area which the Edinburgh Decision said was to be settled solely with reference to Member States' national law (nationality decisions).' Nor is the Decision necessarily permanent: 'Neither the Decision nor the Conclusions claim that the Decision is irreversible.'

The House of Commons Library report then breaks down the decision into its separate areas: economic governance, competitiveness, sovereignty, national security, and free movement and social benefits. It outlines the Prime Minister's proposed reforms on 'Economic Governance' as follows. They begin with a simple statement of fact that requires no reform:

- The EU has more than one currency.
- There should be no discrimination and no disadvantage for any business on the basis of the currency of their country.

The next (although the report does not state this) is a statement that both observes and serves to reinforce EU power:

- The integrity of the Single Market must be protected.
- Any changes the Eurozone decides to make, such as the creation of a banking union, must be voluntary for non-Euro countries, never compulsory.
- Taxpayers in non-Euro countries should never be financially liable for operations to support the Eurozone as a currency.

The next tacitly approves politico-economic control by the ECB:

- Just as financial stability and supervision has become a key area of competence for Eurozone institutions like the ECB, so financial stability and supervision is a key area of competence for national institutions like the Bank of England for non-Euro members.

The final reform statement approves and entrenches the power of the EU:

- And any issues that affect all Member States must be discussed and decided by all Member States.

The report adds that 'The provision on non-eurozone countries not facing financial loss due to 'bail-outs' reiterates a previous agreement in summer 2015 that is already included in an EU regulation.' On 'Competitiveness', the Prime Minister's proposals are as follows, and they begin with the notion of targets:

- A target to cut total burden on business
- To fulfil commitment to free flow of capital, goods and services
- A clear long-term commitment to boost the competitiveness and productivity of the EU and to drive growth and jobs for all

The report also outlines the commitment for the EU to 'pursue an active and ambitious trade policy'. The Government, it says '[believes] it has secured a firm commitment on economic reform', saying that: 'As a result of years of UK pressure, working closely with allies, the EU now has an ambitious agenda of economic reform'. It quotes the Prime Minister as saying: 'it means that the cost of EU red tape will be going down, not up'. The House of Commons Library's own report then sets out the Vote Leave view on competitiveness: 'In 2000, the European Council at Lisbon announced... an average economic growth rate of around 3% should be a realistic prospect for the coming years (quoting the Lisbon European Council, 23-24 March 2000)... The Lisbon Agenda is widely acknowledged to have been a failure, with economic growth in the Eurozone averaging 0.7% between 2000 and 2014'. In other words (although again the report does not say this), a Conservative leader is not connecting the fact that Europe is stagnating to the fact that it is less free.

The Prime Minister's demands on 'Sovereignty' are:

- End Britain's obligation to work towards ever closer union 'in a formal, legally-binding and irreversible way'.
- Enhance the role of national parliaments in the EU, with a new arrangement where groups of national parliaments, acting together, can stop unwanted legislative proposals.

- Full implementation of EU's commitments to subsidiarity.
- Confirmation that EU will fully respect purpose of Justice and Home Affairs Protocols in future proposals dealing with JHA matters, 'in particular to preserve the UK's ability to choose to participate' (UK opt-in arrangement).
- National Security must be the sole responsibility of Member States.

On that first, much heralded point about 'ever closer union', the report said this:

> 'An earlier draft of the final agreement clarified that Treaty references to ever closer union 'are not an equivalent to the objective of political integration, even though such an objective enjoys wide support in the Union."

In other words: the political integration of all EU countries will not stop. On 'National security' meanwhile, 'The Decision confirms that national security 'remains the sole responsibility of each Member State". The report says: 'This is not new', because 'national security is the sole responsibility of Member States. But the Decision also recognises the benefits of collective action on issues affecting all Member States.' Finally, on 'Free movement and social benefits', the Prime Minister's demands are:

- When new countries are admitted to the EU in the future, free movement will not apply to them until their economies have converged much more closely with existing Member States (although, as the report doesn't add, the EU decided Greece had 'converged').
- Crack down on abuse of free movement, e.g. tougher and longer re-entry bans for fraudsters and those involved in sham marriages, stronger powers to deport criminals and stop them coming back, addressing the inconsistency between EU citizens' and British citizens' eligibility to bring a non-EU spouse to the UK, and addressing ECJ judgments that have made it more difficult to tackle abuse.
- EU citizens coming to Britain must live here and contribute for four years before qualifying for in-work benefits or social housing.
- End the practice of sending child benefit overseas.

These next demands about freedom of movement deal purely with criminality, avoiding any question of free movement itself. The 2015 Conservative Party's 2016 General Election Manifesto contained the following pledges to tackle criminality and abuse of free movement:

- We will negotiate with the EU to introduce stronger powers to deport criminals and stop them coming back, and tougher and longer re-entry bans for all those who abuse free movement
- We want to toughen requirements for non-EU spouses to join EU citizens, including with an income threshold and English language test
- And when new countries are admitted to the EU in future, we will insist that free movement cannot apply to those new members until their economies have converged much more closely with existing Member States

The manifesto addressed the question of benefits (which very few migrants claim anyway):

- We will insist that EU migrants who want to claim tax credits and child benefit must live here and contribute to our country for a minimum of four years
- A new residency requirement for social housing, so that EU migrants cannot even be considered for a council house unless they have been living in an area for at least four years
- If an EU migrant's child is living abroad, then they should receive no child benefit or child tax credit, no matter how long they have worked in the UK and no matter how much tax they have paid
- We will end the ability of EU jobseekers to claim any jobseeking benefits at all

Following these commitments, the Decision began by clarifying things we could do anyway. On free movement, specifically changes affecting non-EU family members and criminal cases, the Decision, the report said, has 'some clarifications of the interpretation of current EU rules, including that':

- Member States may take action to prevent abuse of rights or fraud, such as the use of forged documents and cases of marriages of convenience

- In assessing whether an individual's personal conduct is likely to represent a genuine and serious threat to public policy or security, Member States may take into account the individual's past conduct, and the threat may not always need to be imminent. Member States may act on preventative grounds as long as they are specific to the individual concerned, including in cases where there is no previous criminal conviction.

The report says 'the free movement rights of non-EU family members of EU citizens will be restricted':

- Firstly, the Commission will propose amending the 'free movement' Directive (Directive 2004/38/EC) so that non-EU nationals who had no prior lawful residence in a Member State before marrying an EU citizen, or who married the EU citizen after the EU citizen had established residence in a host Member State, are not covered by EU free movement rights. Instead, the non-EU family members would be subject to the host Member State's national immigration laws.
- Secondly, a Commission Communication will provide guidelines on applying EU free movement of persons law, which will clarify that:
- Member States can take action in specific cases of abuse, where an EU citizen has been living in another Member State with a non-EU family member with the purpose of evading national immigration rules and without establishing a 'sufficiently genuine' residence there, and the EU citizen then seeks to return to their country of nationality with their family member under the cover of EU free movement law.
- Marriages which subsist in order that a non-EU national family member can have a right of residence under EU law fall under the concept of 'marriages of convenience', which is not covered by EU free movement laws.

Meanwhile 'the scope for expelling EU citizens on public policy or public security grounds, as set out in Directive 2004/38/EC, will be clarified':

- A Commission Communication will clarify that an individual's past conduct may be taken into account when assessing whether they pose a present threat to public policy or security, and that action may be taken on preventative grounds specific to the individual, even if the absence of a previous criminal conviction. The meanings of 'serious' and 'imperative' grounds of 'public policy or public security' will also be clarified.

• The five and ten year residence thresholds for considering whether expulsion is justified on public policy or public security grounds will be examined in the event of a future revision of Directive 2004/38/EC

And that:

• The UK will not have to pay means-tested unemployment benefits to EU nationals who come to the UK as job seekers

The lobby group *New Europeans*, said the report, 'interpreted the deal as a victory for the principle of free movement':

'...the measures designed to limit the rights of third country nationals married to mobile EU citizens to come to the UK. Again this is unpleasant and painful for those families whose lives will be disrupted as a result and it is an issue we will want to take up...'

This implies that an organisation widely believed to be EU-sponsored say it will not let the deal stand. The Chair of Migration Watch, Lord Green of Deddington, 'reflected this view', saying, 'This deal will do virtually nothing to reduce mass immigration'. The report also quotes Jonathan Portes of the National Institute for Social and Economic Research (widely regarded as a left-leaning organisation), 'who said that all those involved in the negotiations, including the Prime Minister, knew that the proposals would have no significant impact on immigration… The irony was, he said, that the whole episode had only acted as a 'massive advertising campaign for the UK benefit system". He added:

'So, even by the standards of the European Union, this has been an Alice-in Wonderland episode. The government has negotiated a watered-down version of something that it knew did not matter very much… Perhaps the real significance of the negotiation is that it has clarified just how fundamental free movement and non-discrimination are to the European Union. And on this, the UK has clearly had to accept the status quo. There is no Treaty change, now or promised, and the main measures the UK is entitled to impose are temporary and/or time-limited.'

On the free movement questions, the specific legislation that would have to be amended is:

- EU Regulation 883/2004: to give Member States the option to index the export of child benefits to a Member State other than that in which the worker resides to the standard of living and level of child benefits applicable in the Member State in which the child resides.
- EU Regulation 492/2011: to take account of a pull factor resulting from a Member State's in-work benefits system, and provide for an alert and safeguard mechanism to respond to situations where the inflow of workers from other Member States is of an 'exceptional magnitude' over a long period of time.
- EU Directive 2004/38/EC: to exclude from the scope of free movement rights third-country nationals who had no prior lawful residence in a Member State before marrying an EU citizen, or who marry an EU citizen after they have established residence in the host Member State.

On the requirements, Steve Peers adds: 'in the renegotiation deal the Member States commit themselves to supporting two of these three proposals (on child benefit and the emergency brake). It's odd that there's no parallel commitment as regards the third proposal (on EU citizens' non-EU family members).' The report states that:

'Referendums might be required in Ireland, some Eastern European States and possibly France and Denmark. Some elements of the Decision (e.g. limiting child benefits, the emergency brake on in-work benefits, stricter rules on marriages of convenience) will have to be passed by separate secondary EU legislation before they can take legal effect. This would be done using the Ordinary Legislative Procedure, involving QMV in the Council and a simple majority of the EP for approval. The Court of Justice could be asked to rule on whether the threshold condition for the emergency brake had been met.'

This 'Settlement', says the report, is 'not 'irreversible''.

BONFIRE NIGHT

> **But, woe the while! Our fathers' minds are dead...**
> **Cassius from bondage will deliver Cassius**
>
> *Julius Caesar*
> *William Shakespeare*

Re-joining the self-governing nations of the world would allow us many possible kinds of relationship with the EU. Norway has an internal market association outside it, Switzerland has a free trade agreement, others have most favoured nation agreements. We would continue to set the rules of trade through the WTO anyway, and outside the EU we would be able to influence it to the good.

Most British business is done with countries outside the EU, which Brussels harms. Yet would the EU start a trade war with an independent Britain? This would be madness. Four million jobs across the channel depend directly on exports to the UK.[dl] A good deal of business, looking for sanctuary from the EU's hyper-regulation, would more likely relocate to Britain than leave. In the realm of defence, some speculate about what we cannot pursue in the EU, a serious Commonwealth peacekeeping force for example. Britain now gives more to our wealthy European neighbours than all our aid to the developing world combined.

But the EU is not static. The notion that we can continue within it without being part of a superstate beyond our control is wrong. The EU cannot be guided anywhere else but federalism, because it has no other purpose. So the body of Britain stands. Like the other member states, the limbs move, the body appears to function, but the political mind is hollowed out as its functions fall under outside control. Yet now we have a second chance.

We have seen that the EU is not only corrupting in its effects, but anti-democratic to its very foundations. 'The Community itself is only a stage on the way to the organised world of tomorrow', said Jean Monnet. Attempts at such utopias have no connection to the Parliamentary traditions of British politics, traditions we do not revere for their own sake, but because they work. Every single autocracy in history has been created because its followers thought it was justified by its ends, and while we may think autocracy is a thing of the past, in European history autocracies have exceeded democracies by far.

On the Right, some Eurosceptics have failed to connect the misdeeds of the EU to the concerns of Britain's enlightened people: trade, poverty, the environment, but the political weather of respectable opinion is made by organisations like the BBC (however the European Scrutiny Committee and Newswatch appear to have made some impact on the degree of impartiality which the BBC brings to bear on the European referendum as it progresses. But time will tell). This is liberalism only in vague sentiment.

Blair, Brown and Mandelson created New Labour to fight a battle that is now far in the past, but the project failed to achieve its aims, being poorly conceived from the outset, due partly to its attitude to Europe. Labour did not just tolerate, but celebrate our loss of control of our borders, while the influx of cheap labour drove down wages while sucking skilled workers away from Eastern Europe. This is to the benefit of only the tiny elite who employ them in large numbers. The majority of the real jobs created by the party of British labour went to immigrant labour. Labour encouraged the influx that undercut the British working class, providing cheap labour for big employers. In the meantime the trade unions were gagged by political correctness and are still as good as silent. But Labour's historic betrayal of Britain's poor was made possible through their co-opting by the EU.

Entrepreneurship meanwhile is part of the engine of wealth creation, but while the situation for Britain's entrepreneurs is better than on the Continent, they are now swathed in EU red tape, as Brussels has wrapped small businessmen in 105,000 pages of regulations, failing even in its meagre objective of simplifying 54 laws a year.[dli] 72.5 percent of the red tape our businesses deal with comes from Brussels. Some small companies have to fork out £850 a year to comply with just one particular directive, as Brussels attempts to regulate every detail.[dlii] In 1995, Jacques Santer's Commission promised to 'do less but do it better', since which time the number of EU directives and regulations has risen from 8,000 to over 30,000, and the number keeps growing. The mechanism of political accountability has also been severed, as our politicians can blame Brussels for bad laws. When people vote for a new government, they want to see change occur, like pulling the lever on a machine. Now they pull the lever and little happens.

The return of our self-government would restore our self-esteem as an independent nation, and nationhood gives something to the poor in particular. The working men and women who have lined the docks to watch their own country's fleet sail out along the Solent have felt pride, because what they saw was *theirs*. Today Britain's poor are ruled, passive and without democratic responsibility. If you're poor in the EU, you're just poor. But in 1782, Carl Philip Moritz, a German visitor to Britain, wrote home:

> 'My dear friend, when one sees here how the lowliest carter shows an interest in public affairs; how the smallest children enter into the spirit of the nation; how everyone feels himself to be a man and an Englishman – as good as his King and his King's minister – it brings to mind thoughts very different to those we know when we watch the soldiers drilling in Berlin.'[dliii]

Democracies' superior ability to defend themselves is considerable. The Greek city-states were history's first consensual governments, and their armies consisted of soldiers who were free property owners, men who had the best possible reason to fight: motivation. In the end, a society needs personal commitment, not just 'harmony'. But when soldiers have little or no shared identity with the people they are asked to protect, history has shown time and again that they use this power to extort and enslave. Few choose wrong because it is wrong, they do so mistaking it for the good they seek. The danger of any 'European army' is quite clear.

***

The Roman Empire, Charlemagne, Napoleon, the Fascists, the Eastern bloc: every attempt at unifying Europe, or a large part of it, has ultimately collapsed. We must accept that the nation state is an inherent and necessary part of being European, while the superstate is the recurring European nightmare. Diversity of nations is the key to the brilliance of Europe, and they have not created war – a lack of democracy has. In 1943, as Stalingrad seemed prophetic Megiddo, and the Japanese massacred their way through China, a young philosopher named Karl Popper looked far ahead. He wrote that

'If we dream of a return to our childhood, if we are tempted to rely on others and so be happy, if we shrink from the task of carrying our cross, the cross of humaneness, or reason, of responsibility, if we lose courage and flinch from the strain, then we must try to fortify ourselves with a clear understanding of the simple decision before us... there is only one way, the way into the open society. We must go on into the unknown, the uncertain and insecure, using what reason we may have to plan as well as we can for both security and freedom.'[dliv]

Despite taking over the trappings of power in Westminster, no real Tory revival in the British people's admirations is possible until their leaders return to these ideals, which have been only cosmetic since Edward Heath. Until then the public will vote with little enthusiasm, knowing they will receive, at best, slightly more effective surrogate managerialism.

With public life ever more cosmetic, the people become vulgarised consumers of politics as a product. Whether refusing to vote, or tuning in to TV's pretend elections for pop stars in preference to the real ones, the British people are abandoning public responsibility for political play-acting. There is an awful logic to this, with their Parliament has become a vessel for the writ of Brussels law. But apathy is not consent. Like the local heads of a multinational conglomerate meanwhile, each state's 'leader' now often flies to HQ in his jet before expressing a position to his electorate. Thus the political class of each nation talk to each other and to themselves. The *coup d'état* we have watched may have been in slow motion, but a *coup d'état* it has been.

As William Gladstone said in 1888, 'we are part of the community of Europe, and we must do our duty as such'. There should be no doubt that Britain has a European vocation. The destruction of the Spanish Armada by the Elizabethan navy and its Dutch allies formed a great stand against tyranny. Come Trafalgar, Nelson's ships held down another dictator, before at a Belgian village called *Waterlō* Wellington's pan-European force of British soldiers and their Dutch and German allies finished Napoleon for good. Britain's bravery turned the twentieth century for Europe in two world wars. If other European countries give up their parliaments, they are alas not giving up the same thing.[dlv] These experiences have made us. So why should we be surprised that it falls to us to blaze the trail out of Brussels? Yet we are nervous in the act. It is NATO which since the end of the Second World War has preserved the peace in Europe, not the EU, and which a European Army never will.

To those who say the alternative to the Union is the historical branch-line of isolationism, we may say that Britain since its very beginnings has never been isolationist. Both our history and contemporary responsibilities tell us that alternatives to the European Union will not include isolationism. The first lines of the first great work in the English language see the writer of Beowulf looking back to the legends of his ancestors before they crossed the sea:

> So. The Spear Danes in days gone by
> and the kings who ruled them had courage and greatness.
> We have heard of those princes' heroic campaigns.[dlvi]

Only once we leave the European Union will we be able to rejuvenate our parliament. When we have connected the dots of our political life once more, it is natural that Britain will seek out cooperation with the like-minded countries of Europe. A new association must be without the protectionism at the expense of the developing world, which is at the centre of the EU's bankruptcy.

This book began by talking about fear and its supporters. The European Union and its supporters in our referendum have flourished by cultivating fear, and are continuing to do so, because Project Fear is all they have to offer. They play upon the emotions of fear and confuse them with the virtues of risk, but risk is a catalyst to competitiveness and achievement, which the European Union and its advocates do not understand, and which lie at the heart of British achievement over many centuries. We have nothing to fear but fear itself. But let us not be afraid. Fear has brought to power those who would dismantle democracy with the tools of bureaucracy instead of the weapons of war, because the directive is mightier than the sword.

Britain's leaders have not found the courage to affect the necessary sea-change, and the fate of peoples is made at such moments. The European Union was designed for ever closer union from the start, and to that it must continue. Make no mistake: either we choose Britain and democracy, or we choose European pseudo-democracy, letting our leaders take our country forward to nothingness. Tomorrow really is another country.

EPILOGUE: PLATO'S GHOST

**Even in the smallest matter a man should stand under leadership.
He should teach his soul, by long habit, never to dream of acting
independently, and to become utterly incapable of it.**

Plato

At the heart of Brussels' European quarter today, the centrepiece is a roundabout called the *Rond-Point Schuman*. This is a node of glass and steel buildings, post-national in their lack of style. Their long, flat faces suck the life off their streets and into the offices above.

These streets in turn are bare, save for some corporate-style cafes whose menus include bee pollen health drinks. Barbed wire X-fence barricades control access to the *rond-point* from the surrounding streets. Numerous police vans, a few scurrying suits, and various pretty assistants are doing the rounds. Over the roundabout hangs a banner with a shining Euro coin, proclaiming '*vers une gouvernance économique européene renforcé*'.

Outside one office block, heavies in neckties ensure passers-by cannot enter the press conference taking place within. The curve of blackened glass around the building ensures we have only their word for what is happening within. This is the *Justus Lipsius*, whose sign proclaims it has stood here since the year 1995. It is the seat of the European Council, whose logo is a huge eye filled with the European stars. A little down the road, a bronze seems to step off its pedestal into the unknown. It is called 'Stepping Forward'.

Hidden behind the vast Justus Lipsius monolith, one thing of beauty remains. The Residence Palace is an art deco conception, golden in resplendent warmth. Surrounded by a building site, the gem will soon be almost completely engulfed by a new giant, *Europa*, another steel cube whose exterior will resemble a conference pear pressed into a pin screen. Today, the Palace is hosting a *Spinelli Group-Steering Group* debate entitled 'Only a European Federal Union can solve the crisis'. At one side of the atrium, the diminutive former Commission boss Romano Prodi can be seen.

Across the *rond-point*, bronzes of happy children gazing at the sky guard the entrance to the home of the European Commission itself. This hugest block of all is a distortion of curves and cuts, providing no visual focal point from outside. Young politicos gather at the entrance in ties and security tags, the uniform of the European chosen. A pair of Prada glasses is having a conversation with an Armani suit; in the style of this international class they compare the 'experience' provided by various national capitals. A police helicopter circles over still more G4S security guards – red bands for their tags, yellow for the Eurocrats.

Beside this horizontal megalith an educational notice tells us about *The Charlemagne*, as the building is known. Charlemagne, we are told, became King of the Franks in 768. 'In 800, he was crowned emperor by Pope Leo III. His reforms in the area of religion and culture have been described as the *Carolingian Renaissance*. But his empire was divided between his three grandchildren. The period of feudal fragmentation which marked the following centuries was followed by the division of Europe into rival nation-states.'

A motorcade speeds away towards central Brussels. One glass wall bears the regionalist slogan '*Catalunya, Europa*'. A blue and white Saltire flutters across the street. The *rond-point* was once one of the finest places in Brussels, a beautiful cluster of townhouses and apartment blocks of gentle Flemish brick and limestone. One remains, but the buildings shoving against it are cold even on a warm summer's day.

A two-block walk from the roundabout, one finds a glorious mess of orange tiles, copper rooftops and whitewashed stone walls, and the visitor knows he has left the harmonised zone. But leaving the European sector down the Rue Froissard there is a police check, so you'll need a pass should you want to go back behind the barbed wire.

On the hill above the nearby park, immense, concrete and potent behind an old farmhouse with delicate turquoise gables, is Europe's parliament. At one metal entrance, a new heroic statue holds a letter 'e' aloft, while other figures, apparently drowning, stretch their sinewy arms towards it. Before leaving through the Schuman metro station we pass an institution announcing itself 'the leading school in protocol studies'. In red paint below an underpass someone has graffiti-ed the words: 'tout pouvoir sera détruit' – all power will be destroyed. We are in what one anthropologist has called a nonplace: generic, international and dystopian.

***

Around 535 BC, a young man named Heraclitus was born in the town of

Ephesus on the coast of Asia Minor, into a noble family of the town's ruling priest-kings. From a young age Heraclitus was prone to outbursts of violent rage. Witnessing the banishment of a delinquent aristocratic friend, he cried in despair that 'the Ephesians ought to hang themselves man by man, all the adults, and leave the city to be ruled by infants'. Although he had no wish to enter the political life into which he had been born, he supported the rule of the priest-king caste. The people, he thought, were too wayward for such burdens as power: 'the law can demand that the will of one man must be obeyed', he insisted, but 'most men are wicked. The mob fill their bellies like the beasts. They take the bards and popular belief as their guides, unaware that the many are bad and only a few are good.'[dlvii]

Heraclitus would come to believe that he had discovered for the people 'an inexorable and immutable law of destiny', the government of the many by a clique of the few. 'It is surprising', Karl Popper tells us, 'to find in these early fragments, dating from about 500BC, so much that is characteristic of modern... anti-democratic tendencies'. It seems Heraclitus died in about 475BC after trying inexpertly to treat an oedema by covering himself in cow dung and lying in the baking sun. By then he was known across the Hellenic world, and where he finished, fifty years later Plato would begin.

Plato himself was born in 428 BC

BC, like Heraclitus a man of the blood royal, from a respected Athenian family descended from the kings of Athens and its neighbour Messenia. Athens was a democratic state, but in Plato's childhood it suffered through the bloody Peloponnesian War against Sparta, the most powerful city in the region which had maintained the strict rule of an elite caste. Plato was born into war, and he would be twenty-four by the time it ended. It brought disease and famine; Athens fell, then fell into civil war, then the terror of the rule of the Thirty Tyrants. Two of these tyrants were uncles of the young Plato, and both were assassinated by democrats.

Athenian society was left traumatised. Democracy was eventually re-established, but for Plato new brutalities would arrive. Despite being free and at peace, Athens took offence at the work of Plato's favourite teacher, Socrates, judged to have corrupted Athenian youth, and, sentenced to death, Socrates chose to die by drinking hemlock. His student fled. Plato would not be the last to suffer the agonies of the age into which he was born, and his thinking changed forever. Not a politician himself, Plato nonetheless tells us

'From the beginning I was most anxious for political activity... but seeing that everything swayed and shifted aimlessly, I felt giddy and desperate. Everything was in a state of flux.'

Believing his age to be one of chaos and degradation, in *The Republic* Plato tells us it was still possible for society to be released from the bondage of its history, and to strike a final political bargain for security. Plato searched for an order without change or decay, free of the weakness of the lesser states before it. In his world in flux, change fascinated Plato, but he desired more than all else the secrets to arresting it. After the traumas he had known, Plato saw a perfectible world, 'the secret of the royal knowledge of politics, of the art of ruling men'.

Plato in particular believed in a who and a whom: natural rulers and the naturally ruled, in the ideal state that could not wither. Was he describing a place he thought had once existed, lost in the prehistoric fug of time? Plato thought he had found a grail, but was no tyrant and did not want to be. Above all, in the breakdown of hierarchy Plato perceived the fall of man. Athenians still cherished their freedom, but Athens had fallen to Sparta, a slave state with a ruling class. So the Athenian elite, he hoped, would succeed in manipulating its opponents to see its own authority rise.

Plato's Delphic desires are becoming real, and the European Union is now a virtual *Noocracy*, an aristocracy of self-appointed experts. In 2005 the Commission admitted as such in a research document whose title was *Towards a Culture of Life*. It said:

> 'If Plato called his conception of governments a 'sophocracy,' then a political system characterized by social experimentation with a scientific institutionalized base could be called a 'noocracy.' Noocracy would not be the reign of the philosopher-king as seen in Plato. But nor would it be governed by science or the scientists. Power, a power acquired and maintained according to the laws of competition, would remain in the hands of the political elites but with these elites being professionally trained, making the most of the analysis, the forecasts and the propositions emanating from a vast array of advisory groups made up of experts from all areas...' [dlviii]

We may ask how it came to this. How, in the decades after the war, a generation of Europeans allowed democracy to be strangled yet again, as the defence of sovereign democracy itself became an act of xenophobia. If you cease to believe in the democratic self-governing nation state, with one law for all made by a sovereign Parliament, then pretty soon you are going to get something else. Today a younger generation finds itself with a strange inheritance, and keeps trying to operate the machine. Some of the true believers among them affect the fears of this older generation: the Union 'keeps us from war'. But no matter how hard its supporters try to bend reality to fit the template, the European Union was built to prevent a conflict that had already happened, and absolve its builders of their sins.

Athens gave us democracy, but Plato nurtured its bitter twin, and it would reach fulminance in Fascism and Communism, the merciless meshuggeners of twentieth century totalitarianism. Sometimes vicious and violent, sometimes bureaucratic and apparently benevolent, diktat can always supplant democracy. We have arrived at the crossroads. So what is the road ahead?

Barack Obama and John Kerry are preparing to follow the mistakes of their forebears since World War Two by imploring us to reinforce a European authoritarian system, thus betraying the most fundamental values of America's forefathers in the mistaken belief that it will bring peace and prosperity. Just as the United States was born of a rejection of overseas authoritarianism, this referendum is now an opportunity for our own Boston Tea Party.

In freeing our country from the new authoritarian system in Europe, we would also re-set and rejuvenate the special relationship, and in so doing return the English speaking world to its true calling, allowing it to lead the world in democracy and free trade. Having set the example, Britain has the opportunity to establish a new European association – based in London – guaranteeing free trade and the sovereign parliamentary democracy of nation states.

If we vote to leave in our referendum, then Britain's leaders are about to be given a truly historic opportunity – to do the only thing that can ever work, and create a system that defends freedom in Britain and Europe. Just as the Renaissance – the explosion of innovation and trade that allowed the emergence of the modern world itself – depended on free and self-governing European states, our opportunity will be no less than to lead the new European Renaissance, under a system of free-trading nation states, secure in their own borders, bound by a pact of peace and brotherhood, and with the guarantee of mutual defence in a re-invigorated NATO.

As Britain has been many times before, we are now called upon to show Europe one simple thing: how much better things can be.

ACKNOWLEDGEMENTS

This book would have been impossible without the help of many fine people.

First among them are our wives, Sidsel and Biddy.

For academic sources and material we are also hugely grateful to Christopher Booker, Richard North, Robin Harris, David Craig, Matthew Elliot, Lee Rotherham, Richard J. Aldrich, Peter Catterall, Alistair Horne, Richard Lamb, R.B. Manderson-Jones, Charles Clover, Roberto Saviano, Stuart Holland, Andrew Roberts, John Laughland, Norman Lewis, Pedro Schwarz, Brendan Simms and Nassim Taleb.

For their encouragement and enthusiasm we are most grateful to our families, as well as to Dr John Slight, Sandeep Rattan, Andrew Abrams, Zeeshan Hashmi, Jonas Twitchen, Alexander Holland, Thomas Oldham, Thomas Smith, Sir Simon Jenkins, Lord Tebbit, Lord Pearson, Robert Oulds, Austin Mitchell and Adam Afriyie. Any errors or omissions are entirely our own.

Appendix

A Very Brief History of the EU

1948: The American Committee on United Europe (ACUE) is formed by the founders of the CIA

1957: the Treaty of Rome creates the European Economic Community (EEC) with six member states (France, Belgium, Germany, Italy, the Netherlands and Luxembourg).

1962: The start of the Common Agricultural Policy (CAP): market and price guarantees and various protectionist measures, coordinated and financed by the EEC.

1973: The UK, Denmark and Ireland join the EEC (Norway decides to stay out).

1979: The first direct elections to the European parliament.

1981: Greece joins the EEC

1986: Spain and Portugal join the EEC

1987: Single European Act in operation

1991: Maastricht Treaty signed

1992: Official start of the European Single Market

1994: Sweden, Finland and Austria join (Norway decides again to stay out)
Maastricht Treaty starts operating officially
The EEC becomes the EU

1995: EU summit in Madrid agrees a time plan for the launch of the single currency

1997: Treaty of Amsterdam signed

1999: The Euro is launched. Its central bank is the European Central Bank (ECB) in Frankfurt
Treaty of Amsterdam becomes operational

2001: Treaty of Nice signed

2003: Treaty of Nice becomes operational
Drafting of the European Constitution begins

2004: Estonia, Latvia, Lithuania, Poland, Czech Republic, Slovakia, Hungary, Slovenia, Cyprus and Malta join the EU

Spain and Luxembourg approve the Constitution in referenda; France and the Netherlands reject it

2007: Romania and Bulgaria join the EU

The European Constitution, adjusted and renamed the Lisbon Treaty, is signed

2008: Ireland votes against the Treaty of Lisbon. Prime Minister Bertie Ahern immediately announces another referendum

2009: Ireland, now in deep recession, votes in favour of the Treaty of Lisbon in a second referendum. The Treaty of Lisbon comes into force

2010: David Cameron becomes Prime Minister as a Conservative – Liberal Democrat coalition government takes power in Britain

2011: David Cameron vetoes a new European Treaty intended to prevent the collapse of the euro. He also orders his MPs to vote against a referendum on EU membership drafted by Bill Cash and brought by David Nuttall.

2013: David Cameron backs bill by James Wharton MP, co-drafted by Sir Bill Cash, for a referendum on EU membership. Most Lib Dem and Labour MPs abstain.

2016: A referendum on Britain's membership of the European Union is held.

BIBLIOGRAPHY

Aldrich, Richard. J. (1997): 'OSS, CIA and European Unity: The American Committee on United Europe, 1948-60'. *Diplomacy & Statecraft*, 8:1, pp.184-227

Almond, Mark: *Europe's Backyard War – The War in the Balkans*. London: Heinemann, 1998

Amis, Martin: *Koba the Dread: Laughter and the Twenty Million*. London: Miramax, 2002

Andreasen, Marta: *Brussels Laid Bare: How the EU Treated its Chief Accountant When She Refused To Go Along With Its Fraud and Waste*. London: St Edmund's Press, 2009

Bache, Ian and Jordan, Andrew (Eds.): *The Europeanization of British Politics*. London: Palgrave Macmillan, 2008

Balanya, Belen, Doherty, Ann, Hoedeman, Olivier, Ma'anit, Adam and Wesselius, Eric: *Europe, Inc.: Regional and Global Restructuring and the Rise of Corporate Power*. London: Pluto Press, 2000

Benn, Anthony: *The Benn Diaries*. London: Random House, 1995

Berlin, Isaiah: *Freedom and its Betrayal: Six Enemies of Human Liberty* (ed. Henry Hardy). London: Pimlico Press, 2003

Bongers, Erik: *Hidden Disaster*. Luxembourg: Publications Office of the European Union, 2010

Booker, Christopher and North, Richard: *The Great Deception: The Secret History of the European Union*. London: Continuum, 2003

Burke, Edmund: *Reflections on the Revolution in France* (1790) (ed. L. G. Mitchell), Oxford University Press

Butler, David and Kitzinger, Uwe: *The 1975 Referendum*. London: Macmillan, 1976

Cartwright, John: *Evolution and Human Behaviour: Darwinian Perspectives on Human Nature*. London: Palgrave Macmillan, 2000

Cash, William: *Against a Federal Europe – The Battle for Britain*. London: Duckworth, 1991

Cash, William: *Visions of Europe*. London: Duckworth, 1993

Cash, William: *Visions of Europe II*. London: Duckworth, 2016

Cash, William: *It's the EU Stupid*. London: The European Foundation, 2011

Cash, William and Duncan Smith, Iain: *A German Europe: Aspects of a Single State in Europe*. 1997

Catterall, Peter (ed.) *The Macmillan Diaries, Vol. III: Prime Minister and After, 1957-66*. Basingstoke: Pan Macmillan, 2011

Cave, T. and Rowell, A.: *A Quiet Word: Lobbying, Crony Capitalism and Broken Politics in Britain*. London: Bodley Head, 2014

Clover, Charles: *The End of the Line: How Over-fishing is Changing the World and What We Eat*. London: Ebury Press, 2004

Colville, John: *The Fringes of Power: Downing Street Diaries 1939-1945*. London: Weidenfeld and Nicholson, 2004

Connolly, Bernard: *The Rotten Heart of Europe – The Dirty War for Europe's Money*. London: Faber and Faber, 1995

Cooke, Alistair: *Reporting America: The Life of the Nation*. London: Allen Lane, 2008

Craig, David and Elliott, Matthew: *The Great European Rip-off: How the Corrupt, Wasteful EU is Taking Control of Our Lives*. London: Arrow Books, 2009

Dale, Iain: *The Little Book of Boris*. Petersfield: Harriman House, 2007

Davies, Ian, Hirst, Chrissie, Mariani, Bernardo: *Organised crime, corruption and illicit arms trafficking in an enlarged EU: challenges and perspectives*. London: Saferworld, 2001

Davies, Norman: *Europe: A History*. London: Random House, 1997

Dell, Edmund: *The Schuman Plan and the British Abdication of Leadership in Europe*. Oxford: Clarendon Press, 1995

Edgerton, David: *The Shock of the Old: Technology and Global History Since 1900*. London: Profile Books, 2006.

Elliott, Larry and Atkinson, Dan: *Fantasy Island: Waking Up to the Incredible Economic, Political and Social Illusions of the Blair Legacy*. London: Constable, 2007

Elliott, Matthew and Rotherham, Lee: *The Bumper Book of Government Waste 2008: Brown's Squandered Billions*. London: Harriman House, 2008

Forsyth, Murray: *Unions of States: The Theory and Practice of Confederation*. Leicester University Press, 1981

Flinders, Matthew: *Delegated Governance and the British State: Walking without Order*. Oxford University Press, 2008

Flint, Adrian: *Trade, Poverty and the Environment: the EU, Cotonou and the African-Caribbean-Pacific Bloc*. Basingstoke: Palgrave Macmillan, 2008

Freemantle, Brian: *The Octopus: Europe in the Grip of Organised Crime*. London: Orion, 1995

Friedlander, Saul: *Pope Pius XII and the Third Reich: a Documentation*. New York: Knopf, 1966

George, Stephen: *An Awkward Partner – Britain in the European Community* (3rd edition). Oxford University Press, 1990

Gough, Roger and Reid, Anna (Eds.): *The Perfect Union? New Europe and the EU*. London: Policy Exchange, 2004

Grabbe, Heather and Hughes, Kirsty: 'Central and east European views on EU enlargement: political debates and public opinion'. In: Henderson, Karen (Ed.): *Back to Europe: Central and Eastern Europe and the European Union*. London: UCL Press, 1999

Grant, Charles: *Delors: Inside the House that Jacques Built*. London: Nicholas Brearley, 1994

Heaney, Seamus: *Beowulf: A New Translation*. London: Faber and Faber, 2002

Henderson, Karen: *Back to Europe: Central and Eastern Europe and the European Union*. Oxford: Routledge, 1998

Heyde, Maximillian: *The Impact of the Common Agricultural Policy on Food Prices: Consequences for Sub-Saharan Africa*. Saarbrücken: Vdm Verlag, 2009

Hill, Brian: *Studies in Economics and Business: The European Union* (4th edition) London: Heinemann, 2001

Holland, Stuart: *Out of Crisis: a Project for European Recovery*. Nottingham: Spokesman, 1983

Holland, Stuart: *UnCommon Market*. New York: St. Martin's Press, 1980

Horne, Alistair: *Macmillan 1894-1956: Volume 1 of the Official Biography*. London: Macmillan, 1988

Horne, Alistair: *Macmillan 1957-1986: Volume 2 of the Official Biography*. London: Macmillan, 1989

Howard, Michael: *The Invention of Peace: Reflections on War and International Order*. New Haven: Yale University Press, 2001

Howe, Geoffrey: *Conflict of Loyalty*. London: Macmillan, 1994

Hutton, Will: *The World We're In*. London: Abacus, 2003

Jenkins, Roy: *A Life at the Centre*. London: Papermac, 1994

Jenkins, Simon: *Big Bang Localism: A Rescue Plan for British Democracy*. London: Policy Exchange/Localis, 2004

Jordan, A.: *Implementation Failure or Policy Making? How Do We Theorise the Implementation of EU Environmental Legislation?* Working Paper GEC-1995-18. Norwich: University of East Anglia.

Kennan, George F.: *American Diplomacy, 1900-1950.* London: Secker and Warburg, 1952

Kennan, George F.: *Memoirs, 1925-1950.* London: Hutchinson, 1968

Lamb, Richard: *The Macmillan Years, 1957-63: The Emerging Truth.* London: John Murray, 1985

Lawson, Nigel: *The View From No.11 – Memoirs of a Tory Radical.* London: Bantam Press, 1992

Lynggaard, K: *The Common Agricultural Policy and Organic Farming: an Institutional Perspective on Continuity and Change.* Wallingford: CABI Publishing, 2006

Machiavelli, Niccolò: *The Prince* (translated by George Bull). London: Penguin, 2004

Maiskii, I.M.: *The Maisky Diaries: Red Ambassador to the Court of St James's, 1932-1943,* edited by Gabriel Gorodetsky. New Haven: Yale University Press, 2015

Major, John: *The Autobiography,* London: Harper Collins, 1999

Manderson-Jones, R.B.: *The Special Relationship: Anglo-American Relations and Western European Unity 1947-56.* London: Weidenfeld and Nicholson, 1972

Mayer, Arno: *The Persistence of the Old Regime.* London: Croom Helm, 1981

Monnet, Jean: *Memoirs.* London: Collins, 1978

Moritz, Carl Philip: *Journeys of a German in England in 1782.* London, 1795. In Paxman, Jeremy: *The English: A Portrait of a People*: London: Penguin, 1999

O'Neill, Con: *Britain's Entry into the European Union – A Report on the Negotiations of 1970-1972.* London: Frank Cass, 2000

Oborne, Peter and Weaver, Frances: *Guilty Men.* London: Centre for Policy Studies, 2012

Pain, Deborah and Pienkowski, Michael (Eds.): *Farming and Birds in Europe: Common Agricultural Policy and its Implications for Bird Conservation.* London: Poyser, 2002

Pinder, John: *The European Union: a Very Short Introduction.* Oxford University Press, 2001

Popper, Karl R.: *The Open Society and its Enemies, Volume One: The Spell of Plato.* London: Routledge & Kegan Paul, 1945

Roberts, Andrew: *A History of the English Speaking Peoples Since 1900*. London: Phoenix, 2007

Rotherham, Lee: *Ten Years On: Britain without the European Union*. London: The Taxpayers' Alliance, 2009

Saviano, Roberto: *Gomorrah: Italy's Other Mafia*. London: Pan Macmillan, 2007

Schwarz, Pedro: *The Euro as Politics*. London: The Institute of Economic Affairs, 2004

Scrase, Ivan and MacKerron, Gordon (eds.): *Energy for the Future: a New Agenda*. London: Palgrave Macmillan, 2009

Simms, Brendan: *Unfinest Hour: Britain and the Destruction of Bosnia*. London: Penguin, 2002

Smith, Adam: *The Theory of Moral Sentiments* (1759)

Sulík, Richard: *European Financial Stability: A Road to Socialism*. Bratislava: Strana-SaS party paper, 2011

Taleb, Nassim N.: *The Black Swan: The Impact of the Highly Improbable*. London: Allen Lane, 2007

Thatcher, Margaret: *Statecraft: Strategies for a Changing World*. London: Harper Collins, 2002

Thatcher, Margaret: *The Downing Street Years*. London: Harper Collins, 1992

Wallis, Andrew: *Silent Accomplice: the Untold Story of France's Role in the Rwandan Genocide*. London: I. B. Tauris, 2006

Watson, Peter: *The German Genius: Europe's Third Renaissance, the Second Scientific Revolution and the Twentieth Century*. London: Simon & Schuster, 2011

Wilkinson, Richard: *Mind the Gap: Hierarchies, Health and Human Evolution*. London: Weidenfeld and Nicholson, 2000

Wilson, Theodore A: *The First Summit*. Boston: Houghton Mifflin, 1970

Young, Hugo: *The Hugo Young Papers: Thirty Years of British Politics – Off the Record*. London: Allen Lane, 2008

Young, Hugo: *This Blessed Plot: Britain and Europe, From Churchill to Blair*. London: Routledge, 1998

Young, John W.: *Britain and European Unity 1945-1999* (2nd Edition). British History in Perspective series. London: Macmillan, 2000

NOTES & REFERENCES

i   Horne, Alistair: *Macmillan 1894-1956: Volume 1 of the Official Biography*. London: Macmillan, 1988

ii   *Ibid.*, p.167

iii   *Ibid.*, p.168

iv   *Ibid.*, p.169

v   *Ibid.*, p.170-1

vi   *Ibid.*, p.171

vii   *Ibid.*, p.171

viii   *Ibid.*, p.172

ix   *Ibid.*, p.172

x   Maiski, I.M. *The Maiski Diaries: red ambassador to the court of St James's, 1932-1943* / edited by Gabriel Gorodetsky, p.483

xi   Horne, Alistair: *Macmillan 1894-1956: Volume 1 of the Official Biography*. London: Macmillan, 1988, p.172-3

xii   *Ibid.*, p.180

xiii   *Ibid.*, p.180

xiv   *Ibid.*, p.182-3

xv   Maiski, I.M. *The Maiski Diaries: red ambassador to the court of St James's, 1932-1943* / edited by Gabriel Gorodetsky, p.469

xvi   Horne, Alistair: *Macmillan 1894-1956: Volume 1 of the Official Biography*. London: Macmillan, 1988, p,184

xvii   *Ibid.*, p.184

xviii   *Ibid.*, p.185

xix   *Ibid.*, p.185

xx   Young, John W.: *Britain and European Unity 1945-1999* (2nd Edition). British History in Perspective series. London, Macmillan, 2000, p.8-9

xxi   Horne, Alistair: *Macmillan 1894-1956: Volume 1 of the Official Biography*. London: Macmillan, 1988, p.187

xxii   *Ibid.*, p.187-8

xxiii   *Ibid.*, p.188

xxiv   *Ibid.*, p.188-9

xxv   *Ibid.*, p.189

[xxvi] Maiski, I.M. *The Maiski Diaries: red ambassador to the court of St James's, 1932-1943* / edited by Gabriel Gorodetsky, p.33; p.55

[xxvii] Davies, Norman: Europe: a History. London: Random House, 1997, p.1065

[xxviii] Roberts, Andrew: *A History of the English Speaking Peoples Since 1900*. London: Phoenix, 2007

[xxix] Cash, William and Duncan Smith, Iain: *A German Europe: Aspects of a Single State in Europe*, 1997, p11

[xxx] Horne, Alistair: *Macmillan 1894-1956: Volume 1 of the Official Biography*. London: Macmillan, 1988, p.353-4

[xxxi] Young, John W.: *Britain and European Unity 1945-1999* (2nd Edition). British History in Perspective series. London, Macmillan, 2000, p.6

[xxxii] *Ibid.*, p.6-8

[xxxiii] *Ibid.*, p.20

[xxxiv] *Ibid.*, p.37

[xxxv] *Ibid.*, p.12

[xxxvi] *Ibid.*, p.190

[xxvii] *Ibid.*, p.190

[xxxviii] *Ibid.*, p.37

[xxxix] *Ibid.*, p.17

[xl] *Ibid.*, p.40

[xli] *Ibid.*, p.15-16

[xlii] Young, John W.: *Britain and European Unity 1945-1999* (2nd Edition). British History in Perspective series. London, Macmillan, 2000, p.35-37

[xliii] Manderson-Jones, R.B.: *The Special Relationship: Anglo-American Relations and Western European Unity 1947-56*. London: Weidenfeld and Nicholson, 1972, p.41-42

[xliv] *Ibid.*, p.42

[xlv] *Ibid.*, p.45

[xlvi] *Ibid.*, p.49

[xlvii] *Ibid.*, p.51

[xlviii] *Ibid*, p.56

[xlix] *Ibid.*, p.43

[l] Davies, Norman: *Europe: a History*. London: Random House, 1997, p.1083

[li] *Ibid*, p.1083.

[lii] This was described in detail in a doctoral thesis by F.X. Rebattet at

the University of Oxford in 1962, opened to the public in the 1990s. F.X. Rebattet was the son of George Rebattet, Secretary-General of the European Movement. The study was carried out with complete access to the European Movement's internal papers, and in cooperation with its senior figures. In Aldrich, Richard. J. (1997): 'OSS, CIA and European Unity: The American Committee on United Europe, 1948-60'. *Diplomacy & Statecraft*, 8:1

liii   Aldrich, Richard. J. (1997): 'OSS, CIA and European Unity: The American Committee on United Europe, 1948-60'. *Diplomacy & Statecraft*, 8:1, p.185.

liv   *Ibid.*

lv   NSC 10/2, 'National Security Directive on Office of Special Projects' [the Office of Special Projects was the temporary name of the OPC], 18th June, 1948, reprinted in Thomas H. Etzold and John L. Gaddis (eds.), *Containment: Documents on American Policy and Strategy, 1945-50* (New York, 1978), pp.125-8. In *Ibid.*, p.187.

lvi   Cord Meyer, *Facing Reality: from World Federalism to the CIA* (New York, 1982), pp.66-7. In *Ibid.*, p.188.

lvii   *Ibid.*, p.189

lviii   Ronald L. Filippelli, *American Labour and Postwar Italy: A Study in Cold War Politics* (Stanford 1989), p.134. In *Ibid.*, p.192

lvix   *Ibid.*, p.192

lx   ACUE directors list from details of a visit by Robert Schuman, 20th September 1950, folder 5, ACUE records, Special Collections, Lauinger Library, Georgetown University, Washington, D.C. In *Ibid.*, p.193.

lxi   'Report to the Executive Directors of the American Committee on United Europe', by William P. Durkee, May 1952, ACUE file 2, box 4, Walter Bedell Smith Papers, Dwight D. Eisenhower Library, Abilene, Kansas. In *Ibid.*, p.194

lxii   *Ibid.*, p.202

lxiii   Churchill to Donovan, private, 4th June, 1949, folder 90, ACUE records, Special Collections, Lauinger Library, Georgetown University, Washington, D.C. In *Ibid.*, p.195

lxiv   John Pomian (ed.), *Joseph Retinger: The Memoirs of an Eminence Grise* (Sussex, 1972), p.237; Aldrich, R.J., 'European Integration', p.165. In *Ibid.*, p.194

lxv Braden to Bedell Smith, 28ᵗʰ December, 1949, in Walter Bedell Smith Papers, Dwight D. Eisenhower Library, Abilene, Kansas. In *Ibid.*, p.196

lxvi *Ibid.*, p.196

lxvii 'Report to the Executive Directors of the American Committee on United Europe', by William P. Durkee, May 1952, pp.9-10. ACUE file 2, box 4, Walter Bedell Smith Papers, Dwight D. Eisenhower Library, Abilene, Kansas. In *Ibid.*, p.197

lxviii Confidential Memorandum in Braden to Bedell Smith, 27ᵗʰ June 1950, in Walter Bedell Smith Papers, Dwight D. Eisenhower Library, Abilene, Kansas; and Retinger to Sandys, 31ˢᵗ March 1950, European Movement Archives, in Rebattet, F.X. 'The European Movement 1945-53: A Study in National and International Non-Governmental Organisations working for European Unity' (D.Phil. thesis, St. Anthony's College, Oxford, 1962). In *Ibid.*, p.197.

lxix 'Report to the Executive Directors of the American Committee on United Europe', by William P. Durkee, May 1952, ACUE file 2, box 4, Walter Bedell Smith Papers, Dwight D. Eisenhower Library, Abilene, Kansas. In *Ibid.*, p.222.

lxx *Ibid.*, p.193

lxxi Confidential Memorandum in Braden to Bedell Smith, 27ᵗʰ June, 1950, in Walter Bedell Smith Papers, Dwight D. Eisenhower Library, Abilene, Kansas. In *Ibid.*, p.198.

lxxii Memorandum of a conversation between Acheson, Kennan, Spaak and Silvercruys, 19ᵗʰ January, 1950. In *Ibid.*, p.201

lxiii Acting Secretary of State to Donovan, 29ᵗʰ September 1950, Exhibit 6, Appendix 4, May 1952, Walter Bedell Smith Papers, Dwight D. Eisenhower Library, Abilene, Kansas. In *Ibid.*, p.201

lxxiv Memorandum of meetings of US ambassadors in Paris. In *Ibid.*, p.201

lxxv Folder 7, file 2, group 7, Mackay Papers, British Library of Economic and Political Science; and Aldrich, R.J., 'European Integration', p.168. In *Ibid.*, p.202

lxxvi Donovan, report from Strasbourg, 5ᵗʰ December 1951, folder 58, ACUE records, ACUE records, Special Collections, Lauinger Library, Georgetown University, Washington, D.C.; 'Report to the Executive Directors of the American Committee on United Europe', by William P. Durkee, May 1952, pp.6-7, 14-15, Walter Bedell Smith Papers, Dwight D. Eisenhower Library, Abilene, Kansas. In *Ibid.*, p.203

lxxvii   Rebattet, F.X., 'European Movement', p.308. In *Ibid.*, p.203.

lxxviii   Walter Bedell Smith Papers, Dwight D. Eisenhower Library, Abilene, Kansas. In *Ibid.*, p.203

lxxix   Braden, 'Activities of the ACUE', p.13, April 1950, folder 20, ACUE records, Special Collections, Lauinger Library, Georgetown University, Washington, D.C.; Braden to Langer, 12th January 1950, file: ACUE, box 9, Langer papers, Harvard University Archives. In *Ibid.*, p.204-5

lxxx   'Report on the College of Europe', P.C. Dodd (ACUE Scholar) June 1951, folder 1, ACUE records, Special Collections, Lauinger Library, Georgetown University, Washington, D.C. In *Ibid.*, p.205

lxxxi   Rebattet, F.X., 'European Movement', p.34. In *Ibid.*, p.205

lxxxii   'Report to the Directors', Foster, p.13, October 1959, folder 100, ACUE records, Special Collections, Lauinger Library, Georgetown University, Washington, D.C. In *Ibid.*, p.210

lxxxiii   'Statement of General William J. Donovan, ACUE to Committee on Foreign Affairs, House of Representatives', 3rd March 1950, folder 56, ACUE records, Special Collections, Lauinger Library, Georgetown University, Washington, D.C.; Appendix IV Exhibit 4, ;Material Published by the ACUE and Publications Distributed', in ACUE records, Special Collections, Lauinger Library, Georgetown University, Washington, D.C. In *Ibid.*,p.204

lxxiv   Minutes of the Meeting of the Executive Committee of ACUE, 11th October 1950. In *Ibid.*,p.206

lxxxc   Donovan to Bedell Smith, 25th July, 1951, Walter Bedell Smith Papers, Dwight D. Eisenhower Library, Abilene, Kansas. In *Ibid.*, p.206.

lxxxvi   Minutes of the Meeting of the Executive Committee of ACUE, 11th October 1950; BE/M/8, Luxembourg, 21st May 1948, p.2; and BE/M/14, Paris, 23rd November 1953, p.3, in European Movement Archives, in Rebattet, F.X., 'European Movement', p.201, in *Ibid.*, p.207

lxxxvii   European Youth Campaign, 1953, CCS/P/2, box 1, ACUE collection, Hoover Institute, Stanford University. In *Ibid.*, p.208

lxxxviii   'Reports to the Directors of ACUE', William P. Durkee, July 1951 and May 1952, Walter Bedell Smith Papers, Dwight D. Eisenhower Library, Abilene, Kansas. In *Ibid.*, p.208

lxxxix   Geoffrey Warner, 'Eisenhower, Dulles, and the Unity of Western Europe', *International Affairs*, lxix (1993), pp.320-23. In *Ibid.*, p.208

xc   Meeting of the Board of Directors, 6th June 1956, folder 91, ACUE records, Special Collections, Lauinger Library, Georgetown University, Washington, D.C. In *Ibid.*,p.209

xci   Pisani, S. *The CIA and the Marshall Plan* (Edinburgh, 1991), pp.47-52. In *Ibid.*, p.209

xcii   Correspondence from François Duchêne to Richard J. Aldrich, 3rd February 1995. In *Ibid.*, p.225

xciii   Rebattet, F.X., 'European Movement', pp.314-15. In *Ibid.*, pp.212-11

xciv   Connelly to Bedell Smith, 16th February 1952, Walter Bedell Smith Papers, Dwight D. Eisenhower Library, Abilene, Kansas. In *Ibid.*, p.211

xcv   Rebattet, F.X., 'European Movement', pp.208-10. In *Ibid.*, p.214

xcvi   'The Labour Party and European Cooperation', Ernest Davies Memorandum, 25th April 1950, folder 31, 9/9, Hugh Dalton Papers, British Library of Political and Economic Science. In *Ibid.*, p.215

xcvii   Young, John W.: *Britain and European Unity 1945-1999* (2nd Edition). British History in Perspective series. London, Macmillan, 2000, p.27-8

xcviii *Ibid.*, p.24

xcix   *Ibid.*, p.32

c   Horne, Alistair: *Macmillan 1894-1956: Volume 1 of the Official Biography*. London: Macmillan, 1988, p.325

ci   *Ibid.*, p.326-7

cii   *Ibid.*, p.329

ciii   *Ibid.*, p.356

civ   *Ibid.*, p.49

cv   Young, John W.: *Britain and European Unity 1945-1999* (2nd Edition). British History in Perspective series. London, Macmillan, 2000, p.32

cvi   Manderson-Jones, R.B.: *The Special Relationship: Anglo-American Relations and Western European Unity 1947-56*. London: Weidenfeld and Nicholson, 1972, p.93-4

cvii   *Ibid.*, p.91

cviii   *Ibid.*, p.95-6

cix   *Ibid.*, p.35

cx   *Ibid.*, p.36

cxi   Manderson-Jones, R.B.: *The Special Relationship: Anglo-American Relations and Western European Unity 1947-56*. London: Weidenfeld and Nicholson, 1972, p.97

cxii   Horne, Alistair: *Macmillan 1894-1956: Volume 1 of the Official Biography*. London: Macmillan, 1988, p.330

cxiii   Manderson-Jones, R.B.: *The Special Relationship: Anglo-American Relations and Western European Unity 1947-56*. London: Weidenfeld and Nicholson, 1972, p.99

cxiv   *Ibid.*, p.108

cxv   *Ibid.*, p.114

cxvi   *Ibid.*, p.118-9

cxvii   *Ibid.*, p.123-4

cxviii   Manderson-Jones, R.B.: *The Special Relationship: Anglo-American Relations and Western European Unity 1947-56*. London: Weidenfeld and Nicholson, 1972, p.124

cxix   *Ibid.*, p.128

cxx   *Ibid.*, p.328

cxxi   *Ibid.*, p.322-3

cxxii   Bernard Porter in *The Times Literary Supplement*, 8th February 2002. In Roberts, Andrew: *A History of the English-Speaking Peoples Since 1900*. London: Phoenix, 2007, p.12

cxxiii   Colville, John. *The Fringes of Power: Downing Street Diaries 1939-1945*. London: Weidenfeld and Nicholson, 2004, p. 625-7

cxxiv   *Ibid.*, p.362

cxxv   *Ibid.*, p.41

cxxvi   Horne, Alistair: *Macmillan 1894-1956: Volume 1 of the Official Biography*. London: Macmillan, 1988, Vol. 1, p.370

cxxvii   *Ibid.*, p.371

cxxviii   *Ibid.*, p.393-4

cxxix   *Ibid.*, p.394

cxxx   *Ibid.*, p.60-1

cxxxi   BBC Radio Four, *The Today Programme*, 2007

cxxxii   Wilson, Theodore A: *The First Summit*. Boston: Houghton Mifflin, 1970

cxxxiii   Horne, Alistair: *Macmillan 1956-1986: Volume 2 of the Official Biography*. London: Macmillan, 1989, p.29

cxxxiv   E. Bruce Geelhoed and Anthony O. Edmonds (eds), *The Macmillan-Eisenhower Correspondence, 1957-1969* (Basingstoke: Palgrave, 2005), in *The Macmillan Diaries, Prime Minister and After, 1957-66*. Peter Catterall (ed). Basingstoke: Pan Macmillan, 2011.

cxxxv   Lamb, Richard: *The Macmillan Years, 1957-63: The Emerging Truth*. London: John Murray, 1985, p.125

cxxxvi   *Ibid.*, p.134

cxxvii   *Ibid.*, p.132-3

cxxxviii   9th July 1960, Catterall, Peter (ed) *The Macmillan Diaries, Vol. III: Prime Minister and After, 1957-66*. Basingstoke: Pan Macmillan, 2011, p.313

cxxxix   *Ibid.*, p.258

cxl   Young, John W.: *Britain and European Unity 1945-1999* (2nd Edition). British History in Perspective series. London, Macmillan, 2000, p.68

cxli   *Ibid.*, p.306

cxlii   *Ibid.*, p.299

cxliii   Horne, Alistair: *Macmillan 1956-1986: Volume 2 of the Official Biography*. London: Macmillan, 1989, p.307

cxliv   *Ibid.*, p.300

cxlv   *Ibid.*, p.330

cxlvi   1st January 1961, Catterall, Peter (ed) *The Macmillan Diaries, Vol. III: Prime Minister and After, 1957-66*. Basingstoke: Pan Macmillan, 2011, p.351

cxlvii   Diary entry, 29th November 1961. In Horne, Alistair: *Macmillan 1956-1986: Volume 2 of the Official Biography*. London: Macmillan, 1989, p.319

cxlviiii   13th March, 1960, in The Macmillan Diaries, Vol. III: Prime Minister and After, 1957 – 1966, Peter Catterall (ed), 2011. Basingstoke: Palgrave Macmillan.

cxlix   Diary entry, 29th November 1961. In Horne, Alistair: *Macmillan 1956-1986: Volume 2 of the Official Biography*. London: Macmillan, 1989., p.428

cl   *Ibid.*, p.429

cli   *Ibid.*, p.429

clii   *Ibid.*, p.430

cliii   Lamb, Richard: *The Macmillan Years, 1957-63: The Emerging Truth*. London: John Murray, 1985, p.302

cliv   *Ibid.*, p.437

clv   *Ibid.*, p.439

clvi   Horne, Alistair: *Macmillan 1894-1956: Volume 1 of the Official Biography*. London: Macmillan, 1988

clvii   *Ibid.*, p.320

clviii   *Ibid.*, p.78

clix   Booker, Christopher and North, Richard: *The Great Deception: The Secret History of the European Union*. London: Continuum, 2003, p.115

clx   *Ibid.*, p.161

clxi   *Ibid.*, p.165

clxii   Lamb, Richard: *The Macmillan Years, 1957-63: The Emerging Truth*. London: John Murray, 1985, p.163

clxiii   In The Macmillan Diaries, Vol. III: Prime Minister and After, 1957 – 1966, Peter Catterall (ed), 2011. Basingstoke: Palgrave Macmillan, p.468.

clxiv   Lamb, Richard: *The Macmillan Years, 1957-63: The Emerging Truth*. London: John Murray, 1985, p.172

clxv   *Ibid.*, p.174

clxvi   *Ibid.*

clxvii   The Macmillan Diaries, Vol. III: Prime Minister and After, 1957 – 1966, Peter Catterall (ed), 2011. Basingstoke: Palgrave Macmillan, p.474.

clxviii   *Ibid.*, p.494

clxix   In Roberts, Andrew: *A History of the English-Speaking Peoples Since 1900*. London: Phoenix, 2007, p.12

clxx   Lamb, Richard: *The Macmillan Years, 1957-63: The Emerging Truth*. London: John Murray, 1985, p.176

clxxi   *Ibid.*, p.176-7

clxxii   *Ibid.*, p.181

clxxiii   The diplomat was Sir Michael Butler. In *Ibid.*, p.190

clxxiv   *Ibid.*, p.189-192

clxxv   *Ibid.*, p.199

clxxvi   4th February, 1963, The Macmillan Diaries, Vol. III: Prime Minister and After, 1957 – 1966, Peter Catterall (ed), 2011. Basingstoke: Palgrave Macmillan, p.539-540.

clxxvii   *Ibid.*, p.197

clxxviii   *Ibid.*, p.202-3

clxxix   *Ibid.*, p.201

clxxx   Lamb, Richard: *The Macmillan Years, 1957-63: The Emerging Truth*. London: John Murray, 1985, p.197

clxxxi   Horne, Alistair: *Macmillan 1956-1986: Volume 2 of the Official Biography*. London: Macmillan, 1989, p.447.

clxxxii Catterall, Peter (ed) *The Macmillan Diaries, Vol. III: Prime Minister and After, 1957-66*. Basingstoke: Pan Macmillan, 2011

clxxxiii Lamb, Richard: *The Macmillan Years, 1957-63: The Emerging Truth*. London: John Murray, 1985, p.166

clxxxiv Peyrefitte, Alain. *C'etait de Gaulle*, Vol. 1 (Paris, Fayard), p.33, in Booker, Christopher and North, Richard: *The Great Deception: The Secret History of the European Union*. London: Continuum, 2003, p.117

clxxxv Quoted in *Ibid.*, p.84

clxxxvi Young, John W.: *Britain and European Unity 1945-1999* (2ⁿᵈ Edition). British History in Perspective series. London, Macmillan, 2000, p.96

clxxxvii *Ibid.*, p.100-101

clxxxviii Booker, Christopher and North, Richard: *The Great Deception: The Secret History of the European Union*. London: Continuum, 2003, p.138

clxxxix *Ibid.*, p.137

cxc Cash, William and Duncan Smith, Iain: *A German Europe: Aspects of a Single State in Europe*, 1997, p.2

cxci Booker, Christopher and North, Richard: *The Great Deception: The Secret History of the European Union*. London: Continuum, 2003. p.137

cxcii *Ibid.*, p.142

cxciii *Ibid.*, p.142

cxciv *Ibid.*, p.144

cxcv *Ibid.*, p.145

cxcvi *Ibid.*, p.149

cxcvii *Ibid.*, p.149

cxcviii *Ibid.*, p.151

cxcix Dahrendorf, R. In Holland, Stuart: *UnCommon Market*. New York: St. Martin's Press, 1980, p.9

cc Roberts, Andrew: *A History of the English-Speaking Peoples Since 1900*. London: Phoenix, 2007, p.12

cci Booker, Christopher and North, Richard: *The Great Deception: The Secret History of the European Union*. London: Continuum, 2003, p.155

ccii *Ibid.*, p.156

cciii Cash, William: *It's the EU, Stupid*. London: The European Foundation, 2011

cciv Hansard, 17ᵗʰ February 1971, Cols. 272-274

ccv Young, John W.: *Britain and European Unity 1945-1999* (2ⁿᵈ Edition). British History in Perspective series. London, Macmillan, 2000, p.105

ccvi   Booker, Christopher and North, Richard: *The Great Deception: The Secret History of the European Union*. London: Continuum, 2003, p.161

ccvii   *Ibid.*, p.161

cxviii   *Ibid.*, p.162

ccix   *Ibid.*, p.163

ccx   Jenkins, Roy: *A Life at the Centre*. London: Papermac, 1994

ccxi   Booker, Christopher and North, Richard: *The Great Deception: The Secret History of the European Union*. London: Continuum, 2003, p.166

ccxii   *Ibid.*, p.166

ccxiii   Young, Hugo: *The Hugo Young Papers: Thirty Years of British Politics – Off the Record*. London: Allen Lane, 2008, p.41

ccxiv   Booker, Christopher and North, Richard: *The Great Deception: The Secret History of the European Union*. London: Continuum, 2003, p.169

ccxv   *Ibid.*, p.171

ccxvi   *Ibid.*, p.171

ccxvii   *Ibid.*, p.170

ccxviii   Elliott, Larry and Atkinson, Dan: *Fantasy Island: Waking Up to the Incredible Economic, Political and Social Illusions of the Blair Legacy*. London: Constable, 2007, p.220

ccxix   Booker, Christopher and North, Richard: *The Great Deception: The Secret History of the European Union*. London: Continuum, 2003, p.145

ccxx   *Ibid.*, p.145

ccxxi   *Ibid.*, p.152-153

ccxxii   *Ibid.*, p.147

ccxxiii   *Ibid.*

ccxxiv   *Ibid.*, p.148

ccxxv   *Ibid.*, p.148

ccxxvi   *Ibid.*, p.154

ccxxvii   Young, Hugo: *The Hugo Young Papers: Thirty Years of British Politics – Off the Record*. London: Allen Lane, 2008, p.149

ccxxviii   Booker, Christopher and North, Richard: *The Great Deception: The Secret History of the European Union*. London: Continuum, 2003, p.326

ccxxix   *Ibid.*, p.305

ccxxx   *Ibid.*, p.305

ccxxxi   *Ibid.*, p.305

ccxxxii   Clover, Charles: *The End of the Line: How Over-fishing is Changing the World and What We Eat*. London: Ebury Press, 2004, p.265

ccxxxiii   *Ibid.*, p.265

ccxxxiv   *Ibid.*

ccxxxv   Clover, Charles: *The End of the Line: How Over-fishing is Changing the World and What We Eat.* London: Ebury Press, 2004, p.264

ccxxxvi   *Ibid.*, p.265

ccxxxvii   Craig, David and Elliott, Matthew: *The Great European Rip-off: How the Corrupt, Wasteful EU is Taking Control of Our Lives.* London: Arrow Books, 2009, p.277

ccxxxviii   Clover, Charles: *The End of the Line: How Over-fishing is Changing the World and What We Eat.* London: Ebury Press, 2004, p.266

ccxxxix   *Ibid.*, p.266

ccxl   *Ibid.*, p.30-40

ccxli   *Ibid.*, p.194

ccxlii   Craig, David and Elliott, Matthew: *The Great European Rip-off: How the Corrupt, Wasteful EU is Taking Control of Our Lives.* London: Arrow Books, 2009, p.280

ccxliii   *Ibid.*, p.273

ccxliv   Rotherham, Lee: *Ten Years On: Britain without the European Union.* London: The Taxpayers' Alliance, 2009, p.28

ccxlv   Craig, David and Elliott, Matthew: *The Great European Rip-off: How the Corrupt, Wasteful EU is Taking Control of Our Lives.* London: Arrow Books, 2009, p.271

ccxlvi   *Ibid.*, p.290

ccxlvii   Clive Potter: 'Europe's Changing Farmed Landscapes'. In Pain, Deborah and Pienkowski, Michael (Eds.): *Farming and Birds in Europe: Common Agricultural Policy and its Implications for Bird Conservation.* London: Poyser, 2002, p.25

ccxlviii   Pain, Deborah and Pienkowski, Michael (Eds.): *Farming and Birds in Europe: Common Agricultural Policy and its Implications for Bird Conservation.* London: Poyser, 2002, p.9

ccxlix   *Ibid.*, p.336

ccl   José A. Danázar, Miguel A. Naveso, José L. Tella and David Campión: 'Extensive grazing and raptors in Spain'. In *Ibid.*, p.132

ccli   Cliver Potter: 'Europe's Changing Farmed Landscapes'. In *Ibid.*, p.39

clii   Pain, Deborah and Pienkowski, Michael (Eds.): *Farming and Birds in Europe: Common Agricultural Policy and its Implications for Bird Conservation.* London: Poyser, 2002, p.9

cliii   OECD figures, in Hill, Brian: *Studies in Economics and Business: The European Union* (4th edition) London: Heinemann, 2001, p.52

ccliv   Freemantle, Brian: *The Octopus: Europe in the Grip of Organised Crime.* London: Orion, 1995.

cclv   Flint, Adrian: *Trade, Poverty and the Environment: the EU, Cotonou and the African-Caribbean-Pacific Bloc.* Basingstoke: Palgrave Macmillan, 2008, p.28

cclvi   Jenkins, Roy: *A Life at the Centre.* London: Papermac, 1994, p.463

cclvii   Booker, Christopher and North, Richard: *The Great Deception: The Secret History of the European Union.* London: Continuum, 2003, p.188

cclviii   *Ibid.*, p.190

cclix   Thatcher, M, The Downing Street Year, p.543, in *Ibid.*, p.193

cclx   *Ibid.*, p.199

cclxi   Daily Telegraph, 15th September, 2003

cclxii   *Ibid.*, p.201

clxiii   *Ibid.*, p.206-7

cclxiv   *Ibid.*, p.202

cclxv   *Ibid.*, p.207

cclxvi   *Ibid.*, p.229

cclxvii   *Ibid.*, p.213

cclxviii   Ad Hoc Committee for Institutional Affairs, *Report to the European Council*, SN/1187/85 (SPAAK II), Brussels, 29-30 March, p.1. In *Ibid*, p.213

cclxix   *Ibid.*, p.216

cclxx   *Ibid.*, p.216

cclxxi   *Ibid.*, p.217

cclxxii   *Ibid.*, p.221

cclxxiii   *Ibid.*, p.222

cclxxiv   *Ibid.*

cclxxv   Thatcher, Margaret: *The Downing Street Years.* London: Harper Collins, 1992, p.701

cclxxvi   Moravcsik, A.: *The Choice for Europe: Social Purpose and State Power from Messina to Maastricht.* Cornell University Press, 1998, p.367, in *Ibid.*, p.233

cclxxvii   Booker, Christopher and North, Richard: *The Great Deception: The Secret History of the European Union.* London: Continuum, 2003, p.235

cclxxviii   Hutton, Will: *The World We're In.* London: Abacus, 2003.

cclxxix   Rotherham, Lee: *Ten Years On: Britain without the European Union*. London: The Taxpayers' Alliance, 2009, p.103

cclxxx   Simms, Brendan: *Unfinest Hour: Britain and the Destruction of Bosnia*. London: Penguin, 2002, p.55

cclxxxi   *Ibid.*

cclxxxii   *Ibid.*, p.65

cclxxxiii   *Ibid.*

cclxxxiv   *Ibid.*, p.47

cclxxxv   *Ibid.*, p.23

cclxxxvi   *Ibid.*

cclxxxvii   Sir Dudley Smith, in *Ibid.*, p.110

cclxxxviii   *Ibid.*, p.113

cclxxxix   Young, Hugo: *The Hugo Young Papers: Thirty Years of British Politics – Off the Record*. London: Allen Lane, 2008, p.589

ccxc   Simms, Brendan: *Unfinest Hour: Britain and the Destruction of Bosnia*. London: Penguin, 2002, p.107

ccxci   Young, Hugo: *The Hugo Young Papers: Thirty Years of British Politics – Off the Record*. London: Allen Lane, 2008, p.414

ccxcii   Craig, David and Elliott, Matthew: *The Great European Rip-off: How the Corrupt, Wasteful EU is Taking Control of Our Lives*. London: Arrow Books, 2009, p.140

ccxciii   *Ibid.*, p.270

ccxciv   Nigel Lawson in *Ibid.*, p.237

ccxcv   Nigel Lawson in *Ibid.*, p.238

ccxcvi   *Ibid.*, p.239

ccxcvii   *Ibid.*, p.239

ccxcvii   Booker, Christopher and North, Richard: *The Great Deception: The Secret History of the European Union*. London: Continuum, 2003, p.240

ccxcix   *Ibid.*, p.241

ccc   Thatcher, *op. cit.*, p.746, in *Ibid.* p.241

ccci   *Ibid.*, p.244

cccii   *Ibid.*, p.245

ccciii   Lawson, N. *The View from Number 11: Memoirs of a Tory Radical.*, p.913

cciv   *Ibid.*, p.248

cccv   *Ibid.*, p.249

cccvi   Cash, William: *Against a Federal Europe – The Battle for Britain*. London: Duckworth, 1991, p.136-8 cccvii   Booker, Christopher and North, Richard: *The Great Deception: The Secret History of the European Union*. London: Continuum, 2003, p.252

cccviii   *Ibid.*, p.256

cccix   *Ibid.*, p.256

cccx   *Ibid.*, p.256

cccxi   Grant, Charles: Delors: *Inside the House that Jacques Built*. London, Nicholas Brearley, 1994, p.151

cccxii   Cash, William: *Against a Federal Europe – The Battle for Britain*. London: Duckworth, 1991, p.115

cccxiii   Booker, Christopher and North, Richard: *The Great Deception: The Secret History of the European Union*. London: Continuum, 2003, p.275

cccxiv   Craig, David and Elliott, Matthew: *The Great European Rip-off: How the Corrupt, Wasteful EU is Taking Control of Our Lives*. London: Arrow Books, 2009, p.82

cccxv   Gorman, Teresa (1993). *The Bastards: Dirty Tricks and the Challenge to Europe*. Basingstoke: Pan Macmillan, p.125-6

cccxvi   *Ibid.*, p.129

cccxvii   *Ibid.*, p.202

cccxviii   *Ibid.*, p.205

cccxix   *Ibid.*, p.206-7

cccxx   Cash, William: *Visions of Europe*. London: Duckworth, 1993

cccxxi   Booker, Christopher and North, Richard: *The Great Deception: The Secret History of the European Union*. London: Continuum, 2003, p.277

cccxxii   Laughland, John: *The Tainted Source: The Undemocratic Origins of the European Idea*. London: Warner Books, 1997, p.141-2

cccxxiii   Booker, Christopher and North, Richard: *The Great Deception: The Secret History of the European Union*. London: Continuum, 2003, p.287

cccxxiv   Time Magazine, 31st May 1993, p.22. in *Ibid.*, p.289

cccxxv   Laughland, John: *The Tainted Source: The Undemocratic Origins of the European Idea*. London: Warner Books, 1997, p.136

cccxxvi   Craig, David and Elliott, Matthew: *The Great European Rip-off: How the Corrupt, Wasteful EU is Taking Control of Our Lives*. London: Arrow Books, 2009, p.90

cccxxvii   Booker, Christopher and North, Richard: *The Great Deception: The Secret History of the European Union*. London: Continuum, 2003, p.284

cccxxviii   Cash, William and Duncan Smith, Iain: *A German Europe: Aspects of a Single State in Europe*, 1997, p.7

cccxxix Cash, William: *Against a Federal Europe – The Battle for Britain*. London: Duckworth, 1991, p.32

cccxxx Booker, Christopher and North, Richard: *The Great Deception: The Secret History of the European Union*. London: Continuum, 2003, p.324

cccxxxi House of Commons Foreign Affairs Committee, Session 1995-1996, 3rd Report, *The Intergovernmental Conference*. HC 306, para. 25. In Booker, Christopher and North, Richard: *The Great Deception: The Secret History of the European Union*. London: Continuum, 2003, p.328

cccxxxii Hansard, 21st March 1996, col. 541

cccxxxiii Booker, Christopher and North, Richard: *The Great Deception: The Secret History of the European Union*. London: Continuum, 2003, p.335

cccxxxiv *Ibid.*, p.340

cccxxxv Craig, David and Elliott, Matthew: *The Great European Rip-off: How the Corrupt, Wasteful EU is Taking Control of Our Lives*. London: Arrow Books, 2009, p.84

cccxxxvi Booker, Christopher and North, Richard: *The Great Deception: The Secret History of the European Union*. London: Continuum, 2003, p.340

cccxxxvii Craig, David and Elliott, Matthew: *The Great European Rip-off: How the Corrupt, Wasteful EU is Taking Control of Our Lives*. London: Arrow Books, 2009, p.83

cccxxxviii Balanya, Belen, Doherty, Ann, Hoedeman, Olivier, Ma'anit, Adam and Wesselius, Eric: *Europe, Inc.: Regional and Global Restructuring and the Rise of Corporate Power*. London: Pluto Press, 2000, p.58

cccxxxix Young, Hugo: *The Hugo Young Papers: Thirty Years of British Politics – Off the Record*. London: Allen Lane, 2008, p.638

cccxl Jenkins, Simon: *Big Bang Localism: A Rescue Plan for British Democracy*. London: Policy Exchange/Localis, 2004, p.106

cccxli *Ibid.*

cccxlii *Ibid.*

cccxliii *Ibid.*, p.41

cccxliv *Ibid.*

cccxlv *Bild*, 25th March, 1998, In Booker, Christopher and North, Richard: *The Great Deception: The Secret History of the European Union*. London: Continuum, 2003, p.355

cccxlvi *Ibid.*, p.363

cccxlvii M. Everson, G. Majone, L. Metcalfe, A. Schout: *The Role of Specialised Agencies in Decentralising Governance: Report to the Commission* (1999).

In Flinders, Matthew: *Delegated Governance and the British State: Walking without Order.* Oxford University Press, 2008, p.9-10

cccxlviii Flinders, Matthew: *Delegated Governance and the British State: Walking without Order.* Oxford University Press, 2008, p.290

cccxlix *Ibid.*, p.236

ccl Booker, Christopher and North, Richard: *The Great Deception: The Secret History of the European Union.* London: Continuum, 2003, p.361

cccli *Ibid.*, p.361

ccclii The Daily Telegraph, 30th November, 2000. In *Ibid.*, p.388

cccliii Booker, Christopher and North, Richard: *The Great Deception: The Secret History of the European Union.* London: Continuum, 2003, p.361

cccliv Craig, David and Elliott, Matthew: *The Great European Rip-off: How the Corrupt, Wasteful EU is Taking Control of Our Lives.* London: Arrow Books, 2009, p.89

ccclv Young, Hugo: *The Hugo Young Papers: Thirty Years of British Politics – Off the Record.* London: Allen Lane, 2008.

ccclvi Young, Hugo: *The Hugo Young Papers: Thirty Years of British Politics – Off the Record.* London: Allen Lane, 2008, p.677; p.696

ccclvii *Ibid.*, p.659-660

ccclviii Booker, Christopher and North, Richard: *The Great Deception: The Secret History of the European Union.* London: Continuum, 2003, p.397

ccclix *Ibid.*, p.398

ccclx *Ibid.*, p.398

ccclxi *Ibid.*, p.400

ccclxii Rotherham, Lee: *Ten Years On: Britain without the European Union.* London: The Taxpayers' Alliance, 2009, p.66-68

ccclxiii Schwarz, Pedro: *The Euro as Politics.* London: The Institute of Economic Affairs, 2004, p.199

ccclxiv Booker, Christopher and North, Richard: *The Great Deception: The Secret History of the European Union.* London: Continuum, 2003, p.402

ccclxv Gough, Roger and Reid, Anna (Eds.): *The Perfect Union? New Europe and the EU.* London: Policy Exchange, 2004, p.55-56

ccclxvi Letter published in the Baltic Times, 11th May, 2007

ccclxvii Gough, Roger and Reid, Anna (Eds.): *The Perfect Union? New Europe and the EU.* London: Policy Exchange, 2004, p.20-21

ccclxviii Grabbe, Heather and Hughes, Kirsty: 'Central and east European views on EU enlargement: political debates and public opinion'. In:

Henderson, Karen (Ed.): *Back to Europe: Central and Eastern Europe and the European Union*. London, UCL Press, 1999, p.185; p.192

ccclxix   *Ibid.*

ccclxx   28th November 2002, www.number-10.gov.uk

ccclxxi   Booker, Christopher and North, Richard: *The Great Deception: The Secret History of the European Union*. London: Continuum, 2003, p.414-415

ccclxxii   Craig, David and Elliott, Matthew: *The Great European Rip-off: How the Corrupt, Wasteful EU is Taking Control of Our Lives*. London: Arrow Books, 2009, p.105

ccclxxiii   *Ibid.*, p.104

ccclxxiv   *Ibid.*, p.104

ccclxxv   *Ibid.*, p.99-100

ccclxxvi   *Ibid.*, p.99-100

ccclxxvii   Cash, William and Duncan Smith, Iain: *A German Europe: Aspects of a Single State in Europe*, 1997, p.18

ccclxxviii   *Ibid.*, p.102

cclxxix   *Ibid.*, p.109

ccclxxx   Cash, William: *It's the EU, Stupid*. The European Foundation, 2011

ccclxxxi   Craig, David and Elliott, Matthew: *The Great European Rip-off: How the Corrupt, Wasteful EU is Taking Control of Our Lives*. London: Arrow Books, 2009, p.86

ccclxxxii   *Ibid.*, p.114

ccclxxxiii   *Ibid.*, p.95

ccclxxxiv   *Ibid.*

ccclxxxv   Oborne, Peter and Weaver, Frances: *Guilty Men*. London: Centre for Policy Studies, 2012

ccclxxxvi   Craig, David and Elliott, Matthew: *The Great European Rip-off: How the Corrupt, Wasteful EU is Taking Control of Our Lives*. London: Arrow Books, 2009, p.36

ccclxxxvii   *Ibid.*

ccclxxxviii   *Ibid.*, p.11

ccclxxxix   *Ibid.*, p.31

cccxc   Craig, David and Elliott, Matthew: *The Great European Rip-off: How the Corrupt, Wasteful EU is Taking Control of Our Lives*. London: Arrow Books, 2009

cccxci   *Ibid.*, p.296

cccxcii   Tindemann, K., cited in Cash, William: *Against a Federal Europe – The Battle for Britain*. London: Duckworth, 1991. p.28

cccxciii Craig, David and Elliott, Matthew: *The Great European Rip-off: How the Corrupt, Wasteful EU is Taking Control of Our Lives*. London: Arrow Books, 2009, p.267

cccxciv   *Ibid.*

cccxcv   *Ibid.*

cccxcvi   *Ibid.*, p.290-291

cccxcvii *Ibid.*, p.267-268

cccxcviii *Ibid.*, p.51-52

cccxcix   Cash, William: *Against a Federal Europe – The Battle for Britain*. London: Duckworth, 1991, p.116

cd   Craig, David and Elliott, Matthew: *The Great European Rip-off: How the Corrupt, Wasteful EU is Taking Control of Our Lives*. London: Arrow Books, 2009, p.168

cdi   *Ibid.*

cdii   Christopher Booker, Daily Telegraph, 16th January, 2010

cdiii   Craig, David and Elliott, Matthew: *The Great European Rip-off: How the Corrupt, Wasteful EU is Taking Control of Our Lives*. London: Arrow Books, 2009, p.282

cdiv   Balanya, Belen, Doherty, Ann, Hoedeman, Olivier, Ma'anit, Adam and Wesselius, Eric: Europe, Inc.: *Regional and Global Restructuring and the Rise of Corporate Power*. London: Pluto Press, 2000, p.47

cdv   *Ibid.*, p.4

cdvi   Craig, David and Elliott, Matthew: *The Great European Rip-off: How the Corrupt, Wasteful EU is Taking Control of Our Lives*. London: Arrow Books, 2009, p.129

cdvii   Cave, T. and Rowell, A.: *A Quiet Word: Lobbying, Crony Capitalism and Broken Politics in Britain*. London: Bodley Head, 2014. p.136.

cdviii   Balanya, Belen, Doherty, Ann, Hoedeman, Olivier, Ma'anit, Adam and Wesselius, Eric: Europe, Inc.: *Regional and Global Restructuring and the Rise of Corporate Power*. London: Pluto Press, 2000, p.4

cdix   Vaubel, Roland: *The Political Economy of Labor Market Regulation by the European Union*. University of Mannheim Working Paper, 2007.

cdx   Eichener, V. and Voelzkow, H. (1994). *Europaische Regulierung im Arbeitsschultz*, in Volker Eichner and Helmut Voelzkow (eds.). *Europaischer Integration und verbandliche Interessenvermittlung*, Marburg: 385-417

cdxi   David Harrison, Daily Telegraph, 6th November, 2005

cdxii   Craig, David and Elliott, Matthew: *The Great European Rip-off: How the Corrupt, Wasteful EU is Taking Control of Our Lives*. London: Arrow Books, 2009, p.137-138

cdxiii Rotherham, Lee: *Ten Years On: Britain without the European Union*. London: The Taxpayers' Alliance, 2009, p.40

cdxiv   Davies, Ian, Hirst, Chrissie, Mariani, Bernardo: *Organised crime, corruption and illicit arms trafficking in an enlarged EU: challenges and perspectives*. London: Saferworld, 2001, p.30

cdxv   Craig, David and Elliott, Matthew: *The Great European Rip-off: How the Corrupt, Wasteful EU is Taking Control of Our Lives*. London: Arrow Books, 2009, p.43

cdxvi   Young, Hugo: *The Hugo Young Papers: Thirty Years of British Politics – Off the Record*. London: Allen Lane, 2008, p.335

cdxvii Cash, William and Duncan Smith, Iain: *A German Europe: Aspects of a Single State in Europe*, 1997, p.6

cdxviii Hutton, Will: *The World We're In*. London: Abacus, 2003

cdxvix Balanya, Belen, Doherty, Ann, Hoedeman, Olivier, Ma'anit, Adam and Wesselius, Eric: Europe, Inc.: *Regional and Global Restructuring and the Rise of Corporate Power*. London: Pluto Press, 2000, p.49

cdxx   *Ibid.*

cdxxi   Craig, David and Elliott, Matthew: *The Great European Rip-off: How the Corrupt, Wasteful EU is Taking Control of Our Lives*. London: Arrow Books, 2009, p.222-223

cdxxii *Ibid.*, p.283

cdxxiii Rotherham, Lee: *Ten Years On: Britain without the European Union*. London: The Taxpayers' Alliance, 2009, p.47

cdxxiv Wolfgang Münchau, *The Financial Times*, 28th September, 2009

cdxxv   Cash, William: *Against a Federal Europe – The Battle for Britain*. London: Duckworth, 1991, p.35

cdxxvi Schwarz, Pedro: *The Euro as Politics*. London: The Institute of Economic Affairs, 2004, p.176

cdxxvii Vanthoor (1996, p.133) in *Ibid.*, p.176

cdxxviii Balanya, Belen, Doherty, Ann, Hoedeman, Olivier, Ma'anit, Adam and Wesselius, Eric: Europe, Inc.: *Regional and Global Restructuring and the Rise of Corporate Power*. London: Pluto Press, 2000

cdxxvix Europa Press Releases *RAPID*, 10th November 2011

cdxxx   Jeremy Warner, Daily Telegraph, 24th November 2011

cdxxxi   Cash, William: *Against a Federal Europe – The Battle for Britain.* London: Duckworth, 1991

cdxxxii *Ibid.*

cdxxxiii Berlin, I. *Freedom and its Betrayal: Six Enemies of Human Liberty.* London: Pimlico, 2003. p.55

cdxxxiv *Ibid.*, p.57

cdxxxv   Watson, Peter: *The German Genius: Europe's Third Renaissance, the Second Scientific Revolution and the Twentieth Century.* London: Simon & Schuster, 2011, p.532

cdxxxvi *Ibid.*, p.532-5

cdxxxvii Laughland, John: *The Tainted Source: The Undemocratic Origins of the European Idea.* London: Warner Books, 1997, p.113

cdxxxviii *Ibid.*, p.114

cdxxxix *Ibid.*, p.115

cdxl   *Ibid.*, p.116

cdxli   *Ibid.*, p.117

cdxlii   Broszat, M. *200 Jahre Deutsche Polenpolitik. Frankfurt am Main: Suhrkamp, 1972, p.220*

cdxliii *Ibid.*, p.120-1

cdxliv   Berlin, I. *Freedom and its Betrayal: Six Enemies of Human Liberty.* London: Pimlico, 2003. p.66

cdxlv   *Oeuvres de Saint-Simon 1868-1875*, Vol. 1, p.197. In Laughland, John. *The Tainted Source: The Undemocratic Origins of the European Idea.* London: Warner Books, 1997, p.209

cdxlvi   *Ibid.*, p.210

cdxlvii *Ibid.*, p.210

cdxlviii Laughland, John. *The Tainted Source: The Undemocratic Origins of the European Idea.* London: Warner Books, 1997, p.121-2

cdxlix   Ebeling, F.: Geopolitik: *Karl Haushofer und seine Raum Wissenschaft 1919-1945.* Berlin: Academie Verlag, 1994, p.89. In Laughland, John. *The Tainted Source: The Undemocratic Origins of the European Idea.* London: Warner Books, 1997.

cdl   *Ibid.*, p.124

cdli   Mackinder, H.J.: *The Scope and Methods and the Geographical Pivot of History.* (1887). In Laughland, John. *The Tainted Source: The Undemocratic Origins of the European Idea.* London: Warner Books, 1997, p.123

cdlii   *Ibid.*, p.124

cdliii   Von Lösch, K.C.: *Der Kampf für das Recht im Osten*. In *Zeitschrift für das Geopolitik*, 1941-1942, pp. 246-8. In Laughland, John. *The Tainted Source: The Undemocratic Origins of the European Idea*. London: Warner Books, 1997, p.124

cdliv   Ganzer, K.: *Das Reich als europäischer Ordnungs-macht*, in *Reich und Reichsfeinde*. Schriften des Reichsinstituts für Geschichte des neuen Deutschland, Hamburg, 1942, pp.7-97. In Laughland, John. *The Tainted Source: The Undemocratic Origins of the European Idea*. London: Warner Books, 1997, p.125

cdlv   Weingartner, Arnold: *Jenseits des Nationalismus*. In *Nation und Staat*. Vienna: Werner Hasselblatt, 1942-3, pp.258-60. In Laughland, John. *The Tainted Source: The Undemocratic Origins of the European Idea*. London: Warner Books, 1997, p.125-6

cdlvi   Otto Muck, 'Der Großeuropäische Wolhfahrtstraum', in Zeitschrift für Geopolitik, 1943, p.16-22. In Laughland, John. *The Tainted Source: The Undemocratic Origins of the European Idea*. London: Warner Books, 1997, p.126.

cdlvii   Wolfgang Höpker, 'Die Ablösung Zwischeneuropas' in Zeitschrift für Geopolitik, 1940/41, p.189. In Laughland, John. *The Tainted Source: The Undemocratic Origins of the European Idea*. London: Warner Books, 1997, p.126

cdlviii   Ebeling, F.: Geopolitik: *Karl Haushofer und seine Raum Wissenschaft 1919-1945*. Berlin: Academie Verlag, 1994, p.182. In Laughland, John. *The Tainted Source: The Undemocratic Origins of the European Idea*. London: Warner Books, 1997, p.127.

cdlix   *Ibid.*

cdlx   Herwig, M. *Post-War Lies: Germany and Hitler's Long Shadow*, London: Scribe, 2013.

cdlxi   Laughland, John. *The Tainted Source: The Undemocratic Origins of the European Idea*. London: Warner Books, 1997, p.132-3.

cdlxii   Karl Megerle, 'Positive Themes for Press and Propaganda' In Laughland, John. *The Tainted Source: The Undemocratic Origins of the European Idea*. London: Warner Books, 1997, p.128

cdlxiii   Joachim von Ribbentrop, 'Speech on the Prolongation of the Anti-Comintern Pact', *Monatshefte für Auswärtige Politik*, 1941, pp.1055ff.

In Laughland, John. *The Tainted Source: The Undemocratic Origins of the European Idea*. London: Warner Books, 1997, p.129

cdlxiv Friedrich Grimm, 'Allemagne et France: hier, aujourd'hui et demain', Les Conférences du Groupe 'Collaboration', Paris, January 1941, p.9. In Laughland, John. *The Tainted Source: The Undemocratic Origins of the European Idea*. London: Warner Books, 1997, p.129

cdlxv *Das Neue Europa*, No. 1, 15 October 1941, p.4. In Laughland, John. *The Tainted Source: The Undemocratic Origins of the European Idea*. London: Warner Books, 1997, p.129

cdlxvi Dr Reinhald Hoops, op. cit. No. 9, 1st May, 1942, p.6; Walter Freund, op. cit. No.13, 1st July 1942, p.5. In Laughland, John. *The Tainted Source: The Undemocratic Origins of the European Idea*. London: Warner Books, 1997, p.129

cdlxvii Arnulf Baring, *Unser Neue Gröenwahn: Deutschland zwischen Ost und West* (Our New Megalomania: German between East and West), Stuttgart, 1989. In Cash, William: *Against a Federal Europe – The Battle for Britain*. London: Duckworth, 1991, p.75

cdlxviii *Ibid.*, p.81

cdlxix Watson, Peter: *The German Genius: Europe's Third Renaissance, the Second Scientific Revolution and the Twentieth Century*. London: Simon & Schuster, 2011, p.776

cdlxx *Ibid.*, p.763

cdlxxi *Ibid.*, p.789-790

cdlxxii *Ibid.*, p.779

cdlxxiii *Ibid.*, p.713

cdlxxiv *Ibid.*, p.703

cdlxxv *Ibid.*, p.787

cdlxxvi *Ibid.*, p.725

cdlxxvii *Ibid.*, p.780

cdlxxviii *Ibid.*, p.787

cdlxxvix *Ibid.*, p.757

cdlxxx *Ibid.*, p.784

cdlxxxi *Ibid.*, p.824

cdlxxxii *Ibid.* p.821

cdlxxxiii *Ibid.*, p.821

cdlxxxiv *Ibid.*, p.832

cdlxxxv *Ibid.*, p.840

cdlxxxvi *Ibid.*, p.840

cdlxxxvii Cash, William: *Against a Federal Europe – The Battle for Britain.* London: Duckworth, 1991, p.58

cdlxxxviii Watson, Peter: *The German Genius: Europe's Third Renaissance, the Second Scientific Revolution and the Twentieth Century.* London: Simon & Schuster, 2011, p.819

cdlxxxix Herwig, M. *Post-War Lies: Germany and Hitler's Long Shadow* p.23

cdxc *Ibid.*, p.23

cdxci *Ibid.*, p.17-18

cdxcii *Ibid.*, p.156

cdxciii Cash, William and Duncan Smith, Iain: *A German Europe: Aspects of a Single State in Europe,* 1997, p.1

cdxciv Laughland, John. *The Tainted Source: The Undemocratic Origins of the European Idea.* London: Warner Books, 1997, p.148-9

cdxcv Neue Zürcher Zeitung, 10th July 1998

cdxcvi Laughland, John. *The Tainted Source: The Undemocratic Origins of the European Idea.* London: Warner Books, 1997, p.141-3

cdxcvii Laughland, John. *The Tainted Source: The Undemocratic Origins of the European Idea.* London: Warner Books, 1997, p.152

cdxcviii *Ein gemeinsamer Währungsraum,* mentioned by Edgar Meister in a speech to the Friedrich Ebert Stiftung, Trier, 24th October, 1995, in Auszüger aus Pressearitkeln, Deutsche Bundesbank, No. 73, 27th October 1995, p.6. In Laughland, John. *The Tainted Source: The Undemocratic Origins of the European Idea.* London: Warner Books, 1997, p.153

cdxcix Le Monde, 6th February, 1996

d CDU/CSU Bundestag Parliamentary Party, *Reflections on European Policy,* Section II, 'Germany's Interests'.

di Garton-Ash, Timothy: *In Europe's Name: Germany and the Divided Continent.* London: Jonathan Cape, 1993, p.97. In Laughland, John: *The Tainted Source: The Undemocratic Origins of the European Idea.* London: Warner Books, 1997, p.135.

dii Catterall, Peter (ed) *The Macmillan Diaries, Vol. III: Prime Minister and After, 1957-66.* Basingstoke: Pan Macmillan, 2011, p.77

diii Handelsblatt, 15th September, 1998

div The European, 28th September 1998

dv Lange, T. and Shackleton, J.R. *The Political Economy of German Unification.* Oxford: Berghahn Books, 1998, p.5-6.

dvi Blunden, Margaret. 'The Germany Europe Deserves', in *The Political Economy of German Unification*, eds. Lange & Shackleton, Berghahn Books, Providence and Oxford, 1998, p.15

dvii *Ibid.*, p.16

dviii Cash, William: *Against a Federal Europe – The Battle for Britain*. London: Duckworth, 1991, p.82

dvix The Economist, 30th July 1988. In *Ibid.*, p.32

dx Cash, William: *Against a Federal Europe – The Battle for Britain*. London: Duckworth, 1991, p.31

dxi *Ibid.*, p.33

dxii *Ibid.*, p.139

dxii Trager, Frank N: 'On Federalism'. In *Why Federations Fail*, ed. Thomas Franck, New York, 1968. In *Ibid.*, p.84

dxiv *Ibid.*

dxv Pelletier, Rejean: 'Federalism and Upper Houses: Searching for a Solution'. In *Ibid.*, p.85

dxvi Cash, William: *Against a Federal Europe – The Battle for Britain*. London: Duckworth, 1991

dxvii Nipperdey, Thomas. '*Wie das Bürgertum die Moderne fand*', 1988. In *Ibid.*, p.87

dxviii Saalfeld, Thomas, 'The West German Bundestag after 40 years', in *Western European Politics*, July 1990, In *Ibid.*, p.62

dxvix Cash, William: *Against a Federal Europe – The Battle for Britain*. London: Duckworth, 1991

dxx Winock, Michel: 'Les français et la tentation anti-parliamentaire', *Histoire* (137) October 1990. In *Ibid.*, p.52

dxxi Reh, Christine. 'Is informal politics undemocratic? Trilogues, early agreements and the selection model of representation.' Journal of European Public Policy, 29th May 2014.

dxxii Bedock, C., Mair, P. and Wilson, A. (2011) 'Institutional change in advanced democracies: an exploratory assessment', Paper presented at the ECPR General Conference, Reykjavik, 25–27 August. In Reh, Christine. 'Is informal politics undemocratic? Trilogues, early agreements and the selection model of representation.' Journal of European Public Policy, 29th May 2014.

dxxiii *Ibid.*, p.65.

dxxiv   Laughland, John. *The Tainted Source: The Undemocratic Origins of the European Idea*. London: Warner Books, 1997, p.149

dxxv   Cash, William and Duncan Smith, Iain: *A German Europe: Aspects of a Single State in Europe*, 1997, p.2

dxxvi   Sir James Dyson, 21st November 2014, in Hill, Stephen, Spears' Blog 357: 'Bald Assertions and Bald Watching Eagles'.

dxxvii   Cash, William: *Against a Federal Europe – The Battle for Britain*. London: Duckworth, 1991, p.36

dxxviii   Laughland, John. *The Tainted Source: The Undemocratic Origins of the European Idea*. London: Warner Books, 1997, p.155

dxxvix   EP, Activity Report on Codecision and Conciliation, 14 July 2009 - 30 June 2014 (7th parliamentary term), presented by Gianni PITTELLA, Alejo VIDAL-QUADRAS, Georgios PAPASTAMKOS.

dxxx   EU Law Analysis, 10 January 2016, On knowledge as power: transparency of EU law-making procedures, Päivi Leino (University of Helsinki). See also House of Lords Report with Evidence, Codecision and national parliamentary scrutiny, HL Paper 125 (2009) 15-16.

dxxxi   Päivi Leino "The Politics of Efficient Compromise in the Adoption of EU Legal Acts" in Marise Cremona (Ed.), *EU Legal Acts: Challenges and Transformations, Collected Courses of the Academy of European Law* (Oxford University Press, forthcoming 2016.)

dxxxii   Bunyan, 'European Parliament: Abolish 1st [and 2nd] reading secret deals – bring back democracy 'warts and all'', Statewatch analysis available at: http://www.statewatch.org/analyses/no-84-ep-first-reading-deals.pdf

dxxxiii   House of Lords Report with Evidence. Codecision and national parliamentary scrutiny, HL Paper 125 (2009) 15-16.

dxxxiv   European Movement International. 28th September, 2015. 'Abolish backroom deals'.

dxxxv   Marissen, V. Background memo for the public hearing 'Trilogues and transparent law-making', 28th September 2015, organised by the EU Ombudsman, Emily O'Reilly. Blog.activ, 30th September, 2015.

dxxxvi   *Ibid.*

dxxxvii   Dolan, Carl. 'Trialogues: What goes on behind closed doors?' EurActiv, 15th September 2015.

dxxxviii   Berthier, Anaïs. 'Trade Secrets trialogue underlines the EU's democratic deficit.' EurActiv, 17th September 2015.

dxxxix   European Parliament, 2012b. In Reh, Christine. 'Is informal politics undemocratic? Trilogues, early agreements and the selection model of representation.' Journal of European Public Policy, 29th May 2014.

dxl   Rasmussen, A. and Shackleton, M. (2005) 'The scope for action of the European Parliament negotiators in the legislative process: lessons of the past and for the future', Paper presented at the EUSA Biennial International Conference, Austin, 31 March–2 April; and Ostrom, E. (1986) 'An agenda for the study of institutions', *Public Choice* 48: 3–25. doi: 10.1007/BF00239556. In Reh, Christine. 'Is informal politics undemocratic? Trilogues, early agreements and the selection model of representation.' Journal of European Public Policy, 29th May 2014.

dxli   Bressanelli, E., Costa de Sousa, J., Detourbet, C., Kramer, G., Pirnay, E., Vasco, R. and Villari, F. (2009) *Etude sur le système d'attribution des rapports dans les Commissions parlementaires: 6ème legislature 2004–2009*, Brussels: Directorate for Relations with the Political Groups, European Parliament. In *Ibid.*

dxlii   Yordanova, N. (2011) 'Inter-institutional rules and the division of power in the European Parliament: allocation of consultation and co-decision reports', *West European Politics* 34(1): 97–121. doi: 10.1080/01402382.2011.523547, p.100. In *Ibid.*

dxliii   Corbett, R., Jacobs, F. and Shackleton, M. (2011) *The European Parliament*, 8th ed., London: John Harper., p.158, In *Ibid.*

dxliv   Fox, Benjamin, 'Secret EU lawmaking: the triumph of the trilogues'. EUObserver, 4th April, 2014.

dxlv   European Scrutiny Committee, 2009, in *Ibid.*

dxlvi   Fox, Benjamin, 'Secret EU lawmaking: the triumph of the trilogues'. EUObserver, 4th April, 2014

dxlvii   Rotherham, Lee: *Ten Years On: Britain without the European Union.* London: The Taxpayers' Alliance, 2009, p.58-60

dxlviii   House of Commons Library Briefing Paper Number 7524, 8th March 2016, 'EU Referendum: summary and analysis of the new settlement for the UK and the EU' (Arabella Lang, Vaughne Miller, Daniel Harari, Steven Kennedy, Melanie Gower).

dxlix   Vaubel, Roland. 'Disproportionately Undemocratic'. The Wall Street Journal, 30th July 2007.

dl   Rotherham, Lee: *Ten Years On: Britain without the European Union.* London: The Taxpayers' Alliance, 2009, p.83

dli   Craig, David and Elliott, Matthew: *The Great European Rip-off: How the Corrupt, Wasteful EU is Taking Control of Our Lives.* London: Arrow Books, 2009, p.267-268

dlii   Rotherham, Lee: *Ten Years On: Britain without the European Union.* London: The Taxpayers' Alliance, 2009, p.91

dliii   Paxman, Jeremy: *The Political Animal: An Anatomy.* London: Michael Joseph, 2002

dliv   Popper, Karl R.: *The Open Society and its Enemies, Volume One: The Spell of Plato.* London: Routledge & Kegan Paul, 1945

dlv   Cash, William: *Against a Federal Europe – The Battle for Britain.* London: Duckworth, 1991, p.67

dlvi   Heaney, Seamus: *Beowulf: A New Translation.* London: Faber and Faber, 2002

dlvii   Popper, Karl R.: *The Open Society and its Enemies, Volume One: The Spell of Plato.* London: Routledge & Kegan Paul, 1945

INDEX